PUTIN'S
SLEDGEHAMMER

PUTIN'S
SLEDGEHAMMER

THE WAGNER GROUP AND
RUSSIA'S COLLAPSE
INTO MERCENARY CHAOS

CANDACE RONDEAUX

PUBLICAFFAIRS

New York

PublicAffairs
Hachette Book Group
1290 Avenue of the Americas, New York, NY 10104
www.publicaffairsbooks.com
@Public_Affairs

Printed in the United States of America

First Edition: April 2025

Published by PublicAffairs, an imprint of Hachette Book Group, Inc. The PublicAffairs name and logo is a registered trademark of the Hachette Book Group.

The Hachette Speakers Bureau provides a wide range of authors for speaking events. To find out more, go to hachettespeakersbureau.com or email HachetteSpeakers@hbgusa.com.

PublicAffairs books may be purchased in bulk for business, educational, or promotional use. For more information, please contact your local bookseller or the Hachette Book Group Special Markets Department at special.markets@hbgusa.com.

The publisher is not responsible for websites (or their content) that are not owned by the publisher.

Print book interior design by Bart Dawson

Library of Congress Cataloging-in-Publication Data

Names: Rondeaux, Candace, author.
Title: Putin's sledgehammer : the Wagner Group and Russia's collapse into mercenary chaos / Candace Rondeaux.
Other titles: Wagner Group and Russia's collapse into mercenary chaos
Description: First edition. | New York : PublicAffairs, 2025. | Includes bibliographical references and index. |
Identifiers: LCCN 2024035099 | ISBN 9781541703063 (hardcover) | ISBN 9781541703087 (ebook)
Subjects: LCSH: Russia (Federation)—History, Military—21st century. | Wagner Group. | Prigozhin, Yevgeny, 1961–2023—Military leadership. | Russo-Ukrainian War, 2014– | Russian Invasion of Ukraine, 2022. | Putin, Vladimir Vladimirovich, 1952– —Military leadership. | Mercenary troops—Russia (Federation)—History—21st century. | Private military companies—Russia (Federation)—History—21st century.
Classification: LCC DK510.764 .R643 2025 | DDC 947.706/21—dc23/eng/20250203
LC record available at https://lccn.loc.gov/2024035099

ISBNs: 9781541703063 (hardcover), 9781541703087 (ebook)

LSC-C

Printing 1, 2025

*For my family
and in memory of my guardian angels,
Mary Florence, Lois, and John*

CONTENTS

PART THREE: EXPANSION

PART FOUR: OUT OF THE SHADOWS

Photographs follow page 216.

PRINCIPAL CHARACTERS

IN RUSSIA

Vladimir Putin—President of Russia

A former KGB agent turned politician and architect of Russia's post-Soviet authoritarian state, Putin revived a national vision of imperial Russia. He rode to power amid a violent political transition that was shaped by the nexus between the country's criminal underworld and the state security apparatus that ultimately birthed the Wagner Group. As a longtime patron of Wagner chieftain Yevgeny Prigozhin since their days in 1990s St. Petersburg, Putin played a pivotal role in Prigozhin's rise and fall.

Kremlin Power Brokers and Putin Insiders

Sergey Chemezov—CEO of Rostec

A former KGB agent and a longtime ally of Putin, Chemezov led Rostec, Russia's state-owned defense conglomerate. Under his leadership, Rostec and its export arm Rosoboronexport expanded its share of the global arms market, cementing military-cooperation agreements with top Wagner Group strongman clients in the Middle East and Africa.

Nikolai Patrushev—Secretary of the Russian Security Council

A close confidant of Putin from their KGB days, Patrushev played a central role in Russia's national security apparatus as head of the FSB intelligence agency and top adviser to the president. He supported Putin's strategic goals, including the use of paramilitary forces like Wagner to further Russia's interests abroad.

Igor Sechin—CEO of Rosneft

A former KGB officer, former aide-de-camp, and close Putin ally, Sechin led Rosneft, which benefited from Russian paramilitary operations abroad. He played a major role in orchestrating the takeover of Yukos, clashing with Mikhail Khodorkovsky over control of its assets.

Vladislav Surkov—Former Kremlin Aide

A political strategist and longtime adviser to Putin, Surkov served as deputy chief of the presidential administration and was instrumental in designing the Kremlin's authoritarian playbook. An archconservative ideologue known as the "Gray Cardinal," Surkov oversaw Russia's Ukraine and Georgia policy, deploying agents provocateurs to stir up pro-Russian separatist sentiment.

Anton Vaino—Chief of the Presidential Administration

A longtime trusted aide to Putin, Vaino initially served as chief of protocol in the presidential administration, where he oversaw event management and catering, then was elevated to chief of staff. Vaino's function as presidential gatekeeper made him a key contact for Yevgeny Prigozhin.

Influential Oligarchs

Oleg Deripaska—Russian Metals and Mining Tycoon, Former CEO of RUSAL and EN+

A wealthy Russian oligarch, Deripaska was deeply involved in Russia's metals and mining sectors, and his company RUSAL enjoyed close business ties with Glencore, a global commodities brokerage firm. Though primarily known for his industrial ventures, Deripaska maintained close ties to the Kremlin and benefited from Russia's paramilitary operations abroad, including those linked to Wagner's predecessor the Moran Security Group and competitor Redut.

Mikhail Khodorkovsky—Former CEO of Yukos Oil Company and Founder of Open Russia

Once Russia's richest man, Khodorkovsky became a vocal critic of Putin after his arrest and the dismantling of Yukos. He founded Open Russia, a pro-democracy organization, and from exile financed investigative outlets that exposed the ties between Putin's inner circle and paramilitary operations. He became a leading antagonist of Yevgeny Prigozhin after Wagner was implicated in the killing of three journalists from one of those outlets.

Konstantin Malofeev—Chairman of Marshall Capital and Founder of Tsargrad TV

A well-connected pro-monarchist businessman, Malofeev founded Tsargrad TV, a media group promoting ultranationalist and extreme Christian

Orthodox views. Malofeev financed pro-Russian ultranationalist movements in Ukraine and reportedly supported Igor "Strelkov" Girkin and Alexander Borodai's paramilitary activities in Donbas, aligning with his vision of restoring the Russian empire.

Gennady Timchenko—Volga Group Chief and Stroytransgaz Stakeholder

An associate of Putin since the 1990s, Timchenko is one of the world's top business leaders in the energy and commodities trade. His controlling stakes in Volga Group, an investment vehicle for heavy industry and logistics, and the energy-engineering company Stroytransgaz made him one of the leading investors in the Syrian energy-infrastructure projects guarded by Wagner- and Redut-linked paramilitary forces.

St. Petersburg Hustlers, Businessmen, and Political Players

Alexander Beglov—Governor of St. Petersburg

Once closely tied to Yevgeny Prigozhin, who supported his electoral campaign, Beglov later fell out with Prigozhin in a public feud. The dispute revolved around accusations of corruption and the treatment of the Wagner Group dead, as well as Beglov's alleged obstruction of Prigozhin's business ventures in St. Petersburg.

Vladimir Kumarin—Head of the Tambov Mafia

A notorious crime boss and leader of the Tambov mafia, Kumarin was a powerful figure in St. Petersburg's criminal underworld during the 1990s. He was involved in smuggling and racketeering operations, and had connections with prominent business and political figures, including patrons of Yevgeny Prigozhin.

Mikhail "Misha" Mirilashvili—Russian-Israeli Businessman

A former business partner of Yevgeny Prigozhin, Mirilashvili invested in Prigozhin's restaurants, casinos, and grocery businesses. Mirilashvili's close ties with St. Petersburg mayor Anatoly Sobchak gave Prigozhin his entrée to Putin's circle.

Anatoly Sobchak—Former Mayor of St. Petersburg

A prominent political figure during Russia's post-Soviet transition, Sobchak was the first mayor of St. Petersburg and a mentor to both Vladimir

Putin and Dmitry Medvedev. He was a regular at Yevgeny Prigozhin's Old Customs House eatery, where he mingled with the rising political elite, including Putin, whom he helped introduce to influential circles.

Roman Tsepov—Russian Businessman and Chief of Baltik-Eskort

A prominent figure in St. Petersburg's underworld, Tsepov provided personal-security services to Putin in the 1990s and founded the influential private-security company Baltik-Eskort. Tsepov was a key broker between political elites and organized crime, forging connections that made him a powerful figure in the city. He befriended Yevgeny Prigozhin during this time, but his rise ended abruptly with his mysterious death by poisoning in 2004.

Security State Elites, Siloviki, and Ultranationalist Agents Provocateurs

Vladimir Alekseyev—First Deputy Chief of the GRU Military Intelligence Service

As the leading overseer of military-intelligence operations and the top manager of Russian expeditionary-force operations, Alekseyev coordinated the deployment of paramilitaries like Redut and Wagner Group operations in Ukraine and Syria.

Alexander Borodai—Former Prime Minister of the Donetsk People's Republic

A Russian political figure and close associate of Igor Girkin, Borodai served as the first prime minister of the self-proclaimed Donetsk People's Republic during the early stages of the conflict in Ukraine. He played a key role in coordinating Russian-backed separatist efforts in eastern Ukraine and had ties to Russian paramilitary groups, including Wagner.

Dmitry Bulgakov—Deputy Defense Minister and Chief of Military Logistics

As a high-ranking defense ministry official, Bulgakov oversaw Russia's military logistics. A top patron of Yevgeny Prigozhin, Bulgakov played a role in supporting Wagner's operations through logistical support, particularly in Ukraine and Syria, before he was ultimately sacked for mismanagement of logistics during Russia's 2022 invasion of Ukraine.

Alexander Dugin—Russian Philosopher and Ultranationalist Ideologue

Known for his ultranationalist and Eurasianist ideologies, Dugin, particularly in his book *Foundations of Geopolitics*, resonated with military elites and nationalist movements. His ideas influenced paramilitary and separatist efforts, earning him the sobriquet "Putin's Brain." Dugin maintained close ties to figures in the Russian military and intelligence communities, and he was a vocal champion of the Wagner Group.

Alexey Dyumin—GRU Deputy Chief and Governor of Tula

Putin's former bodyguard Dyumin served in the presidential protective service and was second in charge of the GRU military-intelligence wing from 2014 until his promotion to regional governor of Tula in 2016. Considered a potential Putin successor and an influential figure in Yevgeny Prigozhin's rise, Dyumin served as top commander of Russia's special forces, spearheading the invasion of Crimea and the deployment of Russian paramilitary detachments to Ukraine in 2014.

Valery Gerasimov—Chief of the General Staff of the Russian Armed Forces

Gerasimov was Russia's top military officer, its leader of military operations, and an influential figure in the evolution of Russia's irregular-warfare strategy, including the deployment of Wagner Group mercenaries and other expeditionary paramilitaries to expand the Kremlin's influence abroad. Accused of war crimes in Ukraine, Gerasimov was one of the few to survive a defense ministry purge after the mutiny.

Igor "Strelkov" Girkin—Former FSB Officer and Ultranationalist

A leading figure in the 2014 Russian-separatist movements in Donbas, Girkin played a central role in the early stages of the conflict. Despite his nationalist views, he became a vocal critic of Yevgeny Prigozhin and Wagner, denouncing their tactics and influence on Russia's military operations.

Konstantin Mirzayants—Executive Director of Redut

Reportedly linked to Moscow's Podolskaya mafia, Mirzayants served as deputy to airborne intelligence chief Pavel Popovskikh and was an active member of the Union of Paratroopers. As the executive director of Redut, a private-military company and competitor to Wagner, he played a significant role in securing Russian interests abroad, particularly in conflict zones like Syria and Ukraine, often working with Russian intelligence and energy companies.

Pavel Popovskikh—Former Head of the VDV Airborne 45th Guards Spetsnaz Reconnaissance Brigade

An influential and well-connected paratrooper colonel and intelligence chief whose ideas about covert military doctrine and deception operations shaped the early development of Russia's private-military industry, Popovskikh was a leader of the Union of Paratroopers, a veterans' organization that was a major feeder for private-military company formations, including Wagner competitor Redut.

Sergey Rudskoy—Chief of the Main Operations Directorate of the Russian General Staff

A senior Russian military officer, Rudskoy played a crucial role in overseeing Russia's military operations, including campaigns in Syria and Ukraine. He was involved in the coordination of military strategies and paramilitary efforts, including those linked to Wagner Group activities abroad.

Sergey Shoigu—Russian Minister of Defense (2012–2024)

Shoigu directed Russia's military-industrial complex and oversaw defense agencies that contracted with Yevgeny Prigozhin and supported Wagner Group deployments. He clashed with Prigozhin regularly before the 2023 mutiny that led to Wagner's implosion. Accused of war crimes in Ukraine, Shoigu resigned amid a sweeping purge of the defense ministry a year after the mercenary uprising.

Viktor Zolotov—Director of the Russian National Guard (Rosgvardia)

A former bodyguard to Vladimir Putin, Zolotov befriended both Putin and Yevgeny Prigozhin in the 1990s in St. Petersburg. He later rose to head Rosgvardia, a powerful internal-security force, playing a role in securing Russia's domestic control and later inheriting remnants of the Wagner Group.

The Wagner Group, Concord Network, and Affiliates

Andrey "Tramp" Bogatov—Wagner Field Commander

A former Moran Security Group mercenary and senior field commander in Wagner, Bogatov played a key role in operations in Libya, Syria, and Ukraine.

Pyotr Bychkov—Internet Research Agency and Back-Office Lead for Project Lakhta

The former public-relations manager for the governor of Pskov and the top manager of Yevgeny Prigozhin's Internet Research Agency, Bychkov supported Russia's disinformation propaganda machine abroad, including the massive online influence campaign aimed at disrupting the 2016 US presidential election that catapulted Donald Trump into the White House.

Valery Chekalov—Wagner Group Logistics Chief

A Russian Navy veteran, Chekalov was an employee of Prigozhin's Concord Consulting and Management company, and was the Wagner Group's logistics chief. He was the mastermind behind the web of front companies that facilitated Wagner's covert operations, including the transport of military equipment to Ukraine, Africa, and the Middle East, until his death in 2023.

Oleg Erokhin—Former Director of Concord Front Company Evro Polis

A veteran *spetsnaz* officer and irregular-warfare mercenary, Erokhin was a member of the Concord network security team and was a front man for Evro Polis, a holding company linked to multiple Wagner Group operations in the Middle East and elsewhere.

Alexander "Ratibor" Kuznetsov—Wagner Commander

Kuznetsov led Wagner's 1st Assault Detachment in several high-profile operations in Ukraine, Libya, Sudan, and Syria. Known for his battlefield leadership, he played a major role in Wagner's combat strategy and execution in conflict zones.

Alexey Milchakov—Commander of Sabotage Assault Reconnaissance Group "Rusich"

A St. Petersburg native and veteran of Russian special forces, Milchakov was the commander of the Sabotage Assault Reconnaissance Group Rusich, a neo-Nazi paramilitary unit that operated in coordination with the Wagner Group. Known for his extreme ultranationalist views, Milchakov and Rusich were implicated in war crimes in Ukraine and Syria, including the torture and killing of prisoners.

Yan "Slavyan" Petrovsky—Deputy Commander of Sabotage Assault Reconnaissance Group "Rusich"

A Russian-Norwegian citizen and deputy commander of the neo-Nazi paramilitary unit Rusich, Petrovsky was involved in combat operations alongside Wagner forces in Ukraine and Syria. He is known for his far-right extremist views and connections to the Nordic Resistance Movement. Petrovsky has been implicated in war crimes alongside Rusich.

Mikhail Potepkin—Regional Director of Wagner Front Company M-Invest

A former Internet Research Agency employee, Potepkin was a leading stakeholder in M-Invest, a Wagner-linked front company, and its subsidiary Meroe Gold, the primary conduit for Wagner's gold-mining operations in Sudan.

Yevgeny Prigozhin—Founder of Wagner Group (2014–2023)

Known as "Putin's Chef," Prigozhin was an ex-convict turned caterer and serial entrepreneur. Leveraging his ties to Putin's inner circle, Prigozhin financed the Internet Research Agency and led the Wagner Group's paramilitary network in Ukraine, Africa, and the Middle East.

Maxim Shugaley—Russian Political Consultant and Operative

A political consultant linked to Yevgeny Prigozhin, Shugaley was involved in Wagner-affiliated political operations across Africa and the Middle East. He was arrested in Libya in 2019 for alleged election interference while working to support Saif al-Islam Qaddafi's political comeback. Shugaley's work extended to influence operations across various countries on behalf of Russian interests.

Dmitry Sytii—Founder of Wagner Front Company Lobaye Invest

A polyglot, Sytii started out as an employee of the Internet Research Agency, quickly earning trust as a translator after joining several advance-scouting team trips for the Wagner Group to the Central African Republic. As a top stakeholder in Lobaye Invest, Sytii played a leading role in shaping Wagner's gold- and diamond-mining enterprises and other businesses.

Leonid Teyf—Former Deputy Director of Voentorg

A leading defense ministry official and critical contact for Yevgeny Prigozhin, Teyf managed the awarding of defense procurement and contract awards to Prigozhin's Concord network that financed Wagner's operations. The FBI arrested Teyf in 2018 amid a sweeping investigation into Russian interference in the 2016 elections, charging him with bribery and other offenses in an unrelated case and ultimately deporting him from the United States after he served time in prison.

Andrey "Gray-Hair" Troshev—Wagner Group Executive Director

A veteran officer who fought in the Soviet War in Afghanistan and a former rapid-response team leader for a ministry of internal affairs police unit, Troshev was the top administrator for Wagner, managing everything from recruitment to internal security. After the mutiny, Putin selected Troshev to manage recruitment and mobilization of paramilitary forces in coordination with Wagner competitor Redut.

Dmitry "Wagner" Utkin—Lead Wagner Group Field Commander (2014–2023)

Also known as "the Ninth," Utkin was a seasoned special forces veteran with several tours in Chechnya under his belt before entering the mercenary business and cofounding the Wagner Group. A founding member of the paramilitary and a fan of Hitler who was obsessed with Nazi lore and regalia, Utkin adopted the call sign "Wagner" between deployments as a mercenary commander in Syria and Ukraine.

Anton "Lotus" Yelizarov—Elite Airborne Paratrooper and Former Commander of the GRU Intelligence Wing's 10th Separate Special Purpose Brigade

Yelizarov led Wagner operations in Syria, Libya, and the Central African Republic, where he served as base commander in Bambari, near where three Russian journalists were killed. In Ukraine, Yelizarov served as commander of the Wagner Group's Seventh Assault Detachment, playing an instrumental role in capturing Soledar and Bakhmut during the first half of 2023.

IN UKRAINE

Petro Poroshenko—Former President of Ukraine (2014–2019)

Poroshenko opposed Russian paramilitary forces, including Wagner, during the early years of the Donbas conflict. His administration struck a deal with Putin to halt Russian support for paramilitary groups like Wagner, but the ceasefire agreements repeatedly fell apart.

Viktor Yanukovych—Former President of Ukraine (2010–2014)

Ousted after the Euromaidan protests, Yanukovych fled to Russia, where he maintained close ties to the Kremlin. Although he was not directly linked to Wagner, his ouster marked a turning point in Russia's shift toward using irregular and paramilitary strategies to influence Ukraine.

Volodymyr Zelensky—President of Ukraine

A onetime comedian and television and film producer, Zelensky was elected in 2019 amid a wave of disenchantment with Ukraine's corrupt political leadership and frustration over Kyiv's stalled bid to join the EU. He spearheaded the country's defense in the face of Russia's February 2022 invasion, actively pushing for Prigozhin and Wagner leaders to be tried for war crimes.

INVESTIGATORS AND CITIZEN SLEUTHS

Eliot Higgins—Founder of Bellingcat

A self-taught internet sleuth, Higgins played a critical role in the investigation of the July 2014 destruction of Malaysian Airlines flight MH17, exposing the chain of command that supported Russian paramilitary operations in Donbas, including Wagner's handlers. Along with Bellingcat researchers Aric Toler and Christo Grozev, Higgins conducted several penetrating investigations into the connections among Wagner operatives, Yevgeny Prigozhin, and the Kremlin.

Denis Korotkov—Investigative Journalist

A former cop turned journalist, Korotkov was one of the first to break the news about the Wagner Group's exploits in Syria and Ukraine while writing for the St. Petersburg–based online news outlet *Fontanka*. Korotkov received death threats in response to his coverage of Prigozhin's business dealings for *Novaya Gazeta* and later went to work for the Dossier Centre.

Omer Meisel—FBI Special Agent, Office of the Special Counsel

A veteran FBI agent, Meisel played a critical role in the FBI's investigations into Russian interference in the 2016 US elections, including the role of Yevgeny Prigozhin's Internet Research Agency.

Kirill Mikhailov—Russian Defense Analyst at the Conflict Intelligence Team

Cofounder in 2014 of the Conflict Intelligence Team, an independent research organization focused on Russian military affairs, Mikhailov was the first to link Wagner fighters near Palmyra, Syria, to the infamous sledgehammer execution video, playing a critical role in exposing Russian paramilitary activities abroad.

Vladimir Osechkin—Founder of Russian Prisoners' Rights Site Gulagu.net

An ex-convict turned prisoners' rights advocate, Osechkin founded the online platform Gulagu.net, which focuses on exposing abuses in Russia's sprawling prison system and security-agency misconduct. Exiled in France, Osechkin has been a vocal critic of the Russian government and the Wagner Group, and his efforts to aid Wagner defectors have provoked controversy.

Jeannie Rhee—US Federal Prosecutor, Office of the Special Counsel

A top member of former FBI director Robert Mueller's investigation team and seasoned attorney, Rhee led "Team R" and the prosecution against Yevgeny Prigozhin's Internet Research Agency, investigating Russian interference in the 2016 US presidential election.

Andrew Weissman—US Federal Prosecutor, Office of the Special Counsel

A leading member of the Mueller investigation team and a veteran prosecutor, Weissman led "Team 600," which was tasked with investigating allegations that Donald Trump obstructed justice. Weissman worked with Rhee and other members of Team R as they traced Yevgeny Prigozhin's involvement in online influence campaigns and in interference in the 2016 US presidential election.

IN THE MIDDLE EAST AND AFRICA

Bashar al-Assad—President of Syria

A loyal regional ally of Putin in the Middle East and a top recipient of Russian security assistance, al-Assad authorized a brutal crackdown on democratic uprisings during the Arab Spring that sparked a civil war, paving the way for the deployment of Wagner mercenaries in exchange for access to mineral resources.

Omar al-Bashir—Former President of Sudan

A longtime client of the Kremlin and accused war criminal, al-Bashir relied heavily on Russia for security assistance to protect his authoritarian regime, offering the Wagner Group access to Sudan's gold resources in exchange for military support before his ousting in 2019.

Mohammed "Hemedti" Dagalo—Leader of the Rapid Support Forces (RSF) in Sudan

A crafty paramilitary chieftain who gained influence during the Sudanese government's genocidal campaign in Darfur, Dagalo collaborated closely with Wagner forces in exploiting Sudan's natural resources, particularly gold, and financing paramilitary operations in Africa.

Saif al-Islam Qaddafi—Son of Former Libyan Leader Muammar Qaddafi

The younger Qaddafi engaged with Wagner-affiliated political consultants, such as Maxim Shugaley, to shape his political comeback in Libya following the fall of his father's regime in the aftermath of the Arab Spring.

Khalifa Haftar—Libyan Warlord and Leader of the Libyan National Army

A Soviet-educated Libyan military officer and onetime right-hand man of dictator Muammar Qaddafi turned CIA asset, Haftar received backing from the Kremlin and relied on Wagner forces in his military campaign to control Libya, granting Russia access to the country's mineral resources.

George Haswani—Syrian Businessman and Owner of HESCO

Haswani acted as an intermediary between the Assad regime and Russian companies, including Gennady Timchenko's Stroytransgaz. He facilitated energy and infrastructure deals in Syria that relied heavily on protection from the Wagner Group, and he worked Russian military forces to secure oil and gas assets during the civil war.

Fayez al-Sarraj—Former Prime Minister of the Government of National Accord (GNA), Libya

Al-Sarraj led the UN-recognized government in Libya during the Tripoli offensive, defending against Khalifa Haftar's Libyan National Army (LNA), which was supported by Wagner Group forces. Al-Sarraj worked to secure international support amid the escalating conflict.

Faustin Archange-Touadéra—President of the Central African Republic

A mathematics professor turned strongman politician, Touadéra served as prime minister before the Central African Republic sank into a chaotic civil war in 2012 that cleaved the country between Muslim and Christian fighting factions. Touadéra signed a military-cooperation agreement in 2018 that seeded the Wagner Group's expansion of operations across the country.

PROLOGUE

On June 30, 2017, a retired American Marine, blogging as "Josh," posted a two-minute video on Funker530.com, a site popular with military veterans. The video, titled "Breaking: Terrifying Footage of Russians Torturing Prisoner with Sledgehammer," began with a warning: "THIS VIDEO CONTAINS SCENES OF GRAPHIC VIOLENCE THAT MAY NOT BE SUITABLE FOR SOME AUDIENCES. VIEWER DISCRETION IS ADVISED."[1]

The footage, shot on a mobile phone in what appeared to be a desert, showed a bloodied man in a striped shirt and track pants writhing on the ground. A masked man in military fatigues repeatedly struck his arm with a sledgehammer. Nearby, another man's severed head lay on the ground. The scene was brutal. Rivulets of blood and urine stained the soil near a heap of what looked like twisted corrugated sheet metal. Two men with assault rifles slung casually over their shoulders filmed the ordeal with their phones, capturing the screams of the victim as the hammer struck again and again. Hard-rock music played in the background, with lyrics in Russian: "I am a Russian *spetsnaz*. I don't give a fuck. With a rifle in hand, I am coming to kill."

Off-camera, several men laughed and joked in Russian. One who stepped briefly into the frame wore a patch featuring the evil clown face of Joker, the villain from *Batman*, with the words "I'm just going to hurt you very, very badly." Then a short man in a green uniform with a closely shaved head who was wearing a black-and-white-checked Middle Eastern kaffiyeh scarf stepped in closer while two others cursed and laughed maniacally. "Go fuck yourself!" one shouted. The screen went black.

The video had no obvious identifiers, making it unclear when and where it was shot or how Funker530.com had obtained it. Despite the mystery, the gory clip quickly went viral on Reddit and Twitter, sparking horror and a rush to identify the perpetrators. Most who tried failed. But a Russian blogger in Kyiv, Kirill Mikhailov, suspected that the assailants were members of the Wagner Group, a Kremlin-backed mercenary outfit formed with the tacit support of Vladimir Putin amid Russia's annexation of Crimea in 2014.[2]

Known for their cruelty, Wagner's commandos had vaulted from obscurity to global attention under the energetic leadership of Yevgeny Prigozhin, an ex-convict turned hotdog salesman and serial entrepreneur. Tied to the Kremlin on a long tether, Prigozhin was a central player in Russia's unconventional warfare strategy.

By 2017, when the video cropped up, Prigozhin was also rapidly on his way to becoming one of the most sanctioned men in the world. He had earned that dubious distinction after reinventing himself as a caterer and restaurateur and serving for more than two decades as chief maître d' to the Kremlin and to Russia's rich and powerful. His connections to Putin and his inner circle, dating back to their days in St. Petersburg in the 1990s, gave Prigozhin ready access to the titans of Russian industry who rebuilt the country after the collapse of the Soviet Union. Mafia ties and government patronage catapulted him into the country's elite social stratosphere.

Prigozhin boasted of hosting state dinners for kings, queens, and prime ministers. He catered birthday celebrations and inauguration dinners for Putin and former Russian president Dmitry Medvedev. Most notably, former US president George Bush and his wife, Laura, dined several times at Prigozhin's high-end St. Petersburg eateries. Prigozhin's career encompassed grocery retail, casinos, hotels, luxury dining, catering services (earning him the sobriquet "Putin's Chef"), real estate development, construction, and eventually defense contracting.

He became the Kremlin's top pitchman for deploying irregular paramilitary forces worldwide. With covert support from Russian intelligence agencies, Prigozhin provided arms and mercenaries to dictators in exchange for profits from oil, gold, diamonds, timber, and other resources. Wagner's military operations spanned three continents, stretching from Europe to the Middle East and Africa, making Prigozhin's mercenary army a force to be reckoned with in conflicts around the world.

Reviled by many elites in the West, he was larger than life and beloved by the Russian man in the street. Many who followed his lead into battle had criminal backgrounds. They saw in Prigozhin and the Wagner Group a chance at redemption, a path to become heroes and make Russia great again.

His propaganda exploits and experiments in media manipulation targeted dozens of countries, including the United States. Prigozhin's Internet Research Agency, operating on the fringes of Russia's hybrid warfare, ignited a firestorm in Silicon Valley. The disinformation machine he built exposed the Achilles' heel of tech giants such as Facebook and Twitter, forcing them into an uncomfortable reckoning over unchecked platforms and the viral spread of lies.

Prigozhin's operatives masqueraded as journalists, curious tourists, and social media activists, worming their way into the psyche of millions of Americans and Europeans who were already suspicious of their own governments but would—click after click on Twitter and Facebook—become even more suspicious of one another. All the while, Putin denied knowing what Prigozhin was up to, saying that the Kremlin was not involved in the Wagner Group's operations.

From its inception, the Wagner Group was designed to insulate the Kremlin from direct responsibility for its actions. Plausible deniability was the sine qua non of the Wagner's operations, allowing Russia to project power covertly while officially maintaining a distance from the paramilitary's nefarious activities. For the better part of a decade, Prigozhin would—with the Kremlin's express consent—deploy the Wagner Group to great effect, smashing through limits imposed on Russia and its allies by international sanctions. Wagner operations would succeed in expanding the market for Russian arms exports and military know-how in more than a half dozen countries. The Wagner Group's role was not merely auxiliary but an integral instrument in the construction of Russia's strategy for reshaping the world order.

The Wagner Group's covert operations, whether fragmentary tall tales or outright missions, were legendary. Under the energetic leadership of the paramilitary's titular lead field commander, Dmitry "Wagner" Utkin, they did not just hit targets; they also scrambled the pieces on the chessboard of geopolitical competition between Russia and the West. From providing equipment and intelligence to boot-camp–style training, they turned motley militias and hollowed-out armies into formidable forces that were loyal to the autocrats whom Putin sought to cultivate in the Middle East and Africa. Their logistical prowess kept proxy fighters supplied and ready while their infrastructure protection locked down vital assets. They were essential to Putin's strategy of conducting war on the cheap while countering the influence of the United States and its NATO allies.

The mercenaries in Prigozhin's employ extended the Wagner Group's reach from Ukraine and Syria to the Central African Republic, to Sudan, and eventually snaking their way to Libya and Mali. And when years later, in early 2022, Russian forces invaded Ukraine and things got dicey, the Wagner Group would emerge as the backstop, the safety net that ensured the Kremlin could pursue its aims, no matter the odds. These maneuvers were key to Russia's strategy for managing escalation, keeping adversaries guessing, and keeping allies on edge. Prigozhin's mercenaries were critical players in a game of brinkmanship, where Wagner's actions—or the fear of them—played a crucial role in shaping Russia's global standing.

Over the eight years leading up to Russia's massive incursion into Ukraine, Wagner operations had succeeded in expanding the market for Russian arms exports and military know-how. In that span, Prigozhin had built the paramilitary into an advertisement for a more muscular Russia, one determined to rewrite the rules of the international order to its advantage. The men who worked for him embraced with gusto the Wagner Group's informal marketing motto: "Death is our business and business is good." Prigozhin was the Kremlin's number-one pitchman for the Russian way of war.

A few months before Wagner's first sledgehammer video made its splash in 2017, the US Treasury Department sanctioned Prigozhin for his role in constructing military bases near Russia's western border with Ukraine. Prigozhin had by then already rocketed to the top of the FBI's list of suspects behind a wide-ranging online influence campaign aimed at disrupting the 2016 US presidential elections, damaging the candidacy of the former US secretary of state Hillary Clinton and propelling Donald Trump to the White House. Meanwhile, authorities in Kyiv had named Utkin, a former paratrooper, as the suspect in the downing of a Ukrainian military transport plane in the summer of 2014 that killed all forty-nine high-ranking Ukrainian officers who were on board.

That was about the time when Kirill Mikhailov, the Russian blogger, first picked up the Wagner Group's digital trail. Mikhailov was one of a small group of independent Russian researchers at the Conflict Intelligence Team, an online investigative outlet that specializes in sifting through the wide expanse of the internet to unearth the hidden secrets of Russia's military operations. Before the snuff film popped up in his social media feeds, Mikhailov had spent several bleary-eyed nights mapping the Wagner Group's movements around the ancient Syrian city of Palmyra, where fierce battles had raged for almost two years between fighters allied with the terrorist group Islamic State of Iraq and al Sham (ISIS) and government forces loyal to the country's strongman president, Bashar al-Assad.

In a message posted on Facebook a few hours after plunging headlong into an investigation into the origins of the video, Mikhailov had worked out roughly where the footage was shot. The revelation came after he had analyzed another video that had surfaced on the Telegram social media app two weeks earlier showing a Wagner Group fighter carrying a 1970s-era AK-74 rifle as he inspected the bodies of several dead Syrians in a rocky landscape.

"Hi everyone, from Wagner ☺," the cheeky caption on the Telegram video read.

Mikhailov noticed that one of the Russian-speaking men in the sledge-hammer video was also carrying an old AK-74 rifle. Another had an RPK-74 machine gun: a Soviet-era weapon that suggested that it came from the kind of old surplus stock typically provided to Wagner forces in Syria.[3]

Analysis of satellite imagery and press accounts of ISIS battles to control Syria's energy resources later revealed the execution spot as a natural-gas facility located a short distance from Palmyra, where Wagner Group forces had dug in. These were the first clues that a hidden profit motive was likely at work, one that extended far beyond Prigozhin's sprawling network of enterprises. But the victim's identity, how he was captured, and the full extent of Wagner's operations in this remote part of Syria would remain a mystery for another two years. Even more time would pass before the identities of the assailants would be revealed.

The sledgehammer video marked a watershed moment for the Wagner Group, transforming it from a battlefield rumor to an internationally recognized brand and symbol of Russian power. The clip's viral spread on VKontakte, Russia's version of Facebook, led to the creation of memes, T-shirts, and other merchandise featuring an image of a hammer-wielding soldier taking a swing at a horned black demon lying prone on the ground. The sledgehammer, once an icon of Soviet industry, was reborn as a badge of Russia's resurgence.

Until then, Wagner had been an open secret, an entity with no official status or address. It enriched Prigozhin, the Kremlin, and Putin's inner circle through a web of shell companies. Russia's use of irregular paramilitary forces blurred the line between state and private actors. The Kremlin's strategy of deploying irregular paramilitary forces under the guise of private-military companies (PMCs) exploited a vulnerability in international law. The international community has struggled to address the legal implications of the blurred line between state and private actors in conflict.

The law is even less clear about the arm's-length arrangements between state-run companies and ostensibly private entities that profit from the plunder and pillage of proxy wars. Prigozhin's paramilitary force thrived in this legal gray zone, enabling Russia's smooth transition from a member in good standing in the international community to a rogue-state champion of autocracy.

Wagner's psychological impact extended beyond the battlefield. The group's violence, amplified through media and propaganda, instilled fear in Russia's adversaries, enhancing the Kremlin's influence. This broader impact was central to Russia's strategy, projecting power without direct confrontation.

Wagner's brutality sparked outrage, inspiring a new generation of detectives who scoured social media to uncover Prigozhin's rise and the mercenary empire he had built. The viral sledgehammer video exemplified modern warfare, where battles unfolded both on the ground and online.

Indeed, Wagner's emergence mirrored the internet's transformation from a force for good to a battleground where tech giants such as Facebook and Twitter vied for market shares while Russia, China, and the United States competed to shape the rules of global governance in the digital sphere. Prigozhin's rapid ascent was intertwined with the internet's evolution as his network exploited digital platforms for both propaganda and profit.

His downfall, however, was hastened by journalists, investigators, and dissidents who sought to expose the Kremlin's crimes. Part of a growing movement in open-source intelligence (OSINT), these sleuths used public information to challenge official narratives and hold powerful actors accountable.

This was the paradox of Prigozhin's path to infamy. Even as he helped Russia try to win back its Great Power status, Prigozhin left a trail of destruction in his wake that invited ever-greater scrutiny. The higher he flew toward the sun, the more visible were the contrails of his ruinous band of mercenaries. Eventually, the scale of the atrocities attributed to the Wagner Group drew not only sanctions from the United States and Europe but also strong admonitions from the United Nations.

Yet Prigozhin and Putin were not deterred from their quixotic crusade to reshape the global balance of power. Prigozhin skillfully marketed Wagner, turning it into a brand as recognizable as Stolichnaya is to vodka drinkers. Just as Stolichnaya conjures images of Russia and its hard-drinking culture, Wagner's emblem—a skull in crosshairs—became infamous, with the sledgehammer as its unmistakable symbol.

But in the summer of 2017, when the gruesome video gained wide attention, few could convincingly explain how Prigozhin had come to oversee a clandestine army of mercenaries. How and why did this happen? What on Earth had compelled the masked men to whip out their phones to record their ritual torture of an unarmed man on camera and then send it out into the wide expanse of the internet for all the world to see? How did Russia—a nuclear-armed nation with a top-ranked military—come to rely on the personal army of a mafia-connected billionaire convict with no apparent military experience to advance the Kremlin's strategic aims?

This book is an effort to answer those questions and more. It charts the rise of Prigozhin and the Wagner Group, tracing their origins from Russia's reentry into the global economy after the Soviet Union's collapse to the group's implosion in 2023. Along the way, the narrative touches on the lives of the intrepid journalists, activists, information brokers, dissidents, and detectives who sought to expose the hidden tentacles of Russia's unconventional warfare tactics and in so doing exposed the Wagner Group enterprise.

The chronicle that follows is an attempt to contextualize and explain how the merger of interests among Kremlin-connected power brokers, the castoffs of Russia's war machine, and the foot soldiers of the country's shadow economy forged a private army into a global juggernaut that for a moment in the summer of 2023 brought Putin's tyrannical regime to a standstill. Putin's reinvention of Russian power and his push for a new balance where multiple nations, including Russia, could pursue their interests unchecked by the constraints of international law was more than just a strategic pivot; it was a theatrical production with Prigozhin as its unsmiling stage manager. Or, at least, that is how Prigozhin seemed to imagine himself.

But he was just one name in a long line of dramatis personae in the epic saga of the fall, rise, fall, and rise again of Russia as a Great Power. Starting with the 1917 Bolshevik revolution, which unseated Russia's last tsar, the country's most ambitious political visionaries had always relied on useful brigands to stake Moscow's claims through covert and overt means far beyond the state's official borders. In the years before and during World War II, the acts of that play mostly centered on Europe.

During the Cold War, a succession of autocratic Kremlin leaders secretly deployed elite *spetsnaz* officers to back proxy forces in the Middle East, Africa, and Latin America. After the Soviet collapse, some of the earliest hints of the Kremlin's reinvestment in proxy-warfare strategies emerged in the 1990s in the breakaway territories that had once formed part of the Soviet empire.

Those misadventures seeded the careers of a generation of professional soldiers, spies, provocateurs, and entrepreneurs—many of whom, by 2014, filled the ranks of the Wagner Group. Putin's dramatic achievement is that he managed to harness the egos and avarice of many of them in the service of reclaiming Russia's place on the world stage. At the same time, it was a lucrative business for all sides.

Like Putin, Prigozhin and Wagner's field marshal, Dmitry Utkin, represented a slice of Russians who saw themselves as the generational architects of an imperial revival. They envisioned the Wagner forces as modern-day Valkyries, guiding Russia's fate through their militaristic ambitions. This vision crystallized with Russia's full-scale invasion of Ukraine on February 24, 2022, a campaign they believed would secure their place in history.

The massive Russian incursion brought the Wagner Group spectacularly out of the shadows, thrusting Prigozhin, Utkin, and their mercenary commandos into the klieg-light glare of a world stunned by the audacity of Putin's war of aggression. The Wagner Group became notorious the world over for being the shock troops of Russia's invading forces in Ukraine, for recruiting hardened convicts from penal colonies to plunder cities and villages already scarred by years of conflict, and for the devastating human toll that the paramilitary left in its wake. And it was over Ukraine that the marriage of convenience between the former KGB officer and the ex-convict would eventually end in betrayal on both sides with an abortive mutiny and fiery plane crash near Moscow. But we will get to that part of the story later.

Fittingly, toward the end of the line, Prigozhin's life shrank into a procession of ugly news headlines and internet memes that ping-ponged across social media sites after Russian security services raided his luxurious St. Petersburg estate as Prigozhin ordered thousands of his Wagner mercenaries to launch an armed "March for Justice" on Moscow on June 23, 2023. His erasure from public view began one night later, after he abruptly ended what he called his "master class" in how Russia's wars should be fought and won.

Broadcast after the fact via state media, the house search was a carefully crafted bit of theater designed to put a final punctuation point on Prigozhin's ignominy. The tableau inside the house unveiled an intimate portrait of a man who for a decade loomed large in the shadows of Russia's transformation. His role in Putin's epic quest to smash through geopolitical norms and redefine modern warfare was palpable in every corner of Prigozhin's opulent lair.

Across the checkerboard marble floors in the entryway, the grandeur shown on camera was immediately striking. Up the winding staircase, past a stuffed alligator in the hall—a macabre trophy symbolizing his predatory instincts— and inside the wood-paneled billiard room stood the emblem that said it all: a gigantic, man-sized sledgehammer with the words "In case of important negotiations" in bold black letters stamped on its silver-colored head.

This was not just decor but a statement of ethos. The sledgehammer, a blunt instrument of force, symbolized Prigozhin's chaotic and brutal approach to both business and conflict. His Wagner Group, notorious for its ruthlessness and lack of discipline, had become a dangerous tool in Putin's arsenal, executing the Kremlin's foreign policy with violence and recklessness. Through it, Putin was able to create a viable strategy for challenging the West.

In another corner of Prigozhin's billiard room was a headless manikin dressed in a formal black tuxedo jacket and crisp white collar bedecked with dozens of glittering medals. Putin had personally awarded several of them, including the Gold Star medal that designated Prigozhin a "Hero of Russia"— the highest honor in the country for valor—and that Putin reportedly pinned on Prigozhin's chest in a June 2022 ceremony after the Wagner Group had broken through Ukrainian defense lines in the eastern region of Donbas.

In the end, though, the glittering notoriety he had achieved was also the force behind Prigozhin's downfall. Just as the sledgehammer struck without mercy, so too did fate—delivering a violent and uncompromising end that mirrored the disorderly legacy he had built.

PART ONE

ORIGINS

CHAPTER 1

BANDIT CITY

They called him Zhenya when he was a boy. He was sharp-tongued and fast with his fists. For a moment, Yevgeny Prigozhin was convinced he was a born champion, fated for gold medals. The campus at Leningrad Sports Boarding School No. 62, where he enrolled at the age of thirteen, had everything needed for the Soviet Union's future Olympians. There were modern gyms, a huge swimming pool, and a wide expanse of land perfectly suited for cross-country ski training.

No photographs have survived from Prigozhin's youth, leaving the young man he was then shrouded in mystery. With hooded eyes, pointy ears, a receding hairline, and a gap-toothed grin, he wasn't handsome, but his long legs and thick torso made him a natural athlete, and his self-confidence seemed boundless.

He loved gliding through the birch trees in subzero temperatures on the long ski courses that stretched for miles. His stepfather, a ski instructor at the elite sports academy, taught him how to grit his teeth through frostbite and focus on the finish line. If it had not been for the injury that left Prigozhin with a limp, he might well have competed in the Olympics. He could have been a modern-day gladiator in the global contest between the Soviet Union and the United States. But athletic excellence would not be his path to the world stage.

Instead, destiny pointed him in a different direction, first to a prison cell as a petty criminal, then hustling in the emerging capitalist markets of Russia, then into the ranks of Russia's ultrarich, and ultimately to serve at the elbow of the country's most powerful man. The code for deciphering his ascent to the inner circle of Russian power lies in the epochal whirl that gripped his hometown before it fully reclaimed its imperial moniker, St. Petersburg, and after the Soviet Union collapsed into memory in 1991.

It was there that Prigozhin forged the connections that would make him, for a time, one of the Kremlin's most assiduous courtiers, the man who greased the wheels for the reconstruction of Russian power. St. Petersburg was the launchpad for Prigozhin and many others who would rise to prominence in politics, industry, the military, and Russia's shadow wars with the West. But Prigozhin's early escapades offered little hint that he would make much of a name for himself. Clues to his rise were for many years hidden away in dusty files and bureaucratic black holes, obscured by time and faded memories.

In 1979, when he was eighteen, he was hustled through the doors of the Kuibyshevksy District People's Court on robbery charges.[1] Prigozhin received a suspended sentence of two and a half years. Sent to live a two-hour drive from home in a halfway house for wayward youths in Novgorod, Prigozhin spent time working in a chemical factory.[2] Never one to be confined by rules or expectations, he slipped back to St. Petersburg, where he adopted the street name "Jacquot" and, with a couple of other street toughs, started his own gang.[3] He soon went on a crime spree that outstripped the first in brutality.

One victim was a friend from the neighborhood. The young woman was not home when Prigozhin and a friend he had met in the Novgorod penal dormitory broke into her family's house in St. Petersburg. But the girl's mother was quick to suspect it was Prigozhin because he had eyed the cache of household treasures during a friendly visit a few days beforehand. The haul included high-end crystal, vouchers, fountain pens, and an imported leather steering-wheel cover.

Other crimes followed a similar pattern, most occurring in the northwestern part of the city, often a short walk from a metro station. During another robbery, Prigozhin and his crew conned a well-to-do businessman into buying contraband jeans and then took his money at knifepoint in an alley. It was only after Prigozhin nearly killed a woman that same evening in March 1980 that the police finally interrupted his tear through the streets.

Flush with cash and in a celebratory mood, Prigozhin and his three-man crew celebrated with a bottle of champagne and a few shots of cognac at Okean, a riverside seafood restaurant and popular mafia hangout. It was around midnight when Prigozhin spotted a woman putting on an elegant coat as she prepared to leave the restaurant. A harsh spring wind was howling across the Gulf of Finland as Prigozhin and his gang scrambled to the street, crammed into a taxi, and ordered the driver to follow her.

When the woman's car finally stopped and she stepped out, Prigozhin and his friends stalked her on foot. Once they were within earshot, someone asked her for a cigarette. When she began rummaging through her purse, Prigozhin, long-legged and barrel-chested, slipped behind her and put her in a choke hold. The woman barely managed to cry for help before she blacked out.

Another of Prigozhin's friends grabbed her gold earrings. They dragged off her boots, leaving her barefoot and unconscious on a desolate side street. The commotion was loud enough to catch the attention of two nearby police officers, who chased and caught the youngest of Prigozhin's accomplices.

Years later, one of his victims would remember how young Prigozhin and his friends seemed and the haughty airs that his mother, Violetta Prigozhina, a doctor, put on when she appeared in court for Prigozhin's second sentencing, in 1981. Barely out of high school, Prigozhin was well on the way to becoming an accomplished street thug. He was about twenty when he notched his second conviction in the space of two years and was sentenced to thirteen years in prison.[4]

There are few official records of his time behind bars, but it was by all accounts a harsh awakening. A prisoner who claimed to have been a cellmate once suggested that Prigozhin became the sexual plaything of an inmate who was part of the mafia underworld. He said prisoners on their block routinely raped Prigozhin. The claim was not outlandish—sexual hazing is a rite of passage in prisons around the world—but it contradicted Prigozhin's version of history.

In Prigozhin's own recounting, he was heroic, a rebel right from the start, and his refusal to heed orders from the prison staff landed him frequent stints in solitary confinement. Long stretches of isolation turned him into a voracious reader, and at twenty-five he began to turn his life around. He became practically evangelical about the prospect of rehabilitation. He started lifting weights and enrolled in vocational-training programs, where he learned to drive a tractor and operate a lathe.

In time, he earned a foreman's spot in the part of the prison colony that was reserved for industrial production, and he picked up a side hustle selling souvenirs to visitors. He had obtained rank within the gangs that dominated prison life, but his peers viewed him as quirky and impetuous. After one memorable visit from his mother, Prigozhin became obsessed with microbiology and finding a cure for AIDS. He was always on the move, always reading, always trying to improve his chances of early release. "He was a very uncharacteristic person for a correctional facility," one cellmate recalled. "He never sat still. We tried not to do what we considered useless work. But he did it. And he always got into every mess for justice. In general, he had some kind of exorbitant sense of justice. We often told him: 'Don't get involved,' but he lost his head and rushed to sort out the mess, for which he was repeatedly punished by the administration."[5]

While Prigozhin was chafing in prison, eager to restart his life, the country outside was teetering. Three Soviet leaders—Leonid Brezhnev in 1982, Yuri Andropov in 1984, and Konstantin Chernenko in 1985—died in rapid succession. Each death raised the same questions: Who would lead the Soviet leviathan? How much longer would it last?

A year after taking power, Chernenko's successor, Mikhail Gorbachev, the charismatic son of a peasant farming family, offered up an unexpected answer to the first question. He proposed in 1986 to abolish nuclear weapons, declared the need for more transparency (glasnost), and said in a memorable speech in the rust-belt town of Tolyatti that the Soviet Union's socialist experiment could not last without radical economic and political restructuring (perestroika). In the cautious lexicon of Soviet politics, "perestroika" was a euphemism for "reform," a term too fraught with revolutionary connotations to be uttered outright. But the changes it brought were anything but subtle. Small-scale cooperative enterprises sprang up, and a freer press began exposing government failures like never before. What began as a cautious fix soon spiraled out of control, igniting political movements and a nationalist fervor that ultimately ripped the Soviet Union apart. The pace of change was head-spinning. In 1987, just one year after the call for perestroika, Gorbachev and US president Ronald Reagan signed a historic agreement that called for the reduction of US and Soviet nuclear stockpiles under the Intermediate-Range Nuclear Forces Treaty.

In 1988 Gorbachev went to New York for the UN General Assembly and dropped more bombshells, announcing that the Soviet Union planned to slash the size of its army by 500,000 and to withdraw some 50,000 troops from Ukraine and several other neighboring Soviet satellites in Eastern Europe.[6] The Cold War was over, and the world, Gorbachev declared, was moving toward global integration and a new order.

A new dawn was also just beginning for Prigozhin in 1988. That year, he caught the first of many lucky breaks when the Russian Supreme Court reduced his sentence to nine years. He was transferred to a penal colony in Komi, where he spent the remainder of his sentence working on a timber farm. For Prigozhin's trajectory, another event that year would be no less significant.

It began with a little-noticed gangland turf battle in Leningrad that sparked a realignment of Russia's criminal underworld that turned card sharks into billionaires and mafia dons into restaurateurs, catapulting Prigozhin's patrons into power. In the square of a small park near the Devyatkino train station in the northern end of the city, a group of muscled twenty-somethings loyal to the city's most energetic mobster, Vladimir Kumarin, gathered to face off against Kumarin's rival and onetime business associate Alexander Malyshev. The battle between Malyshev's gang and Kumarin's Tambov crew left one dead and dozens injured.

Providentially, the fight landed Kumarin in prison, where a courtship between Kumarin's Tambov Brotherhood and prison officials eventually blossomed into a marriage between Russia's most powerful mafia and the KGB, the Soviet Union's omnipresent secret police. Recounted in a gritty history of the city's gangster underground, *Banditsky Petersburg*, the shakeout of the criminal scene would lay the groundwork for Prigozhin to create a continent-spanning criminal enterprise, a global propaganda empire, and an infamous mercenary army. Most importantly, he was eventually able to insinuate himself into the Kremlin's halls of power.

Two pivotal events that followed in close succession after the gangster brawl in St. Petersburg turned the world that Prigozhin grew up in upside down. The first was the fall of the Berlin Wall in November 1989, which set in motion a democratic uprising that soon engulfed Eastern Europe and led to the second: the collapse of the Soviet Union. In Prague that year, students locked arms with dissidents and gave birth to the Velvet Revolution. Across Estonia, Latvia, and Lithuania, some two million people joined hands in a 420-mile "Chain of Freedom" on the fiftieth anniversary of the day that Nazi Germany signed a secret pact with the Soviet Union to carve up the lands along the Baltic Sea. Moscow's monopoly on political power started to end.

For the functionaries of the collapsing system, it was a tectonic shift that would bury some but propel others to new, more prosperous careers. Among the latter was a young KGB agent based in the East German city of Dresden who watched it all unfold in horror: Vladimir Putin.

Like Prigozhin, Putin was a native son of St. Petersburg. But where the ex-con Prigozhin was firmly embedded in St. Petersburg's underground, Putin appeared to be on the straight and narrow. He was born into a working-class family, and Putin's path to the KGB was quite unexpected. As a young boy, he had been a mediocre student with serious discipline problems. An introduction to the sporting life gradually transformed him into the kind of young man who, with time, would be groomed into an agent in the special services. He took up the Russian martial art of sambo and then judo. He binged on spy films, dreamed of becoming a dashing KGB officer, studied German and law at university, and clawed his way into the spy agency in 1975 a few years before Prigozhin tumbled into a life of crime.

Putin set his sights on a glamorous posting in Western Europe as a heroic cloak-and-dagger man. But his penchant for bucking the rules and his reputation for impulsivity put him on a secondary track that found him languishing in a local post in Leningrad, where he monitored the activities of foreigners before he eventually found his way to East Germany.[7] There were conflicting reports about Putin's brief there, but an East German Stasi agent stated that Putin had at one point served as a handler for the infamous neo-Nazi Rainer Sonntag, a far-right vigilante and agent provocateur.[8] The assignment was sometimes tedious, but life in East Germany in the mid-1980s was cushy compared to the cramped quarters that he and his wife, Lyudmila, had shared with his parents back in Russia. However, the abrupt disintegration of the political order in East Germany marked an inflection point for Putin. The fall of the Berlin Wall haunted him; when thousands of East Germans began pouring over the border into the city's free zone, Putin called Moscow for instructions.

There were none.

Out of sorts and unmoored by what he would later call the "greatest geopolitical catastrophe of the century," Putin returned to his hometown and by his own account took up work as a taxi driver before eventually taking up a new post as assistant to the rector at his alma mater, Leningrad State University, in 1990, the same year that Prigozhin was released from prison. The relationship between these two men—Putin, the judo-black-belt-turned-Russian-intelligence-agent, and Prigozhin, the would-be Olympic-ski-champion-turned-gangster-entrepreneur—threads through every chapter of Russia's post-Soviet transformation. They were the yin and yang of a political system that rewarded back-scratching and punished integrity. It was a mutually beneficial relationship until, abruptly and fatally, it wasn't. Behind the scenes and then openly, Prigozhin would facilitate Putin's challenge to four US presidents, succeeding in undermining the world order and ending America's unipolar moment.

For thirty years, both men would tell different versions of the story of how they met, and both would repeatedly lie about the depth of their relationship. Prigozhin insisted that they first met at an elegant state dinner he catered for the Japanese prime minister soon after Putin became president in 2000. Putin, for his part, barely acknowledged even knowing Prigozhin until circumstances forced him to admit publicly that their first contact dated back to the early 1990s.[9] All the known facts indicate that their paths converged soon after Prigozhin was released from prison, likely shortly after he dropped out of Leningrad Chemical and Pharmaceutical Institute, quit his part-time job as a youth sports coach, and married his wife, Lyubov, in 1991.[10] That was also when Prigozhin got into business with one of St. Petersburg's richest men, Mikhail "Misha" Mirilashvili.

Born in the Republic of Georgia, Mirilashvili was only a year older than Prigozhin but was far more sophisticated and better connected. Known on the streets as Misha "Kutaisi," Mirilashvili was described by those who knew him as a breed apart from the young bloods in the tight-knit Georgian clans that competed to control the black markets.

He earned a degree from the Leningrad Pediatric Medical Institute, but he was a mathematical genius, and gambling was his first love. He was obsessed with a trump-card game called Leningrad Preference and had a knack for counting cards. His card-sharking skills earned him clout at the tables in the illegal gambling houses run by the city's godfather of racketeering, Vladimir Feoktistov, and gave Mirilashvili a substantial leg up in the city's burgeoning gray economy.[11]

Car dealerships, shopping malls, real estate holdings, banking, oil, restaurants—Mirilashvili in the early 1990s had a stake in almost every sector of the St. Petersburg economy, including Lomonsov Port, a key byway of the city's maritime commerce. As president of Russian Video, one of the largest media holding companies, he also came in frequent contact with political players and mafia dons.

In the parlance of the street, Russian Video was for a time what was known as an *obschak*, a kind of mutual fund for the criminal underground that was often placed in the service of financing illicit deals, bribing cops, resolving disputes over debts, and covering legal costs for loyal foot soldiers caught in police dragnets. The company owned the local television Channel 11, which was one of the first stations in Russia to broadcast Western fare such as the American soap opera *Santa Barbara* and racy foreign films like *Emmanuelle*. Most crucially, Russian Video also held a substantial stake in the KGB-controlled Rossiya Bank, the nucleus of financial and political power in the city and the country.

Mirilashvili was, in other words, one of the best-connected businessmen in Russia, and Prigozhin made it his mission to get to know him. Although their memories of their earliest days together differed considerably and would become the source of significant controversy, both agreed that it was Prigozhin's schoolmate from the Olympic Reserve Academy, Boris Spektor, who initially introduced them. Prigozhin was hustling between his gig as a car salesman and running a hot-dog stand that he and his stepfather, Samuel Zharkoy, had started shortly after Prigozhin left prison.

The hot-dog business in the heart of Apraksin Dvor—the busy, chaotic, and decidedly dowdy shopping-mall complex near the banks of the Fontanka River—was a surprising hit almost from the instant it opened. With its maze of sprawling interconnected halls, the run-down market was one of the country's largest and oldest. Finns and Estonians traveled across the Baltic Sea to roam its corridors on the hunt for cheap vodka, eager to trade a few pairs of jeans for a couple of bottles. Prigozhin's hot-dog stand was perfectly placed to corner the market of thirsty and hungry shoppers. Set up in an abandoned trolleybus that Prigozhin repurposed, the kiosk brought in big money by the standards of the day, earning about $1,000 per month, a kingly sum that was nearly twice the national average.

One fast-food kiosk grew to two, then three, and then into a mini-empire that spanned the city and attracted the attention of local gangsters with the Malyshev crew who imposed a protection fee of $100 per kiosk per month.[12] As Prigozhin told it, his business was so lucrative that he earned enough money to travel to the United States in 1993, only three years after he got out of prison. He never disclosed where he traveled or what he did or how long he stayed, but he proudly joked that America had embraced him for his entrepreneurial spirit: "At the American consulate, I filled out a form and literally answered questions like, 'Answer honestly—did you ever cooperate with the KGB? Were you involved in prostitution or drug dealing?' I answered—'I sell hot dogs.' So, they ran, not walked, to help me."[13]

America was a magnet for Mirilashvili, too. He fell in love with casino culture in Nevada when he first traveled there in 1991 and became obsessed with the idea of bringing Las Vegas style back home. Upon his return, he would set out to open more than half a dozen gambling houses in St. Petersburg. It was only a couple of years later that Mirilashvili met Prigozhin. Their encounter led to a business partnership that Prigozhin managed to exploit to striking effect over the coming years. Although Mirilashvili told reporters varying versions of the story of how he and Prigozhin first met, one constant is that it was in the early 1990s and that it started with a mutual interest in the food business.

According to one Mirilashvili account, it transpired as follows: "My partner came to me and said: 'I have a childhood friend who has asked me 30 times to introduce us.' I replied: 'If this person is your friend, why did he have to ask 30 times?' And he answered me: 'Because he sells sausages in the market in Leningrad.' In the end, we set up a meeting, and within half an hour, Prigozhin explained to me how he could open a chain of supermarkets."[14]

The idea was as simple as it was radical: Prigozhin proposed an alternative to the city's stodgy Soviet-style mono-market shops: shiny replicas of Western retail efficiency. No more long lines and surly service for a single loaf of bread—instead, customers would be able to stroll through the aisles and pick what pleased them, a luxury that would appeal to the nouveau riche, curiosity seekers, and foreign tourists, who were beginning to stream into the country's proverbial window on the West.

With Spektor as majority partner, Prigozhin's skills as a pitchman paid off, giving birth to the Contrast grocery chain, which perfectly blended his talent for retail and Mirilashvili's connections in the city's import-export trade and halls of power. "I decided to support this initiative and subsidize it, and he went forward with it," Mirilashvili recalled. "This was his success." Where others saw walls, Prigozhin saw doors and windows. Mirilashvili admired that about him, but he often had the sense that Prigozhin's strength and his weakness was his fearlessness. "He was very impulsive, but also very talented."[15]

It is possible that Putin recognized the same qualities in Prigozhin when the two met. Years later, Putin would echo those words in his backhanded eulogy, describing Prigozhin as "a talented man" who had "made mistakes" in his life. Putin and Prigozhin cut their teeth in the new Russia in St. Petersburg, with Vasilyevsky Island as the launchpad. They both took up residence there in the early 1990s, and it was there that their paths first intersected. With its wide avenues and long piers jutting out into the Gulf of Finland, Vasilyevsky was a hustler's paradise. On one side of the island, long rows of eighteenth-century Italianate buildings, commissioned by Peter the Great when the city was founded, claim commanding views of the Neva River. On the other side, massive brutalist-style housing complexes mushroom outward and upward on its flood-prone shores.

For three centuries after the city's founding, most of the country's wealth streamed through Vasilyevsky. Timber, steel, coal, oil—the stuff of shipbuilding and the combustion engine—cored from deep in the center of the country at the base of the Ural Mountains and Siberia flowed from the east toward Europe while ships from the west arrived with luxury goods and the gadgets of a modernizing world.

Shipyard laborers, submarine builders, merchant marines, and gangs of smugglers clung like barnacles to the island's darker underside. It was once the heart of tsarist imperial power, was where Vladimir Lenin plotted the course of the Bolshevik revolution, and was for a long period Russia's naval headquarters. For anyone looking to get into business or politics or both in Russia, Vasilyevsky was the gateway.

Putin and Prigozhin carried on that great tradition. However, it is unlikely that anyone who knew either of them in those days could have predicted quite how influential both men would become in Russia and eventually the world. For those who did not know Prigozhin well, it was probably not yet obvious that in his quest to reinvent himself, he would also end up helping Putin reset the trajectory of Russian history. But, back then, in what would be forever known as the "Wild 1990s," anything was possible—especially if you knew the right people. That was one of the many other things Prigozhin held in common with Putin.

Though born about a decade apart, they both came of age behind the Iron Curtain and grew into men just as their country began to fall apart around them. Both grew up in the shadow of a state withered by corruption, a malignant bureaucracy that had terrorized the people, and a city haunted by the most extreme privation. Putin's father, Vladimir Spiridonovich, was a World War II veteran who had served on the front lines first with an NKVD battalion and then with the regular army. After the war, the elder Putin, an ardent Communist Party man whose own father had served for a time as Josef Stalin's chef, worked in a railway industrial plant. Putin's mother was a menial laborer who had lost her first child to the privations of the war and survived starvation when the city was under German siege for nearly three years. Prigozhin's father, Viktor, who was a mining engineer of Jewish descent, died when his son was nine years old; little else is known about him other than the fact that his father had fought in the Red Army.

Prigozhin was raised by his mother, Violetta, and grandmother until Violetta remarried. It was his stepfather, the ski instructor Samuel Zharkoy, who taught Prigozhin to fight his way through adversity.

As children of the Cold War, Putin and Prigozhin grew up in a world stretched between two opposing poles—the United States and the Soviet Union. What they ate, the movies they watched, the books they read, the clothes they wore, and their waking dreams were dictated in no small measure by the competition between the world's two superpowers over the rules of modern industry, how wealth was distributed, and how and when states were permitted to wield violence against their enemies and their own citizens. Three generations of Russians and Americans grew up to the beat of close shaves, near misses, and battles fought indirectly in remote regions at the far ends of Moscow's and Washington's reach. Putin and Prigozhin were among them.

It was a time of big armies and small wars fought by proxies under the long shadow cast by the prospect of global nuclear annihilation. The last and most significant of those shadow wars took place thousands of miles from where the White House and the Kremlin plotted out how to best each other: in the remote Hindu Kush mountains. More than a million Soviet citizens churned through the Kremlin's decade-long military intervention in Afghanistan. But for Prigozhin, who had spent almost the entirety of the war behind bars, and for Putin, who had spent the 1980s on assignment for the KGB in East Germany, the Afghan war was little more than an abstraction. Everything around them was imploding.

But the retreat from Afghanistan and the return of battle-worn veterans changed the calculus of their careers. The war left a crater-sized hole in the national economy, hollowed out the army, and scarred the psyche of the country. For the first time since the Bolshevik uprising almost a century earlier, new rulers were taking over the old imperial capital. The public was debating whether to change the city's name from Leningrad back to its prerevolutionary St. Petersburg. The city was hungry. Bread, butter, meat, produce—everything was in short supply. Although the country had recorded a historically high yield for its grain harvest in 1990, Russia's second city was hurting badly. Government mismanagement of the privatization of state-run collective farms had led to angry strikes, slow-burning sickouts that left factory floors empty, failed harvests, and fallow fields. Local markets were paralyzed, and rationing ruled the day.

Amid the upheaval, Prigozhin began to try his luck as a serial entrepreneur while Putin took his first tentative steps on his path to power. A year after the last of the Soviet troops left Afghanistan, the geography that the two men had committed to memory as schoolboys was replaced by one that was wholly unfamiliar. Gorbachev signed an agreement with the United States and its Western European allies that allowed for the reunification of Germany. The Warsaw Pact alliance was beginning to unravel while NATO gained new ground.

Statues came tumbling down. Streets were renamed. Maps were redrawn. The men who ran the world and ruled the country that Prigozhin and Putin had grown up in were no longer in charge. The city they returned to was barely recognizable.

In this respect, they found themselves in good company with thousands who returned home from the war in Afghanistan—many of them limbless, shell-shocked, drunk, and dope-sick. The streets were teeming with out-of-work veterans—so-called *Afghantsy*—who mingled in gyms, bathhouses, and bars, scrapping with one another to gain an edge in a town besieged by street violence. They filled slots as bouncers, bodyguards, bagmen, and bandits. They started up their own private-security companies and became protectors of Russia's burgeoning oligarchy.[16]

One of them, Andrey Troshev, would become one of Prigozhin's closest business associates and the trusted hand of the Russian military. It remains unclear to this day exactly how Troshev came to meet Prigozhin and join the security service for Prigozhin's business empire. But in the 1990s their circles overlapped with many *Afghantsy* veterans who served in the city's police and security services, not a few of whom provided protection and served as corporate front men for Prigozhin's business empire.[17]

A St. Petersburg native, Troshev was a proud graduate of the Leningrad Higher Combined Arms Command School, an elite military academy that offered a four-year infantry-officer training course and had long been a feeder for the leaders of some of Russia's most legendary battles. An estimated 250 of its graduates fought in Afghanistan, 38 were killed, and many came back shell-shocked and mentally and physically wounded. Troshev was twenty-three when he was promoted to the rank of captain in the 70th Separate Guards Motor Rifle Brigade.[18]

In 1987, Troshev's second year in combat, Gorbachev called for a drawdown in Afghanistan, calling the war a "suppurating wound" that was bleeding

Moscow's coffers dry. A little more than twelve thousand Soviet troops had been killed in action by then, but because war had never officially been declared, their fate had largely been treated as a secret, albeit an open one.

Soviet soldiers were often poorly equipped and organized haphazardly in clusters in provincial centers across the Afghan countryside.[19] Corruption was rife within the ranks, and it was not uncommon for pay to go missing. Unit commanders, like Troshev, fared a bit better only because their higher status gave them the power to organize all manner of schemes to siphon off military supplies and sell them on the open market.

In this respect, the Afghan war was good training for what awaited men like Troshev when they returned home. Almost every promise made when they signed up was broken upon their return. Army housing was in short supply, salaries went unpaid, and every request for assistance required endless round-trips to the local military commission. The Politburo had promised perks to veterans, but there was no organized system in place to support the demobilized soldiers who returned home to homes transformed by years of privation and privatization.

The only real assurance that veterans of the Afghan war had that they could get what they needed came in the form of the impromptu veterans' associations that began to spring up several years into the war. State-sanctioned bodies like the Russian Union of Veterans of Afghanistan, whose leadership included some of former Soviet premier Mikhail Gorbachev's staunchest army critics, became an important political training ground for former soldiers who before the war would never have dreamed of self-organizing. The veterans' unions would also turn out to be crucial vectors for the birth of Russia's mercenary industry, and eventually the Wagner Group.

Following the withdrawal from Afghanistan and the collapse of the Soviet Union in 1991, the Kremlin cut its military roughly in half, leaving a little over a million active-duty troops. The downsizing created a huge pool of disillusioned and unemployed men trained to kill. They made good couriers and customers of the city's notorious drug trade. They worked as security guards at the pricey mafia bistros and banks that were starting to dot St. Petersburg's landscape. They became cops and intelligence agents who moonlighted as underworld enforcers.

Such was the combustible mood when Troshev returned from the front, Prigozhin came home from prison, and Putin took up a post at the university while still in the active reserves of the KGB. St. Petersburg was broken and lawless. A sign of the times was the history-making municipal election that made reformer Anatoly Sobchak the first elected mayor of St. Petersburg.

On his coattails came Putin. Still on the KGB payroll, Putin went to work in Sobchak's office and was there when the next thunderbolt struck Russia in the form of a coup in Moscow. When Sobchak took over city hall in 1991 and moved the seat of government to the Smolny Institute, a few subway stops away from Vasilyevsky Island, he had unknowingly reached the apogee of his political career.

Tall and trim with a well-coiffed mane of salt-and-pepper hair, Sobchak had been a popular professor of law at St. Petersburg State University, where for a time Putin was his student. Although he was well known in Communist Party circles for his keen legal mind, Sobchak had gained national notoriety only a few years before, when he was tapped to lead a government inquiry into the violent suppression of mass protests in the Republic of Georgia.

An ally of Boris Yeltsin, Russia's first elected president, Sobchak was a rising star among the coterie of reformers that Yeltsin represented. There was talk that Sobchak had presidential ambitions. Important men in Washington like Henry Kissinger, the former US secretary of state, knew Sobchak's name and considered him a comer. Sobchak had a knack for being at the right place at the right time, so when he stepped into office, hopes were high that he could fix what was ailing the city and possibly even the country.

However, two months after Sobchak took office, in late August 1991, tanks rolled along the streets of Moscow as a discontented group of military men threatened to arrest Yeltsin. They had begun an attempted coup against Gorbachev, and it was clear that the Soviet Union was in free fall.

The coup was primarily hatched from within by a cadre inside what were known then, as now, as the state's power ministries: the KGB, the Ministry of Internal Affairs (MVD), and the ministries of defense and foreign affairs. These *siloviki*, or "wielders of force," resented the shuffling of the social order precipitated by Gorbachev's reforms. Many of the Soviet Union's high-ranking military officers and Politburo officials were not yet ready to give in to change, including Putin's boss, Vladimir Kryuchkov.

As head of the KGB, Kryuchkov was considered one of the chief architects of Soviet-Afghan policy and was among the staunchest of the hard-line resisters to any modernization. He had steadily lost his influence as Gorbachev methodically dismantled each plank of the creaky military bureaucracy. By the time the war in Afghanistan was over, Gorbachev had managed to disband the 40th Army and, along with it, the heart of the Russian military's ruling class. That move and Gorbachev's push to replace much of the military's ruling elites with top-performing officers in the Airborne Assault forces, the VDV, had prompted mutterings about a coup as early as 1990.

To the pro-war hard-liners, it seemed that under Gorbachev, disloyalty to Stalin's memory and to the Soviet system's bureaucratic hierarchies had crept into every corner of life. As far as men like Kryuchkov were concerned, it was Gorbachev's loosening of the reins in the Baltic states and in Georgia that spurred uprisings and the need for the military to brutally suppress them. That is why, perhaps, for some in the military it came as little surprise that Kryuchkov joined several other top Russian military officers and Soviet vice president Gennady Yanaev in forming a committee for the state of emergency, known by its initials GKChP, on August 19, 1991.

Technically, Putin was still duty bound to take orders from Kryuchkov because he was drawing a KGB salary while also working for Sobchak on the city council. He remained on the agency payroll when Sobchak appointed him as deputy mayor and the city council's lead liaison for international affairs. Sobchak was not naive about Putin's background. A savvy politician who had dealt with the secret services for years, Sobchak understood that to get anything done, he would need an inside track in the KGB. "He realized he needed experts who know what buttons to push to get things done," Putin told a reporter, adding an immodest shrug.[20] The crisis put Putin right in the center of the action between the coup plotters and the reformers allied with Yeltsin.

It was a set of relationships that would shape the future of Russia: born in the chaos and discontent of the Soviet Union's collapse, burnished by Vasilyevsky Island's revival, and baptized in the fire of St. Petersburg's violent rebirth. The men who would rebuild Russia after the dissolution of the Soviet Union marinated in this toxic brew of political chaos and economic upheaval. Some were supposed freedom fighters, but many more would, over time, join the ranks of the malcontents, including Prigozhin—although his path was long and far from direct.

Yeltsin and Sobchak were together in Moscow on the day the 1991 coup started. Anticipating that St. Petersburg would be quick to fall if the country's security services threw in their lot with the coup plotters, Yeltsin urged

Sobchak to hurry home. By the time Sobchak arrived at the Palace Square in St. Petersburg after negotiating a truce with the local KGB chief, thousands were already streaming into the city's central plaza.

Looking around, in the sunlight of the summer's White Nights, Sobchak took it all in. The assembled crowd carried the new Russian tricolor flags in blue, red, and white, and began to mass beneath the iconic red-marble Alexander Column in the center of the square. "It was as if the city had been touched by God," Sobchak recalled. "People suddenly opened their eyes to what was happening."[21]

What was happening was a revolution. The imminent collapse of the Communist Party–led government loomed, and the planned economy of the Soviet state was in free fall. The formal dissolution of the Soviet Union followed in December 1991. Barely a month after Yeltsin took power as Russia's first post-Soviet president, Sobchak was forced to plead for humanitarian relief from the West.

Hawkish politicians in Western capitals were unmoved and, in some cases, openly hostile to the idea of sending aid to Russia. Cautious pragmatists in Washington, on the other hand, worried that Russia was too big to fail and argued that the cost of aid was greatly outweighed by the risk of Russia's nuclear weapons falling into the wrong hands amid a civil war. As winter descended, television news coverage of empty shelves, starving children, and long lines of the elderly in threadbare winter wear in front of shops quickly shifted sentiment in the West.

A month after Gorbachev formally dissolved the Soviet Union, the situation was so volatile that Secretary of State James Baker III announced that the United States would redirect surplus food and medical supplies from the Persian Gulf War theater to Russia and other newly independent states. Washington viewed the airlift, dubbed "Operation Provide Hope," as part act of mercy, part insurance policy.

Planeload after planeload flew in from west to east in subzero temperatures, provoking comparisons to the Berlin Airlift, which had marked the start of the Cold War two generations earlier. Some 2,300 tons of humanitarian aid flowed to more than twenty cities within the first two weeks of the program; another 25,000 tons would arrive by rail, land, and sea from Europe and North America over the next three years.

Nearly $165 million in aid was sent to St. Petersburg and Moscow alone, although a significant amount was unusable.[22] To prevent pilfering, Salvation

Army workers rode aboard the trucks that delivered aid to military warehouses, but nothing much stood between the storage sites and the black market after that.[23] The airlift was a meager first diplomatic down payment on a post-Soviet future aimed at staving off a violent civil war that could easily upend the global order.

The emergency humanitarian aid did little to resolve the $66 billion in debt that Russia had inherited upon the Soviet collapse. Moscow needed an injection of cash to stabilize the ruble. Within days of taking the presidency, Yeltsin appealed to the International Monetary Fund for membership in order to secure relief and to help with stabilizing Russia's currency.

Although the daunting economic challenges eventually focused minds back in Washington, they also widened the debate between champions of neoliberal economics, who pressed for a "shock therapy" campaign of rapid market deregulation and privatization, and those who advocated for going more slowly, padding in a bit more social-welfare insulation. Harvard economist Jeffrey Sachs fell hard on the side of the shock therapists. He was convinced that the transition from communism to capitalism was bound to be painful no matter how it unfolded, which is why, in his opinion, getting over it faster was the best option. The shock therapy prescription found resonance with Yeltsin's young, reform-minded economic adviser Yegor Gaidar. But the herky-jerky adoption of reforms that followed would come with unforeseen consequences.

The transition of the Soviet Union from full state ownership of nearly every industrial and service enterprise to a free market, along with the economic gyrations precipitated by the flood of men and matériel returning from the Afghan front, created whole new forms of retail. A new and violent market logic ruled the day, as *Komsomolskaya Pravda*, the muckraking daily for Communist Party youth, discovered when it sent a group of undercover reporters into the Moscow streets to see what it would take to purchase weapons. Handguns were on offer for the ruble equivalent of $900 to $1,200; grenade launchers, submachine guns, and even a tank could be bought for a few thousand more.

Crime was business, and business was crime. Kits of killing gear spilled openly from market stalls along with brigades of young men—some ordinary street thugs, others young restless athletes, and many more war-hardened *Afghantsy*—who were available for hire to Russia's most enterprising hustlers. These were Russia's entrepreneurs of violence—the "New Russians." They were the collectors of coupons, ration cards, connections, and favors.

In Russian popular culture of the era and the serialized TV version of *Banditsky Petersburg*, the hustlers spoke loudly and wore bright red double-breasted suits and lots of hair gel. They acted rough in elegant settings. They traveled in Mercedes-Benz sedans driven by muscular men in dark leather jackets who were ex-convicts, war veterans, amateur athletes, or all the above. On screen, they had well-chiseled European facial features and seemed to especially relish ordering the contract killings of swarthy, dark-eyed rival gangsters from the Caucasus.

They were masters of the new black markets that were a product of Gorbachev's reforms. They moved everything from spare auto parts to American-made blue jeans. They were the micro-builders of a macroeconomy of mafia violence—the soft currency of the era. When someone in the city opened a new business or wanted to get a deal done, they offered to erect a "roof" (*krysha*) to protect against rival gangs and city functionaries on the take. Yevgeny Prigozhin was no exception. But what separated him from so many other hustlers was his uncanny instinct for getting the drop on his rivals and picking the right patrons at the right time—yet another thing Prigozhin had in common with Putin.

CHAPTER 2

THE OLD CUSTOMS HOUSE

What Vladimir Putin remembered most from his early tutorials in the politics of the new world order was Henry Kissinger's droopy eyelids; big, thick glasses; and rapier-sharp intellect. They met first in 1992 during one of Kissinger's trips to St. Petersburg. Putin, at forty, was just beginning to hit his stride in city politics as deputy mayor. Kissinger, sixty-nine, had represented America's interests abroad for nearly as long as Putin had been alive. Kissinger dispensed his first lesson to Putin on their drive together from the Pulkovo airport to the city's old aristocratic vacation grounds on Kameny Island, where Kissinger was set to meet with Mayor Anatoly Sobchak. The occasion was one in a series of meetings convened under the auspices of the Kissinger-Sobchak Commission, set up as a vehicle to attract foreign investment to Russia's busiest import-export hub.

Although both men spoke fluent German and no doubt had studied up on each other, their conversation was mediated by an interpreter. Kissinger quizzed Putin on his background, learning of his time as an intelligence agent in East Germany. "All decent people got their start in intelligence. I did too," Kissinger quipped, a comment that resonated deeply with Putin.[1] The conversation took a surprising turn when Kissinger expressed regret over the disintegration of the Soviet Union, a sentiment that shocked Putin, who had assumed the collapse was the very outcome Kissinger had long desired. This unexpected moment of mutual understanding hinted at the complexities of geopolitics that Putin would come to master.

Others present at that first encounter recalled it as a more scripted conversation, but for Putin it was a defining moment. The meeting had been arranged by Yevgeny Primakov, the head of Russia's foreign-intelligence service, who initially saw in Putin a protégé worthy of guidance, although they would later become rivals. Primakov understood the value of Kissinger's influence, hoping that the veteran diplomat's insights would sharpen Putin's understanding of global power dynamics.[2]

Kissinger expressed his bafflement over Gorbachev's sudden decision to dismantle the Soviet Union, citing the violent aftermath in Yugoslavia, Crimea, Georgia, and Chechnya as evidence of the breakup's hasty and costly nature. For Putin, it was a surprising alignment between a key figure of America's Cold War strategy and a Russian soldier of the ideological battle, leaving him astonished: "I never imagined I would hear something like that from Henry Kissinger."[3]

The Kissinger-Sobchak Commission was a golden opportunity for Putin. The commission, packed with CEOs from companies like Procter & Gamble and Gillette, was a classroom for Putin, a place where he could learn the art of dealmaking and showcase his business acumen. Whereas Sobchak's approach was often blustery, Putin's calm, focused demeanor earned him admiration from Western business leaders. His ability to get things done solidified his role as Sobchak's right-hand man and paved the way for his rapid rise.

The early 1990s in Russia were a time of blurred lines and murky morals. The collapse of the Soviet Union had created a post–Cold War Eldorado, where organized crime, ambitious politicians, and opportunistic businessmen all vied for control. In this volatile environment, Putin and Prigozhin emerged as kindred spirits, each determined to seize every opportunity.

The first game changer arrived in 1992, when Boris Yeltsin lifted the government price controls that had strangled the Russian economy since the 1920s. Yeltsin also cut state investment in military-industrial goods and heavy industry. Inflation skyrocketed as a result. Cash was king. But Russian rubles were worthless. Dollars—especially crisp, new ones—were the new currency of power. To eat well and prosper in the city of five million, at least one of three essentials was necessary: access to hard currency, access to food, or connections with the right people. Prigozhin had all three.

Prigozhin's Contrast grocery chain, launched with Misha Mirilashvili and Boris Spektor, was a hit, raking in a 15 percent cut of profits for him and his commercial director, Kiril Ziminov.[4] The chain thrived partly because of a critical oil-for-food barter deal, where Russia traded oil for Western food imports to stave off famine. In St. Petersburg, Putin, as head of External Affairs, was key, overseeing deals that straddled the line between legitimate business and the city's growing black market. Rumors swirled about Putin's role in distributing import-export licenses that conveniently stocked Prigozhin's stores and fueled other business ventures. A city council inquiry into a $90 million–plus contract brokered under Russia's so-called oil-for-food deal with a German company for a huge shipment of meat that never arrived reinforced those suspicions.[5]

The scandal over the oil-for-food deals almost torpedoed Putin's political career before it even started. At the heart of the controversy was a contract with KINEX, the foreign trade arm of the Kirishi oil refinery, managed by Putin's associate Gennady Timchenko. City council members were particularly eager to investigate this contract, sensing that it held the key to unraveling the murky web of alliances that underpinned the city's power dynamics.[6]

Timchenko was slim and blond with an aristocratic bearing, and his entry into the city's power structure was no accident. Raised in a military family, Timchenko had muscled his way into St. Petersburg's elite circles during the late eighties, securing a coveted spot at the Soviet Foreign Trade Ministry. He broke into the international commodities trade after honing his language skills in East Germany, where his father was stationed.

Timchenko was an engineer by training, and his was a calculated ascent that would position him as a pivotal figure in Russia's post-Soviet economy, tying into the fortunes of both Putin and Prigozhin. Timchenko was key to getting Russian oil into global markets, where it could be sold for higher prices. His role didn't stop there. In 1991 he relocated, moving across the gulf, where he took up residence in Finland just as Putin and Sobchak took power in city hall. It was then that Putin and Sobchak began traveling regularly from Russia to Finland for long weekend outings and business trips. That same year, Timchenko went to work as deputy director for a Finnish company called Urals Finland Oy, which purchased oil from KINEX under a cooperation agreement with the Leningrad Committee on Foreign Economic Relations, which, of course, was helmed by none other than Putin.[7]

When, a few years later, Timchenko was suddenly tapped to head the Finnish company, which was subsequently renamed International Petroleum Products Oy, the promotion gave him the running room he needed to establish Gunvor, a commodities brokerage in the hydrocarbon and minerals trade whose global reach is rivaled only by a few at the top of the pyramid, like the

Swiss-based multinational Glencore. The oil-for-food black-market ventures; Putin's alliances with figures like Timchenko, Gorbenko, and Mirilashvili; and the symbiosis among the KGB, city hall, and organized crime were all pieces of the puzzle that would eventually lead to Russia's resurgence as a dominant player in international energy and commodities markets and, in turn, the creation of a global mercenary empire, with Prigozhin at the helm.

But in those early years, it was Mirilashvili's tight relationship with Sobchak and his unparalleled wealth that made him the heavy in the equation. As chair of the Export-Import Bank, Mirilashvili was one of the leading lights of the city's international trade.[8] Euroservice, one of a half-dozen companies Mirilashvili held a controlling stake in, started out selling clothes, carpets, and computers in the city's department-store malls and then ballooned into a wholesale supplier of food and agro-industrial products with more than a dozen processing plants.[9]

Mirilashvili also held a controlling stake in several entities that Putin helped privatize, including the Samtrest liquor factory and distribution company. Restrictions on alcohol sales—another Gorbachev-era reform—had turbocharged the demand for homemade hooch and expensive black-market bottles of vodka and wine. As a result, the Samtrest factory had been quite a prize until it all but sputtered to a halt during the last-gasp days of the Soviet Union. The particulars of the company's resurrection are murky. But Putin's rivals would allege that Mirilashvili purchased the factory at a deep discount through a kickback scheme, and the deal became the subject of one of several legal investigations launched by the city prosecutor into business-licensing deals overseen by Putin.[10]

The factory was a shambles when Mirilashvili took it over in 1992.[11] However, it wasn't long before Samtrest vodka and wine stocked nearly every major restaurant, hotel, specialty shop, and casino bar in St. Petersburg, including several in which Prigozhin and Mirilashvili held stakes.[12] For much of the time they were in business together, the primary vehicle for alcohol distribution in the city was the Nevsky Union, a restaurant-investment firm that Mirilashvili, Prigozhin, Spektor, Gorbenko, and their mutual business partner Kiril Ziminov held stakes in for years.[13]

Charged with overseeing the licensing of city businesses and connected at every level, Putin held purview over practically every aspect of Prigozhin's enterprises. That included CJSC Spektr, a holding company that Prigozhin managed jointly with Gorbenko and Spektor, which along with Contrast

Consulting and another company called CJSC Viking knitted together a small empire of ventures in the gaming, restaurant, marketing, alcohol distribution, and construction sectors.[14] The centerpiece of those ventures was the glitzy Conti Casino, and it was there, after Sobchak tapped Putin to head the city's Supervisory Council on Casinos and Gaming Businesses in 1991, that Prigozhin's world collided with Putin's, and their interests began to intertwine.

Housed in a massive auditorium called Gigant Hall, which dominated the busy city roadway Kondretevsky Prospect, the casino was a nighttime hot spot. Spektor and Gorbenko spent lavishly in their efforts to deck the place out. With its rows of slot machines, cavernous banquet rooms, and glittering neon lights, the gambling hall was a central hub of St. Petersburg's mafia culture and a magnet for tourists who ferried in from Finland and Estonia to enjoy a night out on the town.

The gaming industry was the nerve center of another of St. Petersburg's fast-growing trades: money laundering. Casinos in St. Petersburg acted as the black banks of the black market. With Putin as overseer, city casinos became critical cogs in the political and economic machinery behind Russia's nascent national banking industry. Gambling houses like Conti brought in much-needed hard currency from across the Gulf of Finland and beyond, making them vital partners for Russia's embryonic financial institutions. Bank Rossiya, Sberbank, VTB—all of Russia's major financial institutions—had a foot in the gambling industry. Some big investors in the gaming trade only dipped a toe in by backing restaurants that set up a couple of slot machines. Other institutions, notably the city-owned Neva-Chance Casino holding, became major stakeholders.

Established in July 1992 by municipal decree, Neva-Chance took a 51 percent stake in St. Petersburg's estimated 180 gambling houses and 1,600 gambling machines in exchange for free rent in municipally held real estate. The whole setup was part of the "Russian Macau" dream that Sobchak hoped to sell to potential foreign investors. Putin tapped his friend Gorbenko to serve as the director of the city-backed casino holding company. One authoritative account suggests that Putin also received anywhere from $100,000 to $300,000 for each casino license issued. However, the value of any alleged kickbacks pales in comparison to the leverage that Putin would gain from the Neva-Chance Casino.[15] The city's gambling venture was critical in helping Putin engineer the expansion of his influence, and it also brought Prigozhin closer to Putin's orbit.

Russians' hunger for conspicuous consumption, their taste for luxury imports, and the casino boom upped the stakes for St. Petersburg's mafia and ultimately led to a deadly shakeout of the city's rivalrous criminal underworld. After a short stint in prison following the Devyatkino park fight, Vladimir Kumarin, head of the Tambov mafia faction, returned to the city in 1993. Like Prigozhin, he had changed. He adopted his mother's maiden name, Barsukov, and tried to reorient his enterprises. But his nickname—the "Night Governor"—stuck, along with many of his old feuds. Armed battles between Kumarin's Tambov cadre and rival crews routinely broke into the open, leading to daily stabbings, shootings, and even a rocket attack on the Palace Bridge, the primary link between Vasilyevsky Island and the city's central business district.

Yet none of that stopped Kumarin. He frequently made a show of arriving at the Conti Casino in his sleek Mercedes with an armed entourage. He broke the habit, briefly, only after assassins lying in wait fired a fusillade of bullets from a Kalashnikov rifle at his car in 1994. The assault killed Kumarin's driver and a bodyguard, and it left Kumarin so gravely wounded that his arm had to be amputated.

It was a dangerous time for gangsters but a boom for the bodyguard business. One of the first to benefit was Roman Tsepov, head of the country's first registered private-security company, Baltik-Eskort. Physically tough and highly intelligent, Tsepov was a biathlete sharpshooter turned mid-level officer in Russia's Internal Affairs Ministry (MVD). He built his reputation as a frontline borders and customs agent, and he managed prison security in St. Petersburg before retiring with the rank of captain in 1992.[16] As part of a surge in domestic private-security firms following Yeltsin's decree legalizing them, Baltik-Eskort quickly landed its first major client: the city-managed Neva-Chance casino company.

Staffed almost entirely from a special police task force out of the Latvian port town of Riga and the Lithuanian capital, Vilnius, Tsepov's company was also the primary provider of security for shipments of luxury cars and imported goods transported eastward from Ukraine to St. Petersburg along the notoriously dangerous "Highway of Death," where violent hijackings were a daily occurrence in the 1990s.[17]

A first-of-its-kind private-security service, Baltik-Eskort offered what was at the time called "striped protection," drawing on the talents and muscle of a mix of enforcers from the KGB and MVD who simultaneously guarded St. Petersburg's rich and powerful while retaining their security-agency posts, drawing double pay and blurring the boundaries between the protection of state and private interests. Among Baltik-Eskort's first important hires was Boris Yeltsin's presidential bodyguard, Viktor Zolotov, another police veteran who had also served in the 9th Directorate of the KGB. Under Tsepov and Zolotov's guidance, the security firm quickly earned a strong reputation, in part because of its celebrity clients. At the top of that list were heavies like mobster Alexander Malyshev, media magnate Boris Berezovsky, and the city's mayor, Anatoly Sobchak.

Crucially, Baltik-Eskort provided security for both Neva-Chance and the Baltic Sea Shipping Company (BMP), Vasilyevsky Island's main economic engine and a vital link among the city's titans of industry. With offices in Vyborg and Kaliningrad, BMP operated a vast fleet of merchant and passenger vessels, handling most of the city's seaborne freight. Once controlled by the KGB, the company had forty-six thousand workers, making it one of the city's largest employers.[18] The privatization and reorganization of BMP under Putin's direction, following the ousting of two hundred KGB agents in 1990, triggered violent power struggles.[19] The turmoil culminated in the jailing of BMP's head and the murder of a corporate director, leading Putin to hire Baltik-Eskort for his personal security. From that point on, Putin rarely traveled without Zolotov or another member of the team by his side, bringing Tsepov and Zolotov in close and frequent contact with budding entrepreneurs like Prigozhin.

WHILE PRIGOZHIN AND Putin were cementing their ties in St. Petersburg, Yeltsin was battling to keep control in Moscow. After the Soviet collapse, Yeltsin gutted the KGB, slashing the secretive agency's personnel rolls from 137,000 to 75,000, a move that triggered a wholesale reorganization and the agency's replacement with the Federal Security Service (FSB).[20] The move ignited a firestorm of debate in Russia's parliament, the Duma, a political tinderbox that was simply waiting for a match light.

Yeltsin's political running mate and vice president, Alexander Rutskoy, sparked the first flames. The trouble started when Rutskoy traveled to Crimea in April 1992 to visit what constituted the most strategically important military installation in the region. It became a new flashpoint after Yeltsin inked a deal with his presidential counterpart in Ukraine, Leonid Kravchuk, that called for the division between Russia and Ukraine of what remained of the Soviet armed forces on the Crimean Peninsula. This included the prized Black

Sea naval fleet based in Sevastopol, where, in a preview of the playbook that Russia would run again in 2014 and 2022, a group of disgruntled *Afghantsy* veterans combined forces with officials from a GRU military-intelligence front company called Impex-55 to launch an irredentist political party called the Republican Movement of Crimea.[21]

Rutskoy's trip was meant to cement a deal for Russian gas exports to Ukraine with Kravchuk's newly installed government in the Ukrainian capital, Kyiv. But it quickly ignited a political donnybrook with lasting geopolitical consequences after Rutskoy declared that Russia would never accede to the division of the Black Sea Fleet and called for Crimea to secede from Ukraine. When a few weeks later, in May 1992, the Duma moved to overturn the 1954 transfer of Crimea from Russia to Ukraine, Kravchuk reacted with anger, pronouncing the vote a breach of the agreement to dissolve the Soviet Union and an affront to Ukraine's territorial integrity.

What started as a slow-burning nationalist putsch in Crimea soon morphed into a challenge to Yeltsin's presidential authority. Fueled by a powerful fusion of interests among Crimean mafia figures, local political notables, and covert Russian intelligence operatives linked to Impex-55, the turmoil over the strategically important Black Sea gateway lay at the heart of a vast region of the world that, as Kravchuk once said, was "torn apart by contradictions, its people exhausted by crises, conflicts, wars, and lines."[22]

Yeltsin's attempts to manage the crises only widened the political divide. His decision to suspend Rutskoy over corruption charges escalated tensions further. The Supreme Council, which then served as Russia's parliamentary body, declared Yeltsin's actions unconstitutional, triggering a full-blown confrontation. On September 21, Yeltsin dissolved the parliament and called for snap elections. In retaliation, Rutskoy announced impeachment proceedings against Yeltsin and dismissed Defense Minister Pavel Grachev, a hard-boiled paratrooper, fueling the tumult. Thousands of protesters answered the call to action, marching on government buildings. Inside the White House, Rutskoy, Parliamentary Speaker Ruslan Khasbulatov, and their hard-line supporters barricaded themselves, unfurling red Communist banners from the windows.

Inside, opposition leaders and volunteers who slipped through the cordon set around the building armed themselves and prepared for a shoot-out. The next day, demonstrators broke through militia cordons surrounding parliament and, egged on by opposition leaders and KGB agent provocateurs loyal to right-wing reactionaries, took over the mayor's offices and attempted to storm the iconic Ostankino television center. The standoff escalated, ending on October 4, 1993, with Yeltsin ordering the military to storm the White House. The rebellion was crushed, but Yeltsin's grip on power was shaken, and the embers of Russia's nationalist fervor were far from extinguished. The ultranationalist zeal that stoked the flames of what became known as "Black October" served as a critical crucible for hard-right political entrepreneurs and provocateurs who would soon spark an authoritarian counterrevolution that would loft Putin into Russia's political stratosphere.

The Russian national mood darkened further in early 1994, when an official government study commissioned by parliament declared that organized crime controlled almost every aspect of life. One Western estimate at the time placed the number of criminal gangs operating in the country at 5,000 and the number of businesses controlled by organized crime at 40,000. Hostage taking and kidnapping were rife. At $10,000 to $18,000 apiece, ransom payments far outpaced average monthly salaries, and more people were killed by mafia violence in one year alone than soldiers were killed in the decade-long war in Afghanistan.[23] Meanwhile, capital flight climbed into the billions in the face of all the violence, while contradictory tax and property-protection laws wreaked havoc on the country's brittle economy. Another round of national and local elections loomed.

In St. Petersburg, Yeltsin's ally Anatoly Sobchak was facing troubles of his own. The reverberating effects of the national crisis were keenly felt in the city, where crime was up, Sobchak's popularity was down, and corruption scandals dominated the daily headlines. Undeterred, Sobchak embarked on a reelection campaign, appointing Putin as his campaign manager. Together, the two would spend some of their time plotting Sobchak's 1996 campaign at a splashy new restaurant that Prigozhin had opened on Vasilyevsky Island.

The idea to open an upscale bistro for the city's rich and powerful grew partially out of the success of Prigozhin's experiment with a new venue in 1995 that would appeal to local bon vivants. It was called, rather uncreatively, the Wine Club. For this venture, Prigozhin knew enough to know he didn't know enough, so he turned to someone with more refined tastes for help.

Tony Gear was a plump, cherub-cheeked British expatriate with a nose for good wine. By his own account, he grew up in a working-class home in Liverpool.[24] He learned the ins and outs of the hospitality business at London's Savoy Hotel and trained as a sommelier. It was those skills that brought him to St. Petersburg's Grand Hotel Europe, the storied and ornate hub of luxury located in the center of town on busy Nevsky Prospect. Poaching a well-trained Briton from the city's most iconic hotel to run the Wine Club was only one of several of Prigozhin's significant business maneuvers. The same year, he launched Concord Catering, the business that made Prigozhin the toast of haute cuisine in St. Petersburg.

The Old Customs House was not much to look at when Prigozhin and his partner, Kiril Ziminov, first contemplated opening a restaurant there. Once white, the building's exterior was stained with gray mildew. Inside, the cavernous warren of bare brick halls was dank and musty. Built in the early nineteenth century, the neoclassical building had pride of place on the riverfront of Vasilyevsky Island. Like many of the wedding-cake–style buildings that lined the Neva River embankment, the Old Customs House had fallen victim to years of neglect. Much like the empire that conceived it, the building seemed well past its glory days. But if there was one thing Prigozhin loved almost as much as making money, it was the challenge of turning the detritus of faded power into gold.

The location was ideal. Lined by a cluster of ornate buildings along the Neva River on Vasilyevsky Island, Staraya Tamozhna, the Russian name for the Old Customs House, sat at the juncture of Russia's imperial ambitions. The customs depot's caverns were situated on University Embankment, in the same building complex as the Kunstkamera, the first museum ever erected in Russia and one of the oldest in the world. Chock-full of weird and wild anthropological curios collected by Russia's great explorers, the gallery halls were constructed on orders of Tsar Peter the Great and were a huge draw for the tourists who began flocking to the city in the 1990s.

With financial backing from Mirilashvili, Prigozhin gambled big that the food industry was the best place to capitalize on the city's reopening to the world and the newly acquired taste for foreign fare. "There were huge changes at that time, everything was changing in the 90s, and I think Prigozhin realized that there was not a single real gourmet restaurant in St. Petersburg," Gear remembered.[25] The opening required a massive overhaul that took about a year to complete. Gear brought in a French chef to help design the menu and trained a team of young kitchen and waitstaff in the fine art of silver service.

A tough and exacting taskmaster, Prigozhin busied himself with every detail of the restaurant's design and management. "He had no tolerance for things like a chipped coffee cup. He would say 'What is this, Tony? There's a crack here!' He wanted to be the best and he treated these types of things very, very harshly," Gear recalled. "He even had a special spotlight that illuminated the floor at every angle—the lighting was such that every speck of dust was immediately visible after a night's cleaning, and every day before the establishment opened he would check to make sure the hall was clean."[26]

Despite the attention to detail, the restaurant was a flop in the first few months after it opened in 1996. Not even the strippers Prigozhin hired to attract big spenders did the trick. With inflation sky-high and the local economy still in free fall, only a limited clientele in St. Petersburg could afford to indulge in foie gras with caviar over lentils or chateaubriand steaks.

Luckily for Prigozhin, Putin and Sobchak—two of his most prominent patrons—did not mind the prices. They dropped by regularly, often with their head of security, Viktor Zolotov, in tow, who along with Baltik-Eskort chief Roman Tsepov became fast friends with Prigozhin. The Old Customs House was a place to see and be seen, a gathering spot for members of Putin's rapidly expanding circle, who noshed on truffles and guzzled expensive imported wine while mapping out how to carve up state assets among themselves.

Whether it was the restaurant's well-connected clientele or the rave reviews it started to receive, the Old Customs House eventually became a tremendous success, drawing celebrity visits from pop stars such as Suzi Quatro and the Pet Shop Boys. During its first year of operation, it reportedly earned a million dollars, an unheard-of sum of money for a restaurant in an era when most were struggling just to get by. But ordinary citizens were at best a distant concern of the powerful men who ran the city and who used Prigozhin's pricey eatery as a place to display their wealth, burnish their reputations, and jockey for power.

Sobchak lost his bid for reelection, but the power transition in St. Petersburg opened doors for Putin, who arrived in Moscow as a clearly rising star in 1996 when he went to work for Yeltsin at the Presidential Property Management Department. If Prigozhin felt the loss of one of his highest-profile patrons of the Old Customs House, he did not say so publicly. Getting by was not a problem; Prigozhin had already cultivated ties with Sobchak's campaign rival, Vladimir Yakovlev, who assumed the role of regional governor for St. Petersburg after winning the election. The restaurant profits were so sizable that even as Putin prepared to decamp for the Russian capital, Prigozhin opened another popular eating establishment, Na Zdrovye! Two others—Russky Kitsch and 7:40, a kosher restaurant—soon also joined the lineup.

A year later, Putin moved up in rank again when Yeltsin appointed him deputy chief of the presidential staff. The post became the springboard for his move to the KGB's successor agency, the Federal Security Service (FSB), and eventually to national political prominence. But Putin's heart never really left St. Petersburg, and as his influence grew, so did Prigozhin's ventures. Their ascent was a sign of things to come—a new era where the lines between state power and personal gain would blur even further, reshaping the future of Russia.

CHAPTER 3

NEW ISLAND

The seduction of Michel Camdessus began late one June evening in 1999 on the banks of the Neva River in St. Petersburg.[1] The electrifying pale light of the White Nights suffused the sky. Always at its most vibrant in the summer, the city hummed with the sounds of late-night reverie as Camdessus, the managing director of the International Monetary Fund (IMF), strolled alongside Russia's prime minister, Sergey Stepashin. Boris Yeltsin had asked Stepashin to plan a charm offensive in advance of Camdessus's arrival for the St. Petersburg International Economic Forum. Everything was riding on convincing the head of the powerful financial institution that Russia was still a good investment. If Stepashin and the rest of Yeltsin's team in St. Petersburg succeeded in persuading Camdessus to grant the government's request to the IMF to lend $4.5 billion, it was possible that the Kremlin might just be able to pull the country back from the brink of yet another economic crash.[2] It fell to Yevgeny Prigozhin, restaurateur to the city's power elite, to pull off the seduction of the Frenchman.

A bailout from the IMF was not going to be an easy sell. That summer, Russia, like much of the rest of the world, was staggering out of one of the worst economic tailspins of the century. The precipitating cause was Thailand's unexpected default on its loans two years earlier and the sudden devaluation of its currency against the US dollar. The move set off a recessionary brush fire that incinerated the economies of half a dozen countries in Asia and then spread to Eastern Europe. At the same time, an internecine battle inside OPEC between Venezuela and Saudi Arabia over oil-production output was roiling world markets. The immediate impact was a falloff in demand for Russia's primary export. In the spring of 1998, the combined effects of the Asian financial crisis and OPEC infighting had already pushed down oil prices by 40 percent, from $17 per barrel to $10.[3] On top of that, Russia was once again drowning in debt. A grinding conflict in the mountainous republic of Chechnya added more strain on the national economy. By the summer, Russia was forced to default on some $40 billion to $50 billion in sovereign debt, a move that shredded the savings of millions of citizens.[4]

The inflationary spiral that followed the default made the situation so unstable that Yeltsin, worried that he might soon have another coup on his hands, sacked the head of the Federal Security Service (FSB), the newly renamed successor agency to the KGB, and replaced him with Vladimir Putin. Putin's subsequent appointment as secretary of the Russian Security Council in March 1999 effectively placed him in charge of managing security for visits of dignitaries like Camdessus. It also sent a sharp signal to anyone paying attention that Stepashin, who had briefly held the same post while overseeing the bungled Russian response to the First Chechen War, was on his way out and Putin was on his way up.

Putin's steady climb up the Kremlin ranks coincided with the first signs of global recovery from the Asian crisis. Russia's economy was slowly sputtering back to life when Camdessus arrived for the opening of the St. Petersburg Economic Forum. World oil prices had rebounded. But the road ahead still looked rocky. Russia was staring down the possibility of defaulting on hundreds of millions in existing loans. It was up to Stepashin and Putin to convince the IMF chief that the Russian government knew how to smooth the way to a more certain economic future.

Then only in its third year, the St. Petersburg International Economic Forum was a by-product of the foreign-investment flows to Russia stimulated in part by the Kissinger-Sobchak Commission. In time, the old imperial capital's annual forum would become a crucial vehicle for Putin's consolidation of domestic and international power. But in 1999, the summit was still very much in its infancy. Modeled on the World Economic Forum in Davos, Switzerland, the event had all the same trappings. Political leaders and business chieftains from dozens of countries flew in on chartered jets. There were big-tent events featuring speakers from multibillion-dollar investment firms. Russia's glitterati showed up in tuxedos and sequined dresses for lavish banquets hosted by the country's newly minted billionaires.

Russia had sealed some of its biggest foreign-investment deals in the first two years of the St. Petersburg forum. The year that Camdessus was guest of honor, it was held at the legendary Tauride Palace. It was a fitting location given that the palace—one of the grandest in the entire country—had once been the estate of Prince Grigory Potemkin, the general who famously built a fake portable village in Crimea to convince his lover, Catherine the Great, of her empire's might.

Whether a sentimental tour of the faded glamour of the tsarist past would convince Camdessus that the Kremlin could reverse the damage to its economy was open to question. There was little doubt that the global situation had dented the economy badly, but the IMF chief, a savvy numbers man known for his disarming wit, was also keenly aware of Russia's gross mismanagement of national tax revenues, rampant corruption, and pilfering of government assets that had led to the political and financial chaos on Yeltsin's watch.

The calculus for Yeltsin's cabinet was simple: if Camdessus was well handled, there was a chance of an IMF bailout. Therefore, the press was barred from attending any of the major meetings at the St. Petersburg forum. No thorny questions would be asked, and few public comments would be made about the ongoing negotiations to retrieve the economy from the ash can. Only Ukraine's prime minister, Valery Pustovoitenko, ignored the unspoken taboo, complaining bitterly that an extension of new IMF loans did little to help Russia's creditors in the region.[5] Why, Pustovoitenko asked, should Russia be treated any differently than Ukraine?

Camdessus did not offer a public response. He was already walking on eggshells. After the disastrous fallout from the East Asian economic crisis, he had come under withering fire from critics of the IMF. With a price tag of $35 billion for Indonesia, Korea, and Thailand combined, the IMF's bailout of the so-called East Asian Tigers had resulted in sharp economic restrictions across the region that triggered violent protests and had knock-on effects in every corner of the globe. The Asian financial crisis demonstrated what could go wrong when the IMF made a bad gamble by lending developing nations more than they could reasonably hope to repay.

It was a major personal comedown for Camdessus because he had been one of the principal backers of the IMF's debt bet. Before joining the IMF, he had headed the Bank of France, a position that made him one of Europe's preeminent and most influential economists. By the time he arrived in St. Petersburg that summer, he had been at the helm of the IMF for twelve years. During that time, Camdessus had essentially midwifed the dollarization of a newly globalized economy. It was a distinction that won him more enemies than friends in the developing world. At one point at the peak of the East Asian meltdown, Camdessus was burned in effigy in Bangkok, a fact that he was likely to want to forget as he strolled the banks of the Neva with the prime minister and his retinue.

The wooing of Camdessus centered on a lavish banquet on Prigozhin's riverboat restaurant. It is unclear who suggested the venue—Stepashin, Putin, or another member of Yeltsin's cabinet. But with its gleaming white hull, soldierly rows of elegantly appointed tables, and chairs upholstered in blue velvet, the floating restaurant offered an ideal setting to show how far Russia had come. Prigozhin had convinced his business partner Kiril Ziminov to open the restaurant after a trip to Paris, where he first got a glimpse of the city's famous flat-bottomed Bateaux Mouches boats. Soon after his return, he purchased and refurbished a rusted-out boat as his own riverboat restaurant, christening it the New Island in 1997. It was an instant hit with St. Petersburg's nouveau riche and powerful. Putin even celebrated one of his birthdays on board.[6]

As the New Island floated down the Neva past the golden-domed watchtowers of the Peter and Paul Fortress, translators narrated the history of the city for Camdessus. The pressure was on to impress. Guards from the Federal Protection Service (FSO) stood watch on the boat deck, scanning for possible threats. Inside the cozy and elegant dining room, Prigozhin worked to keep the mood light and festive, directing tuxedoed waitstaff to keep the libations flowing. About midway through the tour, Stepashin suddenly received an urgent call from Yeltsin. "Seryozha," Yeltsin boomed, calling the prime minister by his diminutive, "don't come back without a loan!"[7]

At least, that is the way Prigozhin remembered the conversation.[8] Less than a decade since his release from prison, Prigozhin's family was prospering, and his business empire was booming. Then married with two children—a girl, Polina, and a boy, Pavel—Prigozhin was thirty-eight, and in a few years his wife, Lyubov, would have a third, Veronika. He had not only managed to get the attention of the Kremlin with the opening of New Island; he also continued to win accolades for the cuisine served at his string of restaurants.

For the next several months, it seemed as though all the wining and dining of the IMF team on New Island had had a positive effect. After returning to the IMF's headquarters in Washington, Camdessus continued to hint that a loan could be in the offing as long as Yeltsin was able to convince enough members of the Duma, Russia's lower house of parliament, to hike taxes on alcohol and gasoline, a condition that Camdessus knew would meet with resistance.

By midsummer, it seemed that the Kremlin was on the verge of success. But the mood in the West shifted a few months later after an outbreak of insurgent violence in the restive North Caucasus prompted a brutal response. The trigger for the IMF's change of heart came in early August, when Shamil Basayev, a Chechen warlord, led an army of almost two thousand local and foreign Islamist extremists in an assault on the neighboring region of Dagestan. The surprise attack represented a massive intelligence failure for Russia's security agencies, including the FSB, where Putin was still in charge. Paradoxically, this failure would pave the way for his rise to power. Russia immediately announced the start of a special military operation in Chechnya in response to the violence. A few days later, on August 9, Yeltsin installed Putin as prime minister, replacing Stepashin.

Once in charge, Putin held nothing back. The fact that Basayev had apparently plotted the offensive with the help of Samir al-Suwalim, a Saudi-born veteran with close ties to Osama bin Laden, made Putin even more eager to exact revenge and prove his mettle. Known as Ibn-al Khattab, or simply Emir Khattab, al-Suwalim was a direct product of Moscow's long proxy war with Washington at the outer edges of the Soviet empire. He had trained and fought in Afghanistan among the Arab mujahideen as a teenager during the waning days of the Soviet conflict. His Islamic International Brigade attracted a fierce and loyal following of Chechen, North African, and Turkish volunteers who fought alongside him throughout the 1990s in skirmishes with Russian troops that spanned from Tajikistan to Chechnya and Bosnia.

Among his first moves as prime minister, Putin ordered hundreds of MVD internal-affairs red-beret troops into Dagestan and unleashed a vicious bombing campaign. The brutality of the military response to Basayev's assault on Dagestan shocked many in the West. But in just a blink, attention shifted again after a series of four explosions struck apartment buildings in several cities over a two-week period, killing more than three hundred and wounding at least a thousand.[9] The first, on September 4, was a car bomb that went off in front of a five-story residence for the families of security personnel in the Dagestani town of Buynaksk. Two others followed in quick succession on September 9 and September 13 in Moscow, decimating two multistory buildings and damaging others nearby. The fourth destroyed an apartment building in the southern city of Volgodonsk on September 16. Putin vowed to hunt down those responsible, famously promising "to wipe them out in their outhouses." Officially, Emir Khattab was the number-one suspect behind the bombings. But the circumstances and timing of the attacks left lingering questions about whether the attacks had been designed to boost Putin's tough-guy image.

Putin's aggressive tone about Chechnya did not go over well in Washington, where the IMF is headquartered. With the campaign for the US presidential election in 2000 already under way, George W. Bush, the leading Republican Party challenger for the White House, was keen to signal that he would take a tough-love approach toward Russia. "Even as we support Russian reforms, we cannot support Russian brutality," Bush intoned during a campaign speech in California. "When the Russian government attacks civilians, leaving orphans and refugees, it can no longer expect aid from international lending institutions."[10]

Bush's foreign-policy adviser for the presidential campaign, Condoleezza Rice, had helped shape the candidate's speech on Russia, and like her mentor, Brent Scowcroft, she advocated a hawkish stance toward the Kremlin that would make clear the distinction between Bush and his Democrat rival, Vice President Al Gore. Scowcroft, who had served for years as national security adviser to President George H. W. Bush, famously plucked Rice, a fluent Russian speaker, from her perch at Stanford University, where she was one of only a few Black professors on campus. She served under Scowcroft on the White House National Security Council during the tricky negotiations between Washington and Moscow over the reunification of Germany and had a front-row seat on the end of the Soviet Union and the transfer of power from Mikhail Gorbachev to Yeltsin.[11] That experience informed Rice's tough and pragmatic stance on Russia and China, and her distaste for mincing words when dealing with Moscow.

Still, for a moment in late September 1999, even as Russian forces waged a relentless aerial bombing campaign against the Chechen city of Grozny, it seemed that the warm reception and the memories of floating down the Neva on Prigozhin's New Island riverboat banquet hall had not yet faded for the IMF chief. At the annual meeting in Washington that month for the Bretton Woods financial institutions, Camdessus urged his counterparts in the World Bank and International Bank for Reconstruction and Development not to overreact to the situation in Russia. "Interdependency has arrived," Camdessus said. "In the new world of globalization cooperation is a must."[12] The Bretton Woods group's system of debt bailouts in exchange for market-driven liberal economic reforms had achieved remarkable gains and weathered the worst storms, Camdessus reminded his colleagues.

It was true that, however imperfectly, Russia had embraced the gospel of the "Washington Consensus," ushering in an unprecedented era of fiscal discipline, market-driven interest rates, privatization of state enterprises, lowering of tariffs, removing barriers to foreign direct investment, and liberalization of trade. Eight years after Yeltsin came to power, almost every factory, potato farm, and oil well from St. Petersburg to the far eastern city of Vladivostok had passed from the state to private hands. Russia, Camdessus said, was turning a corner. Whatever the situation in Chechnya, turning away from Russia and withholding funds could undo all the gains achieved. He leaned over the podium at the front of the packed hotel ballroom and paused for effect. "Amid all the recent controversy, we should not lose sight of the progress that has been made in Russia's journey to a market economy," Camdessus said, pumping his hands downward as if to calm a rising wave. "It would be the height of irresponsibility to turn our back on this great nation. We. Will. Not. Do. It!"[13]

Only a few weeks later, Camdessus appeared to change his mind. Perhaps remembering the sting of the withering criticism directed at the IMF when it had extended loans to Russia during the First Chechen War, he now said he was duty bound to weigh his decision more carefully. He seemed to be waiting for a green light from the White House, but no such signal was forthcoming. In the run-up to the 2000 presidential elections, caution was the prevailing state of mind in Washington.

As it was, tensions between Moscow and Washington were still high because of NATO's bombing campaign against Serbian positions in Kosovo. An air of mistrust hung over the UN Security Council following the Clinton administration's decision to enforce a no-fly zone over parts of the Balkans despite the lack of UN authorization and in the face of objections from both Russia and China. Washington's NATO-backed move also further aggravated long-standing concerns about the transatlantic alliance's growth. The acrimony only increased in the late fall of 1999 after Putin announced that Russia was preparing to spend $115 million of what many in the West saw as borrowed money on its military operations in Chechnya. Reports coming out of the Chechen capital of Grozny of torture and human-rights violations did not help matters. "We cannot go forward with the financing if the rest of the world does not want to," Camdessus said.[14]

All the careful overtures to the IMF seemed to fizzle at that precise moment. Mikhail Kasyanov, Russia's finance minister, likened the IMF threat to withhold funding until the Chechen conflict was resolved to political blackmail. "We do not quite understand [the] statement by Michel Camdessus linking the IMF's financial support for Russia and the antiterrorist operation which is being carried out," Kasyanov shot back.[15] From a Kremlin point of view, rich countries in the West, and by implication Washington, were yet again moving the goalposts. When Camdessus announced in early November that he would be retiring in the new year, it appeared that the question of the IMF loan to Russia was dead.

If anything, the IMF's intransigence only burnished Putin's reputation at home as a tough negotiator who looked out for Russia's interests first and chimed well with the image of strength, competence, and incorruptibility that Putin's backers hoped to sell to the Russian public. The timing also was propitious. On New Year's Eve, as a new millennium was dawning, Yeltsin took the world by surprise and announced he was stepping down and making Putin acting president. A few months later, in March 2000, Putin was elected president.

Russia's wooing of the international financial establishment may have come to naught. But the riverboat banquet did succeed in launching Prigozhin. During Putin's first several years in office, Prigozhin welcomed dozens of dignitaries aboard the New Island restaurant. Presidents, prime ministers, kings, queens, princes, princesses—a veritable who's who of the global elite—enjoyed views of St. Petersburg.[16] They dined on black caviar, pan-fried duck foie gras with a caramelized mango sauce, and more traditional Russian dishes such as cold borscht and pelmeni dumplings stuffed with beef and cabbage. White-gloved waiters glided up and down the dining area's long banquet tables with dessert plates heaped with pavlova meringue, crème brûlée, and slices of fluffy tiramisu. Before and after dinner, guests were invited to lounge on leather couches in the wood-paneled cabin. All the while, Prigozhin hovered in the background, often demonstrating his flair for drama by dressing in formal coattails or a dark, neatly tailored suit with a crisp white shirt.

Prigozhin would later say repeatedly that the night he hosted Putin and Japanese prime minister Yoshiro Mori was one of the most memorable. Mori's state visit to Russia in late April 2000, shortly after Putin's election, marked a moment of triumph for the Russian leader. Mori, a gaffe-prone politician who often wore a clueless expression, had become the leader of his country seemingly by accident, and he had a lot to prove. He was named prime minister in an emergency cabinet meeting in Tokyo only days after a stroke had suddenly incapacitated his predecessor. In an uncharacteristically bold move for a Japanese politician, Mori had decided to break with tradition and make Russia the first stop on his round of state visits instead of the United States. The move signaled Moscow's growing importance for the global economy ahead of the G8 summit of the world's wealthiest nations, which Mori was scheduled to host in Okinawa later that same year. It did not go unnoticed that Mori, when asked his thoughts ahead of the trip about the ongoing war in Chechnya, dismissively waved away questions about the scorched-earth campaign in the Caucasus. This was, he said, a "Russian internal problem."[17]

The trouble for Putin and the Kremlin was that Russia's "internal problem" was starting to look more international. Only a few weeks before Putin broke bread with Mori on Prigozhin's riverboat bistro, units of the Russian rapid-response special police forces from the Otriad Militsii Osobogo Naznachenia (OMON) had descended on the suburbs of Grozny and summarily executed sixty civilians. A few months later, Human Rights Watch issued a report saying that witnesses had seen contract soldiers—*kontraktniki*—from St. Petersburg shoot dozens at point-blank range while conducting house-to-house searches for Chechen rebel fighters in the towns of Aldi and Chernorechie. Part of a sweeping series of "cleansing" operations, the OMON police raids left a trail of destruction and grisly mass killings in their wake, prompting the UN Commission on Human Rights to call for a special independent commission of inquiry into the Russian campaign in Chechnya.[18]

Russian authorities at first suggested that Chechen soldiers dressed in OMON uniforms had carried out the massacre as part of a psychological "false-flag" operation aimed at turning the local population against liberating Russian forces. Eventually, an investigation led by Russian prosecutors confirmed that the contract soldiers behind the attack had come from OMON units based in St. Petersburg and the central Russian town of Ryazan. Public condemnation followed, but the operation offered an early glimpse of the terrorizing tactics that would become the go-to tool of Russia's irregular paramilitary forces during the Second Chechen War, the primary crucible for the hard-boiled veterans who would come to run Russia's future wars and serve in Prigozhin's mercenary army.

While the war in Chechnya raged on, Prigozhin was getting to know Putin's inner circle better and branching out into new territory. Concord Management and Consulting drew up blueprints for the development of a

$150 million luxury real estate complex called Northern Versailles on the shores of Lake Lakhta.[19] Situated at the edge of a pristine nature preserve in St. Petersburg's Primorsky District, the high-end gated community was part homage to Peter the Great, part living monument to the age of imperialism. Plans called for the construction of fifty mansions modeled on mini-versions of British palaces, French châteaus, and knockoffs of the Hermitage.[20] With commanding views of the Gulf of Finland, they were to be purpose-built on 14 hectares of shorefront land for the ultrarich, perfect for commuting to the office and upscale flats downtown by day and soaking in gold-trimmed bathtubs by night.

At the same time, Prigozhin decided to open an ironically named fast-food chain called Blin! Donalts. In English the restaurant's name translates to "Damn Donalds," and it offered traditional sweet and savory versions of traditional pancakes known as blini. Playfully modeled on McDonald's, the fast-food chain was Prigozhin's initial foray into what commentators called at the time "democratic cuisine," where customers called the shots while servers responded politely rather than growling at them per Soviet custom. The chain was the subject of a bubbly write-up in the local business weekly *Delovoy Petersburg*, which in just a few years' time would add Prigozhin to its list of the city's wealthiest individuals.

He became even wealthier when, in early 2001, his business partner Misha Mirilashvili was convicted of kidnapping two men involved in the abduction of his father and sentenced to eight years in prison.[21] As it happened, the trial coincided with an ongoing business dispute between Mirilashvili and Prigozhin over their shared stakes in several restaurants and firms, including the Old Customs House. Mirilashvili was suspicious of the timing. "He wanted to take with him everything that he claimed belonged to him," Mirilashvili bitterly recalled, referring to Prigozhin. "We are talking about ten percent of the business's revenue. I then went to prison and my partners were the ones who managed these lawsuits against him. Even then he had political influence within the system. I have a gut feeling that I went to prison because of Prigozhin, but I have no proof."[22] The split, which left Prigozhin owner of a vast array of holdings, would also ensnare Prigozhin's longtime business partner, Kiril Ziminov, who was reportedly shorted several hundred thousand dollars in the bargain.

With nothing left to restrain him, Prigozhin began to reach even higher. His reputation in the haute cuisine business made him a favorite of one of the world's most famous classical musicians, Mstislav Rostropovich. A cellist and conductor, Rostropovich had studied under Dmitry Shostakovich and early in his career earned a reputation for being a vocal and iconoclastic human-rights defender. After Rostropovich and his wife, the opera soprano Galina Vishnevskaya, gave shelter in 1970 to Aleksandr Solzhenitsyn, the dissident writer and historian of the prison gulag, Soviet authorities slowly squeezed them out of public life, and they left for the United States in 1974. They were rehabilitated during perestroika, and their return to Russia after twenty years in exile was front-page news.

Along the way, Rostropovich had also managed to become close friends with Queen Sofia of Spain, another happy connection that would prove fateful for Prigozhin. Rostropovich played for the royal consort of King Juan Carlos II in Madrid on many occasions. Her family tree branched deep into a line that connected her to Britain's queen Victoria and Russia's last monarch, Tsar Nicholas II, and Sofia looked every inch the descendant of Danish and Greek kings. Conservative to the core, she knew her place and her station. But sometimes she liked to travel under the radar when she went to see close friends like Rostropovich.

So it was that the queen of Spain was expected to arrive one day in late July 2001 at St. Petersburg's Pulkovo airport. Rostropovich and his wife planned to meet her and quietly whisk her away to their residence. No press. No fanfare. She wanted only to spend a few relaxing days with friends touring Russia's old imperial city and catching up over intimate dinners. But just before her visit, Rostropovich's household chef suddenly disappeared. A panicked Rostropovich put in a few calls, and eventually the maestro reached Prigozhin's cell phone through an FSB intermediary. "Zhenechka, it's Slava," Rostropovich boomed. "Can you imagine, a real queen has arrived! And I don't know what to feed her at all! My fraudulent cook took the money, went to the market and did not come back, I'm just in despair." Prigozhin was there in a flash with his chef from New Island. "We quickly sorted everything out, and for four days the Queen stayed with the Rostropoviches," Prigozhin said. "During that time, I took her for a ride on the ship, organized a reception in her honor, and after she left, Rostropovich said to me: 'Brother, how much do I owe you?'"[23]

Not long after, $30,000 suddenly appeared in Prigozhin's bank account, proof once again that he was fast becoming a reliable and discrete Mr. Fixit—for a price. Whatever anyone might have remembered or said about Prigozhin's dark past was easily brushed away. Wherever important people gathered, it seemed, he was at their elbow. As dignitaries from around the world made the pilgrimage to Moscow and St. Petersburg to meet with Putin and the Russian president's tight circle of friends and political confidants, Prigozhin was usually on hand to greet them. Britain's prince Charles and prime minister Tony Blair, French president Jacques Chirac, US presidents Bill Clinton and George Bush, Italian prime minister Silvio Berlusconi, German chancellor Gerhard Schroeder, and Anders Fogh Rasmussen, Denmark's prime minister and the future secretary-general of NATO—all would take turns sitting alongside Putin at Prigozhin's table.[24] The care and feeding of the newly wealthy, recently rehabilitated, and lately powerful was good business, and it would turn out to be even better politics for Prigozhin—the man known ever more as "Putin's Chef."

CHAPTER 4

GUNS, GAS, AND OIL

et drunk and forget." It was going to be that kind of night at the Peterhof Palace, Vladimir Putin promised his dinner guests.[1] Out on the palazzo veranda, ballet dancers in shimmering gold costumes pranced and whirled amid the palace's grand cascade of fountains. Water spouted in rainbow arcs all around them. Inside, in the grand dining room, beneath glittering chandeliers, were trays of sumptuous blinis stuffed with caviar and cream, vodka, wine, and, of course, juice for the teetotaling president of the United States, George W. Bush, and his wife.

A lot was riding on the dinner that night in St. Petersburg. Every detail had to be perfect, especially the food. On that score, Yevgeny Prigozhin did not disappoint. Prigozhin mustered a veritable army of cooks and waitstaff for the event, rehearsing them like a drill sergeant for hours on end before the big day finally arrived. A local newspaper reported that Prigozhin had spent nearly two years planning the menus and training his waitstaff on the intricacies of silver-service catering for heads of state.[2] It was all part of the artful diplomatic ballet that Putin and the Kremlin had choreographed as part of Russia's bid to return to the center of the world stage.

Long in the making, the gala dinner was part of a series that kicked off a weeklong festival in celebration of the 300th Jubilee, the anniversary of the founding of Russia's imperial seat of power. Everyone who was anyone was there. The A-list of dignitaries invited by Putin included Bush and his wife, Laura; Britain's prime minister, Tony Blair; France's president, Jacques Chirac;

Germany's chancellor, Gerhard Schroeder; and Italy's prime minister, Silvio Berlusconi. In all, more than forty heads of state had traveled to St. Petersburg for the May 31, 2003, celebration of the northern capital's great comeback. The last time that the Peterhof Palace had played host to so many powerful Western heads of state, Tsar Nicholas II was still on the throne.

The lavish dinner marked the first time since the start of the US invasion of Iraq that principals of the world's Great Powers were seated in the same room. Because it was a prelude to a much-anticipated conclave scheduled to take place a few days later in France among the leaders of the G8 wealthy nations, the international press dubbed the historic gathering in Russia "the summit before the summit." For more than a year prior, the world's Great Powers had been at loggerheads over the breakdown of the decade-long international embargo imposed on Iraq and how to respond to Saddam Hussein's escalating resistance to UN-mandated weapons inspections. In multiple rounds of votes and debates, Russia, France, and Germany lined up in opposition to American and British attempts to persuade the UN Security Council to vote in favor of military intervention. When US forces finally swept into Baghdad in March, Putin openly called the war a "mistake" that would have "the gravest consequences" for international stability.

The Iraq war was a pivotal turning point that presented a dilemma for Putin. He had expended considerable political capital on rapprochement with Washington, embracing greater engagement with NATO and holding back on public criticism when Bush pulled out of the Anti-Ballistic Missile Treaty in 2001—all with the goal of returning to the club of the world's favored nations. But Putin was growing skeptical that the trade-offs matched the payoffs, given the Bush administration's failure to deliver on its promise to rescind US sanctions imposed on Russia and other Soviet republics in the 1970s under the Jackson-Vanik Amendment.

The US ouster of Saddam exacerbated those tensions, threatening to unravel years of carefully cultivated bonhomie between Putin and Bush. As relations between Moscow and Washington soured, the clash of interests bled into arms deals, where Russia's strategy became clearer. Putin had publicly warned Bush ahead of the American incursion that regime change in Baghdad would result in chaos, and it had. A month before Bush's arrival in St. Petersburg, a firefight between US and Iraqi forces in Baghdad had caught a convoy of Russian journalists and diplomats in the crossfire, raising tensions even higher. There was also the matter of an anticipated $40 million Iraq-Russia trade deal, ongoing pipeline construction projects, and the unresolved status of Iraq's $8 billion in unpaid debts incurred for Russian weapons transfers during Iraq's eight years of war with Iran.[3] The Iraq invasion didn't just strain diplomacy; it also exposed Russia's deep involvement in arms trading and its larger game plan.

What truly alarmed the Kremlin was the growing US military footprint in the Middle East and the imminent expansion of NATO, both of which threatened to undermine Russia's influence in the region and Putin's strategic calculus. Russia's historical alliances with strongmen in the region had led to a synergy of interests between Russia's military-industrial complex and Arab armies that relied on Russian weapons to harden their defenses against external and internal threats. In a stern speech delivered to the legislature in May, Putin expressed frustration with the barriers that still lay in the way of Russia's revival. "Our principal task," Putin opined, "should be the return of Russia to the ranks of rich, developed, strong and respected countries. But this return will only be possible when Russia becomes strong economically, when it is no longer dependent on crumbs from international financial organizations."[4] For Putin, the path back to greatness lay straight through the Middle East.

Historically, the region had long been a critical source of trade revenue for Russia's state-run energy and arms corporations. Energy-infrastructure projects in Iraq and weapons sales had generated billions for the Kremlin's state coffers during Saddam's twenty-four years in power. Regime change in Baghdad not only put those cash flows at risk but also potentially jeopardized the price stability of the world oil market.

Oil was both Russia's number-one export and its Achilles' heel. When the global price of a barrel swung high, hard currency gushed into Russia. During Putin's first term in office, high oil prices had progressively helped Russia pay down its debts to the IMF at a much faster rate than expected. Moscow worried that postwar reconstruction and the rejuvenation of Iraq's oil industry would result in a glut in world oil supplies that could drive the price of a barrel below $20. Such an outcome would have made it next to impossible for the Kremlin to balance its books and could drive Russia into a debt spiral.

The Bush White House, for its part, was much more concerned about Russian arms and tech transfers to what it viewed as rogue states. Russia's proposed plan to aid Teheran with the construction of a nuclear facility was one of two urgent items on the agenda for discussion in a separate bilateral meeting scheduled to take place between Bush and Putin the next day in St. Petersburg. The second issue concerned reports that Rosoboronexport, Russia's state arms-export company, had delivered Russian-made Kornet antitank missiles, GPS jammers, night-vision goggles, and Igla shoulder-fired rockets to Iraq via Syria just two months before the start of the war.[5]

Before their St. Petersburg sidebar, Bush, in a tough phone call with Putin, laid out declassified intelligence that exposed the whole shady operation. The names of General Vladislav Achalov and General Igor Maltsev, two of the men who had spearheaded the Soviet coup plot against Gorbachev and joined in the 1993 uprising against Yeltsin, came up, both men knee-deep in the arms-smuggling plot.[6]

Photos of the two grinning and mugging for the camera in Baghdad surfaced, along with letters issued by Russian front companies sealing the deal. Achalov didn't even try to hide it, telling a Russian reporter, "We didn't fly to Baghdad to drink coffee."[7] Adding fuel to the fire, a pro-Saddam website—iraqwar.ru—popped up about six months before US troops hit Baghdad, and Washington had identified the Kremlin's fingerprints all over it.[8] This was a preview of what would later become Putin's go-to move: deploying mercenaries to do the dirty work, a tactic that would eventually fall under Prigozhin's management as part of Putin's grand plan to put Russia back on the map. Putin, of course, played dumb, claiming that he knew nothing about the arms deal. Instead, he flipped the script, blaming the United States for arming Afghan rebels who morphed into al-Qaeda.[9] It was a classic Putin deflection, revealing just how nervous he was about the power dynamics shifting in the region.

The weapons didn't just magically appear in Iraq. Moving them required a team of pros—contract managers, technicians, and logistics specialists. The operation bore the unmistakable signature of the Main Intelligence Directorate of the Russian military, known as the GRU. Traditionally, the GRU's mission included deep reconnaissance behind enemy lines, psychological warfare, and targeted assassinations, particularly in conflict zones and hot spots in Russia's shadow war with the West. But a central strategic concern was facilitating Russia's military cooperation with foreign countries under arms deals made by Rosoboronexport.

Despite his denials, Putin was likely aware that a group of semiretired veterans linked to Achalov's Union of Paratroopers had established a clandestine pipeline for Russian arms transfers to Saddam's regime in the late 1990s, when Putin was head of the FSB. Iraq, cash-poor but oil-rich after years of war and sanctions, needed skilled military muscle to secure its oil infrastructure, whereas financially strapped Russia needed access to cold, hard dollars.

That mutual need catalyzed to Russia's first post–Cold War experiment with covertly supporting private-military ventures to enhance its advantages in the global guns, gas, and oil trade.

Topped by leading generals who had distinguished themselves in the Afghan war, the paratroopers' union acted as a clearinghouse for private-security companies that operated abroad, including a precursor of the Wagner Group called Anti-Terror Oryol. Founded by a former navy veteran turned merchant marine named Sergey Isakov and a semiretired *spetsnaz* paratrooper named Sergey Epishkin, Anti-Terror Oryol billed itself as a security-training consultancy.[10] In reality, it functioned more like a confederation of special-forces airborne assault detachments, providing training and recruitment for Russian contract soldiers of fortune who served the security needs of large Russian enterprises in the energy industry.[11]

In exchange for the security provided by Anti-Terror Oryol for joint oil ventures in Iraq, Isakov's Russian Engineering Company, an affiliate of the state-owned Rosneft oil company, received a slice of the profits from lucrative oil trading deals tied to the UN-backed oil-for-food program in Iraq.[12] It was backed politically by influential figures in Moscow such as Putin's presidential chief of staff, Alexander Voloshin; former minister of energy Yuri Shafranik; and ultranationalist politician Vladimir Zhirinovsky. Anti-Terror Oryol also landed contracts with two other energy construction firms, Technopromexport and Energoengineering, as well as Tatneft, one of the first Russian oil companies to be traded on the Moscow Stock Exchange.[13]

These security deals were just the tip of the iceberg. Isakov's company received $210 million in oil contracts, making the Russian Engineering Company the sixth-largest foreign recipient of contracts under the UN-backed program.[14] With Russian firms controlling nearly a third of all the oil trade vouchers issued by Saddam under the controversial UN program, the Kremlin grew bolder in its campaign to undermine the UN embargo as UN Security Council members became divided over loosening sanctions.

Iraq became the testing ground for Russia's post–Cold War strategy of covertly subsidizing expeditionary paramilitary forces to bypass international sanctions. Over the following years, Anti-Terror Oryol extended its operations to countries such as Nigeria, Angola, Sierra Leone, Cambodia, and India. The model would prove to be as durable as it was mutable. But the one constant thread was the link among Russia's ultranationalist factions, elite special-forces veterans, mobbed-up businessmen, resource extraction, the global commodities trade, and the GRU intelligence service. The flap over Russian arms transfers to Iraq marked the beginning of the end of Putin's attempts at rapprochement with Washington. It was the first of many controversies that would emerge as Rosoboronexport sought to expand its slice of the world arms-trade market by circumventing international arms embargoes. Putin's first presidential term had in fact ushered in a renaissance for Russia's defense-export industry and the emergence in Russia of a whole new kind of market for clandestine military services. NATO expansion amid the disintegration of the Warsaw Pact military alliance made it nakedly obvious that Russia would have to rethink and retool its defense industry. But the transformation had been far from smooth or easy.

Unlike its global rival the United States, where big defense companies like Lockheed Martin could readily tap into available capital, attract investors, and even expand into niche consumer markets by developing technologies, Russia was financially and politically constrained from moving swiftly to diversify its export offerings. The business model that Putin inherited was broken. The entire architecture of defense exports centered on sweetheart arms-sales deals that offered credit and barter arrangements to developing countries that Moscow sought to enlist as Cold War allies in its contest with Washington. With only a few exceptions, most of Moscow's clients were broke. During the 1980s, countries such as Cuba, Angola, and Mozambique often bartered commodities that were hard for Russia to get, like bananas and palm oil, in exchange for arms sold under military technical cooperation agreements.

Whatever could not be covered by barter deals would be supplemented by billions of dollars in what some called "soft loans" because the terms of payment sometimes stretched to thirty or forty years.[15] The setup found Russia's national defense industry drowning in roughly $150 billion of debt accrued from unpaid sales of tanks, aircraft, and small arms delivered to the Kremlin's foreign clients. Before Putin became president, receipts for arms sales did not exceed much more than $2 billion to $4 billion a year, which meant that weapons were being sold at a fraction of their value—tolerable, apparently, because the defense industry was a huge employer. Rosoboronexport was not only the foreign-policy arm of the Kremlin; it was also the engine of an unevenly developed economy that depended on the conversion of raw materials that Russia had in abundance into machine-made finished products and their delivery by air, land, and sea. And Middle East dictators like Libya's Muammar Qaddafi and Iraq's Saddam Hussein, who had plentiful oil and gas revenues, were important cogs in this machine. Their regular cash payments were a critical staple for regime survival, no matter who held control of the Kremlin. This business model would prove enduring, shaping the way for the growth of Russia's private-military–security industry.

To keep the system running, Putin relied on two of his closest colleagues in the KGB, Nikolai Patrushev and Sergey Chemezov. Patrushev, a compatriot from their early days together as intelligence agents in Leningrad, wore many hats, but his primary role was to advise Putin on economic security and Russian grand strategy. One of his first tasks after replacing Putin as head of the FSB was to conduct an audit of Rosvoorouzhenie, the state weapons-manufacturing conglomerate. The review quickly discovered a host of corruption scandals, including the sale of a group of MiG-29 jet fighters to Peru at bargain-basement prices in exchange for a multimillion-dollar bribe to the arms company's director.[16] In the shakeup that followed, Chemezov, Putin's former KGB boss in Dresden, became deputy director of Promexport and eventually head of Rosoboronexport, the firm that emerged from the first wave of industry consolidation in 2000. With a sharp eye on global markets and unwavering loyalty to Putin, Chemezov, who also served on St. Petersburg's External Affairs Committee and followed Putin to the presidential administration in Moscow, turned Rosoboronexport into the powerhouse of Russia's arms exports.

At Chemezov's urging, Russia launched a four-year reorganization of the defense industry in 2002 that renationalized the sector and brought it under the state's full control. The move granted Rosoboronexport exclusive power over foreign arms sales and gave Chemezov, as the Kremlin-appointed CEO, unprecedented freedom to negotiate defense deals with other nations. Crucially, it also put him in charge of the profits from these arms sales, a portion of which flowed into a Kremlin slush fund that Putin, as president, could use at his discretion.[17] But the restructuring did not immediately resolve the challenge of Russia's reduced share of the global defense export market. Although China and India represented more than 50 percent of Russia's foreign arms sales, the maturation of the defense-manufacturing sector in both countries limited Rosoboronexport's ability to grow its sales.

The two factors that spurred growth of Russian arms exports on Chemezov's watch were rising global oil prices and the proliferation of sanctions against emerging economies. During the ten-year interregnum between the Soviet collapse and the September 11, 2001, terrorist attacks on the United States, Washington imposed fresh sanctions against Iraq, Iran, Sudan, Syria, Libya, and Venezuela. All were oil-rich, had plenty of cash, and were steady clients of Rosoboronexport.

But Russia still lagged far behind the West, which counted the United States, France, and Germany as the world's top three arms exporters. The further expansion of NATO after Bush was elected only reinforced this trend. The looming ascension of Bulgaria, Estonia, Latvia, Lithuania, Romania, Slovakia, and Slovenia after the US Senate ratified the treaty for the addition of all seven nations in May 2003 would increase the total number of NATO member states from nineteen to twenty-six the following year. So when Putin and Bush met separately on the sidelines in Russia that same month, they found their incentives more than a little mismatched, to say the least.

St. Petersburg sat at the center of this world drama for three days straight, and Prigozhin had a front-row view. He owed his thanks for his seat at the table of history as much to Putin as to St. Petersburg's governor, Vladimir Yakovlev, who had become a frequent customer at Prigozhin's Old Customs House restaurant. In the run-up to the 2003 jubilee, Prigozhin had become Yakovlev's go-to man for catering events for visiting delegations and had secured a substantial number of contracts with the local and federal governments, including the multimillion-dollar tender to serve as the lead caterer for presidential receptions during St. Petersburg's tercentenary celebration.[18] And that was just for starters.

At Putin's direction, the city had embarked three years earlier on a sweeping initiative of infrastructure revitalization and cultural rejuvenation. The Russian government spared no expense on the city's makeover, earmarking more than 40 million rubles in subsidies for the refurbishment of the cityscape.[19] Extensive efforts were undertaken to overhaul roads, bridges, and public parks. Historic landmarks like the Winter Palace, the Peter and Paul Fortress, and the Mariinsky Theatre underwent meticulous restoration. Overall government expenditures for the preparations of the jubilee celebration amounted to several billion dollars, reflecting the scale of Putin's grand ambitions for the city and the country.

Private donors poured nearly $300 million into restoring the Konstantinovsky Palace, a grand structure on the Strelna that had been ravaged by World War II. Once a battleground between Nazi and Soviet forces, the palace stood in ruins, with only its walls intact, when Vladimir Putin decreed its conversion into a presidential residence in 2001. The ambitious goal was to transform the palace into a symbol of Russia's resurgence, a showcase of Putin's achievements and of the revival of Russian power. During the celebratory events, Putin and his wife, Lyudmila, temporarily resided there, underscoring the palace's newfound significance in the great revival of Russian power that was under way.

A year before the gala dinner at Peterhof, Prigozhin's holding company, Concord Management and Consulting, won special permission from the city to renovate Trezzini House, an eighteenth-century manor on Vasilyevsky Island near the Old Customs House, and convert it into a four-star, forty-room hotel.[20] The dilapidated building, once home to Domenico Trezzini—the architectural mastermind behind the Peterhof Palace and many of St. Petersburg's iconic structures—was granted to Trezzini by Peter the Great in the 1720s as a token of gratitude. Although the building was in disrepair and required over a decade to commence construction, the deal was a lucrative one. Concord was granted a forty-nine-year lease on the property, significantly enhancing Prigozhin's reputation as a savvy businessman adept at leveraging Putin's patronage into profit. For his work during the tercentenary, the Russian government awarded Prigozhin two shiny medals, one for "Service to the Fatherland," and an order in recognition of the 300th anniversary of St. Petersburg. Prigozhin, it seemed, had finally arrived. He was now firmly part of an emergent servant class of cooks, drivers, butlers, personal assistants, and yacht captains who leveraged their service to Russia's nouveau riche as a springboard to personal wealth.

A few months after the gala dinner at the Peterhof Palace, Putin, ever the loyal patron, celebrated his birthday on board Prigozhin's New Island restaurant with a few members of the presidential cabinet and Russian film luminaries. "Putin saw how I grew a whole business out of a small stall," Prigozhin later bragged to a local reporter. "He saw that I am not above personally serving a plate to people of royal standing, because they are my guests."[21] Although Prigozhin was not yet an insider, his role as the president's top events manager cemented his place as a man who could be trusted to serve the Kremlin discreetly. His star was ascendant, Russia's constellation of power was shifting, and the Kremlin's brief experiment with cooperation with the West and tolerance at home was ending.

THE CHANGE BECAME most evident in the summer of 2003 amid a showdown between Putin and Russia's richest man, Mikhail Khodorkovsky. At the center of this tug-of-war was the future of the country's energy industry and the fate of the Yukos Oil Company, the company that Khodorkovsky had founded. With an estimated market capitalization of $21 billion, Yukos ranked among the top 500 companies in the world and was the pearl of Russia's oil industry.

By way of having the funds and the know-how, Khodorkovsky came to orchestrate the purchase of Yukos through a circuitous route that wound from his days as a nerdy student of chemical engineering in Moscow at the Mende-leev Institute for Chemical Technology in the 1980s through the Communist Party's Komsomol Youth League. Together with his good friend Leonid Nev-zlin, Khodorkovsky parlayed his party connections into building a start-up computer import and trade business in 1987. The Center for Scientific and Technical Creativity for Youth (MENATEP) might have seemed an unlikely vehicle for breaking into global finance, but after it was renamed Bank Menatep in 1990 and began gobbling up huge chunks of Russia's state-owned industrial enterprises sold at fire-sale prices, the possibilities seemed endless.

In 1993 Khodorkovsky landed a plum job as a senior-level adviser with the title of deputy at Russia's fuel and energy ministry. The timing was pro-pitious. That same year, Yeltsin issued a decree that seeded the breakup and restructuring of Russia's state-owned oil-production industry and conversion of parts of the fuel and energy ministry assets into the state-owned oil company Rosneft.[22] The reforms paved the way for the merger of two state companies—Yuganskneftegaz and Samaraneftegaz—into an oil-extraction firm and the for-mation of a related holding company called Yukos. Khodorkovsky converted the insights and contacts he gained from his time at the ministry to engineer Bank Menatep's 1995 purchase of a controlling stake in Yukos for $350 million in an auction that many viewed as rigged.[23]

The purchase grew out of a controversial Yeltsin-era compact known as the "loans for shares" deal. Under the scheme, Khodorkovsky and a small coterie of Russian billionaires snapped up controlling shares of newly privatized compa-nies at auction in exchange for loans that facilitated Yeltsin's 1996 reelection. The arrangement favored wealthy insiders like Khodorkovsky, spotlighting the extreme wealth gap between an emergent class of Russian oligarchs and the rest of the country. Khodorkovsky's capture of Yukos not only underscored the bra-zen tactics employed by well-connected power players in the era's privatization frenzy but also exposed the dark underside of the new political dynamics at play in Russia's nascent market economy.

Over the years that followed, Khodorkovsky pulled off a minor miracle. By applying Western-style accounting and management practices, he managed to erase $3 billion in debt on the company's books. The value of Yukos subse-quently increased sevenfold, and the company doubled its annual production output from 40 million tons to twice that amount.[24]

Khodorkovsky and Putin initially shared a vision for Russia's future. Both understood that the country's vast oil and gas reserves were its lifeline to the outside world. But their approaches diverged sharply. Putin's vision for Russia's energy sector was rooted in state control, with a monopoly over the country's natural resources. Putin famously even authored a plagiarized dissertation on the topic of Russia's mineral resources and strategic planning for the oil and gas market while studying for his PhD in economics at the St. Petersburg State Mining Institute.[25] The thesis borrowed heavily from an American textbook on mining—an interesting choice of subject for a lawyer turned spy with little or no formal background in the oil, gas, or mining industry, but it reflected the new national fervency around the dream that Russia's abundant oil, gas, and mineral resources could restore the country's superpower status.

Khodorkovsky, on the other hand, championed free-market principles, favored closer ties with the West, and embraced globalization. Rich, confident, and seemingly untouchable, he launched Open Russia, a civic organization that advocated political and social reforms, shedding his robber-baron image and positioning himself as a liberal reformer—a role that stood in stark contrast to Putin's authoritarian tendencies and his promise to "liquidate" the oligarch class upon taking office.

The country experienced record GDP growth during Putin's first term and appeared poised to shrug off its crippling debt load as he prepared his bid for a second presidential term. But economic growth was relative; Russia's GDP had been in the negative zone for more than a decade before Putin came to power. It was hard to parse out how much of the country's rapid economic turnaround could be attributed to Putin's policies versus externalities such as the high price of oil on the global market.[26] The economy was highly sensitive to dramatic shifts in the petroleum supply-demand curve, as was the Kremlin.

This logic also drove the renationalization of Gazprom, which Putin saw as both an economic powerhouse and a geopolitical tool. Gazprom, one of Russia's largest employers, accounted for about 25 percent of the country's GDP and 10 percent of the national budget.[27]

To tighten control, Putin replaced independent directors with loyalists from his St. Petersburg circle, appointing to Gazprom's board his trusted friend and campaign manager, Dmitry Medvedev, in 2000 and Alexey Miller, another key St. Petersburg hand, in 2001. Like Rosoboronexport, Gazprom was given broad authority over its security, expanding its private army from thirteen thousand to twenty thousand under the leadership of ex-KGB colonel Vladimir Maruschenko.[28] Maruschenko, who trained the agency's leaders and headed a veterans' association, leveraged his connections to recruit *spetsnaz* veterans, setting a trend for staffing Russia's top industries from veterans' associations that handily retained their import-export licenses, making them useful for all kinds of covert activity.

It was against this backdrop of tightening Kremlin control over the trifecta heart of Russia's economy—guns, gas, and oil—that Khodorkovsky dropped a bombshell. In April 2003 he announced plans for a merger between Yukos and Sibneft, a large oil firm then under the control of Putin's close friend Roman Abramovich. Under the terms of the deal, core shareholders of Sibneft agreed to sell a 20 percent interest in the company to Yukos for $3 billion in cash. Combined, the merger deal would give Yukos control of some 19 billion barrels of oil, making it the fourth-largest multinational oil company in the world. Amid the continued meltdown between Washington and Moscow over the US war in Iraq, news of the merger sent a shock through Russia's political system. Khodorkovsky's quixotic quest to turn the company into an engine of social and political change suddenly took on a new significance.

The merger would have granted Khodorkovsky control over the second-largest oil and gas reserves in the world. Once the deal was sealed, Yukos-Sibneft would become a challenger to all comers. Seeing the writing on the wall, the American giant ExxonMobil sought to gain a stake in the merger. The deal ignited a political tempest within the Kremlin and seemed to especially offend Igor Sechin, another St. Petersburg hand with a KGB pedigree, whom Putin had appointed to serve as a presidential adviser on security and energy issues. The crux of the contretemps centered on Khodorkovsky's vocal criticism of a questionable deal that saw the sale of a scandal-plagued oil company called Severnaya Neft to Rosneft for a fraction of the northern oil company's value.

In a televised meeting between Putin and the country's business titans, Khodorkovsky openly confronted the Russian president about the lack of transparency surrounding the agreement, which increased Rosneft's annual oil output exponentially. "At the time I still believed that Putin hadn't yet decided how he wanted to deal with corruption and how to govern the country," Khodorkovsky said in an interview years later. "For that reason, in 2003 I decided to go, and hear the president out and listen to what he had to say. I believed at the time that the decision hadn't yet been made about how to rule the country. But it turned out I was mistaken."[29]

There were other mistakes too, but the cost of Khodorkovsky's testy on-camera exchange with Putin would become apparent only in October

2003, when a team of masked FSB officers with the agency's Sixth Directorate stormed aboard Khodorkovsky's private jet during a business trip to Siberia and arrested him at gunpoint on suspicion of tax fraud and tax evasion.

Khodorkovsky was convinced that Sechin had weaponized the Sixth Directorate to orchestrate his arrest as revenge for the dustup over the Severnaya Neft sale to Rosneft. A holdover from the Soviet era, when counterintelligence agents monitored every aspect of trade and secretly spied on the heads of industrial-production companies, the FSB's Sixth Directorate was charged with conducting counterintelligence investigations in Russia's economic sphere. But through a combination of purges and appointments, Sechin was at the time slowly in the process of transforming the FSB subunit into his own personal fiefdom and a tool of retribution against Kremlin critics.[30]

Khodorkovsky's pretrial detention for more than a year and the lengthy criminal trial upended the lives of dozens of Yukos employees and all but bankrupted the oil giant. Portions of the company were sold off at a fraction of their value to Rosneft, where Sechin was made CEO soon after Khodorkovsky's arrest. Overnight, Yukos became a watchword for Russia's seemingly inexorable drift away from the West and Putin's embrace of the authoritarian past.

The fallout was significant. Legal battles between the Kremlin and Yukos shareholders dragged on for years, leaving a trail of financial and political damage. But the real story was the deepening feud between Khodorkovsky and Putin. Their grudge match, through proxies like Prigozhin and spanning continents, would continue to play out for years. This wasn't just a business clash—it was a personal vendetta with far-reaching consequences.

As Khodorkovsky's influence crumbled, Putin's grip tightened, and new players started to emerge. The system that had catapulted both men into Russia's upper strata was tilting on a new axis. Putin's tight circle of KGB apparatchiks—the so-called men of force or *siloviki*—sharply elbowed aside anyone or anything that got in their way. In the process, Prigozhin inched up a rung, edging out players like Mirilashvili and filling the vacuum left behind after his other erstwhile patron, Roman Tsepov, died mysteriously in 2004 after drinking a cup of tea laced with a radioactive substance. Although Prigozhin's full role was still taking shape, the foundation was being laid for a new kind of Russian power vertical—one that erased the lines between state action and private ambition and that would reshape how Russia exerted influence at home and abroad long into the future.

CHAPTER 5

THE LAST SUPPER

Years after the fact, George W. Bush would barely be able to recall his final encounter with Yevgeny Prigozhin. The man who had served him during his last presidential dinner in St. Petersburg, in July 2006, had since slipped into the recesses of memory. But other moments from that night at the Konstantinovsky Palace remained sharp and vivid: Tony Blair's sheepish grin as he rushed to his seat, Jacques Chirac's eager gulp of wine, and Angela Merkel's wince during Bush's awkward neck massage—a five-second gaffe that was caught on camera and spun into viral internet memes.

The table gleamed under the golden glow of chandeliers, a masterpiece of elegance and significance. The dinner was one in a series orchestrated by Prigozhin, and it marked Russia's first time hosting the G8 summit. Putin, his face set in an inscrutable mask, sat as an equal among the world's most powerful. Yet beneath the polished surface, there was an undercurrent of betrayal, a tension that hummed like the air before a storm. The cracks between Russia and the West, once hairline, had deepened into visible fissures, their rupture seemingly inevitable. It was a gathering of world leaders who still smiled for the cameras, unaware—or perhaps unwilling to acknowledge—that history would soon divide them.

This would be one of Prigozhin's final moments in the orbit of a US president. Years later, his role would take on a different, more dangerous dimension, but that night he was just a man in the backdrop, like Judas at the Last Supper—present in history but not yet infamous. Long after leaving the White

House, Bush was shown a photo of that evening, his proximity to Prigozhin now weighted with the irony of hindsight. What did it mean? All Bush could offer was a wry smile and an ironic quip: "All I know is I survived."[1]

Prigozhin, on the other hand, remembered every detail. Hovering unctuously in the background in a black tuxedo jacket and white bow tie, he tracked every word exchanged between Bush and Putin during the dinner. By then, Prigozhin's habit of meticulously documenting Putin's interactions with world leaders had begun to veer toward the compulsive; he routinely instructed his staff to note who said what and to whom.[2]

Some dismissed the behavior as little more than a quirky obsession, a reflection of Prigozhin's narcissistic tendencies, perhaps tied to his own ambitions to one day write a tell-all memoir. After all, he had already ventured into vanity publishing, writing a colorfully illustrated children's book titled *Indraguzik*. A whimsical story inspired by the bedtime tales he spun for his children, the tale recounts the adventures of a family of tiny people who live in a chandelier that has magical powers to make small things big. Prigozhin was no Dr. Seuss, but he proudly gave away limited-edition copies to family and friends.

Whatever his writerly ambitions, his diaristic compunctions may well have been a useful means for Prigozhin to pick up stray bits of intelligence during diplomatic table talk that might be as valuable to him as it was to Putin. Ever diligent, Prigozhin catalogued his every encounter with Putin and his inner circle in a Palm Pilot diary. In coded shorthand, Prigozhin jotted down his schedule of meetings with Kremlin bigwigs, a revealing record of how well Prigozhin had learned to play the game and of his careful cultivation of relationships with Russia's power players.

For anyone with real clout, he always had a special gift ready for those big moments. For Putin, there was a nicely boxed pair of bottles of 1912-vintage port wine and a few mint-condition issues of the Soviet-era literary magazine *Neva*; for Sergey Lavrov, Russia's notoriously persnickety foreign minister, there was an expensive bottle of French Armagnac.[3]

The dinner at the palace itself, of course, was flawless, and so was the intimate supper Prigozhin prepared for a cozy couples dinner with Bush, Putin, and their spouses that followed, reinforcing the image of a Russia in control. But the signs of discord were impossible to ignore. Whether Prigozhin ultimately delivered an action report to Putin following the G8 summit dinners is unknown, but if he had, it certainly would have been useful.

The summit's agenda was thick with sticky issues—Russia's stalled membership application for the World Trade Organization, Iran's nuclear program, the thorny question of NATO's eastward expansion, and energy security. The last item on the list was especially sensitive because of Ukraine and Georgia. Both were in a battle with Russia over price hikes that had ripple effects in Europe, making Western leaders increasingly wary of Russia's growing assertiveness. Prigozhin's observations, if passed on to Putin, would have provided useful insight into the West's resolve, offering a clearer picture of the diplomatic battleground ahead.

The feeling of unease during the summit was pervasive. Bush, who had once famously declared he could "get a sense of Putin's soul," was now looking into the eyes of a man who seemed increasingly opaque and sphinxlike. Days before the conference kickoff, Russian security agencies had jailed dozens of activists as they traveled to St. Petersburg to join a planned protest at the G8 gathering. In an awkward exchange during a press conference, Bush broached the topic of Russia's authoritarian backsliding, making a clumsy comparison between Iraq and Russia that prompted a sardonic smile and sharp quip from Putin: "I'll be honest with you: we, of course, would not want to have a democracy like in Iraq."[4] The remark drew guffaws and applause from the assembled press corps, but Putin's dripping sarcasm hinted at his growing antipathy toward the United States.

The precipitating causes were many. But the wound that refused to close stemmed primarily from the outbreak of three successive democratic uprisings in what Russia traditionally considered to be its backyard. The first erupted in neighboring Georgia a month after Mikhail Khodorkovsky was jailed, in November 2003. There, amid freezing temperatures, crowds of protesters in the country's capital, Tbilisi, burst into parliament with roses in hand demanding the annulment of fraudulent elections and the resignation of the country's president, Edvard Shevardnadze. His challenger, Mikhail Saakashvili, a brash Columbia University–educated firebrand, rode to power in 2004 on the wave of the Rose Revolution, promising to steer Georgia toward the West and reclaim the breakaway regions of South Ossetia and Abkhazia.

Georgia's uprising was swiftly followed by Ukraine's Orange Revolution in the winter of 2004. Electoral fraud played its part there too, prompting a popular call for the rerun of presidential elections. In Kyiv, young students, elderly veterans, middle-class professionals, and everyone in between merged under the orange banner of Viktor Yushchenko, an energetic, Western-leaning opposition politician whose Our Ukraine Party challenged the entrenched dominance of the Kremlin in Ukrainian politics.

Yushchenko's opponent and Ukraine's incumbent prime minister Viktor Yanukovych and his Party of Regions had received public backing from both his predecessor Leonid Kuchma and Putin. But even that was not enough to hold back the flood tide of public outrage over suspected Kremlin meddling in a vote marred by fraud. Donning orange scarves, sweaters, hats, and jackets, tens of thousands marched peacefully through the chilly streets of the Ukrainian capital and other cities, calling for political change. Widespread popular support for Yushchenko led to his elevation as president of Ukraine in March 2004.

Next came the Tulip Revolution in Kyrgyzstan in the spring of 2005, when anger over fraud in parliamentary elections prompted street protests and the ouster of Askar Akayev, another regional strongman and Kremlin favorite. The third of the so-called color revolutions triggered a visceral reaction from Putin, who saw Washington's shadowy hand everywhere he turned his gaze.

Compounding these tensions was the 2003 launch of construction on the Baku-Tbilisi-Ceyhan (BTC) pipeline, a $3.6 billion, 1,100-mile project designed to bypass Russia and Iran, providing a direct route for Caspian Sea oil to Western markets. The pipeline, which was intended to transport a million barrels of oil per day, was heralded by the Bush administration as a key energy initiative. To ensure its success in an increasingly volatile region, the United States provided substantial aid, including $64 million to train Georgian troops in antiterrorism tactics, with plans to allocate another $100 million for the Caspian Guard, a network of special-operations units tasked with protecting critical oil infrastructure.[5]

Saakashvili hailed the pipeline's construction as a boon for Georgia's moribund post-Soviet economy and a sign of the country's growing importance in the region. Not surprisingly, conservative voices inside and outside the Kremlin took a darker view, casting the project as more evidence of Western encroachment. As tensions between Georgia and Russia escalated over the disputed status of South Ossetia and Abkhazia, the pipeline became a symbol of Russian and Western competition for influence in the region, adding another layer of tinder to an already combustible situation.

Instability had plagued South Ossetia and Abkhazia since the Soviet collapse. In South Ossetia, an initial conflict in the early 1990s left more than a thousand dead and tens of thousands displaced, leading to a 1993 ceasefire and the creation of a multilateral peacekeeping force of Georgian, Russian, and Ossetian troops. A similar scenario unfolded in Abkhazia, resulting in a 1994 UN-brokered ceasefire and the deployment of Russian peacekeepers in Sukhumi. Despite nominal autonomy, both regions became highly dependent on Moscow, existing in a frozen state of legal limbo, unrecognized by any nation, including Russia.

Strategically, these disputed territories were vital for Russia's influence and its military and trade footholds. The mountainous coastal lands of Georgia's Black Sea coastline were crucial for business in the Caucasus, with rivers feeding hydroelectric stations and transit routes for oil, gas, and timber. Control over these areas allowed Russia to dominate the Black Sea and maintain key trade routes. However, the prospect of Georgia and Ukraine joining NATO threatened to restrict Russia's access to its only warm-water sea route, a scenario as unacceptable to Putin as it was to Catherine the Great in 1768.

Although peacekeeping efforts temporarily stabilized the region, energy-transit routes became a point of contention. By 2004, as Putin entered his second presidential term, Gazprom was under pressure to reconcile domestic gas demand with Putin's ambition to transform Russia into an energy superpower. Following the color revolutions, Gazprom imposed price hikes on Ukraine and Georgia, leading to rolling blackouts and energy shortages in Georgia. Putin blamed the pro-Western leaders for the trouble, but the reality was that Gazprom, though powerful, was a financial basket case, and Russia's economy was addicted to gas revenues.

Reforms initiated by Gazprom CEO Alexey Miller did little to shift the company's need to gobble up fresh territory and infrastructure to produce the high rates of return required to keep Russia's economy humming. The potential for reduced access to the southwest corridor along the Black Sea coast in Abkhazia and South Ossetia threatened to put a big dent in Gazprom's bottom line.

In January 2006, Russia's abrupt halt of gas supplies to Ukraine and Georgia marked a new climax in the so-called gas wars. Disputes over price hikes and transit fees exacerbated simmering political animosities between Moscow and Tbilisi and Kyiv. Gazprom demanded that Ukraine's Naftogaz pay more than four times the going rate of $50 per 1,000 cubic feet of gas.[6] Gazprom hit Georgia just as hard, doubling the rate when it hiked the price per 1,000 cubic feet from $110 to $230.[7]

Tensions between Moscow and Tbilisi only worsened when, in late 2006, Gazprom broke ground for the construction of its hundred-mile-long

Dzuarikau-Tskhinvali gas pipeline. Russia's weaponization of energy seemed only to harden Saakashvili's resolve to retake South Ossetia and Abkhazia. Putin, in turn, began to lean hard into his support for the de facto proxy governments in the breakaway regions.

To further complicate matters, the Pankisi Gorge—a remote mountain area on Georgia's border with Dagestan—had become a refuge for thousands of Chechen refugees, along with gunrunners and kidnappers. Putin accused Saakashvili of deliberately turning the region into a terrorist safe haven, a line that echoed concerns from Washington. Following a series of global terrorist attacks, the Bush administration feared that the Caucasus could become a haven for al-Qaeda because of the weak security along the Russia-Georgia border. Those fears whipped up unprecedented US support for a train-and-equip mission aimed at strengthening Georgia's military as a counterterrorism bulwark. Saakashvili, eager to secure continued aid and bolster Georgia's NATO bid, sent thousands of US-trained troops to Iraq and Afghanistan.

The tit-for-tat tensions between Saakashvili and Putin intensified in July 2006, when Georgia's parliament called for the withdrawal of Russian peacekeepers from South Ossetia and Abkhazia following the opening of the US-backed BTC pipeline. Relations hit a new low in September, when Russia's defense minister, Sergey Ivanov, put Russian troops in Georgia on high alert, issuing a shoot-to-kill order after the arrest of four Russian soldiers accused of spying. In retaliation, Moscow cracked down on Georgian-owned businesses in Russia and deported more than a hundred Georgians for alleged visa violations.

Colonel Bob Hamilton, then the US embassy's defense attaché and adviser to the train-and-equip mission in Tbilisi, remembered the period as almost unbearably tense. Saakashvili seemed to be playing a dangerous game of chicken to bolster his waning political popularity on the domestic front. "In the embassy, the message was always very, very clear: we will not help you; we cannot and will not help you if you get yourself into a war with the Russians over Abkhazia and South Ossetia," Hamilton recalled. "We would tell the Georgians, look, you've got to not walk into the trap. And what the Georgians would always say was, look, what's also happening is the annexation of our territory by the Russians, and we have to respond in some way. 'How would you propose that we respond to this creeping annexation that's going on?' In this way, the Russia strategy was very brilliant in a lot of ways in that they had identified this sort of gap between Georgian and Western thinking on the frozen conflicts and exploited it."[8]

Three imperatives drove Putin's strategy as his second term ended. Priority one was suppressing armed rebellions in territories adjacent to Chechnya. The second was to control Caspian and Black Sea trade, transport, and energy routes. The third was to block further NATO encroachment in Russia's traditional spheres of influence. Anything short of these steps would not only heighten instability but would also, from Putin's viewpoint, imperil Russia's rebirth as a Great Power. During Putin's first term as president, the nuances of this line of reasoning were missed by many, including the Bush White House. It was only when Putin issued a much more trenchant warning at the Munich Security Conference in February 2007 that the world pricked up its ears. When Putin declared that the extension of membership to Georgia and Ukraine was a "serious provocation," it sparked fears that further NATO expansion could trigger a more forceful confrontation.

He was drawing a redline, but Washington, as Putin noted sharply when that same month the United States formally expressed support for Kosovo's independence, seemed impervious. "They have not thought through the results of what they are doing," Putin groused in televised remarks after the news broke. "At the end of the day, it is a two-ended stick, and the second end will come back and hit them in the face."[9]

In April 2008, Bush responded in kind with a sharp message of his own, vowing that Russian hostility would not get in the way of Georgia's and Ukraine's eventual ascension to NATO. Delivered on a stopover in Kyiv en route to a NATO summit in Bucharest that was part of a farewell tour of Europe in the final days of Bush's second presidential term, his remarks landed like a gut punch in Moscow: "Russia will not have a veto over what happens next in Bucharest."[10]

Putin flew into a fit of pique, and the Duma began to hold hearings on whether to recognize the independence of South Ossetia and Abkhazia to counter the "Kosovo precedent." In Bucharest the next day, Putin told Bush during a private meeting that Ukraine did not exist as a sovereign nation. Putin was even sharper in the public speech he delivered at the conference, warning that Russia viewed membership in the alliance for Georgia and Ukraine as nothing short of a "direct threat."

Acceding to pressure from Germany and France, NATO ultimately decided to delay its decision on extending a membership action plan to Georgia and Ukraine. But Saakashvili interpreted Bush's pronouncement as a green light for Georgia to continue rattling its saber over the unresolved status of

South Ossetia and Abkhazia. This would turn out to be a costly misreading of the signals coming out of both Washington and Moscow.

The NATO meeting was barely over when the first sparks flew. On April 11, Russia's chief of General Staff, Yuri Baluyevsky, threatened to take military action, hinting that psychological and sabotage operations were on the table. A little more than a week later, Russian forces shot down Georgian reconnaissance drones over Abkhazia in three separate incidents, including one caught on camera. Mutual recriminations between Tbilisi and Moscow followed. Putin—then entering the final days of his second presidential term—next signed a decree calling for closer relations between Russia and Georgia's two breakaway republics. This was followed by a military exercise of eight thousand soldiers—Kavkaz 2008—just across the border, which provided cover for a progressive buildup of additional forces in the region. With each passing day, Moscow and Tbilisi seemed to edge closer to war.

IT WAS AGAINST this backdrop that Alexander Dugin, a hustler of another stripe and the self-anointed soothsayer of Russia's manifest destiny, traveled from Moscow to South Ossetia in late June 2008. His tour of the tiny patch of land along the strategic fault line in the Caucasus Mountains between Russia and Georgia was a personal first. Dugin came as a man on a mission, an evangelist for a political movement that had crept, virus-like, from the far-right fringes of Russia's variegated opposition movements into the central nerve system of Russian military thinking.

Traveling with an entourage for a weeklong youth boot camp sponsored by his International Eurasian Movement, Dugin had planned this trip for months, but it had been years in the making. Organized with financing from a South Ossetian banker eager to curry favor with the Kremlin, Dugin's maiden voyage to the region was part of a whistlestop tour launched three years earlier with what was widely presumed to be quiet support from the Russian government.[11]

The gathering for members of Dugin's Eurasian Youth Movement (ESM) offered lessons in the art of military preparedness, esoteric lectures on mystical bonds between ethnic Ossetians and Russians, and stark warnings about US intentions to replace Russia as the regional hegemon in the Caucasus. Camp attendees included teenage and twenty-something delegates from ESM youth branches in Italy, Romania, Turkey, and Kazakhstan. Several also traveled from Crimea and other parts of Ukraine, where just a year earlier, in 2007, the government had banned Dugin's youth movement because of his insistence that Ukraine should be reabsorbed into Russia.[12]

At the press conference that capped the event in the South Ossetian capital, Tskhinvali, Dugin had promised he was ready for war. This was a stretch. But the main thrust of Dugin's message on his maiden voyage to South Ossetia— that the world order would be set right again only once Russia was able to push back US hegemony, recognize the independence of Georgia's breakaway regions, and bring former Soviet territories back under the Kremlin's yoke— was eerily on point and in tune with Putin's thinking. "If Russia backs down and makes concessions on the issue of recognition of independence, I think Russia will demonstrate its weakness, and this is very bad," Dugin told a rapt audience at a university lecture hall in South Ossetia. "If Russia recognizes the independence of South Ossetia and introduces not peacekeeping forces but Russian border troops, then the issue of admitting Georgia to NATO will either be removed from the agenda for a long time, or it will mean a direct conflict with the United States."[13] The messaging was timely, and although Dugin's prognostication was more a mirror of the moment than a crystal-ball reading, it augured a seismic shift in Russia's grand strategy that would come amid a clash between Russian and Georgian forces only a couple weeks after Dugin's trip to the region.

If Prigozhin was emblematic of a new breed of moneyed loyalists who understood that in Putin's Russia, power was as much about optics and showy displays of fealty to the Kremlin as it was about strategic acumen, then Dugin was their aspiring spiritual guide, channeling the deep currents of Russian nationalism into a coherent, if radical, geopolitical doctrine. In the decade plus since he had penned a best-selling manifesto that called for Russia to annex Georgia, Ukraine, and Finland, Dugin had developed a knack for showing up at the right time in the right place and saying the things that the Kremlin wanted the world to hear.[14] Born in Moscow in 1962 into a well-to-do family, Dugin impressed many who met him in his younger years as an eccentric with an aristocratic bearing that reflected his station as the son of a high-ranking GRU military-intelligence officer. An autodidact with an exceptional talent for languages, Dugin began to carve his own path in the 1980s, when he fell in with a group of Bohemian occult-loving Moscow subalterns who venerated the mysticism of Hitler's Third Reich. A brief turn with the ultranationalist Pamyat faction, then time on the barricades in Moscow during the 1993 constitutional crisis with the putschists who took over Russia's parliament building, catalyzed his career as a professional ideologue steeped in the traditions of the European New Right and Russian chauvinism.

Together with Eduard Limonov, a leading literary light of Russia's ultranationalist cadres, Dugin formed from their circle of proto-fascist rabble-rousers the National Bolshevik Party, which blended Stalinism with the neo-Nazi aesthetic of punk counterculture into a platform for hard-line opposition to liberalism. Another key Dugin influencer was novelist and military propagandist Alexander Prokhanov, whose tight relations with revanchist members of Russia's officer corps earned him the sobriquet "Nightingale of the General Staff."

Those connections and Dugin's messianic musings in Prokhanov's ultranationalist weekly *Den'* and its successor *Zavtra* on how zeal for illiberal authoritarianism and military confrontation with the West could make Russia great again earned Dugin an invitation in the 1990s to lecture at the Russian military's prestigious Academy of the General Staff. The training school for Russia's elite officer corps was a critical vector in the nexus between aggrieved military leaders who resented their slide down the social ladder after the Soviet collapse and the amalgamation of disillusioned "Red" Communist Party members and "Brown" fascist street gangs, intellectuals, and activists who had fueled Russia's two failed coups.

The lectures became the basis for Dugin's 1997 doorstopper of a book, *The Foundations of Geopolitics*, which, among other things, posited the reabsorption of Soviet lands into a reborn Russia. Key to this formula was a showdown between the United States over the future of a multipolar world order as an inevitable step on the path to the resurrection of Moscow as the "Third Rome." Drawing on a thread of thinking that dates back to the early twentieth-century writings of conservative Russian polemicist Nikolay Trubetzkoy, Dugin peppered his analysis with meditations on German philosopher-soldier Ernst Jünger and Sir Harold Mackinder, an obscure British geographer credited with coining the word *geopolitics*. Dugin divided the world into civilizational sectors, conjuring Russia's revival as an empire and the dominant geopolitical center of gravity across the vast terrain that lies between Europe and Asia, or Eurasia, as he conceptualized it.

Fantastical in its claims and pretensions, Dugin's seminal work of political philosophy essentially proposed redrawing the map of the world order, a proposal that would reignite in the minds of some in Russia's military elite a fever dream of resurrecting the Russian empire. The book became required reading for Russian officers and resonated strongly with hard-core nationalists.

Most importantly for Dugin, who strove to insinuate himself into national politics, his tome would gain him entrée into the outer ring of Kremlin influencers striving to gain favor with Putin, like Dmitry Rogozin, who in 2008 served as Russia's ambassador to NATO. Although his influence was often overstated, it was these associations and Dugin's talent for self-promotion and well-timed sound bites that earned him the moniker "Putin's brain."

Holding forth with his vodka-pink cheeks at the gathering in South Ossetia in the summer of 2008, Dugin was positively giddy about the prospect of war and the coming reckoning over NATO expansion: "Our troops will occupy the Georgian capital Tbilisi, the entire country, and perhaps even Ukraine and the Crimean Peninsula, which is historically part of Russia, anyway."[15]

Things would not go nearly that far, but there were other, more covert signs that indicated Russia had been planning for months, if not years, a direct military confrontation with Georgia. One hint was the quiet deployment to Abkhazia of Redut-Antiterror, a contingent of Russian soldiers of fortune hired on contract to backstop the operations of the VDV 10th Guards Airborne Division in the Caucasus during the peak of the crisis in the region.

Redut-Antiterror was a spinoff organization of Anti-Terror Oryol, the paramilitary outfit founded amid the frenzy to secure shady oil-for-food deals in Iraq under Saddam Hussein when several Russian oil majors began doing business there. Russian corporate-registry records showed that one of the paramilitary's founding members, Sergey Epishkin, was still on board with the outfit. Under new management but still linked to the Oryol group's original founders, the new configuration was partially a by-product of the scandal that had exploded into public view when press accounts and government-led investigations in 2005 exposed massive corruption in the UN program.

Several rounds of reorganization would see Redut-Antiterror take on other names, including PMC Shield, when the paramilitary was deployed to protect energy and mining infrastructure for Russian companies, most notably for Stroytransgaz, the energy-engineering company linked to Putin's friend Gennady Timchenko. Variously known also as "Redut Union," "Center R," the "Redut-Center for Operational and Tactical Decisions," or simply "Redut," the new amalgamation of special operators for hire modeled itself on a trade union and touted its training services online.[16]

Technically, Redut would come to be a nongovernmental organization registered with Russia's Volunteer Society for Cooperation with the Army, Aviation, and Navy (DOSAAF) as the Moscow-based arm of the Veterans of Peacekeeping Missions and Local Conflicts. Under a 2005 law passed in response to the color revolutions, Redut was one of several veterans' associations officially charged with providing advice to active-duty units, retraining reserve officers, and training future recruits via youth camps.[17] The paramilitary's shadow mission was to serve as a hub for the recruitment and mobilization of special-purpose detachments that operated under the direction of the GRU. Redut provided support primarily to VDV Airborne units, including the 7th Guards Airborne Division in Abkhazia, among others.

The brains behind the outfit were two of Russia's most notorious military veterans: Colonel Pavel Popovskikh and Major Konstantin Mirzayants. Popovskikh, a highly decorated veteran of the Soviet-Afghan war, was known for his role as the head of military intelligence for Russia's airborne forces and as the founder of the 45th Guards Spetsnaz Reconnaissance Brigade—a first-of-its-kind unconventional-warfare unit designed for covert operations deep behind enemy lines.[18] His right-hand man, Mirzayants, a graduate of the prestigious Ryazan Airborne Academy, had seen action in Transnistria and Chechnya before a battlefield concussion forced him into early retirement.

But their bond went beyond the battlefield. Both men were implicated in the murder of a journalist, a scandal that would dog them for years and ultimately push Popovskikh into retirement in 2006. Far from fading into obscurity, he took up a leadership role in the Union of Paratroopers, the veterans' organization that gave birth to Anti-Terror Oryol and eventually Redut. By 2008, as tensions escalated in the Caucasus, Redut found itself at the forefront of a historic crisis in Abkhazia—a place where Popovskikh had a home and deep personal ties.[19]

Tasked with overseeing Redut's operations in Georgia was Alexander Makhotkin, a battle-hardened veteran of the Second Chechen War. Known as "Srochka" or "Conscript," Makhotkin was a shadowy figure, rarely photographed and always elusive.[20]

But his reputation spoke volumes. Under his command, Redut's mission in Abkhazia was clear: to conduct reconnaissance, to train Kremlin-loyal forces, and to prepare for the inevitable showdown with Georgian troops.[21] Its operations were not limited to the battlefield—Redut also played a key role in disrupting Western interests in the region's energy sector, leaking damaging information about the Georgian government, and facilitating the delivery of military equipment that would soon be put to use in Russia's conflict with Georgia.

In many ways, Redut represented a new chapter in Russia's use of irregular military forces. It was an auxiliary force with a critical role in advancing Moscow's strategic interests, and its leaders, especially Mirzayants, would go on to influence the mercenary landscape in Russia. As Yevgeny Prigozhin rose to prominence, figures like Mirzayants would emerge as his rivals, each vying for control in the cutthroat world of Russian private-military companies.

Redut was a reflection of what was still wrong with the Russian military as Putin rounded the corner at the end of his second presidential term and prepared to hand the presidential reins to his political understudy, Dmitry Medvedev. Although Putin's old KGB colleague Sergey Ivanov had made some strides toward military reform during his five years as defense minister, dysfunction was still rife.

Behind the scenes of Russia's carefully curated image of strength, the reality of its military was far less impressive. The Russian armed forces were a shadow of their Soviet-era selves—bloated, inefficient, and plagued by corruption. The Chechen wars had exposed these weaknesses, but little had been done to address them. The military was large, but it was unwieldy, with outdated equipment, poorly trained conscripts, and a command structure that was more Soviet nostalgia than modern efficiency.

Putin understood these shortcomings, but reforming the military was no simple task. The military-industrial complex was deeply intertwined with the economy, and any significant changes threatened to upend the balance of power among the elite. Yet as NATO continued its eastward march and as color revolutions swept through Georgia, Ukraine, and Kyrgyzstan, the need for a capable, modern military became increasingly urgent, prompting Putin to call for creation of an "Innovation Army" and to hire an outsider to replace Ivanov in February 2007. This high-profile defense job went to tax minister Anatoly Serdyukov, and it was in part a reward for Serdyukov's successful pursuit of the tax-fraud case against oil magnate Mikhail Khodorkovsky and other Yukos Oil executives. In that instance, Serdyukov had shed light on how, through the bureaucratic magic of audits, big political problems could be solved with minimal bloodshed. With the 2008 elections and his nominal transfer of power to Medvedev looming, Putin tasked Serdyukov with performing a similar miracle in the defense sector.[22]

At the time, Russian forces stood at a little over one million strong and were spread across the military's three main branches—army, navy, and aerospace—and its two independent services, the strategic-missile forces and

the airborne forces, which fell under the direct command of Putin as commander in chief. This unwieldy force structure relied heavily on conscript soldiers and an extremely heavy officer corps that was often resistant to change.
High-ranking generals were especially good at throwing up barriers to reform,
and they were highly incentivized to do so because they stood to lose not only
their jobs but also the lucrative perks that allowed them to skim off the top and
sell inventory.

With the potential for a face-off with Georgia a mere heartbeat away, Serdyukov's charge to overhaul the military was all the more urgent and challenging. By midsummer 2008, rumors of war were no longer rumors; they were all
but a certainty. In a demonstration of resolve, Russia flew a squad of Su-24 jet-
fighters over the border into Georgian airspace on July 8, one of several provocative escalatory steps en route to a full conflagration.[23]

On August 1, after a roadside bomb triggered an exchange of gunfire
between Georgian and South Ossetian forces, Russian-backed South Ossetian forces shelled Georgian villages near the border. Saakashvili took the bait,
launching an all-out assault on Tskhinvali six days later, just as the world was
settling in to watch the pageantry of the opening-day ceremony of the Summer
Olympics in Beijing. Only a few hours before the start of the games, Saakashvili
had ordered Georgian troops near the Roki Tunnel pass to unleash a retaliatory
fusillade of artillery on Russian troops.

With some 35,000–40,000 soldiers assembled and waiting in the region,
Russian forces proved they were more than ready to respond.[24] On the third
day, the conflict quickly spilled into Abkhazia, where the Russians attacked
by land and by sea and occupied the Georgian town of Zugdidi. Meanwhile,
hackers mounted cyberattacks on Georgian government and media websites,
marking a first in the history of warfare and all but ensuring total Russian control of the narrative. Heavy fighting displaced close to 200,000, creating one
of the worst humanitarian emergencies in the region's volatile history. Within
five days of the start of the war, Medvedev declared a halt to major military
operations; two weeks later, he signed a decree recognizing the independence of
South Ossetia and Abkhazia from Georgia.

The upshot was that the Georgian troops were caught flatfooted and the
Russians won. But it was not a pretty victory. Equipment failures resulted in
the loss of several military planes and helicopters. Radio communications were
also hampered by poor-quality gear, a lack of interoperability, and even worse
operational security measures. In one instance, a Russian military general

had to borrow a war reporter's cell phone to issue instructions to his troops.[25] GLONASS, the specially designed satellite geo-positioning system that Russia had spent billions on, proved useless. It was as if the Russians were fighting two separate wars in the same theater: one in the sky against their own technology and one on the ground against the Georgians. Russian forces prevailed, but they fell short in every other way possible.[26] The Russians suffered heavily from problems with command, control, computers, intelligence, and satellite reconnaissance. In the end, Russia had won at least two of its objectives: keeping control over Abkhazia and South Ossetia and sticking a thumb in the eye of NATO and the United States. But the "Innovation Army" that Putin had promised was a long way from being realized and would have to wait for another day.

CHAPTER 6

THE NEW LOOK

The rally on Poklonnaya Hill had been advertised for weeks. At the appointed time on a crisp day in early November 2010, squads of men with leathery, creased faces began mustering by fives and tens on the highest point in Moscow. Some had potbellies. Some hobbled on spindly legs. Some strutted around with chests full of medals. Many bore the mental scars of battles brutally fought in Afghanistan, Transnistria, Chechnya, and more recently South Ossetia and Abkhazia. No one was sure exactly what was going to happen. But they all agreed on one thing: Anatoly Serdyukov, Russia's defense minister, needed to resign without delay.

That, at least, was the conclusion reached by the august officers who made up the board and central council of the Union of Paratroopers. The Moscow protest capped a weeklong conference organized by the union's leader, General Vladislav Achalov, the brains behind two failed coup plots and Russia's covert transfer of arms to Saddam Hussein. Achalov had long been an implacable foe of modernizing forces inside the Kremlin, and now he was at it again.

The object of ire this time—Serdyukov—was quite possibly one of the most unpopular government officials in all of Russia. The proximate cause was his introduction of a sweeping set of reforms in the fall of 2008 that triggered a wholesale overhaul of the military and defense sector. Dubbed the "New Look," the plan called for slashing the size of the military from 1.35 million to 1 million by 2012 and a wholesale restructuring of Russia's defense sector.[1] This was to be done within four years. The timeline was as ambitious as the plan was radical. Others before Serdyukov had tried and failed. But because the new reforms had been initiated at the urgent behest of General Nikolay Makarov, chief of General Staff, they carried more weight.

The idea was to make the Russian military more agile and capable of responding to smaller, localized conflicts like the one that had occurred in 2008 between Russia and Georgia. To achieve these ends, the military's six districts would be fused into four, and giant divisions would be abolished in favor of smaller brigades as the prime organizing principle of Russia's forces. By 2012, the officer corps would be cut to a third of its previous size. Logistics and support services would be almost completely civilianized. In short, Serdyukov had called for a top-to-bottom shake-up of everything—pay and benefits incentives, fitness standards for officers, and how soldiers were promoted, fed, transported, housed, cared for, and buried.

The roster of rally speakers arrayed in opposition to the changes that day was a veritable who's who of mutineers and coup plotters. On the platform truck beside Achalov stood Colonel Pavel Popovskikh, vice president of the union, as well as Popovskikh's former adjutant in the airborne forces and cofounder of Redut-Antiterror, Konstantin Mirzayants. Each had quietly played both sides of the fence during the 1993 coup attempt. Yet another figure onstage was Vladimir Kvachkov, a retired GRU military-intelligence colonel implicated in a failed plot to assassinate Russia's energy minister, Anatoly Chubais. All had been sympathetic and active supporters of the hard-right ultranationalists who nearly brought the Kremlin to its knees twice, and now they looked for all the world like they were prepared to make a go of it again.

The proposed changes would hit the hardest those who were most wedded to the creaky system that had prevailed since the Soviet times. The changes meant tens of thousands would be shunted into retirement. Reform would see the wholesale liquidation of the feudalistic patronage networks of untold numbers of bureaucratic functionaries. In Russia, where the military occupies an outsized economic and social role, the New Look plan was radical.

Among the chief complaints mounted against Serdyukov was that he was a civilian bureaucrat whose only military experience was two years of compulsory service as a junior-grade lieutenant in the Soviet Army. Pudgy and awkward, Serdyukov was no more fit than the out-of-shape generals he publicly castigated for their shortcomings. When he started, he was a virtual cipher to the military and to the outside world. What did a desk jockey know about the calculus of mobilizing thousands to the front while synchronizing deliveries of tanks and ammunition? Or organizing hospital beds for the wounded or graves for the fallen? But it was Serdyukov's call for a merger between the regular military and the elite airborne paratroopers force that had produced the loudest howls of dissent inside and outside the military.

Standing in front of the crowd in Moscow that November, Kvachkov embodied that rage. "Not a word about politics," he bellowed into a microphone on the makeshift stage. "Nobody is talking about politics. What politics are we talking about? Our older brothers are accusing us of involving the paratroopers in politics. Were we involved in politics when the 103rd Division responded to the political situation in Czechoslovakia? Look over there, at the banners of the 15th—that is the same detachment that marched through Kabul. In Baku, in Tajikistan, et cetera, was that politics?" Kvachkov paused ever so slightly for dramatic effect. "In all that time we never asked for anything because the army above all is indivisible. We are not involved in politics, my dear respected paratroopers and special operators. We are, in the end, only asking that politics do not involve us."[2]

The crowd rustled. A few heads bobbed up and down in agreement. Dozens of sky-blue regimental banners emblazoned with white parachutes whipped in the air above the assembly. A few placards called for Serdyukov to step down. Black, white, and gold flags bearing black double-headed eagles, the tsarist standard adopted by the St. Petersburg–based Russian Imperial Movement, were scattered throughout, a sign of the growing influence of the far-right monarchists among Russia's special-forces veterans. From Afghanistan to Chechnya, the airborne forces had been the first to run into the line of fire in every one of Russia's military interventions since the time of Khrushchev. Now the new minister of defense was threatening to cut them down to size. They would be damned if they were going to be held down by a furniture salesman, Kvachkov told the crowd.

In the years between its founding in 2002 and the mass protest against Serdyukov in Moscow in 2010, the Union of Paratroopers had become a formidable political force in Russia. No matter what Kvachkov pretended, everything was politics in the military. The union's leaders established its legal headquarters in Ryazan, not far from the airborne command staff college, and built up a solid base of public support in the seat of one of Russia's most important garrison towns. The union provided support to 130 youth organizations where some 10,000 boys and girls ages 12 to 18 were taught the rigors of military fitness, battlefield glory, and how to lead "exemplary patriotic lives."[3] Eight years in, union membership had swelled into the tens of thousands, with more than a hundred participating veterans' chapters across the country. Several of the local organizations would play an important role in building up the country's reserve force of off-book covert operatives for hire, among them the Oryol Regional Public Organization of the Special Forces (ROSA) and the St. Petersburg Club for Airborne Forces Veterans.

Union leaders had been spoiling for a fight since Serdyukov's appointment, and in the fall of 2010 they had found the perfect inciting incident. On obscure online chat boards with names like Desyantura.ru and Spetsnaz.ru, where thousands of paratroopers and special operators anonymously congregated under arcane aliases like "Aggressor" and "Savage," everyone was griping about Serdyukov's latest blunder. The trouble had started on September 30 during the defense minister's visit to the Ryazan branch of the Combined Arms Training Center, one of several that had been reshuffled as part of the New Look overhaul.

As his helicopter swooped around in a lazy circle over one corner of the training grounds, Serdyukov spotted a modestly sized wooden structure that resembled a church. When an aide confirmed that the site was a chapel erected in memory of paratroopers lost in battle, Serdyukov became so incensed that he ordered the church's immediate destruction. As if to add insult to injury, Serdyukov then laid into Colonel Andrey Krasov, a decorated war hero, telling the bewildered head of the training school that the church was a corrupt waste of state money and threatening to demote him. "You live in shit here; you'll die in shit! This school needs to be downsized altogether!"[4]

Shocked by the forcefulness of Serdyukov's tirade, officers on the scene explained to the defense minister that the chapel was the only one for miles around that the airborne forces and their families could attend.[5] Funds raised by the Union of Paratroopers and a grant from the local Christian Orthodox diocese had helped with construction and maintenance of the site, they said. The church even took the name of the paratroopers' patron saint, the Prophet Elijah. In the end, the chapel stood. Union leaders sent an appeal to Russia's president, Dmitry Medvedev, and Patriarch Kirill of Moscow, head of the Russian Orthodox Church, to intercede. Serdyukov had just unknowingly taken on one of the most potent veterans' associations in the country. It was the beginning of his undoing.

On Victory Square, where union leaders tried to stir the spirits of the crowd, the paratroopers issued five edicts:

1. There is no place for boors and amateurs in the army. Serdyukov—resign!

2. We demand that the Supreme Commander of the Armed Forces give a moral assessment of the act of the Minister of Defense.

3. We demand that the State Duma of the Russian Federation take the course of military reform in the army under parliamentary control.

4. We appeal to the authorities, today you assume full responsibility when, with your inexplicable silence, you fence yourself off from solving the problem and push ordinary people to mass protest events.

5. The Union of Russian Paratroopers reserves the right to further protest actions for the fulfillment of its demands.

The authorities stopped Popovskikh as he drove away from the rally on suspicion of drunk driving. Fans of the maverick colonel protested vigorously that rumors that a cleaning lady had found empty bottles of vodka in the conference room were little more than trumped-up evidence. Popovskikh, his loyal fans insisted, had quit drinking years before. The scandal over Popovskikh's arrest, only four years after he'd been cleared of murder, prompted some to call for protesters to block a major Moscow highway. Inside the Kremlin, there were genuine fears that the discontent could snowball into another military mutiny and full-scale rebellion.[6]

The risk was real. The stiffest resistance to reform had come from within the most elite ranks of the military. On the advice of Makarov, Serdyukov had moved to decommission *spetsnaz* units to make space for what would eventually become a consolidated centralized command for special forces. The changes would lead to the elimination of a thousand officer positions in the GRU, the Main Intelligence Directorate, and slash the overall size of the agency by 40 percent, cutting it down from nine to seven brigades. Other adjustments would also lead to the loss of rank for many of the GRU's most seasoned operatives. The proposed reforms prompted an outcry from General Valentin Korabelnikov, the spy agency's longtime head, who threatened to resign in protest and was ultimately fired in 2009.

It would take another three years for the special-forces command concept to transition from a blueprint to reality. The delay was largely a result of the fierce resistance from an officer corps that resented the disruption to its well-established patronage networks. *Dedovschina*, the harsh tradition of hazing that senior soldiers wielded to enforce bribery and racketeering schemes, was so widespread that desertion rates had reached unprecedented levels.

Out on Victory Square, these nuances vanished. Instead, Kvachkov, Popovskikh, Mirzayants, and others up on the rally stage pointed to Serdyukov's proposed plan to fold the VDV Airborne into the ground forces as the strongest evidence of his incompetence. It was as if no lessons at all had been learned from the Georgian war, they complained. Serdyukov's critics claimed that the reforms were too radical and would set the military back a generation. Or, at least, that was one version of the story.

Another, more favorable view was that Serdyukov was not just talking about transforming Russia's military into a fighting force ready to take on NATO. He was making change happen. Laws passed in earlier years to extend the mandatory retirement age to fifty-five were rescinded. Harder lines on age and fitness requirements resulted in more than twenty-six thousand people being dropped from the military rolls instantly. In one of his more dramatic moves, Serdyukov ordered Russia's naval headquarters to be moved from Moscow back to St. Petersburg, which in centuries past had long served as the seat of the country's maritime power.

Significantly, Serdyukov's plan to give the military a "new look" aimed to rebalance the number of conscripts versus volunteer contract soldiers. A professional volunteer-based army, the theory went, would fix two big problems that were exposed during Russia's intervention in Georgia: poorly trained troops and inexperienced officers. The proposed reform broke with nearly a century of orthodoxy in Russian military thinking. Serdyukov's plan rested on the idea that armies are better prepared when the soldiers who fight in them want to be at the front and that when they are trained well enough to survive combat, they are more motivated to stay enlisted. Under the New Look reforms, *kontraktniki* noncommissioned officers and regular officers would be offered better pay, more perks, and more opportunities to advance. The goal was to have 220,000 officers, 425,000 contract soldiers, and 350,000 conscripts by 2011.[7]

Left unsaid when Serdyukov launched the New Look plan was the simple problem of numbers. Russia needed a leaner, more efficient professional fighting force, but it simply did not have enough men of military age to make the mathematics of the makeover work. After national birthrates began to fall off a cliff following the Soviet collapse, it was obvious that there would not be enough military-age men in the near term to fulfill projected recruitment and mobilization targets.[8]

The quality of recruits was also a concern. Even in a highly unlikely medium-term scenario where there were enough fighting-age men available to fill conscription goals, there was a good chance that a substantial number would be suffering from health conditions that made them unfit for service. When Serdyukov came into office, hepatitis and HIV were among the most cited causes of ineligibility. With high rates of intravenous drug use and alcohol abuse, and low levels of government engagement on addiction treatment and prevention, socially stigmatized diseases were so prevalent that some predicted Russia's military would collapse under the strain of trying to reach unobtainable thresholds for mass mobilization.[9] Serdyukov had set the military a Sisyphean task, and many seasoned veterans inside and outside the Russian General Staff knew it.

If many knew, few were ready to confront the stark realities of the situation.[10] But the social dislocation and economic disruptions caused by these changes were largely underestimated.

The Russian military was a state within a state, the country's largest employer. Each soldier supported at least two to three family members. The profits of countless small businesses were tied to military bases and defense manufacturing plants. Entire regional economies depended on the defense trade. Serdyukov's decision to shrink the size and number of military bases threatened to gut hundreds of military towns nationwide. Recession-era austerity measures posed obstacles to paying out severance pay to those sloughed off the rolls, and cost-saving measures left an estimated 118,000 without government-guaranteed housing.[11] Local officials, already stretched thin, complained about the lack of resources and guidance in dealing with the surge of underemployed, homeless, and often alcoholic veterans left adrift.

Discontent grew when it became clear that much of the administrative and logistical work would be outsourced to private firms. The new arrangement would allow external private companies to bid for lucrative defense contracts for everything from designing new uniforms to catering meals ready to eat for a million soldiers. The transition from a government-run, multibillion-dollar military-logistics industry to one driven by free-market competition presented enormous opportunities for private-sector entrepreneurs like Yevgeny Prigozhin. He and Serdyukov were not strangers to each other. Their careers intersected in St. Petersburg's complex power circles and in the murky world of the Tambov-Malyshev mafia. Originally from the Krasnador region, Serdyukov had earned a degree in accounting and economics from the Leningrad Institute of Soviet Trade. After a brief military stint as a conscript corporal, he went to work for a Soviet furniture manufacturer, and he later worked as a junior clerk in Dresden, where, it was widely believed, he had served as a KGB asset.

Serdyukov's career closely followed that of his leading political patron, and Putin's good friend, Viktor Zubkov. As deputy chairman of St. Petersburg's External Affairs Committee, Zubkov was deeply involved in the deals that Putin brokered between the Tambov-Malyshev mafia and Russia's security agencies.[12] Zubkov was also a founding member of the Ozero Cooperative, the dacha vacation spot near St. Petersburg where Putin and his inner circle strategized about Russia's future. Serdyukov's ties to this group further solidified after he married Zubkov's daughter, Yulia, marking a turning point in his career. In 2000 Serdyukov left his role as general director of the rebranded Mebel-Market conglomerate to become deputy chief of the Federal Tax Service for the St. Petersburg region. The position gave Serdyukov considerable influence over the city's largest industries, including restaurants, casinos, construction, and real estate—the core of Prigozhin's empire.

Prigozhin drew closer to Serdyukov's orbit at the end of Putin's second term, in 2008, when Dmitry Medvedev was elevated to the presidency and Zubkov replaced Medvedev as Gazprom's chairman. Prigozhin's Concord company won the bid to serve as chief caterer for Medvedev's inauguration that spring and then in 2009 secured a lucrative contract to run the first luxury-grade canteen for civil servants in the parliament building in Moscow.

Ensconced on the twelfth floor of the White House, the restaurant, Office 1237, was a fantastic source for gossip and insights into who was up and who was down inside the Kremlin's mercurial court. Seizing on the fresh routes into government contracting created by the restaurant's opening, Prigozhin also began providing meals for the military's General Staff and the defense minister himself.[13] With the military's service sector up for grabs, Prigozhin recognized an opening, nimbly navigating the shifting sands inside the defense ministry.

In the weeks following the protest on Poklonnaya Hill, the Kremlin's corridors buzzed with talk of the paratroopers' defiance. The rally had set in motion a series of events that would soon engulf Serdyukov and his allies in a maelstrom of political and military opposition. The seeds of his downfall were sown that day, watered by the collective anger of those who felt betrayed by the defense minister's sweeping changes. The coming months would reveal just how deep the roots of that anger ran, as Serdyukov's enemies—both seen and unseen—closed in around him, eager to reclaim the power they believed was rightfully theirs.

The old guard's political revolt closely coincided with a coming shake-up of a much greater magnitude in the Kremlin. A little more than two years into Putin's tenure as prime minister and during his power-sharing arrangement with Dmitry Medvedev, the once seamless partnership between the two was beginning to fray. The outbreak of the Arab Spring in late 2010 drove their "tandemocracy" toward rocky shoals just as Medvedev began to contemplate running for reelection and Putin started to reconsider his options.

Medvedev, who had attempted to assert more independence during his presidency in his dealings with the United States, increasingly found himself at odds with Putin's tightening grip on Russia's political and economic spheres. Medvedev was already under fire for the failed Skolkovo project, a multibillion-dollar high-tech hub he had championed after an enthusiastic visit to Silicon Valley that turned out to be a white elephant. The reaction among military conservatives to the New Look reforms significantly heightened Medvedev's vulnerability.

In March 2011, Medvedev further alienated Russian hard-liners by allowing a UN vote in favor of a US proposal to impose a no-fly zone over Libya during the Arab Spring uprising against Muammar Qaddafi. Medvedev had never been a fan of Qaddafi, whom he dismissed as lacking legitimacy and being out of touch with reality.

Medvedev saw the no-fly zone as a chance to show the Obama administration that Russia was ready to play ball on big global issues. He wanted to make sure that any decisions on international interventions went through the United Nations, giving Russia a say and a chance to head off unilateral NATO action. He gave the green light for Russia to abstain on UN Security Council Resolution 1973, which allowed for military action in Libya. "All that is now happening in Libya is the result of the appalling behavior of the Libyan leadership and the crimes it committed against its own people," Medvedev said.[14] Hard-liners in the Kremlin disagreed, casting the decision to abstain as a betrayal of a traditional Russian ally.

Worse, certainly for Medvedev, the Security Council decision to intervene in Libya riled Putin, who issued a sharp public rebuke. In remarks made soon after the UN vote while he was touring a Russian missile-manufacturing plant, Putin compared it to NATO's bombing campaign in Yugoslavia and the false pretext that had led the United States to intervene in Iraq and topple Saddam

Hussein. "It resembles a medieval appeal for a crusade in which somebody calls upon somebody to go to a certain place and liberate it," Putin sneered.[15] Putin's comments marked the beginning of the end of Medvedev's brief turn on the throne, as well as the Obama administration's much-hoped-for reset of relations with Russia.

For years after Putin first assumed office, a fundamental tenet of US foreign policy was the belief that Russia, despite its aspirations to reclaim its global influence, remained a regional power lacking the means to do so. During Putin's first two terms and for part of Medvedev's tenure, the risk of a return to the Cold War days of shadowboxing with Moscow seemed relatively remote. The Russian invasion of Georgia changed that thinking in Washington, but in the immediate aftermath there was limited consensus on the right response.

Hawks like Republican senator John McCain advocated taking a harder line with Putin and bolstering support for Georgia and Ukraine. However, when Barack Obama, McCain's rival in the 2008 presidential race, emerged victorious and entered the White House, a different approach took center stage. Obama's policy was rooted in the belief that it was possible to convince Putin that pursuing mutually beneficial outcomes, rather than engaging in zero-sum games, would enhance Russia's global standing and foster more constructive relations between the two nations.

Michael McFaul, an Oxford-trained political science professor at Stanford University who joined Obama's campaign and then served as a White House adviser before becoming ambassador to Russia, pitched the concept as a "reset" of US relations with Russia. The idea was to hold the line on support for democracies in Europe and Eurasia while decreasing the energy dependence of American allies in those regions and, as McFaul put it, to check Russian aggression while at the same time engaging on critical issues of mutual interest, leaving the door ajar for Russia's integration into the global system.[16]

Bold pronouncements about admitting Georgia and Ukraine to NATO were sidelined in favor of incremental steps like more visible engagement with the two countries at the bureaucratic level via special commissions set up by the transatlantic alliance. During Obama's first term, the White House shifted its focus to ratifying the Comprehensive Test Ban Treaty, negotiating a new version of the Strategic Arms Reduction Treaty, and securing Russia's support to prevent Iran from acquiring nuclear arms.

The animating assumption of the reset policy was that Putin could be convinced to embrace the liberalizing forces that had sparked the disintegration of the Soviet Union. McFaul, who had spent time in the trenches with pro-democracy activists in the 1990s, was convinced that the giddy enthusiasm of those bygone days still held powerful sway among the Russian people.

To demonstrate commitment to this new tack, Obama's secretary of state, Hillary Clinton, famously gifted her Russian counterpart Sergey Lavrov a replica of a red "reset" button with the Russian word *peregruzka* ("overcharge") written on its base—a mistranslation that Lavrov immediately noted while White House press cameras were rolling. "You got it wrong," Lavrov smirked.[17] The gimmick and Lavrov's ungracious reaction spoke volumes about how far apart Moscow and Washington were on the fundamentals of the relationship.

The reset policy was pragmatic in its framing but wishful in its thinking. The schism between Putin and Medvedev over the response to the war in Libya and the Victory Square protest against Serdyukov were strong indicators that reactionary forces would continue to have a strong say in how Russia was run. Further proof arrived when in September 2011, Medvedev said he would step aside so that Putin could run yet again for the top position in the Kremlin as Russia rounded the corner to its parliamentary elections at the end of the year and the presidential contest in spring 2012.

SENSING THAT A transition was in the offing, Prigozhin moved swiftly to capitalize on inroads he had made in Moscow. As chief caterer to Moscow's military brass, Prigozhin gained access into a whole new breed of Kremlin elites. Among the most important of his new patrons was the defense ministry's chief of logistics, Colonel General Dmitry Bulgakov. A jowly, potbellied bureaucratic careerist, Bulgakov was one of the leading advocates for the creation in 2009 of Voentorg, the state-managed defense logistics and supply corporation that would become the primary source of government contracts allotted to Prigozhin's multitude of shell companies.

Voentorg was one of several subsidiaries that fell under the umbrella of Oboronservis, the defense-procurement holding company that Serdyukov had established as part of his New Look overhaul of the military-industrial complex. Modeled on big US defense-service contractors like Kellogg, Brown and Root, and Halliburton, Oboronservis brought under one roof everything from jet-fighter repairs to base construction, catering, and laundry service. Born out of high ideals to optimize the defense apparatus, the aim of the scheme was to stimulate market competition in one of the biggest sectors of Russia's economy. In theory, outsourcing logistics, supply, and maintenance service would both create cost savings and allow the military to focus on war fighting and defense production.

In practice, the scheme turned into a massive boondoggle. The presidential decree behind it appointed Serdyukov as chairman of Oboronservis, giving him undue influence over the CEOs of its subsidiaries, including Voentorg. This role gave the defense minister unparalleled power to distribute lucrative civilian jobs, oversee the sale of defense-related assets, and hand out government contracts and property with little oversight. The defense holding company became a magnet for embezzlement and graft. As Serdyukov consolidated his hold on the military-industrial complex, Prigozhin fixed his mind on ways to profit.

The reorganization of Russia's defense sector could not have come at a better time. The global recession had hit Prigozhin's restaurant businesses hard. Although his fast-food restaurant chain, Blin! Donalts, had originally planned to open in at least twenty locations across the city, only about half as many were operational by 2010. Part of the problem stemmed from lower demand for everything everywhere that accompanied the global recession. Higher costs for basic staples that were prompted by a worldwide food crisis from 2007 to 2008 did not help matters.

But Prigozhin's real problem was that the humble Russian blinis offered at his fast-food chain had nothing on the Big Mac and the Whopper. Russian tastes were shifting, and neighbors who lived near Prigozhin's establishments were fed up with Concord's rough way of doing business.[18] As a result, Blin! Donalts eventually folded altogether.

In fact, although Prigozhin's construction business was booming, significant parts of Concord's holdings were underwater, overleveraged, tangled in red tape, or stuck in unprofitable limbo. Ambitious plans to renovate and flip the aging Trezzini House into a luxury hotel ran into all manner of financial and regulatory obstacles, delaying planned renovations for years.[19] A $120 million Concord real estate development project involving the construction of a medical facility on 17.6 hectares of premium land in St. Petersburg's Primorsky neighborhood was snarled in a series of lawsuits between Prigozhin and the city. M-Invest, one of several firms linked to Prigozhin's Concord Holding Company, was listed as the lead investor in the property, one of several coastal tracts that Prigozhin had snapped up ahead of Gazprom's construction of Russia's tallest skyscraper, the nearby Laktha Center.[20]

Even Northern Versailles, the adjacent property and crown jewel of Prigozhin's real estate empire, seemed stuck. Although the gated community boasted palatial villas worth up to $7.5 million with views overlooking the Gulf of Finland, it was hard to find buyers. Only about half of the mansions had been sold by 2008 to a few rich foreigners and to new-money Russians enthralled by the idea of living in a replica of an eighteenth-century château.[21]

Prigozhin persevered nonetheless. He found new avenues to expand his business empire and nurture his high-level connections, concentrating all his efforts on edging closer to Putin. In September 2010, Concord announced the launch of a food-factory operation in Yanino, a suburb on the eastern outskirts of St. Petersburg, after receiving a blessing from Dmitry Medvedev that helped Concord secure an initial $43 million in government bank loans for the opening.[22]

Putin even marked the auspicious occasion with a visit to the site within days of the factory's opening. In photos, Putin can be seen striding around the plant with a white lab coat draped over the shoulders of his black puffer jacket.[23] In every frame, Prigozhin bends obsequiously toward his patron. Sweeping an arm over a conveyor belt brimming with packaged food, Prigozhin invited Putin to try a bit of borscht or porridge. "Later," Putin promised. Turning to another functionary who accompanied Putin on the factory tour, Prigozhin asked, "What do you think?" "Great! You can feed prisons, the army, hospitals."[24]

Within less than a year, Concord started to do just that. After securing an estimated $117 million in loans from the state-owned Vneshekonombank, Prigozhin opened two more factory sites in the Moscow and Krasnodar area.[25] St. Petersburg regional schools were among the first to begin receiving food from the Yanino factory. Moscow came next, and soon other school systems around the country came under increasing pressure to outsource their catering needs to Concord-affiliated firms. The factory fare was a far cry from the delicacies on offer at Prigozhin's high-end restaurants like the Old Customs House. Incidents of food poisoning and sanitation hazards were widely reported. But neither those complaints nor the hundreds of lawsuits lodged against Concord or its affiliates by angry parents and school administrators presented a barrier to the expansion of Prigozhin's government-contracting business.

Fortuitously, Serdyukov's streamlining of Russia's military colossus would create a bonanza of opportunities for crafty hustlers within an inside track.

One initial beneficiary was Serdyukov's secret lover, Yevgenia Vasilyeva. Blond, buxom, and extremely self-assured, Vasilyeva was seventeen years younger than Serdyukov. Her age and relative inexperience in defense affairs did not present as an obstacle to her being appointed in 2010 to head of the ministry's property-relations department. However, it did prove problematic when Serdyukov's wife—the daughter of his patron Zubkov—discovered two years after Vasilyeva was appointed that Serdyukov was having an affair with his subordinate; she filed for divorce in the summer of 2012.

The political tide turned swiftly against Serdyukov shortly after that. In October 2012 an early-morning police raid on Vasilyeva's thirteen-room home turned up diamonds, pearls, assorted jewelry worth hundreds of thousands of dollars, a stash of about three million rubles in cash, and Serdyukov in his pajamas. Authorities accused Vasilyeva and Serdyukov of selling acres of prime government-owned real estate at fire-sale prices to favored bidders, who in turn sold them at or above market value and split the proceeds with the defense minister, his lover, and their cronies. Initial estimates suggested that the kickback arrangements involved defense ministry assets valued at $100 million.[26]

The embezzlement case against Serdyukov's lover was the culmination of a series of investigations that resulted in the conviction of thirty government officials for the fraudulent use of funds meant to purchase and repair military equipment as part of the plan to accelerate the modernization of Russian defense forces. As it turned out, Serdyukov's "New Look" did little to address the old-school patronage and corruption that had long been a hallmark of Russia's defense sector. Instead, it exacerbated the military's problems.

As more details emerged, it became clear Vasilyeva and Serdyukov were not the only players in the game. Some twenty criminal cases were opened in connection with corruption in Oboronservis, and more than a dozen bureaucrats, contractors, and intermediaries were caught up in the net. Estimates vary regarding to the total damage done, but at one point a Russian prosecutor on the case placed the figure at about 5 billion rubles, or about $1.9 billion in contemporary exchange rates.

Meanwhile, Russia's political climate had turned volatile. Putin's political comeback sparked widespread skepticism and discontent, especially among the urban middle class and the younger generations, who were fed up with the sham of political competition. When in December 2011 parliamentary elections once again miraculously placed Putin's United Russia Party in the pole position, Moscow's streets erupted. Suspicions of fraud had long gone hand in hand with Russian elections, but this time evidence spilled forth in an uncontrollable torrent of mobile-phone videos and photos posted online. Reports of ballot stuffing, manipulated counts, and other irregularities flooded the internet, enraging a population that had long ago grown tired of the facade of Putin's so-called managed democracy. In the heart of Moscow, tens of thousands gathered in Bolotnaya Square, where the demonstrations were loud but peaceful with shouts of "Putin, resign!" ringing in the cold winter air until police began wading into the crowds with batons and shields. As the protests escalated over the course of several weeks in cities across the country, so did the government's response. The world watched as Russia's opposition and its citizens grappled with an authoritarian regime unwilling to relinquish control. Hundreds were dragged away as snow continued to fall amid what became known as the Snow Revolution. The scene was reminiscent of what had happened in Kyiv, Tbilisi, and Bishkek only a few years earlier, and the more recent turmoil of the Arab Spring. It spooked Putin. He lashed out at Hillary Clinton, accusing her of "sending the signal" to opposition activists to foment a rebellion and castigating her for calling out election fraud. "She said they were dishonest and unfair," Putin complained. "We need to safeguard ourselves from interference in our internal affairs."[27]

Amid these currents, new voices and faces of opposition to Putin's rule emerged. Alexey Navalny, a charismatic and outspoken lawyer turned political activist, aimed Twitter and YouTube at Putin like a machine gun. Revelations about the extent of rot in the defense sector provided ready ammunition. In his blogs and comments to the press on the Oboronservis scandal, Navalny was especially unsparing in his derision of Serdyukov. The hapless defense minister, Navalny quipped, had broken one of the cardinal rules of Putin's power vertical when he entered an embezzlement scheme with his extramarital paramour: don't cross the family.[28] Navalny's jabs landed hard and resonated with more media- and tech-savvy Russian voters, who were no longer content to be mere spectators in the country's future.

Navalny's growing popularity triggered propaganda countermeasures from the Kremlin's proxies, including Prigozhin. The most conspicuous of these efforts was an elaborately produced fake documentary called *Anatomy of a Protest*. Produced by Prigozhin's loyal young aide, Dmitry Koshara, and aired in 2012 during prime time on NTV, the film was as bizarre as it was beguiling. Shot almost entirely with hidden cameras, it revolved around a conspiracy theory that Putin's opposition was in the pay of the US embassy.

According to the script, Navalny and other members of Russia's "creative class," characterized as soft, effeminate, educated American and European wannabes who were the cause of all that was wrong with the country, secretly conspired to manufacture a fake protest by paying drunks, homeless people, and migrant workers to show up at an anti-Putin rally.

The campaign to undermine support for Navalny and other opposition figures was only a small taste of what was on the chef's menu. In early 2012, ahead of Putin's presidential campaign, Prigozhin began paying young devotees from the ultranationalist patriotic youth organization Nashi to plaster thousands of pro-Putin messages and comments on LiveJournal and other popular websites and social media platforms like VKontakte, a Russian knockoff version of Facebook. Other tactics included setting up fake websites and spying on journalists and activists.

In due course, the enterprise would take on a more formal structure in 2013 in a warren of offices where an army of online trolls were deployed to reshape Russia's image. Housed in a bland-looking office building in Olgino, an affluent neighborhood in St. Petersburg located at the edge of Prigozhin's growing empire on the shores of the Gulf of Finland, the media marketing company was known as "Glavset." But in less than a year, the troll farm would be known the world over as the Internet Research Agency. Prigozhin, the man who had artfully catered balletic scenes befitting a nineteenth-century tsar for Putin, was now offering himself up as the lead auteur of a new kind of Kremlin counterrevolution on the internet.

In step with this paradigm shift in remaking the Kremlin's image, Putin fired Serdyukov in November 2012 as more details of the Oboronservis scandal came to light, replacing him with Sergey Shoigu, the longtime head of Russia's emergency-response agency, EMERCOM, and then the regional governor for Moscow. In Shoigu, Putin gained the most loyal of loyalists. The two had known each other since the 1990s, and in addition to briefly serving as Putin's deputy in 1999, Shoigu was a cofounder of the United Russia Party.

Raised in Tuva near the border of Mongolia and trained as a civil engineer, Shoigu was not a soldier in the traditional sense. But he had spent the better part of twenty years militarizing the country's emergency-response system. As minister of emergency situations, he had crisis-management skills and a loyalty to the regime that made him a trusted figure within the Russian government.

Shoigu had come by way of the emergency-services post in part through family connections. His father, Khuzhuget, was also an engineer, and he had served as the head of Tuva's Communist Party Council. Accordingly, the young Shoigu followed in his father's footsteps, burnishing his political credentials in the Komsomol. Then, after Shoigu moved from Siberia to Moscow for a government post, Boris Yeltsin tapped him as chief of an early iteration of EMERCOM in 1991.

Shoigu gained notoriety one year into that job when he led a daring operation to evacuate Afghanistan's then-president, Mohammad Najibullah. The operation ultimately failed, setting off a chain of events that ended with the Taliban hanging Najibullah in Kabul.

Shoigu had, nonetheless, fared much better in the face of other tough situations, including the 1993 coup attempt, when he volunteered to arm Yeltsin's supporters in the event that the military failed to heed the president's orders.[29] Shoigu, a rugged outdoorsy type, also won high public praise for his handling of natural disasters. Along the way, he turned to retired military generals to help him reshape EMERCOM into a highly militarized hybrid agency that looked to Western eyes like a fusion of the Red Cross and a national guard service. As one of the few Russian officials untainted by major corruption scandals, he was also among the most popular. Pragmatic and low-key, Shoigu knew how to get things done.

The other factor that commended Shoigu for the post was the fact that he was not part of Putin's St. Petersburg circles, and for this reason the president trusted his judgment. Putin even said as much during his televised and tightly scripted remarks upon announcing Shoigu as the country's new defense minister. In a theatrical scene that would become familiar as the years wore on under Russia's perpetual president, Putin adopted a concerned and serious look as he sat across from a poker-faced Shoigu. "The future chief of one of the most important agencies in our country should be a person who could carry forward all the positive accomplishments of recent years, ensure the dynamic development of the armed forces, ensure the implementation of state contracts, and those grand rearmament plans that we have," Putin said. "I think, in fact, that you could be this person."[30] The canned video exchange between the two men led to speculation about whether Putin planned to anoint Shoigu one day as his potential successor.

It also left some wondering whether it was the defense ministry embezzlement soap opera or the drama in Moscow's streets during the Snow Revolution, or both, that finally forced Putin to pull the trigger on a cabinet shake-up. Another theory suggested that Putin had cooked up the Oboronservis scandal as a means of brushing back grasping hands within his close-knit St. Petersburg circle as he made plans to retake the presidency. Rostec CEO Sergey Chemezov had pressed for Putin to appoint a known quantity from St. Petersburg to the defense ministry. Chemezov was apparently angling for the job himself, but he was rebuffed for reasons that were never publicly explained.[31]

Whispers behind closed doors suggested that the influence of Putin's St. Petersburg crew had been weakened by another scandal far beyond the Russian president's control. When news first surfaced about the 2008 arrest and indictment of Gennady Petrov in Spain on charges of money laundering for the Tambov-Malyshev mafia, it gained little traction in the Russian press. But it did not go unnoticed inside Spaso House, the Moscow residence of the US ambassador and the diplomatic corps.

This became apparent in 2010, when Wikileaks began pouring forth reams of diplomatic cables stolen and leaked from US embassies worldwide. As international press coverage of the Spanish investigation into the Kremlin's mafia ties intensified, it was revealed that Spanish investigators had intercepted calls indicating that Serdyukov and one of his deputies had been in regular and close contact with Petrov for years. Suddenly, the theory that Putin had cooked up the Oboronservis scandal to sideline St. Petersburg insiders began to gather force.

Two other notable political appointments during the early months of Putin's third presidential term stand out as indicative of what was to come following his cabinet shuffle. The first was Shoigu's pick to replace Nikolai Makarov as chief of General Staff. Shoigu, as the new defense minister, needed a trusted partner who could assist him in implementing reforms and modernizing the military. For that he turned to Makarov's immediate subordinate, General Valery Gerasimov.

Gerasimov, practically born in uniform, had slashed his way to the top via a tour in the Second Chechen War as the head of the 58th Army and staff officer postings, including stints as commander of Russia's Central Military District and the Leningrad Military District. A respected military strategist with a reputation for a workmanlike approach to the operational arts, Gerasimov was, as Shoigu reportedly described him, "a military man to the roots of his hair."[32] His military experience perfectly complemented Shoigu's management of the defense sector's maze-like bureaucracy. The two cemented their bond in Abkhazia and South Ossetia, where Gerasimov's 58th Army drove thousands out of their homes across the jagged border between Russia and Georgia in 2008. As head of emergency response, Shoigu coordinated regularly with Gerasimov during the conflict. Together, they formed a political tandem of their own, casting themselves as the twin force behind Russia's military transformation in the twenty-first century.

The second major move—the transfer of Putin's onetime bodyguard, Alexey Dyumin, from the Federal Guards Service (FSO) into the service of the GRU military-intelligence wing—was no less consequential, although it received far less attention at the time. Like Gerasimov, Dyumin, then forty years old, came from a military family. His father, Gennady, was a high-ranking military medic, and his mother, a teacher, followed her husband from post to post while Dyumin was in school. Young Alexey excelled as an amateur hockey goalkeeper while the family was posted to Voronezh. His brawny build and discipline gave him an appetite for competitive sport, and he briefly considered going pro before his father persuaded him that the military would provide a more stable career.

Dyumin enrolled in the Voronezh Higher Military Engineering School of Radio Electronics when he was twenty-two years old. Located within the Moscow military district, the school specialized in training its graduates in counter-reconnaissance tactics. After graduating, he worked for two years as an engineer at the Central Unit for Comprehensive Technical Control of the Russian Air Force. But Dyumin quickly soured on the ritual hazing, hard drinking, and slack culture of Russia's conventional forces.

In 1995, at a friend's urging, Dyumin joined the Federal Guards Service, the agency that runs the Kremlin's security detail. His initial mission was to provide secure communications for Russia's president and prime minister whenever they traveled. He worked with former prime minister Viktor Chernomyrdin and accompanied Putin's predecessor, Boris Yeltsin, on business trips a couple of times. Then, in 1999, Dyumin was tasked with providing security to Sergey Stepashin.[33]

This fateful choice would bring Dyumin in direct touch with Prigozhin, propelling him even deeper into the center of Russian military affairs. In June of that same year, as Stepashin's political star was waning and Putin's was waxing, Prigozhin helped coordinate security arrangements with Dyumin for the state dinner on Prigozhin's floating New Island bistro for the head of the IMF, Michel Camdessus. Two months later, when Putin was named acting president,

Dyumin was tapped to serve as Putin's bodyguard and close-protection chief, making him and Prigozhin part of a tiny circle of men trusted to enter Putin's private inner sanctum.

In an interview with the Russian news outlet *Kommersant* after he was named deputy chief of the GRU intelligence service, Dyumin would credit another Putin associate with ties to Prigozhin, Viktor Zolotov, Putin's very first bodyguard and the head of Russia's national guard force, with speeding his swift ascent.[34] Like Serdyukov, Dyumin additionally counted Viktor Zubkov as one of his leading political champions. Putin apparently liked Dyumin so much that not long after Putin became prime minister under Medvedev, in 2008, he invited Dyumin to play hockey with him on the Russian Army's SKA St. Petersburg Club team.

Co-led by Putin's longtime friend Gennady Timchenko, the hockey team was owned by Gazprom and, like the St. Petersburg–based Yewara-Neva Judo Club that Timchenko and billionaires Boris and Arkady Rotenberg also backed, the hockey team served as an oft-overlooked center of political gravity where the country's wealthiest businessmen played hard alongside the leaders of Russia's most powerful security agencies.

Dyumin played goalie, and he also benefited from coaching by Roman Rotenberg, the son of Putin's childhood friend Boris Rotenberg. The younger Rotenberg managed SKA St. Petersburg and got his career start with Gazprom Export, a wing of the state-owned energy giant. And not coincidentally, Dyumin and Shoigu pushed the puck around together with Putin, too. If the world outside of Russia was oblivious to the importance of those ties, Prigozhin most certainly was not. He well understood the benefit of promoting himself as a loyal servant of the Kremlin, and his instincts were rewarded not long after Putin elevated Shoigu, Gerasimov, and Dyumin to their new posts.

Just two days after Serdyukov was sacked, *Novaya Gazeta* wrote a splashy story about Concord winning yet another big government contract—this time for catering meals for the army. Few specifics of the deal were made public beyond the 140 billion–ruble price tag.[35] An investigative reporter who covered the story for the independent news outlet hinted that the deal was the result of a carefully orchestrated maneuver by Leonid Teyf, Voentorg's deputy director, who had long been Prigozhin's inside man at the state-owned defense-logistics company. This, too, would turn out to be an important puzzle piece in the pixilated picture that would eventually form of how Prigozhin came to dominate

Russia's defense contracting and build a business empire that spanned three continents. His ties with key figures like Bulgakov, Shoigu, Gerasimov, and Dyumin were more than just alliances—they were the foundational sources of newfound power. Behind the scenes, Prigozhin was positioning himself as an indispensable player in Russia's military resurgence. With each new agreement, every handshake, he was laying the groundwork for something far greater than anyone outside his inner circle could imagine.

PART TWO

HIDDEN IN PLAIN SIGHT

CHAPTER 7

GERASIMOV'S GHOSTS

On October 18, 2012, the Nigerian Navy raided a ship called the *Myre Seadiver* off the coast of Lagos. A 315-ton roll-on/roll-off vessel designed to carry wheeled cargo like tractors, trucks, and tanks, the *Seadiver* had been added to the security fleet of Russia's state-owned maritime shipping company Sovcomflot earlier that year. After receiving a slapdash paint job to cover decades of wear, she put out to sea from the Russian naval fortress town of Baltiysk in June 2012.

The ship was one of at least three maritime-security transport boats under the management of the Moran Security Group, a newly rebranded military-security company formed from the remnants of the Anti-Terror Oryol Group. When Nigerian authorities searched the ship, they uncovered a cache of weapons that included more than a dozen AK-47 assault rifles, twenty-plus Benelli MR1 rifles, and a total of nearly eight thousand rounds of ammunition—an arsenal sufficient to outfit two or three platoons.

Russian embassy staff in Lagos protested the raid, arguing that the weapons were standard kit and noting that the *Myre Seadiver* had registered with the port authorities weeks before the Nigerian Navy raided the ship. Moreover, the Russians insisted that the Moran Security Group was a known entity in Lagos. The *Myre Seadiver* had already been sitting at port for weeks before the Nigerian Navy boarded it.

The weapons on board had been declared at each port of call along the ship's onward legs from the Gulf of Aden to the inland port town of Toliara,

Madagascar.[1] The ship's master, Andrey Zhelyazkov, had reportedly even sent emails ahead to the sea agent in charge in Lagos detailing all the contents on board the ship. Everything, he insisted, had been cleared in advance.

The Nigerians were unconvinced. Navy officials in Lagos insisted that Zhelyazkov and his mates had been up to no good. One online African news digest about the raid said Nigerian authorities had accused the *Myre Seadiver* crew of being involved in "economic sabotage."[2] All fifteen Russian men on board were arrested and detained on charges of illegal weapons smuggling. Independent researchers had on previous occasions identified vessels linked to Moran Security as "floating armories."[3]

The *Myre Seadiver*'s voyage was one of thousands scheduled that year by Sovcomflot, Russia's state-owned shipping giant. With a fleet of more than 120 seaborne oil tankers and cargo ships, and annual revenues of well over $1 billion, Sovcomflot has dominated Russia's export-shipping trade since its founding in St. Petersburg in 1988. Like its state-owned counterparts Gazprom and Rosneft, Sovcomflot is headed by a presidentially appointed executive, forming a crucial link in the chain between Russia's biggest exporters and world markets. As such, the company's shipping trade has played a foundational role in Vladimir Putin's quest to transform Russia into an energy superpower and top arms exporter.

What made the *Myre Seadiver* distinct from all the others in the Sovcomflot fleet was the crew and cargo it carried. Officially registered as a "security consultancy," the Moran Security Group presented itself on its website as "a group of companies specializing in maritime security, risk assessment, VIP security, and infrastructure protection." That much seemed true.

Less well advertised were Moran's dealings with a shipping company involved in trafficking nuclear-weapons technology for the Pakistan-based A. Q. Khan network to Libya and covertly shipping missiles to Myanmar.[4] Nor did Moran openly tout its connections to a web of Hong Kong shell companies registered in 2009 to mask its transactions, links that ultimately tied back to one of Prigozhin's business intermediaries.[5] Little noticed at the time, this intriguing trail of bread crumbs provided the earliest hint that Prigozhin or someone in his retinue had already started to dip a toe into the mercenary trade. Moran Security was, in fact, the linchpin of a vast logistics network that cloaked the movement of Russia's transfer of arms to countries under international embargo, a tangled skein that Prigozhin would inherit and transform into the Wagner Group within a little more than a year.

The firm dated its origins to 1990s contracting missions in Iraq, Somalia, and Syria. But it was officially established as a stand-alone "security consultancy" only after Russia was forced in 2010 to deploy a naval destroyer to liberate a Sovcomflot tanker filled with $52 million worth of crude oil from Somali pirates who had taken the ship and its crew hostage in the Gulf of Aden.[6]

Initially registered in Moscow under the name of Vyacheslav Kalashnikov, a well-connected retired KGB agent from St. Petersburg, Moran Security was linked to a hidden matrix of shell companies that spanned from Far East Asia to the Caribbean. Kalashnikov, a German speaker with a law degree, had spent years abroad on assignment for the KGB and capitalized on his experience and connections to become an adviser to Alexander Torshin, a figure with connections to Putin's inner circle and an influential member of the Duma and the United Russia Party. Torshin, a former banker, had been alleged to be linked to money-laundering activities and organized crime, specifically the Taganskaya Gang in Spain, and would later be embroiled in the FBI investigation into Russian interference in US elections, a scheme that unfolded concurrently with the Moran Security Group's expansion in 2011.[7]

Company recruitment information posted on the Moran Security site stated a strong preference for seasoned former GRU, VDV Airborne, and naval infantry specialists with English-speaking skills who had been on at least two foreign tours.[8] The company website's gallery included snapshots of older Russian men in loose-fitting olive-green army uniforms and wielding pistols. A short promotional film linked to the site offered a visual testament to the caliber of personnel they were targeting: fit, adept, and action oriented.

One, a strapping, bald, blue-eyed paratrooper named Andrey Bogatov, posed for the camera with a smirk, both hands gripping an assault rifle. A veteran of the Soviet-Afghan war, Bogatov had served for years in the airborne forces, completing tours in Kosovo and Chechnya before retiring and taking a day job as an electrician.[9] The footage of him in the Moran Security promotional reel was shot several years before he would lose an arm in a battle in Syria and would earn a medal—one that Vladimir Putin personally pinned on his chest.

Bogatov and the two other men who made up the operational heart of Moran Security Group's command echelon each had two decades or more of military service under his belt, and all at one time or another had served on the *Myre Seadiver* or one of the three rescue vessels that were contracted to protect Sovcomflot shipments.

Key in this group were Dmitry Utkin and Alexander Kuznetsov, who, like Bogatov, were GRU veterans who joined Moran Security in 2013. They shared much in common with Bogatov. But the crucial link among the core members of Moran Security's operational group who would go on to form the nucleus of the nucleus of the Wagner Group—Utkin, Bogatov, and Kuznetsov—was the time they had spent in combat in Chechnya.

The standout in this group was Utkin. Within a year of joining Moran Security as a company commander, he would go on to become the titular head of Russia's most notorious mercenary army. By the time he signed on with Moran, Utkin had already put in more than twenty years in Russia's military-intelligence service, where he obtained the rank of lieutenant colonel in the GRU's 2nd Guards Special Purpose Brigade.

Born in the Sverdlovsk region of Russia in 1970 to a single mother of modest means, Utkin spent part of his younger years in Ukraine before moving to St. Petersburg, where he enrolled in officer candidate school at the Higher Combined Arms Command School.[10] Utkin was one of the first in for the battle in the Chechen capital of Grozny during the first wave of the 1990s conflict. After flushing Basayev's forces out of Grozny, Utkin's company, the 584th Spetsnaz Detachment, relocated its base of operations to Budyonnovsk in 1996.

While stationed in Budyonnovsk, Utkin spent part of his time leading reconnaissance operations around the Argun Gorge area and on missions in Dagestan. It was during a rotation to the volatile region that Utkin met through mutual friends the first woman he would marry, Elena Shcherbinina, a Budyonnovsk local who was also in the service. Her impression of Utkin then was that he was the reserved, quiet type—more of a doer than a talker. "I didn't pay much attention to him at first," she remembered. "We often just ended up in the same company."[11]

Soon, though, Utkin would distinguish himself as a standout soldier, winning his first medal after he and a few of his comrades managed to secure the release of a Russian officer who had been taken hostage by Chechen separatists. The couple drew closer after Utkin hired her to work in the command headquarters in Starye Atagi. A few years after they married, Utkin won a promotion and was reassigned in 2000 to Pechory, just south of Russia's border with Estonia, where he was tasked with leading the 700th Guards, a subordinate detachment of the GRU's 2nd Spetsnaz Guards Brigade.

Although the assignment was a step up and would eventually earn Utkin the rank of lieutenant colonel, the switch from high-tempo combat operations in the field to staff duty required a comparatively slower pace that he found stultifying. "He had a very difficult time adapting and he was temperamental when he was not in the fight," Utkin's ex-wife recalled. "He wanted a military career as a combat officer. He was not the type to crease his pants and sit around at headquarters."[12] Utkin's restlessness and testy relations between his wife and mother ultimately drove the couple apart.

Beyond these details, Utkin's biography is spotty. But a curriculum vitae he posted online indicates that he had a rudimentary command of elementary German and had completed a private-security training course in 2006.[13] Utkin continued to serve with the GRU until at least 2008, when he marked his twentieth year of active duty. Some who worked with Utkin on the mercenary circuit suggested he began dipping his toe into the private-security business as early as 2010.[14] He listed Pskov as his residence in 2013, the year he reportedly retired from the service and signed up to work with the Moran Security Group.

Kuznetsov's pedigree was similar. Dark-eyed and swarthy, he had the physique of a welterweight boxer. Kuznetsov spent years serving in the GRU's 10th Special Purpose Brigade before he was tried and sentenced to ten years in prison for robbery and kidnapping, although he served only a fraction of his sentence. From there forward, he worked as a contract soldier of fortune.

Many found their way into Moran Security via word-of-mouth recommendations from friends, casual acquaintances, and other *spetsnaz* operators with St. Petersburg ties who had become veterans' rights activists under the wide umbrella of the Union of Paratroopers. One likely common vector for recruitment was the St. Petersburg Regional Martial Arts and Tactical Shooting Complex, which was part of a constellation of training centers operated by veteran cops with ties to Prigozhin's security service. The complex was a magnet for able-bodied adrenaline junkies who—like Utkin, Bogatov, and Kuznetsov— had aged out, flamed out, run afoul of the law, or all of the above.

Like fish out of water, the men hired to work as contract soldiers of fortune for Moran Security were barely able to function when they were not out at sea or on the front lines. But they would shine as proxy fighters in Russia's shadow war with the West over the future of the world order.

Mercenaries in all but name, they were hard to distinguish from the feudal-era warriors for hire who plied their trade under the banners of ambitious lords and princelings bent on expanding their realms into kingdoms. In fourteenth-century Italy, they would have been called *condottieri* because they signed written contracts after agreeing to go to battle for wealthy city-states. In sixteenth-century Switzerland, soldiers of fortune were called *Reisläufer*: "one who goes to war."

In the seventeenth and eighteenth centuries, Britain and the Netherlands called seagoing auxiliary soldiers privateers; for their services they were awarded shares of earnings from ill-gotten booty seized from enemy boats laden with gold bullion. During the American Revolutionary War, Britain rented whole contingents of German Hessians to fight alongside them in battle. Some were poor, indebted farmworkers and artisans, many of them criminals pressed into service by wealthy patrons whose land they lived on.

Modern descendants of the line were veteran special operatives who formed their own corporations and marketed their expertise in warfare and weapons procurement under the heading of private-military companies (PMCs). Largely a product of postcolonial upheavals and the downsizing of militaries around the world that followed the end of the Cold War, PMCs slashed their way across Africa, Asia, Latin America, and the Middle East on contract for government defense agencies, mining concerns, and oil companies for hefty fees.

In the 1990s the most notorious of these was Executive Outcomes (EO). Founded in South Africa by Eeben Barlow, a veteran special-forces officer, the company became infamous for its exploits in war-torn Angola and Sierra Leone. Legendary for its shape-shifting use of holding companies and corporate shells to manage and disguise the nature of its services, EO built its business off the back of millions in oil and diamond concessions.

Its highly adaptive organizational structure and innovative marketing strategy made EO stand out as a model for big-name American PMCs like Blackwater, the firm founded by Erik Prince that emerged at the center of controversy during the US occupation of Iraq. The common thread across the ages is that mercenary armies are products of states that are short on the financial and political capital needed to feed and field a full-scale military, but big on imperial ambitions.

The Russian men who worked for Moran Security held much in common with these antecedents. By any other name they were mercenaries. But what distinguished them from Western counterparts like Blackwater was their complicated history and ever-shifting legal status. In the dirty-war days of gunrunning from Russia's interior to the heart of the Middle East and Africa in the 1950s and 1960s, KGB agents had delivered crateloads of AK-47 rifles and grenade launchers to Soviet-backed rebel forces. They were called "Comrade Tourists" then. Years later, *spetsnaz* veterans who had operated in 1980s hot spots such as Cuba, Nicaragua, and Venezuela began to mingle in entities like Anti-Terror Oryol, Redut, and the Moran Security Group. It was on these Cold War battlegrounds, where Americans and Russians confronted each other in the shadows of a global ideological battle, that the foundations of the Wagner Group's leadership and command structure were first established.

Most of the world was unaware that big state-run companies like Sovcomflot rented the labor of soldiers of fortune through a peculiar set of legal arrangements that made them vassals of the Kremlin. It was not until the *Myre Seadiver* incident that it became clear that Russia's "Comrade Tourists" had morphed from covert soldier-spies into a loosely linked confederation of mercenary contingents. That realization came only gradually as internal debates over how to regulate Russia's burgeoning private-military–security industry began to bubble up within the upper reaches of Russia's state security apparatus.

The very existence of private-military companies in Russia created controversy and confusion. Although thousands of domestic protection agencies proliferated across the country during the anything-goes 1990s, security entities that serviced expeditionary missions beyond Russia's borders were always tightly yoked to Russia's big state companies and government security agencies.

In Russian, the word itself—*mercenary*—carries multiple meanings in military slang. The Russian term for Russian soldiers who work on contract is *naemnik*, and it stems from the root word *nayom*, which means "to hire or engage for a wage." The word came into wider use in Russian security circles in the early 2000s as the Kremlin sought in fits and starts to transition Russia's military from a conscript-based service to a professional volunteer army where officers are paid on a contractual basis for time-limited service. Professional soldiers at the mid-ranking warrant-officer level were often referred to as mercenaries or *naemniki* as a result. The term is essentially colloquial Russian shorthand for military lifers, men who provide expertise in everything from mine clearance to VIP protection, antipiracy operations, and even sabotage operations. As a rule, military lifers were highly concentrated in elite special-forces units in the VDV Airborne and the GRU, where high-tempo, high-risk operations created a unique esprit de corps.

At the political level, the main source of controversy over mercenary activities arose from a series of contradictory Russian laws and decrees issued in the Yeltsin era and during Putin's second presidential term. Moran Security and its

Russian antecedents Anti-Terror Oryol and Redut were neither private nor fully legal in the traditional sense of those words. Russia's criminal code—Article 359, to be precise—bars Russian citizens from fighting abroad in a foreign conflict for profit or personal gain.[15] The law draws on definitions and terms that spell out what combatants can and cannot do under the Geneva Conventions and related international protocols on the conduct of armed conflict.

Yet those laws, and how they are interpreted in distinct parts of the world, have changed over time along with the very character of war itself. As guerrilla-style tactics and irregular paramilitary formations began to proliferate in the Middle East after the 9/11 terrorist attacks on the United States, they triggered a debate over how to treat groups of fighters that operate abroad on contract either overtly or covertly for a given state.

In Russia, legal loopholes abounded. A 1994 presidential decree gave state enterprises wide latitude to staff and manage their own security divisions, granting contract employees a special, if murky, status. A little more than a decade later, Putin progressively turbocharged the power of state enterprises when he signed legislation in 2007 that created entities known as *goskorporatisiya* (state corporations).[16] It was under this framework that the Kremlin fused the assets of Rosoboronexport and some 400 defense subsidiaries into a huge holding company called Rostec. The measure brought more than 780,000 employees under one giant military-industrial umbrella, giving the megacorporation control over wide swaths of Russia's weapons industry, automotive industry, and chemical industry.

Putin further increased the power of state corporations two years later when he issued a presidential decree that designated oil, gas, and arms-related firms "strategic enterprises." Under the new rules of doing business on behalf of the Kremlin, Russian citizens hired to work on contract for the security divisions of strategic state enterprises are permitted to carry arms and defend Russia's national interests abroad. In theory, they remain civilians because they fall outside the Russian military's direct chain of command.

What exactly constituted Russia's "national interests" was not defined, leaving military security contractors in legal limbo and blurring the lines of the rules of engagement in combat situations. Although Putin's edicts permitted big state-managed enterprises like Sovcomflot, Gazprom, Rostec, Transneft, and Rosneft to hire and equip their own armies, it was silent on how that got done and how their soldiers for hire were supposed to be compensated, managed, and disciplined. The Moran Security Group straddled that gray zone, offering a somewhat vague menu of services in "targeted approaches in the world's current hot spots."

Under these new arrangements, Russia's president gained the power to appoint the heads of state corporations—a privilege that Putin exploited to reward his loyalists with control over multibillion-dollar enterprises. One of the most prominent beneficiaries was Sergey Chemezov, who was appointed CEO of Rostec, effectively making him the head of Russia's largest corporate paramilitary.

Chemezov was far from alone. With a few strokes of the pen, lawmakers in the Duma had created a modern Russian equivalent of the British East India Company. Putin's other trusted allies from his KGB days—Alexey Miller at Gazprom, Transneft's Nikolay Tokarev, Rosneft CEO Igor Sechin, and several others—emerged as the leaders of a new super-elite merchant class operating at the behest of the Kremlin. From 2007 onward, these state corporation heads wielded powers akin to those of the royally designated Court of Proprietors of the East India Company.

Like their seventeenth-century British antecedents, Rostec, Gazprom, Transneft, Rosneft, and other Russian firms classed as strategic state corporations held a state monopoly on foreign trade in energy and arms. Much in the same way that British privateers cruised the open seas, grabbing pieces of the defunct empires of Spain and Portugal in the name of Queen Elizabeth I, Putin's cronies were granted a charter to conquer new energy and defense markets in far-off territories.

The task of securing Russian enterprises abroad and colonizing new markets demanded seasoned military expertise. For this, Putin's inner circle drew inspiration from strategies used by other successful monarchies. When news of the new laws broke in the Russian press, comparisons were swiftly made between the powers granted to the paramilitary forces of Tatneft and Gazprom and those of the Landsknecht—the German mercenaries who fought for princes and aspiring emperors in sixteenth-century Europe. Technically, strategic state corporations and Kremlin-aligned joint-stock companies were required to coordinate with Russia's MVD internal-affairs service and the FSB. But the law did not require consultation with the defense ministry.[17]

This did not sit well with the military establishment. Under pressure to march in time with the New Look overhaul, defense officials sounded the alarm, albeit off the record. "They will need helicopters, planes—the need for aviation will definitely pop up and create a parallel to the Air Force, even an alternative to it. By definition, they need watercraft, so a fleet will appear. They will select the best for command positions, luring officers out of the army," one confidential source complained to reporters covering the changes. "They will simply bleed the officer corps!"[18] The panicky prediction was on the mark.

Cuts to Russia's officer corps created a ready pool of talent for Russia's new corporate armies. The defense ministry lost legions of warrant officers, captains, majors, and colonels to less bruising work for state corporations. Intermediary companies for Gazprom, Tatneft, and Rostec picked them up on contract and offered far higher salaries, making it particularly tough for the Russian military to attract and retain *kontraktniki* enlistees and officers. New market opportunities in the quasi-governmental commercial-security sector reduced incentives for *kontraktniki* soldiers who had signed on for an initial three-year term with the military to re-up their contracts.

Once their military terms were up, they stood a far better chance of earning a decent living and enjoying a better quality of life than if they stayed in the service. Contract jobs for state corporations additionally offered a pathway to income for soldiers who had run afoul of military rules or the law. Scores joined Moran Security, which ran missions in the Middle East, Central Asia, and Southeast Asia, and at various points appeared to have parallel front companies registered in the United Kingdom. Older versions of the Moran Security Group company website also listed offices in Bedford, New York, and Bremen, Germany. The addresses listed for those locations matched those of the South Asia and Africa Regional Port Stability Cooperative, a maritime-safety and antipiracy organization also known as SAARPSCO, with offices also listed in Seychelles, and KEAMSCO, a Kenya-based affiliate.[19]

One of Moran Security's top partners was the insurance giant SOGAZ, a onetime Gazprom subsidiary and leader in Russia's war-risk industry that was partially controlled by Bank Rossiya, the Russian finance giant cofounded by Putin's longtime friend Yuri Kovalchuk. The SOGAZ connection would prove critically important for Moran Security because in time the insurance giant would come to hold a controlling stake in Transneft Insurance, a spin-off risk manager for Transneft, Russia's energy-pipeline engineering giant.

Kovalchuk and Tatneft's Nikolai Tokarev, another KGB veteran from Putin's days in East Germany, were invested in the success of Moran Security's mission. Together with the Russian energy-engineering firm Stroytransgaz, a onetime subsidiary of Gazprom partially controlled by Putin's friend Gennady

Timchenko, Transneft and SOGAZ formed the three corners of a cartel-like structure that had a lock on Russia's energy-infrastructure–export market.

The plethora of ties to Putin's close circle of trusted oligarchs, state enterprises, and so-called *siloviki* security heavies from the FSB indicated that Moran Security enjoyed a privileged status that made it all but untouchable under the law. Along with the Moscow-based security firm RSB Group, Moran Security was one of only a few soldier-of-fortune contingents legally allowed to operate outside of Russian territory.

Few outside of a narrow circle of enterprising Russian investigative reporters and military analysts had any understanding of Moran Security's special status when news broke about the arrest of the *Myre Seadiver* crew in Nigeria. The web of offshore companies spun to obscure Moran Security's ownership structure and financing threw up substantial barriers to outside scrutiny.

Vladimir Neelov, a twenty-something graduate student and aspiring military-affairs journalist from St. Petersburg, helped lift the veil. After a little digging, he found that the Belize registry listed the firm as the Moran Maritime Group and named a mysterious company registered in the British Virgin Islands called Neova Holdings Ltd. as a 50 percent shareholder in Moran. Russia's corporate registry indicated that Moran Security was also affiliated with a St. Petersburg company called Energy LLC. Neova Holdings turned out to be another shell within a shell that tied back to yet another holding company called Novaem Group, a Russian energy-engineering conglomerate based in Barnaul, that appeared to be part of a massive constellation of subsidiaries that all linked back to Russia's top arms purveyor, Rostec.[20] Neelov's revelations about the ties between Rostec and Moran Security landed him a seven-year prison term on treason charges.[21]

There were good reasons for all the secrecy. Moran Security was, in fact, the indirect product of discussions between members of Russia's General Staff about deploying contract soldiers of fortune for more aggressive operations that began as the New Look reforms got under way. In 2010 several top leaders in the General Staff met with Executive Outcomes CEO Eeben Barlow, who in a presentation at the St. Petersburg Economic Forum described in detail how he had built his South African private-military company into a top provider on the African continent.

Up to that point, debates about the PMC question carried out among high-ranking members of Russia's ministry of defense—Gerasimov, Shoigu, and others like Alexey Dyumin—had taken place behind closed doors. But

Barlow's lecture on how Executive Outcomes stitched together a string of front companies to circumvent sanctions on the various African paramilitaries and guerrilla groups that it was contracted to train apparently left a deep impression on decision-makers in the Russian defense ministry. Russian defense ministry insiders would later tell the online news magazine *The Bell* that the lecture sparked the idea of deploying mercenaries or so-called illegals to carry out special covert military missions to minimize the risk of political exposure for the Kremlin if the operations failed.[22]

As the controversy over the predicament of the *Myre Seadiver* crew continued in the Russian press, the debate over the unsettled legal status of military-security companies spilled into the open during one of Putin's final addresses to the Duma in November 2012.

In a scripted mise-en-scène dialogue with a member of the conservative Just Russia Party that was later dutifully reported on by *RIA Novosti*, Putin said he was all for using military-security companies as instruments of Russian influence abroad: "[I] believe that this really is a tool for realizing national interests without the direct participation of the state."[23]

All this was surprising news to those tracking the fate of the *Myre Seadiver*. Nigerian authorities kept the *Myre Seadiver* crew in abysmal conditions in overcrowded, sweltering cells and with limited food and water for six months before a trial date was set in March 2013. In an interview with a local St. Petersburg paper, *Fontanka*, Moran's deputy director Vadim Gusev and a founding member of the Antiterror-Redut soldier-of-fortune confederation called on Putin to support a special operation to release the *Myre Seadiver* crew.[24]

The crew's lot improved when they were transferred to the Russian embassy not long after Russia's foreign minister, Sergey Lavrov, threatened to sanction Nigeria and leaned on Lloyds of London, the world's oldest and most powerful maritime and war-risk insurer, to take action against Nigeria. But the crew remained in custody for several months more before the senior executive vice president of Sovcomflot, Evgeny Abramasov, pressed Sovcomflot's partner, the commodities-trading giant Glencore International, to reach out to local contacts in Nigeria in April 2013 to intercede on their behalf.[25] Nigerian authorities dropped the charges against the Russians in October 2013, almost a year to the day after their arrest. By then, the fate of the *Myre Seadiver* crew was already slipping from the headlines amid rising tensions between Russia and Ukraine and nonstop reports of violence across Syria. The Arab Spring was upending everything, and necessity—ever the mother of invention—was changing attitudes in the Russian military about the special utility of soldiers of fortune.

In Moscow, early in the winter of 2013, Valery Gerasimov began planning his first "Z" formation exercise as chief of General Staff. Gerasimov had vigorously participated in two such annual assessments under his predecessor's guidance. In 2011 one dubbed *Tsentr* covered the country's central district across the Siberian tundra. Another called *Kavkaz* stretched across the Kola region of Russia's eastern reaches to the Pacific shore.

Each exercise revolved around an imaginary conflict between Russia and an unnamed foreign adversary. *Zapad*, or "west" in Russian, signaled the European-facing orientation of the formation. What distinguished the *Zapad-2013* exercise from its predecessors was its enormous size, its parallel emphasis on naval power, and its timing just two years into the Arab Spring and an escalating diplomatic contretemps between the United States and Russia over violent protests in Syria that had metastasized into civil war.

Whether it was said aloud or not, NATO was usually the opponent they had in mind. *Zapad* centered on an imaginary scenario designed to test the Russian response to a Baltic-based terrorist group that waged an amphibious assault along the western edge of the Baltic Sea somewhere between Kaliningrad and St. Petersburg. The exercise was massive, spanning from the Arctic to the strategically important city of Voronezh, just south of Moscow.[26] In terms of manpower, the sheer scale of mobilized military force on the Russian side dwarfed the few thousands who were meant to defend NATO countries to Russia's east.

Over the course of six months, from March to early September 2013, Gerasimov ordered some 70,000 ground troops and 2,500 in the navy to jump through hoop after hoop until they were ready for their six-day final exam over September 20–27.[27] There was one major snap inspection and close to a dozen smaller ones that entailed coordinating the movements of tens of thousands of troops and the placement of millions of tons of equipment in strategic locations. The practice sessions leading up to the grand finale were also unusual in that even military psychologists, medical staff, engineers, logisticians, and the MVD internal-affairs troops were in on the action.[28]

It seemed like overkill, but it was classic Gerasimov. Newly in charge of Russia's million-man-strong military forces, Gerasimov was out to prove himself. He was fond of quoting the maxims of the eighteenth-century military strategist General Alexander Suvorov, and Suvorov's "train hard, fight easy" dictum was a favorite, repeated like an Orthodox catechism. Troop strength, command fitness, control systems, weapons, and logistics were all supposed to come together in a symphony conducted harmoniously by the commander in chief, with soldiers as the musicians playing the tune.

In advance of the far-reaching exercise, inklings of Gerasimov's vision of Russia's future conflicts were already raising concerns in Western capitals. In late February 2013, Gerasimov released a speech for reprint in the official military press titled "The Value of Science Is in the Foresight." Published in *Voyenno-Promyshlennyi Kurier* (*VPK*), a quasi-private defense-affairs news outlet, Gerasimov's oratory had an almost biblical zeal that cast the United States as Russia's greatest threat.

Delivered a little more than a year after Putin's government had violently suppressed the Snow Revolution protests over Russia's fraudulent parliamentary elections, Gerasimov's assessment reflected a widely held view among the generation of Russian Cold Warriors who had come of age in the 1960s and 1970s that Russia was still haunted by inadequate military preparedness. The world had since changed dramatically, in Gerasimov's view. Western propaganda, the internet, satellite communications, and smartphones had given a one-two punch to the global order. Color revolutions, Twitter fights over Ukraine and Georgia's push to join the European Union and NATO, and two straight years of unrest that stretched from Cairo's Tahrir Square to Damascus and Benghazi—it was all proof positive in Gerasimov's estimation that America's regime-change wars had set off an almost unstoppable global conflagration of political chaos.

In Gerasimov's interpretation of world affairs, the United States was the chief cause of the instability. Washington's flirtations with Islamist jihadists in Afghanistan, its tendentious meddling in the Balkans, the messy toppling of Saddam Hussein's regime, and the NATO action in Libya that led to the on-camera mob killing of Muammar Qaddafi—all were indicative of America's master plan for total global regime change. Globalization and America's weaponization of sanctions were strangling Moscow's onetime spheres of influence.

Bewitched by social media and prodded into revolt by unnamed external enemies of peace, the world was on fire. This, Gerasimov declared, was "war by other means": "The role of nonmilitary means of achieving political and strategic goals has grown, and, in many cases, they have exceeded the power of the force of weapons in their effectiveness." Gerasimov pointed to the emerging primacy of irregular forces and use of nonmilitary means—most notably deception, sabotage, and information warfare—for the achievement of strategic ends in Russia's new post-reform military doctrine: "We must acknowledge that, while we understand the essence of traditional military actions carried out by regular armed forces, we have only a superficial understanding of asymmetrical forms and means."[29]

Gerasimov's pronouncements landed at an especially tense time. Moscow and Kyiv were driving toward a cliff amid a contentious trade dispute and Ukraine's bid to join the European Union. The revolutionary force of the Arab Spring was upending the world order in ways that would reverberate long into the future. Popular uprisings removed from power three long-ruling regional heads of state: Tunisia's Zine El-Abidine Ben Ali, Egypt's Hosni Mubarak, and Libya's Muammar Qaddafi. Only one, Syria's Bashar al-Assad, managed to hang on, by a thread, through a combination of harsh police crackdowns on protests, patronage politics, and appeals for help to allies such as Russia and Iran.

Politically, supporting Assad enabled Russia to challenge US dominance and bolster its international standing, reinforcing its position as a global power. It also provided Russia a means to reshape its relations with Turkey, which had been rocky for several years. Economically, Syria was a vital node in Russia's energy-export pipeline and critical to trade transit routes.

For Putin, who reportedly had a deeply emotional response to Qaddafi's on-camera murder by mob, the Arab uprisings highlighted the folly of allowing the United States to act unchecked in the region. He drew the line at Syria, signaling through repeated Russian vetoes on UN Security Council resolutions championed by the West that Russia would stand by Assad despite the grave human-rights violations taking place in the country. Putin had cooperated with Obama on the removal of Syria's chemical weapons, but they were at loggerheads over the peace process and Assad's political fate.

The most concrete risk for the Kremlin was the potential loss of access to Russia's naval installation in the Syrian port city of Tartus and the Khmeimim airbase in Latakia. These two gave Russia a foothold in the Mediterranean that had for decades been essential for Russian arms transfers to regional clients, providing a crucial means of extending Russia's reach into the Middle East and Africa and of checking NATO power on Russia's southern flank.

But a tough UN arms embargo imposed against Assad's regime constituted a serious roadblock for long-scheduled deliveries of Russian military gear to the Syrian capital of Damascus. Diplomatic clashes between the United States and Russia in the UN Security Council over the response to the turmoil in the Arab streets were escalating.

Gerasimov's sober assessment of the situation was a rare moment of transparency for Russia's military leadership. The speech was reflective of a mindset that was starting to take greater hold inside the Kremlin. Although it presented a distorted view of the world, it was greeted as a novelty by Russia watchers when it was later dug up and reprinted in English by *Radio Free Europe/Radio Liberty*.

Until that point, Gerasimov had made few notable public pronouncements, let alone appearances. The dearth of concrete specifics about Gerasimov's thinking up until that point left analysts at CIA headquarters in Langley, Virginia, and its British counterpart in London, the GCHQ, poring over Gerasimov's republished oratory like so many tea leaves as they tried to make sense of how Russia's new military leader thought about the world.

Much ink would be spilled in the West on analysis of what would become known as "Gerasimov's Doctrine." A tongue-and-cheek jibe at the pompousness of the speech, the phrase, coined by British historian and Kremlinologist Mark Galeotti, would eventually catch on like wildfire in the Pentagon. But Gerasimov's discourse was as much about genuflecting before the imperium altar that Putin had erected as anything else.

The speech, Galeotti said, was more sales pitch than "doctrine": "In hindsight, this was Gerasimov, whose job is, after all, not just to be the top soldier, but also to be an advocate for continued defense budget spending and so forth, basically saying to the Kremlin: 'look, we know that you're worried about these non-military kinds of attack. But don't worry, we're on it. We're on top of the problem, and we know how to respond.'"[30]

In fact, Russia had already started experimenting with war by other means long before Gerasimov's pronouncements appeared in *VPK*. Anticipating the likelihood of Russian military intervention, the Kremlin quietly green-lit a ramp-up of deliveries to Tartus. Known informally among seafarers as the "Syrian Express," the clandestine arms-transfer route was a financial lifeline for state-owned arms conglomerate Rostec. Once it was out that the Kremlin had begun to use soldiers of fortune to expand its reach abroad, it was only a matter of time before the Russian public and the world would wake up to reality. And what a rude awakening it would be.

CHAPTER 8
SLAVONIC CORPS

The drive from the oasis city of Palmyra to the desert outpost of Al-Sukhnah is not long. But memory of it runs deep in the short history of the Moran Security Group's adventures in the Middle East. Traveling northeast from the colonnaded ruins of the Temple of Baal toward the Euphrates River, the forty-four-mile stretch of road that connects the two Syrian towns is lined on either side by a wide expanse of sand.

In centuries past, when it was a busy trade route for Greek- and Aramaic-speaking merchants, the land around it was known as the place between two rivers, or Mesopotamia. Byzantines and Persians left their mark, and the area became the heart of the first Islamic Caliphate, which emerged after the death of the prophet Muhammed in 632 CE. More than a millennium later, in 2013, violent clashes between forces loyal to Syria's president Bashar al-Assad and fighters with the Islamic State of Iraq and al-Sham (ISIS) made the region the epicenter of a multisided proxy war that all but destroyed the Moran Security Group and would eventually give rise to the Wagner Group.

Assad had tried and failed for two years to suppress a popular uprising. In response to the brutal tactics that he used to stifle antigovernment protests, thousands of Syrian soldiers deserted, and once-peaceful opposition hardened into armed resistance. Assad had managed to escape the dark fate of other Arab strongmen in large part because of the external support he received from Syria's longtime allies, Iran and Russia. But Saudi Arabia, Qatar, and Turkey were also funneling millions of dollars in aid and military supplies to anti-Assad factions, and in 2013 it began to look like all of Homs, the oil- and gas-rich governorate where Palmyra is located, could slip from Assad's control.

Into this cauldron stepped Moran Security. Still reeling from the reputational hit and financial blow to the company's bottom line incurred during the *Myre Seadiver* trial, Moran officials cooked up a way to recover their losses and rebrand. At that time, the leaders of the shadow mercenary army were still concerned enough about revealing themselves—and their connections in Russia's military and political circles—that they created an alter ego. In the spring of 2013, job ads for a mysterious outfit called Slavonic Corps began cropping up in online message boards on the Russian internet, RuNet. A link to a bare-bones Slavonic Corps website, "slavcorps.org," was provided.

In the upper left corner of the site was a large black *kolovrat*, the neo-pagan symbol for the sun and the Slavic equivalent of the swastika, superimposed on a beige camouflage backdrop. Just below, there was a shadowy figure of a soldier hefting an automatic rifle with a helicopter looming on the distant horizon amid a blazing sunset. It was all very "Apocalypse Now." Language on the site resembled in cadence and tone that of Moran Security's chameleon-like antecedents, Anti-Terror Oryol and Redut-Antiterror, suggesting it had been written by the same person or simply copied and pasted from another site.

The elaborate camouflaging and rebranding was carefully crafted to give the Kremlin plausible deniability. Text on the "About Us" page specified that work with the company was carried out in strict accordance with Russian legislation: "Only the 'Slavic Corps' employs reserve officers, professionals of the highest quality, who have unique military professions, as well as experience in Iraq, Afghanistan, East Africa, Tajikistan, the North Caucasus, Serbia, etc."

Applicants who had combat experience with *spetsnaz* forces in the Russian ministry of defense or ministry of internal affairs (MVD) were encouraged to download and complete a form for contract-based jobs that would last from three to six months.[1] Recruiters for Slavonic Corps promised new employees that they could earn up to $4,000 or $5,000 a month, an enormous sum of money in Russia, where the average gross personal income hovered around $15,000 annually.

Vadim Gusev, the deputy director of the Moran Security Group, had registered a company called Slavonic Corps Limited in Hong Kong in January 2012.[2] In March a Russian company based in St. Petersburg and bearing a similar name, "Slavonic Corps LLC," was registered in the name of St. Petersburg resident Sergey Kramskoy. Curiously, the signature of Moran Security's head of office, Alexey Badikov, appeared on the identification cards issued to Slavonic Corps contractors. Those tapped for an interview were told to show up at the Baltic Shooting Center on Alexander Blok Street in St. Petersburg, which happened to be both the registered address of Slavonic Corps LLC and the place where Moran Security's other leading stakeholder, Boris Chikin, worked as a trainer in bodyguard protection services.

If the web of overlapping connections between Moran Security and Slavonic Corps was confusing, that is probably because it was meant to be. Moscow was steadfastly denying that Russian manpower was involved at all in the Syrian morass, so it was in the interest of the security companies to cover their tracks. Multiple corporate registrations listed at the same address, tangled ownership structures that crisscrossed several jurisdictions—these were the common tricks of smuggling rings, drug cartels, and covert special-forces operatives. Although it was not remarked on when Slavonic Corps first burst into the Russian news headlines, a bit of rooting around in Russia's arcane corporate-registry records revealed that the Baltic Shooting Center was one of several across the St. Petersburg region that likely served as vectors for mercenary recruitment. One other, the Federation for Complex Martial Arts and Tactical Army Shooting of St. Petersburg, was linked by mutual business and friendship ties to Andrey Troshev, who at the time served as part of Prigozhin's security service.[3]

The meshwork of social ties and business stakes probably explained how it was that an enterprising *Fontanka* news reporter and former St. Petersburg cop named Denis Korotkov was tipped off to the arrest of several Slavonic Corps employees in October 2013. It was one hell of a scoop and a sea change in the evolution of how the world thought about Russia's irregular forces.

Korotkov, a rail-thin, mustachioed, pipe-smoking beat reporter, had covered cops and crime in St. Petersburg for years, but this story would turn out to be a game changer for him, parting the curtain of denials that Moscow had drawn around the involvement of Russian military contractors in faraway war zones like Syria. He learned about the Slavonic Corps misadventure a few days after the FSB detained Gusev and another Moran Security employee named Yevgeny Sidorov upon their return home to Russia following a harrowing firefight with ISIS forces in Al-Sukhnah.[4] That dustup in Syria left six Russians wounded. Coming as it did just days after the Nigerian authorities had released the *Myre Seadiver* crew, it also attracted even more unwanted attention to Moran Security Group's business practices just as the Kremlin was quietly contemplating sending more contract soldiers into Syria to help take back oil and gas fields seized by ISIS.

The fact that Moran Security was into shady business seemed to be confirmed when Korotkov phoned a Slavonic Corps employee and was directed to talk to none other than Vyacheslav Kalashnikov, the retired KGB agent and FSB reserve officer who had been mired in the whole crisis over the Russian crew detained in Nigeria. It turned out that Slavonic Corps had enticed 267 veterans to sign contracts for two-year stints protecting energy installations in Syria.[5] More than half were Cossacks. About a dozen were from St. Petersburg. And one was Dmitry Utkin.[6]

Like Utkin, many had previously fought as paratroopers and border guards in Afghanistan, Tajikistan, and Chechnya. During the spring and summer of 2013, Slavonic Corps recruits flew first to Beirut, Lebanon, where they were then driven to a guesthouse on the grounds of a defunct horse track in the Mediterranean port town of Latakia, Syria. Unbeknownst to most, Moran Security had cut a deal with a Syrian-Russian businessman and militia chief named Yusef Jaber to coordinate security operations for local oil- and gas-production sites managed by another well-connected Syrian-Russian oligarch.[7] "When we arrived there, it turned out that we were sent as gladiators, under a contract with some Syrian or other, who may or may not have a relationship with the government," one anonymous Slavonic Corps member told Korotkov in an interview for the St. Petersburg daily *Fontanka*.[8]

Slavonic Corps's operational plans called for a force in Syria of about two thousand. Some recruits were assigned to man several old Russian tanks and antiaircraft guns; others were handed ancient World War II–era rifles and told to shoot at anyone who approached the oil and gas facilities that dotted the landscape around Palmyra, Al-Sukhnah, and, most crucially, Deir Ezzor. This swath of land spanning northward to the edge of the Euphrates River contained facilities built with American money by oil majors like Conoco. Now, as the Syrian conflict raged into another year, those properties were up for grabs. But any taker would have to contend with both the messy politics of dynastic preservation, local freebooters, and quite possibly Kurdish forces trained by the US Special Forces. The mission that Slavonic Corps tasked its men with was a far cry from the routine guard duty that had been described to many of the Russians who signed up as contractors with the mercenary outfit. As the situation heated up in the area, they routinely clashed with ISIS and other antigovernment forces that sought to seize control of Homs from Assad's regime.

One of the more intense skirmishes occurred on October 15, when teams of Slavonic Corps contractors were ordered to strike out from near a military air base in Palmyra for the town of Deir Ezzor to the north, in the heart of Syria's largest oil reserves. They didn't get very far before an encounter with a Syrian Air Force helicopter that flew too close to the convoy ended in a fiery crash. Three days later, Slavonic Corps recruits were called up to support a pro-Assad militia that had come under fierce attack from several thousand rebel forces in Homs. A few of the Russians were wounded, but most managed to escape alive.

Gusev's Syrian clients, however, were none too pleased. A loud dispute broke out between Gusev and his Syrian overlords over money before the entire outfit flew back to Russia. When their flights arrived in Moscow, FSB agents were there to greet them. All on board were stripped of their mobile-phone SIM cards, boarding passes, and any other evidence that proved they had been in Syria. Gusev and Sidorov were promptly arrested.

But the elaborate measures taken to keep Slavonic Corps operations in Syria under wraps fell apart when ISIS fighters recovered the backpack of one Andrey Malyuta and his company identification badge bearing the distinctive Moran Security logo—an ethereal-looking blond mermaid in white robes. Eager to capitalize on the propaganda gold mine that the backpack's contents represented, ISIS fighters quickly put together a video montage and claimed on social media that they had killed a hundred Russian mercenaries during skirmishes near Al-Sukhnah.

The artifacts, ISIS claimed, were proof that Assad was little more than a Kremlin puppet and that Russia had infiltrated covert operators into Syria to suppress the popular uprising against the regime in Damascus. ISIS claimed that Malyuta had been killed. Russian authorities naturally denied the claims. But when a video appeared showing Malyuta—alive and well—smashing a cinder block over his head at an encampment near Latakia, the official story fell apart. After *Fontanka* published its scoop on the Slavonic Corps in late October, the Kremlin found itself in a no-win situation. What had once been plausibly deniable was deniable no more.

Possibly, this was the moment that it began to dawn on Russian military planners and businessmen alike that a better cover story was needed to explain the presence of freelance *spetsnaz* operatives in Syria. The idea to rebrand

Moran Security may have even come from Prigozhin or someone in his security team who moonlighted for Moran. Rumors that Prigozhin was involved in the lucrative trafficking business had buzzed around St. Petersburg's ports for months before the Slavonic Corps fiasco. Leaked correspondence definitively confirmed that his involvement in the Syrian Express began at least as early as 2015.[9] Whatever his involvement, it is certain that when the Slavonic Corps brand disintegrated almost on first contact with the enemy, it forced a rethink, because from November 2013 forward, little to no public mention was made of the Slavonic Corps, the Moran Security Group, or the fate of the men who had been briefly detained when they arrived back at Vnukovo Airport in Moscow. Instead, Russian news outlets mostly described both contingents as defunct when, several months later, Gusev and Sidorov were forced to stand trial for their transgressions in Syria.

The FSB charged Gusev and Sidorov with violating Russia's law on the prohibition of mercenary activities and locked both of them up in Moscow's infamous Lefortovo Prison.[10] The two men pleaded guilty, and their boss, Alexey Badikov, later falsely claimed in court that Gusev and Sidorov had left Moran Security Group's employ before cooking up their deceptive Slavonic Corps scheme.

In retrospect, the Kremlin's crackdown on those behind the Slavonic Corps fiasco was entirely in keeping with a management style that would become a hallmark of how Russia's security agencies tried to contain exposure risks. In the upside-down culture of Russian paramilitaries, what was right was wrong, and what was wrong was right. What mattered most was that missions abroad were carried out below the radar. Secrecy and deniability were prized above all. Gusev and Sidorov's mistake was not that they had bumbled the Syria operation but that they got caught doing it by the press. Denis Korotkov's reporting on the mercenary misadventure had inadvertently exposed a truth that the Kremlin did not want known: that Russia was neck-deep in the Syrian conflict and that the Kremlin had quietly launched a covert military campaign to support the Assad regime more than a year earlier, despite official denials to the contrary.

In a subsequent court hearing, the FSB framed the Slavonic Corps episode as a rogue mercenary operation. A judge sentenced Gusev and Sidorov to three years in prison.[11] Gusev apparently got back in the game briefly in 2014, but he retired shortly afterward. Sidorov went on to take up the Redut mantle, registering a company in the same name with an address in Kubinka near the headquarters of the 45th Guards Spetsnaz Reconnaissance Brigade.[12] Whatever Sidorov's transgressions, they were apparently forgiven.

The whole mercenary enterprise—Slavonic Corps, Moran Security, Redut, Anti-Terror Oryol—resembled a set of nesting *matryoshka* dolls, except that it was not always obvious what or who exactly lay at the center of it all.

The intentional obscurity served to hide Russia's substantial material interests and growing involvement in the Syrian conflict. A 2010 version of Moran Security's website indicated that Russian security contractors for the firm had been operating in Syria near the country's border with Iraq at least three years before *Fontanka* unearthed the ties among Vadim Gusev, Boris Chikin, Yevgeny Sidorov, and Dmitry Utkin. When ISIS began to take control of large swaths of territory in Syria in late 2012, Russian military-security contractors evolved their mission to provide the logistical link for the Russian military advisers already on the ground. A core part of their new mission set was to train local militias affiliated with pro-Assad "Tiger Forces" that protected Russian investments in Syria.

The Russian state-run enterprises that formed the less well-advertised parts of Moran Security's client base had joined the Russia-Syria Business Council two or three years before the start of the Arab Spring. A key conduit for many of the contracts that supported Russian private-military–security operations, the hundred-plus-member business council included high-level Kremlin insiders like Rostec CEO Sergey Chemezov. Representatives from the Russian oil major Tatneft, Rostec subsidiary Technopromexport, and Stroytransgaz also claimed membership in the Russia-Syria Business Council.[13] All three Russian corporations backed energy and infrastructure projects in Syria before the civil war and, as a rule, generally insisted on housing their own privatized military contingents separately in the country, according to Syrian engineers and site managers.[14]

At the onset of the uprising against Assad, key Syrian players like George Haswani, head of HESCO Engineering and Construction, leveraged ties with Russian energy firms to carve out a larger slice of Syria's war economy. HESCO and Stroytransgaz teamed up on projects like the repair of the Kirkuk-Baniyas oil pipeline, part of Russian oil major Lukoil's broader effort to revive a deal with Iraq's North Oil Company. The pipeline's transit fees were set to bring Syria more than $1 billion per year.[15]

Haswani, a dual Syrian-Russian citizen with a Soviet PhD, was the Kremlin's leading contact in Damascus for big energy-infrastructure deals. After a stint managing the Baniyas pipeline, he struck lucrative energy deals through HESCO, partnering with Stroytransgaz on projects in Algeria, Sudan, Iraq, and the UAE.[16] Although he denied US accusations of trading oil on Syria's black market, Haswani acknowledged he was deeply involved in deals between Stroytransgaz and Syrian government ministries overseeing oil and gas contracts.[17] With HESCO's backing, Stroytransgaz built infrastructure across Syria, generating millions for Haswani, Timchenko, and their Russia-Syria Business Council allies—illustrating the Kremlin's firm grip on Syria's economy and security.

At the start of Syria's civil war, just before the imposition of major US and EU sanctions against the regime in 2012, the vast majority of Syrian oil exports were sold on the European market.[18] As a result, Russian investment in Syria's energy sector, and its trade in Syrian oil and gas to Europe in particular, came to represent a vital lifeline for the Assad regime and a critical route to reinforcing Russia's position as the dominant provider of Europe's energy needs.

Much of Syria's oil and gas wealth was concentrated near Palmyra in the Hayan gas block and the northeast region near Deir Ezzor, a fact that ISIS commanders were as keenly aware of as Assad's generals and their backers in Moscow were. The Arab Spring's toppling of key Middle East leaders whom the Kremlin had spent years cultivating threatened to reverse the progress that Russia had made in expanding its share of the Middle East energy and arms market during Putin's first two terms in office.

As the Arab uprisings spread like wildfire, questions began to simmer in Moscow. How would Rostec's top clients in the Middle East, now knee-deep in chaos, repay their hefty Russian loans? How would they handle the mountains of military gear sent to prop up dictators like Assad and Qaddafi? The Kremlin's unease turned to alarm when, in early 2011, more than three hundred Tatneft employees had to be evacuated in a rush, fleeing violent attacks in Libya.[19] Yet even as the region burned, Russian weapons flowed relentlessly into Syria.

Syria, now a powder keg of competing forces, became one of the biggest buyers of Russian military hardware. Rostec's arsenal—bullets, rifles, artillery, helicopters, jet fighters—poured into the country, with Rosoboronexport, the Kremlin's unofficial arm for foreign policy, handling the transactions. When Putin reclaimed the presidency in the spring of 2012, the old guard in Russia's security agencies knew it was time to adapt. The region was shifting beneath their feet, and so too must their strategy. In this high-stakes game, Rostec's CEO, Sergey Chemezov, and the commodities magnate Gennady Timchenko found themselves in the driver's seat, navigating the perilous business of keeping their companies afloat while their clients waged multisided war. It also raised questions for some in the Russian government about the long-debated need to create a pathway for private-military companies (PMCs) to provide training to foreign armies that were the recipients of Russian military kit. Although proposed legislation to legalize PMCs foundered, the Duma enacted a law in 2013 that extended special powers to the GRU that in turn allowed the military-intelligence wing to create and mobilize detachments of military reservists in times of both war and peace.[20] The new regulation spelled out terms under which "volunteers" could sign a contract that would place them under the supervision of ministry or other security agencies for a specified period of time. Attitudes toward soldiers of fortune and unconventional warfare were clearly shifting inside the Kremlin.

The Kremlin's moves to set up an off-book mercenary army slipped right past Washington's radar. While Moscow was quietly laying the groundwork for these formations, the White House was too busy grappling with the latest reports of chemical attacks in Syria. Obama had drawn his "redline" on nerve agents, but now he faced the grim reality of backing it up with action.

Then came August 2013. In Ghouta, near Damascus, sarin gas took the lives of about 1,700 people.[21] The images flooded social media—victims with foam at their mouths, their lips turning blue, bodies stacked like firewood. Most were children. Survivors recounted the horror of trying to breathe as the bombs fell.

With the suffering in Ghouta broadcast on social media for the world to see, Navi Pillay, the United Nations high commissioner for human rights, called for a war-crimes investigation. When UN inspectors confirmed what everyone already knew—that forces loyal to Assad had used sarin to crush the rebellion in the capital—Samantha Power, the Obama administration's fiery ambassador to the UN, called the act "barbaric." In a speech at a Washington think tank, she invoked the memories of Ghouta's survivors as she laid out the case for direct US intervention in Syria.[22]

Sharp condemnation from Washington, coupled with the threat of another US intervention in the Middle East, provoked an acid response from Sergey Lavrov, Russia's foreign minister. He claimed during a press conference that the entire situation was a false-flag operation by anti-Assad rebels, designed to garner sympathy and support from Western powers like the United States: "We have a sufficient amount of evidence that the reports about the use of chemical weapons reflect the fact that the opposition regularly resorts to provocations to initiate strikes and intervention against Syria."[23]

The chemical-weapons issue quickly split the UN Security Council, with Russia and China on one side and Britain, France, and the United States calling for Assad's ouster. That, of course, was a nonstarter for Putin. He argued that the Middle East could not afford another power vacuum and insisted that Russian arms shipments to Assad would continue, Obama's redline notwithstanding.

In Washington there were real concerns that Moscow's support for Assad could destabilize the region just as the United States was trying to reduce its presence. Internal debates within the National Security Council intensified when Hillary Clinton, nearing the end of her term as secretary of state, began considering the possibility of using US influence to interdict Russian military shipments to Syria.[24] It was a bold idea but one fraught with the risk of escalation. For decades, the southeastern Ukrainian ports of Oktyabrsk and Mykolaiv were key hubs for exporting Russian and Ukrainian arms, with shipments managed by a web of interlinked firms based in Kyiv and Odessa. This network funneled weapons from Sovcomflot's ships to Rostec's export operations, forming what became known as the "Odessa Network."[25] Although most arms flowed through the Black Sea, more sensitive cargo bound for Syria was sometimes routed through Baltic ports like St. Petersburg and Riga. These ports, along with key players like FEMCO and Westberg Ltd., became vital to the "Syrian Express": a covert smuggling operation that secretly supplied weapons and military equipment to Assad's regime, ensuring its survival in the face of international sanctions and civil war.

The Syrian Express also meant big business for Russia's arms industry, which Rostec's Chemezov was busily building into an export-oriented behemoth. Dollar for dollar, the volume of Rostec arms exports to Syria ranked that country among the biggest recipients in the Middle East region. In fact, most of Syria's weaponry came from Russia. To safeguard this market, Rostec required covert supply routes to ensure secure and, most importantly, discreet delivery.

One of the first Odessa Network–linked companies to be caught in the act of transferring weapons to Syria was Westberg. A year before the Slavonic Corps scandal broke, Westberg chartered a boat full of AK-47 and rocket-launcher ammunition bound from St. Petersburg to Russia's naval station in Tartus. The *MV Chariot* stopped to refuel in Cyprus. Not long after it reached its destination, press reports documented at least three other Westberg-chartered ships that were caught carrying weapons to Syria. As US pressure to interdict shipments increased in 2012, FEMCO, another major contract provider for the Moran Security Group, faced trouble when its cargo ship the *MV Alead* was caught off the coast of Scotland with refurbished attack helicopters. British authorities confirmed that the *MV Alead* had been trailing a Russian naval convoy after departing Kaliningrad, prompting the vessel's British insurer, the Standard Club, to cancel the shipment's insurance, citing concerns about violating EU sanctions. Six FEMCO ships in total lost their insurance.

The loss of a key insurer for such shipments was a serious blow for Sovcomflot and the Russian economy. Russia's economic-growth model, based on dominating energy-export markets and becoming an "energy superpower," required the capacity to transport oil, gas, and minerals to consumers, which in turn required free navigation of the seas and the ability to recover losses from damage and disasters. When British insurers signaled their willingness to accede to US pressure to cut Russian logistics companies out of the global market, the Kremlin was forced to look for alternatives.

This situation created unique opportunities for those with an appetite for high-stakes risks, those skilled in masking the movements of large numbers of weapons and men, and those adept in the art of illusion. The scrutiny of the Syrian Express and the failure of the Slavonic Corps venture on Syria's front lines had set up a perfect storm, forcing the Kremlin to reconfigure how Russia conducted the business of war around the world. Among the first to get in on the action was Yevgeny Prigozhin.

CHAPTER 9

POLITE PEOPLE

It was going to be the greatest show on Earth. A million spectators were expected to troop through the Black Sea resort town of Sochi for the 2014 Winter Olympics. Billions around the world would be watching it all unfold over seventeen days. Pageantry, pomp, patriotic odes to Russian national glory, and athletic feats—all would swell into one grand crescendo.

Months before the opening ceremony, in the summer and fall of 2013, the city hummed with the sounds of construction. Once a modest holiday spot dotted with Soviet-era sanatoriums and pebble beaches, Sochi was undergoing a colossal transformation. After nearly seven years and more than $50 billion spent on new infrastructure along the Black Sea coastline and surrounding alpine hills of the Caucasus, the global spotlight was fixed on Vladimir Putin's Russia again.

But it was not quite for the reasons that Putin had hoped for.

Success had never been assured. Sochi was a subtropical vacation paradise where winter temperatures were usually mild enough to call for only a light coat. Perched on the border with Abkhazia, and only a hop from the still-volatile North Caucasus region, the city was a run-down resort town that had seen its best days in the Soviet era. Sochi's only real selling point was the snow-packed mountains in the nearby town of Krasnaya Polyana, where Putin was known to take his ski holidays, but there were still concerns about whether there would be enough snow.

Meanwhile, politicians in the West and Olympic athletes reacted negatively to new Russian legislation passed by the Duma in 2013 that banned "propaganda of nontraditional sexual relations" and labeled members of the LGBTQ community as "perverted" outlaws and reprobates. The White House also announced that, in defiance of tradition, it would send a delegation of gay athletes to the Olympics as official guests rather than Obama and the First Family. The #Sochi Games were refashioned into the #Gay Games on social media. Putin's attempt to present an idealized and modernized Russia was fraying.

As Olympic athletes around the world prepared to scale the peaks of human performance in Sochi, a parallel drama of geopolitical dimensions was climbing toward its climax some nine hundred miles away in Kyiv. Locked in a tug-of-war between Russia and the European Union over dueling visions of the future for his country, Ukraine's president, Viktor Yanukovych, was dancing on the edge of a political precipice. The root causes of the troubles were many, not the least of which was Yanukovych's refusal to sign on to Russia's Customs Union with Belarus and Kazakhstan.

But things had turned particularly nasty in July, after Russia sparked a trade dispute with Ukraine over its pending plans to sign an association agreement with the EU aimed at drawing Ukraine away from the Kremlin's orbit and closer to the West. Closer integration with Europe would have sharply curtailed prospects for Ukraine's admission into the Eurasian Economic Union on the lopsided terms that Russia had proposed. Sergey Glazyev, Putin's chief economic envoy and a leading architect of the Customs Union, called Yanukovych's pursuit of the EU deal "suicidal," and he all but threatened war if Kyiv signed the agreement.[1]

Ukraine was the linchpin of Putin's vision of reconstituting Russia's prerevolutionary empire as a counterweight to NATO and the West. And Putin had up until that moment found in Yanukovych a pliable if sometimes erratic partner in that quest. Importantly, Yanukovych had agreed to an extension to the year 2042 of Russia's leasehold over military installations and basing rights for Russia's Black Sea Fleet in Crimea. In return, Russia granted Ukraine a 30 percent discount on natural gas that flowed through transit routes that crisscrossed parts of Donbas where Yanukovych's cronies held controlling stakes in the gas industry. The move gave Putin considerable leverage over Yanukovych, who had also agreed to shelve Ukraine's bid to join NATO.

For Putin, the agreement on Crimea was just one step on a long, winding path toward reabsorbing Ukraine into Russia's fold. The Kremlin subsequently dangled a series of carrots in its efforts to win Ukraine over, including a rather fantastical offer for a merger between Gazprom and Ukraine's national energy company, Naftogaz, that never materialized.

Meanwhile, Yanukovych had plunged Ukraine into an economic tailspin through a combination of self-dealing and incautious deficit spending. Although his Party of Regions still enjoyed substantial support in his eastern home region of Donbas despite those problems, an increasing number of Ukrainians in the rest of the country were fed up with his corrupt rule. Many—especially younger Ukrainians, who had little memory of the Soviet era—hungered to enjoy the fruits of closer integration with Europe.

Yanukovych dashed those hopes when in November he abruptly pulled back from signing the EU association agreement one week before he was expected at an EU summit in Lithuania. Within hours, protests erupted at Kyiv's Independence Square, the Maidan Nezalezhnosti, and quickly morphed into a mass movement that cast a long shadow over the upcoming Olympics.

The drama bore echoes of geopolitical contretemps past. A little more than thirty years had passed since the United States had spearheaded a boycott of the 1980 Summer Olympics, a humiliating snub that neither Putin nor Russia had ever quite lived down. He had tried twice after that to bring the games to Russia. His first bid to bring the games to St. Petersburg when he was still in city hall had bombed.

He was luckier the second go-round, in 2007, when Russia beat out Austria and South Korea. Jubilant, Putin had estimated that it would cost roughly $12 billion to ready Sochi for its big moment on the world stage, promising that the games would be a dazzling display of Russia's resurgence. Instead, the Sochi Olympics were turning out to be the most controversial and expensive in history.

Ballooning Kremlin spending on the refurbishment of Putin's favorite vacation spot had generated an unrelenting stream of headlines about sweetheart contracting deals, kickback schemes, and shoddy construction. So many Kremlin cronies had in fact fed at the trough of government-subsidized development projects that it was almost impossible to keep track.

The plethora of corruption scandals had prompted Boris Nemtsov, a Sochi native and staunch Putin critic, to issue a damning report that described the games as "a festival of corruption and mismanagement."[2] Nemtsov calculated that the money spent on building a thirty-mile highway connecting the remote mountain village of Krasnaya Polyana to Sochi could have been spent on housing for 800,000 to 1,000,000 people. At $8 billion, the cost of the roadway was the equivalent of the entire cost of the Vancouver Olympics.[3]

Even Prigozhin had gotten in on the action. In 2013 his subsidiary company, Concord M, rechristened a forty-five-meter, four-deck yacht purchased from Turkish shipbuilders and refurbished in time for the tourist rush to Russia. Workers retrofitted the main deck of the *Palma de Sochi* with an opulent banquet hall capable of hosting a hundred guests. They painted the hull with a garish rainbow-colored array of palm trees, fitting the tropical theme, and Prigozhin acquired a flag of convenience from Sierra Leone to give it official sailing status.[4] The website for the *Palma de Sochi* advertised romantic cruises along the Moscow River and promised guests that once on board they would experience "refined and pleasant emotions" for a price of 5,000 to 20,000 rubles per hour.

Prigozhin's ambitious plans to cash in on Russia's Olympic fever also involved a multimillion-ruble deal in 2012 with the mayor of Sochi for the purchase and refurbishment of the M.V. Frunze Summer Theater. Built in 1937 during the peak of Stalin's iron grip on the Russian imperium, the concert hall evoked the grandeur of imperial St. Petersburg.

As with many of the other architectural gems that Stalin commissioned for his favorite seaside resort, the Summer Theater was built in the classical Italian style. Stout rows of colonnades ringed the open-air coliseum-style auditorium, which offered sweeping views of Sochi's Black Sea coastline. The festival hall added later was adorned with ornate wedding-cake white trim.

The Summer Theater had served for decades as a central cultural hub for locals and the millions of visitors who flocked to Sochi's warm shores every spring and summer from all over the Russian-speaking world. Its glory days ended in the 1980s, when the theater fell victim to the vicissitudes of a Soviet state in free fall. Several attempts to give the property a facelift followed in the early 2000s, but the project of reviving the Summer Theater never quite got off the ground. The building fell into disrepair and became a canvas for local Sochi graffiti artists.

Prigozhin promised Sochi's city leaders that he would change everything, perhaps spurred on by the potential wealth and influence the 2014 Olympics might bring. Architectural renderings revealed ambitious plans for companies linked to Concord to build a dome over the auditorium and install an elaborate ventilation system. But his grand plan was dogged by accusations of corruption, failure to perform, and public outcry over the terms of Prigozhin's deal with the city of Sochi. A convoluted array of transactions among the city of Sochi, two companies that shared the same address as Prigozhin's Concord company headquarters in the northern capital on Lieutenant Schmidt Embankment along the shores of the Neva River, and a Prigozhin-linked company named Buenas Cubanas LLC were all part of the reconstruction plans.[5]

In the end, the deal stipulated that the city would pay rent to Prigozhin's business for a thirty-year lease in exchange for covering the theater grounds' renovation costs. The esoteric nature of the arrangement and the lack of public consultation on the reconstruction plans infuriated some civic-minded activists and journalists. But beyond a handful of arch news stories in the local Sochi press, few were inclined to publicly challenge the man who set Putin's table.

The yacht and the theater were only a few of the intriguing projects and investments Prigozhin became involved in amid all the fervor for the Olympics. In the fall of 2013, as tensions between Moscow and Kyiv grew, employees of Prigozhin registered roughly a dozen nonprofit organizations in Ukraine, according to documents surfaced by investigative reporters Ilya Barabanov and Denis Korotkov.[6] Calendar entries in Prigozhin's Palm Pilot and telephone records indicate that Prigozhin was in regular touch from 2013 to 2014 with Kremlin insiders like Putin's presidential chief of staff, Anton Vaino, and Alexey Dyumin, deputy director of the GRU.[7] Prigozhin's Concord M company was at that point already installed as the primary caterer for the Presidential Property Management Office, and memos that Prigozhin sent to defense ministry officials suggested that he likely had ready access to privileged inside information.[8]

Within the Kremlin's convoluted bureaucracy, the management of state property fell under the expansive domain of the ministry of finance and the presidential executive office, overseen by Vaino. One of the most senior officials in the president's office, Vaino was uniquely positioned to grasp the complex web of relationships that underpinned Prigozhin's business entanglements with the state.

It is not at all clear what Prigozhin planned to do with his Ukrainian enterprises. But given his propensity for opportunism and considering the escalating crisis in Kyiv, the cascade of activities seemed well timed. Prigozhin was already eyeing property for a vacation home in the Black Sea coastal resort town of Gelendzhik, not far from where Putin had built his own palatial getaway. With eleven houses, two swimming pools, a helipad, and a swath of farmland on a partially forested area set back from the coast, Prigozhin's estate was modest in comparison to Putin's Italianate-style palace on the coast, which sat on a 180-acre lot and was valued at nearly $1 billion.[9]

Purchased in 2014 and partially funded by profits from Megaline LLC's winning February 2014 bid for a multimillion-dollar defense contract for building and maintaining military installations across Russia, Prigozhin's luxury getaway underscored his strategic focus on maintaining proximity to Putin.[10] But Prigozhin's schemes were little more than background noise amid the constant drumbeat of media coverage ahead of the opening of the Winter Games.

As opening day grew closer, the Kremlin tried to drown out its critics with the din of happy progress reports and magnanimous gestures. After an amnesty law was passed by the Duma toward the end of 2013, some twenty thousand prisoners were granted release, including several Greenpeace activists and the members of the opposition rock band Pussy Riot. And in an even bigger surprise, Putin pardoned his nemesis Mikhail Khodorkovsky on humanitarian grounds eight months before his prison term was up. Putin's mantra was simple: Russia—civilized, modern, generous—was on top again. The Olympics was a chance, he said, for the world "to see a new Russia, see its personality and its possibilities, take a fresh and unbiased look at the country."[11]

Yet the challenges that had dogged Russia's peripheral regions since Putin stepped into power persisted. Chechen rebel leader Doku Umarov, the self-styled emir of the Caucasus Emirate, angrily promised in a video released over the summer to disrupt the Olympics. In late December 2013, two suicide bombings occurred in the city of Volgograd, located about four hundred miles from Sochi, initially killing at least fourteen people.[12] The incident was just one in a series that occurred in the lead-up to the games, and the involvement of two young Chechen immigrants in the Boston Marathon bombing a few months earlier had elevated concerns about whether Russia could safely pull off scheduled events that winter. Dark memories of the horrific hostage-taking episode during the 1972 Olympics in Munich and the bombing at the 1996 Olympics in Atlanta loomed over Russia's plans to make Sochi secure.

The Kremlin had taken extraordinary steps to secure the Olympics, spending $2 billion on additional manpower and equipment, and tasking Dyumin with overseeing security. Some forty thousand police and special-services officers were deployed to oversee public safety.[13] And those figures represented only what the Kremlin was willing to openly acknowledge. Behind the scenes, an additional twenty-two thousand Russian troops were deployed to Sochi and the surrounding region.[14]

Russia's subsequent rollout just ahead of the Olympics of a new version of its System of Operative-Investigative Measures (SORM) was only one of several indications that the country was becoming a full-on surveillance state. The system for monitoring wireless-communications traffic was so powerful that the US State Department issued a warning to those traveling to Sochi to consider leaving their laptops and cell phones at home. The additional placement of some 5,500 surveillance cameras around Sochi and antiaircraft missile batteries suggested that the Kremlin was concerned about more than just suicide bombers.

With the challenge of securing the Sochi Olympics looming, Russia's chief of General Staff, Valery Gerasimov, had seized on the political opening the games provided to expand Russia's military capabilities. The most critical of those steps was the establishment in March 2013 of the *Komandovanie sil spetsial'nalnykh operatsii* (KSSO), Russia's first ever stand-alone Special Forces Operations Command.[15] Alexey Dyumin was tapped as the first commander of the unit, which initially consisted of roughly a thousand seasoned hands recruited from GRU *spetsnaz* units and the elite Alpha counterterrorism unit of the FSB.[16]

Modeled on elite forces in the West such as the US Special Operations Forces, Russia's new soldier elites were composed of "tip-of-the-spear" light-infantry forces that specialized in conducting reconnaissance, sabotage, counterintelligence, and counterterrorism operations behind enemy lines. Their operational playbook revolved around the Soviet doctrine of *maskirovka*, the fusion of the mundane with the spectacular in large-scale operations. The strategy thrives on the element of surprise and the use of decoys, disinformation, and psychological manipulation to deceive and confuse—all important skills for what lay ahead.

In December the festival-like atmosphere that had marked the beginning of what became known as the Euromaidan movement in Ukraine took a darker turn after Putin announced that Russia had agreed to a $15 billion bailout of the Ukrainian economy. The move, which was accompanied by promises of cheaper gas, prompted accusations from the opposition in Kyiv that Yanukovych had essentially sold his seat to the highest bidder, triggering calls for his resignation.

Yanukovych responded by ordering a police crackdown to clear the streets in Kyiv. The heavy-handed response from Ukraine's truncheon-waving, jackbooted Berkut special police force only galvanized protesters and brought more people to the streets in Kyiv and other cities across the country.

As the opening of the Olympics in Sochi drew nearer and the world rang in the New Year in 2014, Ukraine looked set to boil over. The government passed draconian laws restricting protests and freedom of speech. The measures only further stiffened the resolve of the Maidan protesters, who now numbered in the tens of thousands.

The demonstrations took on an increasingly confrontational tone, with protesters arming themselves with homemade shields and makeshift weapons, and constructing barricades. The government responded with equal force. Clashes became commonplace, and the streets of Kyiv started to look like a war zone, with smoke from burning tires mingling with the winter fog.

For the Kremlin, looking west from Sochi, the scenes of escalating civil unrest in Kyiv resembled nothing less than an existential threat—an echo of the color revolutions and the subversive winds that had overturned one Soviet satellite regime after another in 1989. To Putin, the risk of losing Ukraine to the West was unacceptable. The old wound was open again, bleeding into his vision, coloring the world red.

As the Olympic torch arrived in Sochi, a split-screen reality started to unfold. Even as Russian officials took to the podium at the opening ceremony to announce the birth of a "New Russia" amid all the pyrotechnics, elaborate sets, and Tchaikovsky's *Swan Lake* on February 7, the Kremlin quietly began ramping up its preparations for the worst-case scenario in Ukraine.

Days before the Olympic flame was extinguished, tensions escalated dramatically in Kyiv on February 20, when police opened fire with live rounds on the demonstrators, killing and injuring scores. The violence evoked a sharp rebuke from parliament, which voted by an overwhelming majority two days later to impeach and remove Yanukovych from office.

Realizing that his number was up, Yanukovych fled that night to the eastern city of Kharkiv, where he had traditionally enjoyed strong support. There, Yanukovych recorded a message asserting that he had been the victim of a coup and comparing the Euromaidan uprising to the 1933 Nazi takeover of Germany: "They are trying to scare me. I have no intention of leaving the country. I am not going to resign, I'm the legitimately elected president."[17]

But even as Yanukovych spoke, Putin was huddled in an emergency session in the Kremlin with the heads of Russia's security services formulating a plan to extract the deposed Ukrainian leader and take control of Crimea. Under direction from Dyumin, Russian special forces readied to whisk Yanukovych across the border into Russia, where he would remain an exiled guest of the Kremlin for the rest of his days.

As THE CENTER of gravity of the crisis shifted to Crimea, a new player stepped into the scene. Igor Girkin, a seasoned FSB operative, plunged into action, seizing the spotlight and the moment he had spent half his life rehearsing for.

He had spent two decades backstage, honing his skills as a professional agent provocateur and assassin for the FSB. In his mid-forties, with a career forged in the fires of Russia's dirty wars, he was well-versed in the brutal calculus of Kremlin-sponsored counterrevolution. A native of Moscow, he developed a passion for military history and reenactment as a student at the Moscow State Institute for History and Archives. Those and other martially oriented creative pursuits served him well as he worked to cultivate intelligence assets on the frontiers of Russia's frozen conflicts.

In his twenties, Girkin volunteered to fight in the 1992 conflict over Transnistria, Moldova's breakaway region. It was there, amid the chaos of Russia's efforts to retain rump-state carve-outs at the edge of the Black Sea, that Girkin, by his own account, accidentally fell in love with war.[18] His next adventure took him to the Balkans, where he fought under the banner of the Tsarist Wolves, a group of Russian volunteers who saw themselves as holy warriors defending Christian Orthodoxy in Slobodan Milosevic's genocidal war.

By 1993, Girkin was back in Moscow, ready to put his battlefield experience to use with a regular-infantry unit in the First Chechen War. During the Second Chechen War, Girkin served as a liaison to the VDV Airborne 45th Guards Spetsnaz Reconnaissance Brigade. It was there, during the brutal campaign known as "Operation Wolf Hunt," that Girkin earned his reputation for cruelty. Operating under the code name "Strelkov" (call sign "Shooter"), he became a figure to be feared.

In the mid-1990s, Girkin crossed paths with Olga Kulygina and Alexander Borodai. Both were on the barricades during the 1993 coup and were well acquainted with Alexander Dugin. Like Girkin, Kulygina had served in the FSB's Service for Protection of the Constitutional System and the Fight Against Terrorism—a successor to the KGB's notorious Directorate Z. Borodai, although he denied any official ties to the FSB, had clearly aligned his career with Kremlin interests.[19] He reported for *RIA-Novosti* in Chechnya and

Abkhazia, where Kulygina posed as an aid worker and journalist. All three—Girkin, Kulygina, and Borodai—regularly contributed to the ultranationalist *Zavtra* news outlet, each playing a role in a drama inspired by Dugin's musings and Putin's imperial ambitions.

Just before Ukraine unraveled, Girkin's superiors had dangled a clandestine mission in Dagestan. "Come New Year, I'll be in the Caucasus. . . . Finally, it's hot enough there for the agency to send scumbags like me," he joked darkly to a friend. But by late 2012, with retirement looming and FSB budget cuts biting, his career prospects dimmed.[20] They told him he needed a psychiatric evaluation—that he was too old for the front lines.[21] The promise of new battlefields vanished, leaving him to seethe in the shadows, far from the glow of the frontline glory he craved.

By early 2013, Girkin was growing restless. Frustrated with the bureaucratic grind of the FSB, he began telling friends he was ready to retire, to find new adventures that would satisfy his thirst for action.[22] He started blogging for *ANNA News*, a pro-Russian outlet financed by an Abkhaz separatist that was known for its flashy, war-glorifying coverage of the Syrian front lines. He made regular appearances on Den TV, an online affiliate of *Zavtra*, and served as an informal adviser to Kulygina on mercenary recruitment for the Syrian Express. Now, with Ukraine on the brink, he saw an opportunity to apply his expertise on a larger, more consequential stage.

No longer just an eccentric spook in the shadows, Girkin began to craft a public profile and forge new alliances. In early 2014 he took on a sideline as a security adviser for Moscow-based Marshall Capital, where Borodai had recently joined as a public-relations adviser to the private-equity firm's CEO, Konstantin Malofeev.

Known as the "Orthodox Oligarch," Malofeev was a man of dangerous convictions. Like Girkin and Borodai, he was driven by a fervent desire to resurrect Russia's imperial past. They aligned in all the important ways: rabid anti-Semitism, suspicion of Muslim immigrants, and paranoia over the influence of the LGBTQ-rights movement. But it was Malofeev, fluent in English and well connected to European archconservatives such as France's Marine Le Pen, who had the kind of money and savvy needed to help Putin manifest his vision of reabsorbing Ukraine back into the Russian imperium.

Malofeev came by his wealth and influence through his pious devotion to the restoration of the Russian empire and traditional family values. Notable among his Kremlin connections were Putin's informal confessor, Father

Tikhon, and other ultranationalist Russian Orthodox grandees like former Russian Railways chief and Putin confidant Vladimir Yakunin and Serge de Pahlen, the son of a White Russian émigré.[23]

After graduating from Moscow State University with a law degree, Malofeev spent several years working for Renaissance Capital, an international investment firm with offices in Moscow. His business career took off, and he soon established a reputation as a shrewd negotiator who was good at closing deals. One that gained considerable attention was Malofeev's acquisition of a 10 percent stake in Rostelecom, which did much to boost profits for his equity firm. From real estate to manufacturing and telecommunications, the array of investments assembled under Marshall Capital's umbrella made Malofeev into a billionaire before he reached the age of forty.[24]

Malofeev poured a fortune into his Saint Basil the Great Foundation, catapulting the charity into the elite circle of Russia's richest Orthodox social trusts. Dubbed "Putin's Soros," Malofeev mastered the art of wielding philanthropy like a weapon in Russia's ideological crusade against what he viewed as Western decay.

In 2012 his political savvy was on full display when he spearheaded a movement that pushed through legislation allowing the Russian government to slam the door shut on websites it deemed toxic. The hit list of these digital outcasts was curated by a cadre of civil-society groups, including Malofeev's own brainchild, the League for a Safe Internet. Not stopping there, Malofeev jumped into the media business with Tsargrad TV, a hard-line Orthodox Christian network that he rolled out with the help of Jack Hannick, a maverick former *Fox News* producer. Launched amid the fiery 2013 Euromaidan protests in Ukraine, Tsargrad TV stirred the pot in the style of *Fox News* but with a distinctly Russian Orthodox twist.

Using the clout he amassed from his foundation, Malofeev clinched a deal with the Christian Orthodox patriarchate in Greece for the temporary custody of religious relics for a tour across historic Byzantine locales. With a nod from Russia's Patriarch Kirill, the tour kicked off in Moscow in late January 2014, capturing the spotlight just as the world turned its eyes to Sochi for the Olympic Games.

The exhibit drew massive crowds, first in Simferopol, Crimea, and then in Kyiv's ancient Perchesk-Lavra monastery. There, amid violent clashes downtown between pro-EU protesters and government forces, the Malofeev relics exhibition was offered up as an orderly counterpoint to the unfolding chaos in the city center.

At this juncture, Girkin, tasked with safeguarding the relics, possibly used his role to probe and potentially intensify the unrest in Kyiv, aided by his links within the FSB. Leaked emails hint at Girkin's repeated sorties to Kyiv in February 2014, although the exact details are shrouded in mystery. At one point, he even gloated in an online gaming chat about orchestrating sniper attacks on protesters—an unverified claim that likely danced between fact and fantasy.[25] Whatever the truth, Girkin was undeniably in Crimea when the situation there escalated dramatically in late February 2014.

Under orders from Putin, Russia's security services were already busily readying for military action aimed at seizing control of the peninsula. Weeks of consultations with lawyers and experts in international affairs and a poll showing strong local support in Crimea convinced him that the annexation was the best path forward. A skeleton plan for the Russian takeover of the Crimea was already on the shelf, but under guidance from the defense ministry's Main Operation Directorate, it was fleshed out further as the situation heated up in Ukraine.[26]

The basic outline called for Russian special forces to seize physical control of the local parliament in Crimea and secure military installations across the region. To achieve that goal, Russian forces were tasked with neutralizing the roughly twenty-two thousand Ukrainian troops based at installations across the Black Sea peninsula—preferably without triggering an all-out shooting war.[27]

To ensure secrecy and surprise, orders for the invasion were issued orally, and snap inspections in Russia's Southern Military District and military maneuvers in the Arctic were conspicuously advertised to divert attention from the main thrust into Crimea. GRU special-operations detachments under Dyumin's command were deployed in the interim to Crimea, along with *spetsnaz* from the VDV 45th Guards and VDV 76th Guards Airborne Assault Division, among others.

Putin turned to Vice Admiral Oleg Belaventsev to develop a more detailed blueprint of action, which ultimately called for the dissolution of Crimea's parliament, emergency installation of a puppet interim government headed by a local proxy, and a referendum on the question of Crimea's status once Russian forces had secured the peninsula. Voters would be given a choice between joining Russia and reverting to the 1992 constitution, which granted Crimea autonomy but under the auspices of the rickety Commonwealth of Independent States. The choice, in other words, was no choice. The task assigned to Belaventsev was to create the illusion of grassroots spontaneity and surprise.

A former KGB officer, Belaventsev was well qualified for the job. He had spent years studying in Crimea, where he graduated from the Sevastopol Higher Naval Engineering School. Several tours on Russian nuclear submarines with Russia's 11th Fleet and the Black Sea 5th Fleet followed before a diplomatic posting in the United Kingdom, where in 1985 Belaventsev was outed as a spy and expelled. After a stint in East Germany where he crossed paths regularly with Putin and Chemezov while on assignment, then time at Rosvooruzheniye, Belaventsev's career path closely intertwined with that of Sergey Shoigu.

From 2001 to 2012, Belaventsev ran EMERCOM Demining, a quasi-private corporate arm of Russia's emergency-services ministry charged with ordnance removal, route clearance, and humanitarian-assistance missions. On Belaventsev's watch, EMERCOM also became one of the largest contractors in the notoriously corrupt oil-for-food program in Iraq.[28] It was EMERCOM that awarded some of the earliest and most lucrative contracts for military security to the Anti-Terror Oryol group for pipeline-security work in southern Europe and the Middle East.[29]

When Shoigu was appointed defense minister, Belaventsev followed, taking up a post in 2012 as head of an Oboronservis subsidiary called Joint-Stock Company Slavyanka, the primary commercial arm for the management of defense ministry real estate holdings and infrastructure construction and maintenance. Belaventsev was responsible for the oversight of defense-contract tenders for cleaning, construction, and food-service provision, a position that gave Belaventsev a wide purview over multimillion-dollar contracts awarded to Prigozhin's companies.

Their tangle of shared business interests and a set of shady and highly lucrative contract deals among JSC Slavyanka, Prigozhin's construction company Megaline, and other Concord network firms would in the coming months finance the operations of Prigozhin's paramilitary forces. With conditions set for Russia's takeover of Crimea, Prigozhin's network of firms was poised to win an estimated $1.5 billion in defense tenders over the coming two years.[30]

On February 26, Belaventsev worked with Dyumin and special forces under his command to map out a plan for the takeover of the local parliament building in Simferopol, where clashes between pro-Ukrainian and pro-Russian members of the local government council had erupted. Armed with a list of potential proxies generated by Malofeev's employees, Belaventsev tapped Sergey Aksyonov, a local organized-crime figure turned politician, to serve as Russia's handpicked prime minister of the Crimea Supreme Council and ram through the transfer of power to a proxy Russian government.

After pacing through the final details of the planned assault, several Russian soldiers slipped into plain clothes while others covered their faces with balaclavas and donned new green uniforms without insignia. Early the next morning, before dawn on February 27, they swept into the Supreme Council building, where upon sunrise curious citizens of Simferopol snapped photos on their cell phones of small clusters of "little green men" armed with sophisticated weapons stationed around the perimeter of the parliament building.

Asked who they worked for, the men identified themselves only as Crimea's local self-defense force. Among their number was Girkin, who later would confess that he led raids on the homes of Crimean council delegates, who were forced to vote the Kremlin's puppet leader Sergey Aksyonov into power.

Similar scenes would soon play out as Russian forces swiftly and methodically seized control of military and government installations across Crimea amid electricity disruptions and cyberattacks that made it impossible for Ukrainian forces allied with the new government in Kyiv to counter. Thousands of Ukrainian soldiers and sailors either agreed to disarm or defected. Offered better pay in rubles, some reportedly switched their allegiance to Moscow overnight.[31]

By March 6, Russian forces were in full control, and the Crimean parliament sealed Putin's military fait accompli with a motion to formally join Russia. Executed with almost surgical precision, the operation was more stealth than shock and awe, marking a significant departure from the blunt-force approach that had been a hallmark of Russia's wars in Chechnya and Georgia. The official line from the Kremlin was that the events in Crimea were a purely local affair. Nothing to see here.

In a LiveJournal post that captured the mood of the moment, Boris Rozhin, a pro-Russian blogger who wrote under the handle "Colonel Cassad," recounted how the mystified head of security at the Simferopol airport was "politely asked to leave" by masked men who spoke unaccented Russian, and Rozhin posted a picture of a line of *vezhlivye lyudi*—"polite people"—standing in an orderly array in front of a government building.

On *Russia Today*, Moscow's slick, state-run news broadcast, commentators picked up on the "polite people" theme as footage of crowds of wizened-looking men and women shouting "Rossiya! Rossiya!" and waving enormous red, white, and blue flags played in an endless tape loop. Russian special forces—masked, gently cradling AK-47 assault rifles in their arms—were shown on TV rescuing cats and quietly conferring with each other over which sausages to buy from the local deli.

They barely spoke to reporters on the scene, turning away quietly whenever the camera lens gazed too long in their direction. They were so gentle—those "little green men"—that Voentorg, the Russian ministry's logistics and surplus-goods company, even renamed its flagship store in St. Petersburg "Polite People." The brains behind the promotional campaign for Putin's new party of war fashion line, it turned out, was none other than Prigozhin.[32] T-shirts and sweatshirts with masked Russian operatives bearing the phrase "Polite People" marketed by his phalanx of shell companies and military-surplus stores became all the rage amid jubilation over the Russian military victory in Crimea.

Even then, Putin continued to insist that the soldiers who had helped pull off Russia's historic landgrab were merely "local forces." He denied that Russia's military had had a direct hand in the operation, saying only that the people had risen up in their own self-defense and had chosen to formally integrate into Russia on their own initiative.

In the Russian blogosphere, meanwhile, Putin's critics turned his bizarre denial on its head and began jokingly referring to Russia's "polite people" as the *ikhtamnyeti*. The expression was a play on Putin's political hand wave. When a reporter later asked him whether the "little green men" who had helped the Kremlin take over Crimea were in fact Russian forces, he shrugged and quipped "Ikh tam nyet": "They're not there."

On March 16, barely two weeks after the closing ceremony of the Olympics in Sochi, Russia formalized its reabsorption of Crimea in a hurried and aggressively orchestrated referendum that generated an improbably high majority vote in favor of integrating with Russia. Official figures placed support for integration with Russia at more than 95 percent, but reports of widespread irregularities cast doubts on that figure. The peninsula, which had been gifted to Ukraine in 1954 during Soviet times, was officially annexed by Moscow, sending a stark warning to Kyiv: any further steps toward the West would come at a steep price.

The shock of Russia's Crimea annexation reverberated across the Black Sea and far beyond. In Brussels and Washington, it sparked a prolonged crisis over how to counter Russia's hybrid warfare tactics and aggressive push to reclaim lost influence and territory. European and American leaders voiced their outrage, quickly followed by sanctions. Russia was booted from the G8, a final coup de grace to Putin's long-coveted quest for membership in the club that wrote the rules of the international order. But the overall response was hobbled, disjointed by the sheer speed of Russia's move and the harsh reality of confronting a nuclear-armed state.

Putin marked the occasion with a victory speech at the opulent Grand Kremlin Hall, the gilded room glittering under crystal chandeliers, as he addressed an audience of Russian officials and dignitaries. He ticked off his list of grievances with a mixture of pride and defiance. Western interventions in Kosovo and later Libya. NATO expansion. But the mother of all sins was the West's support for the "neo-Nazi," "Russophobe" forces behind Kyiv's break with Moscow. Russia had no choice but to intervene in Crimea. "If you press a spring too hard," Putin said, "it will recoil."[33]

Later, in a rally at Red Square, the mood was electric. Thousands of supporters, many waving the old black, white, and yellow Russian imperial standard, filled the square as the orchestral strains of the old Soviet classic, the "Sevastopol Waltz," swelled over the crowd and Putin sang with the chorus. The atmosphere was charged, the people buoyed by the swift military victory in Crimea, unaware of the quagmire that awaited in Ukraine. Putin took the stage, his voice carried by loudspeakers across the historic square: "After a long, hard and exhaustive journey at sea, Crimea and Sevastopol are returning to their home harbor, to the native shores, to the home port, to Russia!"[34] Putin's unilateral redrawing of borders represented the most tectonic shift in European geopolitics since the Soviet collapse. But it was only the beginning of the saga.

While the crowd basked in the triumph of Crimea's annexation, another story was unfolding. Girkin, moving with quiet determination, was preparing to march with a band of fifty-two mercenary volunteers from Crimea to Donbas. They reached their first objective, the eastern Ukrainian town of Sloviansk, on April 12, seizing control of government buildings. Financed by money reportedly funneled from Konstantin Malofeev's charity to a local monastery that served as a base camp for Girkin's forces, the operation quickly gained traction. Girkin rallied enough support that the town was soon fully under control of Russian separatist cadres.[35]

Within days, Borodai was at his side as the self-declared prime minister of the so-called Donetsk People's Republic, and soon after, on April 26, Girkin declared on camera that Borodai had named him defense minister of Russia's newest statelet. A virtual cipher for most of his career, Girkin was now one of the most recognizable faces of Russia's movement of mercenary "volunteers." But he would not stay that way for long.

CHAPTER 10

DOWN, OUT, AND UP IN DONBAS

The disaster that would consume his life for years happened on Gerrit Thiry's day off. A detective with the national criminal-investigation service in the Netherlands, Thiry was at home that Thursday, July 17, 2014, when his phone rang.[1] Twitter and VKontakte, the Russian version of Facebook, were crackling with rumors of a downed jet in eastern Ukraine. Air-traffic controllers were reporting that something had gone wrong with a Malaysian Airlines flight that had departed Schiphol Airport in Amsterdam a little after noon local time that day. Details were scarce, but it appeared that about three hours after takeoff, flight MH17 had disintegrated in midair over Ukraine in the middle of an active war zone. On the ground, in a vast expanse of sunflower fields in the eastern region of Donbas, residents of the tiny village of Hrabove, population 1,000, were reporting they had discovered human remains and pieces of the plane. There were 298 people on board, many of them Dutch families on holiday journeys. That's all anyone could tell him.

Thiry ran through all the hypothetical scenarios in his head. Was it an accident, or was it a crime? Was it a terrorist attack from the inside, maybe a suicide bombing? Was it an air-to-air attack? Had another plane shot down the commercial jetliner on purpose? Or had someone shot the plane out of the air from the ground? The fact that MH17 had been cruising at an altitude of about 33,000 feet when it fell from the sky pointed to either Russian-backed separatists or Ukrainian armed forces as the potential perpetrators. It would take a powerful weapon to bring down a commercial passenger plane flying that high.

Cool and methodical, Thiry had developed his habit of rapidly churning through possible scenarios in his head during years on the job, first as a uniformed beat cop and then as a national investigator tackling organized crime and high-profile murder cases. But it was the MH17 case and the Kremlin that would provide Thiry with his final master class in industrial-strength government deception.

As he raced to his office, Thiry sensed that this was no ordinary disaster; it was an international tragedy with geopolitical ramifications. The immediate aftermath of the crash saw a surge in diplomatic tensions. In addition to citizens of the Netherlands and Malaysia, passengers and crew on board the Boeing 777 hailed from all over the world, including Indonesia, Australia, Belgium, Britain, the Philippines, and the United States. Governments worldwide demanded answers, and the victims' families grappled with the shock of the sudden loss. The village of Hrabove, where a substantial portion of the wreckage and human remains were discovered, became a focal point for investigators and journalists alike. Among the sunflower fields lay thousands of pieces of a grisly puzzle that would take years to solve.

Within minutes of MH17 falling to the ground, Igor Girkin found himself at the center of the drama, probably surprising even himself. Much of the crash site fell within a twenty-mile-square area that lay primarily within the borders of the district of Horlivka. Russian separatist forces that fell nominally under Girkin's command controlled the area. On paper, Girkin's 1st Sloviansk Brigade was the primary force in charge. But the loose confederation of commanders assembled under his leadership as the self-appointed defense minister of the Donetsk People's Republic did mostly as they pleased. That included Igor Bezler, aka "Demon," a former *Afghantsy* veteran turned Russian separatist commander who had seized control of the police station in the town of Horlivka. Bezler, a retired GRU lieutenant colonel, had gained a reputation for being cold-blooded and high-strung. He was as loose with his tongue as he was with his fists. Human-rights groups accused him of involvement in extrajudicial killings and high-profile kidnappings of journalists. Although technically Bezler reported to Girkin, the two were constantly at odds.

At 4:18 p.m. local time in Ukraine on July 17, 2014, two minutes before MH17 exploded in the air above an area near Horlivka, Bezler received a phone call from a subordinate on the ground named Valery Tsemakh. "A birdie is flying towards you," Tsemakh mumbled into his mobile.[2] Bezler said he would report it up the chain of command.

This was nothing unusual. Over a five-week period, from early June to mid-July 2014, Russian-backed separatist forces had shot down more than a dozen aircraft, and MH17's west-to-east flight path appeared to be almost identical to the trajectories of planes shot down earlier in Donetsk and Luhansk, the two administrative districts that constitute Donbas. In fact, one day before MH17 exploded in the sky, Russian separatists brought down a Ukrainian Su-25 jet fighter. The rise in pro-Russian attacks on Ukrainian aerial targets intensified hostilities between Moscow and Kyiv over the status of the disputed region, and the fog of war was growing thicker by the day. The stealthy calm that had accompanied Russia's takeover of Crimea three months earlier had dissolved into pandemonium as Ukrainian forces loyal to the provisional government in Kyiv put up stiff resistance in Donbas.

On June 14, a particularly devastating strike in eastern Ukraine signaled a shift in the conflict's dynamics. Russian-backed separatists, equipped with a shoulder-fired antiaircraft missile, downed a Ukrainian IL-76 military-transport jet on its approach to the Luhansk airport. The crash claimed forty soldiers and nine crew members, a tragedy that prompted a vow of swift retribution from Ukraine's newly elected president, Petro Poroshenko.

In the days that followed, the Security Service of Ukraine (SBU) began piecing together the evidence. Among the intercepted communications, they stumbled upon references to a figure known only by his call sign, "Wagner." Initially, the name meant little—another alias in a war full of them. As analysts delved deeper, they connected the dots between "Wagner" and a man called "Dima," the nickname for Dmitry Utkin.

Utkin, now leading remnants of the company that had washed out in the Slavonic Corps fiasco, had leveraged his past failures and lessons learned into a more refined and lethal operation. The downing of the IL-76 was no random act—it was a calculated takedown based on high-level intel and executed by seasoned operatives with a specific goal in mind. The Ukrainian investigation findings pointed to a deliberate escalation, with Utkin and his mercenaries at the heart of it, reinforcing the Kremlin's increasingly aggressive strategy in Ukraine.

A meticulous review of hundreds of hours of intercepted calls revealed that Dmitry Utkin and his associate Andrey Troshev, call sign "Gray Hair," were not operating in isolation. They were acting in concert with Oleg Ivannikov, a GRU colonel who operated under the call sign "Orion." Orion was no rogue operator. His mission set was part of a larger, deliberate strategy that connected the separatists in Donbas with military directives flowing across the Russian border from the Southern Military District in Rostov-on-Don.[3] This revelation would not emerge until more than a year after the battle for the Luhansk. But the discovery of Utkin's identity peeled back the first layer in an elaborate deception operation orchestrated by a clandestine chain of command that led straight to the top in Moscow, all the way to Russia's chief of General Staff, Valery Gerasimov, and Defense Minister Sergey Shoigu.

When Ukrainian signals-intelligence specialists dug down deeper into their rapidly expanding intercept archive, they next discovered that Orion was getting his orders from the top of Russia's 58th Army, the same military division that had overseen Russia's brutal campaigns in the Caucasus. Headquartered in Vladikavkaz and then headed by Major General Yevgeny Nikiforov, the 58th Army was an infantry workhorse and served as the bulwark for Russia's defenses in the Caucasus and areas along the Black Sea coast, all of which fell under the Southern Military District.

Utkin's contingent was one of a dozen or more experimental battalion tactical groups backed by the GRU and deployed to Donbas under orders from the defense ministry's Main Operations Directorate, the ministry's planning and strategy department.[4] Key to that support was the GRU's 15th Directorate, which began assigning tasks to "agent-combat groups" in Ukraine in early 2014 and to the 78th Intelligence Center in Rostov, a social-psychological research laboratory known as Unit 35555 that was designated as the primary logistics hub for Utkin's commandos.[5]

Utkin's unit bore no official name, but his nom de guerre, "Wagner," was already infamous. Pronounced "Vagner" in Russian, Utkin's call sign carried a triple entendre. It was a nod to his neo-Nazi leanings and to Adolf Hitler's favorite composer, Richard Wagner. The name also evoked the famous scene from *Apocalypse Now* where US soldiers attack a Vietnamese village to the sound of the German composer's "Ride of the Valkyries." Utkin, known for his fascination with Nazi history, had an "SS" tattoo and habitually signed his orders with the symbol of Hitler's shock troops. The moniker also drew inspiration from Eduard Wagner, a Nazi general who served as Germany's quartermaster and head of rearguard forces, and who supported the operations of the Einsatzgruppen paramilitary death squad. In his day-to-day communications with the fighters under his command, Utkin simply referred to himself as

Devyatiy ("the Ninth") and affixed the "SS" symbol to orders and reports sent up the chain to Andrey Troshev, Prigozhin, and the Wagner Group's official handlers in the defense ministry's Main Operations Directorate.[6] "The Ninth" was a coded reference to the nascent pecking order at the center of the contingent that placed Prigozhin at the top as "the First."

Initially formed from a ten-man team, Utkin's unit would grow to roughly three hundred over the summer of 2014, eventually reaching five hundred the following year.[7] Training exercises began in May at a field camp near Rostov-on-Don.[8] Soon after training was completed, Utkin and his team were deployed to Luhansk, where one of their first missions was to seize control of critical logistics nodes, including the airport.

The Russian General Staff initially succeeded in cloaking the true extent of its involvement, buying the Kremlin precious time and maintaining a veneer of plausible deniability for its stealth offensive in Donbas in early 2014. But the shooting down of MH17 quickly began to unravel the ruse, inadvertently exposing the connections among Utkin's, Troshev's, and ultimately Prigozhin's role in the formation of the Wagner Group. A former GRU officer implicated in the MH17 shoot-down who served as Girkin's deputy confirmed this version of events, telling Russian reporters years later that Wagner was a "trial group" that had been "thrown into the storming of the Luhansk airport with the Cossacks," almost as an experiment to see if they could break the Ukrainians' hold on the region.[9]

By the summer of 2014, Girkin and Alexander Borodai had become the most recognizable faces of the so-called *Russkaya Vesna*, or Russian Spring, the moniker adopted by partisans of the Kremlin's covert dirty war. Putin's government had quietly provided the two professional provocateurs with sufficient resources to seize control of huge chunks of the coal- and gas-rich areas of Donetsk and Luhansk. Girkin's work as a security adviser for Konstantin Malofeev's Marshall Capital had apparently given him enough credibility that Putin's deputy chief of staff, Vladislav Surkov, decided to use him in the proxy administration in Donbas.

A couple of months before MH17 was shot down, an employee of Malofeev's company added Girkin's and Borodai's names to a list that was forwarded to Surkov and contained the names of those who would eventually serve as the first administrators in the puppet government in Donbas. In time, Surkov tapped Borodai as prime minister of Donetsk. Igor Plotnitsky, a burly, double-chinned Soviet apparatchik type who headed his own local force, the

Zarya Battalion, was Borodai's administrative counterpart in Luhansk. The problem with the three-way arrangement among Girkin, Borodai, and Plotnitsky was that everyone was in charge, so no one was in charge.

The lack of discipline among Russian separatist commanders undermined Moscow's attempts to disguise the links. As they struggled to push back against Ukrainian forces, hints of panic and frustration began to seep into intercepted conversations between Girkin and other so-called Russian volunteers and their backers across the border in Russia. These harried calls would become critical pieces of evidence pointing to the extensive covert campaign launched at the direction of General Staff headquarters in Moscow.

Additional proof of the links emerged in the immediate aftermath of the MH17 explosion from another conversation picked up by Ukrainian intelligence agents eavesdropping on the open airwaves. About twenty minutes after MH17 exploded over the area surrounding Horlivka, Igor Bezler put in an urgent call to the man code-named Orion, the GRU colonel across the border in Rostov-on-Don. The recording was short, but it was loaded with consequences—most immediately for Girkin, technically Bezler's superior.

"We just shot down a plane. It was Miners Group," Bezler stuttered. "It fell in Yenakievo."

"Pilots. Where are the pilots?" Orion snapped.

"They're going to search for them and photograph the plane. It's smoking," Bezler responded.

The two talked over each other excitedly, Orion thinking that the troops under him across the border in Ukraine had captured yet another Ukrainian Air Force pilot while Bezler stood stunned, gazing at the smoldering wreckage of the passenger plane. The realization on both sides of the Russia-Ukraine border that Russian separatists under Girkin's command were behind the attack unfolded like a slow-motion nightmare. Harried calls zigzagged up and down the chain all the way back to the Kremlin.[10]

There was no straightforward way to keep a lid on the situation, and as the horrifying truth dawned on Putin, it became increasingly obvious that the first priority was to remove Girkin from the scene in favor of more pliable proxies. The second objective was to stall and spin until there was time to mobilize an emergency response to what was quickly becoming one of the worst military catastrophes of Putin's leadership. Like the captain of an aged and lumbering iron battleship in choppy waters, Putin turned his attention to damage control, seeking to navigate through the escalating crisis with a mixture of force, deception, and calculated maneuvers.

Prigozhin's role in those machinations was not immediately obvious, nor was it part of any grand design per se—at least, not one that could be easily traced. It was as much a function of Putin's increasingly fragmented power structure as it was of Prigozhin's irrepressible ambition. Although it would take years for anyone to put two and two together, the MH17 incident offered the first clues of the hidden chain of command and tangled mix of interests that bound Girkin and Prigozhin together in common cause for the Kremlin despite their bitter hatred for each other.

Theories abound about how and why Prigozhin became directly involved in Ukraine. One, advanced by a former Wagner Group commander, suggested that "kontor"—slang for the FSB—had blackmailed him into financing Utkin's commandos, hinting at legal troubles stemming from corrupt construction deals or tax fraud. However, beyond lawsuits and regulatory issues plaguing his real estate projects, little evidence supported this. More likely, Prigozhin, with his usual entrepreneurial flair, had seized the opportunity. Leveraging connections to defense insiders such as Alexey Dyumin and Dmitry Bulgakov, he tapped into a network of former Moran Security contractors with which he and Concord's security chief, Yevgeny Gulyaev, were already familiar.

Wagner insiders claimed that Prigozhin traveled to Luhansk as early as spring 2014, signaling that he was already in the loop on the Kremlin's covert plans for Donbas well before Utkin's deployment and that Putin was well aware of what Prigozhin was doing.[11] This claim is at least partially supported by a November 2014 entry marked in Prigozhin's calendar labeled simply "Vaino-PMC-Patrushev"—a reference to Putin's chief of staff, Anton Vaino, and his most trusted senior adviser, Nikolai Patrushev, who became secretary of the Security Council after serving for several years as head of the FSB. Vaino was one of Prigozhin's most consistent high-level contacts in the Kremlin.

Born in Estonia, Vaino came from a distinguished family of Soviet Communist Party notables and studied at the Moscow Institute for International Relations, a feeder school for future diplomats and spies. From there, he went on to serve for five years in the Russian embassy in Tokyo before Putin tapped him to serve as deputy head of protocol for the president's office in 2007. Vaino came to appreciate Prigozhin's talent for orchestrating elaborate events, but there was more to the relationship than that. The two began to meet more frequently after

Putin was reelected to the presidency in 2012 and Vaino was elevated to chief of staff.

Two key entries in Prigozhin's calendar during the summer of 2012 reveal that Vaino and Prigozhin likely met to discuss positioning Prigozhin's firms for plum defense contracts. In August an entry noted that Prigozhin met with Vaino and Sergey Vladimirovich Khutortsev, head of the Military Industrial Commission of the Department of State Defense Orders.[12] Khutortsev's presence suggested a deeper agenda tied to Russia's defense industrial base. Before Putin appointed him as lead adviser on the defense economy in 2009, Khutortsev, a former officer in Russia's strategic missile forces, was trusted with managing the Kremlin's most closely guarded secrets: Russia's nuclear arsenal.

The subject matter and timing of the meetings indicate that Khutortsev and Vaino well understood that Prigozhin had more to offer than just catering services. The meetings were likely linked to Prigozhin's growing involvement in Russia's military-industrial complex, paving the way for the vast expansion of his ventures into the construction, maintenance, and cleaning services for hundreds of military bases and, eventually, logistical support for the delivery of weapons and military equipment to client states like Syria. After winning additional defense construction tenders in 2014, Prigozhin's company Megaline would go on to build several strategically important bases near Russia's borders with Ukraine and Belarus.[13]

Prigozhin's calendar showed an uptick in the tempo of his meetings with Vaino amid the fallout from the MH17 disaster. The November 2014 meeting was one of three listed that month that mentioned Vaino and Patrushev, including one that bore the intriguing label "Vaino–AE:Patrushev–Who is the executor?" The meetings indicated that both Vaino and Patrushev were involved at the outset in discussions about the formation of the Wagner Group and its leadership structure, and hinted that Prigozhin regularly brought Patrushev and Vaino up to speed on Wagner's doings.

In the fall of 2014, the convergence of Prigozhin, Vaino, and Patrushev on the sensitive subject of Prigozhin's private-military company took place during tense backdoor negotiations between Russia and Ukraine over freezing the conflict on the line of contact in Donbas. Together, Vaino's organizational skills, Prigozhin's expanding business interests, and Patrushev's ideological zeal represented a triangulation of power that would prove critical in Russia's post-Crimea military adventurism.

The involvement of top presidential advisers strongly signaled Putin's growing confidence in the Kremlin's high-stakes bid to make covert operations and mercenaries a central tool of Russian foreign policy.

Prigozhin plunged into Donbas, by his own account, in May 2014. A meeting at the Union of Paratroopers offices with Pavel Popovskikh, the former head of the VDV 45th Guards Spetsnaz, reportedly inspired Prigozhin to begin thinking about how he could increase profits made from his contracts with Russia's defense ministry.[14] The consultation between Popovskikh, the brains behind Russia's covert-operations doctrine and intellectual godfather of the Redut constellation of paramilitary contingents, and Prigozhin, the man many knew only as "Putin's Chef" and black-market fixer, reportedly occurred as the Russian General Staff officers began to grasp, somewhat belatedly, that the conflagration in Donbas was out of control and that their proxy-war plan had run aground. The meeting marked an important turning point in the complicated relationship between Prigozhin and Russia's defense minister, Sergey Shoigu. And it heralded a paradigm shift in the Kremlin's strategy.

To gain the edge and prevent the MH17 situation from spiraling out of control, Putin chose to escalate to deescalate. He gave the high sign to Shoigu and Gerasimov, who were facing one of the greatest tests of their political and military acumen, that it was time to bring in a larger contingent of Russian forces. Prigozhin stepped in to help make that happen.

With a veritable mountain of cash and an armada of vehicles at his disposal, and storage sites conveniently scattered in military cantonments across Russia and the vast expanse of remote territory along Russia's southern and western borders with Ukraine, Prigozhin's network of Concord companies offered the best camouflage possible for moving the number of men and weapons that Russia needed to shove into the suppurating wound that was Donbas. Soon, trucks and SUVs marked with a giant white "W" began popping up all over.

This was the seminal moment in the development of the Wagner Group, when Russia's irregular paramilitary forces went from being a blunt instrument in Putin's quest to challenge American hegemony to the tip of the spear in a military strategy that relied on high-level deception for its success. Prigozhin lent his business savvy, capital, logistical skills, and administrative know-how to an effort that had hitherto been chaotic.

Prigozhin's off-book paramilitary diverged sharply in form from the ragtag militias that marauded across Donbas in the spring of 2014. It was neither an official corporate entity nor a unitary enterprise in the common meaning any more than it was a typical private-military company. Instead, Prigozhin's mercenary force was held together by an invisible web of individuals and assets that threaded through a labyrinth of legal entities, lacking any centralized corporate governance. Notably, Prigozhin was not listed as a corporate officer or a shareholder in his myriad front companies.

Instead, he strategically named his family members as company heads and appointed trusted subordinates from his legitimate businesses to serve as figureheads and principals across an opaque network. In internal correspondence, Prigozhin was obliquely referenced only by his alias "Sergey Peterovich."[15] The backbone of the enterprise was the so-called Back Office in St. Petersburg, which would grow to encompass a general staff, a tactical command, an internal security service, and other administrative subunits. Hundreds of companies assembled under the broad umbrella of Prigozhin's Concord network would serve as the Russian defense ministry's primary conduit for surreptitious cash flows and cover for hidden weapons-supply chains that stretched from deep inside Russia out to Donbas and regions far beyond.

Never content to be a mere middleman, Prigozhin took a hands-on approach to the assembling of a clandestine cadre of special operators who would unite under one banner and rewrite the handbook for waging war by other means. Prigozhin kept his role in Putin's scheme hidden then. But years later, after the masking had fallen away, he would recount with pride how he turned the Wagner Group into a force to be reckoned with in Ukraine and around the world. His version of how it all happened was shared in a florid social media post on VKontakte:

> I went to the ranges where the "Cossacks" were gathering and tried to recruit a group that would go and protect the Russians. But very quickly, I realized that half of these "Cossacks" and other paramilitary comrades were crooks. The other half took the money, hired volunteers, and sent them barefoot and bare to their real death. So, I flew to one of the ranges and started working on it on my own. I cleaned the old weapons, sorted out the body armor, and found experts who could help me do it.[16]

Prigozhin, in leaked correspondence with Russia's minister of defense, humble-bragged that Putin himself had directed him to create a covert military-logistics network as part of a secret mission for the Kremlin aimed at sending goods across Baltic, Black Sea, and Mediterranean waterways to Syria and beyond.[17] That was the story that he told for public consumption. But dozens of entries in Prigozhin's electronic calendar for 2012 to 2013 indicate that Prigozhin was already in regular touch with Russia's deputy defense minister, Ruslan Tsalikov, the ministry's lead on coordinating Russian weapons transfers to Russia's foreign clients and oversight of defense logistics and procurement.[18] Wagner Group insiders also marked 2013 as the year that Prigozhin's chief of security for the Concord network, Yevgeny Gulyaev, began an aggressive recruitment campaign.[19]

In 2014, as Putin prepared simultaneously to augment Russian support for Bashar al-Assad's regime in Syria and to seize control of Crimea, the potential windfall in profits for Prigozhin's constellation of business holdings was almost incalculable.[20]

There are different versions of the story of how Prigozhin first came in contact with Utkin. One compelling account published by *Novaya Gazeta* suggests that GRU deputy director Alexey Dyumin reached out to Utkin in early 2014 as Russian forces prepared to invade Crimea and then introduced Utkin to Prigozhin.[21] Another version often repeated by Wagner Group insiders and partially corroborated by leaked personnel records is that after the disastrous Slavonic Corps misadventure in Syria, the GRU listed Utkin as "retired" but then reengaged him as a "reservist" on contract under an assumed identity.

Both versions align with the available evidence. Most of the organization's top operational chiefs and tactical leaders had identity clones and fake passports associated with their dog-tag identification numbers, including Utkin.[22] Most had already forged strong bonds during their deployments in support of the Syrian Express arms-smuggling operation, including Utkin's compatriots Alexander "Ratibor" Kuznetsov and Andrey "Tramp" Bogatov. The difference now was that they were reconstituted as a brand-new organization that was referred to in internal correspondence vaguely as "the Company."

Like its conventional military counterparts, the Wagner formation included infantry, armor, artillery, and specialized teams such as snipers. The organization would evolve, but the one constant was that Prigozhin, Utkin, and Troshev were always at the apex, each managing a distinct operational area. Their partnership proved remarkably successful, at least in the early stages, although it was not without its frictions. Months after the MH17 controversy had begun to fade from the front page, Ukraine's SBU intelligence agency released a recorded telephone intercept of Troshev and Utkin coordinating their operations in Donbas. During the call, Troshev referred to Prigozhin only by his official battlefield nickname, *Perviy,* or "the First."

"The First has assigned me a task. I am leaving, returning back to Molkino, and after that going all around," Troshev told Utkin.

"What? Has something changed? What happened?" Utkin asked.

"He's not giving them the right information," Troshev groused. "They can't understand the situation with the injured. Now the questions are starting: 'Where's our 100 million? One hundred million were allocated. Where's the fucking bonus pay? And now you're just paying 150,000.'"

"Where did that come from?" Utkin shouted on the line. "I never said that to anyone."

"It's total crap," Troshev agreed.

"Bullshit," Utkin said. "I never said that to anyone. And I have no idea where it's coming from. That means the leak is coming directly from inside Molkino."[23]

"Molkino" was a reference to Concord's new and growing base of operations in Russia's southern rust-belt region, adjacent to the GRU's 10th Special Purpose Brigade. The "they" referred to the Wagner Group's chief *kurators* back at the defense ministry. Beyond that, all that could be divined from the conversation and the tone of familiarity between Troshev and Utkin is that they had worked together long enough to keep their references to Prigozhin cloaked in code.

Prigozhin's outfit held significant sway over what happened in the ungoverned frontier region, where smuggling routes ran from Russia into Ukraine and across occupied Luhansk. In coded shorthand, Russian security agents coordinated closely with criminal elements in the transit zone, where Russian weapons and mercenaries flowed into Donbas and Russian bodies flowed back in refrigerator trucks.

In his early years after his prison stint, Prigozhin had learned a lot about the routes that ran through the lawless border areas controlled by local oligarchs and the gangs from leaders of St. Petersburg's underworld who ran the elaborate smuggling networks that crisscrossed Ukraine's eastern regions. Truckloads of "humanitarian aid" arriving from Russia into Donbas during this period were in many cases sourced in St. Petersburg and accompanied by fighters cultivated by the Imperial Legion, the paramilitary wing of the ultranationalist Russian Imperial Movement. Donbas was everybody's playground, but the Wagner Group was gradually becoming one of the biggest players.

The attack on MH17 sparked the change. The multilayered investigations that followed shifted the dynamics among the Russian fighters in Ukraine in significant ways. One of the main casualties was Girkin, whose clumsy efforts to deflect blame for the disaster away from the Russian-backed separatists angered the Kremlin and could not save him from an eventual murder conviction in a Dutch court.

On the ground in Sloviansk, Girkin had initially scrambled to reframe the rapidly emerging media narrative about what exactly happened to the Malaysian Airlines passenger jet. He posted a message online on VKontakte minutes after the crash that appeared to confirm that forces under his command had shot down the commercial jetliner: "In the vicinity of Torez, we just downed a plane, an AN-26. It is lying somewhere in the Progress Mine. We have issued warnings not to fly in our airspace. We have video confirming. The bird fell on a waste heap. Residential areas were not hit. Civilians were not injured."[24]

The message was not online long before Girkin, realizing the heap of trouble he was in, deleted it and replaced it with two successive updates about an hour after MH17 went down. "The Prime Minister of the DNR, Alexander Borodai, has officially confirmed the fact of the falling of the passenger plane near Torez," he wrote, using the abbreviation for the self-styled breakaway Donetsk People's Republic. "At the crash site an investigative team of the general prosecutor's office of the DNR is working. The DNR is interested in an objective investigation of this incident and is prepared to give foreign investigators access to the crash site."[25]

Girkin's incriminating social media posts inadvertently tripped an alarm on the internet. Several thousand miles away, in England, an unemployed stay-at-home dad named Eliot Higgins took notice. From the moment the plane went down, Twitter was awash in a storm of misinformation, dead-end leads, and random guesses about what happened to MH17. Higgins, a part-time blogger, had been tracking every twist in the story.

Three days before the crash, Higgins had launched a website called bellingcat.com with the aim of debunking the kind of false narratives that began proliferating after Girkin's post appeared online. He named the website bellingcat.com after an old fable about a council of mice who gather to cook up a way to outsmart a cat who is giving them trouble. The mice produce a plan to affix a bell to the cat's neck to provide an early warning of coming danger. Although all the mice agree that it is a great idea, they realize the task will be impossible for any one of them to undertake alone. Bellingcat was about taking collective action to solve the problem of disinformation and outright lies promoted by bad actors.

The idea for the name came to him a couple of years after he started blogging about the violence roiling the Middle East under the name "Brown Moses." In 2013 Higgins gained widespread attention for picking through digital detritus to retrieve clues about the origins of the chemical-weapons attack in Ghouta, Syria. Low-key and self-effacing, with the look of a harried adjunct professor—glasses, rumpled attire, and a tousled, graying mane—Higgins was a college dropout and an autodidact in the extreme.

He would be the first to admit that his knowledge of war reporting came entirely from books, magazines, and movies. But even when wars are viewed from a distance, they can have a transformative effect on the human psyche. The situation in Ukraine was no exception. He was about to revolutionize the news business and to teach Gerrit Thiry and the world a thing or two about how to take on Putin.

En route, Higgins and his energetic research partners, Aric Toler and Christo Grozev, would help finger Igor Girkin as one of the leading perpetrators of the MH17 attack, along with three other Russian men who reported up the chain to Moscow. Bellingcat also helped identify Valery Tsemakh, the 1st Sloviansk air-defense lead for Bezler's group, as a person of interest. The first clue was a short snippet of video footage posted on YouTube on July 17, 2014, the day of the attack on the plane.

The video showed a strange-looking, olive-green military-tank–like truck with a stack of missiles on its roof. Higgins quickly confirmed that it was a Buk missile launcher, a Soviet weapons platform that was designed to shoot down incoming aircraft and to defend the airspace overhead. Higgins and his impromptu team of volunteer sleuths were able to confirm within hours of the disaster that the Buk launcher at some point had been located in the small eastern Ukrainian town of Snizhne.[26]

While journalists and international investigators on the ground in Ukraine were still trying to figure out how to gain access to the accident site, Higgins, with the help of crowd-sourced clues culled from social media, had locked in a critical piece of information that would unlock the mystery of who and what shot down the plane. Within hours, Bellingcat had reached a viable working hypothesis that pointed toward Russian separatists under Girkin's control as the potential culprits behind the attack.

Girkin indirectly confirmed the theory the day after the catastrophe when he tried to spin the story in several different directions in an interview with a pro-separatist online outlet called *Russkaya Vesna—Russian Spring*. First, he suggested that a Ukrainian-manned Su-27 jet fighter had shot the passenger plane down in midair. Then he insisted that the attack was a false-flag operation and that there was something suspicious about the corpses found at the site. "Firstly, most of the people on the plane were dead before the fall," Girkin mused morbidly. Witnesses on the ground, Girkin claimed, noted that except for the pilots, many of the dead bodies were drained of blood. "There was also a strong cadaverous smell noted by many local residents—such a smell could not have formed in half an hour in that weather, and the weather yesterday was cloudy, not too hot."[27]

So began the steady drip-drip of lies and exaggerations about MH17. The initial Russian response was to deny all involvement. Even Wikipedia fell victim to the Kremlin's skillful scalpel work, with references to Russian complicity carefully edited out.[28] Russia's official media circulated tales blaming the Ukrainian government and Malaysian Airlines that were buttressed by doctored photos and contradictory visual evidence, claiming that Russia was the victim of a disinformation campaign.

Prigozhin's Internet Research Agency in St. Petersburg took the lead online, amplifying the Kremlin's denials and conspiracy theories until they became a deafening roar.

With input from an array of hired marketing experts, the "Trolls of Olgino" unleashed a barrage of misleading hashtags, bots, and false narratives across social media. On July 18, the day after Girkin's sloppy response to the disaster, the Internet Research Agency kicked into high gear, posting more than 56,000 unique tweets promoting conspiracy theories about what had happened.[29] The torrent marked a critical turning point in the Russian propaganda machine's tactics and signaled Prigozhin's flowering role as the Kremlin's go-to global social media influencer.

Prigozhin's trolls worked tirelessly to undermine Higgins and Bellingcat, but in doing so, they only elevated Higgins's profile, inadvertently positioning Bellingcat as a frontline player in the Kremlin's information war with the West. The fallout over MH17 marked the beginning of a quiet yet significant contest of wills, where Bellingcat's precise digital forensics became the scalpel that cut through the tangled web of narratives spun by

Prigozhin's Internet Research Agency. It became a relentless back-and-forth—Prigozhin's attempts to tighten his hold on the narrative only amplified Bellingcat's ability to shine a light on the shadow army he was building. The smear campaign did nothing to dissuade Thiry's team from taking a closer look at the innovative methods that Bellingcat had used to so quickly flesh out the details of what had happened. Higgins and his compatriots were democratizing the cabalistic art of digital forensics. World dramas unfolded in cascades of bits and bytes online, but the entire culture of the internet was also changing. Although it was getting harder to travel to war zones safely to cover conflicts as they happened, it was getting easier to reconstruct events from digital fragments picked from the internet.

What was once the primary province of computer science geeks and specialized police and intelligence investigators was suddenly accessible to anyone with a laptop and a hankering to solve hard puzzles. Bellingcat would eventually trace the Buk missile launcher to Russia's 53rd Antiaircraft Missile Brigade, but it would take countless bleary-eyed hours for Higgins and Bellingcat's collective of mostly volunteer investigators to piece the links together. "The most amazing thing to me was just how much information they'd left on the internet about it," Higgins said.[30]

It was a David-and-Goliath scenario, only with a few hundred anonymous virtual Davids facing off online with a very real Russian Goliath. No one was more surprised than Higgins when, in October 2014, officials with the British Metropolitan Police Department reached out to him directly. At the prompting of investigators in the Netherlands, Scotland Yard asked him to sit for an interview about Bellingcat's research on the connection among Girkin's forces, the Buk missile launcher that shot the plane down, and Russian military units that might also be implicated in the case.

Higgins remembered his first brush with a real-world international criminal investigation with crisp clarity. It was a little bit like a cross between a Sherlock Holmes story, a John le Carré spy novel, and a Monty Python skit. There were two Dutch and two Australian investigators. They wanted to know everything. So Higgins sat for hours, going line by line through the myriad articles and tweets that Bellingcat had produced about MH17. "They seemed just as interested in finding out what we knew as how we did what we did," he said.[31]

It was obvious from the outset that it was not going to be as simple as joining two interlocking pieces together with a satisfying snap. Bullets were still flying in Donbas. Then there were the bureaucratic obstacles that came with trying to coordinate an investigation with more than two hundred people who represented the interests of at least a half-dozen countries affected by the case. Meanwhile, Russian officials obfuscated and outright lied. The Joint Investigation Team, or JIT, as the multicountry detective squad was called, pulled in dozens of experts from all over the world. Thiry and his colleagues in Amsterdam divided the investigative work into several parts. There was the victim-identification team, the aviation team, the witness-interview unit, the weapons-analysis group, the signals-intelligence unit, and, most critically, the open-source intelligence group.

A core part of the work entailed reconstructing the airframe from thousands of burned and bent remnants scattered across an area that was several miles square and that sat in the center of an active war zone. The team was cautious about the risks of cross-contamination and potential accusations of bias. The key word, according to Thiry, was "validation." Nothing was taken for granted. Nothing could be excluded. Everything had to be confirmed and reconfirmed: "I didn't want to be blamed for tunnel vision."[32]

Unlike a standard murder investigation, the suspect was not a person but a state. Thiry outlined the challenges years later in an antiseptic conference room in the low-slung office building just outside of Amsterdam where the JIT was housed. Thiry recalled in painstaking detail how the Kremlin fought the investigation every step of the way. It was a quintessentially gray, rainy day in March 2023, and over an extremely strong espresso, Thiry became warmer and more animated as he described the impressive resources marshaled to investigate the attack on MH17.

What surprised him most was how the FSB and the mafia outfits that controlled the transit zone worked together hand in glove. Prigozhin's outfit was a standout. "I was quite shocked to see that the criminal world and the intel world were tied so close together. It frightened the hell out of me," Thiry said.

Thiry found himself navigating a labyrinth of Kremlin disinformation, where every piece of evidence seemed to be shadowed by a deliberate falsehood. The Russians put up obstacles at every turn, first pushing the false theory that a Ukrainian jet fighter was in the air at the same time as MH17, then insisting that they did not have access to flight radar data that ultimately confirmed the obvious—that the plane was downed by a surface-to-air missile. It wasn't just a matter of uncovering the truth—it was a battle against a state apparatus determined to obscure it. "For me," Thiry said, "it's still difficult to understand the shamelessness of the lies."[33]

He was two days away from retirement, finally free to move on with life after a Dutch court had convicted Igor Girkin and two other men of murdering the 298 passengers on MH17. It had taken nine years. By that time, the world finally seemed to be catching up with what Thiry had known for years—that Russia was intent on taking Ukraine no matter the cost.

The inquiry into what happened to MH17 and the Western response to its immediate aftermath would also offer hard and bitter lessons to police, prosecutors, presidents, prime ministers, and the public about the changing character of war in the twenty-first century. It was a perfect case study of the risks and costs associated with proxy warfare and the role of information technology in shaping wartime diplomacy.

The destruction of the plane highlighted the dangers of letting Russia's salami-slicing tactics go unchecked. Washington pundits likened the situation to the tense days after Hitler marched into the Rhineland in 1936, then annexed Austria two years later, with Britain's Neville Chamberlain responding with a muddled appeasement strategy. The incident would school Washington on just how far Putin was willing to go in his quest to restore Russia's status as a Great Power.

Maintaining plausible deniability for Russia's role in the MH17 case and everything that came afterward in Russia's rapidly expanding global proxy war with the West soon exerted so much pressure on the Kremlin strategy that centrifugal forces began to push Prigozhin and the Wagner Group into the center of the diplomatic eddies swirling around the conflict in Ukraine.

A day before the passenger flight was shot down, in July 2014, President Obama had announced from the White House podium that new sanctions would be imposed on companies linked to Putin's close associates from his days in the KGB and city hall in St. Petersburg. Commodities magnate Gennady Timchenko, Rostec chief Sergey Chemezov, and Rosneft CEO Igor Sechin were all blacklisted. All three men and the companies they ran were pivotal for Prigozhin's business endeavors. A day after MH17 went down, Obama promised a fresh round of sanctions and called the crash a "wake-up call for Europe." "This should snap everybody's heads to attention and make sure we don't have time for propaganda," he said. "We don't have time for games."[34]

The ground quickly shifted under the feet of Russia's proxies in eastern Ukraine. Although Girkin had succeeded in arming and raising up militias, bedlam reigned even as the Kremlin pressed for greater control as the tempo of battle heated up on the front lines.

The hodgepodge of Cossacks, criminals, and pro-Putin shills who powered the Russian separatist movement in Donbas were shoddily equipped, poorly trained, and not infrequently inebriated. The militias that nominally controlled the area near where MH17 was shot down were composed of disaffected locals and Russian opportunists who streamed across the border after the annexation of Crimea.

One of the largest proxy contingents was the Prizrak Brigade, a force of 2,000–3,000 men. Its commander, Aleksey "Motorola" Mozgovoy, was a local from Luhansk who claimed Cossack roots and had briefly worked as a cook in St. Petersburg. With his ruddy cheeks, middle-aged paunch, ginger-tinted goatee, and black beret, Mozgovoy resembled a swashbuckling Kris Kringle crossed with a Russian Che Guevara. Charismatic yet cruel, he reveled in comparisons to Cuba's revolutionary icon and was a vocal critic of Ukrainian oligarchs, accusing them of exploiting local labor.

Based in Alchevsk, Prizrak quickly earned a fearsome reputation. Mozgovoy's brigade was notorious for its People's Court, where public humiliation and physical attacks were meted out for minor infractions, and harsher punishments included torture or execution. Prizrak attracted young men eager for action, organized into subunits often called tactical battalions—although many were little more than gangs of twenty-somethings with wispy goatees led by grizzled veterans of Moscow's wars in Afghanistan and Chechnya.

In another part of Luhansk, Alexander "Batman" Bednov led a similar force, drawing from cadres inspired by the fascist ideologies of Alexander Dugin. After the MH17 disaster, he became a vocal critic of Russian attempts to broker a ceasefire with Ukraine, particularly as diplomatic talks intensified ahead of meetings in Minsk in the summer of 2014. Although his core group numbered only around two hundred, their impact on the early battles of the Donbas war was significant. A bug-eyed former officer of Ukraine's Ministry of Internal Affairs, Bednov was notorious for his involvement in torturing civilians. Bednov's so-called Batman Battalion became infamous, with offshoots that added to its fearsome reputation.

The most notorious was the Rusich Diversionary Sabotage Assault Reconnaissance Group. Rusich sprang from a neo-Nazi gang of St. Petersburg fight-club rough boys led by a scruffy half-Russian, half-Norwegian sharpshooter with a Viking fetish named Yan "Slavyan" Petrovsky and the contingent's commander, Alexey "Fritz" Milchakov, a baby-faced local obsessed with re-creating a Russian version of the Hitler Youth. They were part of a wave of fighters trained by the ultranationalist Russian Imperial Movement and deployed in the guise of "humanitarian aid volunteers" to support the Batman Battalion and Prizrak.

Born in the year that the Soviet Union dissolved, Milchakov was emblematic of a slice of Russian youth who came of age in a rudderless country. Like Petrovsky, he grew up in a single-parent household, developed an interest in historical military reenactment as a teenager, and jumped into St. Petersburg's neo-fascist scene in 2007. He quickly earned a fearsome reputation after videotaping the beheading of a puppy—an act that solidified his notoriety among local neo-fascists. Later, Milchakov joined the elite VDV 76th Air Assault Guards Division in Pskov, the same unit where Utkin served.

Utkin and Milchakov shared more than just a military background; they were both also drawn to the mystique of Rodnovery, a neo-pagan faith that resonated deeply with their fascist leanings. For them, Rodnovery offered more than ancient Slavic rituals—it was a rallying cry for ethnic purity and a rejection of the modern world's moral decay. The faith's emphasis on a glorified, pre-Christian past and the warrior ethos of their ancestors fit seamlessly into their worldview, which idolized strength, conquest, and the myth of a racially pure Slavic empire. But their connection went beyond shared beliefs; both were on Prigozhin's payroll, and both played prominent roles in the battle for the Luhansk airfield in the summer of 2014.[35]

As international scrutiny intensified, it became clear that the ad hoc leadership among the separatists was no longer sustainable. The MH17 incident had exposed both the extent of the Kremlin's involvement and the fragility of Moscow's control in Donbas. Intense fighting and red tape delayed Dutch and Australian investigators from reaching the crash site for a full two weeks. The exchange of artillery fire along the line of contact was so heavy that it took the investigators six hours to reconnoiter safe routes to the wreckage near Torez.

They finally gained access to the site on July 31, 2014, shortly after the US State Department publicly released satellite images showing that Russian forces on the other side of the border between Russia and Ukraine had been firing Grad rockets in their direction and the surrounding Donetsk area for weeks.[36] Meanwhile, UN human-rights monitors reported that civilian casualty numbers were climbing.

The situation was dire. Nobody could deny anymore that the conflict was spiraling out of control. The whole project of transforming Donbas into another fulcrum in Putin's frozen conflict strategy needed retooling. Prigozhin offered up a hammer.

CHAPTER 11
THE CLEANERS

efore the Wagner Group was a "group" at all, it was a battlefield rumor. That changed after MH17.

Back in Moscow, Putin turned to his adviser, Vladislav Surkov, to manage the fallout. Often called the "Gray Cardinal" for his behind-the-scenes influence, Surkov was the backstage handler for the network of Kremlin-backed separatists in Ukraine. He got his start in the spin-doctor business after a stint in the GRU intelligence wing, when he went to work in the 1990s in the advertising department of Mikhail Khodorkovsky's Menatep Bank and later as a top strategist for the Kremlin. Surkov was pivotal in shaping the narratives surrounding Russia's incursion into Ukraine, leveraging his deep understanding of media manipulation and public perception to stabilize Putin's image during the crisis.

Initially, Surkov's focus was shutting down genuine domestic Russian opposition figures and replacing them with ersatz political cadres and civil-society organizations. Part of his portfolio included managing Russia's separatist proxies in South Ossetia and Abkhazia. After a 2013 embezzlement scandal forced a brief time out of national politics, Surkov became a political adviser and the presidential administration's lead man on managing the politics of countering and containing the color revolutions, including the Euromaidan movement in Ukraine. With Russian separatists under Girkin's command besieged and chaos rising on all sides, Surkov's new assignment in the summer of 2014 was to keep the clandestine operation he had helped Putin set in motion in Donbas from skidding off the rails.

Putin's goal was to freeze the conflict until it could be reignited at a more opportune time. The playbook was like the one employed in Georgia in 2008. The challenge the Kremlin faced was figuring out how to camouflage the huge movement of men and military gear needed to seize and hold territory in Donbas. Plausible deniability was paramount for improving Russia's odds of notching a diplomatic win at the bargaining table in Minsk. The aftermath of the MH17 crash set in motion a recalibration of strategy within the Kremlin, one that would redefine the roles of its operatives and most importantly the roles of the Wagner Group.

For Surkov, it was natural to double down on the narrative that the conflict in eastern Ukraine had grown out of the purely organic drive of local Russian-speaking separatists who wanted greater autonomy from Kyiv. Girkin's frontline stumbles and the hue and cry raised by the new loudmouthed champions of a Kremlin-controlled Donbas—Batman Battalion, Prizrak, and others—only reinforced that notion. Surkov had the grist he needed to kick his spin machine into even higher gear.

With Putin's backing, he worked with public-relations consultants, political scientists, and enforcers to probe Ukrainian vulnerabilities and build popular support for a new semiautonomous statelet. Much as he had with Abkhazia and South Ossetia in Georgia, Surkov cast his net wide for information and spent lavishly on influence campaigns. According to emails leaked from his accounts, his sources had determined that staying in control of Donbas would be particularly beneficial for Russian companies like Rosneft and Rosatom, the state-run nuclear-energy corporation of Russia.[1] To maintain access to Donbas, however, Russia would have to restart the game with an entirely new strategy and roster of players.

Everything would have to be handled with extreme care to avoid sparking Russian antiwar sentiment at home or inflaming anarchy among Russian separatists in Donbas. The "Russian Spring" that Surkov helped orchestrate attracted all manner of ultranationalists from across the border in Russia, and it held broad appeal for Russian-speaking Ukrainians who lived on the margins of the local economy. The most consequential of these included the Russian Imperial Movement in St. Petersburg and the Cossack National Guard of the Don National Army. Foreign fighters inspired by Alexander Dugin's pan-fascist call to arms traveled from conservative enclaves in the United States, Spain, France, Italy, Germany, and Serbia.

What truly held this disparate coalition together wasn't just the ideological veneer of monarchist revivalism in Putin's politics—it was also the intoxicating promise of adventure, glory, and personal reinvention. The conflict in Donbas offered a chance for these people to escape the mundane and embrace a life of purpose, driven by a desire to play a role in what they saw as an accelerating clash of civilizations. The war wasn't just about territorial gains or political ideology; it was, as well, a stage where they could act out their fantasies of heroism, reshape their identities, and position themselves as warriors in a grand, existential struggle.

At the center of this movement was the "Novorossiya project," an ambitious endeavor to resurrect Russian claims to the vast steppe in southeastern Ukraine, once part of tsarist Russia's "New Russia" in the mid-eighteenth century. This territory included the industrial hub of Donetsk in Donbas, the strategic port of Odessa, and the city of Dnipro. Surkov's strategy was to unite a broad coalition under the banner of the "Russian World," or *Russky Mir*, selling the vision of a revived imperial past. For a brief, heady moment in the spring and early summer of 2014, before the downing of MH17, it seemed as though there was enough momentum, money, and firepower to bring those dreams to life.

However, that support quickly evaporated as Russia shifted its focus and resources to the escalating battle in the town of Ilovaisk. On August 14, after losing his stronghold in Donetsk, Girkin announced his resignation as the so-called defense minister of the Donetsk People's Republic. Returning to Moscow, Girkin and the Kremlin were confronted with the grim reality of Russia's messy, undeclared war on Ukraine—a conflict that was becoming increasingly difficult to spin both at home and on the international stage.[2]

Publicly, Russian officials continued to deny involvement in Donbas. Sergey Lavrov, Russia's foreign minister, dismissed Washington's claims of Russian military presence as attempts to incite another color revolution. He argued that plans to send OSCE (Organization for Security and Co-operation in Europe) monitors to the region should dispel any suspicions of Russian troop deployments: "We hope that this will dispel suspicions that are regularly being voiced against us, that those checkpoints controlled by the militias from the Ukrainian side are used for massive troop and weaponry deployment from Russia to Ukraine."[3]

Behind closed doors, the Kremlin continued to back-channel orders and maneuver airborne troops into position in Donbas. The massive size of the contested territory that lay between the Dnipro River and Ukraine's eastern border with Russia required highly experienced tactical fighters and a level of unit cohesion and discipline that was sorely lacking within Russian separatist ranks. Making matters worse for the Novorossiya project, the Kremlin's attention was split between two fronts—Syria and Ukraine. When Russian skirmishes with Ukrainian forces reached a feverish peak in the fall of 2014, the crisis in Syria was heating up for Bashar al-Assad's beleaguered regime as the Islamic State began to seize control of more territory. With pressure mounting on the Russian economy from US and EU sanctions related to Syria and Ukraine, Putin began laying the groundwork for a negotiated settlement with Ukraine that would give Moscow a bit of breathing room.

So the two parallel paths that Girkin and Prigozhin traveled to gain the Kremlin's favor over twenty-three years, and that led them both to Donbas in 2014, began to merge and then diverge. Just as he had when he was a young man, down on his luck, out to prove himself in St. Petersburg in the 1990s, Prigozhin stepped into the void left behind as others were toppled.

This was the way—an unspoken code, a nod, a handshake contract, a call, a dictum delivered from on high via couriers, text messages, enigmatic emails, and secure phone lines—and suddenly he was on top again, one rung higher on the ladder. From a hustler in St. Petersburg to a multimillionaire with a mansion and yacht, Prigozhin had transformed himself over two decades from a caterer and court jester to a defense contractor extraordinaire and the cleanup man for Putin. But the true scale of the unfolding mess was beyond anyone's grasp.

ON AUGUST 24, 2014, ten days after Girkin and Borodai had abruptly quit their posts in Donbas, an intriguing message popped up in the inbox of Lev Schlosberg, a local politician in Pskov, the same Russian garrison town where Dmitry Utkin and Rusich commander Alexey Milchakov had been posted for several years when they were with the VDV 76th Airborne Assault Division. A paratrooper from the unit posed a question that was on everyone's lips in Pskov: "What is happening? Why are the commanders silent? Why is *everyone* silent?"

Schlosberg, a somber-eyed, clean-shaven human-rights activist who had, against all odds, won a seat a few years earlier in the local constituent Assembly of Deputies in Pskov, read further. "Why are the Airborne Forces command and politicians hiding what is happening now in the Luhansk region, Donetsk, etc. in Ukraine? Why are paratroopers sent on the 15th–16th and later already returning to their unit in zinc coffins? In particular, Leonid Kitchatkin from the 234th regiment. I don't know the rest, but they exist!"[4]

Schlosberg was something of a novelty in Russian politics. Elected to Pskov's local legislature in 2011, he was, at fifty-one, old enough to remember life before and after the Soviet Union's dissolution. But he was far more internet savvy than many of his political peers. He knew how to use Facebook and YouTube to build up a grassroots political following. He had picked up his skills in large part while serving as the local Pskov branch head of Russia's liberal Yabloko Party and running his own online news publication, *Pskovskaya Guberniya*. Schlosberg's news outlet was part personal bully pulpit, part genuine local tribune; as such, it had become a magnet for citizen complaints about the way that Putin was running things and for Schlosberg's own critiques of Russia's role in the Donbas conflict.

In video posts regularly uploaded to his Facebook account over the spring and summer of 2014, Schlosberg made his distaste for the war abundantly clear. Everything that could have possibly gone wrong with Putin's first attempt to bring Ukraine to heel by force had gone wrong. By August, Putin's "little green men" were popping up everywhere in eastern Ukraine, along with widespread reports of well-equipped paratroopers turning up at the battle in Ilovaisk.

Because many of the airborne troops in Pskov were technically categorized as active reservists, there was considerable confusion about whether they had traveled to the front lines of their own accord on a patriotic whim or they were "volun-told" to go fight in Ukraine. There were rumors that the heads of local veterans' affairs associations in Pskov were pressuring reservists to join up and that some had been enticed by promises of high-paying work. On VKontakte and Odnoklassniki, a clunky Russian knockoff of MySpace, hundreds of mothers, wives, girlfriends, and sisters of Russian "volunteers" killed in Donbas posted sentimental snapshots of a candle with the caption *Vechnaya Pamyat*— "In Memoriam." But no one in the airborne headquarters or Moscow offered an explanation for why so many paratroopers were turning up dead or missing, or why so many trucks loaded with dead Russian soldiers in zinc coffins were returning to Pskov.

"At first, with the deaths that occurred in the spring and summer, it looked like they were just the result of fighting in local conflicts [in the Caucasus]. But when dozens die in one battle, it's noticeable," Schlosberg recalled in an interview later. "All of Pskov saw what was going on. After all, all previous military operations of the Soviet Union outside the Soviet Union happened in the same way. Those killed in Afghanistan were also buried, some openly, some secretly. There were military operations in Egypt and other countries. The shock here was just that this was Ukraine, that this is not somewhere distant like in Africa and in Asia, it's nearby."[5]

A day after receiving the enigmatic email, Schlosberg attended the burial ceremony for the fallen soldier, Leonid Kitchatkin, and another VDV paratrooper at the request of the soldiers' friends and family. After a group of paratroopers also in attendance physically attacked him, Schlosberg published a scathing column about Putin's secret war in Donbas titled "The Dead and the Living." In it, he railed against Russia's long history of covering up its casualty counts and surreptitiously burying the war dead. "Defense Minister Sergey Shoigu and Airborne Forces commander Vladimir Shamanov claim that the 76th division does not take part in hostilities on the territory of Ukraine and, accordingly, did not suffer combat losses. Meanwhile, everyone who came to the funeral could see that the division buried the dead," Schlosberg griped.[6] The covert burials were a far cry from the elaborate state burials granted after the VDV 76th suffered one of its worst losses in history in Chechnya in 2000, Schlosberg noted. "In 2000, it was still possible to openly bury dead soldiers. In 2014, this is no longer possible. This is how the wars waged by the Russian state have changed. In essence, this is all the same war— against the people."[7]

Schlosberg and another reporter at *Pskov Guberniya* launched an investigation into reports that nearly a hundred Pskov paratroopers had been killed on the front. But their plan to expose the growing human costs of Putin's clandestine war just across the border was nearly derailed when two unidentified men assaulted Schlosberg one night in late August as he walked from the newspaper's offices to meet one of his reporters. Bloodied, badly concussed, and barely able to remember what happened, Schlosberg was near death and had to be hospitalized for days.

The attack was one in a string against journalists who reported on the rising number of secret military burials across parts of Russia's Western and Southern Military Districts, where many of Russia's forces were highly concentrated. Schlosberg's revelations hinted at what was already well-known among mercenaries who joined up for the fight: that top officers in the airborne forces in Pskov were deeply involved in facilitating the covert movement of Russian operatives deep into Donbas and beyond.

Undeterred, Schlosberg continued to cover the story. In early September he published excerpts of conversations between Pskov paratroopers about heavy losses in Donbas. It was becoming more obvious by the day that Putin was determined to avoid the mistakes made by his predecessors in the 1980s, when increasingly critical coverage of the Soviet war in Afghanistan brought mothers and wives of the war dead out into the streets by the thousands. The only problem was that journalists were not the only ones talking openly about Russia's stealthy mobilization and battlefield losses in Donbas.

In November 2014, Girkin publicly confessed to his leading role as an instigator of Russia's covert Donbas offensive in a blog posted on *Zavtra*, the far-right weekly outlet where he and Borodai first got their start as professional propagandists. With a mix of pride and bitter regret, Girkin recounted to *Zavtra*'s editor in chief, Alexander Prokhanov, how he had seized Sloviansk with only a small group of about fifty under his command and how Russian failures to resupply his forces after the MH17 crash left him no choice but to abandon the fight. "I pulled the trigger of war," Girkin said. "If I had not crossed the border with my contingent, in the end everything would have ended, as it did in Kharkiv, as it did in Odessa. There would have been several dozen killed, burned, and arrested. And that would be the end."[8]

The situation got dicey after the MH17 crash, Girkin explained, when he was ordered to hold Sloviansk even as the Ukrainians began pounding the area with heavy artillery: "The 'tourists' were supposed to arrive in 40 days. There was no way we could have held out until they arrived. We wouldn't even have enough food," Girkin said.[9] The "tourists" reference was a throwback reference to the secret Soviet operatives who plied their covert trade during the Cold War and yet another hint that the Kremlin was more deeply involved in managing the conflict in Donbas than Putin cared to publicly admit. Further proof of that fact came soon after Girkin's public confession.

In late December 2014, a convoy of armored Russian Vystrel vehicles, tanks, and military trucks streamed westward across Russia's border with Luhansk toward the besieged town of Debaltseve in eastern Ukraine, known as "hell town" to Ukrainian soldiers. Clad in a mix of forest green and snow-pattern camouflage, they assembled near the crossroads between Horlivka and

Bakhmut. Arriving just as diplomatic negotiations in Minsk between Russia and Ukraine were under way, they soon encountered fierce resistance from Ukrainian troops.

The battle of Debaltseve unfolded in deadly cold conditions at a crucial railway and road junction, making it a critical strategic target for both sides. Russian forces aimed to bridge their strongholds in Donetsk and Luhansk, while the Ukrainian Army pushed aggressively to maintain control over the region. The fighting was fierce. In short order, Utkin's unit lost at least fifty men, prompting him to make a frenzied call to Andrey Troshev for help that was intercepted by Ukraine's SBU intelligence service.[10] In an exhausted voice, Utkin said that he had not slept for days and that he could no longer keep track of all the losses. "Get me out of here, Nikolayevich. My people will soon shoot me," Utkin grumbled.[11]

It was amid this maelstrom that the very first public mention of Dmitry Utkin's Wagner contingent first surfaced. The trigger was a deadly ambush in Luhansk on January 1, 2015, that killed Alexander Bednov and several other Russian separatists with Bednov's Batman Battalion. Like Girkin, Bednov was a Novorossiya diehard. As the struggle to take control of Luhansk stalled, he became increasingly vocal about the way Moscow was handling support for the anti-Ukrainian insurgent forces under his command. He complained loudly that Voentorg, the ministry of defense's logistics arm, was diverting critical humanitarian supplies into the black market, an allegation that pointed a finger indirectly at Prigozhin's Concord as one of the primary sources of high-level corruption in Luhansk.

At one point, just before he was killed, Bednov even went so far as to publicly accuse the Kremlin's handpicked administrator for Luhansk, Igor Plotnitsky, of being in on the scheme, and Bednov vowed to challenge Plotnitsky in elections scheduled for the spring of 2015. All these details might have been lost if it hadn't been for the fact that the Wagner Group was named as a prime suspect in Bednov's apparent murder.

A day after news of Bednov's death surfaced, Boris Rozhin, a well-known ultranationalist Russian LiveJournal blogger, posted a digest about the ambush and claimed that an unnamed Russian military veteran at the helm of a private-military contractor called PMC Wagner was behind the strike on Bednov's convoy. Writing under the handle "Colonel Cassad," he named Alexey Milchakov, the neo-Nazi commander of Wagner Group affiliate Rusich, as a lead source for the allegation.

Chock-full of innuendo, the blog post also linked to a news brief by none other than Marat Musin, founder of *ANNA News*, which said that Bednov's killers had used flamethrowers to incinerate the bodies.[12] The next day, Rozhin, who was based in Crimea, posted another update about Bednov's death that alleged that a certain retired Russian special-forces officer with the Russian MVD Vityaz counterterrorism wing named "Evegeniy Wagner" was the culprit behind the fatal ambush on the Batman Battalion.[13]

The chorus of blog posts about the mysterious commander named "Wagner" hinted that Russian subterfuge might be in play. The vagueness of the narratives, the overlapping ties among ultranationalist FSB-linked influencers—Borodai, Girkin, Musin, and Milchakov, the sadistic wunderkind paratrooper—and the circuitous sourcing bore all the hallmarks of a classic disinformation campaign. It seemed to be a page torn from the instruction manual for deception that Borodai and Girkin had first crafted two decades earlier in Transnistria and Chechnya.

Girkin would years later own up to knowing all along that the Wagner Group was behind the attack on Bednov and the deadly car-bomb attack that killed Prizrak's commander, Alexey Mozgovoy, several months later.[14] The two killings were part of a string of "wet jobs" conducted by Utkin's team. Known colloquially as "the cleaners," the core cadre of assassins may have numbered close to thirty-one.[15] Most had arrived from Russia in May 2014 along with two detachments—Luna and Steppe—that were formed under orders from General Vladimir Alekseyev, deputy chief of the GRU intelligence wing.

A decorated VDV Airborne officer, Alekseyev was a stout bulldog of a man who often wore a squinty smile on the rare occasions when he let himself be caught on camera. He was born and raised in Ukraine in a middle-class family in a small rural village in the central western region of Vinnitsiya. Bookish and gawky as a teenager, he obsessed over joining the military from an early age, according to his classmates.[16] After fulfilling his two years of mandatory military service, Alekseyev clawed his way upward into the prestigious Ryazan Higher Airborne Command School in the mid-1980s, and from that moment forward he began living the secretive life of an intelligence officer. It was in Ryazan, where Russia's airborne elite staff officers typically train for five years, that Alekseyev would get married and then cross paths with many of the high-ranking *spetsnaz* officers who would come to play central roles in the Wagner Group's evolution.

Following a stint as head of intelligence in Russia's Far East Military District, Alekseyev was called to Moscow, where he served as head of the GRU's 14th Directorate, the department tasked with managing Russia's secretive special-purpose brigades. The job placed Alekseyev, for a time, at the top of the direct line of command over several of the Wagner Group's leading operatives, including Dmitry Utkin and Alexander Kuznetsov. Alekseyev gained more public prominence in 2011, when he took the number-two role under the GRU's director, Igor Sergun. The timing of Sergun's and Alekseyev's parallel promotions in the GRU coincided with the creation of a cross-agency intelligence fusion cell that reportedly brought under one unified command deep reconnaissance *spetsnaz* operatives and agents with Russia's Foreign Intelligence Service (SVR).[17]

This would turn out to be propitious because only three years later, in 2014, Sergun would rely on Alekseyev to help launch an all-purpose hub for training Russia's foreign allies in guerrilla tactics and clandestine reconnaissance and sabotage operations in Ukraine and Syria. But the full details of Alekseyev's involvement in those military misadventures and his interactions with Prigozhin and the Wagner Group would remain hidden for nearly a decade.

The GRU's reasoning behind the elimination of rogue Novorossiya commanders was clear: in the winter and spring of 2015, Putin quite simply needed to extinguish any threat to his bigger-picture strategy, and loose cannons like Bednov and Mozgovoy posed just such a threat. What the Wagner Group offered was a chance to wipe the slate clean, consolidate pro-Russian separatists in Donbas, buy time to regroup, and redirect the energies of Russia's military-industrial complex toward its escalating proxy war with the United States and its allies in the Middle East.

With Islamic State fighters inching ever closer to seizing control of huge chunks of the oil- and mineral-rich area around Palmyra in Syria, few inside the Kremlin questioned the logic of the need to pivot back to the protection of Russia's one solid foothold in the Mediterranean. Most importantly, the Wagner Group's operations gave Putin the running room he needed to control the narrative about who exactly was doing what in Russia's name abroad. Putin could ill afford to trigger more opprobrium from the EU or, worse, stumble into a direct confrontation with US forces running counterterrorism operations in Syria. Moreover, although many in the West cast Putin as a lawless dictator, he demonstrated time and again his keenness to project an image of himself at home as a forthright, wise leader who operated in strict accordance with Russian law.

Putin's desire to maintain the veneer of proceduralism and insulate himself from political blowback at home while also projecting power beyond Russia's borders despite limited military means presented a serious strategic dilemma. Troops were needed in both Ukraine and Syria, but Russian law placed heavy restrictions on the president's ability to call for a general mobilization of forces and deploy conscript forces outside of Russia without a formal declaration of war.

A public announcement that Russia was initiating full-scale combat operations could trigger a military response from the United States. With oil prices dipping to historic lows at under $40 a barrel, the Kremlin could ill afford to tangle directly with Washington, making it even more important for Putin to avoid the use of words like *war, mobilization*, and *soldiers*.[18] And because Russian law also technically prohibits its citizens from fighting in wars abroad for foreign armies for personal profit, it was equally important to lean into words like *volunteer* and *patriot* when referring to private citizens involved in the security business—or even better, in the case of Prigozhin, not to say anything publicly at all.

Fragmentary stories about the Wagner Group nonetheless persisted, and online rumors about the cleanup jobs in Donbas began to take on a viral quality. In June 2015 an online news site called *Ukraine Media Crisis* published an article that repeated a garbled version of the story about Bednov's killing and claimed that a Russian special-forces colonel named "Evgueni Wagner [*sic*]" was responsible.[19] A few months later, on October 15, 2015, one of the very first mainstream Russian-language news accounts mentioning the Wagner Group appeared in the St. Petersburg news outlet *Fontanka*.

After Denis Korotkov, *Fontanka*'s enterprising lead reporter, wrote his first series of stories about the Slavonic Corps, the newsroom was inundated with emails and calls from dozens of unemployed men who either wanted to find out how to get into the mercenary business or had bitter stories to tell about their time in the trenches working for the private-security industry. Korotkov said that the same names kept cropping up so often in the calls and messages that he could piece together the main characters of the burgeoning mercenary operations:

> Then when I was asked to look into what was happening in Ukraine, in Donbas, suddenly somebody said the word "Wagner." From someone else, I got the family name "Utkin." Then, from a third source,

someone said, "Dima." Dima, Dima, Dima—Dmitry Utkin. Someone mentioned he was *spetsnaz*. From there, it was easy enough to figure out who exactly Dmitry Valeryivich Utkin is. Then someone mentioned the name Prigozhin. I just got lucky. I had no idea at the time that I would end up chasing the story for years after that. I was just a beat reporter covering local affairs in St. Petersburg.[20]

No express mention was made of Utkin himself, only oblique references to his Nazi obsession and that the commander of the contingent adopted the name "Wagner" sometime between his misadventure with the Slavonic Corps in Syria and his secret deployment to Crimea a few months later. There were no details either about the Moran Security Group connection and the contingent's roster of heavy-duty clients such as Sovcomflot, SOGAZ, and Rosneft affiliates. But Korotkov's scoop offered plenty of other juicy details. The Wagner Group offered new recruits 80,000 rubles a month—the rough equivalent of $5,000—in exchange for signing a one-year contract that started with one month of training at the Molkino base near Krasnodar Krai, next to the 10th Special Purpose Brigade's main base.[21]

The newsy revelations invited more backbiting from Girkin. Back in Moscow by then, he tweeted and vlogged about the fragmentary rumors that the Wagner Group mercenaries had sustained high numbers of casualties in the fall of 2015 in renewed battles with Islamic State forces in Syria over control of oil and gas facilities near Palmyra in the mineral-rich region of Homs.

Meanwhile, stories about the Wagner Group took on a life of their own online. As *Fontanka*'s stories leaped the language barrier, making their way into English-language outlets like *The Guardian* and the *New York Times*, what started out as battlefield scuttlebutt from the foggy front lines of Donbas suddenly became headline news in London, Washington, and New York. What went unnoticed at the time by most outside of a small circle of obsessive investigative journalists in Russia was that real-time updates about the Wagner Group's deployments in Syria and beyond were driving huge volumes of traffic to a handful of sites on VKontakte. Russia's mysterious mercenaries were quickly becoming social media sensations.[22]

One of the earliest detectable references to the Wagner Group on VKontakte was shared in 2016 among followers of an ultranationalist fan-boy group account unironically dubbed Soldiers of Fortune, *Soldat Udachi* in Russian. The owner of the Soldiers of Fortune VKontakte account referred to himself only as "Andrey," and the account's origin date is unknown. But the account's profile image bore the distinctive red beret associated with Russia's MVD special-forces gendarmerie troops. Although the account had only a few hundred followers when it was registered two years earlier, it soon became a crucial node in a tightly knit network of real and aspiring Wagner fighters connecting to Prigozhin, the Internet Research Agency, and a broader covert Kremlin influence campaign. It was yet another sign that leaders in the upper reaches of Russia's vast security apparatus were becoming more confident that the nascent shadow army that Prigozhin was building held the solution to the operational challenges they faced in Ukraine and Syria.

Behind closed doors, Prigozhin and Putin's gatekeepers in the Kremlin were already beginning to negotiate a more expansive remit for the mercenary forces under Dmitry Utkin's command. A leaked April 2016 memo marked "Top Secret" underscored the unusual nature of the arrangement between the president's office and Prigozhin. The report confirmed not only that Wagner forces had targeted top-level pro-Russian separatist leaders for assassination in 2015 but also that Wagner was one of several covert contingents deployed by the GRU. The memo referred to forces under Utkin's command as "Battalion Tactical Group V," noting its successful efforts to seize control of the oil- and gas-rich territory between Palmyra and Deir Ezzor in northeastern Syria. At the time, Wagner's Battalion Tactical Group V (BTG-V) had approximately 1,200 to 1,300 fighters in Syria, with 70 killed in action and 372 wounded—revealing the heavy toll of their mission.[23]

The memo also made clear that Prigozhin's employees well understood that there was still some trepidation in the Kremlin about the Wagner Group's fuzzy legal status and the murky nature of the relationship among the paramilitary, the GRU, and the defense ministry. Prigozhin's patrons in the defense ministry recognized both the risks and the benefits of extending Wagner's role as a proxy force operating at arm's length: "It is necessary to consider the high potential of BTG V in the context of covert or illegal influence operations in international conflicts, as well as the negative effect that will arise when specialists with extensive experience in combat operations, training, and waging guerrilla-sabotage wars are 'thrown out onto the street.' At the same time, BTG 'V' is financed entirely from private funds and does not require any government funding. The decision is up to you."[24]

The prediction that unleashing a clandestine paramilitary could lead to blowback would turn out to be incredibly prescient. But in the moment, the higher-order goal of conducting covert operations on the cheap in parts of the world where Russia was engaged in a shadow war with the West apparently won the day. The identity of the "you" addressed in the memo wasn't immediately clear. But the phrasing and the metadata hidden in the document pointed to a high-level Kremlin official and suggested that the document might have been written on a device belonging to an official who worked in the Federal Agency for State Property Management, the body that serves as a steward for state-controlled enterprises like Rostec, Sovcomflot, and Gazprom. The document also offered insight into how Battalion Tactical Group V—the precursor to the Wagner Group—fit into an emerging strategy that intertwined public and private enterprises into a covert network of shell companies, money launderers, logistics hubs, information brokers, and mercenaries, all providing military protection abroad for Russia's state monopolies and firms tied to Putin's inner circle.

The first incontrovertible public evidence of those links surfaced several months later in late December 2016. The occasion was an extravagant gala dinner within the opulent confines of St. George Hall in the Kremlin palace on a frosty winter night in Moscow. Inside the gilded great room, tables heaved with silver trays laden with fruit, sparkling dinnerware, and glistening glasses of golden champagne. Putin orchestrated the grand spectacle to commemorate Russia's revered Day of Heroes of the Fatherland—colloquially known as "Heroes Day." Amid the illustrious assembly of several hundred distinguished honorees, a singular figure seated at one of the round banquet tables loomed large in the crowd as a chipper female state TV newscaster described the scene behind her. For those who knew him, the profile of Utkin's bare pate and jutting jaw would have been instantly recognizable amid the sea of gray-haired military personnel and civilians that Putin had summoned.

But the money shot was the snapshots of Putin standing alongside Utkin and his Wagner Group compatriots Andrey "Tramp" Bogatov, Alexander "Ratibor" Kuznetsov, and Andrey "Gray" Troshev, complete with swag bag in hand. Bogatov was missing an arm, and next to him, Troshev stared back at the camera with a blank stare. To Putin's left, in black suits and dark ties, were Kuznetsov and Utkin, their chests bursting with red-ribboned silver medals. The lightning-bolt Nazi "SS" neck tattoo that would transform Utkin's scowling countenance into an internet meme years later was not yet visible in any of the images.

And other than a confirmation from Putin's spokesman, Dmitry Peskov, that Utkin had indeed been pictured alongside Putin at the awards ceremony, no one stepped forward to make an official or even unofficial statement about why the president of the world's second-most-powerful nuclear power was handing out medals to mercenaries. The captions on the photos published in *Fontanka* and picked up by media outlets around the world indicated that Putin had awarded all four men Russia's highest military award for their service in Syria. Next to Putin, their poses in the now-famous photo looked a bit stiff and stilted. But in another photo from that day, featuring just Utkin and his comrades, there was an undeniable intensity, an electric energy that hinted at both deep camaraderie and a readiness to return to the fight.

PART THREE

EXPANSION

CHAPTER 12

SONG OF THE SLEDGEHAMMER

The Hayan Gas Plant in Syria looked like a scene out of Hell. A raging plume of black smoke and orange flames spewed upward from a damaged wellhead. More than half the plant had been destroyed early in the winter of 2017, when Islamic State fighters detonated a string of explosive charges beneath the plant's foundations, and parts of it were still burning uncontrollably.

Within weeks of their festive celebration with Putin in the Kremlin Grand Palace, the Wagner Group's top commanders were back on the front lines in Syria. They arrived in early 2017 to find the harsh desert landscape as unwelcoming as the last go-round and also experienced an irritating sense of déjà vu. For the second time in less than a year, Syrian Arab Army and militia forces loyal to the Assad regime had lost control of Palmyra. The objective for Wagner was the same as on the last deployment: retake the oil and gas fields around Palmyra from ISIS. But this time the stakes were higher, and the way ahead was more fraught.

From the outset of the civil war in Syria, control over the country's major oil and gas facilities emerged as one of the most critical strategic objectives for forces on all sides. The revenues generated from Syria's energy assets funded military operations, propped up the regime's finances, and kept essential services running. For Assad's government, regaining control over these resources was a matter of survival.

In the two decades leading up to the Arab Spring uprisings, family members of the Assad regime and close allies of the government's predominantly

Allawite elites controlled the government's crude-oil exports to Europe, which historically had been a primary market for Syria's particular grade of heavy sour crude oil. During that same time, Russian energy majors—most of which were either fully controlled by the state or counted Gazprom as a parent investor—came to dominate a hefty portion of Europe's energy sector.

Expert estimates placed Syria's prewar oil-production numbers around 385,000 barrels per day.[1] The Syrian Petroleum Company facilities generated about half of those oil flows. Although those levels represented only a fraction of the oil produced daily in neighboring Iraq, Syria's niche hold on a substantive portion of European imports was a highly prized source of guaranteed income for Damascus and an important cog in the globe-spanning machinery of Russia's energy trade.

Control of Syria's energy-production sites became even more crucial after Russia officially announced that it would lend military support to the Syrian Army in the fall of 2015. The Kremlin's calculus was simple: Syria's port of Tartus was not only home to Russia's single most strategic naval base in the Mediterranean; it was also a major energy-transit hub for the Middle East. As such, it was a pivotal plank in the foundation of Russia's strategy for maintaining a dominant position in world energy markets and fending off the pinch of sanctions.

The oil, gas, and mineral reserves near Palmyra were an important source of revenue for Assad's regime and a crucial source of energy for Syria's military as well as electricity for the country. About 80 percent of Syria's gas-production capacity was in the Homs-Palmyra region.[2] The forces that maintained a hold over a prize of that size were likely to win the war.

For Russia, maintaining the political status quo in Damascus was paramount: Syrian government control over energy infrastructure directly affected the financial interests of Russian industry giants like Gazprom and Stroytransgaz, the energy-engineering powerhouse tied to Putin's longtime associate Gennady Timchenko. For opposition forces and terrorist groups like ISIS, seizing these facilities was crucial—not just to cripple the Assad regime's revenue but also to fund their own operations and solidify control. Throughout much of 2016, ISIS forces made significant gains by targeting key installations in Homs, including the strategically vital Hayan Gas Plant.

Despite significant backing from Russia, the Syrian Arab Army and Russian-trained militias like the al-Nimr, or "Tiger" forces, struggled against relentless attacks from ISIS. Desperate, Assad's government turned to the

Kremlin for additional support. In late 2016 a deal was struck in Moscow between a Syrian delegation and Russia's energy minister, Alexander Novak. The Kremlin agreed to aid in the recovery and reconstruction of Syria's energy infrastructure. In return, the Syrian Petroleum Company granted Russian firms a stake in the Hayan block.

One of the first beneficiaries of this arrangement was Evro Polis Ltd., a St. Petersburg company linked to Oleg Erokhin, a former *spetsnaz* officer and a trusted member of Prigozhin's security team. By December 2016, the Syrian Petroleum Company guaranteed Evro Polis 25 percent of the revenues from the Hayan block's production in exchange for retaking these assets from ISIS.[3] In the interim, Russia's parliament had also laid the legal groundwork for the expansion of the Wagner Group's global remit in December 2016 with the passage of a new law that allowed Russian reservists to serve short stints of six to twelve months on counterterrorism missions.[4] The legislation and Syrian concessions granted to Prigozhin's Concord network would pave the way for a massive expansion of the Wagner Group's forces. Prigozhin's web of front companies stood to gain billions from the bargain. Within three years, Syria's government would grant two other Prigozhin-linked companies—Merkury and Velada—oil-exploration rights. However, the web of deals was not without complications.[5]

Winning back control of the Hayan block would require the Wagner Group to train up a whole new cadre of Syrian militia fighters, then cross a wide-open desert valley where they were highly vulnerable to enemy fire. They would then need to take control of the Hayan Gas Plant before rolling onward to another nearby gas-field installation called al-Shaer.

Located about 90 miles northwest of Palmyra, the al-Shaer gas plant and storage facilities sat astride part of the Jabal Shaer field in the Hayan block. With the capacity to produce an estimated 106 million cubic feet per day, the al-Shaer facility was one of the most significant energy-production sites in Syria. But parts of al-Shaer had also fallen victim to the vicissitudes of the war.

Utkin and Alexander Kuznetsov, the Wagner Group's leading tactical commander and head of the paramilitary's 1st Assault Detachment, plotted out a plan for a counteroffensive. Working alongside elements of the Syrian Arab Army (SAA), the newly formed Russian-backed 5th Assault Corps group of local militias, and a specially trained special-forces unit called the ISIS Hunters, Kuznetsov mapped out a plan that called for the amalgamated forces to first seize control of the surrounding heights overlooking the dust bowl of the Hayan block.[6]

Wagner forces fought for nearly three months to reach the outer edge of their first objective, the Hayan Gas Plant. As they picked their way toward the perimeter, ISIS met them with a fierce onslaught. When the dust settled, there were corpses all over the place, some belonging to Wagner and others to ISIS or Syrian regime forces. The counteroffensive was a success and imposed a high cost on ISIS. A leaked document prepared by Wagner staff for Utkin's nomination for four Orders of Courage detailed his leadership during the grueling assault on the Hayan oil field. It highlighted his "skillful management of ground forces and coordination of air strikes," reporting that Utkin's forces killed approximately 180 ISIS fighters and destroyed several tanks and trucks. The document praised Utkin for his strategy, which enabled the "capture of ISIS strongholds at commanding heights in the shortest possible time with minimal losses" and ultimately secured control of the Hayan oil field.[7] But the price Wagner paid was significant.

The list of Wagner's casualties would take days to compile. The dead were kept in cold storage for weeks, and in some cases months, before being discreetly shipped home to Russia. Prigozhin's logistics chief, Valery Chekalov, Andrey Troshev, and members of Wagner's administration team carefully recorded their identities, including their names, birth dates, and hometowns, and made note of whether their bravery had merited a death bonus for their families or whether a state medal for bravery should be posthumously issued.

Notes were added to each column of the copious spreadsheets about who served where and when. In the warren of riverside offices near the Neva that served as the administrative nerve center of Prigozhin's Concord Management and Consulting company, a small group of mostly female accountants and secretaries in the St. Petersburg "back office" processed the payments.

Spreadsheets labeled "200"—the Russian military's coded abbreviation for "killed in action"—contained the names of dozens of fallen soldiers along with their four-digit dog-tag "M-number." This was the sequential token that each Wagner fighter was given, along with a five-digit "B-number" that corresponded to an alias cover identity that appeared on each soldier's government-issued fake passport.[8] Further names appeared on separate sheets marked "300"—military code for the wounded.

Over time the casualties would mount and become increasingly difficult to hide. When Chekalov, a potbellied forty-year-old military veteran, officially signed on as Wagner's business manager–cum–quartermaster in May 2016, the Wagner Group's head count was about 2,300. A year later, as spring turned to summer at the paramilitary's new base of operations at the Hayan Gas Plant, Wagner's ranks had swelled to nearly twice that number, and its forces were divided into at least four separate detachments.[9]

Chekalov, a Vladivostok native who was born into a military family and was a graduate of the Gorky Higher Military School of Logistics, brought considerable experience to the job of overseeing the Wagner Group's supply chains. Also known by his call sign, "Rover," Chekalov had spent eleven years in the Kamchatka Territory in the 311th Special Forces Detachment for Underwater Sabotage Forces and Means, where he served on a naval patrol ship.[10] After leaving the army, Chekalov moved to St. Petersburg, where he became one of Prigozhin's most trusted business associates and the leading point man for oversight of the Concord network's defense ministry contracts, including one that provided canteen services to Russia's Black Sea Fleet in Sevastopol shortly before Moscow's seizure of Crimea.

The quartermaster job entailed tracking hundreds of millions of dollars' worth of monetary transactions, setting up front companies, inking contracts, arranging payroll, and managing procurement deals that involved the surreptitious movement of thousands of men and weapons into combat zones. In one memo on the Wagner Group's transport inventory, Chekalov tallied about 536 tanks, trucks, and armored vehicles that would eventually be transferred from Syria to Wagner's forward operating bases in Libya; that single shipment represented only a small slice of Wagner's total ground fleet at the time.[11] All of it had to be done covertly so that Russian forces could operate below the radar. It was a complex undertaking, given the exponential growth of Prigozhin's overseas business empire.

Prigozhin benefited handsomely from his careful cultivation of high-level contacts. In an open letter to Shoigu, Prigozhin later claimed that Concord had a long-standing relationship with the defense ministry dating back to 2006 and that part of the $1.7 billion earned from army catering contracts had been used to finance Wagner's operations.[12] This raised critical questions: Who was really funding Wagner? Who else profited from Prigozhin's wheeling and dealing?

According to one former Wagner insider, the defense ministry supplied tanks, combat helicopters, grenade launchers, armored vehicles, artillery, rifles, ammunition, and antiaircraft batteries. The average Wagner mercenary earned 250,000 rubles a month ($4,000), whereas a commander made about $5,000. With an estimated 2,000 to 2,500 Wagner fighters in Syria, monthly salaries added up to about $8 million. Add to that the cost of food, shelter, and fuel, and monthly costs ran up to the tens of millions. It was an unsustainable amount of spending. The math did not add up. Prigozhin was a clever businessman, but not that clever.[13]

Although Prigozhin's shell companies profited, it was Rosoboronexport that negotiated the military-cooperation agreements with Russia's foreign partners, not Prigozhin. Wagner's stake in Syria's energy wealth also grew in lockstep with that of Stroytransgaz.

The security agreement between Wagner's front company, Evro Polis, and the Syrian government was key to reviving a multibillion-dollar energy venture launched by Stroytransgaz just before the Arab Spring.[14] In 2009 Stroytransgaz secured the deal for the South Middle Area Gas Exploitation Project—the same year that Timchenko expanded his Luxembourg-based Volga Group, which held a controlling stake in Stroytransgaz.[15]

By then, Timchenko had already cofounded Gunvor, an oil- and commodities-trading powerhouse, with Swedish oilman Torbjorn Tornqvist. Through high-volume trades and strategic acquisitions, they transformed the company into a multibillion-dollar energy-trading juggernaut, ranking among the top three global commodity brokerages. Although sanctions eventually forced Timchenko to sell his stake, their partnership was highly profitable. Only Switzerland's Glencore and Singapore-based Trafigura could rival Gunvor's price-setting influence in the global commodities market.

It was that success and the company's significant foothold in Russia's energy-engineering market that gave Stroytransgaz and Novatek, a gas company in which Timchenko also held a stake, a sizable advantage when it came to negotiating energy-production deals. This was particularly true in the Middle East, especially in Syria, where Stroytransgaz held the dominant position in the market.

One of the most significant prewar deals that Timchenko cut was an agreement for Stroytransgaz (STG) to complete the reconstruction of the Kirkuk-Baniyas pipeline across northeastern Iraq and Syria and the Tuweinan gas facility, just sixty miles south of Raqqa, after it had been partially destroyed by US air strikes in 2003.[16] The South Middle Area Gas Exploitation Project in Homs offered STG a path to tap into expanded revenues generated by its investments in Hayan and tap into gas fields that were projected to generate billions of dollars. Along with the deal that gave STG a stake in Hayan, as well as the right to exploit Syria's abundant phosphate reserves and a major stake in offshore gas exploitation near the port of Tartus, Timchenko's firm stood to become the savior of Bashar al-Assad's flailing commodities-trading industry.

However, Russia's path to profitability in Syria was fraught with literal and figurative minefields. The presence of US special forces further complicated matters, increasing the need for secrecy and narrative control. Maintaining plausible deniability about the covert military units securing Russian investments became imperative. This made Prigozhin and the Wagner Group even more indispensable to the Kremlin.

But Wagner was not the only Russian paramilitary in the arena. A leading competitor on the scene was Redut, the PMC contingent formed by Konstantin Mirzyants and linked to the VDV 45th Guards Spetsnaz Reconnaissance Brigade. Mirzayants and his co-commander, Sergey "Salekh" Salivanov, a former *spetsnaz* trainer with the VDV 106th Airborne, were charged with securing several projects linked in press accounts and internal Wagner correspondence to Stroytransgaz affiliates in the region, including a multimillion-dollar phosphate-mining venture.[17]

In fact, a leaked internal memo circulated by Wagner back-office staff indicated that Redut coordinated its security work with Igor Kazak, a onetime STG official who headed a Russian company called STG Logistic and named General Yaroslav Y. Moskalik as a supervisory contact with the Main Directorate of Russia's General Staff.[18]

Officially, STG Logistic was owned by a Moscow-based company with murky origins, but a paper trail unearthed by *The Guardian* suggested that former Stroytransgaz employees had spun up STG Logistic in 2016.[19] Salivanov himself inadvertently confirmed many of these details in two separate secretly recorded conversations, which also revealed that Redut's operations were backed by the Russian insurance giant SOGAZ and that Russian billionaire Oleg Deripaska paid for Redut's military supplies.[20]

SOGAZ was also a top backer of several medical clinics that secretly provided care for wounded mercenaries. In fact, the clinic arrangement was one of the more visible links to the shadow command structure that the GRU had established to manage the operations of irregular Russian forces. The web of connections was, as always, elaborately tangled. But the shared interests of the stakeholders helped explain the GRU's role in backing the Wagner Group and why it was that Redut, Wagner, and Rusich fighters ended up sharing bunk space in an on-site barracks housed at the Hayan Gas Plant after it was wrested from the Islamic State's control in the spring of 2017.[21]

In fact, although Redut differed substantially from Wagner in size and character, there was considerable overlap between the Wagner and Redut missions in Syria. Redut and Wagner operated as separate entities, but it was not uncommon for Russian mercenaries to rotate on contract from one organization to the other. Internal Wagner Group correspondence indicated this was sometimes a source of tension between the two paramilitaries. Mercenaries who left Prigozhin to serve in Redut were immediately blacklisted and often unable to return. Redut, on the other hand, was quite happy to absorb former "Wagnerovtsy" fighters into its fold because Redut was considerably smaller.

All indications suggest that the competition between Redut and Wagner was just one of several irritants in Prigozhin's dealings with the Russian defense ministry and his Syrian counterparts. Mercenaries sent to battle in Palmyra complained bitterly that they had been issued substandard weapons and old ammunition. Prigozhin himself would several years later recount with bravado to the Russian press how after he had swooped into Syria in March 2017 just as Wagner forces seized control of the Hayan Gas Plant, the defense ministry refused to award medals to Wagner fighters for their role in the seizure of the oil and gas fields around Palmyra: "No, none of my fighters received a medal. Why? Out of jealousy. It often happens in our country that history is distorted in favor of individuals who do not take part in the creation of this history, but, taking advantage of their bureaucratic position, try to steal this history. I hope you understand who I'm talking about."[22]

Whatever his complaints, it was clear that Prigozhin was on a fast track to becoming one of the Russian defense ministry's most important contractors. In a letter addressed to Sergey Shoigu, Prigozhin detailed the extent to which Putin had come to rely on the Wagner Group and his Concord network of companies to help fashion the Russian military's deception operations in Syria and elsewhere. In effusive prose, Prigozhin explained how in 2015 he had received a "secret directive about the purchase on behalf of the ministry of defense" of no fewer than eight cargo ships. "Esteemed Sergey Kuzhugetovich!" the memo began. "In fulfilment of this directive 4 resident companies (RestaurantServis Plus LLC, Merkury LLC, ASP LLC, Glavnaya Liniya LLC) acquired 4 cargo ships."[23] All four of the ships had played an important role in the so-called Syrian Express, secretly moving weapons and equipment for energy production into the Russian-controlled port of Tartus. They were eventually placed under the control of the Russian Navy, he said. Therefore, Prigozhin argued, taxes related to the multimillion-dollar purchase of the ship should be substantially reduced.

More public proof of Prigozhin's outsized role in Russia's military intervention arrived one month after Wagner forces overtook ISIS forces at the al-Shaer gas facility in the late spring of 2017. In May, Putin's political nemesis, Alexey Navalny, published a damning report that detailed a Ponzi scheme involving fake loans to a dizzying array of shell companies under Prigozhin's control that led to the acquisition of some $3.2 billion worth of defense contracts through Russia's military-logistics arm, Voentorg.[24] The exposé shed light on how Prigozhin constantly shuffled the deck to disguise Wagner's true paymasters.

Corporate-registration records indicated that Oleg Erokhin had registered Evro Polis in 2016, only three years after his involvement in the Slavonic Corps fiasco. That same year, Utkin was briefly listed as general director of Prigozhin's Concord Management and Consulting Company, and Erokhin and Wagner's executive director, Andrey Troshev, registered a separate entity, the League for the Defense of the Interests of Veterans of Local Conflicts and Wars, in St. Petersburg. Known as "Liga" for short, the veterans' association was another central link in the chain of command that oversaw the Wagner Group's recruitment and retention operations. It played a substantial role in organizing the burials of Russian paramilitaries killed in action as well as ensuring that wounded were cared for and death benefits were paid.

The game of musical chairs confirmed what intelligence agencies in Washington had already long known. Prigozhin had popped up on the radar of the US Treasury's Office of Foreign Asset Control (OFAC) as early as 2014. But it was the series of investigative exposés published by *Novaya Gazeta* and *Fontanka* about Prigozhin's connections to Voentorg, and other evidence that came to the fore in 2015 and 2016, that finally tipped the scales in favor of more decisive action in Washington, according to Brian O'Toole, a former senior adviser at OFAC.

An expert in illicit finance whose pedigree included stints at the CIA and the global accounting firm Pricewaterhouse Cooper, O'Toole was one of the lead architects of the US and EU sanctions brought against Russia in the immediate aftermath of the Kremlin's annexation of Crimea. He remembered the December 2016 sanctions announcement as the moment when the US government started what would become a years-long game of whack-a-mole with Prigozhin.

Days after the Russian press published pictures of Putin posing alongside Dmitry Utkin and the Wagner Group's three other top commanders in December 2016, Treasury officials in Washington announced that the United States had placed Prigozhin on its sanctions list for the Wagner Group's involvement in Ukraine.[25] Sanctions against Utkin soon followed. The measures placed anyone connected to Prigozhin or the Wagner Group directly in the crosshairs of the US government.

On the day that Treasury went public with its announcement, an undated photo of Prigozhin and Putin together that looked to have been taken in the early 2000s began circulating in press accounts about the sanctions. An iconic portrait that could have easily been titled "The Chef Serves the New Tsar," the photo showed Prigozhin dressed in a crisp black suit, starched white shirt, and silver tie bending obsequiously toward Putin as he served him a dish at an elegantly set banquet table.

To O'Toole, it was obvious that Prigozhin had been working for years as a cutout for Putin and other Kremlin insiders.[26] But O'Toole was skeptical that sanctions against Prigozhin would do much to constrain the Wagner Group. He pointed to the long battle to capture Viktor Bout as a case in point.

Known as the "Merchant of Death," Bout, a polyglot who had served in the Soviet military as a translator, was a legend in Russia's underworld. Years before Prigozhin came along, Bout had a sixty-plane fleet that delivered weapons to most of Africa's major war zones. From 1999 to 2008, the year that Bout was detained in Thailand as the result of an FBI sting operation, he topped the agency's most-wanted list.

With billions of dollars in arms sales to countries under UN embargo, Bout was also, for a time, one of Russia's richest men until a US federal court in Manhattan convicted him in 2011 on charges of conspiracy to kill American citizens. He had sold shoulder-fired rocket launchers to FARC rebel forces in Colombia and Iranian-backed Hezbollah leaders, which led to the proliferation of hundreds of such weapons around the globe. At one point, Bout counted Libya's Muammar Qaddafi as a client, and he even quipped to a *New York Times* reporter that "maybe I should start an arms-trafficking university and teach a course on U.N. sanctions busting."[27]

Bout's example had indeed been quite instructive for those who followed in his footsteps after he was sentenced to twenty-five years in a US prison on four felony counts in 2011. The close timing of the FBI takedown of Bout and Prigozhin's rocket-like ascent starting in 2012 was probably a simple matter of chance. But the one thing they did have in common was that they relied on the same "Odessa Network" arms-smuggling connections that had served Russia's covert operators for years.[28]

"It's a mistake to assume that we can just wipe them out. You know Viktor Bout was designated for a very long time, and the only way we took him off the map was to go snag him in Thailand," O'Toole said. "That's essentially the model. You could pursue that model with Wagner. The only problem with that is you're essentially playing whack-a-mole. It's hard to get out in front of them. Sanctions are, in large part, reflexive."[29]

Treasury's delayed action against Prigozhin, O'Toole said, was as much a result of bureaucratic inertia as it was misplaced blind faith in the power of the West's "rules-based order" to win Russia over to the right side of history. "I think we just held on to this hope that Russia was going to become a more responsible global actor—especially during the time when Medvedev was in power—and holding out hope that Putin was going to disappear from power, which, you know, was always a fantasy. And doing that means you ignore problems, and you don't take things like Prigozhin seriously."[30] But soon it would become impossible to ignore the Wagner Group's operations in Syria.

IN LATE JUNE 2017, a gruesome video clip surfaced unexpectedly in the WhatsApp feed of a reporter at *al-Jessr Press*, a Syrian dissident news outlet.[31] The footage, set against a chaotic industrial landscape in the desert, showed masked men brutally severing a man's head with a large hunting knife and an entrenching spade. The scene was raw, violent, and chillingly matter-of-fact—another horrifying chapter in Syria's ongoing nightmare.

The clip was just one piece of a larger, grisly puzzle. It was one in a series ricocheting across the internet. Another segment had bounced from the Telegram social media app to dozens of obscure websites. One of the segments—a nearly two-minute-long video of several unidentified men brutally beating the same man with a sledgehammer—gained widespread attention after it had been posted on a military blog popular among combat veterans. This ignited a wave of horror and speculation about its origins. In the third segment, the victim's dismembered corpse was suspended upside down from a tall metal structure while two of the assailants doused the body with an accelerant and used an improvised torch to set it aflame. Someone off-camera speaking in Russian grumbled loudly in frustration: "Come on! The wind is blowing hard."

As the dismembered remains swung in the breeze, the letters "VDV 31" were faintly visible on the torso. Presumably, VDV 31 was a reference to the 31st Separate Guards Order of the Kutuzov 2nd Class Air Assault Brigade, a Russian paratrooper brigade based in Ulyanovsk. One of several airborne units that were reorganized during Russian efforts to reform its military after the Soviet collapse, the VDV 31st Brigade fought in the Second Chechen War and the Russo-Georgian War in 2008. During the start of the Ukraine crisis in 2014, elements of the brigade were in Crimea, and in the summer the brigade's units began washing up on the front lines in Donbas.

The fourth segment, though, was the revelation. In it, a pudgy-faced man with a kerchief over his face and dressed in a trademark paratrooper blue-and-white-striped *telnyashka* undershirt mugged cheerily for the camera after setting the legless, armless torso on fire. In the background, someone could be heard laughing and howling while the man in the dirty paratrooper uniform made a hand signal of bull horns—the universal skydiving sign for "check your arm position." "Jambo!" he giggled. "Yeah! This will be the sign for mercenaries."[32]

Another, longer segment showed several of the men laughing and kicking the victim's head around like a soccer ball. In the backdrop of the videos, pipes on the ground and a tall chain-link fence line indicated that the incident likely took place at an industrial plant. Satellite-imagery analysis and press accounts pinpointed the execution site as al-Shaer, the gas facility that was a substantial source of revenue for companies linked to Prigozhin and Stroytransgaz.

The victim was a thirty-four-year-old Syrian man named Muhammad Taha Ismail al-Abdullah. Al-Abdullah, who sometimes went by the nickname "Hamdi Bouta," grew up in a small village called Al-Khoraita, west of the Euphrates River, in the oil-rich governorate of Deir Ezzor. Syrian authorities had detained Bouta as he and several friends from his village crossed into Syria from Lebanon on the way back home to his village. Bouta was charged with deserting his duties as a reservist in the Syrian Army and was subsequently handed over to them.

Bouta's family discovered he had been taken to the al-Draij military camp near Damascus, where Iranian, Russian, and Hezbollah advisers trained the 4th and 5th Assault Corps—units composed largely of press-ganged prisoners like Bouta. According to relatives, Bouta managed to escape but wandered the desert until Wagner forces captured him again at the al-Shaer gas plant in April 2017. Although the story seemed far-fetched, VKontakte posts on soldier-of-fortune channels later confirmed it. "We picked up this fuck in late February or early March with his bare ass hanging out in the desert when we were sweeping retaken territory," one anonymous user wrote. "He said his unit retreated, and he fought back, shadowing our positions for weeks."[33]

The matter might have ended there but for the news coverage of the incident. Revelations about the identities of the perpetrators prompted internal-affairs investigators with Wagner's "Special Department" to open an investigation into the incident. The concern was not for the victim so much as it was for the fact that the videos had been shot on contraband cell phones and that media coverage of Bouta's on-camera murder had prompted inquiries from the Kremlin.

The perpetrators, it turned out, were fighters in the Wagner Group's 4th Assault Detachment. According to an internal memo produced by Wagner's Special Department, the organization's counterintelligence unit, the detachment's commander, "Bes," had ordered several of his men to make an example out of the victim. Under questioning by polygraph examiners, one of eight men implicated, Vladimir "Iceman" Kitaev, admitted to torturing and killing the Syrian captive but insisted that he had not filmed the execution.

Instead, the credit for that dismal act went to Stanislav Dychko, a former police officer from Stavropol who had joined up with Wagner in 2016. Dychko told investigators that he taped the grisly episode under direct orders from the detachment commander. Internal memos on the Special Department investigation revealed that two other Wagner fighters—Andrey "Stropa" Bakunovich and Vladislav "Wolf" Apostol—who were also involved shot additional portions of the video on mobile phones while Vladislav "Roger" Panchuk and Jahongir "Pamir" Mirazorov mercilessly attacked the victim.

Eventually, the video found its way onto the hard drive of another perpetrator from the detachment, Oleg "Kong" Kongin, who edited the video back at the Molkino training base in Russia, where it was then uploaded to Telegram. In all, polygraph examiners eventually collected confessions from eight Wagner fighters involved in Bouta's killing and the creation of the snuff film. But only one—a certain Mikhail Masharov—would be punished and fired for violating Wagner's strict prohibition on using social media.[34]

The sledgehammer video marked a pivotal turning point for the Wagner Group, taking it from an elusive war-zone myth to an international emblem of Russian influence. The clip's viral spread on VKontakte ignited a flood of memes and merchandise. In a surreal twist, perpetrators would go on to become icons in the virtual world as hundreds of Wagner's online fans swapped out their own profile photos for mugshots of the perpetrators snapped from stills of the torture video.

It was exposure that Prigozhin could ill afford. But true to form, he embraced the maxim "There's no such thing as bad publicity" and turned the buzz generated by the sledgehammer video into fuel, using the shock it caused to further entrench his image as Russia's untouchable power broker, thriving in the chaos he helped create.

With high stakes in Syria, Prigozhin grew increasingly aggressive in ensuring that the profits flowed. Wagner didn't just deploy fighters; it also flew in geologists, engineers, and fire-control experts to restore the Hayan block's damaged facilities. Meanwhile, political-marketing specialists and Arabic-speaking sociologists on Evro Polis's payroll flooded Facebook with pro-Russian and pro-Syrian propaganda. Leaked contracts showed that Wagner's operations at gas fields near Palmyra generated $162 million in revenue in just the second half of 2017. Total revenues for 2017 from Evro Polis's contract for the Hayan block, including services like oil and gas storage and gas condensates, amounted to approximately $301 million.[35] It was big business, and the Wagner Group would pay a heavy price to keep it going.

CHAPTER 13

CLASH AT CONOCO

The shooting began on a cold half-moon night in the Syrian desert on February 7, 2018. For hours, US Marines and Green Beret special forces and their Syrian rebel allies had been tracking the trouble that was moving their way. Hunkered in an observation post at the edge of a natural-gas plant, the US team of coalition forces watched warily as hundreds of Russian-backed pro-regime fighters crossed to the west bank of the Euphrates River. As the Americans assessed the situation, more and more spectral green figures appeared in their night-vision goggles. It looked as if the column of advancing fighters was about to punch through the arduously negotiated deconfliction line that was meant to separate Russian and American ground operations.

As night deepened, the US commandos also noticed a cluster of Russian-made military vehicles gathering at the outskirts of the small Syrian farming town of Khasham, about a mile from the gas plant. Toward 10 p.m., there was movement. A column of Russian-made armored vehicles growled to life in the darkness and rumbled forward. The Russian and pro-Assad forces moved in the direction of the gas plant—and toward the Americans. Then came a single rocket, next a fusillade of bullets, followed by the thunderous roar of artillery. At least thirty artillery rounds shook the ground around the gas plant. The shelling from Russian tanks at one point became so intense that the Americans were forced to dive for cover in makeshift foxholes from where they could safely return fire. One of the Green Berets called in their coordinates to a distant command base. US warplanes scrambled in response, countering the Russian assault with a blistering, hours-long aerial bombardment. It was the first time since Vietnam that the US military had directly fired on Russian forces.

About a thousand miles away in Kuwait, Colonel Dave Milner had been watching with growing alarm the grainy black-and-white drone feeds on the enormous computer screens in his windowless office at Camp Arifjan.[1] One of the biggest American forward military-logistics hubs in the world, the base was the nerve center of support for US special-forces tactical operations during the American-led counteroffensive against the Islamic State. Even before the shooting started, it was obvious to Milner, the chief US Army liaison officer during the Russian ground operations in Syria, that the columns were headed toward the gas plant. They appeared to be targeting the exact spot where American and Kurdish forces had established their temporary base of operations in northeast Syria.

The gas plant—locals still referred to it as the Conoco plant, after the American energy company that originally built it, even though Conoco had long since abandoned it—was an irresistible prize. Everyone knew that whoever could seize and hold Conoco would have leverage over Syria's economic and therefore existential future. The Conoco plant was modest by comparison with some of the oil and gas production facilities just across the border in Iraq. But as one of the few reliable sources of cooking gas in Syria—a vital source of black-market and war-economy income for all sides—it was a strategic asset for any force strong enough to secure it. Control of the giant bulbous storage tanks and warren of pipes at the Conoco gas plant had switched hands among various rebel and jihadist groups at least half a dozen times since the start of the uprising against Assad.

After the US-backed Syrian Democratic Forces (SDF) had taken control of the Conoco plant with help from American special forces, the Assad regime was dead set on taking it back. Russia, for its own geopolitical reasons and as the largest foreign investor in Syria's prewar fossil-fuel industry, was just as determined to see and help that happen. The Conoco plant was thus one of the hottest of flashpoints on the Syrian front lines. In fact, only four months earlier, on September 10, 2017, a Russian air and artillery assault on the eastern side of the Euphrates, near the Conoco plant, had wounded ten SDF soldiers who had been fighting alongside US troops. It was exactly the kind of accident that the Russia-US Deconfliction Cell that Milner worked for was set up to prevent, yet the arrangement had still failed.

American generals at the Pentagon and at US Central Command headquarters in Tampa had set up the hotline with the Russians after several near-miss collisions between American and Russian allied forces. The aim was to prevent a tactical blunder from escalating into an all-out shooting war on the ground. As the United States ramped up its plans for the assault on the Islamic State, US Central Command established the Deconfliction Cell in Kuwait as a complement to an ongoing dialogue between Russian and American forces on air sorties that had been launched in nearby Qatar, set up after Turkish F-16 jets shot down a Russian SU-24 supersonic attack craft over Latakia as it edged into Turkish airspace in late November 2015.

As he watched the blurry images beamed from a drone over the Conoco plant that winter night, Milner was sure he was witnessing yet another failure of the system that the United States and Russia had so arduously worked to put in place to prevent the possibility of a clash and an escalation of hostilities that could lead to World War III. It was the second time that Wagner Group fighters had pushed Syrian contingents to capture the Conoco gas plant for Assad's regime. As his small Deconfliction Cell team worked the phones nonstop, trying to get a clearer picture of the assault on the Conoco plant, the contingent of forces on the east side of the Euphrates snaked its way toward the perimeter of the plant.

Nearby American forces on the ground confirmed for Milner what he already suspected: they had picked up Russian chatter on the radio, a sure sign that Russians were leading the assault. Milner had already been on the phone for several hours with Russian officers at the air base near the Syrian port city of Latakia, which served as command headquarters for Russian operations in Syria. Years into Syria's civil war, every country with pieces on the chessboard knew each player's position. The Russians knew where the Americans were. The Americans knew where the Russians were. However, the creeping assault on the Conoco plant was different. Was this an intentional Russian assault on an American-held position or another Russian blunder?

In the weeks before, America's Syrian allies had fought their way south from Raqqa, where they had routed thousands of Islamic State fighters in Iraq and Syria. Russian and pro-Assad regime units on the west bank of the Euphrates had pushed Islamic State fighters out along the opposite side all along the way. In fact, the Russian contingent that fought that night had begun moving eastward from Aleppo after near misses with the Americans there.

The prospect of a miscalculation in Syria was top of mind in Washington and Moscow. The Syrian war had entered a new phase. With help from the Russians, Assad's forces succeeded in retaking the country's strategic oil and gas infrastructure near Palmyra. Now they were pressing north and east to seize control of oil and gas fields on the border with Iraq. Russia's proxy war with the United States in Syria and the military campaign against the Islamic State had metastasized fast.

Back in Kuwait, drone footage on the screen that Milner was watching confirmed his suspicions that the Russians were making a grab for the Syrian gas plant. It made good strategic sense, an asset that the Kremlin could pawn to keep itself liquid and its sovereign wealth accounts stable at a time when the Russian economy had been rocked by sanctions. But even as his team of Russian-speaking US soldiers fielded a flurry of calls about the Russian-led assault on the Conoco plant, Milner began to sense there was something off about the whole scenario. After his third or fourth call to his Russian counterpart at the Kheimim Airbase in western Syria, Colonel Alexander Zorin, Milner began to suspect that Zorin knew it as well.

Zorin was a fixture of Milner's daily routine in Kuwait. Every morning, after meeting with his own team in Camp Arifjan to review the positions of US special-forces movements and the situation on the ground in Syria, Milner would talk by phone or video conference with Zorin and his team of Russian officers. Zorin was sober, serious, and unusually athletic for a Russian officer of his age, and his American counterparts widely assumed that he had ties to the GRU. None of the Americans were able to confirm much about Zorin's background beyond the fact that he had served as Russia's military attaché to Japan just before being tapped for the Syria job. If not always a straight shooter, Zorin at least took seriously the job of preventing skirmishes between Russian and American allied forces on the ground in Syria from escalating into a major conflagration.[2]

On the line with Milner, however, Zorin repeatedly insisted that he knew nothing about the movement of Russian troops anywhere near the Conoco plant. Even as the first rounds of US artillery fire ripped above a column of attackers—soldiers who, Milner had presumed, were Zorin's—the Russian officer continued to deny any knowledge of what was going on near the gas plant. But hours into the counterattack, Zorin suddenly switched direction and said that the Russians who were reportedly part of the operation were not actually under his command.

"We don't know who that is," he said coyly. Milner's jaw dropped. "If they're not yours," he replied, "then who in the hell are they, and what are they doing on our side of the river?"[3] He passed up the US military chain Zorin's message that the forces advancing toward Conoco were not under official Russian command, and soon word came back from the Joint Chiefs of Staff at the Pentagon: permission granted to annihilate them.

It is likely that the nighttime assault on the Conoco plant was anticipated by the Russian military command in Latakia. Although Milner thought he detected a bit of genuine confusion when he put in his first call to Zorin, it was obvious the Russians had a fairly good idea of who was leading the assault, despite their denials. It was classic Kremlin obfuscation, the kind of stonewalling that Milner, a West Point graduate who was fluent in Russian, had grown accustomed to. After Milner moved on from Camp Arifjan to his next posting as America's defense attaché in Moscow, and long after ISIS had been flushed out of Syria, he would remember his frustration that night: "The Russians professed for a couple hours not to know anything about it, then they came back and Zorin says, 'Looks like you might have some terrorists in your area.' They knew that we knew but they just kept on . . . saying, 'We don't know anything about it but if there are any messages you'd like us to pass on, we will.' It was unbelievable."[4]

Even before the Wagner Group set out to cross the Euphrates River that night, Marat Gabidullin had a sense of foreboding. Gabidullin, a leather-faced VDV Airborne *spetsnaz* veteran who had joined up with the paramilitary during the early days of the Donbas campaign, had lost faith in the judgment of Andrey Troshev, the Wagner Group's executive director for operations and the chief liaison to Russia's command center in Latakia. Troshev was a drunk who was out of step with what was needed on the ground in Syria. Mistrust had become kind of a watchword among Wagner's men after the heavy losses sustained during the heated clashes over control of the gas fields near Palmyra. The Syrians assigned to the Russians to train were, in Gabidullin's words, unreliable, lazy, and ill-qualified for combat.[5] But it was his job to train them to survive.

Gabidullin had the surly, serious bearing of a drill sergeant, and he was known around Wagner's barracks at the Hayan Gas Plant as "Ded" or "Gramps." He had joined the Wagner Group via a route familiar to most mercenary commanders: he graduated from the elite Ryazan Airborne Higher Command Military Academy as a lieutenant in the late 1980s, where he first met Konstantin Mirzayants, whom he remembered as an ambitious if charmless hustler with an entrepreneurial streak. After the academy, Gabidullin took command of a paratrooper unit in Chisinau, Moldova. There he also fell in love, married, and had a daughter.

But the settled life never really suited his tastes. Just before receiving a desk job in military intelligence in 1993, he resigned because of the monotony of the mission. Although he would never openly admit it, Gabidullin had a pedigree similar to that of a man who had spent considerable time around officers in predecessor units of the VDV 45th Guards Spetsnaz Reconnaissance Brigade. He seemed to know or be familiar with most of the key leaders of the Union of Paratroopers, and he had met Pavel Popovskikh, the legendary VDV commander, a few times. But that was "ancient history," Gabidullin said. Unable to rejoin the service because of new rules, Gabidullin went on to work with a local mafia boss, for which he was eventually arrested and imprisoned in Krasnoyarsk for three years. For several years afterward he struggled with severe depression and alcoholism, then sobered up and went to work for a local private-security service in Russia. But there he got into trouble again and argued with his boss, which put him directly in the crosshairs of the police. He wrote that he had trouble adjusting to civilian life and was unable to hold a job, a source of friction with his wife, Natasha.

There are many inconsistencies in Gabidullin's stories, and because Prigozhin personally edited Gabidullin's first set of published memoirs, it was hard to separate fact from convenient fiction. But one constant that Gabidullin's narrative shared with other, more senior Wagner fighters who would come forward to publicly tell their version of their encounters with Yevgeny Prigozhin and Dmitry Utkin was the overlap in ties among the officers Gabidullin came up through the ranks with in the VDV and the mercenaries he fought alongside while he was with the Wagner Group in Ukraine and Syria. The time that Gabidullin spent working for Redut after leaving Wagner was another common factor. He explained that one reason for this was that contingents under the command of Mirzayants and those under Prigozhin's control in the Wagner Group drew from the same small pool of *spetsnaz* officers who had seen combat in Central Asia and the Caucasus, and that once hired, they shared the same or similar missions. They often, as a result, also wound up sharing the same barracks or bunk space.

Gabidullin's retelling of what happened in the lead-up to the havoc at the Conoco plant agreed in many respects with accounts that others would share in the weeks and months that followed. He remembered how morale had soured after Wagner's victory at Hayan when word of what happened at al-Shaer spread in the summer of 2017 and the sledgehammer snuff film began circulating. Although Prigozhin conducted a number of field visits to Syria during this period, he rarely interacted with the rank and file, and he was referred to only as "the First." "Many mercenaries had never seen his face. For a long time, Prigozhin remained a ghostly figure, disembodied but endowed with the power to govern their existence," Gabidullin wrote.[6]

Corruption was rampant within the Wagner Group, and a lack of discipline was rife in the field. Those in charge seemed to strive only to one-up each other in their cruelty to their subordinates and during encounters with enemy captives. Valery Chekalov, the Wagner Group's quartermaster, was particularly notorious for the abuse he heaped on back-office staffers in St. Petersburg and low-ranking fighters in the field. When Gabidullin went to work for several months as a strategic planner and administrator in the Concord network's main offices in St. Petersburg, he saw up close how Chekalov seemed to strike fear in those around him: "To be honest, I was not at all impressed by him. First of all, he seemed to copy diligently the manner of his boss and the way he communicated with people. There was a lot of rudeness; he was unrestrained in cursing, and he was tough on his subordinates. Even the presence of women did not seem to stop him from cursing."[7]

Poor morale, backbiting, and mistrust—even Dmitry Utkin seemed cowed by it. Gabidullin recalled that in late January 2018, when talk of a big operation in Deir Ezzor began to bubble up at Wagner's tactical headquarters in conversations among Utkin, Troshev, and other Wagner commanders, Utkin often seemed to wear a skeptical expression, but he never openly challenged the idea. One reason for this could have been that the pressure to mount the assault on American positions at the Conoco plant originated in Moscow. Intercepted recordings of Prigozhin's conversations with Syria's minister of presidential affairs, Mansour Fadlallah Azzam, suggested that he had received a green light from an unidentified high-ranking Russian government official to move forward with the offensive, and Prigozhin apparently promised to deliver a "good surprise" to Assad by capturing the Conoco plant.[8]

The plan of attack was thoroughly flawed. Gabidullin recalled that Utkin looked on impassively and did not say much when Davor "Wolf" Savicic, a Serbian mercenary accused of committing war crimes in the Balkans and of instigating the sledgehammer snuff film video, mapped out the operation.[9] Wagner's 5th and 2nd Assault Detachments and a group of Syrian militiamen fighting under the banner of the Wagner-trained ISIS Hunters were tasked with leading a combined arms assault. Savicic, according to Gabidullin, insisted that tribal leaders in the area who were more loyal to Assad would rise up and bolster the attack. Plus, Savicic said, if the plan was successful, it would also be payback against the Syrian Defense Force (SDF) and the Americans for shelling Russian positions during a skirmish that had resulted in the death of a VDV Airborne general.[10] When Viktor Rekhman, aka "Dnepr," the regional deputy chief of staff for Russian mercenary operations, and Andrey Troshev showed enthusiasm for the plan, Utkin shrugged his shoulders, signaling that he would not get in the way of letting it move forward. "All of this made me uncomfortable," Gabidullin would recall in his own written account of what happened. "But when I heard that my men would have to attack the Kurdish outposts, I became outright fearful for my life."[11]

The plan assumed—mistakenly, it turned out—that the ISIS Hunters could mount a frontal attack on SDF forward positions near the Conoco plant and that US special forces would not intervene. The assumption was based on the fact that the Americans had not directly retaliated when, a few months earlier, in the fall of 2017, Russian mercenaries and their Syrian and Afghan counterparts crossed the Euphrates and took up positions in what was technically demarcated as the American zone. Eager to both prove his worth and secure a prize that could potentially result in a huge windfall of profits for Evro Polis and its chief corporate partner, Stroytransgaz, Prigozhin waved away any reservations. "Out of his excessive self-confidence, he decided that the Americans would not interfere and that we would quickly drive the Kurds out of there," Gabidullin said.[12]

Prigozhin's assurances from General Sergey Surovikin, Russia's lead commander in Syria, may have contributed to his overconfidence. Surovikin, a Novosibirsk native, had begun his military career in the Soviet Army. A combination of honors and scandals marked his ascent up the ladder, including an incident early in his career in 1991 involving the killing of protesters during the coup attempt that ultimately propelled Boris Yeltsin to the presidency of Russia. A graduate of the prestigious Frunze Military Academy, Surovikin had completed combat tours in Tajikistan and Chechnya before serving in Russia's Central Military District.

Trouble followed him all along the way, with accusations of human-rights violations lodged against units under his command and the suicide of a subordinate whom Surovikin had allegedly treated harshly. Surovikin's relative success with helping to establish the first military-police unit for the armed forces seemed to give a boost to his otherwise rocky career. Soon after Valery Gerasimov appointed Surovikin as chief of operations in Syria in 2017, he was also given command of Russia's Aerospace Forces, a position that earned him the nickname "General Armageddon" because of the unrelenting hellfire that Russian forces rained down from above on Assad's adversaries. Surovikin was, in fact, widely credited with the successful seizure of phosphate and gas fields near Palmyra that would generate millions of dollars for companies linked to both Prigozhin and Gennady Timchenko.[13]

Surovikin was one of forty-two high-ranking military and government officials who were accorded honorary membership in the Wagner Group and given a military-identification number that marked them as VIPs. Two others—General Rustam U. Muradov and General Andrey N. Serdyukov—also appeared on the Wagner VIP list. A native of Dagestan, Muradov had served from 2015 to 2017 as Russia's liaison to the joint coordinating body for the ceasefire in Donbas, where he likely would have first encountered Wagner forces, and Muradov was sent to Syria in 2017 as a military adviser. His time there earned him Russia's highest military award, which Putin bestowed on him at a Kremlin awards ceremony.[14] Serdyukov had also played a decisive role in setting Wagner's trajectory, directing troop movements to Crimea in 2014 from his perch as deputy chief of staff for the Southern Military District in Rostov.[15]

The relationships provided mutual benefits. Wagner staff regularly exchanged sensitive battlefield intelligence with their counterparts in Russia's conventional forces, and vice versa. Some of what was shared was accidentally discovered in June 2017, when an inebriated Andrey Troshev was found passed out on the streets of St. Petersburg with a briefcase full of tactical maps and packets of cash.[16] It would have been surprising if Prigozhin had not consulted first with Surovikin and his primary backers before the Wagner assault on the Conoco plant.

Indeed, Prigozhin later claimed that he had discussed the operation in advance with Russia's chief of staff, Valery Gerasimov, just a few days before the offensive in early February.[17] Commanders at the Kheimim Airbase had promised to provide two Su-35 fighter jets to patrol the skies above Khasham and to ready air-defense batteries ahead of the assault. It was those assurances, Prigozhin said, and the green light from Russian high command that convinced him to proceed with the operation, believing they had the full backing of Moscow's military leadership for what would be one of Wagner's most ambitious strikes in Syria.

Down on the ground, a few hundred meters from the Deir Ezzor gas plant's perimeter, Vladislav Apostol, one of several Wagner Group fighters caught up in the pandemonium, found himself ducking for cover as American Hellfire missiles rained down from above. Apostol and a squad of Syrian and Russian fighters armed with AK-47s, sniper rifles, and rocket launchers had rumbled forward in big pickups across the dark desert landscape. Up until that moment, Apostol's path to Syria had followed a trajectory that mirrored that of quite a few others in the Wagner Group. He grew up scrappy in a single-parent household in Moldova and a Russian border town near Ukraine, and like many others in the Wagner cohort, he was a *Suvorovtsy*, an alumnus of Russia's state-run military boarding schools for boys.[18]

Beyond that, not much is known about Apostol's brief foray into mercenary operations in Donbas during the summer of 2014, but he had served for a time as an airborne paratrooper in the 24th Brigade Detachment of the GRU before his path somehow wound its way from Ukrainian coal country in Donbas to the oil- and gas-rich province of Homs in central Syria, where he, like his commander, was caught on camera beating Hamdi Bouta bloody with a sledgehammer at the al-Shaer plant.

By the time that Apostol arrived in Deir Ezzor at the edge of the Conoco plant that night, he had already been in Syria fighting for the Wagner Group for at least a year. For a while, just a handful of people—mostly Apostol's family—even knew that he had secretly gone to fight in Syria. That changed after an American AC-130 gunship lit up Apostol's position and incinerated everything on the ground around him.

Gabidullin recalled that he barely had time to register what was happening. He and his lightly armed platoon of ISIS Hunters had been sheltering in an abandoned building waiting for the go signal when orders suddenly came from the Wagner command to charge straight into the line of fire. The Americans continued to pound the ground from above, destroying in the process a tank near where Gabidullin stood.[19] Fires from the artillery strikes blazed high all around them. "Fall back! Fall back!" came the cry. Those left standing beat a retreat away from the Conoco plant, back toward the river. The barrage continued for hours as the night sky turned pale, mowing down dozens of Russians and their Syrian allies. It was a total rout of the Wagner Group.

At sunrise the next morning after the battle near the Conoco gas plant, the extent of the damage became horrendously apparent. The US counterstrike on the Wagner Group and forces supporting the Assad regime had left hundreds of bodies lying around in the rubble, Apostol's among them. Before the bodies were catalogued and moved, American intelligence officers carefully picked through the bonanza of charred cell phones, laptops, maps, notebooks, and debris for sifting and collating later. It was a devastating blow on multiple levels, one that marked a dangerous escalation of force between Russia and the United States and delivered unprecedented insights into how Wagner worked.

In the aftermath, the clash at Conoco emerged as a battle of perceptions as much as it was a skirmish over territorial control. How many combatants on the ground were ultimately killed that February night, and their names and nationalities, instantly became a matter of dispute. The Kremlin denied any knowledge of the battle at first. But the internet told a different story.

Igor Girkin claimed in a Twitter post that as many as six hundred might have been killed. Media reports in the immediate aftermath estimated the number at three hundred. The real casualty figure would come closer to two hundred killed in action that night, but the number of wounded was unknown. The one other question that remained unanswered was why Surovikin or someone else on the ground with more authority in Syria hadn't ordered in Russian air support to protect the Wagner Group. If the mercenaries were not fighting on behalf of Russia's interests or under direct military control, then who exactly was in charge?

Online clubs popular with Russian mercenaries, commando wannabes, and military veterans on the popular Russian social media platform VKontakte buzzed with rumors that Sergey Shoigu had ordered Russian commanders on the ground to step back from intervening to save the Wagner Group. There were rumors that Dmitry Utkin himself might have been killed, suggesting that American forces had either purposefully or accidentally decapitated the Wagner Group.

A showdown between Prigozhin and Sergey Shoigu at a Kremlin function in Moscow after the incident seemed to corroborate the allegations that bad blood between Prigozhin and the defense minister had gotten out of hand. When Prigozhin confronted Shoigu about the military's failure to provide air cover during the Conoco offensive, the defense minister gave him the cold shoulder. "You wanted to play the hero?" Shoigu sniffed. "We did. All the heroes are in this room."[20]

Gabidullin, who was caught up in the chaotic retreat and sustained a leg wound, said the hours-long battle of Khasham was nothing short of a massacre. "The Russian army abandoned us. The Syrians did not support us either,"

Gabidullin wrote in his second memoir. "Conclusion: we fought for the wrong people." Disillusioned and shattered by the experience, Gabidullin said he quit Wagner not long afterward and took up a new job working as a mercenary for Mirzayants in Redut.[21] This was to be the first of many significant defections that would progressively tear down the carefully constructed walls of secrecy that Prigozhin and other Kremlin insiders had worked to erect around the Wagner Group's clandestine role in Russia's grand strategy.

Often, though, it was Russian soldiers of fortune themselves who gave away the kinds of details that would make it possible to pin down their whereabouts and who exactly was doing what, where, and when. Three weeks before the battle, a trio of VKontakte members started a new user group called "The PMC Wagner Group–Military Review." The acronym was short for "private-military company," and the profile page initially carried a photo of a makeshift burial marker somewhere in Syria.

A few days after the Kremlin issued the first of many denials about what happened at the Conoco plant and less than one month into the VKontakte group's existence, a February 11, 2018, post attracted 183 comments. Many commenters claimed to have direct ties to the Wagner Group. "I have an acquaintance with the PMC in Syria," wrote one user. "Second tour. 5th assault detachment. There is no news about deaths." A user named Ivan Mezentsev posted two audio recordings of unidentified male speakers describing the rout of Wagner forces. "The 5th were all wiped out," said one. "The guys didn't stand a chance."[22] The post instantly went viral.

The shock factor of the clash at Conoco rippled for days on VKontakte. Right after the air strike, another anonymous Wagner fan uploaded a post headed with three words: "Who served where?" The post appeared alongside a photo of an iconic metal statue of a Russian "volunteer" soldier shielding a small child that had been erected in the center of the Hayan Gas Plant after the Wagner Group retook Palmyra. It was a calling card of sorts, a wink and a nod to anyone who had fought in Syria on contract for Prigozhin's outfit. "Looking for co-workers?" the post continued. "Tell us where you served—so it will be easier for your comrades to find like-minded people among this thread of discussions." Responses from more than a hundred users appeared within a few hours, and hundreds more would post replies in the weeks that followed.

Several asked where they could sign up to fight as mercenaries. Other users directed them to call a number in St. Petersburg or travel to the Wagner Group base in the Russian garrison town of Molkino—across from the GRU's 10th

Brigade headquarters. Dozens more simply offered up the names or identification numbers for their current or former military units, the vast majority listing special-forces detachments in Russia's VDV Airborne Assault forces, the counterterrorism wings of the MVD and the FSB, or the GRU. Users named detachments that disproportionately represented motor-rifle brigades composed of the most highly trained scout reconnaissance rangers, snipers, artillery specialists, and air-defense troops.

The cluster of social media postings provided an X-ray snapshot of the Wagner Group's recruitment pool. The kinds of men who raised their hands proudly even after the disaster at Conoco were no ordinary volunteers. Most were hard-core lifers, trained in elite units for offensive operations. Dozens who responded to the post appeared to be at the very heart of the group of pro-Russian Donbas combatants that coalesced on the battlefield as the first Minsk Protocol ceasefire agreement between Russia and Ukraine collapsed in January 2015. Many said that they had fought in pro-Russian separatist units led by Donbas-based commanders who at the time strongly objected to Moscow's attempts to strike a bargain with Kyiv.

Their online profiles marked many as teetotaling, hard-right Orthodox Christian monarchists. A significant number were online followers of the Russian Imperial Movement (RIM), the St. Petersburg–based antiglobalist, white-supremacist, ultranationalist group that had trained hundreds of Russian teens for the war in Donbas via camps run by the movement's paramilitary wing, the Imperial Legion. The movement's leaders—Denis Gariev, Stanilav Vorobyev, and Nikolay Truschhalov—cultivated ties with high-flying members of the Union of Paratroopers who had supported the 1993 coup against Yeltsin, and Western intelligence agencies suspected that RIM had built up a quiet cadre of Russian officers who were sympathetic to the movement's monarchist cause. There was also considerable overlap between diehard followers of RIM and Rusich, the neo-fascist ultranationalist paramilitary backed in Donbas by Alexander Borodai.

All three—the Wagner Group, RIM, and Rusich—had established substantive followings on VKontakte. But after the Conoco clash, the Wagner Group's online subscriber base grew exponentially, from a few thousand to tens of thousands.[23] It was almost as if coverage of the high casualty counts in Syria had acted as an advertisement. The more media reporting there was about the Wagner Group and Prigozhin's exploits—good, bad, or ugly—the more online interest the paramilitary generated.

What was even more notable was how big the Wagner Group's fan base outside of Russia and Ukraine became after the Conoco incident. Thousands indicated that they resided in Germany and the United States, including a small number who said they served with units in America's armed forces. Within just a couple of years, the Wagner Group's online following on VKontakte would balloon even more, with subscribers reaching well into the hundreds of thousands. US special forces may have stopped the Wagner Group in its tracks in Syria, but the buzz generated by the deadly showdown in Syria instantly catapulted the Wagner Group into the virtual stratosphere.

In the immediate aftermath of the battle of Khasham, debates swirled in the international press about the causes and implications of the clash between Wagner and American forces. But what mattered to the Pentagon was that after more than a year of grappling with soldiers that the Kremlin refused to acknowledge, US forces had decisively altered the narrative surrounding Putin's so-called hybrid ghost warriors in Syria. The Pentagon, which had often taken a more cautious approach under both the Obama and Trump administrations, was now trying to assert more control over the unfolding story. The Dunford-Gerasimov line had previously contained risks of miscalculation between Russian and US forces, but after the Wagner assault, the Pentagon seemed to signal this to Moscow: cross the line again, and the response will be overwhelming and unambiguous.

After his stint with the KGB in East Germany, Vladimir Putin (*right*) returned home to St. Petersburg in 1990, where he served as deputy mayor under Anatoly Sobchak. Pictured here together in the summer of 1994, Sobchak and Putin were regulars at Yevgeny Prigozhin's upscale eatery, the Old Customs House. (AP Photo/Dmitry Lovetsky, file)

In a 2006 photo, Russian president Vladimir Putin (*left*) and US president George W. Bush attend a G8 working dinner in St. Petersburg as Yevgeny Prigozhin hovers in the background (*right*). Bush would later express shock on learning that the man who had mounted a violent mutiny against Putin had served him food, saying "All I know is I survived." (Sergei Zhukov, Sputnik, Kremlin Pool Photo via AP, file)

President Vladimir Putin (*left*) and Defense Minister Anatoly Serdyukov walk in front of the Czar Cannon in the Kremlin in 2007. Serdyukov's "New Look" reforms opened the way for Yevgeny Prigozhin to become the defense ministry's leading contractor in 2010 and resulted in a multimillion-dollar scandal that led to Serdyukov's ouster. (AP Photo/RIA-Novosti, Presidential Press Service, Mikhail Klimentyev)

In this photo taken in September 2010, Yevgeny Prigozhin (*second right*) shows Vladimir Putin around his Concord Catering factory near St. Petersburg, which produced school lunches. Prigozhin went on to open another factory, subsidized with tens of millions in preferential government loans, that produced meals for the Russian military. (Alexei Druzhinin, Sputnik, Kremlin photo via AP, File)

In this iconic 2011 photo, Yevgeny Prigozhin (*left*) serves Prime Minister Vladimir Putin during dinner at Prigozhin's restaurant outside Moscow. (AP Photo/ Misha Japaridze, Pool, File)

Alexander Borodai (*center*), prime minister of the self-proclaimed "Donetsk People's Republic," and Igor "Strelkov" Girkin (*left*), defense minister of the breakaway region, listen during a news conference in Donetsk, Ukraine, on July 12, 2014. The photo was taken shortly before forces under Girkin's command shot down Malaysian Airlines flight MH-17, killing all 298 civilians on board. (Photo/Max Vetrov)

President Vladimir Putin (*center*), escorted by Defense Minister Sergei Shoigu (*right*) and Chief of General Staff Valery Gerasimov after attending a defense ministry meeting in Moscow in December 2021. In May 2024, about a year after the Wagner Group mutiny, Shoigu resigned his post amid a weeping Kremlin corruption probe and purge of the defense ministry. (Mikhail Metzel, Sputnik, Kremlin Pool Photo via AP, File)

Russian president Vladimir Putin (*right*) talks to Sudanese president Omar al-Bashir during their meeting in Russia's Black Sea resort of Sochi in November 2017. The talks produced a cooperation agreement that granted Yevgeny Prigozhin's company M-Invest gold-mining concessions in Sudan in exchange for Wagner Group protection. (Mikhail Klimentyev, Kremlin Pool Photo via AP)

Miners in the Ndassima gold mine, 40 miles north of Bambari in the eastern part of the Central African Republic. The mine, originally owned by Canadian mining company Axmin, had an estimated value of $1 billion to $2.8 billion. Wagner Group forces seized control of it after establishing a nearby base of operations. In early 2020 the government transferred Axmin's mining permits to Yevgeny Prigozhin's front company, Midas Resources. (Photo by Thierry Bresilion/ Anadolu Agency/Getty Images)

Flowers laid near photos of the three Russian journalists killed in the Central African Republic in July 2018 while making a documentary on the Wagner Group: Orkhan Dzhemal (*right*), Kirill Radchenko (*center*), and Alexander Rastorguyev (*left*). (Ekaterina Chesnokova/Sputnik via AP)

Russian president Vladimir Putin (*left*) and president of the Central African Republic Faustin-Archange Touadéra pose in October 2019. (Mikhail Metzel, Sputnik, Kremlin Pool Photo via AP)

A tank driven by Wagner Group fighters in Rostov-on-Don after Yevgeny Prigozhin agreed to halt his so-called March for Justice on Moscow late in the evening of June 24, 2023. (Sergey Pivovarov/Sputnik via AP)

A worker removes an advertising banner for the Wagner Group in Volgograd, Russia. After Wagner troops deployed to the front in Ukraine in early March 2022, Prigozhin's companies plastered the country with recruitment billboards. Russian authorities ordered the banners taken down after Putin accused Prigozhin of treason on national television as the June 2023 mutiny unfolded. (Kirill Braga/Sputnik via AP)

After the mutiny, Prigozhin kept up a frenetic travel schedule, in a bid to salvage his business empire. In this photo, one of the last taken before he was killed in an August 23, 2023, plane crash, Prigozhin poses with an assault rifle in an unspecified location believed to be Mali. In footage shared on Telegram, Prigozhin said that the Wagner Group had made Russia "even greater" on all continents, including Africa. (Photo by Wagner Telegram Account/Anadolu Agency via Getty Images)

A portrait of Dmitry "Wagner" Utkin, the titular head of the paramilitary Wagner Group, at a makeshift memorial in Novosibirsk in 2023. When the news broke that Utkin had been killed in a plane crash along with Yevgeny Prigozhin and eight others, mourners erected impromptu memorials. A decorated officer in the elite VDV Airborne forces before forming the Wagner Group, Utkin was buried with full military honors. (Photo by Vladimir Nikolayev/AFP via Getty Images)

Former Wagner Group members who joined an artillery unit of the Akhmat special forces prepare a mortar before firing at a training ground in the course of Russia's military operation in Ukraine. After Prigozhin's rebellion, the defense ministry placed Wagner forces under its direct control, and thousands joined under new contracts with newly created units, including the Africa Corps and Akhmat Battalion. (Stanislav Krasilnikov/Sputnik via AP)

Even Prigozhin's funeral was a covert affair. Fearing that the spectacle would draw crowds of mourners, Russian authorities barred the press and the public from entering the grounds of the Porokhovskoye Cemetery in St. Petersburg, where he was buried between his father and stepfather. Roughly a year after Prigozhin's rebellion, small crowds showed up to his gravesite to honor a lifelike metal statue of Prigozhin erected in his memory on what would have been his sixty-third birthday. (Photo by Artem Priakhin/SOPA Images/Sipa USA)

CHAPTER 14
PROJECT ASTREA

About a week after the Wagner Group clashed with US special forces in Syria, a federal grand jury in Washington charged Yevgeny Prigozhin and the Internet Research Agency with interfering in the 2016 presidential election. The indictment named twelve additional Russian citizens as coconspirators, saying that they had been assisted by an unnamed accomplice. Several had traveled to the United States in the guise of tourists in the summer of 2014 just as the Wagner Group was ramping up operations in Donbas. All those implicated were Russian citizens in the pay of Prigozhin's St. Petersburg–based Concord Management and Consulting. All played leading roles in an elaborate conspiracy aimed at putting Donald Trump in the White House.

The litany of crimes enumerated in the 37-page charging document, filed on February 16, 2018, laid bare Prigozhin's starring role in an audacious Kremlin-directed plan to stack the electoral deck against Trump's opponent, Hillary Clinton. Federal prosecutors explained how Prigozhin's employees divided up the work of creating and animating a virtual army of hundreds of online fake personas who looked, sounded, and acted like Americans. "Matt Skiber" offered money to an American citizen to recruit rally goers to join a "March for Trump" in Florida. "Josh Milton" sent out press releases to thirty media outlets promoting a "Down with Hillary" rally at Trump Tower in New York.[1]

On a warm day late in May 2016, a US citizen was unknowingly pulled into Prigozhin's web of intrigue. Under the guise of an innocuous request, they found themselves standing in front of the White House and holding a sign that read, "Happy 55th Birthday Dear Boss." What seemed like a simple gesture was, in fact, a carefully orchestrated stunt by operatives in the supervision of Prigozhin's lead public-relations man, Pyotr Bychkov.

Unbeknownst to the individual, the "boss" referred not to some local figure but to Prigozhin. The date of the ruse revealed the connection—Prigozhin had been born on June 1, 1961, and this strange display of public homage was a veiled nod to the man who had quietly funded and orchestrated multiple online influence campaigns that spanned from Ukraine to the Middle East, Africa, and Europe.

For Prigozhin, the birthday prank was a modern application of *aktivnye meropriyatiya*, or "active measures," a Soviet-era tactic designed to spread chaos and confusion. During the Cold War, the KGB used the same methods to influence public opinion and sow distrust in Western institutions. Through his troll farm, Prigozhin took this old playbook and updated it for the digital age, using social media to manipulate people into actions that fit his agenda, which dovetailed neatly with that of the Kremlin and wealthy Putin loyalists. It was all about causing disruption without getting caught, just like in the old days of Soviet disinformation.[2]

The grand jury also accused the Internet Research Agency (IRA) of stealing the identities of US citizens and buying stolen credit-card and bank-account information from brokers on the dark web. Operating under the auspices of Glavset LLC, the corporate heart of the agency, IRA employees in St. Petersburg used the stolen information to set up fake email accounts under names like "staceyredneck@gmail.com" and "allforusa@yahoo.com," and to purchase online ads on Facebook and data-storage space on computer servers located in the United States. Gmail, Yahoo!, Facebook, Instagram, YouTube, Twitter—Prigozhin's virtual army was active on every major US platform. All of this was done in the service of what one employee characterized as "information warfare." Viewed in the aggregate, the indictment stated, the operation was nothing short of a criminal conspiracy that aimed at sowing discord in the United States.

The charges against Prigozhin's company and employees were the culmination of years of intelligence collection at agencies overseen by the Office of the Director of National Intelligence (ODNI).[3] Separately, the Justice Department's National Security Division opened its own line of inquiry into Russian meddling in 2016. Then, in May 2017, the Justice Department was forced to appoint a special counsel to investigate the scheme after Trump, in a fit of pique, fired the head of the FBI, James Comey, for failing to cooperate with his request to drop the inquiry into Russian interference. That was when Robert S. Mueller III was asked to step in.

A by-the-book former Marine, Mueller was initially reluctant to take the special counsel job, but he was coaxed out of retirement because of his sense of duty. A Republican with Ivy League credentials, he'd had tough jobs before—a tour in the Vietnam War and twelve years as director of the FBI amid the peak of America's hunt for al-Qaeda and ISIS terrorists—but leading the federal investigation into Russian meddling was a test of a different order. The special counsel's remit was to pin down the who, what, where, when, why, and how of an alleged set of crimes involving dozens of accused coconspirators, many of whom were far out of reach in Russia. It was a gargantuan undertaking.

Russia's three-pronged strategy of assault on the American electorate entailed cyberattacks on voting machines and a hack-and-dump email-leak campaign that targeted the Democratic National Committee (DNC) and the Democratic Congressional Campaign Committee. Topping that off was an intricately woven social-influence campaign that simultaneously tapped into vulnerabilities emanating from Silicon Valley's freewheeling tech industry, harnessed Trump's narcissism, and leveraged the insatiable hunger of top Trump campaign staffers for power, money, and fame.

The specific charges brought against Prigozhin's companies and employees in February 2018 were the product of a six-month obsessive hunt for evidence spearheaded by Jeannie Rhee, the energetic senior prosecutor whom Mueller appointed to lead the task force known as Team R. One of three prosecutorial teams set up at the special counsel's bland, cavernous office in Washington as spring turned to summer in 2017, Team R was responsible for unraveling the mysteries surrounding the two separate but related Russian cyberattacks on the US electoral system. Mueller tasked the other two—Team M and Team 600—with investigating the links between the Kremlin and Trump's campaign chairman, Paul Manafort. A central task was to evaluate allegations that Trump and others in the White House might have tried to impede the Justice Department's investigation.[4]

Initially, it was Manafort's business relationships with Ukraine's exiled president, Viktor Yanukovych, and Russia's billionaire "Aluminum King," Oleg Deripaska, that attracted the greatest scrutiny from the FBI. A seasoned Republican political operative, Manafort had spent decades honing his skills as a Washington lobbyist, catering to authoritarian tyrants and wealthy oligarchs like Deripaska, whose holdings spanned every corner of the globe. Manafort began working with Deripaska in 2004 at the height of the Orange Revolution in Ukraine, where RUSAL, the aluminum megacorporation that Deripaska had founded, held a controlling stake in an aluminum-refinery plant.[5] Deripaska's other holdings included a substantial stake in RUSAL's parent company, EN + Group, which at the time counted as a major shareholder the commodities-trading giant Glencore.

Manafort earned tens of millions of dollars and acquired an appetite for high-end luxury goods, like jackets made of ostrich and python leather, that made him the butt of late-night comedy television jokes after news of his arrest became public. But federal agencies treated Manafort's relationship with Deripaska and Deripaska's close ties with Putin as a deadly serious matter.

Over time, Manafort's relationship with Deripaska would become mired in financial disputes, but not before Manafort helped Yanukovych, the candidate strongly favored by Vladimir Putin and billionaire Russian and Ukrainian oligarchs alike, get elected to the Ukrainian presidency in 2010.[6] Work that Manafort did to promote Deripaska's interests in several countries in Africa also came under scrutiny.

After the Treasury Department sanctioned Deripaska, federal prosecutors in New York opened a corruption investigation into allegations that Glencore had paid $52 million to two intermediaries in Nigeria who paid bribes to government officials in Lagos to secure oil contracts.[7] Those charges and others would eventually be settled when Glencore entered guilty pleas and agreed to pay a $1.1 billion fine. But as the Mueller team's investigation into Manafort unfolded and more emerged about his connections to a GRU agent named Konstantin Kilimnik, who ran Manafort's Kyiv office and served as Manafort's primary liaison to Deripaska, the enormity of the Kremlin's influence campaign and Prigozhin's own role in the wider Kremlin plot began to make more sense.

Clearing a path for a US presidential candidate who would be more amenable to rolling back US sanctions brought against Russia in response to the military incursions in Donbas and Crimea was one Kremlin objective. The other was to obscure the Kremlin's role in helping well-connected Russian businessmen circumvent Western sanctions stemming from conflicts in Ukraine and other war zones where the Wagner Group was beginning to burrow deep into illicit commodities-trading gray markets that stretched from the Middle East to Africa. Maintaining narrative control over who exactly was doing what on

Putin's behalf was critical to his regime's survival, and Prigozhin understood this instinctually because much of his own wealth was bound up in it too.

Rhee, like her boss, Mueller, a hard-charging stickler for details, seemed to have strong instincts of her own when it came to prosecuting the case against Prigozhin. Born in Seoul, South Korea, she had emigrated with her family to the United States in 1977, when she was five years old. Growing up in the Midwest, Rhee was the first child in her family and learned English fast. As a result, her mother, who struggled to keep up in English with the demands of American life, relied on Rhee to serve as the family's chief translator and advocate.[8] After graduating from Yale and then earning a degree from Yale Law School, she followed a well-trodden path of many of the elite school's alumni, clerking for the District Court for the District of Columbia and the US District Court of Appeals for the District of Columbia Circuit, and then becoming a federal prosecutor in Washington.

It was a background that prepared her well for a short spell as a US Senate fellow and later a job at the Office of the Legal Counsel under the Obama administration.[9] Like Mueller, she had also spent time at the Washington offices of the prestigious WilmerHale law firm, where she specialized in white-collar criminal defense and gained a knack for litigating complex cybercrime cases. That role and a case she took up as a defense attorney for the Clinton Foundation did not endear her to Trump and his conservative followers, who pilloried Rhee on Twitter when they found out she had been picked for Mueller's team.[10]

As far as Mueller was concerned, though, she was the perfect fit to take on Prigozhin. An exceptionally quick study, Rhee rapidly memorized the long list of complicated Russian names at the center of her team's inquiry into Russia's efforts to swing the 2016 election.[11] She was aided in the case against Concord and Prigozhin's troll farm by Omer Meisel, a wide-eyed, wisecracking, street-savvy investigator who, like Rhee, had a background in investigating cybercrime. Before joining the Mueller investigation team as a senior investigator, Meisel had headed the cyber and counterintelligence branches at the FBI's field office in San Diego, California. Meisel had at one point also served as a legal attaché at the US embassy in Israel, a position that taught him the tricky diplomacy of working with foreign governments to dig up evidence of espionage.[12]

He cut his teeth as the top federal investigator on the federal fraud and conspiracy case against Enron, a Texas-based energy company. It was then that Meisel became especially close with Andrew Weissmann, chief of the Justice

Department's Fraud Division and Mueller's pick to lead Team M. The trio—Rhee, Meisel, and Weissmann—were often of the same mind and, along with more than a dozen FBI agents and federal prosecutors, formed the informal brain trust behind the prosecution of Prigozhin and the Internet Research Agency.[13]

Rhee knew when she launched the investigation that chances were slim to none that Prigozhin or any of the other Russians indicted would ever be fully brought to account for what the IRA had done.[14] The investigation was more a classic name-and-shame endeavor. She believed that a win for the United States would be to air out all the Kremlin's dirty laundry instead of allowing details of the conspiracy to molder in classified documents held on dusty government computer terminals. Cybercrime was, Rhee said, "the new normal"—the way that nations conducted warfare against their rivals. Exposing the tools, tactics, and techniques used by the IRA and the Russian hackers was a practical way to take on Prigozhin, and by association Putin.

The case was highly sensitive. Trump's vocal opposition to the special counsel's probe into Russian election meddling placed Mueller's team in a delicate position, and rumors that Trump planned to fire Mueller and his staff ran rampant. This was one reason why it took Rhee months to convince FBI agents to pursue potential investigative leads. Some were fearful of Trump's wrath, and at least one would turn out to be secretly cooperating with Russians implicated in the plot.[15]

Tech corporations were also generally uncooperative. Facebook employees had initially discovered Russian efforts to target US politicians on the platform in 2016. Soon afterward, ahead of the 2017 presidential election in France, batches of suspicious posts cropped up that bashed Emanuel Macron and trumpeted the unique qualities of Marine Le Pen, a hard-right candidate whose family-led political party had taken out a loan from a Russian bank and had close ties with Konstantin Malofeev, the ultranationalist Orthodox Christian who helped finance Igor Girkin and Russia's seizure of Donbas.

Hundreds of Emanuel Macron's emails mysteriously spilled into the public domain as a result of a Russian cyber operation. In a scenario that mirrored the DNC hack that eventually led Wikileaks to publish hundreds of Clinton campaign-staff emails, the operation targeting Macron started with phishing attacks in early 2017. But it was only months later, after Facebook CEO Mark Zuckerberg learned about the breadth of the Russian meddling in US elections and realized the extent of the potential legal exposure the tech giant faced as a result, that Facebook finally decided to alert the FBI, just as Rhee's Team R was being formed.[16]

Until that moment, few inside the Justice Department understood just how much Prigozhin's media holdings had grown since he began his early experimentation with industrial-scale disinformation campaigns during Russia's troubled elections in 2012. In the years that followed, Prigozhin's troll farm evolved into a highly sophisticated media and marketing machine. Glavset and the web of other Concord-linked front companies that financed the IRA had an annual budget that ran into the tens of millions of dollars. Its social media arm was run like a modern advertising agency. There was a management group to administer the IRA's hundreds of employees and to supervise the finance department. Other departments included a graphics division, a data-analysis team, and an IT department that kept all the infrastructure humming.

Concord's media investments had also expanded to encompass the Federal News Agency, a propaganda site masquerading as an online news portal. The website, which was better known by its initials, RIA-FAN, was a rebranding exercise aimed at redirecting growing public scrutiny away from the IRA's Orwellian experiments in harnessing the power of large-scale data analysis to manipulate public opinion via platforms like Facebook and Twitter. When curious reporters came calling in 2015 at the IRA's famed headquarters at 55 Savushkina in St. Petersburg, they were told that RIA-FAN was an entirely separate, unrelated entity, despite sharing the same address.

Then, in early 2018, shortly before Wagner forces launched their ill-fated offensive on the Conoco gas plant in Syria, the entire operation—IRA and RIA-FAN—moved to the nearby Lakhta-2 business center on prime real estate near Gazprom's shiny new headquarters, earning workers at Prigozhin's media factory the moniker "Lakhta trolls." Work in the new office building with its tall facade of blue-glass windows did not last long, though; a string of anonymous bomb threats against the IRA would eventually force the building's owners to evict Prigozhin's propaganda machine to a new location.[17]

Despite those troubles, work continued throughout 2017 and 2018 with the same briskness that had accompanied the IRA's first information offensive in 2016. This was partially attributable to the IRA data-analysis department's fluid mastery of a marketing technique known as psychographic segmentation, whose origins were deeply rooted in American capitalism and the Silicon Valley tech boom.

A Harvard social scientist first articulated the concept after observing during demographic research that basic traditional demographic information about a potential business customer—gender, age, race, education level—was a poor predictor of what people liked and disliked and would therefore be willing to buy. Marketing campaigns were likely to be far more successful if they also considered personal preferences like whether a potential customer preferred chocolate ice cream versus vanilla or whether they liked ice hockey more than football.

Information like that could then be used to slice and dice, or "segment," customers into different categories of potential buyers. When combined with the power of computers, which counted clicks, likes, dislikes, and time spent on millions of websites and platforms like Facebook, psychographic segmentation gave advertisers a powerful edge. It also allowed Prigozhin's IRA to identify and gather more intelligence about the Facebook and Twitter users who liked or spent time looking at provocative content posted by Prigozhin's employees in St. Petersburg.

The IRA's data-analysis department then used that information to produce polarizing messages tailored to audiences on the Far Right or Far Left and create algorithms that would push those messages to receptive target audiences. The IRA's methods capitalized heavily on the built-in bias of Facebook and Twitter algorithms toward promoting and amplifying sensational content that provoked outrage and anger. The more that users clicked, liked, and reposted links, memes, and messages posted by fake IRA personas, the further the Kremlin's disinformation campaign spread.

The IRA's internet alter ego, RIA-FAN, took those techniques one step further by attempting to grow the customer base for Russian propaganda by a technique known as astroturfing. The term was a reference to fake grass at sports stadiums, but what it really meant was using deceptive means to orchestrate a marketing campaign that used the same kind of data-mining techniques, then repackaged the same sales pitch in a new wrapper to build up a larger customer base for Russian political messaging.

RIA-FAN borrowed heavily from the stylistics of similar Russian state-run news outlets like *Sputnik News* and *RT*, which were big on flashy visuals and sensational headlines, except it was more louche. Targeted toward a middlebrow Russian-speaking audience, RIA-FAN offered tabloid digests with splashy headlines. Favorite topics included diatribes about the folly of US and EU policy on Ukraine, breathless coverage of the latest signs and portents of the decline of Western power, and random articles on how experts were thinking about the future of oil extraction in Madagascar. A highlight on the portal was its slickly packaged videos shot by RIA-FAN war correspondents dashing around the front lines atop Russian T-72 tanks and gadding about with masked Wagner Group mercenaries and Russian special forces in Syria.

In the spring of 2018, a couple of months after Prigozhin was indicted in Washington and one month after the US Treasury Department lodged a new set of sanctions against Prigozhin and targeted IRA employees indicted in the case, RIA-FAN announced it was going on the offensive against the American government. A press release posted on the RIA-FAN site promised the launch of a new sister web portal called "USAReally" that was going to tell Americans the "real truth" about what was going on in their country: "The Federal News Agency is not going to put up with the hegemony of the US authorities in the information field and announces the launch of the project 'Wake up, America!,'" the RIA-FAN announcement declared.[18] USAReally headlines exposed the naked absurdity of the website's premise. Daily updates to the site offered an assortment of click-bait "news" teasers with headlines like "Mother tried to kill her baby and hide her in a diaper box" and splashy adverts dressed up as new digests on Trump's triumphantly confrontational brand of politics.[19]

As if all that was not strange enough, USAReally's English-speaking, goateed hipster editor in chief, Alexander Malkevich, traveled from Russia to Washington on a tourist visa and invited local reporters to meet for a "media roundtable." The event was scheduled to take place at a WeWork space he rented shortly after the launch of the site. It was a weird and utterly irresistible story for the growing bevy of reporters in Washington sucked into covering the Mueller investigation and who were forced as a result to follow Prigozhin's every move.

Amy MacKinnon, the reporter who broke the news and cowrote a story about Malkevich's bizarre antics for *Foreign Policy*, remembered feeling a mix of curiosity and revulsion upon contacting Malkevich. "A former Russian colleague said that this guy was coming to Washington, and that there had been a lot of fanfare that he was going to open, like, a fake news bureau blocks from the White House," MacKinnon recalled.[20]

Dressed in a T-shirt with the face of Russia's foreign minister, Sergey Lavrov, on it, Malkevich gabbled on in his interview with MacKinnon about the high-minded mission that Prigozhin had apparently sent him on, and he half-jokingly told her and a colleague that he thought he might be awarded a Pulitzer Prize one day.[21] "He very enthusiastically spoke about how censorship was just rampant in America and how he'd come to test the limits of American freedom," MacKinnon wrote.[22] Her interview with Malkevich had barely concluded before FBI agents visited the downtown Washington WeWork space that Malkevich had rented, detained him, searched his computer and phone, and then ordered him out of the country for violating his visa terms.

Every part of the RIA-FAN and IRA machinery appeared to be powered by money that sloshed through a constellation of front companies linked to Prigozhin. The funds came via hidden transactions involving the Concord network of firms; Wagner Group contracts with a long list of despotic regimes facilitated by the Russian defense ministry's logistics arm, Voentorg; and the Kremlin. But Mueller's team made no direct mention of the Wagner Group in its 2018 indictment of Prigozhin.

Instead, the case hinged on the connection between Concord financing of disinformation campaigns and how the IRA deployed the deceptive techniques used to gull millions of Facebook, Twitter, and Instagram users into believing that Trump was a better choice for president than Clinton, or to sit out the election altogether because it was "rigged." The money part of the Justice Department's case against Prigozhin centered on financial transactions involving PayPal and an unnamed American bank that were initiated by several IRA employees, which federal prosecutors said constituted wire and bank fraud. It was an extraordinarily complex case animated by a legal theory that Prigozhin had directed employees linked to Concord to use false advertising, identity theft, and money-laundering techniques to defraud the United States.

To win a conviction, Jeannie Rhee and her Team R investigators would need to explain to a judge and jury how Prigozhin and twelve of his IRA employees used social media marketing tools to pull off the caper. They would then need to demonstrate beyond a reasonable doubt that Prigozhin was in the driver's seat, that the IRA was the vehicle, and that Concord put fuel in the tank at the direction of the Kremlin. However, the point of the case was not to put Prigozhin and his coconspirators behind bars. Rhee, Weissmann, and Meisel argued in their closed-door debates with Mueller that the only way to lift the fog of disinformation that Prigozhin had unleashed on the American public was to get the story about what had happened out into the open in court, where facts still mattered.[23] Mueller's investigation team knew that the case was a long shot. There was no immediate likelihood that Vladimir Putin would approve Prigozhin's extradition to face a US court trial.

So it was surprising when Prigozhin turned to Reed Smith, a Pennsylvania-based multinational law firm and one of the biggest in the nation, to appear in court on Concord's behalf. It was strange, and there was no immediate explanation of how Prigozhin had managed to find Eric Dubelier, Reed Smith's lead attorney on the case, and convince him to enter a not-guilty plea for Concord. Why go to trial at all if there was no risk of extradition, let alone punishment? Why now? What did federal prosecutors have over Prigozhin or the Kremlin or both that could possibly motivate Prigozhin to spend millions of dollars on lengthy trial proceedings?

The first inkling of what was behind Prigozhin's decision to fight the charges appeared during an early pretrial hearing in May. One motive appeared to be political and was predicated on pleasing Putin. The second reason, unsurprisingly, was purely monetary. At least one of Prigozhin's top contacts based in the United States had used American banks to launder money linked to shady financial transactions that traced back to Russia's defense ministry. The third reason for Prigozhin's eagerness to make a public spectacle of taking on Rhee and her team would become apparent only with the passage of time, as more and more of Putin's adversaries became determined to take Prigozhin down. Some in that number included GRU and FSB insiders who quietly waged a shadow turf war against one another that was discernible only to the most practiced of eyes. Others, like the US Treasury Department, were more bold in their targeted actions against Prigozhin.

Sanctions imposed on Prigozhin and Concord, first in 2016 and then in 2018 in connection with the federal indictment against the Internet Research Agency, jeopardized Prigozhin's ability to do business almost everywhere in the world. US Treasury officials had not only named Concord but also targeted Beratex LLC, the Seychelles front company used to register one of the private jets that Prigozhin used to shuttle around the world.[24] Treasury officials also singled out a Cayman Islands–registered Hawker 800XP jet and Isle of Man–registered Embraer Legacy 600 plane tied to a GRU shell company registered in the Seychelles and a similarly named company in the Czech Republic. The estimated combined value of both private jets ranged anywhere from $4 million to $11 million. The US crackdown on the constellation of front companies linked to Prigozhin also targeted the $3 million multi-deck superyacht that Prigozhin had purchased in 2013.

The practical effect of the sanctions was that any bank, company, or person caught doing business with Prigozhin, Concord, or one of the dozens of corporate fronts erected over the years to shield his dealings with the Russian defense ministry and the Kremlin also risked being frozen out of the global financial system. Washington was sending a signal that doing business with Prigozhin was toxic for any parties that did not have a foolproof means of hiding their transactions. Spooked by the implications, Prigozhin became obsessed with clearing his name. His every move became predicated on preserving the billion-dollar empire that Putin had helped him build, and he would soon prove that he was willing to go to extreme lengths to preserve the secrecy surrounding the Wagner Group's covert operations.

All the while, Prigozhin's businesses were constantly dogged by hacks, leaks, and probing news coverage. In response to revelations from the reporting, the US State Department and the Pentagon began casting around for ways to throw a wrench into the machinery that made it possible for Prigozhin to keep his business ventures humming. Studies were commissioned, expert consultants hired, and task forces set up, but for the most part the US government's actions took place well out of public view and often seemed disjointed. Still, the bureaucratic maneuvering in Washington, though sometimes lumbering, marked the start of the first concerted US counterstrike against the most vulnerable nodes in the Kremlin's clandestine networks and a further progression in the escalating information warfare between the United States and Russia.

Evidence of the first of those moves surfaced in December 2018, when the FBI arrested in North Carolina one of Prigozhin's most important US-based contacts. Leonid Teyf was the deputy chief of Russia's Voentorg logistics agency and a leading source of the Russian defense contracts that had earned Prigozhin billions of dollars. The indictment filed against Teyf named several other accomplices, including Teyf's wife, Tatyana, and described Teyf's involvement in an elaborate money-laundering and bribery scheme aimed at disguising millions of dollars in kickbacks paid in exchange for Russian defense contracts.[25]

In 2010, the same year that Prigozhin's Concord network won one of its first big Russian defense-logistics contracts, Teyf became a resident of North Carolina while still working at the defense ministry back in Russia. Shortly thereafter, Teyf and his wife moved into a $5 million mega-mansion near a country-club golf course in an upscale part of Raleigh. FBI agents learned much of this during an April 2014 interview with a confidential informant, identified in an FBI interview transcript as a "security guard" who had worked for Teyf in Russia.

The FBI informant described how he had served as a bagman and money courier for Teyf while Teyf oversaw contracting at Voentorg and shuttled between Russia and the United States. At the time, Teyf also headed a giant defense-logistics–contract clearinghouse called RBE Group, which provided the Russian military with catering, cleaning, construction, and uniform-manufacturing services.[26]

He was the primary go-between in a money-laundering and kickback arrangement between Russia's disgraced defense minister Anatoly Serdyukov and contractors like Prigozhin, who paid millions in bribes in exchange for preferential treatment. Despite Serdyukov's firing, the corrupt scheme continued unabated once Serdyukov was appointed as a high-level manager at Rostec, the Russian arms conglomerate headed by Sergey Chemezov.

From January 2011 to October 2013, roughly $39.4 million was wired to four US accounts at Bank of America that belonged to Teyf and his wife. Nearly all the funds were sent from 293 shell companies registered in the British Virgin Islands, Belize, Hong Kong, Panama, Seychelles, and Cyprus. In all, over a two-year period about $150 million was paid from Russia to some seventy bank accounts held in the name of Teyf and his wife in the United States, federal prosecutors said.[27]

There was so much cash sloshing around, Teyf's security guard told the FBI, that it was a routine occurrence for huge boxes packed with dollars to be delivered on secret nighttime runs to recipients in a money-laundering network that spanned from St. Petersburg to Siberia.[28] Along the way, sizable sums of protection money were regularly paid to at least two major Russian mafia outfits.[29] One group, the informant said, was a Chechen faction controlled directly by Putin.

The other was the Moscow-based Podolskaya mafia, the same organized-crime group at the center of the 1994 murder plot involving the VDV 45th Guards Spetsnaz Reconnaissance Brigade that Redut chieftain Konstantin Mirzayants had been implicated in. That faction, the informant explained, was controlled by a GRU general.[30] Teyf's federal case seemed to join the dots in a web that stretched deep into Russia's murky military underworld, all leading back to the same cadre of mobbed-up paratroopers that had fueled the quiet rise of Russia's mercenary industry.

These allegations were only part of what FBI agents unearthed while investigating Teyf. Much more came to light after federal investigators charged him with offering a $10,000 bribe to an undercover Homeland Security agent in

Raleigh to deport his wife's suspected secret paramour, the son of their house-keeper.[31] As part of the plot, federal agents said, Teyf planned to move with his family back to Russia, where he hoped to use his considerable influence to have his wife arrested and her lover and his family killed.[32]

FBI agents placed Teyf under surveillance sometime in 2014 or 2015, the same year that Serdyukov was named chairman of the board of the state-run United Aircraft Corporation, a key supplier of the jets and helicopters flown by the Wagner Group that was soon after absorbed by Rostec in a merger deal.[33] The estimated $606 million in defense contracts awarded to Prigozhin three years after Teyf and Serdyukov's departure from the defense ministry raised questions about whether Prigozhin had sent money to US bank accounts held in the name of Teyf and his accomplices. Prosecutors made no express mention in their initial filings about the links between Prigozhin and Teyf. However, the case against Teyf left little doubt that Prigozhin's primary contact at Voentorg had greatly enriched himself during the same period when the IRA's election-interference campaigns began to accelerate along with the Wagner Group's expansion into the Middle East and Africa.

All this came as a complete surprise to many of the Teyf family's friends and neighbors in North Carolina's Research Triangle. Some who knew Teyf and socialized with him and his wife, however, suspected that Teyf might have been on the FBI's radar well before his 2018 arrest. Dmitri Mitin, a North Carolina State University professor and Russian émigré, first met the Teyfs at a friend's birthday party.

He remembered how the Christmas holiday parties that Teyf threw for the small Russian émigré community in north Raleigh were always tastefully understated. It was almost as if Teyf, aware of perceptions that rich Russians are loud and showy with their wealth, was trying extra hard to fade into the background. "He was fairly inconspicuous. I remember thinking at the party that they were unusually ordinary. Even the way they dressed was out of character," Mitin recalled. "But the house was enormous. You know you go to Moscow, and you will see that kind of splendor among the very, very rich."[34]

A month before FBI agents moved to execute the warrant for Teyf's arrest in North Carolina, an altogether different kind of operation was under way at the headquarters of the US Cyber Command in Fort Meade, Maryland. The White House had just given the green light to General Paul Nakasone, the chief of the agency, to go on the offensive against Russia and other US rivals. Soon after that, Cyber Command hackers launched a multiphase offensive against

Prigozhin's media factory in St. Petersburg. Defense and intelligence officials told a *Washington Post* reporter that the agency's cyber assault took the IRA offline. "Part of our objective is to throw a little curveball, inject a little friction, sow confusion," one unnamed defense official said.[35] The first wave of attacks consisted of text messages sent to the phones of Prigozhin's employees from spoofed mobile-phone numbers with African country codes, urging RIA-FAN workers to rethink their actions. Then America's hackers managed to gain control of the iPhone of a top RIA-FAN employee and briefly managed to shut down the IRA's servers on November 5, one day before the US polls were set to open for the 2018 midterm elections. RIA-FAN suggested in its own account of the episode that data obtained in the cyberattack from the USAReally portal were also copied onto computer drives located in Sweden and Estonia as evidence of a Western conspiracy aimed at censoring the media.[36]

The bevy of Treasury sanctions, the spate of US cyberattacks on Prigozhin's media enterprises, the FBI takedown of Teyf and his money-laundering ring in North Carolina and other states—all of it hinted at Washington's slow awakening to the problems that Prigozhin posed for US interests. But Prigozhin's courtroom defenders in Washington consistently displayed a deft touch as they parried legal challenges from Jeannie Rhee and other Team R prosecutors.

Eric Dubelier, the defense attorney that represented Concord, had worked as a prosecutor himself in Louisiana, Florida, and Washington before earning a spot at Reed Smith, where he took on the defense of individuals and firms charged with taking bribes from foreign governments. Characterized by his colleagues as an aggressive, sharp-tongued courtroom brawler, Dubelier defended Concord based on a combination of impugning Rhee and her team, undercutting the legitimacy of the special counsel's legal mandate, deriding the charges as a "make-believe crime," and eviscerating any chance that secret US intelligence information could be used against Concord in court.

Over the course of the pretrial proceedings, Dubelier filed several motions aimed at suppressing information contained in the Treasury sanction dossiers and other classified sources.[37] He argued that "the reason is obvious and is political: to justify his own existence the Special Counsel has to indict a Russian—any Russian."[38]

A couple months later, Dubelier would try again to convince the Trump-appointed judge in the case, Dabney Friedrich, that the charges against Concord should be tossed, claiming in a separate motion that there was no law on the books preventing outside interference in US elections or using platforms like Facebook or Twitter to get a political point across to the public: "Just as critically, there is no federal election law or regulation prohibiting any person or group of persons, whether American or foreign, acting independently of a political candidate, from conveying political speech on social media, at political rallies, or in advertisements available for viewing in the United States."[39]

Although the judge did not buy the argument and allowed the federal government's case to move forward, Dubelier's contention that there were few real constraints on what big tech companies can allow to be published on their sites was on point. Facebook, Twitter, YouTube, and others had for years relied on legal protections under an obscure but sweeping immunity clause known as Section 230. Section 230 holds that tech companies that act as intermediaries on the internet cannot be held liable for content posted on their sites by third parties. US law at the time was also fuzzy about how tech companies should deal with situations where sanctioned actors such as the Wagner Group, ISIS, or Hamas used their platforms to promote violent content.

Sensitive to potential liabilities and reputational risk, companies like YouTube learned to act quickly when the federal government inquired about graphic content posted online by Islamist groups such as ISIS. But they typically dithered when it came to Russian propaganda and the often bizarre videos and images uploaded by the Wagner Group and neo-Nazi affiliates like Rusich and the Russian Imperial Legion. It was obvious that online content moderation was at best a selective endeavor guided by the biases of platform algorithms and the squishy guidelines set by tech and policy teams in Silicon Valley office parks.

While Prigozhin's American lawyers were making their arguments in federal court, his Russian legal team and the Kremlin were making a much bigger political point to Washington. In affirming Concord's defense against charges of foreign interference in US elections, Prigozhin, and by association Putin, appeared to be thumbing their noses at the US legal process and Team R's contention that foreign-influence operations could be cast as criminal.

Pouring salt on the wound, Putin, in a flash of sarcastic irony during a state trip to Australia in the summer of 2018, insisted that Prigozhin was no different than the Hungarian-born philanthropist George Soros, whose US-based Open Society Foundation had funded antiauthoritarian activist groups for years: "There's Mr. Soros in the US and he meddles in all sorts of situations around the world, and our American friends often say the US as a country doesn't have anything to do with Soros's private endeavors. And if you take us, that's Mr. Prigozhin's private endeavor."

What Putin meant by "private" clearly departed from the common definition of the term, but that was a nuance that he finessed easily. Putin laughed off the idea that his longtime caterer had somehow managed to best the US government:

> Regarding Mr. Prigozhin, I'd like to ask you to draw a distinct line between the government of the Russian Federation or Russia as a state and corporate entities. You said Mr. Prigozhin is called "Putin's chef." It's true that he works in the gastronomical sphere and has a restaurant in St Petersburg. Do you really think a restaurant owner, even if he has the ability of a hacker and owns a company in the IT sphere— and I don't actually know what he is doing there—do you really think a man of this kind can affect elections in the US or in any European country?[40]

Behind the scenes, Prigozhin's advisers at Capital Legal Services, a leading Russian law firm with offices in Moscow and St. Petersburg, seemed to have a firm understanding of Prigozhin's importance to the Kremlin. Under the auspices of a multipronged legal campaign dubbed "Project Astrea," they used all the legal levers at their disposal to try to slow-roll the federal case against Concord in Washington. Analysis of a cache of leaked email from the law firm revealed that Project Astrea centered on a three-part strategy, each named with a literary flourish, to debunk claims made about the connections among Prigozhin, Concord, the IRA, and the Wagner Group.

The first layer, "Project Shakespeare," involved an aggressive effort to blunt the effect of sanctions and legal cases brought against Prigozhin and his companies. The campaign involved, among other things, the registration of hundreds of front companies that moved military goods across international borders, often under the cover of food shipments. It also included efforts to rebut the federal indictment and troll Team R as Rhee tried to press the case against Concord in court.

Prigozhin's Russian legal team gave him the code name "Capulet" and circulated regular updates about how reporting by Western media outlets on the court case against the IRA was shaping up. In their emails to one another, Prigozhin's Russian attorneys mentioned their suspicions that their communications were being monitored while passing along English-language news clippings about the courtroom duel between Rhee and Dubelier, which seemed to please Prigozhin to no end. "Currently, Capulet is quite satisfied with the project dynamics and information provided to him," one of Prigozhin's Russian attorneys noted.[41]

Project Hamlet focused on fighting US and UK sanctions against Prigozhin and convincing Interpol to cancel a "Red Notice," an international warrant for Prigozhin's arrest. An email addressed to "CLS_Hamlet" marked "No Metadata" included Prigozhin's full appeal document and a lengthy bullet-pointed bio describing Prigozhin's climb from prison convict to decorated Kremlin insider. The document listed no fewer than forty heads of state whom Prigozhin had hosted state dinners for with Putin, and one of the bullet points noted that Prigozhin counted himself as "politically indifferent" up until 2012, when "after slanderous articles by *Novaya Gazeta* [he] almost lost his business and was forced to sell personal assets to restore it."[42]

This seemed to explain the third layer of the strategy, Project Bread and Butter, which entailed bringing defamation lawsuits against journalists who reported on Prigozhin's ties to the Wagner Group. The most conspicuous target was Eliot Higgins at Bellingcat.[43] But Prigozhin seemed more interested in trolling his most potent adversary in the media than winning his defamation case against Higgins. Soon after filing the suit, Prigozhin's lawyer Pavel Karpunin told his partner legal counsel in London that Prigozhin was eager to issue a splashy press release about targeting Bellingcat for libel. Lawyers in London pushed back, warning in a series of back-and-forth email exchanges in August 2021 that a public statement about the proceedings would be "a public relations disaster in the west" and might prejudice the British court against them. Prigozhin seemed quite energized by it all.[44]

In one of the many communications about Project Astrea, Prigozhin's lawyers in Russia and Washington circulated a letter penned in Russian and translated into English at Prigozhin's behest. Dated April 23, 2019, five days after Mueller's team published a multivolume report on Russian meddling and it was announced that Mueller would soon step down, Prigozhin's four-page letter was addressed to Trump; Trump's attorney general, Bill Barr; Speaker of the House Nancy Pelosi; several leading members of Congress; and the US ambassador to Russia, Jon Huntsman Jr. Although it was apparently never sent, the letter was pure Prigozhin, dripping with sarcastic humor, pompous, and factually inaccurate.

"Dear Sirs and Madam," the letter began. "First of all, I would like to express my deep respect for the American people and my admiration for the United States system of government as established by the Founding Fathers of the American republic, and in particular for the rights of criminal defendants under the United States Constitution." Prigozhin said he was relieved to learn that he might finally have his day in court. The indictment of Concord would be his chance to finally defend himself against all the rumors, innuendo, and media reporting that surrounded his relationship with Putin.

"To my amusement and dismay, however, Mr. Mueller also indicted 'Concord Catering,' an umbrella brand name my food services companies used together with various partners over the years. But there was no company called Concord Catering, so this was like indicting the Michelin Man alongside the Michelin tire company, and it only reinforced my impression from the outrageous claims in the indictment that Mr. Mueller was operating under incomplete, mistaken information." [45]

Back in Washington, meanwhile, Prigozhin's American defense lawyers asserted a similar line of argument in a strategy that appeared to rely heavily on a tactic known in courtroom legalese as "graymailing." Used often in high-stakes legal battles involving charges that rely on sensitive state secrets, the maneuver entails a formal request by a defendant's attorney to gain access to secret intelligence, which places prosecutors in a bind over whether to release the information or drop the case. Rhee's team and Prigozhin's defense team filed numerous motions and counter-motions related to the process by which discovery should proceed. As a result, the court case against Prigozhin proceeded slowly as the teams debated whether and how to share two terabytes of evidentiary records with Prigozhin's lawyers in Russia. Rhee said during one hearing that federal prosecutors worried that if they sent sensitive files to Prigozhin's lawyers in Russia, it would be tantamount to handing them over to the GRU.

Those concerns would turn out to be well-founded. A few months after the judge in the case issued a protective order to seal discovery materials disclosed by federal prosecutors to Prigozhin's legal team, a Twitter account called @HackingRedstone posted an enticing offer: "We've got access to the Special Counsel Mueller's probe database as we hacked Russian server with info from the Russian troll case Concord LLC v. Mueller. You can view all the files Mueller had about the IRA and Russian collusion. Enjoy the reading!" The tweet, according to a court filing, also included a link to a webpage located on an online file-sharing portal that contained a weird jumble of junk mail and more than a thousand sensitive case files.[46] When Rhee's Team R reached out to Prigozhin's defense lawyers for clarification, they were waved off brusquely: "I think it is a scam peddling the stuff that was hacked and dumped many years ago by Shaltai Boltai [*sic*]," Dubelier said.

The reference to Shaltai B0ltai was telling, reflecting the strong Kremlin influence on Prigozhin's legal defense in the United States. Shaltai B0ltai was the blog site of the hacking collective known as Anonymous International, which for several years had splashed the details of Kremlin insiders' personal communications on the internet for the world to view. The hacker site's name, Shaltai B0ltai, was a sly reference to the Russian name for Humpty Dumpty and hinted at the hope that cyber hacks might contribute to the fall of Putin's regime. In January 2017, around the time Trump was sworn in as president and just before Rhee's probe into the IRA began, Russian authorities charged several FSB agents with leading the Shaltai B0ltai hack-and-dump ring and working for Western intelligence agencies, accusations that resulted in treason charges. The truth would turn out to be much more complex: the Shaltai B0ltai case was a sign of growing infighting within and between the GRU and the FSB over how best to conduct Putin's undeclared shadow war against the West.[47]

Concerns over data security were not the only delaying tactic employed to stall the case. Back in the courtroom, Judge Friedrich admonished Dubelier, threatening him with contempt if he failed to comply with subpoenas filed by Rhee and her team to produce documents relevant to the case against Concord. As the federal case dragged on into its second year, it became apparent that Dubelier's defense strategy, combined with the IRA and RIA-FAN internet fog machine and the tricks employed by Prigozhin's lawyers in Russia, was starting to have the desired effect.

One month before the opening of the trial, federal prosecutors announced plans in March 2020 to call an unnamed star witness who would offer damaging testimony about Prigozhin's intent to interfere in the elections of another unnamed country. Dubelier moved forcefully to cut Rhee's team off at the pass when in the same court hearing prosecutors asked the judge to allow the witness to testify under a pseudonym to protect him from possible retribution. "I would not be comfortable with that," Dubelier told the judge.[48] It was unclear which witness was being referred to: the federal prosecutor who made the argument to the judge bent himself into a pretzel in an effort not to let classified information slip out in open court.

A few days later, on March 16, 2020, federal prosecutors on Rhee's team cited Concord's failure to comply with subpoenas and a determination by unnamed federal agencies that evidence in the case against the IRA would have to remain classified. With no protections for the prosecution's secret star witness and no way to present potentially damaging information held in classified files, Mueller's team was forced to drop the case against Prigozhin. It seemed that the need to maintain secrecy about the sources and methods that the United States had used to obtain information about Prigozhin's business had trumped Rhee's ambition to expose the contours of Russia's influence campaign. The federal case against Prigozhin was withdrawn, and the charges against him thrown out. By then, though, Prigozhin had already shifted his gaze to new horizons.

CHAPTER 15

AFRICA OR BUST

Early on the morning of July 31, 2018, a squad of UN peacekeepers in the Central African Republic (CAR) made a grim discovery: the bodies of three Russian men on the roadside. The only identification found at the scene was their press cards. Dawn had just broken over the town of Sibut, the nearest security outpost and the last place the three men had been seen alive.

The three journalists had set out the day before for the Ndassima gold mine, the latest object of conquest in the Wagner Group's expanding area of operations. Instead, for reasons that remain unclear to this day, the truck they were last seen traveling in had taken a detour toward a town that lay far off the path of their intended destination. At around 7 p.m. on the night before their bodies were discovered, local army soldiers had waved their car through a checkpoint after radioing back to their Russian advisers in Sibut. Witnesses recalled that an SUV carrying two locals and three white men had just passed through the checkpoint moments beforehand.

Their driver, a local named Bienvenue Duvokama, somehow miraculously escaped. He would later tell Russian authorities that their car had been ambushed at around 8 p.m. by a group of Arabic-speaking men dressed in turbans. But his story was chock-full of contradictions, and before anyone could press him further, he disappeared into the ether.

It was either a highway robbery gone wrong or a targeted assassination that had been made to look like one. There were hints of a struggle, but strangely the victims' valuables were left untouched. One of the murdered men, Orkhan

Dzhemal, was lying face down in the grass, his back pierced with AK-47 bullets. Another, Alexander Rastogurev, had also been shot and was lying near his traveling companion. The third man, Kiril Radchenko, was also shot and left to bleed out a few meters away from the other two.

A team of investigators and forensic specialists hired by the man who had funded their reporting trip, former Yukos CEO Mikhail Khodorkovsky, would later indicate that their corpses had been lying where they were discovered for several hours.[1] They were dumped there as a warning message, one received loud and clear as the news of the murders spread beyond the Central African Republic.

The three had ventured into the heart of Africa on assignment for Khodorkovsky's start-up media outlet, the Investigation Management Center, with the goal of tracing the murky threads of Wagner's operations. Dzhemal, a bull of a man with thick arching eyebrows, was at fifty-one at the pinnacle of his career. A seasoned war correspondent with a history of pitting himself against Russian military machinations in Donbas and Chechnya, he had long been marked by the Kremlin.

Rastogurev, forty-seven, an award-winning filmmaker with a penchant for exposing the underbelly of subaltern Russia, had founded his own production studio after stints at NTV and the US-government–funded independent news channel Radio Liberty. His raw, edgy portrayals of anti-Putin protests led by Alexey Navalny and Ksenia Sobchak ruffled the feathers of Russian authorities. His documentary on the war in Donbas, featuring Kremlin provocateur Alexander Borodai handing out military medals to Russians fighting in Ukraine, further solidified his reputation. Known for his painterly camera work, Rastogurev captivated viewers, earning him a legendary status in Russia's art-house film circles.

It was this very style that had inspired the youngest of the crew, Radchenko, thirty-three, to pursue filmmaking after working as an art-house projectionist in Moscow. He had briefly worked as a videographer for *ANNA News*, the ultranationalist outlet tied to Russia's militarist movement, although he wasn't driven by ideology. Thrilled by the daring escapades of Rastogurev and Dzhemal, Radchenko followed Russian troops in Syria, where his obsession with making a documentary on the Wagner Group first took hold. It was through this ambition that he crossed paths with the RIA-FAN reporter linked to Prigozhin, who would ultimately lead the trio to their deaths on a red dirt road in the Central African Republic's gold-mining heartland.

Word of their plans had already reached Wagner's man on the ground, Valery Zakharov, weeks before their arrival. A former intelligence agent with an undercover unit of Russia's Ministry of Internal Affairs, Zakharov had spent years working in St. Petersburg, honing his skills in surveillance and tracking threats to Putin's regime.[2] Then he went to work for Prigozhin's security team.

Officially, Zakharov's title was presidential security adviser to the Central African Republic's president, Faustin Archange-Touadéra. Unofficially, Yevgeny Prigozhin had placed Zakharov on the payroll of his front company, M-Invest, months before Putin struck a military-cooperation agreement with Touadéra that elevated Zakharov to the position of chief political liaison for Wagner Group operations in the country. Zakharov made it his business to know who was coming and going.

Touadéra was one of the Wagner Group's most important new clients in Africa. A mathematician and former university rector, he had briefly served as the country's prime minister until his presidential predecessor and onetime political patron, François Bozizé, was ousted in 2013. The chronicle of mad monarchs, coups, countercoups, and massacres that had led to Touadéra's election three years later was so brutal and epic that it verged on the biblical.

The short version was that the Central African Republic was a landlocked, resource-rich country located smack in the center of a region mired in ethnic clashes and postcolonial power struggles that respected few borders. Conflict between a predominantly Muslim coalition called the Seleka and a Christian-led countermovement known as the anti-Balaka cleaved the country into factions that spawned more than a dozen militias with variable allegiances. Along the way, troops from Libya and Rwanda, along with Chadian and Sudanese mercenaries, salted the conflict with their own flavor of brutality as Bangui, the CAR's capital, became a breeding ground for organized crime and endless cycles of violence.

After Bozizé was ousted by the Seleka rebel coalition, his successor, Michel Djotodia, lasted less than a year before resigning amid rising conflicts between Seleka loyalists and anti-Balaka factions. The international community, alarmed by the humanitarian catastrophe caused by all the convulsions, yet perennially out of step, passed an array of UN resolutions that led to the imposition of an arms embargo and then the establishment in 2014 of a ten-thousand-member–strong peacekeeping mission called MINUSCA that was meant to bolster security operations led by African Union and French troops.

Hopes were high for change when Touadéra came to power. But with limited control outside the capital, his government faced constant threats from rampant criminality and rebel militias. Insecurity fueled widespread corruption and vice versa, driving his crony government into ever more dysfunctional paroxysms. Chaos in the country acted like a magnet for gold-digging grifters, diamond smugglers, mafia fixers, terrorist money launderers, and wannabe warlords, making it an ideal location for Russia to make fresh inroads and for the Wagner Group to launch a new base of operations.

Wagner had already begun making inroads on the continent as early as 2017. Advance scouting teams composed of geologists, linguists, sociologists, pollsters, social media marketers, and professional gunslingers employed by Prigozhin's front companies crisscrossed the continent to identify new business opportunities.

Prigozhin's whirlwind tours took him to at least a dozen of the twenty African countries that signed military-cooperation agreements with Russia from 2015 to 2018. Madagascar, Zimbabwe, Mozambique, Burkina Faso—the list of touch points on Prigozhin's travel itinerary was dizzying. However, none on that list were as important in this new phase of the Wagner Group's evolution as the Central African Republic and Sudan, the crown jewels at the center of Prigozhin's fledgling transcontinental empire. Both would turn out to be critical linchpins in Putin's long-game strategy for offsetting the pain of sanctions and retaking Ukraine.

Key to that plan was the cultivation of trade and military ties with autocratic African leaders who needed Russian arms to vanquish their rivals and Russian expertise in the extractive industries to maintain their exclusive hold on sources of rent from lucrative mineral deposits. Defense exports—Russian weapons and the men who knew how to use them—represented the most durable means to achieving that end.

But because many potential African client states were financially strapped, direct cash payments for military assistance often proved challenging. Instead of cash for guns, Russian intermediary companies would be compensated with mining concessions for military services. To edge out Western competitors, Russia often sweetened the terms of its bargains by offering to renegotiate loans or to outright cancel debts owed to the Kremlin. As France's president,

Emmanuel Macron, would later aptly put it: the Wagner Group was the "life insurance of failing regimes" in Africa.[3]

As recompense for its largesse, Russia gained preferential treatment on trade deals and infrastructure projects that would generate income that would help offset the bite of Western sanctions imposed in response to Russia's annexation of Crimea. An ancillary benefit of such deals was that gold and gems could easily be smuggled to the United Arab Emirates, where it could be converted into hard currency or gold ingots to bulk up Russia's reserves, a critical source of ready revenue and a hedge against the risk of escalating Western sanctions.

In a February 2018 memo sent to the Main Operational Directorate of Russia's General Staff, Prigozhin's employees mapped out in detail how "the Company" could be employed in the service of those goals. Careful, as always, not to mention the Wagner Group or Prigozhin's Concord company expressly, the strategy note elaborated on a plan for deploying political influence campaigns in twenty-one countries and "gradually squeezing out" US and EU influence in Africa in favor of Russia's expansion on the continent.[4]

The cast of characters Prigozhin enlisted in this quest came from all walks, and they frequently worked hand in glove with Russia's foreign ministry. There was Mikhail Potepkin, a Nashi youth party leader with a hipster goatee, who worked for the Internet Research Agency in St. Petersburg and then was recruited to serve as regional director of Prigozhin's front company M-Invest in Sudan.

Potepkin's comrade, Dmitry Sytii, a shaggy-haired, reed-thin graduate of St. Petersburg State University and a polyglot translator at Prigozhin's troll farm, started out as a French interpreter but quickly emerged as the friendly corporate face of Wagner enterprises in Bangui. From his perch as an employee of Prigozhin's other front company, M-Finans, and founder of Lobaye Invest, the corporate arm of Wagner's gold-mining operations in the CAR, Sytii would come to wield outsized influence in the country.

Sytii's counterparts in Bangui, Yevgeny Khodotov, a former agent with the RUBOP organized-crime bureau, served as regional head of Lobaye Invest along with Alexander Kuzin, another Concord network employee. Another M-Invest man, Ivan "Miron" Maslov, was chief of security for Wagner's advance scouting parties.[5] A native of Russia's far-eastern Pacific Rim region who had earned his stripes as a lowly driver during the battle for the Luhansk airport in 2014, Maslov was part of a new generation of younger Wagner commanders who had somehow managed to survive and thrive in the cutthroat environment that reigned among Prigozhin's mercenaries in Syria.

Behind the scenes on the diplomatic front, Prigozhin's ground team in Africa relied on advice and expertise provided by Nikolai Dobronravin, a professor at St. Petersburg State University who specialized in local African languages and cultures. An author of several papers on the politics of oil and mineral extraction in Africa, Dobronravin was one of the first in a long line of academics from the university's international-affairs faculty lured by the promise of travel, adventure, and contract pay from Wagner Group front companies.

In September 2017, Dobronravin traveled as a consultant with Sytii and two others from Russia to the CAR on a scouting trip for M-Invest.[6] The purpose of the trip was twofold: to set up logistical lines between the Central African Republic and Sudan, and to gather intelligence on prospects for Wagner's expansion. During his tour of the country, Dobronravin took copious notes on potential avenues for setting up shop, taking special note of the country's virgin redwood forests and who was who in the gold- and diamond-mining business. The trip would prove useful in more ways than one for Dobronravin and the Wagner Group.

At Sochi in October 2017, Touadéra shook hands with Russia's foreign minister, Sergey Lavrov, on the outlines of the military-cooperation agreement between Russia and the Central African Republic that smoothed the way for Wagner's entry. Toward the end of that year, the UN Security Council agreed to grant Russia an exemption to an arms embargo, allowing Russia to donate small arms and ammunition to the country.

Wagner's new assignment in the Central African Republic was to transform the country's national army, the FACA, into a cohesive fighting force. A base camp was set up for this purpose at Berengo Palace, not far from the country's war-scarred capital. Once serene and stately, the palace grounds had served forty years earlier as the seat of power for the country's late self-declared emperor Jean Bedel-Bokassa, who earned the nickname "Cannibal Emperor" for feasting on the flesh of his political enemies in the gilded dining hall of the palace. For a brief time after Bokassa's ouster, local gangs with wooden rifles trained by French peacekeepers made camp there, surviving on a diet of rat meat while the country sank into anarchy.

By the time that the first waves of Russian military instructors and crates full of AK-47 rifles began arriving in early 2018, though, all that remained of the estate's previous occupants were the rats. The first wave of Russians to arrive by air in January 2018 numbered 175; that number quickly doubled. Soon, jumbo cargo jets loaded with Russian-made military gear chartered by Flight Unit 223, the Russian defense ministry's aviation wing for irregular cargo, began landing on a regular timetable in Bangui as even more Russian instructors also arrived by convoy from neighboring Sudan.

The CAR agreement was one of two concluded in 2017 that would turn Wagner into a force to be reckoned with on the African continent. The second was the result of a headline-grabbing meeting in Russia that November between Putin and Sudan's president, Omar al-Bashir, one month after the Trump administration lifted a long-standing US trade embargo against the war-torn country. Under indictment for genocide by the International Criminal Court, al-Bashir traveled to Sochi to plead with Putin, as he put it, "for protection from the aggressive acts of the United States."[7]

Technically, al-Bashir could have been arrested on the spot when he landed. The Hague tribunal had issued warrants for him in 2009 and 2010 because of his role in facilitating atrocities committed in Sudan's Darfur region by a band of ethnic Arab mercenaries known as the Janjaweed. Rostec's export arm, Rosoboronexport, had been the Janjaweed's chief military supplier during the peak of al-Bashir's Darfur campaign under a three-way oil-for-arms deal with Russia's Tatneft. But Russia was not a party to the international statute that gave the International Criminal Court its mandate, and in any case, Putin was not much inclined to have him arrested.[8]

Putin's public alignment with al-Bashir represented a high-stakes maneuver, yet it resonated positively across the African continent. Here, the International Criminal Court (ICC) was often derided as the "International Caucasian Court." Many Africans viewed the ICC as a neocolonial instrument of the West, primarily because it disproportionately targeted African leaders. Putin's meeting with al-Bashir was not just a casual diplomatic engagement but also a calculated provocation aimed at the Western powers. It served as a clear demonstration that the traditional "rules-based international order" championed selectively by the United States was under pressure from emergent multipolar dynamics and new world order.

Russia's strategy in Africa was twofold. First, it aimed to weaken Western influence by showing solidarity with nations and leaders who felt marginalized or victimized by Western policies. Second, it was an attempt to stitch together a coalition of states that were seeking alternatives to the Western-centric world order. This coalition building was not just about political alliances but also about creating economic and security ties that could operate outside the purview of Western sanctions and diplomatic pressures.

Putin's bold move with al-Bashir was a declaration, almost a proclamation, that Russia was positioning itself as the patron of the world's rogue states. By aligning with controversial figures like al-Bashir, Putin was testing the resolve of international institutions and gauging the elasticity of international law. The maneuver was part of a larger Russian narrative that portrayed the country as a defender of national sovereignty against what it perceived as the overreach of international bodies.

Under the bargain with al-Bashir's government, Russian funds, arms, and training would flow more or less directly to a battle-hardened former Janjaweed commando named Mohammed Hamdan Dagalo. Better known as Hemedti, Dagalo had been appointed head of Sudan's Rapid Support Forces (RSF) after al-Bashir disbanded the Janjaweed. He would serve as the Wagner Group's primary military liaison in Sudan and critical interlocutor for the gold-smuggling trade.

The Sochi summit produced a host of cooperation agreements on trade and development, including a promise to open the way for Russia to construct a naval station on the Red Sea coast at the Port of Sudan, where a Gazprom subsidiary was beginning offshore oil exploration. At a parallel meeting attended by Dmitry Medvedev, Mikhail Potepkin signed an agreement granting M-Invest a gold-mining concession in Sudan, entitling the company to 30 percent of the proceeds from its mining operations.[9]

The accord formalized a deal that Potepkin had reached earlier in the summer of 2017 as a representative of Meroe Gold, the regional subsidiary of Prigozhin's M-Invest company in Sudan. Under this agreement, M-Invest would pay a $200,000 retainer plus $100,000 monthly to Aswar Multi Activities, a company controlled by Sudan's military-intelligence wing, for immigration assistance for employees and for help in importing weapons and ammunition.[10]

In the interim, Wagner Group commanders began setting up the physical infrastructure and intelligence architecture required to run a vast chain of logistical hubs across four countries: Syria, Sudan, the Central African Republic, and Libya. Makeshift encampments were erected at several junctures along treacherous smuggling routes between Bangui, the Wagner Group's logistical hub near the Sudanese capital of Khartoum, and infiltration routes in Libya.

To defend against the risk of penetration by Western intelligence agencies and more embarrassing leaks of communications intercepts, Wagner staff also set up a crude cipher and separately established an encrypted communications channel. In cryptic missives, Wagner's chief of operational intelligence, Viktor Bondar, aka "Bonya," mapped out transfers of weapons and men to "the brigade" field stations.[11] Syria received the code name "Pesky," which translates to "sands" in English. Sudan was referred to as "Solnechnoye" or "Sunny"; the CAR was assigned the code name "Tsaritsyno" or "Tsaritsa's property"—a likely reference to the famous Tsaritsino palace area in Moscow. Libya was coded as "Lipetsk," a reference to the city in western Russia.

A list of contacts labeled "VPN-Telephone 2018" was circulated with details on how to reach top-tier contacts in the nerve center of the Wagner Group's operations via secure encrypted channels.[12] Essentially a coded phone book, the list contained 530 names that revealed the extent of Prigozhin's connections with the GRU and officials with the FSB's Center for Combating Extremism. It also made clear that despite growing dissatisfaction among Wagner's rank and file with the group's chief executive officer, Andrey Troshev, he was by far the most central operational leader, second only to Prigozhin himself.

For his part, Prigozhin seemed to relish the cloak-and-dagger aspects of the work. He donned beards, hairpieces, and exotic garb as he moved from one clandestine meeting to the next in this or that African capital. On some trips he traveled on a Russian passport issued under the assumed name of "Dmitriy Isaackovich Geyler." On others he proffered the fake credentials of his body double, occasionally flashing a company certificate for Sewa Security, Wagner's front company in the Central African Republic.[13]

Russia's pivot to Africa opened vast opportunities for the Wagner Group and the Russian conglomerates it served. Each new spot that Wagner mercenaries were able to secure on the African map represented windfall profits for Rosoboronexport, which shipped crates of small arms, grenades, armored trucks, helicopters, and jets out to Africa in short order after Prigozhin and his representatives landed in country.

By 2018, the Wagner Group's head count had swelled to about 4,300.[14] A substantial number remained in Syria, but the bulk of forces were deployed forward to Africa in ad hoc formations spread across Sudan, Libya, and the CAR. Whereas terrain and conditions on the ground dictated the size, capabilities, and organizational structure, each of Wagner's ten assault detachment groups typically had its own drone, antiaircraft, signals, engineering, repair, and medical units.

Modeled on the nimbler battalion tactical groups adopted by Russia's conventional forces following the New Look reforms, Wagner assault detachments were slightly smaller, with head counts ranging from 300 to 500 men. Ground-unit commanders regularly received additional support from about 150 helicopter and fixed-wing pilots who were on contract with Prigozhin's front companies.[15]

In almost every possible way, the Wagner Group resembled in size, shape, form, and command culture a full-scale airborne paratrooper assault brigade, albeit a covert one.[16] And in internal memos, "the company" was often used interchangeably with "the brigade" in situation reports and equipment requests.

But whenever pressed to explain the Wagner Group's presence in the Central African Republic, Valery Zakharov denied any connection. He insisted that the Russian-speaking men at Berengo Palace and the ones who strolled the aisles of local markets in camouflage with their faces covered and sidearms on their hips were civilian "instructors" on short rotations, not soldiers of fortune. "Wagner? What Wagner? This is just an urban legend," Zakharov once wisecracked to an *Al Jazeera* reporter. "These men are Russian reservists nothing more."[17]

There was some truth to this assertion, though only a half-truth. Wagner deployments were managed by the Officers Union for International Security (COSI), a parallel front organization established in the Central African Republic by Alexander Ivanov, a semiretired Russian military officer. Ivanov also insisted that there was no connection between the Russian instructors and the Wagner Group. But Wagner personnel records suggested otherwise.

Many of the Russian commandos at Berengo Palace and other forward operating bases farther afield in the country had previously served in the VDV Airborne or MVD Internal Affairs units, and several of the leading Wagner commanders had served in GRU special-purpose detachments. Several Wagner platoon leaders who distinguished themselves in Syria obtained the rank of detachment commander as they rotated to Sudan and the CAR before later being called up for action in Libya.

In Sudan, for instance, Alexander Kuznetsov, the former GRU officer who had made his mark during the battle for Palmyra, led the 1st Assault Detachment, overseeing security training and gold-transport operations. Kuznetsov's opposite number in the CAR, Boris "Zombie" Nizhevenok, also did a brief tour in Sudan before taking charge as head commander for Russian military-training operations in the Central African Republic.

Like Kuznetsov, Nizhevenok was a former GRU officer who had served in Chechnya, where he earned a reputation for toughness. As chief of Wagner's

3rd Assault Detachment, Nizhevenok had duties in the CAR that included overseeing the operations of the roughly 2,300 to 2,600 Wagner fighters who would eventually rotate through the country.[18] He spent his days logging hours of training with FACA army troops and local gendarmes. But Nizhevenok was no desk jockey. He regularly led motorcycle patrols deep into thick forests, and he was a hard disciplinarian.

One step below Nizhevenok in the pecking order was Anton "Lotus" Yelizarov, who led Wagner's clearing operations around the gold mines in the Bambari area and was the base commander there. A swaggering paratrooper with graying hair and thick eyebrows, Yelizarov was one of several in Wagner's leadership echelon who had graduated from a Suvorov military boarding school as a teenager, then went straight into service with the VDV Airborne. He completed officer-training school at Ryazan Guards Higher Airborne School, specializing in the operation of multipurpose tracked and wheeled vehicles, a useful skill in the Central African Republic's muddy forests.

Early in his military career, Yelizarov rotated through several tours in the North Caucasus before he was assigned as a senior warrant officer to the GRU 10th Special Purpose Brigade in Molkino. Like so many in Wagner's band of misfit brothers, Yelizarov ran into his share of disciplinary problems while working odd jobs on the side in carpentry and interior design.[19] In 2016, during his third year of service at Molkino, he was busted down to captain and forced to quit the service after he was charged with illegally trying to sell his state-issued apartment. It was then that he joined up and went to Syria on Prigozhin's payroll.

Formally, Yelizarov was the low man on the totem pole under the chain of command that led from Troshev to Utkin downward. But his post in the eastern town of Bambari and its proximity to the famously rich Ndassima gold mine signaled that Yelizarov had quickly gained the trust of the small circle of leaders who constituted Wagner's operational command.

Others in Wagner's employ had been equally quick to earn Prigozhin's confidence.

Three months after Wagner formally set up shop in Bangui, Dobronravin was appointed to a UN sanctions-monitoring panel for Sudan in March 2018. The appointment, which followed a failed bid to serve on a similar panel for the Central African Republic, gave Dobronravin a catbird seat over the leading UN body responsible for monitoring the security sector as well as human-rights and arms-embargo violations in Sudan.

Dobronravin denied that his consultancy for M-Invest influenced the Russian foreign ministry's push to get him seated. But leaked documents showed that he continued to relay information to Sytii, Potepkin, and other Prigozhin employees.[20] The posting was a perfect perch for cultivating ties with locals in Sudan while back-channeling situation reports to the Wagner Group's office in St. Petersburg. And there could be no denying that the timing of Dobronravin's appointment to the Sudan panel was exceptionally useful.

It was around this time, early in the spring of 2018, that the three Russian reporters had set out for Molkino, where they secretly shot footage at Wagner's training camp in Russia. A trip to Syria was debated next, but nixed as too dangerous. Intrigued by reports that Wagner was expanding its reach, the trio of journalists began casting around for entry points for their story in Sudan and the Central African Republic. That was when Kiril Romanovsky, the RIA-FAN correspondent in Prigozhin's pay, stepped into the picture.[21]

In April, Romanovsky offered to connect them with a local UN aide named "Martin," who could help show them around and find them a driver in Bangui. On Romanovsky's recommendation, the documentary crew arranged via WhatsApp text messages to work with "Martin," who connected them with their driver, Bienvenue. But "Martin" never materialized at the airport in Bangui as promised because "Martin" did not exist.

Eyes were on the three-man documentary crew from the instant their flight touched down early on the morning of July 28 in Bangui. A Wagner-trained local gendarme named Emmanuel Tuaguende Kotofio was assigned to shadow their every move. He would trail them right up until the moment they met their end.

Unable to connect with the fixer or driver that Romanovsky had set them up with, the journalists taxied to their temporary digs at the Hotel National, near the center of town. Eventually the driver turned up, and on their first full day in country, the Russian film crew gamely attempted without success to gain access to Berengo Palace. Masked Wagner fighters at the perimeter brusquely turned them away.

Undeterred, the Russian journalists set out late the next morning (July 30) for Bambari, where Wagner had set up camp on the perimeter of a gold mine, one of several under the control of Prigozhin's front company Lobaye Invest. For an unknown reason, which their driver was unable to explain, when the journalists arrived in Sibut around dusk, they took a detour north instead of east to Bambari. They would never reach their destination.

Phone records unearthed by Mikhail Khodorkovsky's investigators months later would reveal that Kotofio, the local gendarme assigned to track their movements, had followed them to Sibut. All along, he was in constant contact with a Wagner commander named Alexander Sotov, who in turn was in touch with Zakharov—the Kremlin's man in the presidential office.

Putin pronounced the deaths of the three journalists a tragedy.

But in a backhanded dig in December 2018, he seemed to suggest that they had brought it on themselves by nosing into the Wagner Group's affairs in the first place. "As far as I know, your colleagues travelled to Africa as tourists, not even as journalists, without notifying local authorities," he said.[22] The killer or killers were never charged, and the Russian government investigation predictably dragged on for about a year before it dead-ended.

As far as Khodorkovsky was concerned, Prigozhin had either ordered the hit against the three journalists himself, or someone close to Putin had pushed Prigozhin to silence them permanently. "I consider Prigozhin to be a thug who is fully capable of murder," Khodorkovsky said in an interview years later. "What he did in his youth when he got arrested reflected the psyche of a thug."[23]

In fact, the story of what led up to the murders was much more complicated. One branch of the narrative trail seemed to lead all the way back to the bitter rivalry that had erupted between Putin and Khodorkovsky over Yukos, which dated back to 2003, when Rosneft took control of the Yukos assets. A year before the three journalists traveled to the Central African Republic, Khodorkovsky's investigative outlet had dug up information about the suspicious death in 2004 of a passenger on board Prigozhin's floating New Island restaurant who had fallen overboard. The story was quite sensational, but some suspected instead that it was a controversial documentary about Putin's close friend and Rosneft CEO Igor Sechin produced by Khodorkovsky's team and released only four months before the journalists were killed that reignited the bitter enmity between Khodorkovsky and Putin and placed the documentary crew in the direct line of fire.

The film traced Sechin's improbable rise from little-known KGB flunky to Putin's personal secretary in St. Petersburg, then to head of Rosneft after Khodorkovsky was imprisoned. The film explained how Sechin co-opted the FSB's 6th Directorate into his own private fiefdom and used it to jail Putin's challengers. The big reveal centered on a fancy private hunting preserve that Sechin erected in Tula, where Alexey Dyumin had been appointed as governor after his successful tour as deputy chief of the GRU. Highly provocative, the film was an instant hit, garnering more than a million views on YouTube.

But likely more galling for both Sechin and Putin was the fact that Khodorkovsky's charitable foundation, Open Russia, had financed the entire series even though Russian authorities had banned the organization. More irritating still, no doubt, was the fact that Khodorkovsky continued to live freely and to pursue his vendettas against the Kremlin despite a 2018 Russian arrest warrant for him in absentia for his alleged role in a murder-for-hire plot. That charge was never proven, and Khodorkovsky maintained that the case was trumped up and politically motivated. The Kremlin was clearly determined to thwart Khodorkovsky's activism, a fact that placed anyone even tangentially associated with his enterprises at risk.

Years later, Kiril Radchenko's brother Roman could not shake the suspicion that his brother and the other two journalists killed in the Central African Republic had somehow gotten snagged in this tangle of twisted yarns and vengeful intrigues. "I didn't really think about it much for a long time, but this fixation in the news with 'Prigozhin. Prigozhin. Prigozhin' all the time got me thinking," he recalled. "When I reviewed all these materials again, at some point I started to make the connection with all this. I think there's just some kind of—again, these are all assumptions—but Sechin, the Tula region, Alexey Dyumin, the governor of the Tula region, who is already associated with Prigozhin. I see such a chain here now. But, of course, it cannot be proven."[24]

Khodorkovsky admitted he had been "naive" and maybe even glib about the risks involved in trying to expose Prigozhin's links to the Wagner Group. The murders, Khodorkovsky said, were as much a sign of Prigozhin's moral depravity as they were of Putin's fecklessness: "For me, the question is: how can a guy with that kind of biography be put in charge of two such disparate businesses? One business is a troll farm, and the other is a mercenary operation. In my view, he is both financier and front man for GRU."[25]

Khodorkovsky's ten-year odyssey in Russia's prison system had aged but not beaten him. The thick head of dark hair he had sported when his grudge match with Putin over Yukos and Russia's future had started had given way to a close crewcut flecked with white streaks. He spent years ruminating over the missteps that had led him to believe that Putin would do things differently than his autocratic predecessors. Sitting in the drawing room of his well-appointed London townhouse, he was coolly philosophical about his ongoing battle with Putin's regime and Prigozhin. "By the rules I live by if Prigozhin or Prigozhin's guys detained these journalists and arrested them for trying to film and then sent them to jail I would have complained but I would have said, well, that's OK," Khodorkovsky mused. "Even if they had shot them in the legs I would, of course, have also responded strongly but that would have been within the bounds of the game. But to kill three people because you don't want them to investigate something about you? Well, that's a violation. That's a violation of the rules of the game."[26]

However, the winners and losers of the game would not be revealed for several more years. But Khodorkovsky would soon make it clear that he intended to be on the winning side against Prigozhin. Revenge took the form of a new organization, the Dossier Centre, which doggedly pursued inside information about the Wagner Group and Prigozhin's dealings with the Kremlin.

In the interim, Russia continued conducting business as usual. Three weeks after the murders, in August 2018, Sergey Shoigu and his Central African Republic defense ministry counterpart Marie-Noëlle Koyara signed a military-cooperation agreement on the sidelines of a Moscow arms exhibition. Over the months that followed, Touadéra became more and more dependent on the Wagner Group. Through an arrangement widely believed to have been brokered by Prigozhin's intermediary in Africa, Konstantin "Mazay" Pikalov, the Russians were put in charge of running the presidential guard.[27]

Pikalov, a grizzled graduate of the Leningrad Naval College, had entered the private-security sector nearly a decade earlier, completing bodyguard-training courses in the 1990s. By 2009, he and fellow mercenary Vasily Yaschikov were offering their services through the St. Petersburg Konvoy Cossack Society, eventually forming a connection with Orthodox oligarch Konstantin Malofeev. Leaked documents revealed Pikalov's presence in Sudan in 2017, where he provided security for a Russian delegation of political technologists.[28] However, his involvement with Wagner's top commanders on the front lines in Donbas had begun as early as 2014.

Wagner Group front companies gained ever-greater access to mining sites across the country. Within a year of Wagner's arrival, local media sources in the CAR would report that Lobaye Invest had added at least four new mining sites in the towns of Ndele, Bria, Birao, and Alindao to its roster of gold- and diamond-mining concessions.[29] Meanwhile, Wagner operatives reportedly ferried planes full of gold over the border into Sudan, where it was refined and then shipped onward by Meroe Gold to the United Arab Emirates for laundering.[30]

Within two years, Wagner had set up nearly fifty bases across the Central African Republic, according to a map created by Prigozhin's team. Wagner's widespread presence made it a critical security ally for UN peacekeepers, who were outgunned by local militias, although the unspoken partnership would wither as Wagner's mounting civilian casualties drew greater public scrutiny and strained relations with the UN mission ahead of pending elections.

Much of this success was attributable to the decisive steps that Zakharov began to take to negotiate deals with insurgent leaders who maintained a chokehold on mineral-rich parts of the country. The biggest breakthrough came in February 2019, when Prigozhin reportedly took on as his personal mission the negotiation of an agreement between Touadéra's government and fourteen armed groups during a week of negotiations in Khartoum.[31]

Bribes paid to rebel leaders as part of the bargain were apparently not enough to keep the arrangement glued together for long, however. The deal would fall apart within six months amid frictions between Touadéra and his former political patron François Bozizé over Bozizé's exclusion from the upcoming national elections in 2020.

Still, in the excitement of the moment, the deal represented a win that Prigozhin could take to the bank with his sponsors in the Kremlin. He had pulled every lever of influence at his disposal to hand Moscow a diplomatic victory over its rivals in Paris. The Khartoum accords gave Touadéra and his FACA forces more sway over the country's war economy while earning the Wagner Group considerably more political cachet. More importantly, the accords opened new avenues for the expansion of the Concord network's business empire.

Along with Lobaye Invest, Dmitry Sytii expanded the Concord network's reach into the diamond-mining industry with the 2019 registration of a company called Diamville. Together, the two companies anchored the conveyor-belt–like gold- and diamond-smuggling operation that snaked its way through nearby Cameroon and Sudan and had touch points in Madagascar and Gabon, where Touadéra's clannish retinue did its banking.[32] In time, researchers would also identify Bois Rouge, a timber company, as part of the growing galaxy of firms linked to Sytii in the Central African Republic.

But it was Midas Resources that would become the primary corporate vehicle for the Wagner Group's takeover of the country's biggest prize, the Ndassima gold mine. Acquisition of the mine would catapult the Concord network's earnings in Africa from the tens of millions of dollars into the hundreds of millions. Located about forty miles north of the Wagner Group's joint base with FACA forces at Bambari, Ndassima was the only industrialized gold mine in the country. The total value of its gold deposits hovered near the $2.8 billion mark, according to one estimate.[33]

War and roving bands of militias had forced Axmin, the Canadian mining company that originally owned the mine, to curtail operations there in 2013. Over the four years that followed, a splinter faction of the Seleka, the UPC, exerted nominal control over the vast stepped tiers of pitted, yellow earth where the mine lay. Together with FACA soldiers, the Wagner Group launched an aggressive campaign to retake control of the mine almost immediately upon their arrival in 2017.

Two years later, Axmin company officials were surprised to learn that officials with the CAR ministry of mines had rescinded Axmin's license and that the government had transferred control of Ndassima to Midas Resources.[34] The government's grant of the concession to the Russian company made Dmitry Sytii one of the most influential men on Prigozhin's payroll on the African continent.

In record time, Sytii had wired the CAR from top to bottom. In his role as Russia's soft-power impresario and head of Maison Russe, the cultural-exchange center financed by Prigozhin's companies in Bangui, he applied lessons learned from previous influence campaigns on an industrial scale. Free flags and T-shirts bearing the Russian red, white, and blue tricolor were readily available for Maison Russe visitors. Russian-language lessons were on offer, along with carousel rides and day camps for children.

At one point, Zakharov even played master of ceremonies at a glitzy "Ms. Centralafrique" beauty pageant there. At bars around town, Africa Ti L'Or, the beer distributed by Sytii's locally owned brewery, would become one of the biggest sellers, and Russian-distributed Wa-Na-Wa vodka flew off the shelves of local markets.

Even more intoxicating, though, was Radio Lengo Songo—"Build Solidarity"—an FM and shortwave radio station that was launched to great fanfare with funding from Lobaye Invest soon after Sytii's arrival. Company earnings paid for the installation of more than a dozen reception towers, making Lengo Songo FM the most popular station in the country.

On Facebook, which served as the main internet gateway in much of Africa, hundreds of Internet Research Agency sock puppets promoted Russia's outreach as a revival of Soviet-era brotherly ties, crediting Moscow with helping

African allies defeat European colonial powers and counter US interference. The Russian sales pitch was bluntly axiomatic: Russia equals stability. The West equals chaos. It was an argument that resonated widely in a part of the world where centuries of colonialist plunder and Europe's imposition of divisive segregationist regimes that cleaved along ethnic and linguistic lines had impoverished and embittered generations.

Combined with mercenary muscle and plenty of graft, the Russian counterinsurgency campaign turned out to be incredibly effective for a time. There could be no denying that the Wagner Group had succeeded in building a genuinely devoted and loyal fan base in the Central African Republic. Two years into Wagner's expansion of operations on the continent, the question was whether Prigozhin's outfit would be able to sell the rest of Africa on its future with Russia.

Across the border in Sudan, the picture was decidedly more mixed. In early 2019 the country exploded into turmoil as mass protests against President Omar al-Bashir's thirty-year regime transformed into a full-blown uprising. What started in December 2018 as outrage over the tripling of bread prices swiftly escalated into a nationwide demand for al-Bashir's resignation. The grievances were many, rooted in decades of economic decline, rampant corruption, and severe repression.

By early April 2019, the situation was white-hot. Thousands of Sudanese citizens flooded the area around the military's headquarters near the presidential compound in Khartoum, demanding al-Bashir's ouster and the installation of a civilian-led government. It was no fringe movement; it was a vast uprising drawing strength from every corner of Sudanese society.

A little more than a week after the protests erupted, on April 11, the military deposed al-Bashir and placed him under house arrest under its authority, raising alarm bells in the Kremlin. Suddenly, Russia's planned capture of the Sudanese government looked to be on very shaky ground. Within days, Prigozhin was on board a plane with a high-level Russian defense ministry delegation bound for Khartoum, according to flight records examined by *Novaya Gazeta* reporters.[35]

Leaked documents from M-Invest shared with CNN by Khodorkovsky's Dossier Centre indicated that Prigozhin apparently arrived in Sudan armed with an elaborate disinformation-campaign plan aimed at discrediting pro-democracy protesters and handing back control of the government to Sudan's intelligence services.[36] In addition to the usual smear tactics, one bullet point in the strategy document apparently called for "public executions of looters and other spectacular events."[37]

The Transitional Military Council installed after al-Bashir's ouster did not act on the advice. But the presence of Wagner Group fighters during the protests suggested that Prigozhin's commandos in Khartoum still exerted considerable influence inside Sudan's security institutions. With boots on the ground and a hand in Sudan's gold mines, they were deeply entwined in the country's military and political fabric.

The turning point in the crisis came on June 3, when RSF troops under Hemedti's command launched a savage crackdown on a peaceful sit-in. At least a hundred demonstrators were massacred, and countless more were injured. The brutality generated sharp rebukes from Western capitals but little in the way of concrete action, even as Wagner's footprint began to expand farther across the African continent.

CHAPTER 16

ONWARD TO TRIPOLI

In November 2018, Libyan strongman General Khalifa Haftar flew to Moscow to meet with the Russian defense minister, Sergey Shoigu. There was much to discuss. Ravaged by civil war, Libya was in free fall. In the hopes of gaining an edge in its bid for greater influence across Africa, for three years Russia had been covertly arming Haftar's Libya National Army (LNA) in contravention of a UN embargo.

The encounter between the two men—a former CIA asset turned Russian military proxy and Moscow's top man in charge of defense—was already newsworthy, but it was Yevgeny Prigozhin's cameo appearance that set off a feeding frenzy in the international press after a video of the meeting surfaced on Twitter.

The official line from the Kremlin was that Prigozhin was simply there to cater the event. "He arranged an official dinner and took part in the discussion of the cultural program of the Libyan delegation's visit," an anonymous source told Russia's state news agency, Interfax. The claim beggared belief. The Kremlin was offering the Wagner Group to help Haftar trounce his rivals in Tripoli in the hopes of securing lucrative energy, arms, and infrastructure deals.

Dressed in a sharp-looking navy-blue suit, crisp white shirt, and dark tie, Prigozhin sat alongside Shoigu and Russia's chief of General Staff Valery Gerasimov, looking very much at home in their company. The meeting, which was also attended by Sergey Rudskoy, chief of the Russian military's Main Operations Directorate and head man in charge of Russia's foreign-arms transfers, provided the first visual confirmation of Prigozhin's increased stature within the Kremlin. It also affirmed the Wagner Group's growing importance in Russia's quest to use Africa as a springboard for reestablishing its Great Power status.

With the prospect of elections in Libya looming in December 2018, the Kremlin and Haftar saw a window of opportunity opening. Shoigu had been in talks with Haftar for more than a year about a potential transfer of Russian-made fighter jets and weapons. Valued at $2.4 billion, the military-aid package reportedly included ten Sukhoi-35 fighter jets, six Yak-130 combat aircraft, and several Kilo-class submarines—in other words, enough to blow Haftar's competitors in Libya quite literally right out of the water.[1] More importantly to Russia, and concerning to the United States and NATO, the deal would grant Russia access to two eastern port cities, Tobruk and Benghazi, within striking distance of Europe's southern flank.

Libya's collapse into civil war in 2011 had cost Russia dearly. During the chaos that erupted amid the NATO intervention that led to the violent ouster and killing of Muammar Qaddafi, unrest across the country had forced Tatneft to evacuate more than three hundred of its workers from the country's oil and gas fields. Losses for the state oil company were estimated in the region of $100 million in the immediate aftermath.[2] Moscow officials placed total revenue losses from potential Rosoboronexport arms sales to Libya at well over $4 billion.[3] As the conflict spiraled out of control, Russian Railways also found itself out of pocket and unable to execute on plans to build a much-anticipated rail line from the eastern city of Benghazi southward to Sirte.

During the first three years of the conflict, Russia had hedged, keeping diplomatic channels open with leading Libyan factions while cranking up its anti-NATO propaganda. The Kremlin changed its stance in 2015, after Haftar seized control of the eastern half of the country following divisive parliamentary elections the previous year that found the Government of National Accord (GNA), a grouping aligned with the Muslim Brotherhood, nominally in control of the western half, surrounding Tripoli, but besieged by ISIS and al-Qaeda–aligned extremists. The country was effectively lawless.

At this stage the crisis in Libya evolved into a high-octane international proxy war that saw Qatar and Turkey support the GNA's prime minister, Fayez al-Sarraj, and the United Arab Emirates, Egypt, Saudi Arabia, France, and Russia on the side of Haftar. With an estimated 47 billion barrels in oil reserves and

52 trillion cubic feet in proven gas reserves, Libya represented a huge potential bonanza for all the players at the table.

Haftar, the Kremlin's choice of champion in this high-stakes geopolitical poker game, was risky. For much of his professional life, he had survived on a diet of cunning, betrayal, and opportunism. He was a central player in the 1969 military coup that first brought Qaddafi to power, then had studied for several years in Moscow at the elite M. V. Frunze Military Academy in a Soviet program for foreign officers that was famous for training future autocrats. The LNA's chokehold on Libya's eastern oil terminals and Haftar's access to billions in oil, gas, and mineral concessions made him an especially attractive target.

However, other parts of Haftar's résumé were less reassuring to the Kremlin. In the 1980s, during Libya's border war with Chad, Haftar had been captured along with four hundred Libyan troops under his command. Qaddafi's public disavowal of the incident eventually pushed Haftar into the arms of the CIA, which financed the establishment of the LNA and a botched attempt to topple Qaddafi in the 1990s.

Over the next two decades, Haftar led a quiet life in relative obscurity in the leafy suburbs of Virginia near the Pentagon and the CIA headquarters in Langley, where he worked on contract as a paid adviser to US intelligence agencies. The Arab Spring uprisings paved the way for his eventual return to Libya, where fortune eventually favored him on the battlefield.

His success was due in no small measure to substantial support from the Emiratis, who supplied Haftar's forces with sophisticated Russian-made military equipment through an elaborate covert-arms pipeline that spanned from Russia's military-industrial heartland to Abu Dhabi, the center of the Emirates' defense complex. Russia had subsequently backed Haftar with surreptitious shipments of weapons into Benghazi, along with more than $1 billion in counterfeit Libyan dinars printed by Goznak, Russia's state mint, from 2016 to 2018.

In addition to outfitting Haftar's troops with Rostec-made weapons, military spare parts, Russian technicians, and military advisers attached to the Wagner Group, Moscow had authorized the Wagner Group's ostensible competitor in the military security–contracting business, RSB Group, to contract for a de-mining mission at a cement factory in Benghazi. But these initial investments were more a hedging strategy than a ringing endorsement of Haftar, whose mercurial ways raised doubts about his long-term viability as a political proxy in Putin's increasingly aggressive drive to turn Libya into the linchpin of its dual-track strategy of asserting Russia's dominance in Africa and challenging NATO.

Instead, Putin harbored a stronger preference for Saif al-Islam, Qaddafi's son, despite the inconvenience of a standing International Criminal Court warrant for his arrest on charges of committing crimes against humanity. Held in captivity by an Islamist militia for years, Saif had also been separately sentenced to death by firing squad in a war-crimes trial held in absentia by a GNA court in Tripoli in 2015. When Saif was released from captivity under a deal brokered with the GNA's rivals in Tobruk two years later, the Kremlin hoped for his return to power in Tripoli and for a political marriage of convenience with Haftar.

It fell to Prigozhin to help broker the accord and to strengthen the hand of both Haftar and Saif ahead of anticipated negotiations for a political settlement and elections. Here, Prigozhin's back office employed the usual tricks. RIA-FAN trolls got to work on mounting a massive influence campaign, buying online ads on Facebook and setting up fake accounts there and on Twitter, where bots were employed to push anti-GNA and pro-Saif and pro-Haftar propaganda that received millions of views. Prigozhin's outfit also paid off the debts of Jamahiriya TV, the Qaddafi regime's defunct broadcast mouthpiece, in a bid to revive nostalgia for the good old days, when Saif had been poised to inherit his father's political mantle before the revolution knocked the station off the airwaves. With production studios in Cairo, the station hired a "network of people's correspondents" to reach an estimated six million viewers.[4]

On the military front, while the Kremlin continued to harbor doubts about Haftar, his utility as a proxy in the conflict trumped all other considerations. Seeking to capitalize on the stronger foothold gained by Wagner forces across Africa's Sahel region in the Central African Republic and Sudan, the Russian defense ministry authorized an increase in the number of Wagner forces in Libya to bolster Haftar's forces, a move that would eventually see more than 1,200 Russian mercenaries surge into the country. Soon after the 2018 Moscow summit among Prigozhin, Haftar, and Russian defense officials, fresh contingents of *Wagnerovtsy* were inserted into eastern Libya.

Within weeks of their arrival, Haftar's amalgamated army captured the massive El Sharara oil field in southwest Libya in February 2019. Situated just a three-hour drive west from the small town of Sabha in the oil-rich region of Fezzan, the El Sharara field supplied the GNA-controlled National Oil Company with an estimated 315,000 barrels of oil per day. The LNA's seizure of the field signaled the opening salvo of "Operation Flood of Dignity," the code name for Haftar's blitzkrieg-style offensive aimed at toppling the GNA and capturing Tripoli.

Haftar's alliance with Prigozhin alarmed UN staff charged with monitoring the arms embargo against Libya and the human-rights situation in the country. Equally troubling was the fact that the Wagner Group had drawn Syrian fighters into the conflict. An estimated 2,000 Syrian fighters recruited to work on contract with the Wagner Group arrived in Benghazi on dozens of flights organized via Syria's Cham Wings airline. Most were paid on average $800 to $2,000, a fraction of what their Russian counterparts earned, according to a UN expert report.[5] Tasked with digging trenches, building improvised roads, and guarding sensitive Wagner Group positions, the Syrians were little more than cannon fodder, and many would not survive the Tripoli campaign. Those who did would go on to fight on the front lines of Wagner's next frontiers.

In St. Petersburg the information-warfare part of the campaign was rolled out. Plans were made to parachute into Libya a political technologist from the Foundation for the Protection of National Values, the research arm of the Concord network's back office that had designed the pro-Trump website USAReally. Officially, Maxim Shugaley traveled to Tripoli as an independent researcher and election observer for the foundation. Unofficially, Shugaley's primary goal was to prep Saif al-Islam for his political comeback and to cement the Kremlin's hoped-for coalition between al-Islam and Haftar.

Like so many others affiliated with Concord and Russia's industrial-scale influence campaigns, Shugaley had found his way into Prigozhin's circle via the ultranationalist Rodina Party, which had sponsored Shugaley's failed candidacy for the St. Petersburg city council in the early 2000s. By the time that he and three other foundation consultants arrived in Tripoli in late March 2019, Shugaley had already hopscotched across Africa on Prigozhin's dime many times. The most notable of his trips was a six-month stop in Madagascar, where Shugaley served as an electoral consultant to one of at least six different presidential candidates backed by Russia in a tight race for the presidency of the resource-rich country. In exchange for the help, Prigozhin's front company Ferrum Mining was awarded a concession for chromite mining.[6]

The plan for Libya was more of the same. But the number of players on the board, the mix of motivations at play, and mistrust all around greatly complicated Shugaley's mission. A lengthy situation report prepared by Prigozhin's political consultants laid bare their reservations about Haftar, noting that he intended to keep his US citizenship and—somewhat ironically—complaining about his transactional style of politics: "Russian specialists are restricted in their work, meanwhile Haftar is using the assistance of the Russian Federation to boost his own profile and as a bargaining chip. There are serious grounds to believe that, in the event of his military-political victory, Haftar would not be loyal to the interests of Russia."[7]

To tip the scales back in Moscow's favor, the Wagner Group secured assurances from the Sudanese warlord Hemedti in Khartoum that thousands of his rapid-support forces would be at the ready to cross Sudan's porous border with Libya to assist the LNA takeover and provide support to Libyan tribes that could serve as a check on Haftar's ambitions when it came time to broker a political settlement. From there, it would be up to Saif al-Islam to hold the shaky two-way coalition with Haftar together under one big political tent. The plan was pure bubblegum and baling wire, but it was the best that Prigozhin's team was able to come up with on the quick.

Days before Haftar formally announced his intention to seize Tripoli in early April, Shugaley and his colleague Alexander Prokofiev traveled to meet with Saif al-Islam in his Zintan redoubt to lay out the plan. But their interactions with Putin's preferred partner were no more reassuring. Armed with a colorful PowerPoint slideshow written in slick English and labeled "Libya's Rebirth-Strategy," Prigozhin's team of political technologists laid out an eleven-point plan to buff up Saif's image.

Apart from the idea of a "Safe with Saif" flash mob in support of Saif at The Hague, the menu of recommended actions was standard management-consultancy fare.

Holed up in his living room with television news of Haftar's march on Tripoli blaring in the background, Saif seemed anxious, distracted, and unconvinced by the proposal to share power with Haftar. He told his Russian guests that he was intrigued by their proposal—especially the online propaganda—but was skeptical about big-tent party politics being the answer. "Libyans vote for a leader, not a party," he quipped.

"His behavior shows clear signs of narcissism. He is convinced that as soon as he goes public the majority of the people will support him at once, and that Haftar's people will come over to his side," Prokofiev noted. "In contrast to his supporters, who see the Muslim Brotherhood as their main threat, he considers Haftar to be the biggest threat." The talks bore little fruit; there was too much bad blood between Haftar and the Qaddafi dynasty's political heir apparent.[8]

Instead, the caper had served to attract the attention of US intelligence agents operating in Libya, who tipped off GNA government officials about Prokofiev and Shugaley's agenda. In May 2019, just days after Prokofiev flew back to Russia, GNA authorities detained Shugaley and his Arabic translator, Samir Seifan, on charges of espionage. The arrests led to the capture of thousands of internal documents that revealed the scope of Prigozhin's plans to conduct psychological operations across Africa in tandem with Wagner Group deployments in resource-rich parts of the continent.

In Libya, Prigozhin's trademark one-two-punch combo of deploying disorienting disinformation campaigns and deception tactics to paper over Wagner's links to the Kremlin would initially prove quite effective. But as Wagner operatives on the ground began to make contact with their adversaries and civilian casualties began to mount, the presence of Russian mercenaries became undeniable.

Working side by side with the LNA, Wagner operatives set up camp at the al-Jufra air base, conducting frontline reconnaissance runs to improve the accuracy of LNA artillery and drone strikes. Wagner forces set up an array of air defenses around the airbase perimeter, most notably including expensive Russian-made Pantsir S1 antiaircraft rocket launchers that had been specially shipped in by air from the United Arab Emirates.

One intriguing aspect of the arrangement was that the manufacturer of the Pantsir batteries, the KBP Instrument Design Bureau, was headquartered in Tula, where Alexey Dyumin, Prigozhin's longtime acquaintance, had been appointed governor by Putin in 2016. Tula, a major center for arms manufacturing, was also central to Rostec's enterprises, including production of Russia's iconic AK series assault rifles. Dyumin took up the governorship after serving briefly as deputy defense minister and head of construction and property management at the ministry.[9] During Dyumin's tenure at the defense ministry, Prigozhin's company, Megaline LLC, and related affiliates won several lucrative construction and cleaning contracts worth millions, including one for the construction of a military village in the Belgorod region.[10]

Companies linked to Prigozhin also won several construction tenders for projects commissioned by Tula's regional government, including a sports stadium, a kindergarten, and Patriot Park, a local outdoor museum of Russian-made military gear. Megaline was also the lucky winner of construction and cleaning contracts for a similar but larger Patriot Park in Moscow. These were doled out by General Timur Ivanov, another ally of Dyumin and the defense ministry patron of Prigozhin.[11] Those connections likely explained how it was that Prigozhin's mercenary outfit emerged as the leading recipient of Pantsir platforms and associated military equipment sent to Libya.

The coordination between the Emiratis and the Wagner Group in Libya was as much a product of Prigozhin's entrepreneurial schemes as it was a reflection of broader Kremlin strategy. An analysis of customs data for 122 shipments from Russia to the UAE in 2019 and 2020 showed that UCS Holdings, a Russian logistics firm linked to military shipments in Donbas, played a key role in transporting to the UAE Pantsir-related materials valued at nearly $8 million.[12] Flight-tracking data further indicated that some equipment destined for Wagner forces arrived through covert flights from Abu Dhabi to Libya. Additionally, a network of air-logistics companies, such as FlySky Airlines and Azee-Air, helped facilitate Wagner's operations, transporting military cargo across airfields in Libya, the Central African Republic, Mali, and Syria.[13]

Further confirmation that the UAE had a hand in backing Wagner's operations in Libya surfaced in a dense 100-page Pentagon report published in November 2020 that said the US Defense Intelligence Agency had assessed that the UAE "may provide some financing for the group's operations."[14] This was truly a revelation. For years, the UAE had played host to thousands of US military forces, providing critical basing for and support of an air force expeditionary wing at the Al Dhafra Airbase near Abu Dhabi. The partnership between Moscow and the UAE's defense industry in Abu Dhabi was a blatant violation of international sanctions against Wagner and UN resolutions calling for peace in Libya. A September 2019 Wagner report detailed the group's close collaboration with Emirati forces, noting how UAE air strikes, guided by coordinates from Wagner drone operators, successfully hit pro-GNA positions, forcing them to retreat.[15] The Arab Spring uprisings and the subsequent rise of ISIS had apparently shifted the Emiratis' priorities and allegiances.

The combination of Wagner's expertise, Russian weaponry, and Chinese-made Wing Loong drones purchased by the Emiratis proved effective in helping the LNA punch holes in the GNA defenses. Aided by Wagner's targeted strikes and crack teams of snipers fielded by the contingent's neo-Nazi reconnaissance and sabotage detachment, Rusich, Haftar's forces were advancing fast toward Tripoli by September 2019.

At military headquarters in Tripoli, the fear among the forces loyal to the UN-endorsed government that Haftar could breach the capital's defenses was palpable. Fred Wehery, a former US defense attaché who served in Libya after Qaddafi's overthrow, witnessed the sheer terror that gripped the city when he met with GNA military officials at the time: "I could see on the faces of those GNA commanders utter shock, utter exhaustion and the panic that the front-lines could actually collapse, that Haftar for the first time might be able to push into Tripoli. And it was all because of Wagner. It spooked the GNA. Snipers suddenly got more accurate. Mortar rounds got more accurate. The LNA was gaining territory."[16]

The gains would not come without cost. An April 2019 situation report described how heavy casualties had prompted Haftar to beg Russia's senior VDV Airborne commander on the ground, Lieutenant General Andrey Khol-zakov, to deploy more Russian drones to shield the LNA from attack. The tides began to turn even more sharply against Wagner and Haftar's forces when Tur-key agreed in the fall of 2019 to step up its military support for the UN-backed GNA government.

Among other things, the military aid came with artillery support from a Turkish naval destroyer loitering off Libya's coast in the Mediterranean, mili-tary advisers, and mercenaries shipped in from Syria. However, it was the fleet of lethal Turkish-made Bayraktar drones that would prove to be pivotal. From September 2019 to July 2020, at least a hundred Wagner mercenaries assigned to mount air defenses were killed by Turkish missiles that struck Russian Pan-tsir antiaircraft batteries.[17] In response, Wagner began aggressively recruiting Syrian mercenaries to join in the fray.

Hundreds more wounded Wagner fighters were shipped back to St. Petersburg, where they recovered from their injuries at medical clinics run by SOGAZ. The most notable of those treated was Wagner's salty 1st Assault Detachment commander Alexander Kuznetsov, who told a Reuters reporter who caught him—arm in sling—smoking casually outside the clinic that he had just returned from fighting in Libya.[18]

Wagner's high casualties in Libya augured for tough times ahead. Within a year of the start of the battle for Tripoli, Haftar's forces and his Russian advisers would be forced to beat a quick retreat. Videos and images from Libya's front lines shot during the offensive on Tripoli showed Wagner forces scattered and scrambling into defensive positions across the Sirte-Jufra line.

In their wake, they left a trail of atrocities, including the murder of three members of a Libyan family who were taken captive by Russian fighters near the town of Espiia. Unexploded Russian-made mines and booby-trapped

munitions in houses and buildings that the mercenaries occupied led to dozens of casualties, leading UN investigators to accuse Wagner of war crimes.[19]
The battlefield reversals and the publicity surrounding Wagner-linked atrocities would eventually set the stage for a ceasefire agreement that called for the
expulsion of foreign mercenaries from the country. However, it turned out that
Libya was not the only place where the Wagner Group found itself on the back
foot in hot spots where Russia had overextended itself.

In Mozambique, where Russia had signed a military-technical cooperation agreement with the government of President Felipe Nyusi in 2017, Prigozhin had managed to edge out other high-profile private-military contractors
like Erik Prince and South Africa's Eeben Barlow in large part because of a
promise from Russia to write off 95 percent of the debt that Mozambique
owed to Russian state banks and a planned Gazprombank-financed offshore
liquefied-natural-gas project. Besides, Russia was at the time still Mozambique's
largest trading partner, and Mozambique's flag, after all, still bears the image of
a Kalashnikov rifle, a symbolic remnant of Mozambican reverence for Soviet
support given to anticolonial rebel forces during the Cold War era.

But despite the warmth between Maputo, the capital, and Moscow, Wagner forces received a much colder welcome when two hundred of them deployed
in September 2019 to Mozambique's restive, ruby-rich province of Cabo Delgado on the Indian Ocean seaside to help local forces fight a homegrown ISIS
contingent. Wagner forces were simply outclassed. "A lot of the fighting was
being done by the police. They were totally out of their depth," a longtime
Western security adviser based in Maputo remembered. "They clearly were not
expecting to fight a guerrilla war with a full-on insurgency."[20] This became very
clear when in early October, ISIS rebels killed two Wagner mercenaries in an
ambush and then beheaded them. An internal Wagner Group assessment of the
incidents in Cabo Delgado attested to this view.

The incidents involving Shugaley and Wagner in Mozambique were hardly
ringing advertisements for Wagner's services. But Prigozhin would soon apply
his peculiar panache to the narratives of Wagner's PR disasters and turn them
into Hollywood-style screen gold. Produced by Aurum LLC, Prigozhin's
film-production company, the first of these, *Shugaley*, told a wildly romanti-
cized story of Shugaley's capture and imprisonment in Libya. The feature-length
adventure film generated hundreds of thousands of views when RT, Russia's
state propaganda broadcast network, released the version dubbed into English
on its YouTube channel.

It would be one of three in a series of "Shugaley" features, in which the eponymous hero is a weird cross between James Bond and Indiana Jones as he takes on all comers: his Islamist captors, CIA agents, and a shady London-based Russian oligarch who is clearly modeled on Mikhail Khodorkovsky. Punctuated with gun battles, loud explosions, torture scenes, choppy flashback scenes from Shugaley's life in St. Petersburg, and interludes featuring cameos by Saif Qaddafi and Haftar's arch-nemesis Fathi Bashaga, the Shugaley series flips everything about Russia's involvement in Libya on its head, fingering the GNA for war crimes suspected of being committed by LNA and Wagner fighters.

The films formed part of a wider Prigozhin-financed PR campaign orchestrated by the Foundation for the Protection of National Values to secure Shugaley's release from prison in Libya. Complete with Facebook and Instagram pages, the films were promoted as documentaries, and they veered from the surreal to the darkly comic when real-life Hollywood movie stars Charlie Sheen and Dolph Lundgren recorded encouraging video messages calling for Shugaley's release on the pay-to-play app Cameo.[21] For his troubles, Prigozhin would pay Shugaley $245,000 after he and his translator were finally returned back to Russia in late 2020.[22]

All of these machinations were fine-tuned to align with Putin's carpe-diem push to capture hearts and minds in Africa.

His efforts reached a new peak in March 2019, when some forty-three heads of state showed up to the Olympic Village in Sochi for the first-ever Russia-Africa Summit. Cohosted with Egypt's president, Abdel Fattah el-Sisi, Putin's two-day charm offensive drew thousands of delegates from all fifty-four of the continent's nations. A soft-power extravaganza, the event featured a promise from Putin to double Russia's Africa investments to $40 billion. Additional highlights included speeches from such notable Russian luminaries as the ultraconservative oligarch Konstantin Malofeev, who had recently been named the head of Russia's International Agency for Sovereign Development, a brand-new aid agency modeled loosely on its American and Chinese counterparts.[23]

It was a major diplomatic coup for Russia, which claimed to ink $12.5 billion in trade deals during the summit, including several agreements for Rosoboronexport to sell military gear. Nearly five years after the West had shunned him as the head of a pariah state in response to Russia's invasion of Crimea, Vladimir Putin was an international statesman again, glad-handing African leaders whom Washington had ignored. "We see how a number of Western states resort to pressure, intimidation and blackmail of the governments of sovereign African countries," Putin told his African guests. It was truly a remarkable turnaround, and Putin hammed it up in a lengthy interview, declaring with his characteristically dry understatement that Russia was eager to "open a new chapter" in Africa, "a continent of opportunity."[24]

CHAPTER 17

MIX-UP IN MINSK

The first thing that seemed off about the thirty-two Russian men who arrived at the Belorusochka spa hotel near the Belarus capital of Minsk on July 27, 2020, was that they showed no interest in drinking. Dressed in a mix of tracksuits and camouflage fatigues and toting duffel bags, they did not say much when they checked in, other than that they did not plan to stay long. Once settled, they mostly kept to themselves, strolling in pairs around the leafy perimeter of the suburban waterside resort and claiming to be "tourists" on a short layover en route to Istanbul.

A few hotel staff found the timing of their arrival—just ten days before the upcoming presidential election—suspicious. The country had been on edge for months, rocked first by protests against the presidential incumbent, Aleksandr Lukashenko, over his mishandling of the COVID-19 outbreak and then by widespread public discontent over the disqualification of several opposition candidates. Faced with an unprecedented challenge to his twenty-six-year rule, Lukashenko had ordered a harsh crackdown that seemed only to spur the active opposition and propel the popularity of his most potent challenger, Sviatlana Tsikhanouskaya.

A stay-at-home mom with two kids, Tsikhanouskaya was as unlikely a presidential candidate as they come. She had reluctantly stepped up as a candidate and into the international spotlight after her husband, Sergey, a popular pro-democracy blogger, was barred from running and then arrested on trumped-up charges. Plainspoken and unpretentious, she often joked on the campaign trail that she was "the accidental candidate." The close bond she built with the wives of other disqualified candidates earned her a tremendous following. Her rallies drew as many as sixty thousand people in Minsk—the kinds of crowds that had not been seen in the streets since the collapse of the Soviet Union.

With his characteristic comb-over and thick mustache, Lukashenko was the polar opposite of his opponent. Often referred to as "Europe's last dictator," he embodied a bygone era of Soviet-style leadership. Lukashenko hailed from the Belarusian countryside, and his political journey began with his lone vote against the dissolution of the Soviet Union, culminating in his first presidential victory in 1994. From then on, Lukashenko meticulously crafted what he termed a "managed democracy": mirroring Putin's Russia, manipulating laws to prolong his rule, and stifling political opposition.

Despite his authoritarian baggage, Lukashenko sought with limited success to position Belarus as a mediator between Russia and the West in the years leading up to the 2020 elections. His neutrality on Russia's annexation of Abkhazia and South Ossetia garnered him favor with the European Union. His outright refusal to recognize the Kremlin takeover of Crimea and role as middleman in the Donbas conflict earned him additional room for diplomatic maneuvering.

Lukashenko even found himself courted by the Trump administration, with Secretary of State Mike Pompeo pledging to restore diplomatic ties between Belarus and the United States during a February 2020 visit. These developments hinted at a potential thaw in Belarusian relations with the West, prompting speculation about the future of the country's economic ties with Russia.

In the run-up to the election, Lukashenko had taken great care to lean into the ambiguity, making a great show out of publicly rejecting a proposal from Putin to integrate Belarus into a formal union with Russia in exchange for energy discounts. But concerns that Lukashenko would cave to pressure from Putin to more closely intertwine the economies of their two countries continued to roil the electorate. With towns across Belarus electrified by labor strikes and clashes between police and protesters, it was hard to avoid comparisons with the color revolutions and the Euromaidan crisis in Ukraine that had set Putin on a warpath with the West and led to the annexation of Crimea. The sudden appearance of a platoon-size cadre of Russian "tourists" with a notably military bearing in the suburbs of Minsk just a few days shy of the vote produced an eerie sense of déjà vu.

The thirty-two men at the Belorusochka appeared to be unperturbed by the political situation unfolding in the country until a squad of black-clad Belarusian KGB agents swooped into the resort late on their second night there. The surprise raid on their rooms turned up multiple passports and crisp bundles of US currency as well as currency from Sudan and Syria. The morning after the raid, on July 29, the Belarus state news channel played scenes of the raid on an endless loop, showing half-dressed, stunned-looking men lying face-down in bed with their hands cuffed behind their backs as a few others were led away to an armored police van.

While in custody, the men continued to insist that they were only tourists, saying that they had planned to spend time in Istanbul visiting the legendary Hagia Sophia cathedral. Unconvinced, the authorities in Minsk said the men at the resort and one other man arrested separately in a town to the south all worked for the Wagner Group and had been detained on suspicion that they had traveled to Belarus at the Kremlin's behest to interfere in the elections.

Lukashenko was even more specific, accusing Russia during a speech to parliament of hiring more than two hundred Wagner Group mercenaries to carry out terrorist attacks aimed at destabilizing Belarus. "Russia is afraid of losing us, because it has no truly close allies left except us," Lukashenko told members of parliament. With typical theatrical bravado, he next staged a tele-vised meeting with members of his cabinet, ordering security officials to hunt down the remainder of the Wagner contingent, who he claimed had slipped into the country covertly to carry out a plot ordered by Vladimir Putin to replace Lukashenko with Tsikhanouskaya.[1]

It was a laughable claim, at least the part about Putin backing the Bela-rusian pro-democracy leader, and Kremlin spokesman Dmitry Peskov natu-rally denied that any such plot existed. In a rare moment of semitransparency, though, Russian officials acknowledged in a statement released by the Russian embassy in Belarus that the men detained did indeed work for a private-security company but that they simply were passing through Minsk on their way to an undisclosed location via Istanbul. This much turned out to be true. When ques-tioned by Belarusian authorities, the Russians explained that the brief stop at the resort was the result of a logistical snag.

Those tantalizing tidbits set off a whirlwind of online speculation about what the real story might be. Southfront.org, a Russian propaganda outlet of dubious provenance that focused on military affairs, confirmed the story, or at least part of it. An article published on the site carried copies of flight tickets for Belarus to Turkey booked in the names of several of the Russian mercenaries arrested. The Southfront piece claimed that all of the thirty-three men had signed up on contract with a small St. Petersburg–based military-security company called PMC MAR that had been hired by Rosneft to protect the Russian oil company's production installations in Venezuela. Online chatter among ultranationalist bloggers in the Grey Zone, a popular VKontakte and YouTube channel that had gained a wide following with the Wagner Group's growing online fan base, seemed to back up the claim.

The news was hardly surprising. It had long been an open secret that Minsk served as a transit hub for Wagner Group contingents. Leaked paperwork suggested that Concord network employees en route to Africa, the Middle East, and other regions had routinely passed through Minsk since at least early 2017.[2] Russian mercenary traffic through Belarus intensified after rounds of sanctions imposed on Prigozhin's companies made travel through parts of Europe and the Middle East especially tricky. After the onset of the COVID pandemic placed even more restrictions on flights out of Russia, overland transfers and flights out of Minsk provided the best guarantee of catching an onward long-haul commercial flight to Wagner's far-flung hubs in the Central African Republic, Syria, and Libya.

Belarus was also an important logistical hub for Wagner Group supplies and a friendly port of call for members of Yevgeny Prigozhin's back office. Customs records indicated that Prigozhin's company Broker Expert LLC had at one point during 2017–2018 shipped from Belarus to Sudan heavy construction equipment made by a Minsk-based joint-stock holding company called OAO Amkodor. Additional supplies for Wagner's operations included boxes loaded with flash-bang grenades for crowd control that were shipped through Minsk on behalf of a state-managed defense-research institute in Russia.[3]

However, most of the details about the Wagner Group's long-standing dependence on Belarus for logistics support got lost in the media storm when, a few days after the arrests, the Ukrainian Prosecutor-General's Office demanded the extradition from Belarus of twenty-eight of the detained men. Ukraine claimed that the mercenaries were wanted on war-crimes charges stemming from their time fighting in Donbas on the side of Russian separatists. Ukrainian prosecutors said there was evidence linking more than a dozen of those detained to the shooting down of a Ukrainian military-transport plane that had famously launched Dmitry Utkin's career as Wagner's commander and also to the downing of flight MH17.

Lukashenko announced that he was contemplating acceding to Ukraine's request for extradition. It was a strange twist to an already surreal story that would only get weirder as the days ticked by. Although Lukashenko had traditionally made a big show of his independence, he had always been a steadfast supporter of Putin. The only logical reason that Lukashenko could have for antagonizing Putin amid so much political unrest was that it presented a welcome diversion from the constant drumbeat of negative headlines about the government crackdown in Belarus and giddy reporting about Tsikhanouskaya's candidacy.

It later became clear that there were multiple motivations in play. However, fallout from the elections quickly overshadowed the controversy over Ukraine's claims about the mercenaries and Lukashenko's contentious remarks about the Kremlin's involvement in the plot. Following the closing of the polls on August 9, Lukashenko declared himself the victor, claiming to have secured over 80 percent of the votes. This boldly false assertion sparked even more public rancor. Hundreds of thousands of people poured into the streets, demanding fair elections and Lukashenko's resignation. When Tsikhanouskaya showed up at the electoral commission to file a complaint a day after the election, officials in Lukashenko's cabinet told her to shut her campaign down and then forced her into exile. The moment of change all of Belarus seemed to be waiting for never arrived; darker times were to come.

Many in the contingent arrested in Minsk, it would turn out, had indeed served on previous tours in Donbas on contract for irregular Russian contingents during the initial stages of the conflict in 2014 and 2015. Among the most notable on the list of mercenary detainees was Anton Bakunovich, one of 122 Wagner snipers named in a UN expert-panel report on Libya that linked Prigozhin's outfit to several war crimes.[4] The Russian recruiter who hired Bakunovich and the others—a certain "Sergey Petrovich"—had purposefully set out to cultivate operatives with a proven track record of fighting in Ukraine. He had promised to pay each man $5,000 per month, more than enough to offset the debts and bills that they had accrued since their last tour abroad with the Wagner Group. After submitting their paperwork to another intermediary, they had traveled by bus over the border from Russia into Belarus on July 25. They were part of an anticipated wave of 180 Russian mercenaries scheduled to arrive in Minsk that week. Or at least that was what they had been made to believe.

The arrests in Belarus had set off a panic in Kyiv inside the office of Ukraine's president, Volodymyr Zelensky. The sudden appearance of the

Russian mercenaries in Minsk and the Ukrainian request for their extradition was no coincidence. It was a sting operation that had taken Ukrainian intelligence agencies more than a year to set up, and it had just blown up in President Zelensky's face. Dubbed "Project Avenue," the Ukrainian scheme called first for duping dozens of Russian mercenaries suspected of involvement in war crimes into signing a contract to work for a private-military–security company, then convincing them to travel by bus to Minsk. Upon arrival, their onward flight out of the Belarusian capital to Istanbul would be diverted as it flew over Ukrainian airspace for a "medical emergency" that would force the plane to touch down in Kyiv, where they would be promptly arrested. Once the men were in custody, Ukrainian authorities planned to either try the mercenaries in court or use them to sweeten the terms of a prisoner exchange with Moscow.

The seeds of the clandestine Ukrainian scheme grew out of another covert action that led to the capture in June 2019 of a leading suspect in the downing of Malaysia Airlines flight MH17. The target, Volodymyr Tsemakh, a Russian separatist fighter with Igor Girkin's 1st Slovyansk Brigade, confessed on camera to helping hide the Russian-supplied Buk missile that killed all 298 passengers on board. Posing as friendly neighbors, Ukrainian agents nabbed Tsemakh by drinking him under the table at a house party. Then they wheeled the inebriated fighter out and smuggled him across the line of contact in Donbas for "urgent medical care." Ukrainian insiders would later tell Bellingcat that the success of the Tsemakh rendition gradually convinced Ukraine's chief of military intelligence, Vasyl Burba, that it might be possible to pull off an even bigger caper.[5]

The initial idea was to trick a targeted list of Russian mercenaries into sharing details of their role in suspected war crimes, then use their confessions to expose the Kremlin's role in backing mercenary operations in Ukraine. The vehicle at the center of the deception was PMC MAR, one of several paramilitaries spun up in St. Petersburg with the support of Russian security agencies to help with surreptitious cargo transfers into Syria and Ukraine. Part of the hub-and-spoke model for mercenary recruitment that Russia's intelligence services had erected in advance of the annexation of Crimea, PMC MAR had a flashy online presence and an established social media following. A small task force of agents within Ukraine's GUR military-intelligence wing tapped into this vulnerability, setting up a look-alike PMC MAR website and posting help-wanted ads on internet job sites. "Sergey Petrovich" was in fact a Ukrainian intelligence asset posing as a Russian recruiter.

The scheme was risky. Incredibly, though, it had unfolded without a hitch right up until the Russian mercenaries arrived in Minsk. The plan imploded amid a turf war between Burba, Ukraine's military-intelligence chief, and Zelensky's chief of staff, Andriy Yermak. The problem was the timing. A day before the mercenary contingent's scheduled departure from Russia, Zelensky had finalized a deal with Russia for a ceasefire in Donbas and a prisoner exchange that had been brokered with the help of Switzerland's president, Simonetta Sommaruga. When Burba briefed Zelensky on July 24, the covert rendition operation was already well under way, but the deal had not yet been fully ratified.[6] Fearful about the potential for blowback, Zelensky, at Yermak's urging, ordered a temporary halt to the operation, a decision that set off a chain of events that led to Burba's firing and the plan's exposure.

For a moment, it almost seemed like the Ukrainians had convinced Lukashenko to hand over the Russians, but Kyiv's hopes were quickly dashed. Facing unrelenting pressure from street protests and threats of sanctions from the West over his handling of the elections, Lukashenko suddenly found himself in need of Putin's help. The Belarusian dictator agreed to send the Russian mercenaries back to Russia on August 14. The matter did not end there, though. Instead, it ballooned into a diplomatic contretemps between Zelensky and Putin, and also into a domestic political scandal that badly dented Zelensky's government.

As it was, Zelensky, a little more than one year into his first presidential term, was already on shaky ground on the domestic front. A political newcomer, he had rather improbably taken Ukraine by storm when he jumped into a crowded presidential election contest in late 2018. Zelensky was a comedian and television and film producer who had grown up in an industrial town called Kryvyi Rih in a part of southern Ukraine that was predominantly Russian speaking. His wildly popular television show, *Servant of the People*, which told the story of a humble high school teacher turned accidental president, had made Zelensky a household name. Once a sideshow in a national election that with forty-four candidates seemed to be more of a demolition derby than a political race, Zelensky quickly shot to the top of the polls in early 2019 in what ultimately became a three-way race against an older wealthy incumbent, Petro Poroshenko, and a scandal-plagued also-ran, Yuliya Tymoshenko.

During the campaign, Zelensky positioned himself as the "anti-candidate." He was neither part of the #Euro-Optimist bloc nor part of the old-school oligarchy that had run Ukraine for decades. He remained coy throughout the race about where he stood on Ukraine's bid to join NATO, hewing closely to the line that the priority was to peaceably resolve the ongoing conflict with Russia. He openly mocked the country's plutocratic billionaire class, although he counted one of Ukraine's richest men among his backers. He eschewed terms like "campaign manager," preferring instead to direct official inquiries to his team of "advisers," a whiz-kid gaggle of Ukraine's best and brightest—well-bred English-speaking lawyers, businesspeople, university professors, and urban intelligentsia. With millions of Instagram followers, he was everything that Poroshenko and Tymoshenko were not: young, affable, and tech savvy.

Zelensky's strategy was to present himself as a perfect answer to Ukraine's political malaise and vacuum up the protest vote. In the spring of 2019, that part of the electoral pie seemed to be growing by the day. Fractured by an escalating proxy war with Russian-backed separatists in Donbas in which the Wagner Group had initially figured prominently, and paralyzed by corruption, Ukraine seemed unable to break from its Soviet past. Six years after the Russian incursion, the country's eastern regions remained a tinderbox. Roughly thirteen thousand people had been killed in the fighting in Donbas up to that point. Hundreds of thousands more were internally displaced. Russia's construction of an eleven-mile bridge into Crimea over the waters of the Kerch Strait had crippled Ukraine's ability to ship goods out of its two busiest eastern seaports, Mariupol and Berdiansk, badly damaging the Ukrainian economy.

So when Zelensky rocketed to victory with 73 percent of the vote in an April 2019 runoff against Poroshenko, the mood in Kyiv was ecstatic. The glow wore off fast when two months after taking office, on July 25, 2019, Zelensky found himself in a conversation with Donald Trump that plunged the two men into an international imbroglio of epic proportions. Billed as a routine call aimed at congratulating Zelensky on his win, the call quickly became something else entirely. During the conversation, Trump urged Zelensky to investigate spurious allegations that Trump's main political challenger, Joe Biden, had used his political influence to help his son, Hunter, win lucrative business deals in Ukraine. In exchange, Trump promised to reward Ukraine with an invitation to the White House and much-needed military aid.

For Zelensky, the fallout from the call was immediate and far-reaching. Caught between the demands of a powerful ally and the need to maintain Ukraine's independence and integrity, he faced intense pressure from both sides. He denied that there had been anything improper about his call with Trump. But Zelensky's handling of the situation raised questions about his political acumen. When in the fall of 2019 the imbroglio over the White House phone call metastasized into a congressional impeachment trial of Trump, Zelensky found himself increasingly vulnerable to jabs from the sidelines from Poroshenko, who was still hoping for a comeback and looking to score political wins for his party.

Meanwhile, promises that Zelensky had made on the campaign trail to battle corruption, implement reforms, and bring fresh faces into government ran into serious headwinds. A complicating factor in this messy mix was Yermak, whose relationship with Zelensky dated back several years, to when both had business ties to a local TV channel, but had become a lightning rod for controversy when Zelensky stepped into the presidency. A lawyer by training, Yermak, like Zelensky, had a background in film production and had successfully founded his own media company. Once ensconced in Zelensky's cabinet, Yermak had proven himself an adept negotiator, although his chummy personal relations with well-connected power brokers like Russian business tycoon Roman Abramovich led some in Ukraine's loyal opposition to cry foul.

Yermak's ties to the historically pro-Russian Party of Regions had also made him suspect in the eyes of many civil servants. Suspicions were further inflamed when Yermak arranged a prisoner swap in September 2019 that entailed the release of twenty-four Ukrainian sailors who had been taken prisoner by Russia in exchange for the release of Volodymyr Tsemakh, the one suspect in the MH17 case whose testimony could have been most damning for Putin. The move enraged Ukrainian intelligence agents in the GUR and investigators with the SBU who had collaborated on Tsemakh's capture.

It was within this context that the fight between Yermak and Burba over the exposure of the plan to kidnap the Russian mercenaries unfolded. It had taken the GUR more than a year to cultivate and entice their targets to walk into the trap set for them in Minsk. Incensed by what he viewed as Yermak's betrayal, Burba told anyone who would listen that he was worried that Russian moles in Zelensky's cabinet had tipped off the Belarusian authorities. The indiscretions and messy fallout from the operation led to Burba's firing. The scandal that followed—dubbed "Wagnergate" by the Ukrainian press—took on a life of its own after that.

Meanwhile, Wagner staff scurried to head off any blowback, firing off a memo in August addressed to Sergey Rudskoy, head of Russia's Main Operational Directorate of the General Staff. The report confirmed that at least twelve of those arrested had indeed worked for Wagner in the past but stated that they had been let go variously for drinking on the job, for using drugs, or for unspecified health problems.[7]

A few days after their return home, on August 16, 2020, two of the Russian mercenaries explained in a lengthy interview on Russia's state television channel how they had been unknowingly duped by Ukrainian intelligence agents into signing a contract to work for the fake PMC MAR. In Belarus the men were stuck, they said, because the woman handling the logistics of their trip told them she couldn't book flights for such a large group. The following day, on August 17, an official with Ukraine's national anticorruption bureau, NABU, affirmed that version of events and openly accused Zelensky's chief of staff, Yermak, of purposefully thwarting the Ukrainian rendition plan and leaking details to the Belarusian KGB.

The story snowballed when on the same day a popular Ukrainian newscaster, Yanina Sokolova, posted copies of official documents confirming that Zelensky had been briefed on the contours of the rendition scheme in advance and separately played excerpts of recorded phone calls between the Ukrainian intelligence agents behind Project Avenue and their Russian mercenary targets.[8] Sokolova hinted darkly without presenting much proof that Burba had traveled to Washington just before Project Avenue had reached its culmination phase.

Putin did not miss a beat. A week after Sokolova's "Wagnergate" report hit the airwaves, he claimed that the entire scheme had been cooked up by Ukrainian intelligence agents in cooperation with the CIA with the aim of destabilizing the region. The strategy of turning the Wagner Group into an international bogeyman had once again turned out to be a very useful one indeed. Bypassing questions about the Wagner Group's existence and status, Putin said that the men had traveled to Minsk for "perfectly legal reasons."[9] Three weeks later, Lukashenko fired the KGB chief who had initiated the arrests of the Russian mercenaries and replaced him with one far more friendly to the Kremlin. There would be no more mix-ups in Minsk.

CHAPTER 18

PRELUDE TO SPRING

The description on the FBI most-wanted poster was clinical. There was no press conference, no fanfare, just the facts. Name: Yevgeny Viktorovich Prigozhin. Alias: "Yevgeny." Hair: Bald. Eyes: Brown. Race: White. Nationality: Russian. Prigozhin, the FBI poster noted, had ties to Russia, Indonesia, and Qatar. He was wanted for perpetrating fraud against the United States: purchasing space on American internet servers and paying for the creation of hundreds of fictitious personas and websites that promoted disinformation about US presidential candidates.

Issued in March 2021, some nine months after Interpol rescinded its international warrant for Prigozhin's arrest, the FBI notice offered a reward of $250,000 to anyone with information that would lead to Prigozhin's apprehension. There was no mention of Prigozhin's connections to the Wagner Group. But the FBI move was the closest that the United States had come to declaring open season on Vladimir Putin's most visible and trusted agent of chaos.

Only months into Joe Biden's first term as president, the FBI warrant was one of several indicators that the tides were once again turning in relations between Russia and the United States. In the White House, members of Biden's National Security Council were busy fine-tuning the language in a series of sanctions against Russian spies, hackers, and proxies implicated in election-interference operations, cyberattacks, and the military occupation of Crimea.

When the measures were officially announced, the White House expressly named Russia's GRU and SVR foreign-intelligence agencies as the facilitators of a crippling 2020 cyberattack against SolarWinds, an American software company, that led to breaches of sensitive federal government computer systems and affected tens of thousands of ordinary internet users. The Biden administration said that it was also expelling ten diplomats at the Russian embassy in Washington on suspicion of espionage.[1] And in another slap at Prigozhin, the sweeping set of measures issued by the US Treasury took aim at Prigozhin's network of front companies and operatives in Africa, blacklisting leading members of the back office in St. Petersburg, the Foundation for Protection of National Values, and the AFRIC project.[2]

Sensing the potential threat from the changing of the guard in Washington, Prigozhin sought to get out ahead of it. Soon after the FBI listing was made public, Prigozhin gave his first-ever major interview to the English-speaking press. In his interview with the London-based *Daily Telegraph*, Prigozhin claimed that he was a "pacifist." He strenuously denied having any links with the Internet Research Agency. He waxed philosophical about the rift between Moscow and Washington, insisting that he had nothing to do with Russia's election-meddling scheme. "I have never served in the Russian government and, it bears repeating, I am not closely acquainted with President Putin," Prigozhin told the *Telegraph*.[3] Later, in a statement posted to his company's VKontakte social media account, Prigozhin was even more adamant. "Fraudsters are fraudulently trying to accuse me, a squeaky-clean person, of fraud," the statement read.[4] Prigozhin also added that he would pay up to $500,000 to secure the capture of Mikhail Khodorkovsky.

The feud between Khodorkovsky and Prigozhin had obviously become quite personal. A few days later, Khodorkovsky obligingly issued a rejoinder of his own: "Putin's chef Prigozhin was so worried about the trouble caused to him by the FBI that he put out a bounty on my head," Khodorkovsky said in a videotaped statement posted on his own website, Khodorkovsky.com. "As you can see, Prigozhin has matured. He is no longer about boots and earrings, but a proper contract for either kidnapping or murder," Khodorkovsky coldly quipped. "You can take a guy out of a St. Petersburg back alley. But you can't take the back alley out of him."[5]

Prigozhin and Khodorkovsky were like the poles of two opposing magnets, simultaneously attracted and repelled by forces unleashed by Putin and the Kremlin. Whenever there was a geopolitical quake between Moscow and

Washington, Prigozhin and Khodorkovsky pressed toward the epicenter of the action. After Khodorkovsky's Dossier Centre published its findings from its investigation into the killings of the three Russian journalists in the Central African Republic, Khodorkovsky's team of investigators methodically began to turn up the heat against the Wagner Group.

Leaks of sensitive internal files culled from Prigozhin's interlocutors grew from a trickle into a gushing river. Much of the information came from sources on the dark net or was dumped out in the open by anonymous hackers. Taken together, the streams of leaked flight records, passport numbers, contract payments, and personnel lists revealed the Kremlin's deep involvement in shoring up the international criminal cartel under Prigozhin's management.

Prigozhin responded by cranking up his propaganda machine while mounting attacks against journalists and researchers who reported on the Wagner Group's covert operations. In March a mysterious noxious chemical substance was dumped at the entryway of *Novaya Gazeta* a couple of weeks after the investigative news outlet published a series of exposés about the Wagner Group. Dmitry Muratov, the paper's editor in chief, noted that the incident occurred on the same day that Russian and Syrian lawyers for the family of Hamdi Bouta, the Syrian citizen bludgeoned to death by sledgehammer-wielding Wagner soldiers, cited *Novaya Gazeta*'s articles in the legal suit they filed that called for the criminal prosecution of six Wagner fighters in Russia.

Two months later, in May, government officials in Bangui rolled out the red carpet for the stars and producers of *Tourist*, a Russian action film shot on location in the Central African Republic and produced by Prigozhin's film company Aurum. Billed as the cultural event of the year, the open-air premiere screening featured a cameo appearance by none other than Maxim Shugaley. The event drew a crowd of more than ten thousand excited fans who were handed free T-shirts featuring the movie's main character as they entered the city's national stadium.

A confection of propagandistic puffery and Hollywood-style action, the film centered on the Rambo-style adventures of one Grisha Dmitriev, aka "Tourist," a heroic Russian cop who signs up for a military-training mission with a group of Russian instructors in the Central African Republic, only to find himself doing battle with renegade bandits bent on toppling the government in Bangui. The through-the-looking-glass, fun-house–style narrative had something for everyone: shambolic Western UN peacekeepers, a stern-looking Central African military general, and a thinly veiled doppelganger of Dmitry

Utkin, who is portrayed as a tough-as-nails bald Russian military instructor, minus the Nazi tattoos.

The film's debut was a sharp contrast to what was really happening in the country. Shortly before *Tourist* was released, a UN expert panel on mercenary activity sounded the alarm about the Wagner Group's targeting of journalists and human-rights workers who had documented atrocities linked to Russian operations in the Central African Republic. A separate report prepared for the UN Security Council detailed a series of Wagner offensives in January and February where Russian military instructors had looted motorcycles, gold, and diamonds, and tortured and killed several civilians in the Bambari area. In one instance, at least six civilians were killed when Wagner operatives stormed into a mosque and began shooting indiscriminately.[6]

Meanwhile, the Wagner Group's general staff began bulking up and mapping out plans for the recruitment and outfitting of two new detachments that would soon be bound for Mali. Rumors that Russian mercenaries might deploy to the war-torn country had started percolating months earlier after three high-ranking military officers in Mali's army who had spent a year training at Moscow's Higher Military College overthrew the government of Mali's president, Ibrahim Boubacar Keita.

Russia had already begun to lay the groundwork for Wagner's expansion in 2019, when Sergey Shoigu signed a military-cooperation agreement with Mali that included terms for the sale and maintenance of two Mi-35 helicopters.[7] Plans for Wagner's deployment to Mali began taking more concrete shape after Russia's newest strongman client in the Sahel, Colonel Assimi Goïta, spearheaded a second putsch in May 2021 and deposed interim president Bah Ndaw following a cabinet reshuffle that elicited deep frictions between the military and transitional civilian leaders. Goïta's forces encountered little to no resistance as they secured key military and strategic locations in the capital, Bamako, indicating a significant consolidation of power within the military ranks loyal to Goïta.

Goïta's display of force so soon after his time in Russia was an embarrassment for the United States and Europe, which had also supplied and supported his training in counterterrorism tactics at military academies in Germany and the United States. Condemnation from the international community was swift. But it did little to change the trajectory of the country, which would fall increasingly under Russia's sway. Within a few months the Wagner Group would seal a deal with Mali's new military rulers that called for Prigozhin's front companies to be paid an estimated $10.8 million per month for their services.[8]

However, events farther afield would prove even more pivotal for Prigozhin's future. In April the Biden administration announced that it would go through with the deal that Donald Trump had inked with the Taliban. In a videotaped address from the Roosevelt Room in the White House, Biden told America and the world that he intended to bring the twenty-year US war in Afghanistan to a close. Biden said he was the fourth American president to preside over the war, and he would not bequeath that ignoble legacy to a fifth: "I simply do not believe that the safety and security of America is enhanced by continuing to deploy thousands of American troops and spending billions of dollars a year in Afghanistan." By September 11, 2021, the United States would withdraw all but 2,500 troops from Afghanistan.

"We cannot continue the cycle of extending or expanding our military presence in Afghanistan—hoping to create ideal conditions for the withdrawal and expecting a different result," Biden said.[9] The speech was unnervingly like the one given by Mikhail Gorbachev thirty-five years earlier, when the Russian premier had called for the drawdown of Soviet troops, which signaled the end of the Kremlin's shadow war with Washington and the imminent collapse of the Soviet system. Delivered just months after hundreds of angry supporters of Donald Trump stormed the Capitol in an event that bore the unmistakable signs of an authoritarian putsch, Biden's announcement of the US exit from Afghanistan carried haunting echoes of history. It mirrored the mood that had accompanied the Soviet withdrawal from Afghanistan thirty-two years earlier—two superpowers, decades apart, facing existential crises over their role in the world, their withdrawals underscoring the fragility of Great Powers in decline.

Confirmation of the US withdrawal from Afghanistan was the green light that Putin had been watching and waiting for. Publicly, Russia had for years paid lip service to its support for US efforts to broker a settlement of the Afghan conflict. But through subtle and unsubtle means, the Kremlin sought to undermine the negotiating process that the United States had set up between the Taliban and Ashraf Ghani's emissaries in Doha, Qatar.

Months before Biden took office, rumors and reports swirled about a secret Russian program to pay Taliban fighters to target US and coalition forces in Afghanistan. Then, while Washington was still reeling from the fallout from the violent January 6 riot and mob attacks on Congress, Moscow announced that it planned to host a peace conference of its own, inviting the

Taliban and representatives from other Afghan political factions to meet in Russia.

In May the White House released declassified intelligence confirming that operatives with the GRU's special expeditionary Unit 29155 had rewarded Taliban fighters for mounting attacks on US and NATO troops.[10] Although the CIA had initially expressed only low to medium confidence levels about this information, the intelligence suggested that other agencies were more confident that Russia's legendary kill team was in on the scheme. The news arrived as debates raged inside the Biden administration about the credibility of additional intelligence assessments suggesting that US Afghan forces were likely to be able to survive for only a few months after the American pullout. But they would not even hold out for that long.

On August 16 the worst fears about the possibility of a chaotic US pullout were realized when Taliban fighters took over the Presidential Palace in Kabul only hours after President Ashraf Ghani fled the country. Across the Afghan capital, Taliban commandos careened triumphantly down the streets while thousands of fearful Afghans mobbed the gates of the city's only airport. Harrowing scenes of young Afghan refugees clamoring to grab onto the wings and wheel wells of departing American military cargo jets and the bloody carnage left after a suicide-bomb attack at the airport were beamed around the world on the evening news.

Meanwhile, politicians in European capitals carped that the Biden administration had not sufficiently consulted its allies about the pace of the pullout. Twenty years after the United States had invoked NATO's all-for-one and one-for-all call to arms in the face of al-Qaeda's attacks on New York and Washington, the transatlantic alliance had never looked more divided, and the United States had never looked weaker.

As if to underscore the point, Prigozhin's favorite man of action, Maxim Shugaley, suddenly showed up in Kabul with an offer of assistance to the Taliban. A day after a suicide bomb ripped through a crowd at the gates of the city's airport and killed 13 US soldiers and 170 Afghan civilians, a photo of Shugaley in a black T-shirt posing awkwardly alongside the Taliban's bearded and turbaned spokesman Zabiullah Mujahid cropped up on social media.

Two weeks later, amid escalating tensions between Washington and Moscow over NATO's invitation to Ukraine to participate in a Black Sea naval exercise, Russia launched its massive Zapad 2021 military exercise, mobilizing some 200,000 troops and 760 pieces of military equipment just across Ukraine's borders with Russia and Belarus.[11] The mask was off and the gauntlet thrown.

Putin had already all but declared war on Ukraine in June, when he published a 7,000-word essay titled "On the Historical Unity Between Russians and Ukrainians." Brimming with romantic allusions to Ancient Rus and chauvinistic reinterpretations of the events that had led to Ukraine's 1991 declaration of independence, the diatribe was chilling in tone and substance. Invoking lessons learned from his old law-school mentor, Putin tried to build the legal case for Russian intervention in Ukraine:

> You want to establish a state of your own: you are welcome! But what are the terms? I will recall the assessment given by one of the most prominent political figures of new Russia, first mayor of Saint Petersburg Anatoly Sobchak. As a legal expert who believed that every decision must be legitimate, in 1992, he shared the following opinion: the republics that were founders of the Union, having denounced the 1922 Union Treaty, must return to the boundaries they had had before joining the Soviet Union. All other territorial acquisitions are subject to discussion, negotiations, given that the ground has been revoked.
>
> In other words, when you leave, take what you brought with you. This logic is hard to refute. I will just say that the Bolsheviks had embarked on reshaping boundaries even before the Soviet Union, manipulating with territories to their liking, in disregard of people's views.[12]

Soon after Putin's speech, a few astute internet sleuths who worked for a Washington think tank called New America noticed that chatter was picking up on an Instagram account that belonged to the neo-Nazi Wagner Group affiliate Rusich. Rumblings about Rusich's possible return to the Ukrainian front for a "Russian Spring 2.0" in Donbas appeared in posts on the group's account in January 2021.[13]

Months later, on September 27, 2021, Rusich indicated in another post, one that included a stylized selfie of its members atop a Russian armored vehicle, that they were training for military exercises. "BMP stands for 'Boyevaya Mashina Pehoty' meaning 'infantry fighting vehicle'—is a type of armored fighting vehicle used to carry infantry into battle and provide direct-fire support," the post declared.[14]

Then, in late October, another Instagram post made clear that the soldier-of-fortune contingent had designs on a return to Kharkiv. In comments posted in response to the battlefield selfie, a user named @anton_lvr asked if Rusich planned on another deployment to "DNR/LNR," shorthand for the Donetsk People's Republic and Luhansk People's Republic, the two Russian-separatist–controlled districts of Donbas.

The reply from Rusich was brief: "@anton_lvr хнр, кнп, и т.д." The reference to "KhNR" was an allusion to the abbreviation for Kharkiv, the scene of multiple, protracted bloody battles from 2014 to 2015 during the Kremlin-backed separatist onslaught in Donbas. "KhNR" was short for "Kharkiv People's Republic," which pro-Russian separatists briefly proclaimed in 2014 before Ukrainian forces reasserted control over the city.

Rusich had acquired a reputation for exceptional brutality. In September 2014 it attacked a column of Ukrainian volunteer fighters near the Donbas town of Metallist, killing dozens, according to Ukrainian news reports.[15] Afterward, local sources said that Rusich members mutilated and set fire to the dead.[16] Throughout their 2014–2015 deployment, Milchakov, Petrovsky, and other Rusich members courted infamy, posting images of atrocities and selfies with dead bodies, again according to Ukrainian media.[17] Ukrainian human-rights groups also accused the contingent of torturing prisoners of war. Rusich's outsized social media footprint served as useful propaganda, hyping members as fearsome warriors and belying their relatively small numbers in Ukraine during the 2014–2015 period.

A year before Rusich tipped its hand about its planned infiltration of Kharkiv, another video uploaded to the paramilitary's Instagram account showed its recruits conducting firing drills with members of the Union of Donbas Volunteers (SDD), an organization for Russian veterans of the Donbas war that enjoyed close relations with Putin's United Russia Party. The video featured an interview with SDD leader Alexander Borodai, the former prime minister of the self-proclaimed Donetsk People's Republic in eastern Ukraine. In the video, Borodai called the participants "real Russian patriots" and emphasized the importance of such groups for Russia's national interest.

Instagram posts showed that Rusich returned regularly to what appeared to be the same firing range, its telltale blue-roofed gazebos most recently appearing in a post on the group's account on January 15, 2022. The Partizan Center, the fighting wing of the ultranationalist Russian Imperial Movement, appeared to train at the same facility. A Partizan Center post referred to the range as the "shooting range of the Ministry of Emergency Situations," known internationally as EMERCOM, the Russian government agency formerly run by Sergey Shoigu.[18]

The location of the shooting range in the center of the special district reserved for EMERCOM operations and administration in the St. Petersburg region was significant. Long a sinecure of Russia's *siloviki* security elites, EMERCOM was among the first Russian agencies to experiment with quasi-private military contingents. The agency's contracting offshoot EMERCOM Demining played a substantial role in the evolution of Russia's military-security industry.

Other photo posts to the Rusich Instagram account showed members carrying out parachute jumps from an Antonov An-2 aircraft, which the Russian military has historically used as a training aircraft for the airborne divisions. Some of those photos were geotagged to the city of Pskov, where the 76th Guards Air Assault Division paratrooper unit was garrisoned. Just as in 2014, at the old stomping grounds where Rusich commander Alexey Milchlakov and Wagner's commander Dmitry Utkin had trained with Russia's elite paratrooper force, Pskov was once again buzzing. Taken together, Rusich's apparent access to government facilities and links to other far-right organizations painted a picture of a militia with at the very least tacit Kremlin backing and friendly ties to the state, if not a militia that was under direct state control. Although unnamed sources would come forward to say that the Wagner Group was caught unawares by brewing trouble on the border between Russia and Ukraine, it would have been surprising if Utkin was not already anticipating a shift in mission.

After the October 2021 Instagram comment in which Rusich hinted at a return to Kharkiv, the group's account went silent, a chilling sign of what was to come. In late January, amid Pentagon warnings of the potential for an escalation of the conflict between Russia and Ukraine, Alexander Borodai told Reuters that Russia's parliament was preparing to recognize the independence of two breakaway regions in eastern Ukraine: Donetsk and Luhansk.

PART FOUR

OUT OF THE
SHADOWS

CHAPTER 19

ORCHESTRAL MANEUVERS

About two weeks after Russia invaded Ukraine on February 24, 2022—this time openly, in contrast to the stealth incursion in Crimea eight years earlier—the Wagner Group began shrugging off its camouflage. Twitter vibrated with rumors that Prigozhin's paramilitary had changed its name to "Liga" ("the League") in a bid to attract new recruits for the war. A thinly veiled reference to the St. Petersburg veterans' association run by Wagner's chief of staff, Andrey Troshev, it was the first hint that the Wagner Group was preparing to step fully out of the shadows. Another post on the Telegram channel for Reverse Side of the Medal coyly dropped coded references to Wagner's insider nickname—"the orchestra," displaying a portrait of Hitler's favorite composer Richard Wagner above a cryptic text that verified that a new recruitment drive was under way: "The philharmonic known as Wagner has decided to take part in the Great World Concert and is holding auditions to select for its touring musical troupe."[1]

The post drew hundreds of ebullient thumbs-up and hang-loose emoji replies, and even more responses that hinted at the enormity of the shift in the Wagner Group's official status. Those who asked about the salary received a variety of estimates ranging from $3,000 to $5,000 per month; one Telegram user suggested that the going payout rate if a new Wagner recruit was killed in action was 5 million rubles, about $45,000, close to twice the annual median income for most Russian citizens.[2]

While social media apps blew up with news of the Wagner Group's every wiggle, snapshots of the landing page for a Wagner Group recruitment website,

"Join-Wagner.com," started to circulate on Twitter. Written in English and French, the splashy website was registered in November 2021, only three months before the Russian onslaught began. It was tailor-made to attract foreign recruits and bore all the hallmarks of other campaigns linked to Prigozhin's influence operations—provocative images, simple catchphrases, and the dark symbology of Russian militarism.

The landing page carried a colorful poster image of the iconic Wagner Group memorial statue erected in Russia soon after the devastating clash with US forces in Syria. The site also included a tab for a French translation of the content and maps of Wagner's bases of operation across Africa. Visitors interested in learning more were encouraged to enter their contact information in an online form so they could "Join PMC Wagner to protect the peace and tranquility of civilians from terrorists and bandits!" Another poster image on the site showed an eagle in flight above a trio of soldiers and the words "We stop terror," also written in English. Below the form, the site carried a line from the classical treatise on military strategy *Epitoma Rei Militaris*: "If you want peace, prepare for war."

The slogan echoed Putin's spin on his undeclared war in Ukraine—a "peace through strength" narrative masking the ruthless offensive. In a masterstroke of Orwellian doublespeak, Putin called the invasion a "special military operation" meant to "liberate" Ukraine from "terrorists" and "Nazis." This clever label built a rhetorical bridge between all-out war and a peacekeeping mission. By framing it as a limited, targeted operation, Putin dodged the domestic and international fallout of declaring war while reaping the benefits of military aggression that muddied the boundaries between legitimate targets and actors. It was a sleight of hand—one of many Putin had mastered—that allowed him to claim no ties between the state and the Wagner Group, despite its clear role as an auxiliary force bundled with state-managed extractive ventures and Russian arms deals. This approach fed into a broader strategy of narrative smoke and mirrors, a hallmark of Putin's regime and Russian military doctrine since the assault on Georgia in 2008.

As Russian missiles pummeled cities across Ukraine, mercenary detachments from the Wagner Group and its competitor Redut slipped across the border from Belarus and Russia. In Kyiv, Russian operatives advanced in stealth mode toward the heavily guarded government quarter of the Ukrainian capital. Their destination: the office of Ukraine's president, housed in a colossal Soviet-era building on Bankova Street, where just hours into the invasion,

Volodymyr Zelensky defiantly declared his intent to remain, telling the West that he needed ammunition, not a ride.

On the twelfth day of the Russian onslaught, Zelensky issued a bold challenge that almost dared the Russians to come for him. He posted a video on Twitter of him calmly strolling through the gilded hallways adjoining the presidential suite: "I stay here in Kyiv. I am on Bankova Street. I'm not hiding. And I'm not afraid of anyone."[3]

Zelensky issued the challenge mere days after a contingent of fifty Russian mercenaries came within a block of the presidential building before Ukrainian forces intercepted and gunned them down.[4] However, the deadly skirmish marked only the beginning of Russian attempts on Zelensky's life. Raids conducted by Ukraine's national police and intelligence agencies across Kyiv turned up dozens of collaborators and would-be Russian saboteurs and assassins within the first week of the war.

Ukrainian intelligence officials presented as evidence of Wagner's involvement in the assassination plot against Zelensky a pair of dog tags discovered in the street near the heart of the capital. The tags bore a message in English, Arabic, Persian, and French: "Please help and call us." The reverse side had a phone number for a mobile phone in Syria, an email address, and a website, www.200300.info. An examination of an archived version of the website revealed a cryptic message that offered corroboration of what had been suspected for months—the Wagner Group had a new mission in Ukraine: "Keep this man alive, and you will be rewarded. If the man is wounded, provide him with first aid and you will be rewarded. If the man is dead, bring his remains back and you will be rewarded."[5]

The dog-tag find came a couple of days after reports surfaced that Russia had recalled some four hundred members of the Wagner Group from Africa before the invasion began and redeployed them to Kyiv from Belarus in January with kill orders.[6] In addition to Zelensky, Kyiv's famous mayor and former world heavyweight boxing champion Vitaly Klitschko and twenty-two other boldface names in the Ukrainian government were on the Russian target list. It was not a surprise that Putin wanted Zelensky dead. Putin had said from the outset that the goal of Russia's so-called special military operation was to secure Russian control of the breakaway eastern region of Donbas and to replace Zelensky's government with pro-Russian leadership.

Details about the assassination plot would turn out to be much more complicated. The Kremlin had in fact dispatched mercenaries from Redut, the

GRU-managed hub for paramilitary recruitment established at the headquarters of the 78th Intelligence Center in Rostov-on-Don, to kill Zelensky and decapitate his government. Set up in the summer of 2021 under the direction of the Wagner Group's original sponsor, GRU deputy director General Vladimir Alekseyev, the latest iteration of Redut was conceived as a covert mechanism for rapid mobilization of auxiliary forces. Often referred to only obliquely in official documentation as the Regional Center for Socio-Psychological Research (RSPLI) or Unit 35555, the military-intelligence unit was the same one that issued the Wagner Group one of its very first cache of weapons and ammunition when the paramilitary deployed to Donbas in 2014.[7]

In the lead-up to the invasion, Prigozhin had reportedly tried without success several times to reach Alekseyev by phone just before the start of the euphemistically named "special military operation." Analysis of phone-record information conducted by *The Insider* suggested they finally connected on the eve of the invasion, although the conversation was short, and it is uncertain what the two talked about.[8] Defense ministry insiders suggested that Alekseyev had brushed Prigozhin off on orders from Shoigu, who had long held a dim view of Prigozhin and his management style. As it stood, Prigozhin's companies were embroiled in several legal disputes with the defense ministry over failures to perform and accrued debts.

Alekseyev had reportedly turned to a relative and former Wagner security lead, Anatoly Karazi, to expand the Redut enterprise and manage its operations out of the VDV Airborne 45th Guards Spetsnaz Reconnaissance Brigade headquarters in Kubinka. On learning of Karazi's entry into the mercenary market, Prigozhin threatened to thrash his competitor, a move that was entirely in keeping with his thuggish instincts. But the frictions well predated Karazi's entry on the scene.

At least twenty distinct Redut detachments were established within the first year of Russia's war in Ukraine, attracting thousands of former Wagner Group fighters who had deployed on previous missions for Prigozhin's outfit.[9] The conflation between the two—Wagner and Redut—would prove a useful means of masking the maneuvers of Russian special operatives, creating confusion on the ground about who exactly was doing what on behalf of the GRU.

But what caught the world's attention in the heat of the moment in the initial weeks of the invasion was that Putin had chosen the Wagner Group to execute the Kremlin's most sensitive covert and dramatic mission. Russia's invasion of Ukraine marked a significant turning point in the Kremlin's approach to marketing its phantom army. Once labeled "Keystone Cossacks," the private army that Prigozhin had built for Putin over the course of nearly a decade had morphed from a shadow force of adventuresome bumblers into a slickly advertised Praetorian Guard, tasked with carrying out Russia's most sensitive missions in enemy territory. The Kremlin's links to Wagner Group mercenary forces had suddenly emerged as critical assets in Putin's bid to topple Zelensky's government and to restore Ukraine as the centerpiece of its strategy to reconstruct the Russian empire and challenge the primacy of NATO in Europe.

Wagner's value added for the Russian military was that its well-established reputation for brutality had turned it into one part instrument of psychological warfare, one part diversionary force, and one part deniable proxy. The stylized, rifle-toting gangster lean adopted by Wagner's masked commanders on camera projected an image of insider cool, competence, and bravery unmatched by any other element of the Russian military. Everywhere Wagner went, eyes followed, making it an object of obsession for Russia's enemies. And Prigozhin's talented band of propagandists ensured that it stayed that way: posing provocatively on the battlefield and marking every meme it popped onto Telegram with its signature skull-in-crosshairs insignia.

The Wagner Group was evidently undergoing a wholesale rebranding. Once the invasion kicked off, Wagner Group social media marketing rapidly emerged as an essential element in Russia's mobilization efforts and the Kremlin's information war against Ukraine and the West. The war ignited a surge in growth in the paramilitary's online fan base that was accompanied by a concerted push to establish local online groups in dozens of Russian cities with the explicit aim of recruiting new fighters to the Wagner Group. After the Russian onslaught in Ukraine began in 2022, the spike in interest in the Wagner Group propelled exponential growth in the fan base, catapulting the membership in the Wagner Group's single most popular channel on VKontakte from about 64,000 in February 2022 to more than 355,000 by the year's end.[10]

As Ukrainian forces began to push Russian troops out of areas surrounding Kyiv and the center part of the country, online clubs based in several cities across Russia bearing the Wagner Group handle also began to proliferate. Each group bore identical profile images: a band of masked soldiers with rifles slung over their shoulders, posing with a stand-up bass, a saxophone, and a tuba as if they were ready to strike up Richard Wagner's "Ride of the Valkyries" against the backdrop of a Syrian desert-scape. Combined, some twenty-nine Wagner-branded VKontakte groups carrying standardized landing pages would claim an aggregate total membership of 1.3 million users within the first year of the war.[11] Prigozhin, with apparent help from Russia's intelligence agencies, had turned his paramilitary into a walking advertisement for Russia's new way of war. But despite the obvious expectation in Russia of a quick victory, it did not materialize.

In Kharkiv, Russian forces encountered fierce Ukrainian resistance, bogging down in weeks of intense urban combat. Mariupol, a strategic port city in southeastern Ukraine, also became a focal point of heavy fighting. Ukrainian defenders held off Russian advances even as the city was bombarded with unrelenting rocket fire. In the North, the battle for Kyiv turned into a protracted and brutal affair as Ukrainian forces repelled assaults from Russian paratroopers who had swarmed by helicopter into Antonov International Airport in the nearby town of Hostomel. The initial strategy of rapid advancement proved overambitious for Russia. Logistics faltered, morale among Russian troops waned, and Ukrainian resistance turned Putin's intended blitzkrieg into a quagmire.

As time passed, the magnitude of Putin's miscalculation became obvious. He had expected NATO to fracture over how to respond to the invasion. Instead, the United States and Europe presented a united front, sanctioning Russia harshly and funneling sophisticated weaponry to the Ukrainian military that stymied the Russian advance. Although Kremlin war planners had convinced Putin that the Russian Army would handily crush the Ukrainians, high Russian casualty numbers made it quickly apparent that Russia would need reinforcements. But for Putin to call for a full-scale mobilization would have been tantamount to admitting failure, that the war was a war, not a "special military operation," and that victory would not come as swiftly or cheaply as he had promised.

The Wagner Group provided an expedient solution to Russia's manpower problems. In early March, after news of the assassination plot broke, Putin told members of Russia's security council that he had approved a proposal made by Sergey Shoigu for the defense ministry to recall Wagner fighters and to redeploy them in Ukraine alongside Russian-trained fighters from Syria, Libya, and the Central African Republic. Shoigu confirmed that an additional sixteen thousand fighters trained by the Wagner Group were prepared to join the fray.[12]

Putin explained the mercenary involvement as "people who want to come on a voluntary basis, not only for money, but to help the people who live in the Donbas," and said that Russia was prepared to "meet them halfway and help them move into the combat zone."[13] Suddenly, what had seemed to be one of the Kremlin's most closely guarded secrets—the fact that Russia had raised a mercenary army with global reach—was now being openly touted not only via anonymous posts on social media channels but also by the Russian president himself. Putin and Shoigu, who had studiously avoided public mention of Russian mercenaries for years, were publicly calling for help from Prigozhin.

Putin's rhetorical shift on the Wagner Group came as the world learned of a horrific massacre in the Mopti region of Mali, where Wagner mercenaries, alongside Malian forces, brutally killed around five hundred civilians over five days near the village of Moura in early March 2022, according to a UN investigation.[14] The rolling campaign of summary executions left a trail of mass graves and blew the lid off the Kremlin's clandestine support for a paramilitary that had become notorious around the world for its involvement in war crimes.

Meanwhile, sightings and signs of Wagner irregulars were cropping up everywhere. In early April, news broke of mass killings in the Kyiv suburb of Bucha. Local eyewitnesses said that regular Russian troops and contract soldiers of fortune had pushed into Bucha three days after the start of the offensive.[15] By then, many of the town's thirty-nine thousand residents had fled as Russian troops streamed over the Ukrainian border from Belarus. However, an estimated four thousand remained; most were too old, disabled, or poor to flee.

Serhii Shepetko, Bucha's deputy mayor, remembered bitterly how the Russian occupation unfolded. "The Russians thought we would greet them with flowers. They were mistaken," Shepetko said.[16] Disbelief had all but paralyzed the city council as hurried arrangements were made to gird for the onslaught. Even as the warning signs mounted that Putin intended to go all in with the Russia invasion, Bucha City Council members were convinced that most of the fighting would take place farther to the east, in Donetsk, Luhansk, and Kharkiv. A massive barrage of artillery strikes quickly disabused them of the illusion that the Kyiv region would remain untouched. On February 27, Russian forces launched a full-on assault against Bucha, overwhelming a hastily assembled, poorly armed contingent of local territorial-defense forces. Hundreds of Russian national guard soldiers flooded the streets, forcing city officials to surrender to the Russian occupation almost immediately.

The situation in Bucha deteriorated rapidly after that. Russian troops looted abandoned homes, stealing appliances, underwear, and other personal items. At checkpoints set up all around Bucha, Russian soldiers subjected locals to rough treatment, conducting strip searches and examining local men for signs of bruises on their shoulders or burns on their hands that might indicate they had fought on the side of local defense forces.

Armed with a list of names of local city officials and residents who served at nearby military installations, Russian contingents began house-to-house searches. It was then that it became clear, Shepetko said, that the Russians had relied on a shadow network of collaborators who had taken up residence in Bucha and other nearby suburbs to plot the takeover of the Kyiv region. "They had lists of local politicians and they had lists of military officials who lived in town. They knew exactly who lived where," Shepetko remembered.[17]

For a full month after the Russian takeover, town officials tried to bargain with their Russian captors to let them bury the dozens of bodies of the dead left moldering on Yablunska Street, Bucha's main thoroughfare. But the head of the VDV Airborne regiment that occupied the town initially refused, relenting to a request to bury some of the bodies in the cemetery at St. Andrew's Orthodox Church only when the stench of death became too overwhelming even for the Russians.

Initial reporting indicated that Russian soldiers had detained, in some cases tortured, and then summarily executed about 278 residents. But as Ukrainian troops began to liberate Kyiv's surrounding suburbs, the scale of the carnage snapped into sharper focus. The bodies of many of the Ukrainian civilians killed had their hands tied behind their backs and showed signs of mutilation. More than 1,300 were initially reported killed, and many of the victims' bodies were either tossed into mass graves, incinerated, or left to rot on the street. It was a cleansing operation, pure and simple, one of historic proportions.

Moscow's response to the devastating scenes of corpses strewn about like so much trash after Russian troops retreated in late March was as chilling as it was telling. The Russian foreign ministry's chief spokesperson, Maria Zakharova, accused Ukraine of staging the massacre in Bucha, claiming that the release of film footage from the crime scene was a Western ruse aimed at staining Russia's image.[18] But as more reporters arrived and local authorities, foreign forensic experts, and investigators from the International Criminal Court combed through the wreckage, it was obvious that the Russians were responsible. Further confirmation came when Ukrainian officials announced that intercepts of Russian communications revealed that the targeting of civilians in Bucha had been deliberate.

The first hint of suspected Wagner Group involvement came from survivors of the massacre in Bucha themselves. Eyewitness accounts suggested that the corpses of hundreds of Russian soldiers were left behind with pocket litter that identified their names and affiliations. It was also noted that several Ukrainian civilians had been beheaded; the gruesome markers, witnesses said, were mostly the work of *kontraktniki*—contract soldiers. Many of the *kontraktniki* seemed to be ethnic minorities from some of Russia's most economically depressed rust-belt regions in the center and remote eastern regions of the country.

One other telling sign that the Russian soldiers who stormed into Bucha that spring were no ordinary soldiers was a corpse booby-trapped with explosives that was discovered after Ukrainian forces reseized the town. Three years earlier, in Libya, Wagner Group fighters had also employed this signature defensive tactic: booby-trapping corpses and stuffing teddy bears with live ordnance as they scrambled in retreat during their failed offensive on the Libyan capital of Tripoli.

As more details of the carnage began to emerge, the messaging out of Moscow suddenly shifted again. Russian authorities claimed that Ukrainian forces had concocted the entire incident as a false-flag operation. In a lengthy television interview conducted a few days after the news about Bucha broke, Putin's chief spokesman, Dmitry Peskov, refuted claims of Russian involvement. Confronted with satellite imagery and video taken while Russian forces occupied Bucha, Peskov gave a dismissive shrug of the shoulders and accused Ukraine, the United States, and NATO of manufacturing evidence. He insisted that the imagery was fake, saying that Maxar, the American commercial satellite company that had released the photos, was part of a wider US campaign to undermine Russia. "We know Maxar is in very tight cooperation with the Pentagon," Peskov said.[19]

Amid the Russian denials, international journalists and investigators continued to turn up evidence of Russian war crimes in Bucha. Cases of ammunition marked with the unit number for the 104th and 234th Airborne Assault Regiments, subunits of the 76th VDV Airborne Division, were found near a site where eight Ukrainian men were summarily executed. Surveillance-camera video showed Russian-made BMD armored vehicles marked with a big white "V" on the side, suggesting that the troops had made their way to Bucha from Belarus. Other video footage posted online revealed how Russian paratroopers wearing padded leather helmets and white armbands had marched the group of men through the streets before shooting them and leaving their bodies to rot in the open.[20]

Several days into Ukraine's formal investigation, the town's local prosecutor, Ruslan Kravchenko, discovered a cache of information about the Russian soldiers who swept into the town on a computer server that the Russians had abandoned during the fray. Soon after that, Ukrainian authorities released the identities of several Russians whose names turned up in the server files, on cell phones left behind, or both. Most served in subunits of the 76th VDV Airborne Division out of Pskov. This hinted at the strong possibility that contract soldiers with the Wagner Group had also been present in Bucha because Wagner forces had frequently shadowed elements of the 76th VDV in other conflicts, most notably in Donbas in 2014 and then in Syria. Many of the paramilitary's earliest recruits were also veterans and *spetsnaz* reservists who had served in elite units based in Russia's Western Military District.

Suspicions about the Wagner Group's involvement only deepened when German intelligence officials confirmed early reports that Ukrainian intercepts of Russian radio communications that were traced to areas near Bucha indicated that contract soldiers were responsible for the atrocities. In one recorded intercept, two Russian men cursed and complained that they had been abandoned without air support as tens of thousands of Ukrainian troops boxed them in. Frustrated, an unidentified man on the line shouted forcefully in Russian, "Fucking kill them all for fuck's sake!" "Got it," the other replied. "What the fuck is wrong with you motherfuckers?! Civilians—slay them all!"[21]

Not long after the telephone intercept and computer server turned up, more evidence surfaced at the site not far from Yablunska Street, where some of the ugliest violence had occurred. Investigators found a love letter from the girlfriend of a Russian airborne officer who served in a unit of the 76th VDV Airborne Division in Pskov. Eight more paratroopers with the 234th and 104th Assault Regiments of the 76th VDV were additionally implicated when reporters dialed the numbers logged on the cell phone of a Bucha resident that Russian soldiers had commandeered during the town's occupation.[22]

History seemed to be repeating itself. From Afghanistan to Chechnya to Syria, "cleansing" operations and collective punishment had been a hallmark of Russian warfare. In Ukraine the same scorched-earth tactics were apparent everywhere. In nearby Irpin, a community that borders Bucha, the situation was similar. Angela Makeevka, Irpin's deputy mayor, remembered how panic had set in during the first twenty-four hours of the war as Russian forces descended on the Kyiv region. She evacuated her entire family from the capital, thinking that the suburbs would be safer. She was wrong.

By February 25, Russians controlled more than half of Irpin, cutting off most routes of escape.

The first days were chaos. Thousands of residents fled on foot on a collapsed highway overpass over the Irpin River that became known as the "bridge of life" because Ukrainian forces had blown it up to keep Russian forces out. Inexperienced young Russian conscripts who had been told little by their superiors about the Russian invasion plan shot at everything and everyone. It was impossible, Makeevka said, to get around Irpin safely. "It was like a post-apocalypse movie. There were bodies in the streets everywhere. As we were driving, we came across a sniper so we turned back around and started to back up the road," she said. "That's when we saw a dog was in the middle of the road eating something and when we got a little closer we saw it was eating a body."

About two weeks into the occupation, as Ukrainian defense forces began to chip away at Russian positions around Kyiv, the conscripts were reinforced by more experienced Russian soldiers. "There were Buryatis, Kadyrovtsy, Wagnerovtsy," Makeevka said. "You could tell them apart because of the insignia they wore on their shoulders. They had better uniforms. They had better weapons, and they had night vision goggles. They carried themselves with more confidence."[23]

A similar pattern was evident in Motyzhyn, a small farming village dotted with sunflower fields and dairy farms located about an hour's drive west of Kyiv, where Wagner forces were also sighted. The Russians had picked the spot because it was the highest point in the Kyiv region, making it perfect for the 24/7 drone-reconnaissance operations they had been tasked with running when they received their orders to muster in Belarus a little more than three months before the invasion.[24]

The Russian paratroopers who rumbled into town on February 27 in a massive column of armored vehicles with old Soviet military maps in hand found attitudes in Motyzhyn largely unchanged since the last time Russians had tried to occupy the town, during World War II. One Motyzhyn resident, a retired pensioner in her seventies who began surreptitiously relaying information about the Russian movements to Ukrainian forces shortly after the Russians arrived, apparently became particularly troublesome. According to a local human-rights organization, the woman—whose name was not initially released—was killed when the town's Russian occupiers firebombed her house.[25]

The town's mayor of more than ten years, Olha Petrivna Suhenko, subsequently came under immense pressure from the Russians to rein in Motyzhyn's rebellious residents. A stout woman with a warm smile that belied a no-nonsense attitude picked up from years of teaching kindergarten, Suhenko was not inclined to take orders. On the day the Russians arrived, she posted a message on Facebook: "There are foreign bastards in our village. Take care. Don't leave your homes. Keep calm."[26]

Russian troops commandeered a house at the far end of Motyzhyn's old military road near the banks of the forested hill and converted it into a torture chamber where at least twenty locals suspected of collaborating with Ukrainian troops were held and beaten mercilessly. Several of the Russians said they had fought in Libya and Syria on contract before being redeployed in Ukraine and knew how to deal with traitors; two would later be identified by Ukraine. Nonetheless, Suhenko and other town residents carried on quietly running the town's underground resistance, slipping information to the Ukrainian military, and running supplies to local defenders hidden around the village.

Mykola Kurach, head of the village's local defense forces, had been hiding out in Suhenko's house the night before the Russians came for her and her husband, Ilhor, on March 23. He recalled how the Russians, incensed at the villagers' betrayal, tore the house apart but promised Suhenko's son, Oleksandr, that the couple would be returned after a brief interrogation. The promise was not kept. A few hours later, the Russians returned for Oleksandr and took him to the torture chamber.[27]

On April 2, six days after Ukrainian forces liberated the village, the bodies of all three members of the mayor's family were found riddled with bullets and dumped in a shallow mass grave near the edge of the forest in Motyzhyn. A month after their bodies were discovered, Ukrainian prosecutors named three members of the Wagner Group—Alexander Stupnitsky, Sergey S. Sazonov, and Sergey V. Sazonov—in connection with the murders.[28] The charges marked the first but not the last time that members of the Wagner Group were formally charged with war crimes in Ukraine.

As Ukrainian forces beat back the enemy onslaught in the north and center of the country, the Russians began to direct their focus to the east. In mid-April, a post on the Telegram channel for the popular pro-Ukrainian website Inform-Napalm claimed that Ukrainian soldiers had found banknotes from Libya, Syria, and the Central African Republic on the bodies of several Russian fighters found heaped together near the eastern railway town of Popasna in Luhansk.

A handwritten note that was part of the pocket litter found at the site included several hastily scrawled telephone numbers. Beneath the name "Khavtar" was a number for a mobile in Novosibirsk and just below that a mobile number that started with "+223," the country code for Mali.[29] When a call was made to the number a few hours after the first mention online, however, the line had been disconnected.

Videos posted on Telegram confirmed that Wagner Group fighters had closely coordinated their battlefield maneuvers in Popasna with elements of the VDV 76th Airborne Division and the 40th Marine Brigade of the Pacific Fleet. The footage and the clues found at the grisly gravesite provided the first clues that Prigozhin's forces might be somewhere nearby. Wagner's first assault detachment commander, Alexander Kuznetsov, had in fact arrived on the scene in early March, working alongside the deputy commander of the 40th Marine Brigade. It was tough going at first.

A Wagner fighter recounted for Prigozhin's RIA-FAN correspondent, Kiril Romanovsky, how heavy Ukrainian shelling and drones overhead had pinned the Russian mercenaries down during one memorable skirmish in Popasna: "I watched as our guys, regular riflemen, were in the trenches, and just above them hovered an enemy quadcopter, which at the time seemed impossible to shoot down. The quadcopter hovered over our guys and then immediately started tearing them apart with mortars, cannon artillery, 122–152 caliber."[30]

Confirmation that Prigozhin had also been on the scene for one of the war's pivotal opening battles eventually came in April, when photos posted on pro-Russian social media channels showed him dressed in neat-looking khaki cargo pants and a camouflage jacket alongside Vitaly Milonov, an ultranationalist Russian MP from St. Petersburg, posing in front of a run-down building.

Prigozhin claimed in an online post that the photo with Milonov was taken during a chance meeting in St. Petersburg: "I was strolling along Nevsky Prospect. I saw Milonov walking. I approached him and said hello. That's the whole story. There's nothing to tell. Why does everything in the background look broken down? Well—that's just the way it is in our city—St. Petersburg."[31]

The only thing true about Prigozhin's story was that he had known Milonov for years. Milonov had climbed through the ranks of St. Petersburg's ultraconservative power circles around the same time that Prigozhin was getting into the catering business and Putin was the city's deputy mayor. One of the more colorful members of Putin's United Russia Party, Milonov, who had recently gained new fame for hosting a bizarre antigay reality TV show, was like so many in Prigozhin's St. Petersburg clique: a masterful manipulator of language and culture.

The license plate affixed to a truck pictured in the background of the photo of Milonov and Prigozhin revealed the black, blue, and red flag of the Donetsk People's Republic.[32] As more details about the Russian offensive at Popasna emerged, several other online sleuths pieced together the specific location of Prigozhin's rendezvous with Milonov, an elementary school in a nearby town that was doubling as the temporary headquarters for a mobile propaganda operation spearheaded by none other than Maxim Shugaley. Ukrainian intelligence officials would later use the photo and a series of others to triangulate the position of the Wagner detachment's temporary headquarters in Popasna and fire a fusillade of artillery rockets that killed an estimated hundred mercenaries in one day.

As the battle for control of Popasna raged on, Wagner Group casualties reached record peaks, but by mid-May, the Russians had gained control. The Wagner Group's prominent role in Russia's overall strategy for Ukraine had changed the facts on the ground for Russia's military. They stormed next into the towns of Lysychansk and Severdonetsk, and edged ever closer to strategic crossroads near Soledar and Bakhmut.

The paramilitary's documented trail of destruction stretched across Donbas. But it was the massacre in late July of dozens of Ukrainian prisoners of war that exposed anew the depth of Wagner's cruelty. The incident occurred at a detention center in the Donetsk region that Wagner forces controlled in the eastern town of Olenivka. At various points leading up to the incident, as many as 2,500 Ukrainians—a mix of soldiers and civilians—were held there. But the number surged when 2,000 Ukrainian soldiers with the Azov Regiment who were taken captive during the epic eighty-day siege of the Azovstal Steel and Iron Works in Mariupol were transported to Olenivka for holding as part of a negotiated surrender with Russian forces.

The Azov Regiment's origins in Ukraine's far-right nationalist movement had been a point of controversy since its founding as a territorial militia during the first Russian incursion in 2014. A highly effective fighting force known as "the little black men," the regiment was folded into Ukraine's national guard. But its reputation was tainted by its links to its founder, Andriy Biletsky, an ultranationalist affiliated with Ukraine's neo-fascist Right Sector coalition. The regiment's complicated history made it a convenient target of Russia's information war, and an ideal bête noire for the Wagner Group.

When Wagner forces took over control of the prison compound from local separatists on contract for Russia's defense ministry, they would routinely drag Azov Regiment prisoners from their cells for lengthy torture sessions. Prisoners were poorly fed in general, but Azov inmates, many emaciated and in poor condition after the Mariupol siege, often went days without food or proper care.

On the night of July 27, about two hundred wounded Azov fighters were moved to a makeshift barracks in an industrial workshop on the compound. Late the next evening, the Russians set up a Grad missile launcher next to the barracks that they fired twice before the barracks suddenly exploded, according to prisoners who witnessed the incident and barely escaped with their lives. Flames consumed the wounded, the defenseless, and the desperate, leaving little but charred human remains in a heap of twisted metal. Initial reports indicated that at least 53 died immediately and that another 130 were left injured.[33]

Russian officials denied responsibility, saying that Ukrainian forces had fired HIMARS rockets on the compound, a claim that the Ukrainian government vigorously denied and countered with accusations against the Kremlin. A UN investigation would later debunk the claim, buttressing accounts given by survivors that suggested that the explosions had been caused by Wagner fighters.[34]

A separate investigative report released by Ukraine's General Staff a few days after the incident suggested that the Russian mercenaries had deliberately fired on the barracks to destroy evidence of the prisoners' maltreatment ahead of an anticipated inspection by the Federal Security Service of the prison grounds after complaints that Wagner had embezzled defense ministry funds. The massacre and the Ukrainian government's preliminary findings prompted demands for the International Committee of the Red Cross to be allowed to inspect the site. Months of haggling with Russian authorities over access to the prison ultimately derailed the Red Cross fact-finding mission, leaving the question of responsibility unresolved.

However, there was no debate about who oversaw the Wagner Group's battlefield operations at the time. Prigozhin remained the company front man, but Dmitry Utkin retained the title of brigade commander, directing operations from a position in the rear across the border in Russia. And however dimly he was viewed by the rank and file, Andrey Troshev managed to stay in charge as chief of what Wagner referred to in its own internal memos as the general staff.

Before the start of the war, in 2021, Wagner's general staff consisted of fourteen tactical commanders who held supervisory authority over everything from intelligence to communications and field operations. Ten others under Troshev and Utkin's direct chain of command fell under the heading of administration, which included oversight of combat deployments, logistics, and instructional education among other, more mundane management tasks.[35]

In 2022 the size of the organization would grow exponentially, from a few thousand to tens of thousands, as Prigozhin's back office hurried to coordinate a splashy billboard recruitment campaign across Russia and take in applicants who flocked to Wagner's new website—wagner2022.org—where an enticing offer awaited: "Do you want to write your name in the history of military glory, but don't want to fight with bureaucracy and inspections? Then good news for you—the orchestra needs musicians in Ukraine! Embark on your first combat campaign with living legends of the industry!"[36]

CHAPTER 20

GULAG NO, GULAG YES

The charred and twisted ruins of Lysychansk and Severodonetsk were still smoldering when Prigozhin took his first official steps into the limelight. The earliest witnesses to the moment were prisoners held at the IK-8 prison colony in Tambov. It was a clear summer day in early June 2022. A helicopter swooped into the prison compound. Prisoners were ordered to muster in the penal colony's wide-open courtyard square. They watched with a mix of awe and confusion as Prigozhin, dressed in a tan khaki flight jacket with medals pinned to his chest, alighted from the chopper with a small retinue of armed men and strode to the center of the square. Prigozhin introduced himself as the head of the Wagner Group and told the prisoners assembled in a wide circle around him that he had an offer they would be foolish to refuse. Anyone who agreed to sign up to fight on the front lines in Ukraine for six months would be paid handsomely. If they survived, they would be granted amnesty and would be free to live normal lives.

The visit was unprecedented, and the offer seemed too good to be true. Until that moment, life had been for the most part a monotony of TV watching and trying to keep up with family from afar. Lucky breaks for the 430,000-plus men and women entombed in Russia's vast prison system do not happen often.[1] For those who are fortunate enough to secure a coveted spot on one of the prison work crews, their twelve-hour days are spent mostly on their feet. Some stitch together uniforms that will be worn by their captors. Others clear forests, do construction work, or undertake other heavy labor. Still more can and package food. All are at the mercy of the country's Federal Penitentiary Service.

Known as FSIN, the national penitentiary service is the apparatus that governs Russia's archipelago of "smothered opportunity," as Russia's most famous prison memoirist, Aleksandr Solzhenitsyn, called Russia's 869 penal colonies.[2] With an estimated 352,000 employees, the FSIN prison bureaucracy is run like a veritable army. Its penal settlements are concentrated in areas that are forested or rich in natural resources, a legacy of Soviet economic-development experiments that relied heavily on forced labor. The prison-labor scheme is exceptionally lucrative; some 26,000 prisoners work for approximately 1,700 state and private companies across the country, yielding nearly $192 million in annual revenue for the government in 2022, and that is only the official reported number.[3] It also feeds a thriving gray market husbanded by FSIN employees who pad their paltry civil-servant salaries with bribes paid by inmates for special privileges and by criminal networks that operate inside and outside the prisons.

Just beneath the official FSIN layer of control sits the prisoners' committee (*blatkomitet*). The *blatkomitet* is part of the shadow administration that oversees the complex codes of honor governed by the old-school mafia heavies who are the leading enforcers of organized-crime groups such as the Tambov Brotherhood. *Blatkomitet* members informally enforce the written and unwritten rules of the penal colony and are often richly rewarded with access to contraband cell phones, booze, and drugs. It is this layer of Russia's prison culture that had schooled the young Prigozhin.

He apparently never forgot the most important lesson learned: it's not who you are but who you know that gets you through the rough times. Analysis of phone records, calendar entries, and internal documents revealed that Prigozhin had reestablished connections with federal prison officials long after his own prison stint. Numerous meetings with FSIN officials were logged in Prigozhin's electronic scheduler from 2012 to 2019, including at least two with FSIN director Gennady Alexandrovich Kornienko.[4] This potentially suggested that Prigozhin's strategy of pulling from the ranks of the incarcerated was not a last-ditch effort, as once thought, but rather a long-established practice that fed directly into Wagner's core ethos of leveraging desperation and criminality for profit and power. If true, it would suggest an even deeper integration of state-sanctioned criminality in Wagner's operations, with prisons becoming recruitment centers for mercenaries long before this became public knowledge.

When he strode into the courtyard where IK-8 prisoners had gathered, a jolt of electricity surged through the crowd. "We couldn't believe our eyes," one inmate—a convicted murder serving a twenty-three-year sentence—told a reporter for *The Guardian*. "But there he was standing in front of us: Prigozhin, in the flesh, urging us to join the Wagner private-military group and fight in Ukraine."[5] Barely more than sixty years old, Prigozhin had achieved the unthinkable. A convicted street hustler and hooligan had become a billionaire who had half the Kremlin on speed dial: he was living proof of the possible in Putin's Russia.

Prigozhin's prison visits had been generating buzz for weeks. He cut a striking figure as he joked with prisoners and guards alike. He dove into his pitch with gusto and didn't sugarcoat the risks. The war was brutal. There was only a slim chance of survival, and many would come home in zinc coffins—if there were any remains to recover at all. But, Prigozhin promised, signing up with the Wagner Group would be a once-in-a-lifetime chance to turn their lives around and do something of value for their country and their long-suffering families. They would get paid for their time in the trenches, and if they managed to survive, they would be granted a pardon for their crimes—perhaps signed by President Vladimir Putin himself.

Social media posts about the Wagner Group's prison-recruitment drive began circulating online early in the summer of 2022 as Wagner Group forces began to puncture Ukrainian defenses near the Azovstal plant in Mariupol. Relatives of prisoners at the IK-6 Obuvkhovo and IK-7 Yabloneva prison colonies near St. Petersburg offered the first concrete details, telling Russian journalists that in an early-July visit, Wagner Group representatives promised that the prisoners could earn about $3,200 in exchange for six months of service on Ukraine's front lines. Service "contracts" were little more than a verbal agreement, a token, but a promise of a death payment to prisoners' families of roughly $80,000 was a potentially life-changing amount if it was delivered—enough to buy a car, start a new business, or find a new life.[6]

Known as "Project K," the prison-recruitment drive picked up momentum as word spread. About forty signed up in the initial round, according to a report submitted to the UN by two human-rights organizations.[7] Relatives discovered that about fifty inmates were transferred to the Rostov region, bordering Ukraine, only after prisoners asked family members for passport details and signatures authorizing the transfer of prisoners' salaries to their families. In one prison, Wagner recruitment posters were pinned to the community bulletin board. East of St. Petersburg, in the city of Tula, a prison official at the IK-4 penal colony described July visits from Wagner Group representatives, several of them armed. In all, 270 prisoners from Tula signed up to fight at the Ukrainian front during the opening days of the recruitment campaign. In the republics of Moldovia, Mari El, and Komi, where Prigozhin himself had once served time, hundreds more joined.

Initially, Wagner Group representatives tried to recruit as many former military and law enforcement officers as they could. Prisoners were told that anyone physically fit and below fifty could volunteer for the front if they had not been convicted of sexual offenses or acts of terrorism. As Russian casualties mounted in the drive toward Bakhmut, Wagner recruiters became less discerning. In at least one instance, an entire unit was formed from a pool of sexual offenders. No one could say for sure whether the unit had been given a special mission. By early August, human-rights groups estimated that prisoners from seventeen penal colonies had joined and that the number of volunteers had reached at least a thousand.[8]

The total number of prisoners sent to the front, wounded, or killed remained a mystery. Statistics cited by journalists and human-rights groups were consistently untrustworthy, and oft-cited references to estimates that placed the number of prisoners sent to the front at 40,000–50,000 relied on flimsy sources and faulty methodologies that likely grossly overestimated the number. Reports also circulated that Prigozhin's representatives had delivered death payments to prisoners' families in person, but few specifics were on offer in those cases either. In one account, locals said they glimpsed Prigozhin visiting the grave of a fallen convict fighter at an old cemetery in St. Petersburg.

As Russian troops pushed to secure the northeastern corridor of Donbas, Wagner commanders stationed at training grounds in the Rostov region began dispatching prisoner units to serve as diversionary forces and to dig defensive trench lines. Russian news stories began to proliferate about Prigozhin's appearances at correctional facilities across Russia and about poorly trained fighters in Rostov, while photos began to crop up on Telegram showing long lines of white trucks bearing the remains of the dead from the front lines of Soledar and Bakhmut. In an information coup, a group of security-agency defectors from the FSB's counterintelligence units made it clear that the surreptitious mobilization of thousands of convicted criminals was a systematic, top-down directed effort to feed what would soon become known as "Operation Bakhmut Meat Grinder."

A chief source of the information about the FSB's role in the scheme was a YouTube channel and website called Gulagu.net. This social media vertical was the brainchild of Vladimir Osechkin, a former convict turned human-rights activist who had fled Russia several years earlier for fear of retribution from the Russian government. Born in Samara, he grew up in a middle-class family that flourished during the Soviet era, with a journalist father and cardiologist mother. So steeped was his family in the elite culture of Russia's *nomenklatura* that Osechkin, as a kid coming of age in the Wild 1990s, fantasized about joining the FSB. They were the good guys, he thought, while the mafia-connected bandits and hooligans that shook him and his friends down for their walking-around money were on the wrong side of Russian history.[9]

Osechkin's naivete and teenage idealism led him to enroll in Samara University's law faculty, hoping to follow Putin's path to an FSB officer's badge. He said those dreams were shattered when he was falsely accused of murder.[10] Detained for three months and pressured to confess, he learned the harsh truth about Russia's corrupt legal system—where guilt was assumed and innocence came with a price tag. After his family's lawyer got the charges dropped, Osechkin moved to Moscow and started a successful car dealership. But profitable ventures in Russia attract unwanted attention. In 2007, after refusing to pay a bribe to local authorities, he was arrested on fraud charges and spent four years in prison, where he documented the rampant corruption and abuses.

After his release in 2010, Osechkin formed a bond with Russian journalist Olga Romanova, whose husband, Alexei Kozlov, had also clashed with the law. Kozlov, a Moscow finance entrepreneur, was charged with financial crimes after a business dispute and became a well-known prison blogger during his eight-year sentence, exposing the abuses within Russia's prison system. Kozlov's Butryka blog inspired Osechkin in 2011 to launch Gulagu.net, a prisoners' rights website. Although Osechkin would later have a falling-out with Romanova, his growing influence led to his appointment to a government working group on prison reform.

Despite his success, Osechkin's activism and information brokering stirred controversy. He faced heavy criticism from human-rights activists and the independent Russian press for his role in a prison-insurance scheme that was intended to shield inmates from abuse. But his massive online following and extensive network of tipsters within Russia's prison system and among prisoners' families made him an undeniably influential figure, despite the backlash.

Even as his activism gained momentum, Osechkin, by his own admission, lacked nuance when it came to Russia's foreign policy. During the Euromaidan crisis and Russia's annexation of Crimea in 2014, he openly supported the Kremlin's actions. Like many Russians, Osechkin disliked the corrupt system that Putin had created but initially failed to see the contradiction between his disdain for the abuses of Putin's vertical of power at home and his support for Russia's aggressive moves abroad.

That realization came only gradually and much later for Osechkin, not long after he was forced to flee Russia and after he settled in France's famously picturesque resort town of Biarritz.[11] From there, Osechkin gained greater notoriety inside and outside of Russia in 2021, when he published several video clips culled from a forty-gigabyte cache of prison-surveillance footage showing the physical and sexual abuse of inmates in Russian prisons. Osechkin had gained access to the video archive when a former prison inmate contacted him not long after his release from a notoriously abusive prison unit in the Russian city of Saratov.

The inmate, Sergey Salevyev, a thirty-one-year-old Belarusian citizen, surreptitiously smuggled copies of hundreds of torture videos. Soon after, Osechkin helped Salevyev secure asylum in France, and the FSB placed Osechkin on Russia's most-wanted list. Both men—Osechkin and Salevyev—wound up in Biarritz in large part because of their connections to another Russian émigré and anti-Putin human-rights activist named Pierre Hafner.

Hafner and Salevyev briefly captured headlines worldwide in March 2022 when, a few weeks after Russia's invasion began, they broke into the Biarritz mansion of Putin's youngest daughter and released a videotaped tour of her luxurious residence after unfurling a Ukrainian flag from a balcony over the street.[12] The trio—Hafner, Osechkin, and Salevyev—formed one node in a growing cluster of activist anti-Putinist Russian émigrés scattered across France and other parts of Europe who emerged as a kind of anti-imperialist resistance front. They probed Europe's ultra-wealthy enclaves to expose the spots where rich Russian oligarchs parked their yachts and summered in high-style mansions.

Their on-camera antics often bordered on the campy, and the tone of their citizen journalism verged on the conspiratorial, but they were highly effective communicators. And, in time, their twenty-first-century reprisal of a kind of World War II–era underground resistance movement began to act as a magnet for disillusioned FSB and MVD security officers and eventually Wagner Group defectors.

Osechkin, more than any other, would be credited with fleshing out the full story of Prigozhin's prison-recruitment campaign. The story's seed was a video that began circulating on Telegram in early September just as the battle for control of Soledar was heating up. Shot on a mobile phone from a distance, the video showed Prigozhin enjoining a crowd of prisoners to sign up to fight with the Wagner Group. "Do you have anyone who can get you out of prison alive?" he shouted. "There are two, Allah and God. I am taking you out of here alive. But it's not always the case that I will bring you back alive."[13]

The clip was downloaded thousands of times after a reporter found it on an anonymous Telegram channel called Kremlin Whispers. Although it was quickly deleted, Alexey Navalny's Anti-Corruption Foundation posted a copy of it. Because there were no immediately recognizable markers of its provenance, however, it was initially unclear if the man depicted in the video was really Prigozhin.[14]

The video did make one thing apparent: Russia's war planning was woefully insufficient. Before the invasion started, in the winter of 2022, Russia massed an estimated 190,000 troops along Ukraine's borders.[15] The vast majority were conscripts on short-term rotations and thus ill-equipped to take on a well-armed, well-trained, and highly motivated Ukrainian military equipped with donated weaponry from the West. A lack of coordinated command structures further undercut their effectiveness. Six months in, the net result was high rates of attrition on both sides of the front and a near stalemate between Russian and Ukrainian forces in several parts of the country.

The video confirmed that the Russian military and the Wagner Group—Russia's premier fighting force—were both very short on manpower. Putin's reluctance to call for a general mobilization of forces and put the country on a full war footing constrained the Russian military's ability to solve problems on the battlefield. As Ukrainian forces pushed back the Russian onslaught, however, Prigozhin began rooting around in the bowels of the country's labyrinthine penitentiary system for fast solutions.

By early fall, as the contours of Russia's prison-recruitment scheme came into fuller view, the Russian military was struggling to cope. Russia needed an urgent intervention to get things back on track, and it looked like Putin had once again tapped Prigozhin to supply a quick fix. Still, the leaked prison-recruitment video left many analysts scratching their heads. Why now? What was behind the timing of the video's release?

It turned out that the "leak" was probably not a leak at all. Its content and timing were strategic. Evidence suggested that Prigozhin or someone linked to him posted the video in order to counter claims by prison-rights activists like Osechkin that the Russian government was turning prison inmates into cannon fodder. The "leak" came on the heels of a heated but indirect exchange between Osechkin and Prigozhin. Days beforehand, in early September 2022, a site called Gulagu-da.ru cropped up on the internet. It was classic Prigozhin. Gulagu-da, or Gulag-yes in Russian, was a witty rejoinder to Osechkin's cleverly named Gulagu.net, or Gulag.no.

A banner at the top of Prigozhin's site emblazoned the words "Stories of Heroes Who Made the Right Choice!" over a video of a Russian flag billowing in the wind high above what looked like a smokestack at the Azovstal steel plant. Videos of prisoners who signed up to fight in Ukraine offered cheery testimony about their time on the front. In one video a convict-unit commander, Kalashnikov in hand, squatted in front of two dozen men clad in tan military uniforms and smiled sunnily. Using a derogatory Russian slang term for Ukrainians, he declared with a smile, "We are on our way to go crush the khokols." In another, a convict-fighter with a military medal pinned to his chest and seated atop a hospital bed alongside several other wounded Wagner soldiers joked, "It's true there were a lot of Nazis there. But we still managed to kick some ass all the same."

The Gulagu-da.ru site was registered on September 6, 2022, and the videos posted on it were created and posted over the three subsequent days.[16] The domain registry did not list the site owner, but further checks revealed that it was hosted by a St. Petersburg–based tech company called TimeWeb Ltd. The trail of clues seemed to end until September 9, when Prigozhin filed a letter of complaint with Russia's prosecutor general.[17] In a three-page screed posted on the VKontakte account for Concord Managment and Consulting, Prigozhin accused Osechkin of waging a disinformation campaign against him and called for Russian authorities to list Osechkin's YouTube channel as the product of an extremist organization.[18]

No sooner had Prigozhin's letter of complaint been posted than the video depicting him urging prisoners to join up began to circulate on Telegram. Released on the heels of devastating Russian battlefield losses, the video hit the English-language press, and its location soon became clear. High above a clump of concrete cell blocks, a green-roofed church and a red-brick smokestack loomed distantly in the backdrop.[19] The distinctive landmarks and a survey of satellite imagery yielded the penal colony's location: the old Russian frontier town of Yoshkar-Ola in the heart of the Mari El Republic.

Once one of the first military outposts on the frontier of an expanding tsarist empire, Yoshkar-Ola is one of many tiny ethnic enclaves that managed to maintain its distinct character despite centuries of Russian repression. Known as Red City in the Finno-Ugric tongue of the locals, the town became home to a strategic-missile unit on the list of the Russian military's "shock troop" forces, making Yoshkar-Ola one of the most important cogs in the machinery of Putin's war in Ukraine. The town supplied Russian forces not only with missiles but also with a steady stream of cannon fodder: convicts culled from the barracks of the IK-6 penal colony, which was where the Wagner Group recruitment video was shot.

Yoshkar-Ola is also home to the People's Memorial Museum of the History of the Gulag, a kind of living memorial to Aleksandr Solzhenitsyn's classic prison exposé *The Gulag Archipelago*. Built on the grounds of a former prison-execution complex, the museum contains material evidence of terror wrought by the Soviet secret police and stands as a vivid reminder of the horrors visited on the prisoners of Yoshkar-Ola's penitentiary and other prisons across the country. Convicts in every country come with a mythos of their own; in Russia they are known as the *zakluchennyi*, or *zeks*, the castoffs who rise, fall, and rise again. They are made stronger by the beatings and privations they suffer. Their bonds are as martial as those of any army. Resourceful and resilient, *zeks* can make something out of nothing.

Inside, they survive by a code that is quite literally written on the body with tattoos. Saints, angels, and cathedrals express devotion to thievery. Skulls and coffins signal a conviction for murder. Safecrackers and money launderers sport bow-tie tattoos. Rank is sometimes indicated by stars etched in blood and flesh.[20] Prigozhin himself had acquired the markings of his rank when prisoners tattooed a woman on his back, a sign of subjugation and being "owned" by an inmate of higher rank.[21] The lifers are the would-be secondary sovereigns of the system, after the prison guards. Some are thieves-in-law with mafia fiefdoms that hum along inside and outside their cell walls. Others are political prisoners, hung out in the public eye as irredeemable until they emerge again with a determination to expose all the rot of the gulag.

Gulag is an acronym. The *Glavnoye Upravleniye Ispravitelno-Trudovykh Lagerey*, or Main Directorate of Correctional Labor Camps, was shortened to GULAG almost as soon as it was created under control of the Soviet secret police in 1930. As Solzhenitsyn noted, the gulag was simply a new iteration of a system for political repression built by the Bolsheviks in 1918 until it was disbanded and reorganized in 1956, a few years after Stalin's death. Harsh winters, starvation, hard labor, and torture of political dissidents killed millions caught up in the penal system.

The open feud between Prigozhin and Osechkin threatened to expose anew every black corner of the Stalinist regime that Putin was striving to re-create. Both Osechkin and Prigozhin joined the long tradition of *zeks* who entered prison naive about the harsh repressions of the state only to emerge as the most radical catalysts for social change. The two men were a generation apart, but both shared the lived experience of Russia's castoff class, and both were transformed by their prison experiences. Prigozhin emerged as a determined social climber eager to scale the rungs of power; Osechkin became a human-rights hustler, leveraging his obsessive documentation of the Russian state's worst abuses to build a career as an online personality. Both were part of a long Russian tradition that divides the popular imagination between the imperial and the revolutionary.

This freighted history was the backdrop to Prigozhin's entrance to the IK-6 penal colony in Yoshkar-Ola in September 2022. Once inside, Prigozhin confirmed what Osechkin and others had reported, telling the crowd of men in black prison jackets that the first wave of prisoners to be sent to the Ukrainian front was recruited from a penal colony in St. Petersburg. Forty convicts were dispatched in June with guns and a modicum of training to the embattled perimeter of the Vulhedar thermal power plant in Donbas.[22] Three were killed, and several more were injured, Prigozhin said. "They died heroes," he told the crowd.

He knew better than anyone else how the word *hero* sounded to those deemed beyond redemption. Prigozhin leaned hard into his *zek* credentials: going to the Ukrainian front was beyond risky, and chances were high, Prigozhin said, that anyone who volunteered would soon meet their maker. But there was also a chance that those who signed up might survive. "I have everything that is needed—planes, tanks. We have everything that is needed to fight this war efficiently," Prigozhin reassured the captives. Anything, he said, was better than dying a coward's death in prison. "If you are killed you will be buried with honors in Goryachi Klyuch alongside other Wagner Group heroes," Prigozhin promised.

That the cemetery at Goryachi Klyuch would be offered up as a Valhalla for the afterlife of Russian soldiers of fortune was as significant as it was surprising. It marked the first time that Prigozhin mentioned the memorial compound since it was built in the fall of 2018. For years, he had dodged questions about Wagner fighters killed in action and the resting place for Russia's fallen paramilitary fighters. Initially, the only semiofficial acknowledgment of the site was published by the Russian-language daily *Kommersant* after a chapel was erected there—by Prigozhin's company Megaline LLC—behind a walled-off compound in October 2018.[23]

Due south of the Wagner Group's main training base in Molkino, the Goryachi Klyuch compound sits near the town's famous hot-spring resort. The head and torso of a statue of a brawny Russian paramilitary soldier looms over the high slate-gray walls as he cradles a military assault rifle in his muscular arms. Inside the verdant green courtyard surrounding the chapel, an elaborate bronze memorial reportedly depicts a confrontation between two Wagner Group fighters and ISIS attackers in Syria.[24]

A St. Petersburg–based company called Exclusive Technology LLC, linked to Prigozhin's business enterprises, purchased the 1.6-hectare lot, eventually transferring ownership in December 2018 to Andrey Troshev's League for the Protection of the Interests of Veterans of Local Wars and Military Conflicts. The site was likely the brainchild of Troshev and Troshev's longtime comrade in arms Andrey "Tramp" Bogatov, another *Afghantsy* veteran and Liga member.[25]

For Wagner commanders who were there from the very start, Goryachi Klyuch was hallowed ground. The rich black earth along a tributary of the Kuban River where the memorial lay was salted with the blood of Wagner's fallen. So when Prigozhin called it out during his sales pitch to the prisoners of IK-6 in Yoshkar-Ola that day, he spoke with his heart. Anyone—murderer, rapist, thief—who signed up for the fight would be absolved of their sins and guaranteed a vaunted place alongside real heroes, Prigozhin told the crowd. Within months, his words became reality for many as the cemetery footprint at Goryachi Klyuch began expanding while the battle of Bakhmut dragged on into the bleak winter.[26]

When Prigozhin confirmed in late September 2022 that he was indeed the man in the infamous prison video in Yoshkar-Ola and acknowledged his ties to the Wagner Group, it sent shock waves around the world.[27] He said that he founded the Wagner Group in 2014 after seeing how poorly Russian separatist fighters were treated during the siege for control of Donbas. Inspired by a sense of patriotism, Prigozhin said, he decided to see for himself what he could do to help prevent what he termed a "genocide of the Russian population" in Donbas. "I, like many other businessmen, went to the training grounds where the 'Cossacks' gathered, and started to squander money on the recruitment of a group that would go and protect the Russians," Prigozhin explained. "But I quickly realized that among all these 'Cossacks' and other paramilitary comrades that half were swindlers who stole the money meant for volunteers and sent them naked and barefoot to their very death."[28]

It was a bold admission, and a puzzling one. The Wagner Group had come under UN scrutiny for war crimes in several countries across Africa and the Middle East—to say nothing of the countless violations of laws of war in Ukraine. Why had Prigozhin chosen this moment to publicly stake his ownership claim?

The reasons for Prigozhin's step into the limelight soon became clearer. The Wagner-run Telegram channel Grey Zone began releasing more and more footage of Prigozhin grandstanding on and off the battlefield. His avowal came two days after Russian media began circulating a video showing him and Wagner commander Anton "Lotus" Yelizarov attending the funeral of a Wagner fighter killed in action during fierce fighting in Bakhmut.

Prigozhin's brief cameo at the memorial service for Alexey Nagin, known as "Terek," was a theatrical display where fiction bled into reality. Nagin, who had starred in and cowrote the feature film *Best in Hell*, a dramatized portrayal of Wagner's bloody siege of Mariupol, became the symbol of Prigozhin's narrative. The film, shot in a bombed-out warehouse in Ukraine, was produced by Prigozhin's studio Aurum, the same company behind the Shugaley series, *Tourist*, and *Granit*, a movie about Wagner's failed mission in Mozambique. Prigozhin's presence at the funeral was more than a tribute—it was a performance aimed at boosting his stature, an act designed to underscore his arrival as a charismatic majordomo and Kremlin insider. Prigozhin was signaling hard that he was untouchable.

His increased visibility coincided with an intensifying political skirmish with Defense Minister Sergey Shoigu over Wagner's ambiguous status. Prigozhin's appearance at Nagin's funeral was not an isolated act of theatrics—it was part of a larger campaign strategy. He had already tested the approach a few weeks earlier in August, when he attended the funeral of Darya Dugina, daughter of ultranationalist ideologue Alexander Dugin, after she was killed in a car bombing. Prigozhin seized that moment to align himself with Russia's ultranationalist fringe, a powerful and growing constituency he sought to court in his bid to demonstrate to his rivals that he could be as formidable in politics as he was on the battlefield. Prigozhin doubled down a few weeks later, acknowledging in an online post that he had backed the Russian troll farm that interfered in the 2016 US presidential election, which put Donald Trump in the White House.[29] With each public admission, Prigozhin seemed once again to be trolling Washington. Coming less than a year into Russia's offensive, these developments raised important questions: Was Prigozhin's sudden grab for the media spotlight coordinated with the Kremlin, or had Putin's attitude toward Prigozhin shifted in some way? Why, after years of carefully distancing itself, would the Kremlin suddenly decide to abandon its long-running strategy of maintaining plausible deniability when it came to Prigozhin and the Wagner Group?

If nothing else, Prigozhin's antics were distracting. The Wagner Group began to dominate news headlines just as it seemed that much of the world was beginning to question Putin's strategic acuity: Russian troops in Ukraine's southern Kherson province and Kharkiv were faltering in the face of a surprisingly effective Ukrainian counteroffensive. The diversionary nature of Prigozhin's increasingly sharp jabs at the West, at Ukraine's president, Volodymyr Zelensky, and even at Kremlin patrons became clearer with the release of yet another controversial video on social media. Where many of Russia's military leaders had failed in driving the narrative of Russia's war of aggression in Ukraine, Prigozhin seemed to be succeeding.

Prigozhin was on a winning streak. Or he at least wanted to create the impression that he was. In early November 2022, the Wagner Group made headlines again with the grand launch of its business center in a sleek, modern skyscraper in St. Petersburg. The event was a media circus, with curious journalists mingling in the airy atrium of the glass-paneled office building alongside bearded Wagner fighters and prominent ultranationalist bloggers like the Grey Zone's Vladen Tatarsky. The celebration, deliberately timed to coincide with Russia's National Unity Day, mirrored a parallel event in Moscow, where Putin led a similarly symbolic ceremony.

The development sparked immediate speculation that Yevgeny Prigozhin might be positioning himself for a higher political role—perhaps even eyeing a move to replace Putin. News that the Wagner Group had formally registered a company address unleashed a torrent of conjecture. Was it an attempt to solidify the mercenary army's legal standing, or was Prigozhin preparing to wield Wagner's influence in the political arena? The reality turned out to be far more complicated.

Emblazoned with a giant "W" on the entry door, the Wagner Group Center was promoted as a cutting-edge hub for IT specialists and innovation. Plans included hosting a hackathon aimed at boosting Russian drone operations on the front lines. But the building was more Potemkin village than tech powerhouse—only about half the floors were occupied, with its grand image masking the hollow reality behind the facade.

The registered company wasn't the Wagner Group but the "Wagner Group Center," with Alexander Tensin, a former Kalashnikov Concern employee, listed as its chief stakeholder—not Prigozhin.[30] The connection to Kalashnikov, based in Barnaul, was no coincidence: Wagner's precursor, Moran Security Group, had deep ties to Rostec subsidiaries there.[31] It was a classic bait and switch, with a touch of three-card monte. Prigozhin had secured the land rights in 2019 but soon clashed with St. Petersburg regulators, and the project became mired in red tape, complicated by his feud with regional governor and former patron Alexander Beglov.[32] Prigozhin was using his newfound fame to settle old scores, flexing his influence where bureaucracy had stalled him.

The rift between Prigozhin and Beglov opened shortly after Beglov's 2019 election. Prigozhin had thrown his weight behind him, deploying his troll farm to disparage Beglov's challengers. Prigozhin claimed he had spent millions only to be abandoned once the election was over. As Wagner forces became bogged down in Bakhmut, Prigozhin unleashed a steady stream of attacks demanding that Beglov be investigated for treason for failing to honor fallen Wagner fighters and for helping his son dodge the draft.[33]

Prigozhin thrived on the fear that his tough-guy persona and the Wagner Group's ruthless reputation inspired. This was driven home when he openly cheered the videotaped ISIS-style execution of Yevgeny Nuzhin, a former Wagner fighter who had defected to Ukraine. The clip, ominously titled "The Hammer of Revenge," was posted on the Grey Zone Telegram channel in mid-November, just two months after Nuzhin confessed on camera to deserting Wagner. It featured a masked executioner in camouflage using a sledgehammer to kill the elderly-looking Nuzhin. In an online post, Prigozhin denounced Nuzhin as a traitor and sneered, "I think this movie is called A Dog's Death for a Dog."[34]

Haggard and emaciated, Nuzhin said he had been serving a twenty-eight-year sentence for murder when he signed up to fight for Wagner.[35] He was one of the thousands who took Prigozhin and Putin up on their joint offer of combat pay and clemency in exchange for joining Russia's mercenary detachments on the front lines. In his execution video, Nuzhin said he believed that he was recaptured by force after Ukrainian authorities released him on his own recognizance, while Russian media reported that Nuzhin was returned to Russia as part of a prisoner exchange. How exactly Nuzhin wound up in the custody of a sledgehammer-wielding Wagner Group executioner after that remains a mystery.

In a well-timed rejoinder to Nuzhin's on-camera execution, the European parliament issued a resolution urging the EU Council to designate the Wagner Group a terrorist organization. Prigozhin responded by circulating a video of one of his company representatives delivering a bloodied sledgehammer embossed with the Wagner Group's iconic skull-and-bones symbol to the EU Parliament.[36] The menacing prank drew quick clapback from Estonia's foreign minister, Urmus Reinslau, a passionate anti-Putin EU hawk who countered with a video of his own, making a display of opening a red case with a shiny pair of handcuffs and promising that they'd be waiting for Prigozhin at the International Criminal Court in The Hague.

Reinslau's stunt and the EU action against Prigozhin and Wagner came on the heels of a similar debate in Washington. After years of little action, several members of Congress advanced a resolution to add the Wagner Group to the US list of foreign terrorist organizations, placing Prigozhin and his paramilitary force on par with Osama bin Laden and al-Qaeda. But as the Russian offensive dragged on toward a year with the close of 2022, the question that loomed wasn't whether Prigozhin would be hauled before a criminal court on organized-crime charges or The Hague for crimes against humanity. It was whether Prigozhin would survive the Ukraine campaign at all.

CHAPTER 21

A STAB IN THE BACK

The year was new. Bakhmut—the cathexis of Prigozhin's ambition and already a smoldering pit of jagged rubble—shimmered like a mirage. Everything that could have gone wrong had gone wrong. Bodies were piling up. Ammunition was scarce. Morale was low. Desertions were through the roof. All the world was watching, eyes fixed on the Wagner Group, waiting to see if Yevgeny Prigozhin would go up in flames.

He had wagered almost everything he had on a bet that the Ukrainians would be unable to resist the lure of claiming victory over the Wagner Group. It was the most pivotal decision of Prigozhin's short-lived career as a conventional military commander. And, so far, he had been right. The Wagner offensive in Bakhmut promised to deliver big for Russia. Prigozhin's mere presence had goaded Ukraine's top general, Valery Zaluzhny, into throwing everything that Ukrainian forces had at the defense of the city. It was a daring gamble for both sides.

Not since World War II had so many given up so much so fast for so little in Russia's name. With estimated average daily death tolls on either side reaching close to two hundred, the months-long clash between Russian and Ukrainian forces for control of Bakhmut and the surrounding area had taken on an outsized significance. The grinding struggle would ultimately waste the lives of roughly ten thousand Ukrainian troops and some nineteen thousand Wagner fighters.[1]

Six months into the offensive, Wagner casualties reached well over ten thousand, a fact that Prigozhin himself attested to in a macabre video postcard uploaded to Telegram in the small hours on the first day of January 2023 that showed him standing in the center of a makeshift morgue in the basement of a bombed-out building as a truckload of corpses arrived behind him in the background.[2] Many, including his own men, had begun to question Prigozhin's sanity.

But on January 10 the Wagner Group had marched triumphantly into the center of the neighboring town of Soledar, and Prigozhin was rewarded with a win that he believed he could finally legitimately claim was his and only his.

Prigozhin was at his most bombastic. Legs spread wide, arms open, face beaming, he posed in Soledar's legendary underground salt mines for the camera alongside his men in full battle rattle—camouflage fatigues, combat helmet, and armored vest. Snapshots of his historic victory generated hundreds of thousands of hearts, happy faces, and thumbs-up emojis from the Wagner Group's growing online fan base.

It was a stunning moment. One of Russia's most visible and vocal critics of Russian military operations in Ukraine was shouting from the virtual rooftop that he had done what no Russian general had yet managed: snatched victory for Russia from near defeat and seized the strategic initiative from Ukraine.

Prigozhin's mercenary army had proved a powerful instrument in the Kremlin's quest to rally Russian public support for a war that in its first year had looked doomed to fail. Prigozhin's clever online marketing campaign and prisoner-recruitment scheme had patched a gaping hole in the defense ministry's poorly prepared force-mobilization plans.

From a purely operational point of view, the Wagner Group, under Dmitry Utkin's stewardship, had repeatedly demonstrated that smaller units led by field commanders who were accorded good equipment and greater autonomy could maneuver and adapt in rapidly shifting circumstances.

At the political level, Prigozhin's showy style had conferred other important advantages. His distinctive public profile as a Kremlin insider-outsider kept the world guessing about Putin's true intentions. From the very beginning, the mystique surrounding the relationship between Putin and Prigozhin was what made the Wagner Group so potent on and off the battlefield. Whether real or imagined, Wagner's exploits fueled the notion that Russia's president had granted Prigozhin carte blanche to act with impunity.

Prigozhin's masterful manipulation of social media and the weaponization of pro-Kremlin disinformation, first during the MH17 crisis in Donbas and then during the 2016 US elections, only enhanced the perception that the revival of Russia's Great Power status could be bought on the cheap. For nearly a decade, Putin had bet big that covert proxies could produce low-cost wins and that any blowback effects could be managed if he could plausibly deny knowing what Prigozhin was up to. But Russia's full-scale invasion of Ukraine changed that calculus.

The war in Ukraine painted a target on the Wagner Group's back, stoking an appetite for vengeance among Putin's closest liegemen and Russia's foreign enemies alike. As more Western military aid arrived and the winter cold set in, the Wagner Group's early advantages withered under the punishing demands of a conventional war where opposing forces were more evenly matched.

Drones, electronic warfare equipment, heavy artillery, and the availability of ammunition set the tempo of action as much as manpower. In a war of attrition, deniable proxy forces were cannon fodder first and soldiers second, making their leader even more expendable.

Prigozhin lacked the military experience and political acumen required to digest those hard facts. He had spared nothing in his campaign to turn the Wagner Group into an internationally recognized symbol of the Russian way of war. Billboards featuring Prigozhin's portrait along with masked Wagner fighters cradling assault rifles in their arms were plastered across Russia.

Even as the Kremlin issued an edict banning official state media from mentioning the Wagner Group in the new year, preparations were under way to open forty-two new Wagner recruitment centers. Poll numbers suggested that Prigozhin was one of the most popular men in Russia, and millions followed his exploits on Telegram, Twitter, and VKontakte. The Wagner Group brand seemed to be as durable as Prigozhin's rise in popularity was unstoppable.

Prigozhin had publicly blamed the defense ministry for abysmally high Russian casualty rates, channeling frustrations heard all along the front lines and across Russia's right-wing ultranationalist factions. After Wagner's win at Soledar, mainstream Russian pundits had transformed Prigozhin into a national folk hero and the Wagner leaders into celebrities, repeatedly interviewing field commanders like Alexander Kuznetsov and Andrey Bogatov.

The buzz prompted a flurry of speculative international press coverage that hinted Prigozhin might be a possible contender to replace Shoigu or even

Putin.[3] He was dazzled by the echo chamber he had created. The glare of the spotlight on the Wagner Group had blinded Prigozhin to the risks he was taking each time he publicly bit the hand that fed him.

The genesis of the discord among Prigozhin, Shoigu, and Gerasimov well predated Russia's invasion of Ukraine. Quarrels over supplies, payments, and lines of authority had first erupted in Syria after the battle for Palmyra and dragged on for years. Although Prigozhin carped privately in memos to Shoigu that the defense ministry had shortchanged him, his complaints only reinforced Shoigu's perception of Prigozhin as a power-hungry ingrate. In a sign of the intensifying acrimony between Prigozhin and Russia's defense chiefs, the ministry's logistics subsidiary, Voentorg, filed a record 560 claims against Prigozhin's companies in 2022 alone.[4]

The crushing losses that the Wagner Group had sustained during the battle with US special forces for control of the Conoco plant in Syria created an irreversible split between Prigozhin and defense ministry leadership. The central tension had always been over who in Russia would reap the greatest share of profits and political rewards from Prigozhin's successes and who would pay the price for his failures.

This likely explained why on the day that the Wagner Group captured Soledar, Russia's defense ministry made no mention of Prigozhin or his paramilitary in its initial official statement. It was only after Prigozhin complained in an interview with Russia's state TV channel that the defense ministry was "constantly trying to steal Wagner's victory" that the official record was quickly amended with a hastily issued press release that praised Wagner's contributions.[5]

The episode poured gasoline on a firestorm of criticism that had already been raging for months among pro-war ultranationalist bloggers who complained that Putin was mismanaging the war. Leading the charge was Igor Girkin, who immediately took to YouTube and Telegram to denounce the Wagner Group's win as little more than a short-lived tactical win and to sharply warn that the Bakhmut offensive was doomed to failure because frictions between Prigozhin and defense ministry leaders risked fracturing the military.[6]

The defense ministry's slight, and its timing, were hardly accidental. The action in Soledar came only days after Putin fired Prigozhin's chief patron in the military, General Sergey Surovikin, and replaced him with Valery Gerasimov as the overall lead commander for the war in Ukraine.

Surovikin was one of the more obvious casualties of the burgeoning factional feud within Russia's power ministries over the future of Russia's irregular paramilitaries. Politically sidelined after the battlefield reversal in Kherson that forced him to order a Russian retreat, Surovikin was considered a contender for the job of chief of General Staff. He had been a steadfast supporter of the Wagner Group right from the start, when the first cadre of paramilitaries arrived in Donbas in 2014. His bond with Prigozhin had grown only stronger during the early stages of the war in Syria, when Surovikin relied on Concord's logistics chains for the supply of critical military gear and on Wagner forces to spearhead Russia's train-and-equip mission for local pro-regime militias and to mount ground offensives in oil- and gas-rich parts of the country.

After Russia's invasion of Ukraine started, Prigozhin and Chechen warlord Ramzan Kadyrov had enthusiastically aligned themselves behind Surovikin's push for Russian troops to take more decisive, aggressive action against Ukrainian forces. All three argued for Putin to call for a general mobilization and to set the country's economy on a full-scale war footing. When in October 2022 Putin appointed Surovikin as Russia's overall operational commander for the war in Ukraine, Prigozhin had hailed the general as a "legendary figure" and the "most competent" leader in the military.[7]

The relationship between Prigozhin and Surovikin had grown so tight that it quite literally would end up changing the landscape of the war in Ukraine: a day after Surovikin's appointment, Wagner forces began digging trenches and fortifications—the so-called Surovikin line—across a huge swath of Luhansk.[8] During Surovikin's brief tenure as lead field commander, calls for the "Wagnerization" of Russia's military had become a kind of rallying cry among ultranationalist influencers who wanted to see Putin empower Russia's irregular forces to take on a bigger role.

Kremlin insiders close to Putin's longtime adviser Nikolai Patrushev and military leaders aligned with Shoigu had debated for months among themselves how to take away Prigozhin's megaphone and shut down the cult of personality that had grown up around him.[9] The Bakhmut morgue video and Prigozhin's public tantrum over the way the defense ministry had reacted to the Wagner Group's win at Soledar provided more fodder to Prigozhin's detractors in Moscow. He was out of control, and the Wagner Group was now not only a threat to Russian unity of command but also a liability for Putin and for the country.

The vulnerabilities that Prigozhin had created for the Kremlin were becoming increasingly apparent outside Russia. US intelligence officials tracked Wagner's movements closely, estimating that Prigozhin spent as much as $100 million per month to keep the paramilitary going.[10] A sizable chunk of the money flowed to munitions-production companies in North Korea and to Chinese space-industry companies that provided the Wagner Group with access to satellite imagery of the Ukrainian front.[11] As the war dragged into its second year, policymakers in Western capitals openly debated whether the Wagner Group should be blacklisted as an international terrorist organization. Under US law, the move would have placed Prigozhin on par with al-Qaeda leader Osama bin Laden, and draft legislation to that effect was advanced by a bipartisan group of Republican and Democratic lawmakers in Congress.

But the proposed measure received a chilly reception in the White House, where influential members of the National Security Council raised concerns about the potential unintended consequences that might come from such a move.[12] Designating the Wagner Group a terrorist group risked inflating Prigozhin's political profile even more among pro-war ultranationalists. Besides, after two decades of a highly destructive "war on terror," the United States had lost considerable credibility in Africa and the Middle East. Biden could not very well order a targeted drone strike against Prigozhin as Donald Trump had done in the case of Iran's general Qassem Soleimani, the head of Teheran's paramilitary Quds Force. The possibility of a sharp Russian retaliation and escalation of the conflict in Ukraine all but ruled out a US terrorism designation.

In January, Treasury and State Department officials began mapping out alternate routes for disrupting the Wagner Group's networks, settling eventually on the idea of designating the Wagner Group a transnational criminal organization.[13] This move, along with a new round of sanctions against Prigozhin and his associated enterprises, essentially elevated the Wagner Group to a status like that of a Mexican drug cartel. In theory, the new designation made anyone who materially aided the Wagner Group, including Putin's strongman allies in Africa and the Middle East, exceptionally susceptible to arrest and prosecution in any number of countries.

At the defense ministry in Moscow, consensus had already started to build around the idea that Prigozhin was more a liability than an asset. To Shoigu, the Wagner Group was a necessary but crude tool, one that needed to be tightly controlled. He believed in the supremacy of the state over private forces, a principle that Prigozhin's growing power directly threatened. Shoigu viewed

Prigozhin's criticisms as a direct assault on his authority. Yet Shoigu could ill afford to be seen as stoking infighting while the fate of Bakhmut hung in the balance, Russian troops in Ukraine were on the back foot, and his own internal support inside Putin's regime was flagging.

There were also other considerations. The G7's imposition of a price cap on Russian oil meant that the Wagner Group's arms deals and mining operations in Africa were vital to the survival of Russia's wartime economy. At one point, defense ministry officials aligned with Shoigu toyed with the idea of launching a public campaign to discredit Prigozhin by proxy by pitting him against a strawman like Igor Girkin. But they struggled to identify a candidate at the same punching weight who could be trusted to remain on the leash. The question for Shoigu was not what to do but how to do it.

Whether by luck or design, a partial answer presented itself two days after Prigozhin stormed into Soledar. On January 12, a twenty-six-year-old former Wagner Group squad leader named Andrey Medvedev slipped across Russia's border with Norway and appealed to Norwegian authorities for political asylum. His dramatic escape on foot across a frozen river high up along the Arctic Circle, as he was pursued by barking dogs and Russian guards, had all the makings of a Hollywood thriller. It was made all the more so by the fact that only two weeks earlier Medvedev had recorded a video denouncing Prigozhin and saying he was prepared to testify in court about the atrocities he witnessed at the hands of Wagner commanders in Ukraine.

The video received more than 500,000 views after Vladimir Osechkin uploaded it to his Gulagu.net video channel. "I fear for my life and well-being at this moment," Medvedev said. "I have committed no crime other than that I refused to participate in all these incomprehensible maneuvers of Yevgeny Prigozhin."[14]

Medvedev's story was patchy and often seemed contradictory, but, overall, it matched much of what was known and suspected about how the Wagner Group operated. According to his video confession, the seeds of Medvedev's disaffection were planted as summer turned to fall during the first year of the war, when waves of prisoners began arriving at staging points near Bakhmut ahead of Wagner's offensive. Medvedev, who served as a conscript in the VDV 31st Guards Assault Brigade in Donbas in 2014, said that he served as a squad leader in Wagner's 4th Platoon, 7th Assault Detachment. "There were insults, beatings," Medvedev said. "Our commanders started giving stupid orders, handing us machine guns, then throwing us like meat at tanks."[15]

The "incomprehensible maneuvers" Medvedev referred to were a critical plank of the Wagner Group's "Bakhmut Meatgrinder" strategy, which centered on human-wave attacks that were supported by drone surveillance and an unrelenting volley of artillery. Ukrainian military-intelligence analysts attributed Wagner's battlefield progress to the fact that its field commanders attenuated their tactics to the low-grade skill levels of their recruits. In the early phase of the Bakhmut offensive, Wagner forces began experimenting with nighttime assaults. Ad hoc units of fifteen to twenty of the paramilitary's more seasoned commanders, equipped with night-vision goggles and thermal scopes, advanced toward positions; then, once they had established a foothold, a wave of fifty or more men—many of them prisoners— would swoop in immediately and start digging trenches.[16] Progress on the battlefield was thus measured in inches and city blocks.

The tactics demanded heavy artillery support for success. But ammunition was in short supply all around, leading Prigozhin to complain bitterly that they were suffering from "shell hunger." Wagner was not the only one struggling to cope with the ammunition shortages. Initially, Prigozhin was able to overcome the challenge by tapping into the strong relations he had forged with the defense ministry's logistics chief, Dmitry Bulgakov, and General Mikhail Mzintsev, who retained the VIP status he had gotten with Wagner during the Palmyra offensives in Syria. But when Bulgakov was fired in September 2022 and Mzintsev began to lose the confidence of his superiors, the Wagner Group had to scrounge like all the other Russian units on the front lines. The situation found Wagner forces increasingly exposed as a result.

Medvedev would later tell a *New Yorker* reporter that when he openly questioned the logic of Prigozhin's plan to charge pell-mell straight into the line of Ukrainian fire in Bakhmut, Wagner commanders punished him by locking him in a shipping container.[17] Senior Wagner commanders told Medvedev and other squadron leaders that they had shoot-to-kill orders for anyone who failed to follow orders or who was caught trying to desert or surrender to the Ukrainians.

Medvedev said that he witnessed the summary execution of two Wagner fighters by Federal Security Service (FSB) officers who were part of the Wagner Group's internal-security team and that he had heard about more than half a dozen other cases where recruits who refused to follow orders were shot at point-blank range. He had seen what happened to Yevgeny Nuzhin, the Russian inmate in his squad who defected to the Ukrainian side, only to be returned to his tormentors and then executed with a sledgehammer in November 2022.

Medvedev decided then that he would quit as soon as his four-month contract was up. But when he tried to leave, he was told that his term would be extended, first to six months and then to eight. When Medvedev protested, he was thrown in a pit and told to prepare for retribution.[18] He said that he escaped the front with the help of a sympathetic Wagner commander. He had been home barely a month when the threats against him from Russia's security services began. It was then, Medvedev said, that he hatched his plan to publicly defect and accuse Prigozhin of ordering his commanders to commit war crimes.

Although Prigozhin's name was the only one Medvedev would publicly mention in his initial video confession and other subsequent public statements, Medvedev provided enough detail to indicate that he had fought under the command of Anton "Lotus" Yelizarov, who was then the head of Wagner's 7th Assault Detachment, and that a split had emerged within the upper echelons of the Wagner Group's command structure. Hints of growing factionalism within Wagner's ranks had bubbled up months earlier on Telegram as Andrey Troshev sought to assert himself as the primary official spokesman for the paramilitary. Medvedev's headline-grabbing escape to Oslo revealed that there were deep cracks beneath the surface.

When soon after Surovikin's demotion and Medvedev's highly public defection Prigozhin publicly acknowledged that he had been forced to end his prison-recruitment drive, it became even more apparent that Shoigu and Gerasimov had finally decided to take the gloves off in their fight to wrest back control of the war narrative. Prigozhin's admissions came during a ninety-minute interview with a popular Russian military blogger named Sergey Pegov on his WarGonzoRu.tube channel.[19]

Conscious that he was fast losing political ground, Prigozhin tried hard to spin his earlier criticism of the defense ministry as little more than casual banter and denied he had any political ambitions. His quarrel, Prigozhin said, was not with Shoigu but with the nameless fat-cat bureaucrats in Moscow who were holding up the supply of equipment and ammunition, a complaint echoed by other Russian generals on the front lines.

What was even more notable, though, was who else was in the room with Prigozhin for the interview. Dressed in a black bomber jacket and black cargo pants, Andrey Troshev played the part of somber straight man to Prigozhin's agitated majordomo, confirming that ammunition shortages had become problematic while carefully avoiding specifics and speaking only in hypotheticals. Yelizarov, too, had a brief cameo and nodded vigorously, and off-camera the voice of Dmitry Utkin could be heard complaining about the Wagner Group's casualties and the perennial problem of "shell hunger."

Others also apparently sensed blood in the water. On the first day of April, in broad daylight, a bomb explosion ripped through an upscale St. Petersburg bistro owned by Prigozhin. The attack instantly killed popular pro-war blogger and Wagner Group champion Maksim Fomin and injured more than forty others who had gathered at the Street Food Bar No. 1 for an event sponsored by a pro-war troll-farm collective called CyberFrontZ.

Located on the banks of the Neva River and just a short walk from the Old Customs House and the Trezzini Palace Hotel, right in the heart of Prigozhin's old stomping grounds on Vasilyevsky Island, the bistro had become a hot-spot hangout for Russia's young pro-war glitterati.

Fomin, who had adopted the pen name Vladen Tatarsky, was a convicted felon from Donbas who was one of the originators of the wildly popular Wagner Group social media vertical called Reverse Side of the Medal (RSOTM). With a following of more than half a million users on Telegram, his acerbic takedowns of Russia's military leaders, insider scoops on Russia's military maneuvers, and shrill critiques of the Kremlin's prosecution of the war had made Fomin one of the most recognizable faces of Russia's increasingly influential ultranationalist *voenkorps* blogger set. He was a walking advertisement for all that the Wagner Group represented.

Video footage circulated by attendees at the gathering who survived the bombing indicated that the explosives had likely been planted in a gold-colored bust fashioned after Fomin's likeness and handed to him as a gift by a young, red-haired woman named Daria Tsepova, who attended the event. Initially, Russian authorities said they suspected that Ukrainian intelligence agents were behind the plot.

Ilya Ponamarev, a former Russian parliament member, claimed that the bomb plot had been carried out in the name of the National Republican Army, a controversial cadre of anti-Putin partisans based in Kyiv.[20] In what looked like a coerced videotaped confession circulated after Tsepova's swift arrest, Fomin's assailant told the FSB during her interrogation that she had been put up to the bomb plot by an anti-Putin opposition activist connected to Alexey Navalny.

The whole episode bore the telltale fingerprints of an FSB setup, and even Prigozhin seemed to understand that the bombing was as much a warning to him personally as it was to the Wagner Group's supporters. He compared Fomin's killing to the car-bomb assassination of Alexander Dugin's daughter, Darya, the previous fall in Moscow, dismissing outright the Russian government's suggestion that Kyiv was behind the plot: "I think that there is a group of radicals that is hardly related to the government that is behind this."[21]

Alexander Dugin signaled support for Prigozhin's assessment, issuing a lengthy letter on Telegram a week later under the heading "The Wagner Factor and the Thesis of Justice." Dubbing Prigozhin "the new Hemingway" of Russia's war, he hailed the Wagner Group as a new "heroic" "military brotherhood" and the "just" standard-bearers of the country's military defense. "They gave this war a style, became its symbols, found the most accurate and most sincere words to express what was happening," Dugin opined. "Wagner's war is a people's war, a war of liberation, a cleansing war. It does not accept half measures, agreements, compromises, negotiations made behind the backs of fighting heroes."[22]

The bombing had backfired. Instead of silencing ultranationalist critics of Putin's mishandling of the war, it seemed only to stoke support for Prigozhin.

A new pattern started to appear. Every time things seemed to start looking up for Prigozhin, a new video or leaked document would surface on Telegram aimed at discrediting him or his allies. No sooner was Dugin's passionate missive published than rumors began flying on Telegram that Prigozhin was secretly receiving backing and supplies on the sly from Mikhail Mzintsev, head of defense logistics for Russian forces and a Surovikin ally.

Then, as if on cue, a few days after that rumor surfaced, Osechkin released a new hour-long video in April featuring two more Wagner defectors from a squad of prisoners who claimed that Prigozhin had personally ordered them to execute dozens of Ukrainian children and to blow up a trench pit full of Russian convict fighters. The two men, Azmat Uldarov and Alexey Savichev, both appeared to be drunk during their interviews, and like Medvedev their accounts were full of conspicuous omissions.[23] Mzintsev was fired a week after the two videotaped confessions about the Wagner Group's war crimes were published. He soon dropped all pretense of loyalty to Shoigu's camp, joining Wagner as a frontline adviser.

Over the remainder of April, Prigozhin was in damage-control mode. He tried to counter the narrative that he was on the back foot politically with a series of cry-wolf threats, suggesting that he would pull Wagner forces out of

Bakhmut if steps were not taken to resupply his troops and remove Shoigu from his post.

One day, he would claim the Wagner Group was inches from victory. The next, Prigozhin would post a rambling screed claiming that there was no way to win in Bakhmut and that the entire war was an American plot to weaken Russia. Prigozhin was spinning so hard that he seemed to be making himself dizzy.

Things reached a crescendo in early May, when Prigozhin aired his grievances in a shocking scene where he berated Shoigu and Gerasimov on camera, standing in a field littered with the bodies of Wagner Group soldiers. Sweeping his arm out behind him where rows of bloodied corpses were laid out like cordwood in the darkness, Prigozhin shouted at the camera: "The blood is still fresh. Show them all!"[24]

As the cameraman dutifully closed in on the gruesome panorama, Prigozhin gritted his teeth and vaulted himself in front of the lens like a wild animal. "And now listen to me you bastards! These are somebody's fathers. These are somebody's sons. And the scumbags who are refusing to give us ammunition will be eating their innards in hell.

"We're 70 percent short on ammo. Shoigu! Gerasimov! Where's the fucking ammo. . . . You scum sit there in your expensive clubs. Your kids are getting off on YouTube recording all the details of their little lives. You think you're the masters of this life, that you can do as you please, that you can dispense with others as you see fit," he growled. "These men came here as volunteers and they're dying so that you can get fat in your mahogany rich offices."[25]

The situation was almost impossible to make sense of. Was Prigozhin speaking for Putin? Was the infighting between the Wagner Group and Russia's conventional forces part of some grand Kremlin design?

Nearly every week since the start of Russia's invasion of Ukraine, there were reports of Russian citizens who were arrested for freely speaking their minds on the internet. Teenagers and elderly grandmothers were jailed for liking and reposting antiwar comments. Poets who recited antiwar verses received five-year prison sentences, and an artist who replaced supermarket price tags with antiwar messages was arrested and sent away for seven years. Opposition activists Alexey Navalny and Vladimir Kara-Murza faced sentences so long that it was doubtful either would come out alive. Yet Prigozhin—profane, petty, and obdurate in his complaints about the men Putin had placed in charge of running the war—remained unscathed.

The situation quickly veered from the incomprehensible to the ominous. In early May, as Wagner forces inched closer to the center of Bakhmut's ruins, Prigozhin threatened yet again to pull his men from the front a day after Victory Day celebrations in Russia. Politically isolated, out of supplies, and facing the very real possibility that the Wagner Group could implode under all the pressure, Prigozhin looked like a defeated man and seemed to be finally turning tail.

It was then that Shoigu saw an opportunity to kill two birds with one stone. A stalemated Wagner Group signaled a vulnerable Prigozhin and a potential path to finally bringing Russia's irregular paramilitary contingent under Moscow's full control. Defense ministry officials in Moscow drew up plans for the Wagner Group and other "volunteer" contingents to be folded under one administrative umbrella. In theory, that could have given Russia's defense leaders the ace in the hole they needed to beat back Ukraine's summer counteroffensive. But it was not to be.

In late May, as rumors that Prigozhin was plotting a coup began to swirl in the open, Prigozhin's messaging began to switch tack again. In a move that seemed designed to counter the coup narrative, he suddenly declared victory in Bakhmut on May 20 in yet another Telegram post. A video circulated widely on Telegram the same day showing Wagner commander Alexander "Ratibor" Kuznetsov waving a Russian flag over his head and shouting "Victory" as the battered ruins of Bakhmut loomed in the background behind him.[26]

Ukrainian officials immediately issued a statement denying that their forces had lost control of the city. Naturally, Prigozhin was undeterred. Dressed in his now-familiar combat uniform and gripping a hand-signed Russian flag in his fists, Prigozhin shouted at the camera: "Today, full control was taken of Bakhmut. We took the entire city completely. We went from house to house so that no one could reproach us and say that there was a piece that was not taken." Pausing briefly to catch his breath he boomed: "We thank you Vladimir Vladimirovich Putin for giving us this opportunity and high honor to defend our homeland."[27]

That could have been the last word, but Prigozhin again went on the offensive two weeks later, in early June, telling a local Russian TV reporter that he intended to file documents with the prosecutor general's office charging Shoigu and the defense ministry with dereliction of duty for failing to resupply Russian troops. Then, in reaction to reports that VDV Airborne forces were going to replace Wagner on the front lines in Bakhmut and that Shoigu was going to take steps to subjugate the Wagner Group and other irregular Russian contingents to the defense ministry, Prigozhin urged Putin to replace Shoigu with Mikhail Mzintsev, warning that Russia could see a repeat of the 1917 Bolshevik revolution if the Kremlin refused to call for general mobilization.[28]

When that message seemed to gain little traction, Prigozhin escalated, accusing the Russian military of laying mines along Wagner's lines of retreat from Bakhmut and firing artillery at Wagner forces as they withdrew from Bakhmut back toward their encampments near the Russian border. The situation escalated when Wagner forces briefly took as a hostage Colonel Roman Venevitin, the commander of the unit that Prigozhin said had fired on his soldiers, forcing him to confess on camera that he had intentionally targeted Wagner troops.[29]

Sensing he was in a do-or-die moment, Prigozhin next began reaching out to his allies in parliament and the military in a bid to convince them to take his side against Shoigu. Although his entreaties to Duma chairman Vyacheslav Volodin received a cold response, he found more sympathetic ears among other longtime allies. Sergey Mironov, head of the hard-right Just Russia Party, reportedly invited Prigozhin to travel to Moscow with Surovikin to deliver remarks at a parliamentary roundtable on the topic of the war and the future status of mercenaries.[30] Surovikin by then was already quietly acting as a go-between for Prigozhin with the defense ministry, holding the thin line that separated the Wagner Group and Prigozhin's growing number of supporters inside the military from open revolt.

But whatever talks there were, they failed to convince Putin to reverse the decision to bring the Wagner Group more firmly under Shoigu's direct line of control. On June 13, Putin told a group of war correspondents that he was siding with Shoigu, insisting that the July 1 deadline for transitioning Wagner forces to defense ministry oversight was the only way forward and hinting vaguely that plans might be in the works to enact a law that would clarify the legal status of irregular contract forces. To drive the point home, Zvezda TV, the military's official news channel, broadcast a report that same day claiming that Prigozhin's onetime ally Vladimir Alekseyev had attended a contract-signing ceremony with several unnamed volunteer paramilitaries.

Late on the evening of June 23, Prigozhin finally threw all his chips on the table. In a move that brought Russia to a virtual standstill, he told his followers in a series of audio messages uploaded on Telegram that he had ordered 25,000 Wagner Group fighters to march on Moscow to demand that Shoigu and Gerasimov publicly explain why they had prosecuted the war so ineptly. "I ask that no one put up resistance. Anyone who tries to resist we will consider a threat, and we will swiftly eliminate them," Prigozhin warned. "This is not a military coup. This is a march for justice."[31] And just like that, with a few clicks of the keyboard, the Wagner Group's war became a battle for survival between Putin and Prigozhin.

In all his twenty-four years in power, Putin had never looked so weak. The man who had set Putin's table for decades was now holding a knife to the president's throat, urging a hired gang of mercenary killers to tear down what it had taken Putin nearly three decades to rebuild. While images of Prigozhin posing defiantly like a modern-day gladiator aspirant in front of the camera ricocheted across millions of mobile phones and TV screens, Putin was nowhere to be seen. Instead, as newscasters around the world breathlessly reported that Russia—the second-most-powerful nuclear-armed country in the world—was on the brink of civil war, the only sign that anyone in the Kremlin was still in charge was the warrant for Prigozhin's arrest issued by the FSB hours after the mutiny had begun.

As the hours ticked by with no official public response from Putin, Alekseyev and Alexey Dyumin, Putin's former bodyguard and Prigozhin's longtime ally, tried to reach Prigozhin by phone, but to no avail. Meanwhile, Prigozhin continued to push for a direct conversation with Putin but was continually rebuffed. It was only when Wagner forces began massing near the outer perimeter of Rostov-on-Don and Prigozhin posted a new lengthy video online that panic started to set in inside the Kremlin.

Sitting in a barren conference room in a beige T-shirt and fatigues, Prigozhin, looking haggard and frustrated, denounced the entire war in Ukraine as little more than a sham mounted by greedy military officials and oligarchs who were trying to deceive Putin and the Russian people. "The war wasn't needed to return Russian citizens to our bosom, nor to de-militarize or de-Nazify Ukraine," he said. "The war was needed so that a bunch of animals could simply exult in glory."[32]

As Wagner forces inched toward Moscow, broadcasters and newswires began playing on a tape loop a video of Prigozhin's onetime GRU patron Vladimir Alekseyev pleading with him to stop the march. Shot in the panicky late-night hours after Prigozhin launched his mutiny, the short clip revealed the depth of fear gripping the Kremlin. Sitting in front of the camera in a white-walled room with his hands folded tightly in his lap, Alekseyev spoke in the wooden tone of a hostage with a gun to his head, calling the Wagner mutiny a "stab in the back."

Without saying his name, Alekseyev reminded Prigozhin of their long, close working relationship and urged him to stand down: "I was shoulder to shoulder with your PMC in 2014, 2015, 2016, working on missions in the name of the national interest. Our country is in a very difficult situation now at a time when the entire Western world has taken up arms against us. At a time when weapons and ammunition are being sent from all over the world, you are doing the very thing that the West wants to do to us." Next, it was Surovikin's turn. Looking as if he was reading from cue cards and cradling an assault rifle on his lap, he moved stiffly as if it pained him to even say the words: "I urge you to stop. The enemy is just waiting for the internal political situation in our country to worsen. Stop the convoys. Return to the bases where you are stationed."[33]

At a little after 7:30 a.m. the next day, June 24, Prigozhin declared in another online video that Wagner forces had secured control of the headquarters for the Southern Military District in Rostov. It was a surreal tableau. Outside on the streets of Rostov, young men and police officers dressed in uniforms waved warmly as Wagner convoys rolled down otherwise empty streets in tanks and armored trucks unobstructed. Inside, on the base, Prigozhin calmly glanced at his watch as he narrated how his men had seized a nearby air base, medical bay, and the district command center on the base while masked Wagner fighters strolled around casually in the background.

A couple hours later, another extraordinary scene unfolded on camera as Prigozhin testily berated Deputy Defense Minister Yunus-Bek Yevkurov for addressing him in the informal "you" and scolded a sheepish-looking Alekseyev for failing to turn Shoigu and Gerasimov over to the Wagner Group's custody.

"Guys are dying because you're pushing them through a meat grinder—without ammunition, without any thought, without any plan. You're just senile clowns."

Yevkurov, looking stunned, stammered, "You think you're doing everything right now? Is that it?"

"Absolutely right. We're saving Russia."[34]

Even as these scenes played out, a separate column of Wagner forces advanced north toward the Russian capital. Photos showed dozens of regular unarmed soldiers standing by passively at a checkpoint located about a hundred miles south of Voronezh as Wagner convoys streaked by unimpeded.

Although the waves of military defections that Prigozhin had undoubtedly been counting on to boost his push to the capital did not materialize, Wagner fighters were still able to drive along the M4 highway virtually unopposed until they reached the outer limits of Voronezh, about three hundred miles south of Moscow.

Tensions escalated there when Wagner fighters shot down a helicopter that had fired on the convoy and missiles struck an oil facility as Wagner forces careened toward a secret nuclear-weapons storage site called Voronezh 45 near midday. Further north, in Lipetsk, authorities ordered construction crews to start digging up the roadways into the city to slow Wagner's rapid advance. Moscow officials placed the capital region on full lockdown.[35] But outside of those steps and the military helicopters and planes that hovered overhead, there were few other visible signs that Russia's security forces were prepared to take action as truckloads of Wagner fighters began streaming into Lipetsk. Putin was missing in action, and so was Shoigu.

When, twelve hours into the crisis, Putin finally took to the podium to deliver a televised emergency address, he looked visibly shaken. Wagner forces by then had reportedly shot down half a dozen helicopters and two military planes, killing at least fifteen members of Russia's security forces. Invoking the memory of the Bolshevik uprising against Russia's last tsar, Putin angrily accused Prigozhin of treason: "This is a stab in the back of our country and our people. This is exactly the kind of blow that was dealt to Russia in 1917, when the country was fighting the First World War. But her victory was stolen. Intrigues, quarrels, politicking behind the back of the army and the people turned into the greatest upheaval, the destruction of the army and the collapse of the state, the loss of vast territories. In the end was the tragedy of the civil war." But Russian citizens, officials, and security services, Putin insisted, had stood fast against the enemy's attempts to spark internal civil strife and had come out even more united: "The organizers of this mutiny have betrayed their own people, their own country. They lied and made them shoot at their own people. This is what the enemy wants to achieve, brother killing brother."[36]

The crisis left Putin few good choices. Bitter memories of the chaotic coups that had convulsed Russia in the 1990s loomed. Removing Prigozhin while Wagner forces were still out in force risked turning him into a martyr, splintering Russia's security forces, and engulfing the country in a full-scale civil war. But inaction was not an option either. Gorbachev. Yeltsin. Their biggest mistake had been letting the master narrative slip from their control. Putin could ill afford a repeat of televised images of Russian tanks rolling in the streets, troops firing on government installations, and bodies strewn in the streets of Moscow while war raged next door. So he did what he had always done best—launch a flood-the-zone information attack.

Searches for Prigozhin's name were blocked on the internet, and Telegram was knocked offline repeatedly in Rostov, Moscow, and St. Petersburg.[37] Putin doubled down on his two-pronged strategy of isolating Prigozhin and undercutting his sway over his subordinates. Calls went out to Wagner commanders urging them to stand down or risk harm coming to their families. State TV news channels began broadcasting live a raid on Prigozhin's palatial St. Petersburg estate by a team of black-clad internal-affairs security forces. Photos from inside his lavish mansion—complete with a helicopter pad, personalized medical clinic, gilded chapel, boxes stuffed with cash, rifles, handguns, stacks of gold bars, fake passports, and a giant sledgehammer—circulated online and were instantly made into memes.[38]

Online, reactions to the mutiny were mixed. Girkin sneered and posted an "I told you so" video. Ramzan Kadyrov dutifully repeated Putin's "stab in the back" phrase and said he had ordered a contingent of his Akhmat Regiment to hunt down Wagner troops in Rostov, but he never delivered on the threat.

Then, almost as suddenly as it started, the mutiny ended on the evening of June 24. Late that evening, Prigozhin announced that he had agreed to an eleventh-hour bargain to halt the uprising. In a recorded message on Telegram, he struck a defiant tone, saying that he had ordered his fighters to turn back to avoid escalation. "During this time, we have not shed a single drop of our soldiers' blood," Prigozhin claimed falsely. "Now, the moment has come when blood may be shed. Understanding the responsibility of shedding Russian blood, we are turning our columns around and returning to the field camps." Lest anyone think his gambit had failed, Prigozhin added a final line: "According to plan."[39]

Brokered with the assistance of Nikolai Patrushev, head of Russia's Security Council, and Belarus president Aleksandr Lukashenko, the deal called for Russian authorities to drop the criminal charges against Prigozhin and to provide immunity for Wagner Group forces in exchange for their withdrawal across Russia's border into Belarus.[40] As news of Putin's grand bargain with Prigozhin spread, enthusiastic crowds came out into the darkened streets of Rostov to cheer, swarming giddily around Prigozhin's SUV as he and his men began withdrawing to their encampments. It seemed that Prigozhin had won by losing.

It was as surprising an outcome as it was anticlimactic. But it was the surest sign that Putin finally understood the full dimensions of the problem he had created by letting Prigozhin off the leash. More proof followed two days later, when Putin announced in another televised address that the Russian government had shelled out $1 billion to finance the Wagner Group's operations in Ukraine from May 2022 to May 2023, adding that Prigozhin's Concord company had received $940 million under a separate contract that called for it to supply the army with food and catering services. "Hopefully, nobody stole anything during these activities or, let's say, stole less," Putin cooed slyly. "We will obviously look into all this."[41]

It was a shocking admission—even if an incomplete one. After nearly a decade of clinging to the fiction that the Wagner Group operated independently as a "private" military company, Putin appeared to abandon all pretense of plausible deniability. Already under indictment by the ICC for crimes against humanity in Ukraine, Putin openly confessed on Russian national television and to the world that his government had paid for the operations of an off-book paramilitary force implicated in widespread torture, illegal detention, extrajudicial killings, and indiscriminate targeting of civilians. During the one-year period Putin outlined in his speech, UN experts and international human-rights organizations had documented scores of incidents linking the Wagner Group to atrocities in Ukraine, Africa, and the Middle East. Most of the payments to Wagner fighters and Prigozhin's Concord network of firms, Putin confirmed, fell under the oversight of Voentorg, the defense ministry's logistics and services arm that had managed Prigozhin's contracts.

Whether intentionally or not, Putin effectively exposed the administrative mechanics behind the Wagner Group's operations, which had generated billions for Prigozhin's network of shell companies. From 2012 until Wagner's 2023 march on Moscow, Voentorg was the main vehicle for Prigozhin's lucrative government contracts and the primary channel for Russia's defense ministry to funnel weapons into Donbas after the 2014 Crimea seizure.

It was via Voentorg that Putin armed pro-regime forces in Syria, Sudan, and the Central African Republic, and mounted mercenary-supported military coups across the Sahel. Voentorg had also been at the center of elaborate defense ministry kickback schemes that spanned from St. Petersburg to Raleigh, North Carolina, and likely financed the Internet Research Agency's meddling in the

US presidential election. No Voentorg, no Wagner Group. It was that simple. This raised a question: Why had Putin bothered to say anything publicly at all?

Putin's speech was both perplexing and paradoxical. He attempted to draw a clear line between the eight years before Russia's February 2022 invasion and the period of overt support that followed. On one hand, his admission seemed designed to reshape the narrative around the Kremlin's backing of irregular paramilitaries, another rhetorical feint born out of strategic necessity to preserve the sanctity of a Russian government challenged by its own lawlessness. On the other, Putin's confession sharply contradicted years of official denials, raising questions about state complicity in alleged war crimes. Notably, however, the timeline of support that Putin outlined conveniently bypassed the early March 2022 incident in Mali, where Wagner forces were implicated in the massacre of five hundred unarmed civilians.

Putin was caught in a head-spinning spiral of his own deceptions, mixing up the facts as he tried to paper over public admissions by his subordinates that Wagner had long coordinated its actions with the GRU, all with the Kremlin's tacit consent. Someone was going to pay for Wagner's trespasses, but it was not going to be him. Hints that Putin had found a possible scapegoat came when Russian media reported that the FSB had placed Surovikin, who had vanished from public view, under house arrest after questioning him about his ties to the uprising. A few other key figures from Wagner's inner circle also went to ground. Rumors of an impending defense ministry purge swirled. Putin had found the paintbrush he needed to smear Prigozhin's accomplices. The only thing that remained unresolved was who would ultimately take the first fall.

CHAPTER 22

ICARUS DOWN

Punishment was swift, but retribution was slower in coming. The first step the Kremlin took after banishing Prigozhin to Belarus was to take away his bullhorn. Five days after the mutiny, Roskomnadzor, the state information monitor, blocked websites run by Prigozhin's troll farm. The next day, Patriot Media, the corporate heart of Prigozhin's propaganda empire, announced that it was shutting down its operations.[1] The dissolution of Patriot Media spelled the end for dozens of websites, including RIA-FAN, the most potent weapon in Prigozhin's disinformation arsenal, and dozens of Wagner Group–related fan-boy channels on VKontakte. Thousands of subscriber accounts linked to the popular Grey Zone and the Wagner Group Military Review went dark. The moves brought to an ignoble and sudden end more than a decade of investment in building up Prigozhin's online influence machine. Talks of a plan for a private media company backed by banker Yury Kovalchuk and linked to Putin's alleged mistress Alina Kubayeva to purchase Patriot Media quickly evaporated. After pouring millions of rubles and hours into building a market for lies in the service of Putin's political agenda, Prigozhin and the Wagner Group brand had simply become too toxic.

Only Telegram offered Prigozhin any real chance of political survival. About a half-dozen channels associated with Prigozhin's Concord Management and Consulting company remained intact following the mutiny. A safe harbor for Russian-speaking critics of Putin's management of the war in

Ukraine on the Right and the Left, the platform emerged as the sole source of information about the Wagner Group's fate.

The prognosis was decidedly mixed. The game was obviously over for Wagner in Ukraine. There were also signs that Wagner forces had begun to rotate out of Bangui amid a brief shake-up of the management hierarchy and reports that government forces in Syria had cordoned off bases where Wagner had once operated. With Assad loyalists fearful at the loss of their security blanket, the Russian military moved swiftly to corral those Wagner fighters who remained, forcing them to either sign new contracts or leave the country.[2] But with forces still scattered all over Mali, Libya, Sudan, and Belarus, many questions remained unsettled about what would happen to the rest of Wagner's global footprint. Then there was the matter of Prigozhin's unresolved status. The fact that he had not "accidentally" leaned too far out of a window or fallen ill from a poisoned cup of tea one week out from challenging Putin was surprising.

Instead, Prigozhin seemed to be constantly on the move, traveling on his private jet from Minsk to St. Petersburg and then Moscow and back. Cast into the political wilderness after a final meeting with Putin in late June and unable to settle back comfortably into his palatial estate in St. Petersburg after denouncing Putin's war of aggression on Ukraine, Prigozhin was now most at home in the sky. Everything else around him had crumbled, but Prigozhin—propelled by boundless energy, grievance, and a sense of destiny—remained convinced that his Midas touch would not fail him.

His faith was partially rewarded when, ten days after the rebellion, authorities in St. Petersburg announced soon after a secret meeting with government officials in Moscow that they had returned to Prigozhin's driver nearly 10 billion rubles—roughly $111 million—in cash stuffed into boxes that had been found during police raids on his properties.[3] Although the money was apparently earmarked for the salaries of Wagner fighters, its return to Prigozhin's staff suggested that some confusion remained about how to respond to the mutiny.

The Kremlin faced several dilemmas. Putin needed to demonstrate he was in control but not at fault for letting things spin into chaos. Prigozhin had unquestionably crossed a redline. He needed to be neutralized, but surgical precision would be needed. The thousands who followed Prigozhin and Utkin into battle had proven themselves to be formidable combatants, and many clearly felt greater loyalty to their brothers in arms than to what they regarded as corrupt and incompetent military leadership. The sense of betrayal and mistrust remained palpable. Although there were signs of an emergent divide among senior Wagner Group commanders, it would not be easy to peel them away and contain the threat from another uprising without significant inducements.

Russia also needed to reassure its client states that it remained committed to their security and capable of providing consistent services, regardless of domestic turmoil. Billions in arms sales, mining enterprises, and energy-production deals were at stake in Africa and the Middle East. Killing off the Wagner Group would be akin to slaughtering the goose that laid the golden egg.

The Kremlin's core strategy of using irregular military formations to project power, mobilize forces, extract valuable commodities, and fulfill military-technical agreements with a growing number of client states had proven to be a winning one. To move forward, the whole enterprise would need to be restructured and rebranded.

Hints that an overhaul was under way arrived in spurts. In early July, analysis of satellite imagery by independent researchers and the international press confirmed online chatter about the Wagner Group's moves in Belarus. Residents near the village of Tsel reported that government engineers and bulldozers had suddenly shown up at a defunct military garrison and begun clearing debris from an open area near the site a few days after the mutiny.

Located in the river-valley district of Asipovichy, about an hour's drive southeast of Minsk, the bucolic setting turned out to be the new base of operations for an estimated 3,000–5,000 Wagner fighters who had signed on to follow Prigozhin to Belarus. Soon, Belarusian military officials invited a select group of reporters to tour the Wagner campsite, showing off neatly arranged rows of sturdy khaki-colored military tents. An embarrassing photo posted online of Prigozhin in his underwear sitting on an army cot confirmed that he was there, too.

On July 17 a flag-retirement ceremony was held at Wagner's redoubt in Molkino. As lines of masked and camouflaged men stood at attention, four commanders retired the Russian national flag and three Wagner Group flags. It was soon revealed that Sergey "Pioneer" Chubko, the onetime commander of Wagner forces in the Central African Republic, would be placed in charge of managing the forces encamped in Belarus.[4] State news channels in Minsk said that Aleksandr Lukashenko had approved a plan for Wagner to train Belarus special forces to defend against an anticipated NATO invasion.

A few days later, a big show was made of Wagner forces and Belarusian troops tromping through a forested area near Brest along the border area of

Poland. The training exercise immediately set off alarm bells in Warsaw. Military officials in Western capitals worried that the Wagner mutiny had been a feint designed to mask the movement of troops in advance of a cross-border sabotage campaign in Poland or a diversionary offensive in Ukraine. "We're tracking and adjusting," one former military official said.[5]

Then news trickled out that Putin had warned Russia's Security Council of an imminent two-pronged Polish attack on Belarus and western Ukraine. In a highly choreographed televised meeting between Putin and Lukashenko two days later, Putin played the part of supreme commander, gesturing to a map of Belarus and pointing to the imaginary spots near Brest where Poland had positioned its invading forces. A clear attempt at psychological intimidation, it seemed that the Wagner Group still had some value for Putin.

Ten days later, as high-level diplomatic delegations from dozens of African countries arrived for a third big Russia-Africa summit in St. Petersburg, photos surfaced of Prigozhin glad-handing African officials at the Trezzini Palace. What was going on? Had Putin decided to live and let live, or was Prigozhin freelancing? The ambiguity was maddening.

It all ended on August 23, 2023, about 30,000 feet above the ground.[6] Initial reports suggested that a military plane had crashed somewhere near the edge of Tver, a town 110 miles northwest of Moscow. Witnesses who spotted the private jet flying overhead just before it crashed at 6:20 p.m. Moscow time said they heard two explosions. A thick white plume streaked the blue sky near the plane's tail as the jet plummeted to the ground. The plane was not, in fact, a military plane but a private jet. As more details from the crash site became available, it appeared that the plane, an Embraer Legacy 600, was carrying two of the world's most wanted men: Yevgeny Prigozhin and Dmitry Utkin.

On one mobile-phone video posted as the jet spiraled toward Earth near the Kuzhenkino railway station just outside of Tver, two women who had witnessed what happened from the back of a residential yard could be heard talking. "There were two pops then it started falling. What is it? Look, it's falling," one of the women gasped. "Damn. Oh fuuuuuuck! It's going down." In another, a woman taking video from the same grassy yard murmured loudly, "Maybe it's a drone? It's probably a drone of some sort."[7] Minutes after the plane dropped below the tree line on the horizon, passersby took shaky handheld videos of the crash site with their mobile phones. Flames and black smoke shot up from a spot where parts of the plane's body, its blue tail, and a crushed part of the wing could be seen strewn across the wide-open grassy field.

Within an hour, online plane spotters and local Russian news outlets had pieced together the flight path of RA-02795. Bound for St. Petersburg, the plane had taken off from Moscow's Sheremetyevo airport a few minutes before 6 p.m. The Brazilian-made executive jet made a few slight dips and climbs as it sped toward Prigozhin's hometown before its signal disappeared. Its last recorded moment was 6:11 p.m., Moscow time. All ten people on board— Prigozhin, Utkin, five members of their entourage, and the plane's three-person crew—were killed. Telegram buzzed with rumors that the plane had been either mistakenly or intentionally shot down by a Russian antiaircraft battery near Tver.

There were reports that a second plane operated by the FSB had taken off from Moscow around the same time as Prigozhin's jet and traveled on a parallel flight path. Speculative theories about whether a bomb might have been planted on board began to ripple across Telegram, VKontakte, and Twitter. For a brief moment, a photo of a packed suitcase and a plate of toast with butter posted by the plane's thirty-nine-year-old flight attendant, Kristina Raspopova, mesmerized the world. It was, according to her brother, her last meal. The flight attendant's brother noted that she had mentioned in a call that the plane had recently undergone unspecified repairs. Then, as online sleuths began to dig through corporate records and social media accounts of the other victims, and reporters began tapping their sources, attention turned to the other less well-known figures on the plane's manifest.

Valery "Rover" Chekalov, the Wagner Group's chief of logistics, was listed as being on board along with four other members of Prigozhin's close-protection unit. For seven years running, Chekalov had served as Prigozhin's logistical right hand, moving money, standing up front companies, and ensuring that the Wagner Group was well equipped. He had helped Prigozhin set up the coded phone book and security protocols that were meant to defend against outside penetration. That Chekalov and Utkin were on the same flight as Prigozhin was more than surprising. It reinforced suspicions that the downing of Prigozhin's jet had been intentional.

In almost every major organization in the world, it is standard practice for high-profile leaders to travel separately from their immediate successors to ensure continuity in the event of a security mishap. Utkin and Chekalov had always been hypervigilant about masking the Wagner Group's movements. Prigozhin had likewise earned a reputation for being fastidious about his security. When at home in St. Petersburg, he often traveled in a small convoy of armored luxury sedans and SUVs. Prigozhin had to be one of the most despised and envied figures in Russia, yet few, if any, had ever come close to puncturing his security bubble. He became even more stealthy and paranoid about being captured or killed after the United States pressed Interpol to issue a red notice for him. Why, then, had Prigozhin, Chekalov, and Utkin traveled together?

In all their years of working together, Utkin and Prigozhin were rarely seen together. The only recent, known public evidence that the two were ever in the same place was the video taken at an unverified location in Belarus that popped up on the "Orchestra Wagner" Telegram channel about three weeks after the Wagner mutiny. It, too, was taken with a cell phone, and the footage appeared to have been shot either in the predawn hours or at dusk.

In the five-minute clip, Prigozhin can be seen in silhouette, wearing his trademark flight jacket and baseball cap, and carrying a small bag. As the blurry camera eye sweeps in an outward arc along the horizon line behind Prigozhin, the outlines of rows of maybe hundreds of men lining the forested field in a square around him come into view. In unison, Wagner troops give a full-throated shout of thanks. "What is happening right now at the front is a disgrace. We should not be part of it," Prigozhin shouts. "We should wait for the moment when we can show ourselves in full strength, then our program will be completed." Belarus is where the Wagner flag will now fly, he tells them. This will be Wagner's new home. "While we are here, I am sure we will make the Belarusian army the second-[best] army in the world, and if necessary, we will stand up for them," he promises.

"I want to ask everyone to pay maximum attention to the fact that the Belarusians have met us not only as heroes, but as brothers. By the way, they say the local girls in the shops whisper lustfully 'Wagner is here!'" A huge roar rises up from men surrounding Prigozhin. A new mission would be opened in Africa for the Wagner Group, he promises. "This is not the end. This is only the beginning. Soon we will begin the most important work in the world, and well." Prigozhin pauses for effect, then shouts in English: "Welcome to hell!" The troops erupt with cheers of excitement. A few seconds later Prigozhin introduces "the man who started it all—Wagner himself."

A man whose lanky form resembles that of Utkin stands tall, in a baseball cap and a loose-fitting polo. He steps forward. "In case you don't know who I am, I'm the one they call commander—I am 'Wagner' himself." The assembly booms in reply: "Huzzah! Huzzah!" Utkin pauses, doffs his dark-colored baseball cap with a theatrical flourish, and takes a bow. "I want to thank you.

Thanks to our work the name 'Wagner' is known around the world!" The speech was short but significant. It offered the first glimpse in nearly a decade of the man who helped the Kremlin build a global shadow army.[8]

From Donbas to Damascus and onward to Bangui, Benghazi, and Bamako, Utkin's call sign had echoed across continents for nearly a decade, rallying thousands to fight in the name of Wagner. In Russia, countless graves adorned with red, yellow, and black wreaths carried Utkin's battlefield nom de guerre. Never once in his nine-year career as head of one of the world's most feared and notorious paramilitaries had Utkin been seen on camera. The long absence from view had made Dmitry Utkin almost mythical to most of the world. Now, for the first time, the sound of his voice—or at least the voice of someone who looked like him—could be heard thanking his troops for their blood, sweat, and tears. This is what differentiated Wagner from ordinary Russian forces. Prigozhin, Utkin, Yelizarov, and others on Wagner's Council of Commanders: they were unafraid to stand on the front lines shoulder to shoulder with their legion.

In contrast, everything about the way the Kremlin handled the narrative of the war reinforced the cold distance that had grown up between the men whom Russia's commander in chief ordered to sacrifice all and the people who made money off their backs. Whereas the Russian government made sentimental news digests about mothers who cheerily showed off the white Lada sedans given in recompense for Wagner troops killed in action, Prigozhin marched around Bakhmut in fatigues on camera. Although the Russian government shelled out billions to the paramilitary's chieftain, it would take almost a decade for Putin to even utter the word "Wagner" on camera. And even then it was in the context of Prigozhin's great betrayal—the mutiny.

In the days following the mutiny, Twitter had crackled with updates and screen grabs of the $10 million Embraer Legacy 600 jet flitting from Moscow to St. Petersburg to Minsk in loops.[9] Even before the mutiny, Prigozhin's jets were popular attractions on aviation traffic-monitoring sites like Flightradar.com and Flightaware.com. But nothing was ever certain when it came to reports about Prigozhin's plane travel. Over the years there were constant sightings, and reported mid-flight accidents, including one where Prigozhin was erroneously reported as being killed over a forest in Congo in October 2019.[10] That same year, press reports indicated that from 2017 to 2019, one of Prigozhin's private jets had flown to Beirut forty-eight times on slingshot routes that took him into Lebanon and then jetted repeatedly from there on to Damascus, Benghazi, or Bangui.[11] The two other executive-style jets he owned—each worth about

$2 million and registered under UK and Czech front companies—meanwhile hopscotched across Africa constantly, making it all but impossible to determine who was on board.

So when Embraer, the Brazilian aviation company that manufactured Prigozhin's jet, issued a statement within hours of the first reports of the crash saying that Prigozhin's Embraer Legacy 600 had experienced no notable mechanical issues in the entire time of its operation, this sent up a red flag.[12] It was the first known confirmation from sources outside Russia that something had truly gone wrong and that the jet may have been intentionally downed. Embraer officials said the airplane manufacturer had not serviced the plane since 2019. They even offered to assist Russian authorities with the investigation to rule out the possibility of a mechanical failure—an offer that the Kremlin flatly rejected.

The plane's Moscow-registered owner and operator, MNT Aero, was predictably cagey in response to inquiries into the crash, and within less than twenty-four hours of the wreck there were indications that the company might go out of business. A search for details on the air-chartering company's background revealed two curious facts. A company with a similar name was registered in the United Kingdom under the directorship of a man named Ninoslav Cucnic in 2011, and the Moscow-based company with the same name, MNT Aero LLC, was registered under the directorship of one Olga V. Gubareva.[13] Perhaps not surprisingly, it turned out that MNT Aero LLC also held contracts with two important clients of Prigozhin's sprawling business empire: Tatneft and Rosoboronexport.[14] Prigozhin had reregistered the plane in the Seychelles under the name of a company called Autolex Transport in February 2018, according to publicly available records.

The move to disguise his private jet just a few days before US prosecutors indicted him, and Wagner's subsequent internal crackdown on cell-phone and social media use, provided tantalizing clues that increasing public scrutiny of Prigozhin's movements, sanctions against him, and tensions between the paramilitary leader and his sponsors in the Kremlin had forced him to make adjustments to his security protocols. Maybe more importantly, published tidbits about Prigozhin's plane fleet indicated that Russia's intelligence agencies had been keeping an equally close eye on Prigozhin's movements for years, a fact of which he was no doubt well aware.

That seemed only natural in Putin's Russia, and a look at available corporate data suggests that Prigozhin expended tremendous amounts of effort on masking his movements and those of his employees and his family members as sanctions squeezed his enterprises in the final years of his life. A news article about Gubareva's links to the company also mentioned that she was the registered director of another Moscow company called Stal Est LLC.[15]

A little digging revealed that one of the original founders of the Stal Est venture was a Latvia-based real estate broker who spent part of his time shilling for Latvenergo, a Gazprom subsidiary that services Latvia. An even deeper dive uncovered a nest of companies that traced back to various administrators and lawyers that Prigozhin had assigned to manage his assets. Further details culled from corporate-registry and flight-path information indicated that Prigozhin's private jet had also flown to Syria on several occasions in May, a month before Prigozhin openly declared war on Sergey Shoigu and marched on Moscow.

The jet-setting was part of a pattern that had emerged as Prigozhin scrambled to keep his empire from crumbling under the weight of US and European sanctions and seemingly crushing demands from the Kremlin to service the needs of the state. Whenever in Moscow, the plane flew in and out of Chkalovsky Air Base where flight crews often filled out manifests with the names of passengers under fake passports. Security concerns meant that the plane's transponder was also typically turned off shortly after takeoff, but for some reason it had been left on during the Embraer Legacy 600's last journey.

Equally suspicious for Prigozhin's loyal fan base on Telegram was the fact that surviving relatives of Prigozhin's bodyguards—Yevgeny Makaryn, Sergey Propustin, Nikolay Matuseev, and Alexander Totmin—reported signs that something had gone wrong just before the flight took off. Normally, when Prigozhin's bodyguards traveled abroad with him, they were rarely in touch because they were often in remote parts of Africa that were out of the range of cell-phone towers. Even when they were able to connect, contact was often fleeting because Prigozhin's bodyguards feared—rightfully, it turned out— that their cell-phone signals and movements could be monitored. By contrast, when Prigozhin's bodyguards traveled on domestic flights within Russia, they were usually in touch with their wives and family members throughout their travels, even sending quick messages from the tarmac before takeoff.[16] This time was different, at least, according to a few breathless Telegram and local Russian press accounts.

Six days beforehand, on August 17, Prigozhin's security detail had flown with Utkin and Chekalov from St. Petersburg to Moscow. The next day,

Prigozhin, Utkin, Chekalov, and their four-man security team flew to Mali on a Russian IL-76 cargo plane via Damascus, Syria.[17] One stop on Prigozhin's final Africa tour included a visit with Wagner fighters and local officials in the Central African Republic.

Meanwhile, Prigozhin's erstwhile defense ministry rivals had kicked off their own tour of the continent with a visit in Libya. From August 2023 to January 2024, delegates from the GRU and the SVR, Russia's premier foreign-intelligence spy agency, would conduct no fewer than eight trips across Africa in a bid to transform Prigozhin's mercenary enterprise into a formal arm of the Russian state.

Before Prigozhin boarded his return flight to Moscow, another video snippet appeared on Telegram. Less than a minute long, the footage showed him dressed head to toe in sandy-colored camouflage fatigues and a floppy camo hat while a couple of armored pickup trucks idled audibly in the background. A few armed men loitered nervously nearby. A wide-open expanse of Sahel desert behind him suggested he was somewhere in Mali, one of the few places other than the Central African Republic where Shoigu had been unsuccessful in fully shutting Prigozhin out. "We are working. The temperature is more than 50 C. Everything is the way we like it," Prigozhin said. "The Wagner Group is conducting reconnaissance and search operations, making Russia greater on all continents, and making Africa free. Justice and happiness for African people. A nightmare for ISIS, al-Qaeda and other gangsters. We hire real heroes and continue to fulfill the promise we made."[18]

The VChK-OGPU Telegram, an online source linked to Russia's security services, reported that Alexander Totmin, an amateur boxer and former *spetsnaz* operator who had fought in Sudan with Wagner, was tasked with accompanying Prigozhin on the August 23 flight out of Sheremetyevo. Totmin was in touch at about 1 p.m. that day and reportedly told his wife that he would be home in the evening. There was an exchange between Totmin and his wife about a friend's wedding, and he told his wife he missed her. The last message from Totmin was at about 5:38 p.m., before the exchange abruptly ended.

In Washington a press gaggle mobbed President Joe Biden as he was leaving the gym. Asked whether he'd heard the news about the plane crash, Biden replied, "I don't know for a fact what happened but I'm not surprised." When someone shouted, "Do you think Putin did it?!" Biden replied, "There's not much that happens in Russia that Putin's not behind. But I don't know enough to know the answer."[19]

A day later a Pentagon spokesman said that rumors that the plane had been taken down by a surface-to-air missile were inaccurate. US intelligence officials instead told the *New York Times* and the *Washington Post* that they suspected a bomb had been planted on the plane or that systems on board had somehow been sabotaged. This theory appeared to align with many of the known facts. There were no eyewitness sightings of a missile or another plane nearby. At the crash site, Russian investigators found that the wings of the jet were mostly intact, confirming that an explosion from within had likely taken it down.

Rumors on Telegram's reliably unreliable channels hinted that explosives could have been planted on board when repairs were done on the plane at Sheremetyevo in Moscow on July 20. In addition to repairing the brakes on the left side of Prigozhin's jet, repairmen were also supposed to replace a broken refrigeration part. Ordered through a third party, the cooling mechanism was manufactured exclusively in the United States.[20] Sometime after it arrived at a warehouse in Sheremetyevo, the part had been damaged when it was dropped. The unnamed supplier took the damaged part back and sent another one of unknown origin in its stead.

Gleb Irisov, a former Russian Air Force lieutenant who served under Prigozhin's patron Sergey Surovikin, leaned toward the bomb-plot theory. An outspoken critic of Putin's regime, Irisov, a former defense reporter for Russia's state media outlet TASS, had gained notoriety after leaving Russia for the United States in the fall of 2022 amid Putin's call for partial mobilization. He took for granted that Putin and Russian special security services were behind the air catastrophe.

The question was how and when Prigozhin had been killed. "There may have already been plans to kill these two reprobates. Perhaps this was even one of the reasons why Prigozhin came forward and became outspoken in the first place. He was probably trying in this way to protect himself, to show that he was still useful, that he could do something, that he had some kind of value," suggested Irisov. "He believed in Putin and his benevolence. But he greatly miscalculated. All the people who supported him also, of course, greatly miscalculated."[21] Irisov ran through the different theories. One was that Prigozhin had faked his death and sent his body double to Chkalovsky Air Base to board the plane in his stead. Another was that Prigozhin and Utkin had been killed soon after the mutiny, possibly somewhere in Belarus, and their bodies were placed on board the plane before it took off. Hours after the plane imploded in midair, this second theory—that Putin had ordered the decapitation of the Wagner command weeks earlier and that the GRU or FSB tried to cover it up with the plane takedown—was churning across dozens of Telegram channels.

It sounded crazy, but that version of the murder theory lined up with other intriguing coincidences. There were hints that Prigozhin's family had begun vying for his estate several weeks before the accident. There had been a strange phone call in mid-July that notified Google Maps that the famous Lakhta Plaza, the Prigozhin family's premier property, was closed indefinitely. Then there was the bizarre photograph of Prigozhin in his underwear in a tent in Belarus and online chatter about Wagner fighters probing a forested area near Lithuania's eastern border with Belarus. That was followed by a suspicious sudden August 11 closing of two border checkpoints in Lithuania, not far from where the photo had likely been taken.[22] Did they all imply that Prigozhin hadn't died on the plane after all?

In early August, about two weeks before the crash, a news alert announced: "Evgeny Prigozhin May Already Be Dead—A Belarusian Opposition Leader [Says]." The article was posted on August 6 on an obscure website purporting to be an Indian news outlet called "The Times Hub."[23] The online site had all the hallmarks of a fake-news site. It was hosted on a server somewhere in British Columbia, and despite an "About" page that claimed it was a leading news source in India, there was scant coverage of local developments. Instead, most of the reporting pertained to the war in Ukraine and European and American government responses to it. All of the articles were written by "Natasha Kumar" in English, and the 1-800 number included on the site led to a phone bot hawking a medical monitoring device. But what was even more interesting was that the story claimed that Prigozhin had been strangled in the Belarusian town of Pinsk, about four hours by car southwest of the Wagner cantonment near the village of Asipovichi.

The improbable source of this story was reportedly Serhi Bulba, the leader of the White Legion, a Belarusian armed-resistance group. The story suggested that Bulba said Prigozhin's body had been dismembered and burned so it would be unrecognizable. It was all part of a planned purge of Wagner's rebellious leadership. Even if it was not true, the story suggested that someone had gone to great lengths to see how far tales of Prigozhin's assassination could go. The flurry of rumors, misdirects, and outright lies that erupted within the first twenty-four hours after the plane crash made it fairly obvious that it was going to be impossible to determine what really happened to Prigozhin.

Before his fall from the sky, Yevgeny Prigozhin had achieved rock-star status. Just as with the grassy knoll and the Zapruder tape, conspiracy theorists would return to the clip of Prigozhin and Utkin talking to Wagner troops in Belarus and the video of the Wagner chieftain's plane tumbling to Earth again and again. They would play and replay footage from Prigozhin's final days in Africa, looking for hints that Prigozhin's killer might be standing somewhere nearby but out of the frame. They would obsessively examine every second of a video shot from inside the Embraer Legacy 600 by two faceless women who had apparently contacted Prigozhin days before his death and asked about purchasing the jet. And, like Elvis Presley, Prigozhin would be resurrected repeatedly. After his death, he walked Jesus-like in cyberspace. Prigozhin would rise, fall, and rise again each time a tremor was felt in the Kremlin; every facet of his last day would be picked over ad infinitum for signs of prophecy. In his final act, the convict turned catering magnate turned internet impresario and warlord had transformed into a forever martyr.

CHAPTER 23

SUCCESSION

Who did it? The question answered itself before it was asked. Whether through a wink or a nod, it was widely presumed that Vladimir Putin had given the order to eliminate Yevgeny Prigozhin and put an end to the Wagner Group affair. Although the "how" part of the plot to take Prigozhin down remained an unresolved mystery, the "why" was obvious: Prigozhin's mutinous march on Moscow constituted the most serious challenge yet to Putin's rule. But the two-month period after Putin's angry disavowal of Prigozhin as a traitor suggested that Putin had been hesitant to act, leaving open the possibility that someone other than the president had finally stepped in more forcefully. Such a drastic decision cut against Putin's innate sense of loyalty, and the delay in moving to contain the threat from Prigozhin reinforced the notion that Putin may have been reluctant to go hard against an old friend who had more than proven his worth.

Putin even looked a bit choked up when a day after Prigozhin's jet went down, he expressed his condolences for the ten people killed on board. Seated in a wood-paneled office with what looked like a set of photos from the crash site, Putin spoke in an unusually soft tone: "If there were people from the Wagner company, as initial reports suggest, I'd like to say they made a significant contribution to our common cause of fighting the neo-Nazi regime in Ukraine."

Putin could not ignore the basic facts. Wagner was, for a while, a bright spot in a very dark time for Russia. It had energized men and imaginations, reviving the Kremlin's reputation for craftiness. "I knew Prigozhin for a very long time, since the early 1990's. He was a man with a complex destiny and he made serious mistakes in his life." Mistakes, indeed. It was hard to even count, let alone calculate, the weight of all Prigozhin's many missteps. But one of the biggest had been his open challenge to Putin's dictatorial grip.[1]

Wagner insiders proffered all manner of theories about how the plot to kill Prigozhin had been carried out. Marat Gabidullin, the Wagner Group defector who had worked in Prigozhin's St. Petersburg office, didn't dismiss the idea of Putin's direct involvement. But he suggested another implausible-sounding plot twist. The multinational energy companies that Prigozhin had succeeded in besting in the Middle East and Africa could have been equally motivated to get rid of him. After all, if it had not been for Wagner, it was doubtful that Transneft, Gazprom, Stroytransgaz, and Severstal would have gotten as far as they had in securing the rights to mine gold and diamonds and drill for oil and gas across the Middle East and Africa.

A couple of months after the plane crash, Putin insinuated in offhand remarks that Prigozhin and his traveling companions had likely been high on cocaine and playing with live hand grenades before the plane exploded. "Unfortunately, no tests were carried out for the presence of alcohol and drugs in the victims' blood," he said. "In my opinion, it would've been important to do that analysis."[2] Putin's claim would have been laughable if it was not so insulting to the public's intelligence.

In reality, of course, the decapitation of the Wagner Group's leadership was most probably an inside job that had been long contemplated by Prigozhin's detractors inside the Kremlin. Sergey Shoigu's months-long campaign to discredit Prigozhin was slow in convincing Putin to act. But more likely, Putin had decided to end Wagner and Prigozhin on the day of the mutiny or very soon after it. The only way to unpack what happened was to focus on Putin and Kremlin insiders. Loyalty, rather than competence, was what mattered most to Putin.

The plane wreck had occurred only a day after the Kremlin announced that Prigozhin's most passionate champion in the upper echelons of the conventional forces, General Sergey Surovikin, had been demoted again. This hardly seemed a coincidence. That Sergey Shoigu and Valery Gerasimov had managed to sideline Prigozhin's chief supporter in Russia's officer corps and that both had somehow come out on top despite increasing indications that their leadership was imperiling the performance of Russia's armed forces immediately raised suspicions of their direct involvement in Prigozhin's killing. Yet their failure to prevent the mutiny in the first place damaged their credibility. Who in the defense ministry could really be trusted with a targeted assassination after a mercenary rebellion?

A former Russian intelligence officer and Western intelligence officials told the *Wall Street Journal* that Putin's right-hand man, Nikolai Patrushev, had ordered the hit.[3] This had the ring of truth. Calendar entries and phone-log data showed that Prigozhin was in touch with Patrushev regularly over the years and kept him abreast of his doings with the Wagner Group. Before the war, the number of people close enough to Putin to command his full faith and respect could probably be counted on one or two hands. During the lockdown and isolation at the peak of the COVID pandemic, a paralyzing inertia seemed to guide the choices he made, and paranoia ran rife in the system he had built.

Once the start of the Russian offensive against Ukraine kicked in, Putin showed an unusual penchant for dragging his feet when making decisions. It had taken nearly a year for members of the presidential cabinet to convince Putin that Prigozhin was out of control. The campaign to discredit Prigozhin had proceeded chaotically, and the government's handling of the mutiny had ended in humiliation for Putin and his allies. Putin could ill afford any more missteps. Patrushev, in his years of service as head of the FSB and chief of Russia's Security Council, had shown himself to be a cool and calculating bishop in Putin's court.

That the price of Prigozhin's betrayal would be death was not really in doubt. The only question was how to get it done. If Putin moved too fast or too publicly by declaring open season on Prigozhin, Utkin, Chekalov, and other Wagner Group leaders, he risked stoking the ire not only of their subordinates but also of those in the conventional forces who were sympathetic to criticisms about the way the war was being run. The arrest of Prigozhin's ultranationalist rival, Igor Girkin, in early July on extremism charges reinforced the impression that the Kremlin was moving swiftly to neutralize any form of dissent, ensuring that both Wagner loyalists and hard-line nationalists critical of Prigozhin were silenced before they could become a broader threat.

This perhaps explained why, for a time, Putin and official Russia went almost mute after the dramatic FSB raid on Prigozhin's mansion in St. Petersburg a week after the mutiny. The Wagner ethos had seeped into so many aspects of the war that it was difficult to disentangle the limited progress on the battlefield in Ukraine from the Wagner Group's success and Prigozhin's outsized personality.

Where others inside the defense ministry had stumbled, Prigozhin had marched straight ahead. He had mobilized tens of thousands of convicts to fight in a war while hundreds of thousands of middle-class Russians fled the country to escape the draft. He had challenged the president of Ukraine to engage in an aerial dogfight and openly mocked Ukraine's backers in Washington and Brussels. He had feted the fallen with medals and elaborate ceremonial burials. However flawed he was as a human being, Prigozhin had resurrected a sense of pride in the military and ignited deep passions in the men who answered his call.

Dismembering Wagner's leadership would take time and care. Like cutting away a cancerous tumor, it would take careful and thoughtful planning to preserve the good tissue and cut away the bad. As long as one or more of the leadership lived and continued to run a parallel army under the Wagner banner, there was a risk of losing control again.

Besides all that, Russia was still short of money, supplies, and men. It would have been impossible to excise the Wagner Group wholesale from Russia's defense plans. Killing Prigozhin or Utkin in the immediate aftermath of the uprising without settling the issue of succession and containment would have been foolhardy. Russia's military-technical agreements with African states were critical to keeping the war going. Absent the gold, diamonds, oil, timber, and gas that Chekalov's schemes generated for both Prigozhin and the Russian industrial giants, the Kremlin would have a harder time paying for the ammunition and other military material that it needed to press ahead against Ukraine's counteroffensives.

The trouble was that Prigozhin had put all this at risk. The mutiny had, more than anything, added insult to injury. In the final stretch of his life, too much had come to be known about Prigozhin's networks. The camouflage that Putin, Prigozhin, and a whole cast of spies, lawyers, bankers, and money launderers had so artfully woven over nine years began visibly fraying just before the invasion of Ukraine. Prigozhin had begun tearing at the tightly stitched fabric of relationships built up with proxies across Africa and the Middle East at least a year earlier. His antics could well have jeopardized Putin's ability to pay off the military's General Staff, potentially paving the way to a full-scale coup.

Gerasimov and Shoigu likely understood this better than most. So—one theory went—they had turned to General Andrey Averyanov, the GRU's chief of reconnaissance and sabotage, for help. Averyanov, who headed a military-intelligence cadre known to most of the world only as Unit 29155, was one of three suspects immediately implicated in the plot to eliminate Prigozhin and the Wagner Group's other two key leaders. Along with two Russian defense officials, General Ruslan Tsalikov and General Yunus-Bek Yevkurov, Averyanov, as the military-intelligence agency's chief of clandestine operations, formed a triumvirate of plotters.

All three were ruthlessly loyal to Gerasimov and Sergey Shoigu. Each in his own manner had been responsible for both running the military's smuggling operations and eliminating threats to that network via a series of assassinations and sabotage missions. Tsalikov's career had tracked closely that of Shoigu for three decades. A thick-waisted military functionary, Tsalikov had spent several years under Shoigu as head of the finance directorate at the Ministry of Emergency Services. When Shoigu became minister of defense in 2012, Tsalikov followed his old friend there, taking up the position of deputy defense minister.

In that role, Tsalikov was the military's head quartermaster, charged with overseeing the management of logistics and supplies. Most importantly for Prigozhin and the Wagner Group, Tsalikov was in charge of overseeing the defense ministry holding company JSC Garnizon, the main conduit for Wagner Group contracts and deployments. A leaked document detailing Tsalikov's interactions with Prigozhin and his many shell companies made clear that if anyone had a vested interest in seeing the Wagner problem dealt with, it was Tsalikov.[4]

Tsalikov's colleague, Yunus-Bek Yevkurov, also had his own reasons for vengeance. After all, it was Yevkurov who was caught on camera simpering before Prigozhin as the warlord addressed him rudely in the familiar vernacular "you." During their brief but tense interchange, Prigozhin threatened to wipe out the air assets that Yevkurov had likely had a hand in deploying during the so-called March for Justice. In addition to overseeing combat training for the military, Yevkurov was charged with aviation safety for state air fleets, a position that put him technically in control of oversight of the hundreds of air cargo runs made by Flight Unit 223, the military-aviation service that frequently transported Wagner's men and matériel to the field in Russia's near abroad. Tsalikov had been the check writer for Prigozhin's Concord network of companies and its many dark-money subsidiaries, but Yevkurov had been chief valet to the Wagner Group.

Then there was Averyanov, the lead suspect behind Prigozhin's killing, the GRU's so-called king of the shadows. A graduate of the Tashkent Higher Combined Arms Academy in Uzbekistan, Averyanov had served as a *spetsnaz* operative in Moldova and at one point with a Serbian reconnaissance detachment during the Balkans conflict, where he picked up fluency in Serbian and apparently a fascination with Ottoman-era weaponry.[5] A decorated veteran of the First and Second Chechen Wars, he obsessed about his personal privacy, and for years the only known photos of him were the handful taken of him strutting proudly down the aisle at his daughter's wedding in 2017.

Trim and fastidious, he appeared to be a man with a healthy appreciation for well-tailored suits. As head of Unit 29155, Averyanov enjoyed the rare distinction of leading the GRU's 161st Intelligence Training Center in Moscow, which for years has specialized in training secret, highly skilled operatives for deep-penetration covert missions in enemy territory.[6] Among the three Putin loyalists who could gain the most from Prigozhin's death, Averyanov stood out. As one former Western intelligence agent explained it in the aftermath of Prigozhin's presumed death, although Averyanov was unlikely to take on the kind of administrative tasks that Tsalikov and Yevkurov had while Prigozhin was in charge, he had other skills that commended him as the new head of Russia's off-book paramilitaries.

Averyanov's reputation as chief of the GRU's "wet-job" assassination teams and lead mastermind of destabilization campaigns that spanned multiple countries made him an ideal candidate to replace Prigozhin. "Ultimately, he's the guy who kicks ass and people know it. That works in his favor," the former Western intelligence agent said.[7] Averyanov's fearsome reputation stemmed from the role he had played in tasking the GRU sabotage teams responsible for several daring attacks on weapons depots, international organizations, and individuals involved in countering Russia's covert thrusts deep within Europe. From 2014 to 2019, investigators in Britain and Europe would link Averyanov directly to several clandestine operations.

One of the first operations entailed the bombing of a well-protected weapons depot in the town of Vrbětice in the Czech Republic in October 2014. Averyanov reportedly flew in ahead of the stealth attack that was perpetrated by three members of Unit 29155 and that led to the destruction of thirteen tons of ammunition, killed two, and wounded several others.[8] About a half year later, in March 2015, similar scenes would play out at the Vazov Machine-Building Plant in Bulgaria. In all, the GRU, under Averyanov's direction, mounted more than a half-dozen sabotage operations against depots storing weapons and ammunition that were to be sent by a Bulgarian arms dealer to anti-Russian forces in Ukraine and Syria.[9] Among Averyanov's most famous GRU missions was the attempted poisoning of Sergey Skripal in March 2016 in the British town of Salisbury.

A former blue beret paratrooper and GRU agent, Skripal had, at the age of fifty-nine, been exchanged as part of a prisoner swap orchestrated by the Obama administration in the summer of 2010. Known as the "illegals spy swap," the deal involved the transfer of ten Russian sleeper agents who had lived under deep cover in the United States for several years. About seven years after the swap, Putin assigned the GRU the job of exacting his revenge against Skripal for serving as a double agent for Britain's MI-6 intelligence service. This made sense. After all, because Skripal had served as head of personnel for the GRU, he was likely intimately familiar with Averyanov and his team of saboteurs and assassins. Skripal reportedly had used his encyclopedic knowledge of the GRU's list of sleeper agents and spies to out at least three hundred undercover Russian operatives.[10] If anyone was truly suited to carrying out a revenge plot, it would have been Averyanov, the very man who had embarrassingly lost hundreds of agents to schemes that Skripal had steered the MI-6 on.

It turned out, in fact, that Skripal was still in the spy business when Averyanov tasked two GRU colonels with taking him out with Novichok, the same rare nerve agent that would be used against Putin's challenger, Alexey Navalny. Bellingcat was the first to publicize the identities of Anatoly Chepiga and Alexander Mishkin, and link them to Averyanov's Unit 29155.[11] Later, UK authorities would identify a third coconspirator operating under the name "Sergey Fedotov" as the man who had tested the poison in an airport hotel room before the two younger men, Chepiga and Mishkin, smeared Novichok on a door handle at Skripal's residence in early March 2016. The assassination attempt sent Skripal and his daughter Yulia to the hospital. It also killed a woman whose boyfriend had found a discarded perfume atomizer that contained the Novichok.

By then, Unit 29155 had also featured in the hacking of the World Anti-Doping Agency and had attempted to steal information from the Organization for Prohibition of Chemical Weapons (OPCW). In short, if there was going to be a hit on the Wagner Group's top leaders, few in the GRU would have been as well positioned as Averyanov and Unit 29155 to execute orders from on high in the Kremlin.

The Kremlin's careful orchestration of the optics surrounding the Russia-Africa Summit held in St. Petersburg seemed to bolster the theory. Held about a month after the mutiny, the long-planned conference drew only seventeen African heads of state, far fewer than at Putin's first high-profile event, before the war in Ukraine. Barred from participating in any official capacity,

Prigozhin worked the sidelines, posing with Central African Republic diplomats at his Trezzini Hotel, making it clear he was still in the game—still relevant. He refused to be silenced. When a coup erupted in Niger in late July, he quickly offered sharp commentary: "What happened in Niger is nothing other than the people's struggle against their colonizers."[12] The sudden appearance of Wagner flags and Russian flags waving in the crowd fueled speculation that another Wagner-inspired takeover was in the works.

This spectacle unfolded alongside one of the strangest reunions of Russia's most notorious spies and black-ops figures in recent history. Among them was Viktor Bout, the infamous arms dealer imprisoned by the United States in 2008 and traded in a headline-grabbing prisoner swap in 2022 for WNBA star Brittney Griner. Bout, now a Duma candidate for the ultranationalist Liberal Democratic Party, spoke at the summit with polished rhetoric about shifting power away from Western dominance and hinted at plans to reenter the logistics business in Africa. "The scales are tipping, and critical mass is shifting to the side with new ideas and fresh approaches to the challenges of the future, which will no longer be orchestrated by Anglo-Saxon domination that's hindered true development unjustly for so long," Bout would later tell a South African defense reporter a day before Prigozhin's plane went down.[13]

Averyanov was also there. If ever there was a signal that the jig was up for Prigozhin, it was when Putin presented Averyanov to the African leaders at the conference as Russia's new head of security for Russian operations on the continent. The subtext was clear: Russia now planned to wield a much bigger stick to ensure that its supply of gold and other precious metals continued to flow to intermediaries in the UAE, Turkey, and China uninterrupted. More importantly, for the first time Russia was prepared to conduct its illicit pillage-for-profit scheme in the open.

Although Prigozhin's social-media–driven influence campaigns had helped Russia achieve important wins during the chaos that ensued with the Arab Spring, as the war in Ukraine dragged on, their utility became questionable. The more the Wagner Group's social habits and networks came into view, the more possible it became for Ukrainian forces and their Western allies to disrupt them. By pushing for paramilitaries to swear their allegiance to the Kremlin and tapping Averyanov to clean up after Prigozhin, Putin was basically gambling that the West did not have a game plan for countering Russia's growing influence across Africa.

He was right.

To interdict or conduct a direct strike against a shipment of Russian goods where declared military operatives were on board in the air or on the high seas would be tantamount to an act of war. When Putin waved vaguely in the direction of Averyanov at the summit, it seemed that the question of who was the primary bureaucratic beneficiary of the plane crash was as settled as it likely ever would be.

That left the question of successors. They fell into two categories, organizational successors and familial successors, and perhaps not surprisingly it would turn out that there was some overlap. On the organizational side, Andrey Troshev once again seemed somehow poised to take the mantle of the Wagner Group's chief transformation officer. Some Wagner fighters perceived Troshev's well-known drinking problem and advanced age as disqualifying traits, but his name and that of Liga, the veterans' association he had formed in St. Petersburg, factored in every conversation about Wagner's succession. Troshev was often referred to in Liga correspondence and on semiofficial Wagner social media channels as the leader of the paramilitary's so-called Council of Commanders, and his number was on speed dial with every element of the GRU and FSB that had supported the Wagner Group's adventures abroad.

Moreover, there were growing signs of tension between Troshev and Prigozhin in the year leading up to the mutiny, resulting in Troshev's ouster as head of Liga and, by extension, the Wagner Group. Dmitry Aleksandrovich Podolsky, a former commander of Wagner's 5th Assault Detachment, emerged as a key figure in the split. In May 2023, Podolsky appeared in a video signing letters to Duma deputies on behalf of fallen Wagner fighters, echoing the narrative that most losses were the result of ammunition shortages caused by Shoigu's incompetence.[14]

A month later, in a Telegram post, Podolsky openly criticized "Shoigu with his bureaucracy" and possibly Troshev himself.[15] He recounted his twenty-one years of military service, witnessing the decay and plunder under Serdyukov and Shoigu, while "favorites, ass-lickers, and storytellers" thrived. By directly confronting Russia's military leadership—something Troshev was unwilling to do—Podolsky aligned himself with the prevailing sentiment among Wagner's field commanders. As a multiple amputee who had lost an arm and two legs during the capture of Bakhmut, Podolsky was ideally positioned for a powerful office role advocating for the rank and file. On June 30, a week after the uprising, Liga announced Troshev's removal as its chief, with Podolsky succeeding him.

Troshev's countermoves were less visible, but one version of the story was that he had falsely agreed to capitulate to Shoigu's demand for all paramilitaries to pledge allegiance to the Kremlin and surrender their arms by July 1. According to this narrative, Troshev had sent letters announcing that Wagner convoys would move northward in an orderly fashion from June 21 to July 5. However, he had allegedly been secretly plotting to push the Trojan Horse convoy straight to the Kremlin's doorstep.

A much more likely scenario was that Troshev had quietly turned on Prigozhin long before the mutiny. The fact that Troshev survived while Prigozhin perished, despite their shared history since the Wagner Group's founding, strongly suggested Troshev's involvement in the plot against Prigozhin. Moreover, Troshev's decision to assume a more public-facing role as Liga's head, just as Russia's offensive intensified in the summer of 2022, further underscored the possibility that he had shifted allegiances months before Shoigu's campaign to discredit Prigozhin fully matured. Marat Gabidullin, the Wagner Group defector who had served under Troshev's direct command, was skeptical of Troshev's prospects as a potential successor to Prigozhin. Waving his hand dismissively during an interview, Gabidullin said that, if anything, Troshev would serve as little more than a "*svadebny general*," a "wedding general" or figurehead. However, Gabidullin acknowledged that he was a bit biased in his views and that he was no fan of Troshev. Still, Gabidullin reluctantly admitted that as the onetime head of the Liga veterans' association and the organization's main registered director, Troshev held important sway within the Russian security bureaucracy.

Additional hints of how the shake-up at the top would play out within Wagner's upper ranks became apparent in the immediate aftermath of Prigozhin's death. On August 26, three days after the plane wreck, the @OrchestraW Telegram channel, one of several semiofficial mouthpieces of the paramilitary, posted a stern message aimed at rebutting rumors that Anton "Lotus" Yelizarov had been picked to replace Utkin.[16] Although Yelizarov was technically considered the highest-ranking member of Wagner's combat commanders, the post noted that his main duty was leading combat missions and training. Still, Yelizarov's long-standing relationships with senior GRU officials from his days with the GRU 10th Special Purpose Brigade in Molkino and the fact that at forty-two he was considerably younger than Troshev made him a strong candidate for either the number-one or number-two position within the Wagner Group's successor cadres.

Besides Yelizarov, two others who stood out as possible replacements for Utkin were Alexander "Ratibor" Kuznetsov and Andrey "Tramp" Bogatov. Of the two, however, it was Kuznetsov who was the more well-known and revered, and the one considered more likely to succeed Utkin as colonel in chief of battlefield operations. "He is a brave man," Gabidullin said with a somewhat awestruck gaze. "He is a very advanced military thinker. He feels the fight. This is a genius of war on a tactical and even operational-tactical level."[17]

Beyond his battlefield prowess, one other thing that commended Kuznetsov as a successor was the fact that he already knew all the players in Redut, the rival paramilitary outfit linked to the VDV 45th Guards Spetsnaz Reconnaissance Brigade. According to Gabidullin, Kuznetsov had crossed paths with Redut's commander, Konstantin Mirzayants, in Syria as early as 2013, when Kuznetsov served as the company commander of the ill-fated Slavonic Corps detachment. However, this likely explained why, in the final analysis, Kuznetsov ended up a year later going his own way and joining Kadyrov's Akhmat Battalion. He promised all the comforts of home: "We will take everyone. Everyone who is with us, everyone who is for the Motherland. Everything will be the same as in the Wagner PMC. One to one. Without any papers or anything else. Our whole kitchen remains the same, nothing changes."[18]

As it now stood, Wagner fighters who had laid down their arms after the mutiny were given the option to join the First Volunteer Corps, a unit specially established to fold Prigozhin's mercenaries into conventional military service under the aegis of the national guard, Rosgvardia. Many did so. Within a few months, Yelizarov would confirm that he had played the hand he was dealt to his advantage, signaling his prominent role as a commander with the new Volunteer Corps in a Telegram post announcing the opening of a new base colocated with the 150th Motor Rifle Division.[19]

Redut ultimately inherited the role of Kremlin-approved conduit for the recruitment of irregulars, and there were signs that Mirzayants had been tapped to smooth the way for the transition. With his strong links to the VDV's 45th Guards military-intelligence wing and the Union of Paratroopers, reported links to the Podolskaya mafia, and years of experience running a paramilitary, Mirzayants was a natural choice.

Plus, Mirzayants, as head of Redut, had already had plenty of experience "managing up" when it came to dealing with mercurial Russian power brokers. Anonymous testimony submitted by a former Wagner fighter and GRU officer to Britain's foreign affairs committee named Putin's close associate and Volga Group head Gennady Timchenko as the "godfather" of Redut and suggested that Mirzayants maintained close ties to members of the military's General Staff.[20] Mirzayants's other great advantage was that he knew well and understood the temperament of General Yaroslav Y. Moskalik, the defense ministry's lead on military technical cooperation for the Middle East and Africa. It appeared once again that affiliation with the Union of Paratroopers had proved to be the best guarantee of surviving the vicissitudes of Putin's power vertical.

However, no one had the kind of charisma and swagger to replace Prigozhin. As news of the crash aftermath began to be subsumed by coverage of impromptu Wagner Group memorials, the churn over succession became more fractious. In the great tradition of empires and revolutions past and present, the question of who would lead the paramilitary next revolved around two opposing poles: dynasty versus merit. There was talk that Prigozhin's son, Pavel, was looked at by some within Wagner's ranks as a more appropriate pick to take over. All mafias run on the logic of dynastic blood ties. In this respect, the crime family that Prigozhin built was no different.

Pavel had, according to his father, fought with distinction in Syria and Ukraine. He knew where his father had secretly socked away cash and Concord company assets. It did not go unnoticed that about two weeks before his father's death, Pavel became the owner of the companies linked to the multimillion-dollar Lakhta Plaza complex in St. Petersburg. But rather than proof positive of Pavel's prospects as the Wagner Group's next successor, the transfer of Lakhta Plaza LLC's ownership from Prigozhin to his son was more definitive proof that Putin's chef was indeed dead.

Pavel was not the only beneficiary of the restructuring of Prigozhin's business empire. Prigozhin's estranged wife inherited full ownership of the Eliseev Merchants Store and Chocolate Museum on Nevsky Prospect. In a surprising twist, Prigozhin's friend and longtime partner in hijinks, Dmitry Koshara, the brains behind the 2012 fake documentary *Anatomy of a Protest*, became the registered director of Agat LLC, the same holding company that had once been the backbone of Prigozhin's failed Blin! Donalts fast-food restaurant chain. With an estimated value of 22 million rubles, or about $227,000, it was a substantial gift.[21] It was another indication that an understanding had been reached between Prigozhin's family and the Kremlin sometime between the end of the Russia-Africa Summit on July 28 and

August 11, the day the first transfer of Prigozhin's assets began, according to corporate-registry records and Russian media reporting. Prigozhin's family members likely already knew that he was a dead man walking.

Soon after Prigozhin's death, Telegram channels circulated a picture of his will, which named young Pavel as heir to most of his late father's assets. This accorded Prigozhin's scion a degree of gravitas that imbued his claim to the mantle of greater legitimacy, but a straight-down-the-line dynastic succession that would accord Pavel the same kind of autonomy that his father had enjoyed was out of the question after all the effort that had gone into neutralizing the Wagner Group as an internal threat to Putin's regime. In the immediate weeks after Prigozhin's death, the mercenary cadre was still reeling and convulsed by internal feuding. At the age of twenty-five, the young Prigozhin was too inexperienced to take the reins of a paramilitary with such a freighted history. To the degree that Putin was willing to countenance Pavel as a successor to his father, his role would turn out to be largely ornamental.

For a moment, there was speculation on social media that the Kremlin had settled on Viktor Bout as Prigozhin's replacement. In the days that followed the plane crash, Twitter and Telegram were rife with rumors that Bout had secretly sealed a deal with Putin to carry the Wagner Group project forward while Prigozhin was scrambling to save his empire. A photo taken of Bout and Prigozhin mugging for the camera at the Russia-Africa conference in St. Petersburg only a few weeks before the crash was pored over by thousands of social media users like so many tea leaves.

Bout had, after all, been an instructive model, and Prigozhin's entry into the arms-smuggling racket soon after Bout's 2011 arrest had raised eyebrows. But Bout's high public profile made him just as much a liability as Prigozhin, and a lot about the business of running a transnational crime cartel had changed during Bout's decade-plus in a US prison. In any case, if there was anything at all to the speculation about the parallel arc of Bout and Prigozhin's luck and misfortunes, it was a secret that Prigozhin likely took with him to his grave.

In the event, the very qualities that alienated Troshev from many Wagner Group field commanders—his dogged willingness to play ball with the Ministry of Defense, even at the cost of untold casualties on the field—were precisely what recommended him to the Kremlin after Prigozhin's death. Although Wagner's senior commanders had reportedly rejected Putin's proffer of retaining

368 · PUTIN'S SLEDGEHAMMER

Troshev as executive director of Liga, it was clear that he had gained the most in the aftermath. A month after the plane crash, in September, Troshev would appear on camera with Putin.[22] Seated at a long table next to Prigozhin's nemesis Yunus-Bek Yevkurov, Troshev was tasked with managing volunteer fighter units in Ukraine. Kremlin spokesperson Dmitry Peskov stated that Troshev now worked for the Ministry of Defense, and it was widely presumed that Wagner's former executive officer would go on to direct newly formed units under the aegis of "PMC Redut."[23]

Yevkurov's presence at the meeting was another indication of who would be heading up the Kremlin's irregular-warfare strategy in a post-Prigozhin world. In the months that followed, Yevkurov would lead regular delegations to Wagner Group client states such as Libya, Mali, and the Central African Republic, formally announcing in the fall of 2023 the creation of a successor organization called the Africa Corps, directly subordinate to the Ministry of Defense.[24] Mirzayants was at his side on several occasions.

Officially established in July on the heels of Prigozhin's mutiny, the Africa Corps subsumed the Wagner Group's mission on the continent. The rebranding was a throwback to a similar outfit established under the command of Nazi Germany's Erwin Rommel during World War II in a bid to boost fascist Italy's challenge to Allied powers with colonialist interests in Africa. Placed under the control of a newly created division of the GRU led by Averyanov called the Special Activities Service, Russia's Africa Corps was slated initially to grow in size to forty thousand troops.[25]

This target would prove ambitious. But the eventual integration of leading Wagner commanders like Anton Yelizarov into the Africa Corps fold would provide continuity for the Russian military's assistance to the Alliance of Sahel States, a mutual-defense confederation formed among key Kremlin clients Mali, Burkina Faso, and Niger.

Although the survival of Wagner's leading commanders in the aftermath of Prigozhin's downfall seemed assured, many other questions remained unanswered, particularly regarding who else stood to benefit politically from the Wagner chief's spectacular exit. Pundits and analysts picked through the flood of commentary that gushed out from *siloviki* notables. Chechen warlord and Prigozhin frenemy Ramzan Kadyrov, who had threatened to thrash Prigozhin and crush the rebellion but never showed up, was one of the first to jump into the fray.

"I asked him to leave his personal ambitions behind in favor of matters of paramount national importance," Kadyrov said. "Everything else could be dealt with later. But that's just the way he was, Prigozhin, with his iron character and his desire to get what he wanted right here and now."[26] If Kadyrov's remarks were a sign of anything, it was that he was at minimum a better card player than Prigozhin.

Another notable voice was Prigozhin's second-most-important patron, and Putin's long-presumed successor, Alexey Dyumin. The subtly defiant tone of Dyumin's elegy for his old friend Prigozhin was striking: "I knew Yevgeny Prigozhin as a true patriot, a decisive and fearless man. He did a lot for the country, and his homeland will not forget him. We mourn for those who died in this disaster, for all the soldiers of the Wagner PMC who fell during the special military operation. You can forgive mistakes and even cowardice, betrayal—never. They were not traitors."[27]

Four days after the plane crash, the Kremlin announced that authorities suspected foul play. State investigators said that DNA tests on the passengers' bodies had confirmed that Prigozhin was killed on board. But few other details about what caused the explosion were offered. Accordingly, the focus started to shift to the question of burials.

The "special funeral operation" for Yevgeny Prigozhin began six days after the plane crash. Early that morning, after the press got wind of Prigozhin's planned burial, reporters all over St. Petersburg were glued to their phones, madly swiping through Telegram. When and where would it take place? Who would be at the graveside of the man who almost toppled Putin's regime? The only thing that was clear as of August 28 was that the Heroes of Russia—Prigozhin and Valery Chekalov—would remain in St. Petersburg. And the only certainty was that how Prigozhin was buried was the best measure of how Putin planned to deal with the Wagner Group. Funerals for Russia's rich and powerful are the Rosetta stones of the country's future. They often become legends in their own right. Speculation about who was there, who was missing, why, and what it portended for Russian politics often outlives memories of what really happened. In the case of Prigozhin's final rites, the funeral, fittingly, unfolded like a covert operation.

Fontanka, St. Petersburg's local paper of record and the chief chronicler of Prigozhin's rise for almost thirty years, dubbed the event "the most private funeral in the modern history of Russia."[28] It might have sounded like hyperbole but for the fact that those who knew the details of the funeral had reportedly been forced to sign nondisclosure agreements by unnamed security-service authorities. As dawn arrived on the appointed day, news-desk editors ordered their reporters to fan out across the city to see if there were signs of unusual activity at any one of St. Petersburg's sixty-five cemeteries. Around 9 a.m., a *Fontanka* reporter noticed unusually heavy traffic in Primorsky District, the upmarket neighborhood near where Prigozhin had erected his palace-like home within the gated walls of the Northern Versailles complex on Lake Lakhta.

There was visible bustling around the gates of the Serafimovskoye Cemetery. *Fontanka* live-streamed updates about competing rumors that there were happenings at the Bogoslovskoye and Northern Cemeteries. Serafimovskoye Cemetery was the burial grounds of many a gloried son and daughter of the northern capital. Included on that list were Putin's mother and father, along with many lesser-known survivors of the brutal siege of St. Petersburg in World War II. Naval officers and the submariners who died in the sunken and abandoned *Kursk* rested there. Briefly, it appeared as if Chekalov might join them. But there would be no burials that day at the church cemetery famous for housing the remains of Russia's military heroes, a reporter was curtly told.

Then suddenly, at about 11:20 a.m., someone standing watch near the Northern Cemetery spotted a black Mercedes SUV that belonged to Alena Mozhar, Valery Chekalov's associate and partner, and the director of one of Prigozhin's shell companies. Two minibuses pulled up to the gate. A bearded Wagner fighter dressed in the paramilitary's trademark tan camouflage and sporting Wagner's skull-in-crosshairs black-and-red insignia strolled up to the cemetery entrance with a bouquet of flowers in hand. In a long line of twos and threes, mourners streamed toward the pristine white chapel on the grounds, saying little as they went.[29] One estimate suggested that nearly two hundred arrived to say their farewells. As a decorated Hero of Russia, Chekalov was entitled to fireworks and all the trappings of a military funeral ceremony, but even his last day ended as it had begun, in quiet obscurity.

At about half past noon, just before the last prayers were said for Chekalov, there was an update from a *Moskovsky Komsomolets* correspondent in Moscow from the Mystichi Cemetery. Nothing was happening there, though, yet. The pomp and circumstance would come two days later, when Dmitry Utkin was buried in Mystichi with full military honors at the Pantheon of Defenders of the Fatherland.[30] Meanwhile, a *Fontanka* correspondent in St. Petersburg who discovered a patch full of graves for Wagner fighters in the Beloostrovskoye Cemetery was told by a groundskeeper that police had been posted at every cemetery in the city. Every move was calculated to keep the world guessing. The final mystery ended at 2:12 p.m., when a *Fontanka* correspondent sighted Prigozhin's black BMW sedan, license plate number O377CA, driving in a funeral procession down University Embankment on Vasilyevsky Island, the place where Putin and Prigozhin's long friendship had begun. The cortege was headed toward Manezh, on the other side of the Neva River in front of Saint Isaac's Square.[31]

There could be no mistaking the symbolism of the place. About 219 years earlier, in 1804, when construction began on the Konnogvardeyskiy Manege, Tsar Alexander I, the one they called "The Blessed," was in power when the first stone of the massive white neoclassical hall was laid. Erected to house the training grounds for the Russian emperor's Imperial Horse Guards, or the so-called Life Guards Cavalry, the Manezh had at one point after the Bolshevik revolution doubled as a car garage for the KGB's predecessor agency, the NKVD.[32] In the late 1970s, as Prigozhin entered his teenage years, local laborers transformed the colonnaded structure once again into the city's Central Exhibition Hall. However, what mattered on this occasion was not the airy external face of its Greek revival halls but its spiritual interior.

This was where the imperial court's most trusted men were trained to defend the royal family against all comers. During the period from the formation of Life Guards Cavalry in 1730 forward to the great Bolshevik convulsion of 1917, the tsar's guard would undergo many changes. The most notable of these was in 1931, when expatriate members of the guard renamed the formation the Imperial Horse Guards during a bicentennial anniversary celebration in Paris. It was the oldest such horse regiment in the royal retinue, the head of the guard held the rank of the colonel in chief, and the position by divine right belonged to the emperor.[33] For a time, early on after Empress Anne established the regiment, the only people other than the men of the Imperial Horse Guards allowed to enter the chamber of the tsar's family without special permission were the imperial maids, footmen, butlers, and, occasionally, the chef.

Garroted in Pinsk? Taken out in a cargo plane on a flight back home from Mali, then boarded feet first into his executive jet before it was blown apart? Killed while horsing around with grenades in mid-flight over Russia? Or maybe still alive? Here in this temple to Russian imperial might, the truth about Prigozhin's life and death did not matter anymore. In death, he had been absorbed into the Pantheon. His family and loyal followers would always maintain that Prigozhin was buried in the city that had paved his way to glory. The only questions that remained unanswered were who would pay the price for all the carnage, and the bitter legacy Prigozhin had left behind.

EPILOGUE

FALLOUT

On May 9, 2024, Russia's Victory Day parade unfolded on Red Square amid a gloomy spring snow flurry, casting a somber contrast to the event's familiar grandeur. Tanks rumbled, jets roared overhead, and row upon row of soldiers saluted as Sergey Shoigu stood in a black convertible, his medals gleaming in the cold, gray light. His face remained impassive, but the weight of his final moment as Russia's grand marshal was unmistakable. This was his last ride in power as defense minister before the Kremlin's post-Prigozhin purge would sweep him aside. The car slowly rolled down the parade route, Shoigu offering salutes in return, but beneath the surface the wheels of his undoing were already in motion.

The crowd in the VIP grandstand, their wizened faces set with looks of stoic resolve, watched unaware—or maybe uninterested—that their defense minister was days away from being ousted. Shoigu had been the face of Russia's military for more than a decade, steering the behemoth through Crimea, Syria, and Ukraine. But on this day, beneath the veneer of pomp, an undercurrent of foreboding rippled through the rows of assembled generals.

Just two weeks earlier, Russian authorities had arrested Shoigu's deputy and a longtime Prigozhin patron, Timur Ivanov, on charges that he had accepted a roughly $12 million bribe in exchange for handing out defense contracts.[1] In the immediate aftermath of the mutiny, Putin had hinted that heads would roll, remarking that he hoped "no one stole anything—or let's say didn't steal much."[2] And he delivered on that hint. From that moment

373

forward the Kremlin systematically isolated Wagner facilitators, neutralized Prigozhin sympathizers, reassured client states, and reorganized Wagner's global network. By the late spring of 2024, the reshuffling had gutted
the ranks of Russia's military leadership, taking down about a dozen officers,
several of whom had facilitated Wagner operations and profited from Prigozhin's rise. The taint of the Wagner mutiny colored every decision that the
Kremlin made.

Even as the parade rolled on, Shoigu knew the unspoken truth—he was no
longer in charge. That privilege now rested with Andrey Belousov, a man with
none of Shoigu's faux-military swagger but with all of Putin's trust. Belousov,
an economist by training, was no ordinary technocrat; he had for years played
a pivotal role as a liaison for Prigozhin to Putin's trusted circle, quietly brokering solutions to bureaucratic and financial challenges that came with running a
covert war through a web of off-book paramilitaries like Wagner.[3] The defense
ministry shake-up marked the Kremlin's tightening grip on its mercenary apparatus, signaling the end of Shoigu's feckless management and the consolidation
of a more state-controlled paramilitary machine.

Moscow's pundits were quick to spin the changing of the guard as a natural outcome of Putin's reelection in March, framing the cabinet reshuffle as
part of the president's plan to bring in fresh leadership for the next phase of his
presidency. But Russian news headlines hinted at deeper turbulence, suggesting
that commodities magnate Gennady Timchenko and metals tycoon Oleg Deripaska might also soon feel the pinch of the Kremlin's crackdown on Wagner
Group enablers.[4]

Belousov's rise reflected a wider strategic reset. His focus would be on
restoring order to a chaotic military-industrial machine that had been hollowed
out by corruption and torn apart by infighting among Russia's traditional military, paramilitary, and intelligence services. The shift underscored Putin's
intent to bring financial discipline and logistical oversight to the military as the
war in Ukraine dragged on and the cost of failure mounted. By reining in Wagner's remnants, rebranded as the Africa Corps, Russia hoped to both stabilize
its influence abroad—in places like Mali, Burkina Faso, and the Central African Republic—and prevent any future challenges to Putin's authority at home.
The African operations, far from being abandoned, had been expanded under
the aegis of the Expeditionary Corps—the official name of Russia's irregular
paramilitary force, now controlled by the GRU military-intelligence wing—
ensuring that they remained under the Kremlin's tighter grip.

A more pragmatic strategy was taking shape, highlighting Putin's growing awareness of the critical role that industrial policy and cash flows play in achieving war goals. This recalibrated approach prioritized economic survival under Western sanctions, emphasizing the need for innovative solutions to maintain pressure on Ukraine over what was anticipated to be a prolonged conflict. The revised playbook marked a more pronounced shift toward balancing military efforts with economic resilience, preparing Russia for the long haul both on the battlefield and in maintaining its broader geopolitical ambitions.

Across Red Square, Valery Gerasimov, the chief of General Staff, stood just as rigid as Shoigu, though with none of the same bravado. Both men knew what was coming. Shoigu had been given the "honor" of leading that year's parade, but everyone knew it was more of a send-off than a tribute. Soon, Putin would name Shoigu secretary of the Security Council, shunting aside his old KGB friend Nikolai Patrushev to make room for a loyalist of a different stripe. It was a demotion in prestige, certainly, but like the elevation of Putin's old bodyguard Alexey Dyumin to secretary of the State Council that May, it also kept Shoigu within Putin's trusted ranks, albeit in a more symbolic position.

But there were other factors, no doubt, that influenced Shoigu's change in title. A little more than a month after the Victory Day parade, Shoigu's fate took a sharp turn on June 24, 2024, when the International Criminal Court issued an arrest warrant for him and Gerasimov on war-crimes charges. The Hague court issued an indictment against the two specifically for directing attacks on power grids and critical civilian infrastructure in Ukraine, delivering a stunning blow to Shoigu's legacy.[5]

The timing was almost poetic: exactly one year to the day after Prigozhin had launched his aborted "March for Justice" on Moscow, demanding Shoigu's ouster. Prigozhin had accused Shoigu of corruption and blamed him for the deaths of Wagner fighters in Ukraine. On Shoigu's watch, an estimated 50,000 to 85,000 Russian military personnel were confirmed killed during the first two years of the war, according to an accounting by *Mediazona*, an independent news outlet.[6] Western intelligence agencies placed the total number of Russian casualties at that time at more than 300,000.[7]

Half a world away from Moscow, the true legacy of Wagner's chaos was starting to unravel. In late July 2024, beneath a blazing sun in Mali, a brutal ambush unfolded. In the northern expanse of the desert, Russian corpses lay scattered on the white sands, their blood darkening the earth. Tuareg rebels, their faces obscured by their signature pale blue and white *tagelmust* scarves, moved silently among the dead. They rifled through the bodies for weapons and pocket litter, showing no urgency, no fear—this was routine.

Then, suddenly, one of the corpses stirred. A Russian soldier, once thought dead, sprang to life, seizing a rock with trembling hands. He lunged at his attackers in a desperate, doomed final stand. The rebels reacted without hesitation—within seconds, their gunfire rang out, cutting him down again. This time, for good.[8]

The scene, captured on video, became a harsh reminder of what the Wagner Group, now the Africa Corps, had become. The skirmish near the outpost of Tinzaouaten was one of the deadliest encounters involving Russian forces on the continent, leaving at least eighty-four Russians dead and several taken captive.[9] Most were ex-Wagner fighters absorbed into new detachments after Prigozhin's mutiny, tasked with securing Russia's foothold in Mali's gold-rich north. A full three years after Wagner detachments first set down in the Malian capital of Bamako, the country was, in the summer of 2024, still a battlefield for Russia's shadow war, where paramilitaries secured valuable resources in exchange for their counterinsurgency efforts.

In the wake of the Wagner mutiny, Russia exerted its influence across the continent—and nowhere more so than in Mali—to reassure its clients of its ongoing commitment to provide agreed-upon security assistance. Bamako was the scene of multiple high-level diplomatic engagements led by top Russian military officials in the aftermath of Prigozhin's rebellion. These diplomatic overtures were also entangled with the broader Russian defense ministry purge. But the impact of the defense ministry overhaul and the efficacy and sustainability of Russia's irregular-warfare strategy across Africa remain uncertain, particularly as Moscow grapples with the competing demand for experienced combatants closer to home.

Mali has emerged as the bellwether of Russia's post-Prigozhin paramilitary strategy. There, the Africa Corps has experienced its most significant recent successes and failures. Outside of Ukraine, Mali is Russia's most active combat zone, with an estimated force of a thousand irregulars—down from a peak of two thousand in early 2023. As the Africa Corps began to engage in large-scale offensive missions in 2023 and 2024, Mali looked set to serve as a crucial test case for the defense ministry's efforts to reassert control over its paramilitaries, ensuring that they never again threaten the state.

As in other countries, Russia is leveraging its military investment in Mali to secure economic advantages. At the Atomexpo-2024 International Forum in

Krasnoyarsk, Mali's minister of mines said that Krastsvetmet, Russia's largest gold refiner and state-owned precious-metals producer, had plans to construct a gold refinery in Mali to process ore from the country and the surrounding region.[10]

A product of the Soviet-era gulag prison-industrial complex erected under Josef Stalin, Krastsvetmet is the same company that produced the gold bars found in Prigozhin's residence following the Wagner Group mutiny. In November 2023 the United Kingdom added Krastsvetmet to its sanctions list, along with twenty-eight other entities and individuals linked to Russia's gold trade.

Western sanctions on Russia's finance sector and bans on Russian gold exports have created perverse incentives for Russia to expand its military footprint in Africa. The Kremlin plans to establish the refinery using a business model similar to the one employed in Sudan, which could allow Russia to exert more direct control over Mali's gold production and exports. The temporary closing of the Wagner-controlled mine in Sudan in September 2023 amid the country's intensifying civil war might explain the aggressive tack Russia has since taken in Mali.

By refining gold locally, Russia could expand its capacity to bypass international sanctions that prevent direct exports of Russian gold to Western markets. Such an outcome would have significant ramifications for the ongoing conflict between Russia and Ukraine, potentially prolonging the war, raising barriers to a negotiated settlement on terms favorable to Kyiv, and imperiling European security in the longer term.

Post-Prigozhin, the Kremlin rebranded and reorganized, but the strategy was the same: use expeditionary forces like the Africa Corps to extend influence in resource-rich regions, providing a lifeline to Russia's war economy as Western sanctions tightened. The rebel ambush, like the parade Shoigu presided over, was more than a military event. It was symbolic of the deeper rot within Russia's global military apparatus. In Mali the Africa Corps continued Wagner's legacy—ruthless, flexible, and ultimately disposable. Yet while the Kremlin worked to reassert control over its paramilitaries, its expeditionary forces in Africa faced growing threats. A coalition of Tuareg separatists, aligned with al-Qaeda, had gained ground, emboldened by the growing instability of Russia's forces.

For the Kremlin, these battlefield setbacks were dangerous, not just for the immediate losses but for the escalating strategic dilemma they represented. The same forces that once brought quick victories were now vulnerable, as Moscow found itself torn between deploying seasoned troops to Ukraine and keeping them abroad to finance the war. The grim video from the Malian desert heralded the unspooling of a long-sustained illusion: that Russia's paramilitary forces could fight wars cheaply, deniably, and with minimal consequences.

The situation in Mali is intricately linked to Russia's war effort in Ukraine, extending beyond calculations of security-assistance costs and benefits. Several Africa Corps units have since been recalled and redeployed to support Russian operations in Ukraine, such as the spring 2024 Kharkiv offensive. The surprise Ukrainian offensive in the Russian region of Kursk in early August 2024 increased the pressure, prompting Russia to recall Africa Corps units based in Burkina Faso for redeployment to the Ukrainian front.[11]

Meanwhile, Ukraine appeared to be stirring the pot. Unverified reports suggest that Ukrainian operatives had thrown support to Tuareg rebels in a bid to frustrate Russia's expansion of influence. These claims echoed consistent reports of Ukrainian special forces potentially orchestrating similar attacks in Sudan and Syria. Although the veracity of these reports remained unproven, Ukraine capitalized on the psychological effects of propaganda about a shadow war, conveying that it retained the capability to challenge Russia far beyond its borders. At the same time, Ukraine's suspected support for anti-Russian forces in Mali and elsewhere generated blowback, which reshaped Kyiv's relations in Africa and the Global South. In August 2024, Niger and Mali cut diplomatic ties with Ukraine following reports of its military-intelligence support of Tuareg insurgents.

But what loomed even larger over Russia's paramilitary ambitions was the unresolved question of accountability for Wagner's atrocities during the Prigozhin era. Between 2014 and 2023, Wagner had left behind a trail of human devastation across Ukraine, Syria, Sudan, Libya, Mali, and the Central African Republic. The violence was systematic—mass executions, rape, torture, illegal detention, and indiscriminate targeting of civilians were woven into the fabric of Wagner's operations.

Andrey Troshev, the hidden hand behind much of Wagner's administrative inner workings and the man in charge of the paramilitary's substantial internal-security apparatus, kept the machinery running, overseeing troop discipline while Prigozhin courted attention. As Wagner expanded its reach, so did its body count. Yet as of the summer of 2024, Troshev remained unscathed—like Anton Yelizarov and other prominent Wagner Group leaders,

Troshev continued untrammeled, safe in the knowledge that little consensus had been reached about how to respond to Russia's deployment of expeditionary forces in the guise of private-military companies, let alone Wagner Group's record of atrocities.

Wagner's structure obscured the lines between state-sponsored violence and mercenary enterprise. This ambiguity was what allowed Russia to act with impunity, even though the chain of command often ran straight back to the General Staff and the GRU intelligence wing. With the formation of the Africa Corps and Wagner's formal absorption into the defense ministry, however, that distance became increasingly difficult to maintain. The General Staff and GRU's more aggressive control over expeditionary forces made the state's ties to paramilitary atrocities more explicit, increasing the potential for criminal liability for high-ranking Russian officials. If international investigators were to pursue accountability, there would now be an even clearer path to linking Russia's leadership to those crimes.

But ten years after Prigozhin teamed up with Utkin to form their mercenary outfit with express backing from the Kremlin, the question remained: Would justice ever be served for the victims of Wagner's actions? The sheer scale of violence and exploitation committed under the banner of Russian paramilitary forces is staggering, but international mechanisms for holding these forces accountable are slow, cumbersome, and fraught with political challenges. Figures like Shoigu and Gerasimov—already under scrutiny for Russia's action in Ukraine—are, for instance, unlikely targets for prosecution for Wagner's past transgressions given that they are already facing charges in The Hague.

Political will permitting, others lower down the chain of command, such as Wagner's honorary VIPs Sergey Surovikin and Mikhail Mzinstev, and well-known leaders such as Troshev and Yelizarov, might be stronger candidates for legal action under universal jurisdiction for crimes committed not only in Ukraine but across the theaters of Africa and the Middle East. Yet as this book went to press, Russia's ability to shield its military and political elite from prosecution had so far proved resilient, and the Africa Corps's ongoing operations showed that Moscow had not given up leveraging paramilitary violence to advance its geopolitical aims.

For the moment, Moscow continues to project power through its paramilitary forces, shielding itself behind layers of bureaucratic deniability. But the world is watching, and the crimes of the Prigozhin era are not forgotten.

With each new battle in Africa, each redeployment to Ukraine, the question of accountability will grow louder. How long can Russia sustain its shadow army before the world demands an accounting?

Meantime, the Wagner Group brand endures, a ghost in Russia's military-industrial machine, kept alive by its symbolic power and the client relationships built by Prigozhin and his network. Recruitment efforts continue, with new fighters headed for Ukraine and Africa.

For months after Prigozhin's death, a Wagner-linked Telegram channel regularly posted user-submitted photos of people proudly displaying Wagner badges and merchandise against the backdrop of far-flung corners of the world. Images poured in from Russia and dozens of countries, including South Korea, Germany, and the United States.[12] The underlying message appears to be one of resilience: despite setbacks, the Wagner Group remains a potent global force, a model for other adventuresome authoritarians. Whether this implicit threat materializes may hinge, in part, on whether international efforts to expose and prosecute Russian paramilitaries for their extensive record of brutality and exploitation gain traction.

The mutiny may have been Wagner's swan song, but the real story is unfolding now—on the battlefields of Ukraine, in the gold mines of Africa, and in the back rooms of Moscow, where the future of global security is being rewritten by men who understand that in the end, wars aren't won by armies. They're won by those who can rewrite the rules and leave others scrambling to catch up.

AUTHOR'S NOTE AND ACKNOWLEDGMENTS

When I first sat down to sketch the outline of this book, in early January 2022, more than one hundred thousand Russian troops were massed on Ukraine's border. An invasion looked all but inevitable. The Pentagon's claims about Russian covert operatives stirring up chaos inside Ukraine as a pretext for war had the whole world on edge. Tensions between the White House and the Kremlin over Ukraine were then already at a boiling point. Yet officials in both Biden's administration and Zelensky's government seemed to be hedging their bets on Putin's true intentions. However, there was little doubt in my mind that whatever the outcome of the coming clash between Russian and Ukrainian forces, the Wagner Group would be a central player in this latest chapter of Russia's relentless push to reclaim its status as a global power.

All signs at the time—just a few weeks before Russia fired its opening salvo—indicated that the Wagner Group was preparing for action. Wagner had already expanded its reach into Mali, and there were hints that Russia had begun putting feelers out to the military junta that took over Burkina Faso in early 2022. But online chatter suggested that at least some Wagner operatives had already been recalled from Africa and the Middle East in preparation for a renewed Russian intervention in Ukraine.

At that point, I had already traveled to Ukraine several times in search of insights into how Yevgeny Prigozhin managed to transform a small force of a few hundred into an army of thousands. But the seeds of the research for this book were planted years before Russia's intervention there in 2014. I was first exposed to Russia's complicated history while living in a run-down student dorm on Vasilyevsky Island as an exchange student at St. Petersburg State University in the mid-1990s. Enchanting and beautiful as it was, St. Petersburg was still visibly scarred by the Soviet legacy. Gripped by mob culture and rampant corruption yet steeped in deep artistic traditions, the city left a lasting impression on me.

I later gained a deeper understanding of how Putin's ambitions played out on the global stage when I traveled on a reporting fellowship to Georgia and Azerbaijan as an aspiring foreign correspondent in 2004. I also saw up close how the Russian way of war played out in Afghanistan, where I covered the US-led intervention there, first for the *Washington Post* and then for the International Crisis Group, a think tank focused on conflict prevention. Those experiences and many others inspired me to begin researching the origins of the Wagner Group in early 2018, just after Wagner's fateful battle with US special forces near the Conoco gas plant in Syria exposed anew the strange relationship between Putin and Prigozhin.

That is how I found myself in the summer of 2018 staring at a laptop for hours on end in the darkened conference room of a London hotel with a group of total strangers digging through social media posts for hints of how the Wagner Group connected to Putin's strategic ambitions. That weeklong training with Eliot Higgins and his team at Bellingcat quickly turned a bit of curiosity seeking into an obsession.

At the time, Washington was only just starting to wake up to the scale of the threat to international security from Russia's export of mercenary muscle to autocratic regimes. When it came to understanding how Prigozhin's paramilitary came to figure so prominently in Russia's grand strategy, much was left to the imagination or, in rare cases, pure speculation without hard evidence.

Early on, however, many clues to how the Wagner Group built its brand were available online in the form of thousands of social media accounts of self-avowed Russian mercenaries on VKontakte, Telegram, Instagram, and YouTube. Many Concord network contractors also maintained accounts on Facebook and LinkedIn. Those accounts were important starting points.

But an inherent challenge in using social media to conduct research is that it is dependably distorted and online data is often ephemeral. With support from a team of gifted researchers and information scientists, I navigated around the obstacles the data presented, gaining an understanding over time about how Wagner grew into a global enterprise. In addition to publicly available information contained in the archive of twenty-five social media accounts collected by my colleagues at New America and Arizona State University from 2018 to 2023, I drew on media reporting, corporate registries, court records, customs records, ship- and plane-path data, and sanctions notices for my research. A substantial number of Wagner Group–linked social media channels have been archived on a dedicated project site: uncoveringwagner.org.

The most critical sources of information came from leaked email correspondence and travel and financial records from Prigozhin's interlocutors obtained by the Dossier Centre and shared with New America. A separate cache of leaked data files from Prigozhin's company Evro Polis and subsidiaries that I was granted access to by C4ADS, a DC-based research organization, was a vital source for gaining insights into how the Wagner Group organized its internal affairs and managed its relations with key stakeholders inside and outside of the Russian government. Leaked email correspondence shared online by the Distributed Denial of Secrets collective was also helpful; notable in this group are the Capital Legal Services and Dark Side of the Kremlin data sets. Combined with more than one hundred interviews conducted from 2018 to 2023 with sources in the Middle East, Africa, Ukraine, Russia, Europe, and the United States, all the above resources and those listed more fully in the notes section below formed a critical part of the research for this book. In many cases, those who agreed to speak to me did so on condition that their names would not be used because of safety concerns; those who agreed to speak on the record are noted in the citations.

Most books are the products of collaboration. This book is no different. Throughout the writing of this book, I have collaborated with many outstanding researchers, almost too many to count and thank here. But Ben Dalton tops the list. I am deeply indebted to him for his support throughout this endeavor. Ben worked with me on all phases of this book: cowriting analysis, sounding out ideas, digging deep into a torrent of data and documents, and recording and transcribing hours of interviews. His knowledge of Russian history, language, culture, and politics was invaluable. He cracked the code on Wagner phone book and calendar data, organized and conducted field research trips, spearheaded photo research, fact-checked, and edited portions of the book. He did it all with grace and good humor, all while leading our team as program manager at New America's Future Frontlines program.

Not enough can be said about the many fearless Russian and Ukrainian journalists, human-rights defenders, and research analysts who have blazed the trail in reporting on Vladimir Putin's repressive regime and how Yevgeny Prigozhin and the Wagner Group fit into Putin's geostrategic ambitions. The world owes a huge debt to the reporters and editors at *Meduza*, *Novaya Gazeta*,

The Insider, and *Fontanka* who daily risk their lives to expose Russia's dark side. Everyone who has ever written anything about the Wagner Group is standing on the shoulders of Denis Korotkov, Ilya Barabanov, Roman Badanin, Kirill Mikhailov, Roman Dobrokhotov, Yuriy Butusov, and Lilia Yapparova. The Dossier Centre team generously shared insights and information that would have otherwise remained hidden. I am grateful to all the above for their courageous work, sharp insights, and generous guidance.

The community of public-interest investigators, human-rights defenders, and independent researchers who have dedicated years to tracking Russian paramilitaries and to holding Putin's regime to account is a potent testament to the energizing force of speaking truth to power. I have benefited greatly from the work of several notable experts in the field, especially Natalie Coburn, Nathalia Dukhan, Christo Grozev, Eliot Higgins, Jack Margolin, Sorcha McLeod, Lou Osborn, Michael Sheldon, Kateryna Stepanenko, and expert researchers at Molfar in Kyiv and the Human Rights Center at UC–Berkeley.

In Kyiv I relied on the expert guidance of Bogdana Bondarenko and Dmytro Zolotukhin to help me navigate my way to the places and people who know the most about the toll that Russia has exacted on Ukraine. Maxim Skrypchenko at the Transatlantic Dialogue Center also provided expert advice and insights. Thanks also to Chris Miller for his generous spirit.

Clive Priddle at PublicAffairs is one of a kind. He is a tremendous editor, and he deserves considerable credit for taking a gamble on a first-time author caught up in the swirl of a story that took several sharp and sudden turns. I owe Clive a special debt for his patient guidance through the publishing process. I am also very grateful to Lara Heimert, senior vice president and publisher of the Basic Books Group, for putting her faith in me and for her enthusiastic support of the book. Thanks also to Anupama Roy-Chaudhury, Jamie Liefer, Ellie Wells, and the entire team at PublicAffairs for all their hard work.

My agent, Gail Ross at WME Agency, is as fierce as they come, and this book would not have seen the light of day without her. I am grateful to Gail for seeing this book through from start to finish and holding my hand all along the way.

It would have been impossible to progress without the wisdom and editorial talents of Vanessa Gezari, Narisara Murray, Susan Sachs, and Robert Templer, who each applied their keen eye to the many tangled knots in the narrative, coached me through rough patches in the writing process, and smoothed away the many rough edges.

The seeds of the research for this book grew out of a joint research project between Arizona State University and the New America Foundation on the future of proxy warfare in the twenty-first century. I count myself lucky to have been able to call both institutions my professional home since 2018.

At New America, I owe special thanks to Anne-Marie Slaughter, Peter Bergen, and Paul Butler for giving me the running room to pursue this challenging project. My colleagues on the Planetary Politics team, Heela Rasool-Ayub, Gordon LaForge, and Riley Rogerson, moved mountains to buy me the time needed to focus on writing; I am very grateful to them for it. Over the last several years, I have benefited from the work of several current and former project researchers at New America. Two standouts in this category are Jonathan Deer and Oliver Imhof, whose investigative skills helped illuminate many a dark corner in the story of the Wagner Group and Rusich. I have also been fortunate to work with a talented roster of student researchers from Arizona State, Princeton, and other universities. They will all understand why I have not expressly named them here, but they can trust that they have my utmost gratitude.

At Arizona State University, I am grateful to Daniel Rothenberg, Jeff Kubiak, and Alicia Ellis at the Future Security Initiative for backing me up on this long journey every step of the way. Michael Simeone and Shawn Walker at ASU's Information Competition Lab have been essential partners; their drive, smarts, and innovative approach to information science made it possible to crack the code hidden in countless terabytes of data collected on the Wagner Group and Rusich over the years. Carolyn Forbes provided sage advice throughout, friendship, and good company. Tom Taylor contributed substantially to the early phases of the research.

The incredible team of researchers and data scientists at C4ADS made the deep dive into the internal workings of the Wagner Group possible. The cache of records and documents they have compiled over the years from Yevgeny Prigozhin's Concord network was an essential resource. Thanks especially goes to Hugh Bradshaw, Denise Sprimont-Vasquez, Varun Vira, Jack Ziebel, and their colleagues at C4ADS, all of whom helped me navigate and plumb the depths of Russia's illicit networks.

Portions of this book evolved out of a series of columns and articles I wrote for the *World Politics Review*. Thanks to Judah Grunstein and Hampton

Stephens for giving me the space to tease out the threads of the Wagner Group's evolution.

Friends and family are the ones who make it possible to push through the ups and downs of writing a book. You can never really thank them enough for all that they do for you. For all the reasons that they already know, I am not naming them here, but I hope they also know I am eternally grateful for the strength, support, and inspiration they provide me every day.

While I am deeply grateful to the many individuals who provided guidance and support during the writing of this book, any errors or shortcomings in this work are entirely my own.

NOTES

PROLOGUE

1. "Breaking: Terrifying Footage of Russians Torturing Prisoner with Sledge Hammer," Funker530.com, June 30, 2017, https://funker530.com/prisoner-sledge-hammer.

2. Interview with Kirill Mikhailov, March 2020.

3. Conflict Intelligence Team, Facebook post, June 30, 2017, www.facebook.com/CITeam .org/posts/815128818640097.

CHAPTER 1: BANDIT CITY

1. Ilya Davlyatchin, "The Stormy Youth of the Kremlin Restaurateur" ("Бурная молодость «кремлевского ресторатора»"), *Rosbalt*, September 21, 2018, www.rosbalt.ru/piter/2018 /09/21/1733712.html, archived version at archive.is/wip/mWBaC; "Prigozhin's Criminal Past Straight from the Source," *Meduza*, June 29, 2021, https://meduza.io/en/feature/2021/06/29 /prigozhin-s-criminal-past-straight-from-the-source.

2. Davlyatchin, "Stormy Youth."

3. Andrei Zakharov, Katya Arenina, Ekaterina Reznikova, and Mikhail Rubin, "Chef and Chief," *Proekt Media*, July 12, 2023, www.proekt.media/en/portrait-en/evgeny-prigozhin.

4. "Prigozhin's Criminal Past, Straight from the Source," *Meduza*, June 29, 2021, www .meduza.io/en/feature/221/06/29/prigozhin-s-criminal-past-straight-from-the-source.

5. "Who Is Yevgeny Prigozhin: Confession of Cellmates and Classmates of an Odious Businessman" ("Кто такой Евгений Пригожин: исповедь сокамерников и одноклассников одиозного бизнесмена"), *Antimafia*, November 20, 2022, www.antimafia.se/news/11651-kto _takoj_evgenij_prigohin_icpovedj_sokamernikov_i_odnoklassnikov_odioznogo_biznesmena.

6. "Address by Mikhail Gorbachev at the UN General Assembly Session (Excerpts), December 7, 1988," Wilson Center, https://digitalarchive.wilsoncenter.org/document/address -mikhail-gorbachev-un-general-assembly-session-excerpts.

7. Philip Short, *Putin* (New York: Henry Holt, 2022), 90–92.

8. Leigh Baldwin and Sean Williams, "Follow the Leader," *Atavist*, June 2022, www.magazine .atavist.com/follow-the-leader-nazi-putin-sonntag-cold-war.

9. Anastasia Yakoreva, Anastasia Napalkova, and Ilya Rozhdestvensky, "A Restaurateur and His Students: Who Supplies 90% of Meals to Moscow Schools" ("Ресторатор и его ученики: кто поставляет 90% обедов в московские школы"), RBC.com, July 18, 2016, www.rbc.ru /business/18/07/2016/57852f819a7947410f6bc75b; Zakharov, Arenina, Reznikova, and Rubin, "Chef and Chief."

10. Yakoreva, Napalkova, and Rozhdestvensky, "Restaurateur and His Students."

11. Details of Feoktistov's biography and his connections to Mirilashvili are recounted in several online Russian publications. Mirilashvili was apparently called as a witness in a legal case involving Feoktistov in 2002. See "The Russian Video Affair" ("Дело о "Русском видео"),

FLB, June 21, 2000, www.flb.ru/info/18936.html; and "Feka Uses a Woman as a Punching Bag" ("Фека использовал женщину в качестве боксерской груши"), *Kommersant*, March 6, 2002, www.kommersant.ru/doc/565689.

12. "I Paid Bandits $100 per Stall" ("С каждого ларька платил по 100 долларов бандитам"), *812 Online*, February 28, 2011, web.archive.org/web/20120604170042/http://www.online812.ru/2011/02/28/014.

13. "I Paid Bandits $100 per Stall."

14. Shirit Avitan Cohen, "'After All That I Suffered in the USSR, How Can I Be Accused of Wanting a Dictatorship Here?,'" *Israel Hayom*, September 18, 2023, www.israelhayom.com/2023/09/18/after-all-i-that-i-suffered-in-the-ussr-i-am-now-accused-of-wanting-a-dictatorship-here.

15. Cohen, "'After All That I Suffered.'"

16. Vadim Volkov, *Violence Entrepreneurs: The Use of Force in the Making of Russian Capitalism* (Ithaca, NY: Cornell University Press, 2002).

17. There is some evidence to suggest that Troshev may have crossed paths on more than one occasion with an Afghan army veteran named Sergey Shabodo, one of Prigozhin's earliest business partners and an active leader of St. Petersburg's vibrant veterans' movement. See Adolph Putler (*sic*), "Is Putin's Friend Poisoning Children?" ("Друг Путина травит детей?"), *Newsland*, November 1, 2011, www.newsland.com/post/835353-drug-putina-travit-detei.

18. A historical association of the 70th Separate Guards Motor Rifle Brigade published an unofficial biography of Troshev several years after news of his association with the Wagner Group became public. An archived version can be found at archive.ph/ZuzM6#selection-4621.36-4621.48.

19. Rodric Bratithwaite, *Afghantsy: The Russians in Afghanistan 1979–89* (London: Profile, 2011), 122–129.

20. Steven Erlanger, "In St. Petersburg Fight over Power and Property," *New York Times*, April 27, 1992.

21. Sobchak's daughter Ksenia Sobchak reconstructed her father's last days in office in a 2018 feature documentary directed by Vera Krichevskaya called *The Case* (Дело Собчака). Sobchak's speech was memorialized in the film.

22. *U.S. Assistance to the Former Soviet Union 1991–2001: A History of Administration and Congressional Action*, Congressional Research Service, January 15, 2002.

23. Thomas L. Friedman, "As Food Airlift Starts, Baker Hints U.S. May Play Role in Ruble Fund," *New York Times*, February 11, 1992, www.nytimes.com/1992/02/11/world/as-food-airlift-starts-baker-hints-us-might-agree-to-role-in-a-ruble-fund.html.

CHAPTER 2: THE OLD CUSTOMS HOUSE

1. Vladimir Putin, *First Person* (New York: Hachette, 2000), 81–82.

2. Harald Malmgren, "What the West Gets Wrong About Putin," *UnHerd*, January 13, 2022, www.unherd.com/2022/01/what-the-west-gets-wrong-about-putin.

3. Putin, *First Person*, 81–82.

4. "Investigation: How Putin's Personal Chef Came to Feed the Army for 92 Million Rubles" ("Расследование: как личный кулинар Путина накормит армию за 92 млрд рублей"), *Forbes.ru*, March 17, 2003, www.forbes.ru/kompanii/potrebitelskii-rynok/235779-rassledovanie-kak-lichnyi-kulinar-putina-nakormit-rossiiskuyu-a?page=0,2.

5. The late Russia scholar Karen Dawisha and Russian journalist Masha Gessen described details of the scandal in their books as recounted and documented by St. Petersburg City Council member Marina Sal'ye. See Dawisha, *Putin's Kleptocracy: Who Owns Russia?* (New York: Simon and Schuster, 2015), 106–126; and Gessen, *The Man Without a Face: The Unlikely Rise of Vladimir Putin* (New York: Riverhead, 2012), 116–119.

6. Dawisha, *Putin's Kleptocracy*, 111–113.

7. "Timchenko, Gennady Nikolaiyevich (bio)" ("Тимченко, Геннадий Николаевич"), TASS, www.tass.ru/encyclopedia/person/timchenko-gennadiy-nikolaevich.

8. "In St. Petersburg, They Shot at Sobchak's Companion, Narusova and Mirilashvili" ("В Петербурге стреляли в компаньона Собчака, Нарусовой и Мирилашвили"), *Fontanka*, December 17, 2012, www.fontanka.ru/2012/12/17/174.

9. "Misha Mirilashvili Returns to His Roots" ("Михаил Мирилашвили возвращается. К истокам"), *Fontanka*, January 22, 2009, www.fontanka.ru/2009/01/22/011.

10. Boris Berezovsky, "New Repatriation: What Is to Be Done?" ("Новый передел"), *Kommersant*, July 24, 2003, www.kommersant.ru/doc/398799.

11. Samtrest Factory website—an archived version of the history page can be found at web .archive.org/web/20010203054900/http://www.samtrest.spb.ru/index1.htm.

12. Mirilashvili contended in a 2023 interview with Israel Haysom that business disputes with Prigozhin led to the division of several commonly held companies after Russian authorities detained Mirilashvili on kidnapping charges in 2001. See Shirit Avitan Cohen, "'After All That I Suffered in the USSR, How Can I Be Accused of Wanting a Dictatorship Here?,'" *Israel Hayom*, September 18, 2023, www.israelhayom.com/2023/09/18/after-all-i-that-i-suffered-in -the-ussr-i-am-now-accused-of-wanting-a-dictatorship-here.

13. Corporate-registry records for Nevsky Union LLC listed Prigozhin as a stakeholder until 2019; see checko.ru/company/nevsky-soyuz-1027806064549.

14. Nina Petlyanova, "Putin's Personal Chef's Recipe for Success" ("Рецепт успеха личного повара Путина"), *Novaya Gazeta*, October 14, 2011, novayagazeta.ru/articles/2011 /10/14/46298-retsept-uspeha-lichnogo-povara-putina.

15. Yuri Felshtinsky and Vladimir Pribylovsky, *The Corporation: Russia and the KGB in the Age of President Putin* (New York: Encounter, 2009), 88–89, 87.

16. Dawisha, *Putin's Kleptocracy*, 73–78.

17. Felshtinsky and Pribylovsky, *Corporation*, 226–227.

18. Sergey Ochkivsky, "The Revival of the Fleet Is the Key to the Stability of Russia's Development: Competition and the Market," *St. Petersburg Offers* 4, no. 60 (2013): 74–85, https://web .archive.org/web/20131029193756/http://www.zerkalospb.ru/arhiv/2011/ofeers_03_11.pdf.

19. Anatoly Sobchak, "How Did Russia Lose Its Fleet in the Baltic and Who Is to Blame?" ("Морского торгового флота России на Балтике—Как Россия потеряла флот на Балтике и кто в этом виноват?"), *Moskovskaya Novosti*, June 10, 1998, archived version at web.archive.org /web/20131029211741/http://datarhiv.ru/51/85.

20. Vadim Volkov, *Violence Entrepreneurs: The Use of Force in the Making of Russian Capitalism* (Ithaca, NY: Cornell University Press, 2002), 131.

21. Ruslan Gorevoi, "Impex-55-Crimea—the Cradle of the RDC" («Импэкс-55-Крым» — колыбель РДК), *Ostrov Krym*, 2000, https://web.archive.org/web/20161121041609/http: //ok.archipelag.ru/part1/impeks-55.htm.

22. Tony Wesolowsky, "Leonid Kravchuk, First President of Independent Ukraine, Dead at 88," Radio Free Europe/Radio Liberty, May 10, 2022, www.rferl.org/a/ukraine-leonid -kravchuk-obituary/31843390.html.

23. Peter Daniel DiPaola, "Criminal Time Bomb: An Examination of the Effect of the Russian Mafia on the Newly Independent State of the Former Soviet Union," *Indiana Journal of Global Legal Studies* 4, no. 1, article 9, supranote 8, 146.

24. See Gear's online biography at tony-gear.ru, archived version at https://archive.ph /wip/dlPDu; and "Ресторанное путешествие длиною в жизнь" ("The Restaurant Journey of a Lifetime"), Peterburg2, August 18, 2017, https://peterburg2.ru/articles/restorannoe -puteshestvie-dlinoyu-v-zhizn-32145.html.

25. "Attention to Detail: Restaurateur Tony Gear Explained How Prigozhin Created the 'Old Customs House'" ("Внимание к мелочам: ресторатор Тони Гир рассказал, как Пригожин

создал «Старую таможню»"), *Argumenty Nidely*, December 5, 2022, www.argumenti.ru
/society/2022/12/802433, archived version at https://archive.is/wip/hlX67.

26. "Attention to Detail."

CHAPTER 3: NEW ISLAND

1. "Michel Camdessus First Takes in the White Nights and Meets with Premier Ste-
pashin" ("Мишель Камдессю впервые увидел белые ночи и встретился с новым премьером
России"), *GazetaLenta.ru*, June 16, 1999, https://gazeta.lenta.ru/daynews/16-06-1999/20camdess
_Printed.htm.

2. Sharon LaFreniere, "Moscow May Get New Loans," *Washington Post*, June 17, 1999,
www.washingtonpost.com/archive/business/1999/06/17/moscow-may-get-new-loans
/a43f8b18-b42d-4ffd-a366-946b65cf2682.

3. Robert Mabro, "The Oil Price Crises of 1998–9 and 2008–9," Oxford Energy Forum, May
2009, www.oxfordenergy.org/wpcms/wp-content/uploads/2010/11/SP10-TheOilPriceCrisisof
1998-RMabro-1998.pdf.

4. "The Russian Crisis," paper prepared jointly by the secretariats of the United Nations Conference on Trade and Development and the United Nations Economic Commission for Europe,
Geneva, 1998, 8, supranote 4.

5. IMF, press release no. 98/31, "IMF Approves Augmentation of Russia Extended Arrangement and Credit Under CCFF; Activates GAB," July 20, 1998.

6. "Yevgeny Prigozhin—'Haute Couture Catering? That's Simple'" ("ЕВГЕНИЙ
ПРИГОЖИН: 'КЕЙТЕРИНГ ОТ КУТЮР? ЭТО ПРОСТО'"), *Viperson.ru*, May 19,
2008, https://viperson.ru/articles/evgeniy-prigozhin-keytering-ot-kutyur-eto-prosto, archived
version at https://archive.is/wip/YnEMo.

7. "Yevgeny Prigozhin—'Haute Couture Catering?'"

8. "I Paid Bandits $100 per Stall" ("С каждого ларька платил по 100 долларов бандитам"),
812 Online, February 28, 2011, web.archive.org/web/20120604170042/http://www.online812
.ru/2011/02/28/014.

9. Mike Eckel, "Two Decades on, Smoldering Questions About the Russian President's Vault
to Power," Radio Free Europe/Radio Liberty, August 7, 2019, www.rferl.org/a/putin-russia
-president-1999-chechnya-apartment-bombings/30097551.html.

10. Simon Shuster, "How the War on Terrorism Did Russia a Favor," *Time*, September 19,
2011, https://content.time.com/time/world/article/0,8599,2093529,00.html.

11. David Plotz, "Assessment: Condoleezza Rice, George W. Bush's Celebrity Adviser," *Slate*,
May 12, 2000, https://slate.com/news-and-politics/2000/05/condoleezza-rice.html.

12. Address by Michel Camdessus, Chairman of the Executive Board and Managing Director
of the International Monetary Fund, to the Board of Governors of the Fund, World Bank, September 28–30, 1999, www.imf.org/external/am/1999/speeches/pr03e.pdf.

13. Address by Michel Camdessus.

14. "Camdessus's 'Dear John Letter' Not Accepted with Good Grace by Russians," James-
town Foundation, https://jamestown.org/program/camdessuss-dear-john-letter-not-accepted
-with-good-grace-by-russians.

15. "Camdessus's 'Dear John Letter' Not Accepted."

16. Prigozhin's New Island restaurant was later sold to a Moscow-based company called
28th Gnome LLC, according to a website for the restaurant, which was renamed Notte Bianca.
See http://teplokhod.moscow/restoran-teploxod.html#restoran, archived version of the site at
https://archive.is/wip/GiUe8.

17. "Japanese Prime Minister Yoshiro Mori flew to St. Petersburg" ("Премьер-министр
Японии Иосиро Мори вылетел в Санкт-Петербург"), 1tv.ru, April 28, 2000, www.1tv.ru
/news/2000-04-28/289527-premier_ministr_yaponii_iosiro_mori_vyletel_v_sankt_peterburg.

18. "UN Calls for Chechnya Inquiry," *Guardian*, April 25, 2000, www.theguardian.com /world/2000/apr/26/chechnya.

19. "Developers Are Building Palaces and Pavilions" ("Рынок осваивает новый сегмент жилья"), *Delovoy Peterburg*, July 1, 2004, www.dp.ru/a/2004/07/01/Developeri_strojat_dvorci.

20. Nick Peyton Walsh, "Russian Super-Rich Turn Back the Clock in Palatial Fashion," *Guardian*, August 28, 2004, www.theguardian.com/world/2004/aug/27/russia.nickpatonwalsh1.

21. Masha Kaminskaya, "Prosecutors Formally Charge Mirilashvili," *St. Petersburg Times*, February 2, 2001, archived version at https://web.archive.org/web/20140306043935/http: //sptimes.ru/index.php?action_id=2&story_id=14216.

22. Shirit Avitan Cohen, "'After All That I Suffered in the USSR, How Can I Be Accused of Wanting a Dictatorship Here?,'" *Israel Hayom*, September 18, 2023, www.israelhayom.com/2023 /09/18/after-all-i-that-i-suffered-in-the-ussr-i-am-now-accused-of-wanting-a-dictatorship-here.

23. "Yevgeny Prigozhin—'Haute Couture Catering?'"

24. An annotated biography of Prigozhin included in a leaked cache of documents from Capital Legal Services (CLS), a Russian firm hired by Prigozhin, listed the names of no fewer than fifty global leaders who attended state dinners hosted by Prigozhin, among them China's Communist Party chairman Hu Jintao, Prince Albert of Monaco, Canadian prime minister Jacques Chretien, Indonesian president Megawati Sukarnoputri, Finnish president Tarja Halonen, and Qatar prime minister Hamad bin Jaber Al Thani. The document surfaced in a cache distributed by the website Digital Denial of Secrets and has been widely cited in the press; see https: //ddosecrets.com/article/capital-legal-services.

CHAPTER 4: GUNS, GAS, AND OIL

1. "Where and How the Presidents Played" ("Где и как гуляли президенты"), *Komsomolskaya Pravda*, June 2, 2003, www.spb.kp.ru/daily/23042.5/110721.

2. "Rich People of St. Petersburg: Yevgeny Prigozhin" ("Богатые люди Петербурга: Евгений Пригожин"), *Delovoy Peterburg*, March 18, 2009, www.dp.ru/a/2009/03/18/Bogatie _ljudi_Peterburga.

3. Peter Baker, "Russia Defends Trade Deal with Iraq," *Washington Post*, August 20, 2002.

4. Gregory Feifer, "Russia: Putin Says Russia Should Become 'Great Power,'" Radio Free Europe/Radio Liberty, May 16, 2003, www.rferl.org/a/1103255.html.

5. Peter Baker and Susan Glasser, *Kremlin Rising: Putin's Russia and the End of Revolution* (Washington, DC: Potomac, 2007), 227.

6. "Gazeta.ru: Iraqi Army Trained by Russian Generals" ("Газета.Ru: Иракскую армию обучали российские генералы"), *Lenta.ru*, April 3, 2003, https://lenta.ru/news/2003/04/03 /generals.

7. Joseph L. Galloway, "Two Former Soviet Army Generals Helped Saddam with War Strategy," Knight-Ridder Newspapers, May 24, 2007, www.mcclatchydc.com/latest-news /article24436009.html.

8. Martin Sieff, "A Russian View of the War," UPI, March 31, 2003, www.upi.com/Defense -News/2003/03/31/A-Russian-view-of-the-war/23721049134006.

9. Ariel Cohen, "U.S.-Russia Relations Threatened by Iraq Arms Sales," Heritage Foundation, April 1, 2003, www.heritage.org/europe/report/us-russian-relations-threatened-iraq-arms-sales.

10. Igor Popov, "Soldiers for Rent" ("Солдаты напрокат"), *Forbes.ru*, September 3, 2010, https://archive.ph/UQOhl#selection-1615.367-1615.374.

11. Details about the Anti-Terror ownership structure can be found in Russian corporate registries; see ООО ЦЕНТР АНТИТЕРРОР (Anti-Terror Oryol Center), registration tax identification number 5753036460, https://spark-interfax.ru/orlovskaya-oblast-orel/ooo-tsentr -antiterror-inn-5753036460-ogrn-1055753015207-39509adcbb1d4e93be02dc4913f79198.

12. Sergey Isakov's dealings in Iraq and the connections between Rosneft and the Russian

Engineering Company are detailed in US government investigations into corruption in the oil-for-food program; see "Oil for Influence: How Saddam Hussein Used Oil to Reward Politicians Under the United Nations Oil-for-Food Program," Hearing on the Permanent Subcommittee on Investigations, Committee on Homeland Security and Government Affairs, United States Senate, May 17, 2005, https://archive.org/stream/gov.gpo.fdsys.CHRG-109shrg21438/CHRG-109shrg21438_djvu.txt.

13. Ivan Konovalov and Oleg Valetsky, *The Evolution of Private Military Companies* (*Эволюция частных военных компаний*) (Tsentr Strategichesky Konyunktury, 2013), 66–67.

14. Independent Committee into the UN Oil-for-Food Program, "Manipulation of the Oil-for-Food Program by the Iraqi Regime" ("Volcker Report"), October 27, 2005, 351–352, https://amlawdaily.typepad.com/amlawdaily/files/paul_volckers_final_oilforfood_report.pdf.

15. "Trade in Russian Weapons on the World Market" ("Торговля российским оружием на мировом рынке"), Scientific Information Agency—Fatherland Research, 2010, http://old.nasledie.ru/voenpol/14_1/article.php?art=23.

16. Yuri Felshtinsky and Vladimir Pribylovsky, *The Corporation: Russia and the KGB in the Age of President Putin* (New York: Encounter, 2009), 236.

17. Stephen J. Blank, "Rosoboroneksport: Arms Sales and the Structure of the Russian Defense Industry," Carlisle, PA: Strategic Studies Institute, January 2007, 7.

18. "Investigation: How Putin's Personal Chef Came to Feed the Army for 92 Million Rubles" ("Расследование: как личный кулинар Путина накормит армию за 92 млрд рублей"), *Forbes.ru*, March 17, 2003, www.forbes.ru/kompanii/potrebitelskii-rynok/235779-rassledovanie-kak-lichnyi-kulinar-putina-nakormit-rossiiskuyu-a?page=0,2.

19. "On the Day of the 300th Anniversary of St. Petersburg, Vladimir Putin Gave an Interview to the City's Media" ("В день 300-летия Санкт-Петербурга Владимир Путин дал интервью городским средствам массовой информации"), Kremlin.ru, May 27, 2003, http://special.kremlin.ru/events/president/news/30199.

20. "Trezzini House Is Being Reconstructed for an Eighth Time" ("Дом Трезини реконструируют по восьмому кругу"), *Fontanka*, September 28, 2010, www.fontanka.ru/2010/09/28/111; "Restaurateur Prigozhin Reconstructs Trezzini's House in St. Petersburg into a Hotel" ("Ресторатор Пригожин реконструирует дом Трезини в Петербурге под отель"), *RIA Novosti*, October 1, 2010, https://ria.ru/20101001/281086299.html.

21. "I Paid Bandits $100 per Stall" ("С каждого ларька платил по 100 долларов бандитам"), *812 Online*, February 28, 2011, web.archive.org/web/20120604170042/http://www.online812.ru/2011/02/28/014.

22. Richard Sakwa, *Putin and the Oligarch: The Khodorkovsky-Yukos Affair* (New York: I.B. Tauris, 2014).

23. David Hoffman, *The Oligarchs* (New York: PublicAffairs, 2002), 100–126.

24. Sakwa, *Putin and the Oligarch*, 175.

25. Igor Danchenko and Clifford Gaddy, "The Mystery of Vladimir Putin's Dissertation," Brookings Institution, March 30, 2006, www.brookings.edu/wp-content/uploads/2012/09/Putin-Dissertation-Event-remarks-with-slides.pdf.

26. Fiona Hill and Clifford G. Gaddy, *Mr. Putin: Operative in the Kremlin* (Washington, DC: Brookings Institution Press, 2013), 159–162, 253–254.

27. Cindy Hurst, "The Militarization of Gazprom," *Military Review*, September-October 2010, 61.

28. Hurst, "Militarization of Gazprom."

29. Interview with Mikhail Khodorkovsky, London, June 2022.

30. Sanshiro Hosaka, "Putin's Counterintelligence State: The FSB's Penetration of State and Society and Its Implications for Post–24 February Russia," International Centre for Defence and Security, Estonian Foreign Policy Institute, December 2022, 3, 15.

CHAPTER 5: THE LAST SUPPER

1. Adela Suliman, "George W. Bush Recalls Dinner Served by Wagner's Prigozhin: 'I Survived,'" *Washington Post*, September 12, 2023, www.washingtonpost.com/world/2023/09/12/george-w-bush-prigozhin-dinner-russia.

2. Irina Tumakova, "Lunch of Silence" ("Обед молчания"), *Novaya Gazeta*, November 26, 2019, https://novayagazeta.ru/articles/2019/11/26/82879-obed-molchaniya.

3. Ilya Barabanov and Denis Korotkov, *Наш Бизнес Смерть (Our Business Is Death)* (StraightForward Foundation, 2024), 73–74.

4. Nick Paton Walsh and Patrick Wintour, "Putin: Don't Lecture Me About Democracy," *Guardian*, July 15, 2006, www.theguardian.com/world/2006/jul/16/g8.patrickwintour.

5. Candace Rondeaux, "A New Direction in Energy: A Pipeline to Promise, or a Pipeline to Peril," *St. Petersburg Times*, May 15, 2005, www.tampabay.com/archive/2005/05/15/a-new-direction-in-energy-a-pipeline-to-promise-or-a-pipeline-to-peril.

6. "Russia Cuts Ukraine Gas Supplies," *BBC News*, January 1, 2006, http://news.bbc.co.uk/2/hi/europe/4572712.stm.

7. "Gazprom Threatens to Cut Gas to Georgia," Radio Free Europe/Radio Free Liberty, November 7, 2006, www.rferl.org/a/1072571.html.

8. Interview with Robert Hamilton, January 2021.

9. "Putin Explained Why the Kosovo Precedent Is Scary" ("Путин объяснил, чем страшен прецедент Косово"), *Korrespondent.net*, February 22, 2008, https://korrespondent.net/world/russia/383916-putin-obyasnil-chem-strashen-precedent-kosovo.

10. Matt Spetalnick, "Bush Vows to Press for Ukraine, Georgia in NATO," Reuters, April 1, 2008, www.reuters.com/article/us-nato-ukraine-bush-idUSL0141706220080401.

11. Charles Glover, *Black Wind, White Snow: The Rise of Russia's New Nationalism* (New Haven, CT: Yale University Press, 2016), 307.

12. Glover, *Black Wind, White Snow*, 307.

13. "Alexander Dugin: 'We Came as Supporters of the Independence of South Ossetia, and We Will Leave It as Fanatics,'" *sojcc.ru*, June 30, 2008, https://web.archive.org/web/20090703055936/http://sojcc.ru/rus/1148.html.

14. Two of the most authoritative accounts on Dugin's role in the rise of Neo-Eurasianism and right-wing ultranationalism in Russia are Glover, *Black Wind, White Snow*; and Marlene Laruelle, *Russian Eurasianism: An Ideology of Empire* (Baltimore: Johns Hopkins University Press), 2008.

15. "The Road to War in Georgia: The Chronicle of a Caucasian Tragedy," *Der Spiegel*, August 25, 2008.

16. The original Redut Antiterror site can be found at http://redut-czentr.narod.ru; the archived version is at https://archive.is/87g5H.

17. A user of Desantura.ru named Scorpion218 provided details about Redut's formation and legal standing in a November 2008 post on a blog followed by a number of Redut members: https://club.desantura.ru/user/184/blog, archived version at https://archive.is/wip/F6Nrn. In interviews and written testimony made public in 2023, Igor Salikov, a veteran of Redut and the Wagner Group, described Redut as a training consultancy that was established by the GRU for the purposes of recruiting and mobilizing veterans for special-purpose units and deployments.

18. Denis Korotkov, "Без «Щита»," *Novaya Gazeta*, July 28, 2019.

19. "In Memory of P. Popovskikh Rus 06 02 18" ("Памяти П Поповских Рус 06 02 18"), YouTube, www.youtube.com/watch?v=tosrkhSuX78.

20. Makhotkin memorialized some of his adventures working as a soldier of fortune in Iraq here: http://artofwar.ru/m/mahotkin_a_w. His email address at one point was listed as redut89@yandex.ru, the same one that was listed on the private-military company's

website. This corporate-registration file lists Makhotkin as the director of the veterans' association and of a firm called Redut-Consulting LLC: www.rusprofile.ru/person/makhotkin-av -402000562396.

21. *Spetsnaz* veterans who had fought with a variety of paratrooper units, including the 2nd Special Purpose Brigade—the same GRU detachment that Dmitry Utkin commanded for years before forming the Wagner Group—made up the core of Redut when it was officially launched as a training center.

22. Dale Hespring, "Tightening the Reins: Russian Military Reform and Anatoly Serdyukov," *Journal of Problems of Post Communism* 55, no. 6 (November/December 2008): 28.

23. Ariel E. Cohen and Colonel Robert E. Hamilton, "The Russian Military and the Georgia War: Lessons and Implications," Strategic Studies Institute, June 2011, 19–21.

24. Cohen and Hamilton, "Russian Military and the Georgia War," 10.

25. Mark Galeotti, *Putin's Wars: From Chechnya to Ukraine* (London: Osprey, 2022), 124.

26. Cohen and Hamilton, "Russian Military and the Georgia War," 35–37.

CHAPTER 6: THE NEW LOOK

1. Mikhail Barabanov, Konstantin Makienko, and Ruslan Pukhlov, "Military Reform: Toward the New Look of the Russian Army," Valdai Discussion Club, Moscow, July 2012, 15, http://vid1.rian.ru/ig/valdai/Military_reform_eng.pdf.

2. A videotaped excerpt of General Kvachkov's speech and others at the rally can be found here: https://voensud.ru/forum28/topic1422-90.html.

3. Soyuz Desyantnikov Rossii (Union of Paratroopers of Russia), "Union of Paratroopers of Russia—We Are 10 Years Old," http://sdrvdv.ru/istoricheskaya-spravka, archived version at https://archive.is/wip/gMKSP.

4. "Defense Minister Anatoly Serdyukov Swore at the Head of the Airborne Forces School for Building a Temple and Ordered His Dismissal," *Novy Den'*, October 18, 2010, https://newdaynews.ru/incidents/305014.html.

5. Viktor Myasnikov, "And, ruins of the chapel . . . ," *Nezavisimaya Gazeta*, October 19, 2010, www.ng.ru/politics/2010-10-19/3_kartblansh.html.

6. "Landing Force Will Block Rublovskoye Highway" ("Десантура перекроет Рублёвское шоссе"), *MR7.ru*, November 10, 2010, https://mr-7.ru/articles/2010/11/10/desantura-perekroet -rubliovskoe-shosse.

7. Barabanov, Makienko, and Pukhlov, "Military Reform," 28.

8. Barabanov, Makienko, and Pukhlov, 27–29.

9. Jeffery Holacheck, "Russia's Shrinking Population and the Russian Military's HIV/ AIDS Problem," Atlantic Council, 2006, www.atlanticcouncil.org/wp-content/uploads/2006 /09/0609-HIV_Russian_Military-Holachek.pdf.

10. Michael Kofman, "Russian Performance in the Russo Georgian War Revisited," *War on the Rocks*, September 4, 2018, https://warontherocks.com/2018/09/russian-performance-in-the -russo-georgian-war-revisited/.

11. Vadim Solovyov, "Military Reform—2009–2012," *Nezavisimaya Gazeta*, December 12, 2008, https://nvo.ng.ru/forces/2008-12-12/1_reform.html.

12. "US Embassy Cables: Russia Is Virtual 'Mafia State,' Says Spanish Investigator," *Guardian*, December 2, 2010, www.theguardian.com/world/us-embassy-cables-documents/247712.

13. Ilya Zhegulev, "The President's Breadwinner" ("Кормилец президента"), *Forbes.ru*, March 2, 2013, www.forbes.ru/forbes/issue/2012-03-1/234794-kormilets-prezidenta.

14. "Putin, Medvedev Engage in Rare Public Split over Libya," Voice of America, March 21, 2011, www.voanews.com/a/putin-medvedev-engage-in-rare-public-split-over-libya-118399039 /136842.html.

15. Gleb Bryanski, "Putin Likens U.N. Libya Resolution to Crusades," *Reuters*, March 21, 2011, www.reuters.com/article/us-libya-russia/putin-likens-u-n-libya-resolution-to-crusades-id USTRE72K3JR20110321.

16. Michael McFaul, *From Cold War to Hot Peace* (Boston: Houghton Mifflin, 2018), 80–81.

17. "Clinton, Lavrov Push the Wrong Reset Button," *Reuters*, March 6, 2009, www.reuters .com/article/economy/clinton-lavrov-push-wrong-reset-button-on-ties-idUSN06402140.

18. "'Concord' Closed the Network 'Damn! Donald's' in St. Petersburg" ("'Конкорд' закрыл сеть 'Блин!Дональт's' в Петербурге"), *Restrano FF*, March 2012, https://restoranoff.ru/news /newsfeed/Konkord_zakriel_set_BlinDonalts_v_Peterburge.

19. "Trezzini House Reconstruction Is Stuck in the Eighth Circle of Hell" ("Дом Трезини реконструируют по восьмому кругу"), *Fontanka*, September 8, 2010, www.fontanka.ru /2010/09/28/111.

20. Nadezhda Zaitseva, "Concord Is Suing Smolny" ("«Конкорд» судится со Смольным"), *Vedemosti.ru*, www.vedomosti.ru/newspaper/articles/2011/04/07/konkord_suditsya_so_smol nym.

21. Dmitry Sinochkin, "On the Asphalt: St. Petersburg Absorbs Low-Rise Buildings" ("На асфальте: Петербург поглощает малоэтажку"), *Vedomosti.ru*, June 9, 2008, www.vedomosti.ru /newspaper/articles/2008/06/09/na-asfalte-peterburg-pogloschaet-malojetazhku.

22. Zhegulev, "President's Breadwinner."

23. "Working Visit of Vladimir Putin to the Northwestern Federal District," *Sputnik*, September 10, 2010, https://sputnikmediabank.com/media/763585.html?context =list&list_sid=list_63428.

24. Zhegulev, "President's Breadwinner."

25. Zhegulev, "President's Breadwinner"; Elena Dombrova and Alexandra Kreknina, "Yevgeny Prigozhin Opens a Gourmet Dining Room," *Vedomosti*, March 10, 2011, www.vedomosti.ru /business/articles/2011/03/10/stolovaya_vysokoj_kuhni.

26. "Russian Defense Ministry Official Charged with Fraud," *Reuters*, November 22, 2012, www.reuters.com/article/us-russia-embezzlement-idUSBRE8AM0MY20121123.

27. Michael Crowley, "Why Putin Hates Hillary," *Politico*, July 25, 2016, www.politico.com /story/2016/07/clinton-putin-226153.

28. Michael Weiss, "Corruption and Cover-Up in the Kremlin: The Anatoly Serdyu-kov Case," *Atlantic*, January 29, 2013, www.theatlantic.com/international/archive/2013/01 /corruption-and-cover-up-in-the-kremlin-the-anatoly-serdyukov-case/272622.

29. Maria Livadina, "The Rise and Fall of Sergey Shoigu," *Novaya Gazeta Europe*, July 4, 2024, https://novayagazeta.eu/articles/2023/07/04/the-rise-and-fall-of-sergey-shoigu-en.

30. "Putin Fires Defense Minister, Names Shoigu to Replace Him," *RFE/RL*, November 6, 2012, www.rferl.org/a/putin-fires-russia-defense-minister/24761953.html.

31. Tatiana Stanovaya, "Four Kinds of Crises for the Putin Regime—and the Begin-ning of Its End," Institute of Modern Russia, November 27, 2012, https://imrussia.org/en /politics/339-four-kinds-of-crises-for-the-putin-regimeand-the-beginning-of-its-end.

32. "Profile: Russia's New Military Chief Valery Gerasimov," *BBC News*, November 9, 2012, www.bbc.com/news/world-europe-20270111.

33. Andrei Kolesnikov, "As It Turns Out in the End, Life Has Changed Dramatically More Than Once" ("В конце концов, жизнь не раз круто менялась"), *Kommersant*, February 9, 2016, www.kommersant.ru/doc/2911780.

34. Kolesnikov, "As It Turns Out in the End."

35. Irek Murtazin, "The Defeat of Voentorg" ("Разгром Военторга"), *Novaya Gazeta*, November 8, 2012, https://novayagazeta.ru/articles/2012/11/08/52262-razgrom-voentorga.

CHAPTER 7: GERASIMOV'S GHOSTS

1. "Kremlin Seeks London Sanctions for Nigeria in Myre Seadiver Case," *PortNews*, March 25, 2013, https://portnews.ru/digest/print/12235/?backurl=/digest.

2. "Nigeria: Russia Seeks Release of Detained Sailors," *AllAfrica.com*, February 17, 2013, https://allafrica.com/stories/201302170087.html.

3. Tom Wallace and Farley Mesko, "The Odessa Network: Mapping Facilitators of Russian and Ukrainian Arms Transfers," C4ADS, September 13, 2013, 60, https://c4ads.org/wp-content/uploads/2013/09/TheOdessaNetwork.pdf.

4. Jack Margolin, *The Wagner Group: Inside Russia's Mercenary Army* (London: Reaktion, 2024), 55.

5. Gigi Lee and Fong Tak Ho, "Public Records Map Wagner Group's Hong Kong Connections," Radio Free Asia, June 27, 2023, www.rfa.org/english/news/china/wagner-hong-kong-06272023131737.html.

6. Ludmilla Danilova, "Russian Forces Seize Oil Tanker from Somali Pirates," Reuters, May 6, 2010, www.reuters.com/article/us-russia-tanker-pirates-idUSTRE64531520100506.

7. Sebastian Rotella, "Russian Politician Who Sent Millions to NRA Has Long History in Spain," *ProPublica*, January 19, 2018, https://www.propublica.org/article/russian-politician-who-reportedly-sent-millions-to-nra-has-long-history-in-spain.

8. Åse Gilje Østensen and Tor Bukkvoll, "Russian Use of Private Military and Security Companies: The Implications for European and Norwegian Security," Norwegian Defence Research Establishment, Chr. Michelesen Institute, September 11, 2018, 23, www.cmi.no/publications/file/6637-russian-use-of-private-military-and-security.pdf.

9. Andrei Bogatov shared details of his biography and made mention of his encounters with the French in Mitrovica, Kosovo, in an October 2022 television interview that was widely viewed as one of his first forays into electoral politics in Russia. "Герой России Андрей Богатов / Ангел русского духа" ("Hero of Russia Andrey Bogatov/Angel of the Russian Spirit"), YouTube, www.youtube.com/watch?v=NOZCZFfaPTM.

10. "Heil Petrovich!" ("«Хайль Петрович»"), Dossier Centre, April 10, 2023, https://dossier.center/utkin.

11. Gennady Zubov, "A Comrade in Arms Is Looking for Wagner" ("Вагнера ищет боевая подруга"), *Gazeta.ru*, December 16, 2016, www.gazeta.ru/social/2016/12/16/10431467.shtml?updated.

12. Zubov, "Comrade in Arms."

13. "Putin's Chef's Kisses of Death: Russia's Shadow Army's State-Run Structure Exposed," Bellingcat.com, August 14, 2020, www.bellingcat.com/news/uk-and-europe/2020/08/14/pmc-structure-exposed.

14. Former Wagner commander and Redut veteran Igor Salikov said in a December 2023 recorded interview with Vladimir Osechkin that Utkin talked about working in the private-military–security industry around 2010; the interview can be viewed at www.youtube.com/watch?v=GMpl2TPNqW8. Former Wagner fighter and ex-Redut Marat Gabidullin corroborated that timeline in a September 2023 interview.

15. The law states that "a mercenary shall be deemed to mean a person who acts for the purpose of getting a material reward, and who is not a citizen of the state in whose armed conflict or hostilities he participates, who does not reside on a permanent basis on its territory, and also who is not a person fulfilling official duties." Criminal Code of the Russian Federation, No. 63-FZ, June 13, 1996, www.wto.org/english/thewto_e/acc_e/rus_e/WTACCRUS48_LEG_6.pdf.

16. Vadim Volkov, "Russia's New 'State Corporations': Locomotives of Modernization or Covert Privatization Schemes?," PONARS Eurasia Policy Memo, No. 25, August 2008, 1–2, https://www.ponarseurasia.org/wp-content/uploads/attachments/pepm_025.pdf.

17. Vladimir Voronov and Anton Tsymbalov, "The Private Armies of Big Corporations," *Novaya Vremya*, December 24, 2007, https://newtimes.ru/articles/detail/5674.

18. Voronov and Tsymbalov, "Private Armies."

19. An archived version of the contacts page for KEAMSCO can be found at https://web.archive.org/web/20170227200509/http://www.keamsco.com/contactus.html.

20. Neova Holdings Ltd. counted as one of its affiliates a public joint-stock company called Novaem Group, a Russian energy-industry, pipe-making, and machine-building conglomerate formed from a merger of Sibenergomash, TM Engineering, Trubmash, and other Russian companies in 2009. Public records and company websites for several Novaem subsidiaries indicate that the holding-company conglomerate had links to multiple Russian-owned companies, including Technopromexport, a joint-stock engineering firm partially owned by Rostec. See "NOVAEM Group Became the Owner of Alapaevsk Metallurgical Plant OJSC" ("Группа НОВАЭМ стала собственником ОАО 'Алапаевский металлургический завод'"), *Altapres.ru*, February 17, 2011, https://altapress.ru/ekonomika/story/gruppa-novaem-stala-sobstvennikom-oao-alapaevskiy-metallurgicheskiy-zavod-63054, archived version at https://archive.is/wip/ahCua.

21. "Military Guru Gets 7 Year Prison Term for Passing Classified FSB Data to German Firm," TASS, July 2, 2020, https://tass.com/defense/1174011.

22. "A Private Army for the President: The Tale of Evgeny Prigozhin's Most Delicate Mission," *Bell*, January 31, 2019, https://en.thebell.io/a-private-army-for-the-president-the-tale-of-evgeny-prigozhin-s-most-delicate-mission/?ref=en.thebell.io.

23. "Putin Supported the Idea of Creating Private Military Companies in Russia" ("Путин поддержал идею создания в России частных военных компаний"), *RIA Novosti*, November 4, 2012, https://ria.ru/20120411/623227984.html.

24. Denis Korotkov, "Заложники Нигерии ждут коммандос от президента" ("Hostages of Nigeria Await Presidential Commandos"), *Fontanka*, February 25, 2013, www.fontanka.ru/2013/02/25/164.

25. Moran Security's run-in with Nigerian authorities emerged at the center of a legal dispute between Glencore and its Nigerian partner, Amazoil, in 2015, when the Nigerian oil company's head, Sir Og Amazu, filed a lawsuit in a British court alleging that Glencore failed to pay Amazu $5 million for his help in the Moran Security crew case. Amazu's claim against Glencore was later dismissed. But in an interview about the strange *Myre Seadiver* case several years later, Amazu said he believed that Glimer was registered in Cyprus. He further contended that the remainder of the payment he was due never came through despite multiple calls to Glencore's Moscow representatives. Amazu claimed that he was unable to find out more about Glimer, and there is very little listed about the company online beyond references to companies with the exact same name that appear to have links to energy firms in Russia and Slovakia. Glencore officials, in interviews given to the press shortly after Amazu filed suit several years after the fact, denied any wrongdoing and called the claim "baseless." See Javier Blass and Jesse Riseborough, "Nigerian Trader Says Glencore Failed to Pay for Rescue Help," *Bloomberg*, June 23, 2015, www.bloomberg.com/news/articles/2015-06-23/nigerian-trader-says-glencore-didn-t-pay-on-help-freeing-sailors?embedded-checkout=true.

26. Stephen Blank, "What Do the Zapad 2013 Exercises Reveal? (Part One)," *Eurasia Daily Monitor* 10, no. 177 (October 4, 2013), https://jamestown.org/program/what-do-the-zapad-2013-exercises-reveal-part-one.

27. Johan Norberg, "Training to Fight: Russia's Major Military Exercises 2011–2014," Swedish Defence Academy, December 2015, 23–37, www.foi.se/rest-api/report/FOI-R--4128--SE.

28. Blank, "What Do the Zapad 2013 Exercises Reveal?"

29. Valery Gerasimov, "The Value of Science in Prediction" ("Ценность науки в прогнозировании"), *Voenno-promyshlennyi Kur'er* 8, no. 476, February 27–March 3, 2013, https://web.archive.org/web/20140630012651/http://vpk-news.ru/sites/default/files/pdf/VPK_08_476.pdf.

30. Interview with Mark Galeotti, October 2023.

CHAPTER 8: SLAVONIC CORPS

1. An archived version of the application instructions on the Slavonic Corps website can be found at https://web.archive.org/web/20130918014923/http://slavcorps.org/ru/vakansii.

2. Evidence of the Hong Kong registration for Slavonic Corps is archived at https://archive.ph/UmLp8/image.

3. Andrei Troshev is listed as one of several beneficiary stakeholders in the Federal Complex Martial Arts and Tactical Army Shooting; see the listing of connections here: www.list-org.com/company/5648607/graph.

4. "Petersburg Sent Landsknechts to Syria" ("Ландскнехтов в Сирию послал Петербург"), *Fontanka*, October 20, 2013, www.fontanka.ru/2013/10/30/099; "The Investigation into Russia's First Mercenary Case Has Been Completed" ("Завершено расследование первого в России дела о наемниках"), *Isvestia*, August 6, 2014, https://iz.ru/news/574852.

5. "Petersburg Sent Landsknechts."

6. Denis Korotkov, "They Fought for Palmyra" ("Они сражались за Пальмиру"), *Fontanka*, March 29, 2016, www.fontanka.ru/2016/03/28/171.

7. Michael Weiss, "The Case of the Keystone Cossacks," *Foreign Policy*, November 21, 2013, https://foreignpolicy.com/2013/11/21/the-case-of-the-keystone-cossacks/; Ilya Barabanov and Denis Korotkov, *Наш Бизнес Смерть (Our Business Is Death)* (StraightForward Foundation, 2024), 46.

8. "Petersburg Sent Landsknechts."

9. A 2015 memo Prigozhin addressed to Sergey Shoigu detailed Prigozhin's involvement in the Syrian Express. C4ADS, Evro Polis and subsidiaries data holdings.

10. "Petersburg sent Landsknechts."

11. Denis Korotkov, "Without Shield" ("Без «Щита»"), *Novaya Gazeta*, July 29, 2019, https://novayagazeta.ru/articles/2019/07/28/81406-bez-schita.

12. Corporate-registry data associated with Yevgeny Sidorov's tax identification indicates that Sidorov launched Redut Security in 2019 after Moran Security Group was liquidated; see www.rusprofile.ru/person/sidorov-eg-503212225365.

13. The Russia-Syria Business Council website was shut down at some point after 2018; an archived version can be found at https://web.archive.org/web/20171027023232/https://www.srbc-sy.com/#home.

14. From January to June 2019, the author collaborated with Syrian researchers at the Omran Center for Strategic Studies on collecting data and interviews about Russian corporate interests and paramilitary operations in Syria.

15. "Russian Firm Signs Deal to Fix Iraq-Syria Pipeline," Reuters, March 26, 2008, www.reuters.com/article/russia-iraq-contract-idINL2673766420080326.

16. Ceren Kenar and Ragip Soylu, "Why Are Russian Engineers Working at an Islamic State-Controlled Gas Plant in Syria?," *Foreign Policy*, February 9, 2016, https://foreignpolicy.com/2016/02/09/why-are-russian-engineers-working-at-an-islamic-state-controlled-gas-plant-in-syria.

17. George Haswani, letter addressed to Ambassador Mark D Wallace, Counterextremism Project, March 23, 2015, www.counterextremism.com/sites/default/files/letter_hesco_03232015.pdf.

18. "Factbox—Syria's Energy Sector," Reuters, September 5, 2011, www.reuters.com/article/uk-syria-oil/factbox-syrias-energy-sector-idUKTRE7841PT20110905.

19. Viktor Feshchenko and Elena Shmeleva, "The Ministry of Emergency Situations Evacuated 481 People from Libya, of Which 330 Were Russian Citizens" ("МЧС эвакуировало из Ливии 481 человека, из них 330 граждан России"), *Rossikaya Gazeta*, February 28, 2011, https://rg.ru/2011/02/28/escape.html.

20. "Federal Law on Amendments to Certain Legislative Acts of the Russian Federation on the Issues of Creating a Mobilization Human Reserve," *Russkaya Gazeta*, January 1, 2013, www.rg.ru/documents/2013/01/11/reserv-dok.html.

21. "Syria War: What We Know About Douma 'Chemical Attack,'" *BBC News*, July 18, 2019, www.bbc.com/news/world-middle-east-43697084.

22. Max Fisher, "Samantha Power's Case for Striking Syria," *Washington Post*, September 7, 2013, www.washingtonpost.com/news/worldviews/wp/2013/09/07/samantha-powers-case-for-striking-syria.

23. "Answers to Questions from the Mass Media by Russian Foreign Minister Sergey Lavrov Summarizing the Results of His Participation in the 10th Conference of the Valdai Discussion Club, 18 September 2013," Russian Federation Ministry of Foreign Affairs, www.mid.ru/es/foreign_policy/news/1627532/?lang=en.

24. Interview with former US State Department official, June 2022.

25. Tom Wallace and Farley Mesko, "The Odessa Network: Mapping Facilitators of Russian and Ukrainian Arms Transfers," C4ADS, September 2013, 4, https://c4ads.org/reports/the-odessa-network.

CHAPTER 9: POLITE PEOPLE

1. Anders Åslund, *How Ukraine Became a Market Economy and Democracy* (Washington, DC: Peterson Institute for International Economics, 2009), 1.

2. Steven Lee Meyers, "Putin's Olympic Fever Dream," *New York Times*, January 22, 2014, www.nytimes.com/2014/01/26/magazine/putins-olympic-fever-dream.html.

3. Meyers, "Putin's Olympic Fever Dream"; Marissa Payne, "Gunned Down Russian Opposition Leader Boris Nemtsov Was Leading Critic of Sochi Olympics," *Washington Post*, February 28, 2015, www.washingtonpost.com/news/early-lead/wp/2015/02/28/gunned-down-russian-opposition-leader-boris-nemtsov-was-leading-critic-of-sochi-olympics.

4. Specifications for the *Palma de Sochi* also state that the boat was eight meters wide: www.vesselfinder.com/ru/vessels/details/9665839. Registry information for the *Palma de Sochi* can be found at https://fleetphoto.ru/vessel/36193, archived version at https://archive.ph/wip/YvNRI, additional photos at https://fleetphoto.ru/photo/428374/?vid=36193.

5. "Fate of the Summer Theater—Drama or Tragedy?" ("Судьба Летнего театра Сочи—драма или трагедия?"), *Sochi-24*, April 15, 2013, https://sochi-24.ru/obshestvo/sudba-letnego-teatra-sochi-drama-ili-tragediya.2013415.62273.html.

6. Ilya Barabanov and Denis Korotkov, *Наш Бизнес Смерть (Our Business Is Death)* (StraightForward Foundation, 2024), 74–75.

7. Independent analysis of Prigozhin's leaked calendar data found that he was in frequent contact with Dyumin, Vaino, and other Kremlin insiders during the 2012–2021 period. See also "Putin's Chef's Kisses of Death," Bellingcat.com, August 14, 2020, www.bellingcat.com/news/uk-and-europe/2020/08/14/pmc-structure-exposed.

8. An independent review of hundreds of leaked files from Prigozhin's Evro Polis company and its subsidiaries archived by the Washington-based research organization C4ADS and sampling analysis of the metadata embedded in several of those records revealed that a substantial number of documents created by Prigozhin and his employees contained markings suggesting a potential link to the Federal Agency for State Property Management (Федеральное агентство по управлению государственным). A 2021 lawsuit brought by Roszagransobstvennost (Росзагрансобственность), the state enterprise charged with managing federal assets abroad, against Evro Polis pertaining to the use of Russian federal property in Syria suggests that the link may be more than coincidental; see Дело NoA41-43516/21, Арбитражный суд Московской области, court decision entered on November 2, 2021, https://kad.arbitr.ru/Card/c66d6a52-f021-4a48-ae6d-63055463eec6. For details about Concord's dealings with the Presidential

Property Management Office, see "Firm Linked to Prigozhin to Make Money on Yunarmiya Supplies" ("Связанная со структурами Пригожина фирма заработает на поставках Юнармии сообщают «Открытые медиа»"), *Otkrytiye Media*, May 30, 2018, https://openmedia.io /investigation/kak-svyazannaya-s-prigozhinym-firma-mozhet-zarabotat-na-yunarmii.

9. "Andrey Bokarev Moved into Prigozhin's Estate" ("В усадьбу Пригожина заселился Андрей Бокарев"), *Antimafia*, December 28, 2023, https://antimafia.se/news/50039-v_ucad jbu_prigohina_zaselilsja_andrej_bokarev; Andrew Roth, "No-Fly Zone over Putin-linked Palace Is Due to NATO Spies, Says FSB," *Guardian*, January 27, 2021, www.theguardian.com /world/2021/jan/27/no-fly-zone-putin-linked-palace-navalny-due-to-nato-spying-says-fsb.

10. Denis Korotkov, "Concord Inherits Oboronservis" ("«Конкорд» наследует «Оборонсервису»"), *Fontanka*, June 14, 2014, www.fontanka.ru/2014/06/09/162.

11. "Putin on Sochi: I Would Very Much Like Sports Not to Be Marred by Politics," *RT.com*, January 19, 2014, www.rt.com/news/putin-journalists-olympics-gays-846.

12. "Second Deadly Blast in Russian City of Volgograd Kills at Least 14," *ABC News*, December 30, 2013, https://abcnews.go.com/Blotter/deadly-blast-russian-city-volgograd-kills-14/story ?id=21365802.

13. Andrei Soldatov, Irina Borogan, and Shaun Walker, "As Sochi Olympic Venues Are Built, So Are Kremlin's Surveillance Networks," *Guardian*, October 6, 2013, www.theguardian.com /world/2013/oct/06/sochi-olympic-venues-kremlin-surveillance.

14. Adam Radomyski, "Security of the Winter Olympics in Sochi," *Safety and Defense Scientific and Technical Journal* 7, no. 1 (June 13, 2021): 98.

15. "A Special Operations Forces Command Has Been Created in Russia" ("В России создали командование сил спецопераций"), *Lenta*, March 6, 2013, https://lenta.ru/news /2013/03/06/specops.

16. Roger McDermott, "Putin's Secret Force Multiplier," International Center for Defense and Security, May 5, 2016, https://icds.ee/en/putins-secret-force-multiplier-special-operations -forces.

17. Shaun Walker, "Ukraine's Former PM Rallies Protesters After Yanukovych Flees Kiev," *Guardian*, February 23, 2014, www.theguardian.com/world/2014/feb/22/ukraine -president-yanukovych-flees-kiev.

18. Igor Girkin, *Bosnian Diary* (Боснийский дневник). Archived version last accessed July 13, 2023, https://archive.org/details/20190731_20190731_1744.

19. For a thorough accounting of the biographies of Girkin, Borodai, and Kulygina, see Pierre Vaux and Michael Weiss, "Vile Bodies: How Fascist Cultists and Spooks Spearheaded Russia's War in Ukraine," Free Russia Foundation, 2023, https://thinktank.4freerussia.org/reports/vile-bodies.

20. Christo Grozev, "The Orthodox Crusaders—Part I," Christo's Blog, May 20, 2014, https://cgrozev.wordpress.com/2014/05/20/the-orthodox-crusaders-part-1/.

21. Grozev, "Orthodox Crusaders."

22. Grozev.

23. Catherine Belton, *Putin's People: How the KGB Took Back Russia and Then Took on the West* (New York: Farrar, Straus and Giroux, 2020), 419–420.

24. Belton, *Putin's People*, 421–422.

25. Christo Grozev, "The Orthodox Crusaders: An Overdue Prologue," Christo's Blog, May 28, 2014, https://cgrozev.wordpress.com/author/christogrozev/page/8.

26. D. S. Ryabushkin, "Crimea Events of 2014: Causes, Chronology, Consequences," *Journal of Slavic Military Studies* 35, no. 1 (2022): 122–131.

27. Mark Galeotti, *Armies of Russia's War in Ukraine* (Oxford: Osprey, 2019), 7.

28. U.S. House of Representatives, Subcommittee on Oversight and Investigations, "Hearing on the United Nations Oil-for-Food Program: Saddam Hussein's Use of Oil Allocations to Undermine Sanctions and the United Nations Security Council," May 16, 2005.

29. Candace Rondeaux, "Decoding the Wagner Group: Analyzing the Role of Private Military Security Contractors in Russian Proxy Warfare," *New America*, November 7, 2019; see also Roman Anin, Olesya Shmagun, and Jelena Vasic, "Ex-Spy Turned Humanitarian Helps Himself," OCCRP, November 4, 2015, www.occrp.org/en/investigations/4565-ex-spy-turned -humanitarian-helps-himself.

30. "The Restaurateur and His Students" ("Ресторатор и его ученики"), *RBC.ru*, July 8, 2016, www.rbc.ru/newspaper/2016/07/19/57852f819a7947410f6bc75b; see also "Yevgeny Prigozhin: The Way from Prison to Russian State-Building," *Molfar.com*, https://molfar.com/en /blog/yevgeny-prigozhin.

31. Ryabushkin, "Crimea Events of 2014," 135.

32. "Firm Linked to Prigozhin to Make Money on Yunarmiya Supplies" ("Связанная со структурами Пригожина фирма заработает на поставках Юнармии сообщают «Открытые медиа»"), *Otkrytiye Media*, May 30, 2018, https://openmedia.io/investigation/kak -svyazannaya-s-prigozhinym-firma-mozhet-zarabotat-na-yunarmii.

33. Steven Lee Myers and Ellen Barry, "Putin Reclaims Crimea for Russia and Bitterly Denounces the West," *New York Times*, March 18, 2014, www.nytimes.com/2014/03/19/world /europe/ukraine.html.

34. Myers and Barry, "Putin Reclaims Crimea."

35. Oleksiy Bobronikov, "The Orthodox Oligarch, His Guard Dog and Their Tsarist Dream," *Kyiv Post*, February 6, 2023, www.kyivpost.com/post/11866.

CHAPTER 10: DOWN, OUT, AND UP IN DONBAS

1. Interview with Gerrit Thiry, Badhoevedorp, Netherlands, March 2023.

2. Bellingcat was among the first to triangulate and verify information culled from an SBU intercept of Valery Tsemakh's conversation with Igor Bezler on the day of the MH17 catastrophe. JIT investigators in the Netherlands also confirmed this account in their own separate analysis. See "A Birdie Is Flying Towards You," Bellingcat.com, www.bellingcat.com/app/uploads/2019/06 /a-birdie-is-flying-towards-you.pdf; and Netherlands Public Prosecution Service, "Investigation into the Main Scenario," MH17 Case, Prosecution and Trial Court Sessions 8–10 June 2020.

3. On June 2, 2018, SBU released a recorded excerpt of a call between Dmitry Utkin and Oleg V. Ivannikov. YouTube, www.youtube.com/watch?v=f7t1y5l1zKs.

4. Internal memos name several leading officials in the Main Operations Directorate as the chief managers of Russia's paramilitary forces, and the department is also referenced in Russian media as the administrative center of the effort; see "A Private Army for the President: The Story of Yevgeny Prigozhin's Most Delicate Assignment" ("Частная армия для президента: история самого деликатного поручения Евгения Пригожина"), *Bell*, January 29, 2019, https://thebell .io/41889-2.

5. Inventory list dated 2014, C4ADS, Evro Polis and subsidiaries data holdings; Estonian Foreign Intelligence Service, "International Security and Estonia—2022," January 31, 2022, 15–16, www.valisluureamet.ee/doc/raport/2022-en.pdf.

6. The Dossier Centre was the first to confirm Utkin's use of Nazi symbols in his day-to-day dealings with the Wagner Group. A subsequent author review of documents contained in the cache of leaked correspondence from Prigozhin's businesses confirmed that Utkin affixed the "SS" Nazi symbol to reports and supply orders. See "Heil Petrovich" ("«Хайль Петрович» История Дмитрия Уткина—человека, который подарил группе «Вагнера» название"), Dossier Centre, April 10, 2023, https://dossier.center/utkin.

7. Internal organizational chart, "Организационная структура на 09.12.2014" ("Organizational Structure on 9.12.2014"), C4ADS, Evro Polis and subsidiaries data holdings.

8. Wagner Group field report dated March 31, 2018, C4ADS, Evro Polis and subsidiaries data holdings.

9. Ilya Barabanov and Denis Korotkov, *Наш Бизнес Смерть (Our Business Is Death)* (StraightForward Foundation, 2024), 31–33.

10. "Intercepted Audio of Ukraine Separatists," *New York Times*, July 14, 2014, www.nytimes .com/video/world/europe/100000003007434/intercepted-audio-of-ukraine-separatists.html. See also "Malaysia Airlines Crash: Intercepted Call Suggests Rebels to Blame," *Telegraph*, July 2014, www.youtube.com/watch?v=gAKPK9d9zVc.

11. Anna Aruntunyan and Mark Galeotti, *Downfall* (London: Ebury, 2024), 104; Ilya Barabanov and Denis Korotkov, *Наш Бизнес Смерть (Our Business Is Death)* (StraightForward Foundation, 2024), 31–35.

12. Notations on the calendar entry suggest that Prigozhin's discussions with Khutortsev and Vaino were focused on an amendment to Russian laws pertaining to insurance claims, the national pension fund, and investment vehicles for financing housing for military personnel. For detailed analysis of Prigozhin's calendar entries and other related leaked data, see www .uncoveringwagner.org.

13. "Prigozhin Picked Up the Remains of the State Defense Order" ("Пригожин подобрал остатки оборонного госзаказа"), *Fontanka*, April 16, 2016, www.fontanka.ru/2016/08/17/153.

14. Yury Nursessov, "Who Cares About Wagner?" ("Кому мешает «Вагнер»"), *ko.ru*, August 25, 2020, https://ko.ru/articles/komu-meshaet-vagner.

15. "Heil Petrovich!"

16. Prigozhin issued the statement about his founding role in the Wagner Group on the VKontakte account for Concord Management and Consulting in late September 2022. The Concord account has since been deleted from the platform, but Prigozhin's remarks were widely reported in the international press. See Pjotr Sauer, "Putin Ally Yevgeny Prigozhin Admits Founding Wagner Mercenary Group," *Guardian*, September 26, 2022, www.theguardian.com /world/2022/sep/26/putin-ally-yevgeny-prigozhin-admits-founding-wagner-mercenary-group.

17. Internal memo dated 2015, C4ADS, Evro Polis and subsidiaries data holdings.

18. C4ADS, Evro Polis and subsidiaries data holdings.

19. Irina Malkova and Anton Bayev, "A Private Army for the President: The Story of Yevgeny Prigozhin's Most Delicate Mission" ("Частная армия для президента: история самого деликатного поручения Евгения Пригожина"), *Bell*, January 29, 2019, https://thebell.io /41889-2.

20. The Syrian Express connection hinted at the intriguing possibility that Prigozhin or someone in his retinue had already been in touch with leading members of the Moran Security Group as early as 2013 and that Prigozhin recognized the opportunity that lay before Concord as the leading logistics contractor for the Russian Ministry of Defense.

21. Irek Murtazin, "The Generals Set the Tasks" ("Задачи ставили генералы"), *Novaya Gazeta*, June 29, 2023, https://novayagazeta.ru/articles/2023/06/29/zadachi-stavili-generaly.

22. C4ADS, Evro Polis and subsidiaries data holdings.

23. Dmitriy "Wagner" Utkin to his Chief of Staff, Troshev (aka Sedoi), Institute for Postinformation Society, October 17, 2017, YouTube, www.youtube.com/watch?v=ahX8BPH8R2A.

24. Eliot Higgins, *We Are Bellingcat: Global Crime, Online Sleuths, and the Bold Future of News* (London: Bloomsbury, 2021), 63–65.

25. Arthur Bright, "Web Evidence Points to Pro-Russia Rebels in Downing of MH17," *Christian Science Monitor*, July 17, 2014, www.csmonitor.com/World/Europe/2014/0717 /Web-evidence-points-to-pro-Russia-rebels-in-downing-of-MH17.

26. Higgins, *We Are Bellingcat*, 63–65.

27. "Igor Strelkov: Some of the People from the Boeing Died a Few Days Before the Disaster" ("«Русская весна», «Игорь Стрелков: Часть людей из «Боинга» погибла за несколько дней до катастрофы»"), *Russkaya Vesna*, July 18, 2014, https://rusvesna.su/news/1405676334.

28. Tom Sear, "#MakeTVShowsAustralian, Maria Sharapova and MH17: Internet Research

Agency (IRA) Russian Troll Activity in Australian Cyberspace," *Journal of the AIPIO* 28, nos. 2–3 (2020): 89.

29. Sear, "#MakeTVShowsAustralian," 89.

30. Interview with Eliot Higgins, November 2023.

31. Higgins interview.

32. Thiry interview.

33. Thiry interview.

34. Paul Lewis, Dan Roberts, Spencer Ackerman, and Julian Borger, "Obama Says MH17 Destruction Is a 'Wake-Up Call' for Europe," *Guardian*, July 18, 2014, www.theguardian.com /world/2014/jul/18/obama-mh17-wake-up-call-europe-ukraine-russia.

35. Review and analysis of leaked documents from Prigozhin's businesses dated 2017 to 2021 showed that Alexey Milchakov's ID number (M-2691) surfaced in at least two instances in early duty-roster documents found in the cache. C4ADS, Evro Polis and subsidiaries data holdings.

36. Michael B. Kelley, "US: These Satellite Photos Prove That Russian Troops Are Shelling Ukraine," *Business Insider*, July 28, 2014, www.businessinsider.com/us-heres-where-russian -troops-are-shelling-ukraine-2014-7.

CHAPTER 11: THE CLEANERS

1. Alya Shandra and Robert Seely, "The Surkov Leaks: The Inner Workings of Russia's Hybrid War in Ukraine," *RUSI*, July 2019, 32.

2. "Who Are You, 'Shooter'?" («Кто ты, «Стрелок»?»), *Zavtra*, November 20, 2014, https://zavtra.ru/blogs/kto-tyi-strelok.

3. "Lavrov: Russia Will Not Respond in Kind to Western Sanctions," *Moscow Times*, July 28, 2014, www.themoscowtimes.com/2014/07/28/lavrov-russia-will-not-respond-in-kind-to -western-sanctions-a37723.

4. Lev Schlosberg, "The Dead and the Living" («Мёртвые и живые»), *Pskov Guberniya*, August 26, 2014, https://web.archive.org/web/20140826213515/http://gubernia .pskovregion.org/number_705/01.php.

5. Interview with Lev Schlosberg, September 20, 2023.

6. Schlosberg, "Dead and the Living."

7. Schlosberg interview.

8. "Who Are You, 'Shooter'?"

9. "Who Are You, 'Shooter'?"

10. Randy Noorman, "The Battle of Debaltseve: A Hybrid Army in a Classic Battle of Encirclement," *Small Wars Journal*, July 17, 2020, https://smallwarsjournal.com/jrnl/art /battle-debaltseve-hybrid-army-classic-battle-encirclement.

11. The SBU recording has since been taken down by YouTube. An excerpt of Utkin's call with Troshev was documented by the Ukrainian press; see "Наемники 'Вагнера' на Донбассе: СБУ обнародовала новое важное аудио," November 2, 2017, https: //apostrophe.ua/news/society/2017-11-02/naemniki-vagnera-na-donbasse-sbu-obnarodovala -novoe-vajnoe-audio/111977.

12. Marat Muhsin, "Six Militiamen Were Burned with a Shmeli, Including Alexander Bednov" ("Из Шмелей сожжены шесть ополченцев, включая Александра Беднова"), *ANNA News*, January 4, 2015, http://web.archive.org/web/20150714061545/http://www.anna-news .info/node/27164.

13. Colonel Cassad, "The Situation with 'Batman'" ("Ситуация с 'Бэтменом'— Промежуточные итоги"), January 2015, https://colonelcassad.livejournal.com/1972757.html, archived version at https://archive.is/wip/0Fwwr.

14. Denis Kazanskyi, "Теперь уже можно это рассказать! Гиркин признал, что Мозгового ликвидировал генерал ГРУ Алексеев" ("Now It's Time to Tell! Girkin Admitted That

Mozgovoy Was Liquidated by GRU General Alekseev"), YouTube, July 4, 2023, www.youtube.com /watch?v=6L-prWks_pM.

15. Candace Rondeaux and Ben Dalton, "Putin's Stealth Mobilization: Russian Irregulars and the Wagner Group's Shadow Command Structure," *Future Frontlines–New America*, February 22, 2023, www.newamerica.org/future-frontlines/reports/putin-mobilization-wagner -group.

16. "#Ukraine: Someone Else's General" ("#ВУкраине: свой чужой генерал"), CurrentTime TV, December 6, 2022, www.currenttime.tv/a/vukraine-svoy-chuzhoy-general/32153784.html.

17. "Russia Will Merge Intelligence Officers" ("Россия сольет разведчиков"), *Moskovskaya Komsomolets*, October 28, 2011, www.mk.ru/politics/2011/10/28/637742-rossiya-solet -razvedchikov.html, archived version at https://archive.is/zYAJ8.

18. US Energy Information Agency, "Crude Oil Prices Started 2015 Relatively Low, Ended the Year Lower," January 6, 2016, www.eia.gov/todayinenergy/detail.php?id=24432#:~ :text=Crude%20oil%20prices%20ended%202015,average%20price%20over%202010%2D14.

19. "Who Killed Major 'Batman'?," Ukraine Crisis Media Center, July 23, 2015, https: //uacrisis.org/en/29663-francais-qui-a-tue-le-commandant-batman.

20. Interview with Denis Korotkov, September 19, 2022.

21. Denis Korotkov, "'Slavic Corps' Returns to Syria" ("«Славянский корпус» возвращается в Сирию"), *Fontanka*, October 16, 2015, www.fontanka.ru/2015/10/16/118.

22. Rondeaux and Dalton, "Putin's Stealth Mobilization."

23. Internal correspondence, C4ADS, Evro Polis and subsidiaries data holdings.

24. Internal memo dated April 2016, C4ADS, Evro Polis and subsidiaries data holdings.

CHAPTER 12: SONG OF THE SLEDGEHAMMER

1. David Butter, "Fueling Conflict: Syria's War for Oil and Gas," Carnegie Endowment for International Peace, April 2, 2014, https://carnegieendowment.org/middle-east /diwan/2014/04/fueling-conflict-syrias-war-for-oil-and-gas?lang=en&center=middle-east.

2. David Butter, "Syria's Economy: Picking Up the Pieces," Chatham House, June 2015, 20, www.chathamhouse.org/sites/default/files/field/field_document/20150623SyriaEconomy Butter.pdf.

3. The Dossier Centre shared a copy of the Evro Polis contract with the author, along with documents containing data about revenues generated under the deal with the Hayan Petroleum Company and Syrian Petroleum. For more details, see Candace Rondeaux, "Inquiry into the Murder of Hamdi Bouta and Wagner Group Operations at the al-Shaer Gas Plant, Homs, Syria—2017," *Future Frontlines–New America*, June 5, 2020, www.newamerica.org/future-security/reports /inquiry-murder-hamdi-bouta.

4. "The State Duma Has Adopted a Law on Short-Term Military Contracts" ("Госдума приняла закон о краткосрочных военных контрактах"), TASS, December 14, 2016, https: //tass.ru/armiya-i-opk/3872222.

5. "Syria Hands Oil Exploration Contracts to Two Russian Firms," Reuters, December 17, 2019, www.reuters.com/article/markets/currencies/syria-hands-oil-exploration-contracts -to-two-russian-firms-idUSKBN1YL0VJ.

6. Abdullah Al-Jabassini, "From Insurgents to Soldiers: The Fifth Assault Corps in Daraa, Southern Syria," European University Institute, May 14, 2019, 21, https://cadmus.eui.eu /bitstream/handle/1814/62964/RR_2019_09_EN.pdf?isAllowed=y&sequence=1.

7. Undated award nomination memo for Dmitry Utkin, C4ADS, Evro Polis and subsidiaries data holdings.

8. From 2018 to 2021, Wagner Group fighters received at least 5,832 such aliases, according to New America's analysis of the data and documents in the C4ADS, Evro Polis and subsidiaries data holdings. For further details, see www.uncoveringwagnergroup.org.

9. Wagner Personnel Dataset, *Future Frontlines–New America*; C4ADS, Evro Polis and subsidiaries data holdings.

10. "Valery Chekalov—Biography," SMI24, https://24smi.org/celebrity/292026-valerii -chekalov.html.

11. Pierre Vaux, "Briefing on the Work of the Repair Brigade from the Russian Federation in Libya," *Insider*, September 12, 2019, www.interpretermag.com/briefing-on-the -work-of-the-repair-brigade-from-the-russian-federation-in-libya.

12. Prigozhin posted the letter to Shoigu in June 2023 on his social media account, which has since been deleted. The letter was widely referenced in the international press. See, for instance, Mary Ilyushina, Rachel Chason, Robyn Dixon, and John Hudson, "After Mutiny, Kremlin Looks to Unwind Holdings Tied to Wagner Mercenary Boss," *Washington Post*, July 1, 2023, www .washingtonpost.com/world/2023/07/01/prigozhin-wagner-businesses-kremlin-russa.

13. Interview with former Wagner commander and ex-Redut fighter Marat Gabidullin, September 2023.

14. Rondeaux, "Inquiry into the Murder of Hamdi Bouta."

15. "Timchenko to Raise Stroytransgaz Stake to 80 Pct," Reuters, June 1, 2009, www .reuters.com/article/russia-stroytransgaz/timchenko-to-raise-stroytransgaz-stake-to-80-pct -idINL16272520090601.

16. Ceren Kenar and Ragip Soylu, "Why Are Russian Engineers Working at an Islamic State–Controlled Gas Plant in Syria?," *Foreign Policy*, February 9, 2016, https://foreignpolicy .com/2016/02/09/why-are-russian-engineers-working-at-an-islamic-state-controlled-gas-plant -in-syria.

17. The phosphate-mine deal is referenced in an internal Wagner Group memo, C4ADS, Evro Polis and subsidiaries data holdings. See also Mohammed Bassiki et al., "A 'Bloody' Trade: Inside the Murky Supply Chain Bringing Syrian Phosphates into Europe," OCCRP, June 30, 2022, www.occrp.org/en/investigations/a-bloody-trade-inside-the-murky-supply-chain-bringing -syrian-phosphates-into-europe.

18. Internal memo dated August 3, 2018, C4ADS, Evro Polis and subsidiaries data holdings.

19. Charlotte Alfred, Mohammad Bassiki, Bashar Deeb, and Oleg Oganov, "'Blood Money': Europe's Secretive Trade in Syrian Phosphates," *Guardian*, June 30, 2022, www.theguardian.com /world/2022/jun/30/europe-syria-phosphates-trade-assad.

20. "The Secret GRU Unit 'PMC Redut' Within the 45th Separate Spetsnaz Brigade of the Ministry of Defense of the Russian Federation, Financed by Oleg Deripaska" ("Секретное подразделение ГРУ «ЧВК Редут» в составе 45 ОБр СпН МинОбороны РФ, финансы Олега Дерипаски"), Gulagu.net, www.youtube.com/watch?v=pKSg7Yt1Z9A.

21. Gabidullin interview.

22. "How Palmyra Was Captured and Why the Fighters of E. V. Prigozhin Were Not Nominated for an Award" ("Как происходило взятие Пальмиры и почему бойцов ЧВК «Вагнер» Е.В. Пригожина не представили к награде"), *Dzen*, March 5, 2023, https://dzen.ru/a /ZASmwnnRki-TwHqJ.

23. Internal memo from Yevgeny Prigozhin to Sergey Shoigu, C4ADS, Evro Polis and subsidiaries data holdings.

24. "Navalny Unmasks a Cartel Allegedly Earning Billions in Russian Defense Deals," *Moscow Times*, May 17, 2019, www.themoscowtimes.com/2017/05/19/navalny-unmasks-a -cartel-allegedly-earning-billions-in-defense-contracts-a58049.

25. US Department of Treasury, press release, "Treasury Sanctions Individuals and Entities in Connection with Russia's Occupation of Crimea and the Conflict in Ukraine," December 20, 2016, https://home.treasury.gov/news/press-releases/jl0688.

26. Interview with Brian O'Toole, former senior adviser to OFAC, U.S. Treasury Deprtment, September 2020.

27. Peter Landesman, "Arms and the Man," *New York Times*, August 17, 2003, www.nytimes.com/2003/08/17/magazine/arms-and-the-man.html.

28. Tom Wallace and Farley Mesko, "The Odessa Network: Mapping Facilitators of Russian and Ukrainian Arms Transfers," C4ADS, September 2013, 4, https://static1.squarespace.com/static/566ef8b4d8af107232d5358a/t/56af8a2dd210b86520934e62/1454344757606/The+Odessa+Network.pdf.

29. O'Toole interview.

30. O'Toole interview.

31. Interview with *al-Jessr Press* staff, February 10, 2020. See also Waleed Abu al-Khair, "Russia, Syria Must Answer for Wagner Group, Lawyer," *Diyaruna*, November 27, 2019, https://diyaruna.com/en_GB/articles/cnmi_di/features/2019/11/27/feature-02.

32. Rondeaux, "Inquiry into the Murder of Hamdi Bouta."

33. Rondeaux.

34. Several internal reports on the incident identified the perpetrators, C4ADS, Evro Polis and subsidiaries data holdings. The Dossier Centre also unearthed details about the aftermath of the internal investigation; see "Wagner's Sledgehammer" ("Кувалда «Вагнера»"), Dossier Centre, February 20, 2023, https://dossier.center/kuvalda.

35. Rondeaux, "Inquiry into the Murder of Hamdi Bouta."

CHAPTER 13: CLASH AT CONOCO

1. Interview with former US Deconfliction Cell chief Dave Milner, August 4, 2022.

2. Interviews with former US Deconfliction Cell chief Robert Hamilton, May 4, 2022, and September 15, 2020.

3. Milner interview.

4. Milner interview.

5. Marat Gabidullin, *In the Same River Twice (Moi, Marat, ex-commandant de larmée Wagner)* (Paris: Michel Lafon, 2022).

6. Marat Gabidullin and Veronika Gorman, *My Truth (Ma Vérité)*, Kindle ed. (Paris: Michel Lafon, 2023), 9.

7. Interview with ex–Wagner Group and former Redut commander Marat Gabidullin, September 2023.

8. Ellen Nakishima, Karen deYoung, and Liz Sly, "Putin Ally Said to Be in Touch with Kremlin, Assad Before His Mercenaries Attacked U.S. Troops," *Washington Post*, February 22, 2018, www.washingtonpost.com/world/national-security/putin-ally-said-to-be-in-touch-with-kremlin-assad-before-his-mercenaries-attacked-us-troops/2018/02/22/f4ef050c-1781-11e8-8b08-027a6ccb38eb_story.html.

9. Savicic is one of several mentioned in a leaked memo written by a member of the Wagner Group's internal-affairs department contained in the C4ADS, Evro Polis and subsidiaries data holdings. Marat Gabidullin, in his September 5, 2023, interview with the author, corroborated the account in the memo. See also Denis Korotkov, "Thugs" ("Головорезы"), *Novaya Gazeta*, November 11, 2020, https://novayagazeta.ru/articles/2019/11/20/82805-golovorezy-21; and Marija Ristic, "Serb Fighters' Mercenary Path from Ukraine to Syria," *Balkin Insight*, April 22, 2016, https://balkaninsight.com/2016/04/22/bosnian-serb-fighters-mercenary-path-to-syria-04-22-2016.

10. General Valery Asapov was killed in Deir Ezzor on September 24, 2017. See "ASAPOV VALERY GRIGORIEVICH 01/01/1966–09/24/2017," Union of Paratroopers, http://sdrvdv.ru/news/asapov-valeriy-grigorevich-01-01-1966-24-09-2017-g/; and "Biography of General-Lieutenant Valery Asapov," TASS, https://tass.ru/info/4589852.

11. Gabidullin and Gorman, *My Truth*.

12. Gabidullin interview.

13. "FBK Investigation About General Surovikin" ("Расследование ФБК о генерале Суровикине"), Anti-Corruption Foundation, November 10, 2022, https://acf.international/ru/news/surovikin.

14. "Major General from Dagestan Became Hero of Russia" ("Генерал-майор из Дагестана стал Героем России"), *RIA Derbent*, December 29, 2017, https://riaderbent.ru/general-major-iz-dagestana-stal-geroem-rossii.html.

15. Alexander Krolenko, "Who Exactly Is Andrey Serdyukov" ("Кто такой Андрей Сердюков"), *RIA Novosti*, September 30, 2016, https://ria.ru/20160930/1478241892.html.

16. "Hospitalised Russian Mercenary in Possession of Syrian Maps and Cash," *Moscow Times*, June 6, 2017, www.themoscowtimes.com/2017/06/06/drunk-mercenary-hospitalised-with-thousands-in-cash-and-syria-maps-a58162.

17. Prigozhin posted a narrative account of the events surrounding the battle for Conoco to his Telegram account in June 2023. See https://telegra.ph/Evgenij-Prigozhin-o-tragedii-8-fevralya-2018-v-Hshame-06-12, archived version at https://archive.is/wip/kWUmD.

18. Alexander Baklanov, "Journalists Identify Two Russian Mercenaries Involved in Brutal Syrian Murder, Including One Who Likely Served with Wagner PMC Leader," *Meduza*, December 13, 2019, https://meduza.io/en/feature/2019/12/13/journalists-identify-two-russian-mercenaries-involved-in-brutal-syrian-murder-including-one-who-likely-served-with-wagner-pmc-leader.

19. Gabidullin and Gorman, *My Truth*.

20. Prigozhin Telegram post, June 2023.

21. Gabidullin and Gorman, *My Truth*, 29.

22. References to VKontakte posts are drawn from a cache of 11,071 publicly available posts to a club channel titled "PMC Wagner—Military Review" that were collected as part of a joint research project between New America and Arizona State University from November 2019 to January 2021. Posts have since been deleted from the VKontakte platform, but a special collection of more than two dozen Wagner-related VKontakte and Telegram accounts can be viewed at www.uncoveringwagner.org.

23. Candace Rondeaux and Ben Dalton, "Putin's Stealth Mobilization," *New America*, February 22, 2023, www.newamerica.org/future-frontlines/reports/putin-mobilization-wagner-group.

CHAPTER 14: PROJECT ASTREA

1. United States v. Internet Research Agency, et al., Case 1:18-cr-00032-DLF, document 1, filed 02/16/18, www.justice.gov/d9/fieldable-panel-panes/basic-panes/attachments/2018/02/16/internet_research_agency_indictment.pdf.

2. Countless scholars have written about Soviet disinformation campaigns and the use of active measures to deceive targets; several have produced compelling analysis comparing Prigozhin's troll farm to Soviet-era KGB disinformation mills. See Vladislav Bittman, *The KGB and Soviet Disinformation: An Insider's View* (McLean, VA: Pergamon-Brassey, 1985), 35–69; and Thomas Rid, *Active Measures: The Secret History of Disinformation and Political Warfare* (New York: Farrar, Straus and Giroux, 2020), 397–409.

3. Minority Staff Report for the U.S. Senate Committee on Foreign Relations on Putin's Asymmetric Assault on Democracy in Russia and Europe: Implications for U.S. National Security, January 10, 2018, www.foreign.senate.gov/imo/media/doc/FinalRR.pdf.

4. Andrew Weissman, *Where Law Ends: Inside the Mueller Investigation*, Kindle ed. (New York: Random House, 2020), 64–77, 90.

5. "Ukrainian Court Freezes Interests of Deripaska Firms in Mykolaiv Alumina Refinery," Interfax, July 1, 2022, https://interfax.com/newsroom/top-stories/80883.

6. Report of the U.S. Senate Select Committee on Intelligence on Russian Active Measures Campaigns and Interference in the 2016 U.S. Election, vol. 5: Counterintelligence Threats and

Vulnerabilities, August 18, 2020, www.intelligence.senate.gov/sites/default/files/documents /report_volume5.pdf.

7. "Glencore Entered Guilty Pleas to Foreign Bribery and Market Manipulation Schemes," US Department of Justice, May 24, 2022, www.justice.gov/opa/pr/glencore-entered-guilty -pleas-foreign-bribery-and-market-manipulation-schemes.

8. Jeannie Rhee recounted details of her biography in an awards ceremony video in 2021. See YouTube, www.youtube.com/watch?v=GpR8NYhshew.

9. Jeannie Rhee bio, https://dcchs.org/wp-content/uploads/2020/06/RheeBio.pdf.

10. Matt Zapotosky, "Trump Said Mueller's Team Has '13 Hardened Democrats.' Here Are the Facts," *Washington Post*, March 18, 2018, www.washingtonpost.com/news/post-politics /wp/2018/03/18/trump-said-muellers-team-has-13-hardened-democrats-here-are-the-facts.

11. Weissmannn, *Where Law Ends*, 90.

12. Omer Meisel and Jeannie Rhee's role in the case against the IRA and Prigozhin is described at length, along with the inner workings of Mueller's team and a full and thorough accounting of the probe, in a memoir written by Andrew Weismannn, one of the lead prosecutors on Mueller's team. See Weissmann, *Where Law Ends*.

13. Weissmann.

14. Rhee shared her take on the federal investigation into the Internet Research Agency in a podcast discussion with Andrew Weissman and others posted to YouTube on October 30, 2023; see "From Russia with Kompromat," Talking Feds with Harry Litman, https://youtube.com /Yk6GdsYHmWo?si=UbVrtbbiZyFuKkr1.

15. "Former Special Agent in Charge of the New York FBI Counterintelligence Division Sentenced to 50 Months for Conspiring to Violate U.S. Sanctions on Russia," US Department of Justice, December 14, 2023, www.justice.gov/opa/pr/former-special-agent-charge-new -york-fbi-counterintelligence-division-sentenced-50-months.

16. Sheera Frankel and Cecelia Kang, *An Ugly Truth: Inside Facebook's Battle for Domination* (New York: Harper, 2021), 117–118.

17. "Office Building Evicts Russian Troll Farm over Repeated Bomb Threats—Reports," *Moscow Times*, January 31, 2019, www.themoscowtimes.com/2019/01/31/office-building -evicts-russian-troll-farm-over-repeated-bomb-threats-reports-a64358.

18. "Wake Up America—FAN Is Preparing to Launch a News Agency," RIA-FAN, April 4, 2018, https://web.archive.org/web/20180408024643/https://riafan.ru/1043445-prosnis -amerika-fan-gotovit-k-zapusku-novoe-informacionnoe-agentstvo.

19. See USAReally.com at https://web.archive.org/web/20180601215622/https://usa really.com.

20. Interview with Amy MacKinnon, February 2020.

21. Amy MacKinnon, "Russian Troll or Clumsy Publicity Hound?," *Coda*, June 15, 2018, www.codastory.com/disinformation/russian-troll-or-clumsy-publicity-hound.

22. MacKinnon interview.

23. Rhee and Weissmann did not respond to requests for comment on the IRA case; however, they did discuss Team R's approach to the case in a podcast in November 2023. See "From Russia with Kompromat."

24. "Treasury Targets Assets of Russian Financier Who Attempted to Influence 2018 U.S. Elections," US Treasury Department, September 30, 2019, https://home.treasury.gov/news /press-releases/sm787.

25. United States v. Teyf (5:18-cr-00452), District Court, E.D. North Carolina, unsealed indictment, November 8, 2018.

26. US v. Leonid Isaakovich Teyf, Tatyana Anatolyevna Teyf, a/k/a Tatiana Teyf, Alexey Vladimirovich Timofeev, Olesya Yuryevna Timofeeva, Alexei Izailevich Polyakov, a/k/a Alex

Norka, No. 5:18-CR-004520FL. See https://storage.courtlistener.com/recap/gov.uscourts
.nced.167685/gov.uscourts.nced.167685.182.3.pdf.

27. *U.S. v. Leonid Teyf et al.*

28. Exhibit E, Homeland Security Investigation, US Department of Homeland Security,
October 12, 2018, https://storage.courtlistener.com/recap/gov.uscourts.nced.167685/gov
.uscourts.nced.167685.182.3.pdf.

29. Another strange twist in Teyf's case was the fact that he shared the same defense attorney
as Felix Sater, a convicted felon linked to a mafia money-laundering scheme, a onetime real estate
business partner of Donald Trump, and a pivotal FBI informant in the inquiry into Russian interference in the 2016 election. A federal court sentenced Teyf to five years in prison after he pleaded
guilty to bribing a public official, visa fraud, and making false statements in relation to foreign
interests, according to a Justice Department press release. When I contacted Teyf's defense attorney, Robert S. Wolf, he initially declined to comment on the record about his client's case but said
he would convey my request for comment to Teyf. After several further exchanges, Wolf said he
would get back to me and would send Teyf a list of questions that I submitted via email in August
2023. "I'm just waiting for sign off from the client on a response," Wolf wrote. But there was no
further word from Teyf's attorney after that.

30. *U.S. v. Leonid Teyf et al.*

31. *U.S. v. Leonid Teyf et al.*

32. Harry Holmes, "Russian National a One-Man Crime Wave, US Prosecutors Say," OCCRP
.org, January 24, 2019, www.occrp.org/en/daily/9157-russian-national-a-one-man-crime-wave-us
-prosecutors-say.

33. "Russian Ex-minister Named Aircraft Group Head After Plane Blaze," *France24.com*,
May 13, 2019, www.france24.com/en/20190513-russian-ex-minister-named-aircraft-group-head
-after-plane-blaze.

34. Interview with Dmitri Mitin, April 2020.

35. Ellen Nakashima, "U.S. Cyber Command Operation Disrupted Internet Access of Russian Troll Factory on the Day of 2018 Midterm Elections," *Washington Post*, February 27, 2019,
www.washingtonpost.com/world/national-security/us-cyber-command-operation-disrupted
-internet-access-of-russian-troll-factory-on-day-of-2018-midterms/2019/02/26/1827fc9e-36d6
-11e9-af5b-b51b7ff322e9_story.html.

36. A US Cyber Command source described parts of the operation to a *Washington Post*
reporter in 2019; RIA-FAN also posted several articles on the subject at the time of some of
the attacks in 2018. See Nakashima, "U.S. Cyber Command Operation"; and "US Cyber
Attack on FAN: Details of the Unsuccessful US Cyber Command Operation," RIA-FAN, February 27, 2019, https://web.archive.org/web/20190227164129/https://riafan.ru/1155441
-kiberataka-ssha-na-fan-podrobnosti-neudachnoi-operacii-us-cyber-command.

37. *U.S. v. Internet Research Agency, et al.,* Case 1:18-cr-00032-DLF, document 46, July 16,
2018.

38. *U.S. v. Internet Research Agency, et al.,* Case 1:18-cr-00032-DLF, document 10, May 14,
2018.

39. *U.S. v. Internet Research Agency, et al.,* Case 1:18-cr-00032-DLF, document 46.

40. "Putin Reiterates His Stance on Russia's Alleged Involvement in US Elections," TASS,
June 5, 2018, https://tass.com/politics/1007957.

41. Pavel Karpunin made this statement in an email dated July 17, 2018, that was part of the
CLS Leaks data set posted on the Digital Denial of Secrets (DDoS) website on April 2, 2022.

42. Line 36 in an undated curriculum vitae for Yevgeny Prigozhin prepared and circulated by
his legal team, Capital Legal Services. The CLS email leaks comprise approximately 200,000 internal emails of Capital Legal Services, a Russian law firm with offices in Moscow and St. Petersburg.

The data set totals 65 GB and covers a period between October 2012 and March 2022. An anonymous hacker or hackers released the emails on the Digital Denial of Secrets (DDoS) website on April 2, 2022. Background on the data set can be found here: https://ddosecrets.com /article/capital-legal-services.

43. The CLS email leaks comprise approximately 200,000 internal emails of Capital Legal Services, a Russian law firm with offices in Moscow and St. Petersburg. The data set totals 65 GB and covers a period between October 2012 and March 2022. A small number of emails predate 2012, but these are automatically generated notifications that contain no body text. An anonymous hacker or hackers released the emails on the DDoSecrets website on April 2, 2022. See Capital Legal Services, https://ddosecrets.com/wiki/Capital_Legal_Services.

44. Pavel Karpunin email correspondence dated August 12, 2021, CLS Leaks, Digital Denial of Secrets, April 2, 2022.

45. Prigozhin's legal team at Capital Legal Services circulated a draft copy of this letter in emails that were leaked as part of the CLS Leaks data set posted on the Digital Denial of Secrets (DDoS) website on April 2, 2022.

46. *U.S. v. Internet Research Agency, et al.,* Case 1:18-cr-00032-DLF, document 94, January 30, 2019.

47. Kimberly Senz, "Infighting Among Russian Security Services in the Cyber Sphere," BlackHat USA 2019, January 15, 2020, YouTube, https://youtu.be/ntwsAxk_Tmw?si=YraVsxQFJSElqXat.

48. Josh Gerstein, "Feds: Mystery Witness Will Implicate 'Putin's Chef' in Election Interference," *Politico*, March 4, 2020, www.politico.com/news/2020/03/04/mystery-witness-russia -putin-election-120508.

CHAPTER 15: AFRICA OR BUST

1. "Final Report on the Murder of Orkhan Dzhemal, Aleksandr Rastogruev and Kirill Radchenko in the Central African Republic," Dossier Centre, July 2019, https://dossier.center /car-en.

2. Denis Korotkov, "The Night Has No Eyes" ("у ночи нет глаз"), *Fontanka*, September 18, 2018, www.fontanka.ru/longreads/68673145.

3. As France's president Emmanuel Macron would later put it best, the Wagner Group was the "life insurance of failing regimes." "France's Macron Calls Wagner Group 'Life Insurance of Failing Regimes' in Africa," Reuters, February 27, 2023, www.reuters.com/world/europe /frances-macron-calls-wagner-group-life-insurance-failing-regimes-africa-2023-02-27.

4. "Стратегия развития «негроидного расового шовинизма» или пригожинский ответ доктрине Герасимова" ("Strategy for the Development of 'Negroid Racial Chauvinism' or Prigozhin's Answer to the Gerasimov Doctrine"), Dossier Centre, https://dossier.center/e-prigozhin /article/prigozhinskij-otvet-doktrine-gerasimova.

5. Maslov's name appeared alongside that of Dobronravin, Potepkin, Khodotov, and Sytii on leaked travel billing documents sent to Concord Management and Consulting obtained by the Dossier Centre and shared with the author.

6. Candace Rondeaux, "How a Man Linked to Prigozhin, 'Putin's Chef,' Infiltrated the United Nations," *Daily Beast*, November, 27, 2020.

7. "Sudan's President Bashir Asks Putin for 'Protection' from 'Aggressive' US," *France 24*, November 23, 2017, www.france24.com/en/20171123-sudan-president-bashir-asks-putin -protection-aggressive-us.

8. "G.I. Joe: Tatneft Links Up with Arms Exporter," *Energy Intelligence*, February 13, 2002.

9. "Meeting Between Dmitry Medvedev and Omar al-Bashir" («Встреча Дмитрия Медведева с Президентом Судана Омаром Баширом»), Russian embassy press release, November 24, 2017, http://government.ru/news/30259.

10. Khadije Sharife, Lara Dhimis, and Erin Lazaar, "Documents Reveal Wagner's Golden

Ties to Sudanese Military Companies," OCCRP, November 2, 2022, www.occrp.org/en /investigations/documents-reveal-wagners-golden-ties-to-sudanese-military-companies.

11. Bondar's signature and title appear in a number of country situation reports and personnel records contained in the leaked document cache from Concord network companies contained in the C4ADS, Evro Polis and subsidiaries data holdings.

12. C4ADS, Evro Polis and subsidiaries data holdings.

13. Details about Prigozhin's fake identification documents surfaced in a number of Russian media reports in June 2023. See "Stash of Fake Documents, Cash, and Unidentified Powder Found at Prigozhin's St. Petersburg Office," *Meduza*, June 26, 2023, https://meduza.io/en /feature/2023/06/27/stash-of-fake-documents-cash-and-unidentified-powder-found-at -prigozhin-s-st-petersburg-office.

14. C4ADS, Evro Polis and subsidiaries data holdings.

15. C4ADS, Evro Polis and subsidiaries data holdings.

16. The technical Russian term for such units was *Boyevoy Armeysky Reserv Strani* (Боевой Армейский Резерв Страны—БАРС).

17. Nicolas Haque, "Central African Republic Calls on Russia to Train Its Army," *al-Jazeera*, November 15, 2018, www.aljazeera.com/videos/2018/11/15/central-african-republic -calls-on-russia-to-train-its-army.

18. C4ADS, Evro Polis and subsidiaries data holdings. Nizhevenok was listed by rank and detachment number in personnel records and internal memos. He corroborated many of the details of his service with Wagner in a February 2023 interview with Vladimir Solvyov. See "Командир 'Вагнер' с позывным 'Зомби': от Африки до Бахмута" ("'Wagner' Commander, Call Sign 'Zombie': From Africa to Bakhmut"), *Amalnews*, February 15, 2023, https://amalantra.ru /komandir-chvk-vagner-s-pozyvnym-zombi, archived version at https://archive.is/wip/sDqmB.

19. "Anton Yelizarov from 'Wagner,'" Molfar.com, https://molfar.com/en/blog/komanduvav -nastupom-na-soledar-vbiv-bagato-nashih-deanon-ielizarova-z-vagnera.

20. Luke Harding, "Revealed: UN Sudan Expert's Links to Russian Oligarch Prigozhin," *Guardian*, November 27, 2020, www.theguardian.com/world/2020/nov/27/revealed -un-sudan-experts-links-to-russian-oligarch-prigozhin.

21. Interview with Roman Radchenko, October 2023.

22. Office of the President of Russia, Transcript of Vladimir Putin's annual press conference, December 20, 2018.

23. Interview with Mikhail Khodorkovsky, London, June 2022.

24. Interview with Roman Radchenko, October 2023.

25. Khodorkovsky interview.

26. Khodorkovsky interview.

27. Interview with a senior Western diplomat, June 2023.

28. A review of correspondence and billing records shared with the author by the Dossier Centre corroborated additional details found in leaked correspondence referencing Pikalov's duties contained in the C4ADS, Evro Polis and subsidiaries data holdings.

29. Matthieu Olivier, "Russia's Murky Business Dealings in the Central African Republic," *Africa Report*, August 23, 2019, www.theafricareport.com/16511/russias-murky-business -dealings-in-the-central-african-republic.

30. "Treasury Sanctions Illicit Gold Companies Funding Wagner Forces and Wagner Group Facilitator," US Treasury Department, June 27, 2023, https://home.treasury.gov/news /press-releases/jy1581; "Architects of Terror: The Wagner Group's Blueprint for State Capture in the Central African Republic," *Sentry*, June 2023, 3, https://thesentry.org/wp-content /uploads/2023/06/ArchitectsTerror-TheSentry-June2023.pdf.

31. John Lechner and Marat Gabidullin, "Why the Wagner Group Won't Leave Africa," *Foreign Policy*, August 8, 2023.

32. "Architects of Terror."

33. Jessica Berlin, David Clement, et al., "The Blood Gold Report," *21 Democracy*, December 2023, 23.

34. "Shadow Men: Inside the Wagner Group, Russia's Secret War Company," *Wall Street Journal*, June 8, 2023.

35. Irina Dolinina, Alesya Marohovskaya, Denis Korotkov, and Jakub Šimák, "The Chef's Global Footprints," *Novaya Gazeta–OCCRP*, December 17, 2019, www.occrp.org/en /investigations/the-chefs-global-footprints.

36. Tim Lister, Sebastian Shukla, and Nima Elbagir, "Fake News and Public Executions: Documents Show a Russian Company's Plan for Quelling Protests in Sudan," CNN, April 25, 2019, https://edition.cnn.com/2019/04/25/africa/russia-sudan-minvest-plan-to-quell-protests -intl/index.html.

37. Roman Popkov, "'Public Executions of Looters and Other Spectacular Events'" ("«Публичные казни мародеров и другие зрелищные мероприятия»: советы людей Пригожина свергнутому диктатору"), *MBK Media*, April 25, 2019, https://mbk-news .appspot.com/rassled/soveti-ludej-prigozhina.

CHAPTER 16: ONWARD TO TRIPOLI

1. "Russia to Arm Libya's Haftar in $2bn Weapons Deal," *New Arab*, January 25, 2017, www .newarab.com/news/russia-arm-libyas-haftar-2bn-weapons-deal.

2. "Russia Tatneft in $100 Mln Libya Capex Loss—Source," Reuters, March 28, 2011, www.reuters.com/article/russia-tatneft/russia-tatneft-in-100-mln-libya-capex-loss-source -idUSLDE72R0J120110328.

3. "Gaddafi Fall Cost Russia Tens of Blns in Rms Deals," Reuters, November 2, 2011, www .reuters.com/article/idUSL5E7M221H.

4. Pierre Vaux, "Jamahiriya TV," *Interpreter*, September 11, 2019, www.interpretermag .com/jamahiriya-tv; Michael Weiss and Pierre Vaux, "Russia's Wagner Mercenaries Have Moved into Libya. Good Luck with That," *Daily Beast*, September 28, 2019, www.thedailybeast.com /russias-wagner-mercenaries-have-moved-into-libya-good-luck-with-that.

5. United Nations Sanctions Research Platform, letter dated May 24, 2022, from the Panel of Experts on Libya established pursuant to Resolution 1973 (2011) addressed to the President of the Security Council, 12, https://sanctionsplatform.ohchr.org/record/20452?ln=en.

6. "Master and Chef: How Evgeny Prigozhin Led the Russian Offensive in Africa," *Proekt Media*, March 19, 2019, www.proekt.media/en/article-en/evgeny-prigozhin-africa.

7. Pierre Vaux, "On the Situation in Libya," *Interpreter*, September 12, 2019, www .interpretermag.com/on-the-situation-in-libya.

8. Alexander Prokofiev made the statement about Saif Qaddafi in a leaked memo dated April 4, 2019, that was translated into English in full by Pierre Vaux; see Vaux, "Report on the Meeting with the Doctor. 03/04/2019," *Interpreter*, September 12, 2019, www.interpretermag.com /report-on-the-meeting/.

9. "Who Is Alexey Dyumin and How Did He Come to Power" ("Кто такой Алексей Дюмин и как он пришёл во власть"), *Secret Firmy*, June 26, 2023, https://secretmag.ru/enciklopediya /aleksei-dyumin.htm.

10. Vladimir Prokushev, "Забыли, кто вас кормит?," *Novaya Gazeta*, June 29, 2023.

11. Sergey Ezhov, "Парк жуликов и воров," *Insider*, April 24, 2019, https://theins.ru /korrupciya/152511.

12. Candace Rondeaux, Oliver Imhof, and Jack Margolin, "The Abu Dhabi Express: Analyzing the Wagner Group's Libya Logistics Pipeline & Operations," *New America*, November 3, 2021, www.newamerica.org/future-frontlines/reports/the-abu-dhabi-express.

13. United Nations Sanctions Research Platform, letter dated May 24, 2022.

14. U.S. Department of Defense Lead Inspector General, "East Africa Counterterrorism Operation, North and West Africa Counterterrorism Operation," Report to the United States Congress, July 1, 2020–September 30, 2020, 36–37.

15. Internal report dated September 19, 2019, C4ADS, Evro Polis and subsidiaries data holdings.

16. Interview with Fred Wehery, January 2021.

17. Rondeaux, Imhof, and Margolin, "Abu Dhabi Express."

18. Maria Tsvetkova, "Russian Clinic Treated Mercenaries Injured in Secret Wars," Reuters, January 7, 2020, www.reuters.com/article/us-russia-putin-mercenaries-exclusive/exclusive-russian-clinic-treated-mercenaries-injured-in-secret-wars-idUSKBN1Z61A7/.

19. UN Human Rights Council, "Report of the Independent Fact-Finding Mission in Libya," forty-eighth session, September 13–October 1, 2021.

20. Interview with Western security adviser, June 2023.

21. Dean Sterling Jones and Amy McKinnon, "How Russia Tried to Weaponize Charlie Sheen," *Foreign Policy*, September 23, 2020, https://foreignpolicy.com/2020/09/23/how-russia-tried-to-weaponize-charlie-sheen-release-operative-libyan-jail.

22. Robyn Dixon, "Russian Political Action Man Sets Up Shop in Kabul in Bid to Win Deals for Moscow," *Washington Post*, January 10, 2022.

23. Evan Gershkovich, "At Russia's Inaugural Africa Summit, Moscow Sells Sovereignty," *Moscow Times*, October 26, 2019, www.themoscowtimes.com/2019/10/26/russias-inaugural-africa-summit-moscow-sells-sovereignty-a67916.

24. "Putin to Hold Series of Bilateral Meetings on Sidelines of Russia-Africa Summit" ("Путин проведет серию двусторонних встреч на полях саммита Россия-Африка"), TASS, October 20, 2019, https://tass.ru/politika/7026554.

CHAPTER 17: MIX-UP IN MINSK

1. "Lukashenko Says Russia Fears Losing Belarus" ("Лукашенко заявил о страхе России потерять Белоруссию"), *RBC*, August 4, 2020, www.rbc.ru/politics/04/08/2020/5f29276f9a794729aae5eca9.

2. According to leaked travel records, billing receipts, and customs information from Evro Polis, Mercury LLC, M Invest, and Broker Expert, four individuals bearing Belarusian passports traveled to and from Minsk at the expense of companies linked to Prigozhin more than a dozen times from January 2017 to December 2018.

3. A customs form signed by Anatoliy V. Dubovets, the head of finance and logistics at the Belarus Internal Affairs Division, indicated that a Russian-based military munitions firm, AO FNPTS, was the shipment's sender. Also known as the Federal Research and Production Center of the Scientific Research Institute for Applied Chemistry, this state-owned enterprise specialized in a range of pyrotechnics products sold by Russia's state-owned arms company Rosoboronexport.

4. Denis Korotkov, "How Lukashenko Was Captured by a Platoon of Wagnerovtsy" ("Как Лукашенко взвод вагнеровцев в плен взял"), *Novaya Gazeta*, July 31, 2020, https://novayagazeta.ru/articles/2020/07/30/86449-kak-batka-vzvod-vagnerovtsev-v-plen-vzyal.

5. "Inside Wagnergate: Ukraine's Brazen Sting Operation to Snare Russian Mercenaries," Bellingcat.com, November 17, 2021, www.bellingcat.com/news/uk-and-europe/2021/11/17/inside-wagnergate-ukraines-brazen-sting-operation-to-snare-russian-mercenaries.

6. "Andriy Yermak: 'It Looks Like a Well-Thought-Out and Planned Disinformation Campaign'" ("Андрій Єрмак: «Це виглядає як добре продумана та спланована дезінформаційна кампанія»"), *LB.ua*, August 19, 2020, https://lb.ua/news/2020/08/19/464172_andriy_iermak_tse_viglyadaie_yak_dobre.html.

7. C4ADS, Evro Polis and subsidiaries data holdings.

8. Interview with Yanina Sokolova, Bucha, Ukraine, June 2022.

9. "Putin Accuses Ukrainian Intelligence Services and the USA of Detaining PMC Fighters in Belarus" ("Путин обвинил спецслужбы Украины и США в задержании бойцов ЧВК в Белоруссии"), *Lenta.ru*, August 27, 2020, https://lenta.ru/news/2020/08/27/putin_zaderzhanie.

CHAPTER 18: PRELUDE TO SPRING

1. "Fact Sheet: Imposing Costs for Harmful Foreign Activities by the Russian Government," whitehouse.gov, April 15, 2021, www.whitehouse.gov/briefing-room/statements-releases/2021/04/15/fact-sheet-imposing-costs-for-harmful-foreign-activities-by-the-russian-government/#:~:text=Today%2C%20President%20Biden%20signed%20a,of%20Russia's%20harmful%20foreign%20activities.

2. US Treasury Department, "Treasury Escalates Sanctions Against the Russian Government's Attempts to Influence U.S. Elections," April 15, 2021, https://home.treasury.gov/news/press-releases/jy0126.

3. Dominic Nicholls, "'Putin's Chef' Breaks Cover to Insist He Is a 'Pacifist,'" *Telegraph*, November 7, 2021, www.telegraph.co.uk/news/2021/11/07/putins-chef-wanted-fbi-denies-links-paramilitary-forces-online.

4. Chris Riotta, "'Putin's Chef' Defends Himself as a 'Squeaky Clean Person' After FBI Adds Russian Oligarch to Most Wanted List," *Independent*, March 24, 2021, www.independent.co.uk/news/world/americas/us-politics/putin-chef-yevgeny-prigozhin-fbi-b1821749.html.

5. "For Few Dollars More: Putin's Chef Offers $500,000 for Capturing MBK in Response to the FBI," Khodorkovsky.com, March 2, 2021, https://khodorkovsky.com/for-few-dollars-more-putins-chef-offers-500000-for-capturing-mbk-in-response.

6. UN Security Council, "Letter dated 25 June 2021 from the Panel of Experts on the Central African Republic extended pursuant to Resolution 2536 (2020) addressed to the President of the Security Council," 23, https://reliefweb.int/report/central-african-republic/final-report-panel-experts-central-african-republic-extended-4.

7. "Russia and Mali Sign Military Cooperation Agreement" ("Россия и Мали подписали соглашение о военном сотрудничестве"), TASS, June 25, 2019, https://tass.ru/armiya-i-opk/6588923.

8. Josh Irish and David Lewis, "Exclusive Deal Allowing Russian Mercenaries into Mali Is Close—Sources," Reuters, September 13, 2021, www.reuters.com/world/africa/exclusive-deal-allowing-russian-mercenaries-into-mali-is-close-sources-2021-09-13.

9. Terri Moon Cronk, "Biden Announces Full U.S. Troop Withdrawal from Afghanistan by Sept. 11," *DOD News*, April 14, 2021, www.defense.gov/News/News-Stories/Article/Article/2573268/biden-announces-full-us-troop-withdrawal-from-afghanistan-by-sept-11/#:~:text=Strategic%20Management%20Plan-,Biden%20Announces%20Full%20U.S.%20Troop%20Withdrawal%20From%20Afghanistan%20by,11&text=President%20Joe%20Biden%20said%20the,20th%20anniversary%20of%20the%20war.

10. Charlie Savage, Eric Schmitt, and Michael Schwirtz, "Russian Spy Team Left Traces That Bolstered C.I.A.'s Bounty Judgment," *New York Times*, May 17, 2021, www.nytimes.com/2021/05/07/us/politics/russian-bounties-nsc.html.

11. "The Main Directorate of International Military Cooperation of the Ministry of Defense of the Russian Federation Held a Briefing on the Preparation of the Joint Strategic Exercise 'Zapad 2021': Ministry of Defense of the Russian Federation" ("Главное управление международного военного сотрудничества Минобороны РФ провело брифинг о подготовке совместного стратегического учения «Запад-2021»: Министерство обороны Российской Федерации"), *function.mil.ru*, August 20, 2021, https://function.mil.ru/news_page/country/more.htm?id=12378427@egNews.

12. Vladimir Putin, "On the Historical Unity of Russians and Ukrainians," July 12, 2021, http://en.kremlin.ru/events/president/news/66181.

13. Credit for the discovery goes to New America researcher Jonathan Deer; see Candace Rondeaux, Jonathan Deer, and Ben Dalton, "Wagner Group Contingent Rusich on the Move Again," *Future Frontlines–New America*, January 26, 2022, www.newamerica.org/future-frontlines /blogs/wagner-group-contingent-rusich-on-the-move-again.

14. On September 27, 2021, Rusich posted a selfie of its members mounted on a Russian-made BMP armored-infantry fighting vehicle on its Instagram account under the handle @rusichpvk. The post referenced a Russian military veterans' club and military-training exercises, and it received 371 likes from account followers. See Rondeaux, Deer, and Dalton, "Wagner Group Contingent Rusich."

15. "5 сентября 2014 года—кровавая дата 24-го отдельного штурмового батальона 'Айдар.' ФОТОрепортаж Источник" ("September 5, 2014—A Bloody Date for the 24th Separate Assault Battalion"), Censor.net, https://censor.net/ru/p350702.

16. Michael Sheddon, "An Untimely Death Reveals the Nature of a Russian Neo-Nazi Unit That Fought in Syria," DFRLab, Atlantic Council, October 7, 2021, https://medium.com /dfrlab/an-untimely-death-reveals-the-nature-of-a-russian-neo-nazi-unit-that-fought-in-syria -5398a7d28e0a.

17. "A Neo-Nazi Militant from Russia Sneered at the Murder of Ukrainians—Photo" ("Боевик-неонацист из России поглумился над убитыми украинцами (фото)"), Bignir .net, September 6, 2014, https://news.bigmir.net/ukraine/4643160-boevik-neonacist-iz-rossii -poglumilsya-nad-ubity-mi-ukraincami-foto.

18. Geolocation analysis of photo stills from a Rusich recruitment video indicates that the shooting range is located at PSK Severyanin (Severyanin Gardening Club) in Kolpino, near St. Petersburg. The site maps to adjacent EMERCOM properties and an undated page on the website for the shooting club mentions that the site is a base for EMERCOM training. See "History of the Creation of PSK Severyanin" ("История создания 'ПСК Северянин'"), http: //whitenightscup.ru/about.php, archived version at https://archive.is/wip/I6Elm.

CHAPTER 19: ORCHESTRAL MANEUVERS

1. The reference to the "philharmonic known as Wagner" was in a post uploaded to the Reverse Side of the Medal (RSTOM) channel on Telegram on March 1, 2022; it has since been deleted. Screenshots of the Telegram post have been preserved by the Future Frontlines program at New America here: https://x.com/NewFrontlines/status/1499101698505203716/photo/1.

2. According to Our World in Data, the annual median income in Russia in 2020 was roughly $20,500. Our World in Data, https://ourworldindata.org/grapher/gdp-per-capita -worldbank?tab=chart&country=~RUS.

3. The video was posted on Zelensky's Twitter account on March 7, 2022; see Volodymyr Zelensky, "Every Day of Resistance Creates Better Conditions for Ukraine in the Negotiations to Guarantee Our Future in Peace," Office of the President of Ukraine, March 7, 2022, www .president.gov.ua/en/news/kozhen-den-sprotivu-stvoryuye-dlya-ukrayini-krashi-umovi-na -73417.

4. Interview with senior Ukrainian security official, Kyiv, Ukraine, September 2022.

5. The website 200300.info was taken down after Ukraine's SBU revealed its existence. A check of internet archives reveals that all recordings of the site for 2022 resolve to a black screen; this may point to the potential of intentional redirection to a site that appears to give a null result.

6. Manveen Rana, "Volodymyr Zelensky: Russian Mercenaries Ordered to Kill Ukraine's President," *Times of London*, February 18, 2022, www.thetimes.co.uk/article/volodymyr -zelensky-russian-mercenaries-ordered-to-kill-ukraine-president-cvcksh79d.

7. In videotaped interviews and written testimony in 2023, former Wagner Group fighter and ex–Redut commander Igor Salikov described in detail how Redut served as a hub for mercenary recruitment and deployment for the GRU over the years, and internal memos from a leaked cache of Concord network documents appear to corroborate the suggestion that there was a degree of fluidity between the recruitment pools for the two organizations. See Salikov's December 2023 interview with Vladimir Osechkin for Gulagu.net on YouTube at: https://youtu.be/GMpl2T PNqW8?si=CLwxylTpz1yzo0zT. A December 2014 memo listing an inventory of weapons issued to Wagner forces by Unit 35555 is also cited in Ilya Barabanov and Denis Korotkov, *Наш Бизнес Смерть (Our Business Is Death)* (StraightForward Foundation, 2024).

8. "The Toad and the Ministry of Defense: How Evgeny Viktorovich and Sergey Kuzhuge-tovich Quarreled," *Insider*, May 12, 2023, https://theins.ru/politika/261683.

9. "The GRU Created a Secret Network of Mercenary Formations Under the Guise of PMC 'Redut'" ("ГРУ создало секретную сеть наемнических формирований под видом "ЧВК "Редут". Расследование "Схем" и "Системы""), *Nastoyashoye Vremya*, October 13, 2023, www .currenttime.tv/a/redut-schemes-systema/32628913.html.

10. Ben Dalton and Candace Rondeaux, "Rebranding the Russian Way of War: The Wagner Group's Viral Social Media Campaign and What It Means for Ukraine," *New America*, February 16, 2023, www.newamerica.org/future-frontlines/reports/russian-way-of-war-wagner.

11. Dalton and Rondeaux, "Rebranding the Russian Way of War."

12. "Putin Called for Help to Those Who Want to Go to Donbas as a Volunteer" ("Путин призвал помочь тем, кто хочет поехать в Донбасс добровольцем"), Interfax, March 11, 2022, www.interfax.ru/russia/827570. See also "Putin Says Russia to Welcome Volunteers from Middle East to Fight Ukraine," CNA, March 11, 2022, www.channelnewsasia.com/world /putin-say-russia-welcome-volunteers-middle-east-fight-ukraine-2557871.

13. "Putin Called for Help."

14. UN Office of the High Commissioner for Human Rights, "Rapport sur les évènements de Moura du 27 au 31 mars 2022," May 2023, www.ohchr.org/sites/default/files/documents /countries/mali/20230512-Moura-Report.pdf.

15. Human Rights Watch, "Ukraine: Russian Forces' Trail of Death in Bucha," April 21, 2022, www.hrw.org/news/2022/04/21/ukraine-russian-forces-trail-death-bucha.

16. Interview with Serhii Shepetko, Bucha, Ukraine, September 2022.

17. Shepetko interview.

18. "Russia Says Footage in Ukraine's Bucha Was 'Ordered' to Blame Russia," Reuters, April 4, 2022, www.reuters.com/world/russia-says-footage-ukraines-bucha-was-ordered-blame -russia-2022-04-04.

19. "Ukraine War: Vladimir Putin's Spokesman Says Images of Bodies in Bucha 'Were Not Victims of Russia,'" *Sky News*, April 7, 2022, https://news.sky.com/video/ukraine-war-vladimir -putins-spokesman-says-images-of-bodies-in-bucha-were-not-victims-of-russia-12584570.

20. Yousur Al-Hlou, Masha Froliak, Evan Hill, Malachy Browne, and David Botti, "New Evidence Shows How Russian Soldiers Executed Men in Bucha," *New York Times*, May 19, 2022, www.nytimes.com/2022/05/19/world/europe/russia-bucha-ukraine-executions.html.

21. Melanie Amann, Matthias Gebauer, and Fidelius Schmid, "German Intelligence Intercepts Radio Traffic Discussing the Murder of Civilians," *Der Spiegel*, April 7, 2022, www .spiegel.de/international/germany/possible-evidence-of-russian-atrocities-german-intelligence -intercepts-radio-traffic-discussing-the-murder-of-civilians-in-bucha-a-0a191c96-634f-4d07 -8c5c-c4a772315b0d.

22. Ekaterina Fomina, "Eight Pskov Paratroopers in Bucha," *iStories*, June 6, 2022, https: //istories.media/en/investigations/2022/06/27/eight-pskov-paratroopers-in-bucha.

23. Interview with Angela Makeevka, Irpin deputy mayor, Irpin, Ukraine, September 2022.

24. Interview with Motyzhyn town council member, Motyzhyn, Ukraine, September 2022.

25. "A Pensioner from Motyzhyn Helped the Ukrainian Military Destroy About a Hundred Pieces of Russian Equipment: The Invaders Killed Her," *Zmina*, May 4, 2022, https://zmina.info/news/pensionerka-z-motyzhyna-dopomogla-ukrayinskym-vijskovym-znyshhyty-blyzko-sotni-odynycz-tehniky-rosiyan-okupanty-vbyly-yiyi.

26. James Marson, "Execution of Village Mayor Becomes Symbol of Brutality in Ukraine," *Wall Street Journal*, April 5, 2022.

27. Interview with Mykola Kurach, Motyzhyn, Ukraine, September 2022.

28. The names of all three mercenaries appeared on the Wagner Group's personnel rolls during the 2014–2021 period, although it was less clear how these men found their way to Motyzhyn in 2022. Interview with senior official in the Prosecutor General's Office in Ukraine, Kyiv, September 2022; see also Lorenzo Tondo, Isobel Koshiw, Emma Graham-Harrison, and Pjotr Sauer, "Alleged Wagner Group Fighters Accused of Murdering Civilians in Ukraine," *Guardian*, May 25, 2022, www.theguardian.com/world/2022/may/25/wagner-group-fighters-accused-murdering-civilians-ukraine-war-crimes-belarus.

29. Ukrainian military blogger Andrei Shtirlitz was one of the first to post photos and information from the scene at Popasna, in April 2022 on Telegram: https://t.me/a_shtirlitz/17714.

30. Kiril Romanovsky, *Кирилл Романовский: Восемь лет с «Вагнером»* (ACT, 2024).

31. Prigozhin's post to his VKontakte and Telegram has since been taken down. The photo of Milonov and Prigozhin in Pervomaisk was reposted on numerous platforms; see https://t.me/mozhemobyasnit/12117.

32. Journalist Samuel Ramani posted commentary on the photo of Prigozhin and Milonov on April 19, a day after several Telegram channels picked up news that the bodies of several Russian mercenaries had turned up near Popasna: https://twitter.com/SamRamani2/status/1516318594900152323.

33. Aleksandra Klitina, "Olenivka Prison Camp Massacre—New Details Emerging," *Kyiv Post*, August 4, 2022, www.kyivpost.com/post/1931.

34. Yulia Gorbunova and Kseniya Kvitka, "One Year Since Death of Ukrainian POWs in Explosion," Human Rights Watch, July 28, 2023, www.hrw.org/news/2023/07/28/one-year-death-ukrainian-pows-explosion.

35. The size of the Wagner Group fluctuated over time, but data culled and analyzed from 160 personnel records suggest that the core number in 2021 hovered between 10,000 and 13,000. However, this number reflects only those trained in Russia; the actual pre-2022 figure is likely higher given that foreign fighters from the Middle East and Africa joined the front lines.

36. Wagner Group recruitment website, archived version at https://web.archive.org/web/20220602134606/https://wagner2022.org.

CHAPTER 20: GULAG NO, GULAG YES

1. Estimates of total numbers imprisoned in Russia vary from year to year. In a March 2023 analysis, Judith Pallot cited FSIN estimates at 433,006 for 2023, whereas a 2019 analysis placed the total number closer to 470,000. See Judith Pallot, "Lies, Damn Lies and Statistics—How Many Prisoners Has Wagner Really Recruited?," *Riddle*, March 7, 2023, https://ridl.io/lies-damn-lies-and-statistics-how-many-prisoners-has-wagner-really-recruited; and Jan Strzelecki, "Russia Behind Bars: The Peculiarities of the Russian Prison System," Osrodek Studiow Wschodnich, July 2, 2019, www.osw.waw.pl/en/publikacje/osw-commentary/2019-02-07/russia-behind-bars-peculiarities-russian-prison-system.

2. Quoted in Strzelecki, "Russia Behind Bars."

3. "Russia's Budget Revenue from Prisoner Labor Doubles from 2016–2022," *Moscow Times*, August 11, 2023, www.themoscowtimes.com/2023/08/11/russias-budget-revenue-from-prisoner-labor-doubles-from-2016-2022-a82126; Strzelecki, "Russia Behind Bars."

4. Two sources of information emerged as crucial in decoding how Prigozhin and his

subordinates operated the Wagner Group. Part of a cache of internal leaked documents provided to New America by the Center for Advanced Defense Studies (C4ADS), the first was a document bearing the innocuous title "VPN phones ALL on_01_06_2018" ("Телефоны VPN ВСЕ на_01_06_2018"). Despite its mundane label, this file proved to be an analytical gold mine, offering unprecedented insight into the Wagner Group's behind-the-scenes activities. A second key source was Prigozhin's personal calendar from July 2012 to April 2022, containing 17,824 appointments after data cleaning. These calendar data and the extensive connections that they show to Russia's military bureaucracy yielded a plethora of insights. New America's analysis of the final four years of entries (2018–2022) revealed a system of coded entries corresponding to the back-office directory. For further details, see www.uncoveringwagner.org.

5. Pjotr Sauer, "'We Thieves and Killers Are Now Fighting Russia's War': How Moscow Recruits from Its Prisons," *Guardian*, September 20, 2022, www.theguardian.com/world/2022 /sep/20/russia-recruits-inmates-ukraine-war-wagner-prigozhin.

6. Zdravko Ljubas, "Russian Mercenaries Recruit Convicts," Organized Crime and Corruption Reporting Project (OCCRP), July 9, 2022, www.occrp.org/en/daily/16553 -russian-mercenaries-recruit-convicts-to-fight-in-ukraine-2.

7. Russia Behind Bars and the European Prison Litigation Network, "Submissions Concerning the Recruitment and Participation of the Russian Convicted Prisoners in the War in Ukraine," September 2022, www.prisonlitigation.org/wp-content/uploads/2022/09 /Submissions_UN-HRC-SpecProc_RBB-EPLN_recruitment-of-prisoners-in-Russia-1.pdf.

8. "New Soldiers of the Russian Army: PMC Wagner Recruited More Than a Thousand Prisoners in 17 Colonies of the Country" ("Новые солдаты российской армии: ЧВК Вагнера завербовала больше тысячи заключённых в 17 колониях страны"), *Verstka Media*, August 5, 2022, https://verstka.media/vagner-verbovka-zakluchennyh-iz-17-koloniy.

9. Irina Chevtaeva, "Vladimir Osechkin: Taking Things to the State Duma" ("ВЛАДИМИР ОСЕЧКИН: С ВЕЩАМИ В ГОСДУМУ"), *SovershenoSekretno.com*, October 28, 2013, https://web.archive.org/web/20210613014711/https://www.sovsekretno.ru/articles/vladimir -osechkin-s-veshchami-v-gosdumu.

10. Interview with Vladimir Osechkin, Biarritz, France, June 2023.

11. Osechkin interview.

12. Interview with Pierre Hafner, Biarritz, France, June 2023.

13. Christiaan Triebert, "Video Reveals How Russian Mercenaries Recruit Inmates for Ukraine War," *New York Times*, September 16, 2022, www.nytimes.com/2022/09/16/world /europe/russia-wagner-ukraine-video.html.

14. "Navalny's Team Posts Video of Man Allegedly Recruiting Russian Inmates to Fight in Ukraine," RFE/RL, September 15, 2022, www.rferl.org/a/russia-prigozhin-prisoners-vagner /32035035.html.

15. Patrick Wintour, "Russia Has Amassed up to 190,000 Troops on Ukraine Borders, US Warns," *Guardian*, February 18, 2022, www.theguardian.com/world/2022/feb/18/russia -has-amassed-up-to-190000-troops-on-ukraine-borders-us-warns#:~:text=Russia%20has %20amassed%20up%20to%20190%2C000%20troops%20on%20Ukraine%20bor ders%2C%20US%20warns,-This%20article%20is&text=Russia%20has%20amassed%20 up%20to%20190%2C000%20troops%20on%20the%20borders,in%20less%20than%20a%20 month.

16. "'Gulag, Yes.' Yevgeny Prigozhin Spoke About the Site Where Prisoners Are Advised to Go to the Front," VotTak, September 10, 2022, https://vot-tak.tv/novosti/10-09-2022-proekt -gulagu-da; the archived version is at https://archive.md/FIF2m.

17. The post was uploaded to the Concord Consulting and Management Press Service and is accessible here: https://vk.com/concordgroup_official?w=wall-177427428_1140, archived version at https://archive.md/wip/CyNdV.

18. A copy of the letter was posted on the Concord Consulting and Management Press Service account here: https://vk.com/concordgroup_official?w=wall-177427428_1140.

19. Triebert, "Video Reveals."

20. Russian artist Arkady Bronnikov famously collected thousands of photos of tattooed Russian prisoners from the 1960s to the 1980s while working as a local police inspector for the Ministry of Internal Affairs (MVD). When it was published, Bronnikov's collection and that of others who contributed to the indexing of prisoners' body art opened a window onto a world rarely seen outside of Russia. See Russian Criminal Tattoo Archive, https://fuel-design .com/russian-criminal-tattoo-archive; and "Decoding Russian Criminal Tattoos—in Pictures," *Guardian*, September 18, 2014, www.theguardian.com/artanddesign/gallery/2014/sep/18 /decoding-russian-criminal-tattoos-in-pictures.

21. Andrei Zakharov, Katya Arenina, Yekateraina Reznikova, and Mikhail Rubin, "Chef and Cook. Part 5. Portrait of Yevgeny Prigozhin, the President of Russia's Personal Sadist" ("Шеф и повар. Часть 5. Портрет Евгения Пригожина, персонального садиста при президенте России"), *Proeckt Media*, July 12, 2023, www.proekt.media/portrait/evgeniy-prigozhin.

22. Triebert, "Video Reveals."

23. "A Chapel in Memory of Russian Volunteers in Syria Opened in Goryachiy Klyuch" ("В Горячем Ключе появилась часовня в память о российских добровольцах в Сирии"), *Kommersant*, October 10, 2018, www.kommersant.ru/doc/3765883.

24. The statue is dedicated to the memory of Roman Zabolotny and Grigory Tsurkana, who were apparently killed in 2017 during hand-to-hand combat while on patrol near the Wagner base of operations in the Syrian city of Palmyra. "Journalists Were Touched by Their Visit to the Memorial Dedicated to PMC Wagner Fighters in Krasnodar Krai" ("журналистов поразила часовня героев ЧВК «ВАГНЕР» в краснодарском крае"), *GlobalKras .ru*, October 9, 2018, https://globalkras.ru/news/id/7962/1; "Ownership of the PMC Wagner Chapel Has Been Transferred to the Organization of Commander 'Gray'" ("Часовня 'ЧВК Вагнера' сменила собственника. Им стала организация командира 'Седого'"), BBC Russian Service, January 14, 2019, www.bbc.com/russian/features-46808417.

25. "Hero of Russia Andrei Bogatov Met with Ulyanovsk Residents: 'Veterans Are Undeservedly Forgotten by the State'" ("Герой России Андрей Богатов встретился с ульяновцами: 'Ветераны незаслуженно забыты государством'"), *73online.ru*, August 23, 2021, https://73on line.ru/r/geroy_rossii_Andrei_bogatov_vstretilsya_s_ulyanovcami_veterany_nezasluzhenno _zabyty_gosudarstvom-93255.

26. "A New Cemetery for the Fallen Soldiers of PMC 'Wagner' Will Be Established in Goryachiy Klyuch" ("Новое кладбище для погибших бойцов ЧВК «Вагнер» появится в Горячем Ключе"), BlokNot Krasnador, April 12, 2023, https://bloknot-krasnodar.ru/news /novoe-kladbishche-dlya-pogibshikh-boytsov-chvk-vag-1591218.

27. Prigozhin's statement was posted on the VKontakte page for his company on September 26, 2022. The original can be found here: https://vk.com/concordgroup_official ?w=wall-177427428_1194; the archived version is at https://archive.vn/CkUkS.

28. Concord Consulting and Management Press Service, statement, September 26, 2022, https://vk.com/concordgroup_official?w=wall-177427428_1194, archived version at https: //archive.vn/CkUkS.

29. "Russia's Prigozhin Admits Interfering in U.S. Elections," Reuters, November 7, 2022, www.reuters.com/world/us/russias-prigozhin-admits-interfering-us-elections-2022-11-07.

30. "Prigozhin Officially Registered the Company 'PMC Wagner Center' in St. Petersburg," *Delovoy Peterburg*, January 17, 2023, www.dp.ru/a/2023/01/17/Prigozhin_oficialno_zareg.

31. Vladimir Neelov, "Private Military Companies in Russia: Practices and Perspectives on Their Use" ("Частное Военное Компании в России: Опыт и Перспективы Использования"), 2013, 26, https://csef.ru/media/articles/4838/4838.pdf.

32. "Prigozhin to Challenge Denial of Permit for Wagner Center PMC Deployment" ("Пригожин оспорит отказ в выдаче разрешения на ввод 'ЧВК Вагнер Центр'"), *Delovoy Peterburg*, November 10, 2022, www.dp.ru/a/2022/11/10/Prigozhin_osporit_otkaz_v.

33. "Prigozhin Complained Twice About Beglov to the Prosecutor's Office" ("Пригожин дважды пожаловался на Беглова в прокуратуру"), *Bumaga*, November 22, 2022, https://paperpaper.io/prigozhin-pozhalovalsya-na-beglova-v-gen.

34. "Ukraine War: Wagner Chief Defends Brutal Killing Video," *BBC News*, November 14, 2022, www.bbc.com/news/world-europe-63623285.

35. Yuri Butusov released the video interview with Nuzhin on September 15, 2022, via the YouTube channel of his social media vertical Butusov Live (Butusov Plus): www.youtube.com/watch?v=t4dJRPHuzFg. *Meduza* published coverage on the Butusov video release on September 16: "'If You Didn't Follow Instructions, They Shot You': A Russian Convict Recruited by the Wagner Group Tells His Story," *Meduza*, https://meduza.io/en/feature/2022/09/16/if-you-didn-t-follow-instructions-they-shot-you.

36. Sophia Ankel, "Putin Ally Says He Sent EU Parliament a Stained Sledgehammer After It Branded Russia a State Sponsor of Terrorism," *Business Insider*, November 24, 2022, www.businessinsider.com/putin-ally-yevgeny-prigozhin-says-he-sent-eu-parliament-sledgehammer-2022-11.

CHAPTER 21: A STAB IN THE BACK

1. Jack Watling, Oleksandr V. Danylyuk, and Nick Reynolds, "Preliminary Lessons from Ukraine's Offensive Operations, 2022–23," Royal United Services Institute (RUSI), July 18, 2024, 11.

2. Peter Beaumont and Pjotr Sauer, "'Every House a Fortress': Wagner Counts Costs as Russia Stalls in Bakhmut," *Guardian*, January 3, 2023, www.theguardian.com/world/2023/jan/03/ukraine-wagner-leader-counts-cost-as-russian-offensive-stalls-in-bakhmut.

3. Mikhail Zygar, "The Man Challenging Putin for Power," *New York Times*, January 26, 2023, www.nytimes.com/2023/01/26/opinion/russia-putin-ukraine-wagner.html.

4. "Voentorg Files Record Number of Lawsuits Against Prigozhin's Companies for Supplying Troops with Poor Quality Food" ("«Военторг» подал к компаниям Пригожина рекордное количество исков из-за снабжения войск некачественной едой"), *Rosinform*, January 24, 2023, https://rosinform.press/voentorg-podal-k-kompaniyam-prigozhina-rekordnoe-kolichestvo-iskov-iz-za-snabzheniya-vojsk-nekachestvennoj-edoj.

5. "Prigozhin Announced an Attempt to Steal Victory from PMC Wagner" ("Пригожин заявил о попытке украсть у ЧВК Вагнера победу"), RBC.ru, January 13, 2023, www.rbc.ru/politics/13/01/2023/63c1501f9a7947704ab114b8.

6. Igor Girkin, Telegram, January 13, 2023, t.me/strelkovii/3730.

7. Andrew Roth and Dan Sabbagh, "Russian General Who May Have Known About Wagner Mutiny Goes Missing," *Guardian*, June 28, 2023, www.theguardian.com/world/2023/jun/28/russian-general-wagner-mutiny-goes-missing.

8. "Wagner Group Founder Claims That Russia Creates Defensive Lines, 'People's Militia' in Belgorod Oblast," *Kyiv Independent*, October 19, 2022, https://kyivindependent.com/wagner-group-founder-claims-that-russia-creates-defensive-lines-peoples-militia-in-belgorod-oblast.

9. Karolina Hird, Riley Bailey, Angela Howard, George Barros, Nicole Wolkov, Layne Philipson, and Frederick W. Kagan, "Russian Offensive Campaign Assessment, March 16, 2023," Institute for the Study of War, March 16, 2023, www.understandingwar.org/backgrounder/russian-offensive-campaign-assessment-march-16-2023.

10. Aamer Madhani and Edith M. Lederer, "White House: Russia's Wagner Group Received Arms from North Korea," Associated Press, December 22, 2022, apnews.com/article/russia-ukraine-business-north-korea-e6a068d91bc9828ecadfb67c929a4162.

11. "Treasury Sanctions Russian Proxy Wagner Group as a Transnational Criminal Organization," US Department of the Treasury, January 26, 2023, www.home.treasury.gov/news/press-releases/jy1220.

12. Interview with former US government official, January 2023.

13. "Treasury Sanctions Russian Proxy Wagner Group."

14. "Former Commander of the Wagner PMC Andrei Medvedev Was Able to Leave the Russian Federation and Requested Asylum/Protection in Norway" ("Экс-командир НВФ 'ЧВК Вагнер' Андрей Медведев смог покинуть РФ и запросил убежище/защиту в Норвегии"), Gulagu.net, January 14, 2023, www.youtube.com/watch?v=vgc-TxCqEsA.

15. "Former Commander of the Wagner PMC."

16. The assessment of Wagner's tactics in Bakhmut was contained in a 2022 report prepared by Ukrainian forces that was shared with the author.

17. Joshua Yaffa, "Inside the Wagner Group's Armed Uprising," *New Yorker*, July 31, 2023, www.newyorker.com/magazine/2023/08/07/inside-the-wagner-uprising.

18. "Former Commander of the Wagner PMC."

19. "The Big Reveal: Prigozhin on Betrayal and PMC Ambitions" ("Большое разоблачение: Пригожин о предательстве и амбициях ЧВК"), *WarGonzo*, May 2, 2023, https://rutube.ru/video/d20159064ae5c074fe194d6e6f3a8e68.

20. "Ponomarev*: The Same People Are Behind the Murders of Tatarsky and Dugina" ("Пономарев*: за убийством Татарского и Дугиной стоят одни и те же люди"), *RIA Novosti*, April 24, 2023, https://ria.ru/20230424/ubiystva-1867326825.html.

21. "Как убивают российских пропагандистов и кто за этим может стоять" ("How Russian Propagandists Are Killed and Who Might Be Behind It"), *Belsat.eu*, May 5, 2023, http://cdn2.belsat.eu/ru/news/09-05-2023-kak-ubivayut-rossijskih-propagandistov-i-kto-za-etim-mozhet-stoyat.

22. Alexander Dugin posted the commentary under his handle @AGDchan on Telegram under the heading "ФАКТОР «ВАГНЕРА» И ТЕЗИС СПРАВЕДЛИВОСТИ" ("The Wagner Factor and the Thesis of Justice"), April 8, 2023. An archived version of Dugin's Telegram post can be found at https://archive.is/wip/dwjZo.

23. Sarah Dean and Josh Pennington, "Two Russians Claiming to Be Former Wagner Group Commanders Admit to Killing Children," CNN, April 18, 2023, www.cnn.com/2023/04/17/europe/wagner-commanders-russia-kill-children-intl-hnk/index.html.

24. "'Shoigu! Gerasimov! Where's the Fucking Ammo?' Evgeny Prigozhin's Obscene Tirade Blames Top Military Officials for the Mercenary Cartel's 'Senseless Losses,'" *Meduza*, May 5, 2023. https://meduza.io/en/feature/2023/05/05/shoigu-gerasimov-where-s-the-fucking-ammo.

25. "'Shoigu! Gerasimov!'"

26. Jack Margolin, *The Wagner Group: Inside Russia's Mercenary Army* (London: Reaktion, 2024), 230.

27. Mark Trevelyan, "Russia's Prigozhin Claims Capture of Bakhmut, Ukraine Says Fighting Goes On," *Reuters*, May 20, 2023, www.reuters.com/world/europe/russias-prigozhin-claims-full-control-bakhmut-2023-05-20.

28. Guy Faulconbridge, "Mercenary Prigozhin Warns Russia Could Face Revolution Unless Elite Gets Serious About War," *Reuters*, May 24, 2023, www.reuters.com/world/europe/mercenary-prigozhin-warns-russia-could-face-revolution-unless-elite-gets-serious-2023-05-24.

29. Anastasia Lotareva and Ilya Barabanov, "PMC Wagner Detained a Lieutenant Colonel of the Russian Army and Forced Him to Apologize. What's Going On?" ("ЧВК 'Вагнер' задержал подполковника российской армии и заставил извиниться. Что происходит?"), *BBC Russkaya Sluzhba*, June 5, 2023, www.bbc.com/russian/news-65812906.

30. Pyor Kozlov, "Hours Before Declaring Mutiny, Prigozhin Secretly Planned Duma Speech to Win Back Putin's Favor," *Moscow Times*, November 21, 2023, www.themoscowtimes

.com/2023/11/21/hours-before-declaring-mutiny-prigozhin-secretly-planned-duma-speech-to
-win-back-putins-favor-a83167.

31. "Prigozhin's Speech Sounds Like an Announcement of a Military Coup (Although, It Seems, That's Not How Coups Begin)" ("Выступление Пригожина звучит как объявление о начале военного переворота [хотя, кажется, перевороты начинаются не с этого]"), *Meduza*, June 23, 2023, https://meduza.io/feature/2023/06/23/prigozhin-ob-yavil-chto-fakticheski -sobiraetsya-osuschestvit-voennyy-perevorot-v-rossii-nazvav-ego-marshem-spravedlivosti.

32. "'A Bunch of Bastards Needed the War to Show Off': Prigozhin Predicts Russian Retreat, Says Ukraine Wasn't Going to Attack Russia in 2022," *Insider*, June 23, 2023, https://theins.ru /en/news/262823.

33. "General Sergei Surovikin Appeals to Wagner PMC Mercenaries, Urges Them to 'Stop the Columns and Obey the Will and Order of Vladimir Putin,'" *Insider*, June 23, 2023, https: //theins.ru/en/news/262844.

34. "Prigozhin Met with the Deputy Minister of Defense and the Deputy Chief of the General Staff in Rostov-on-Don" ("Пригожин встретился в Ростове-на-Дону с замминистра обороны и замглавы Генштаба"), *Meduza*, www.youtube.com/watch?v=YBoYuGxp4Tc.

35. "Wagner PMC Forces Reach Lipetsk Region, Governor Confirms. Excavators Seen Digging Up Roads," *Insider*, June 24, 2023, https://theins.ru/en/news/262892.

36. "Putin Called Prigozhin's Rebellion 'Betrayal' and 'Treason,'" *Meduza*, June 24, 2023, www.youtube.com/watch?v=XsZkbl85PhQ.

37. Vera Bergengruen, "The Telegram Mutiny," *Time*, June 27, 2023, https://time.com /6290378/yevgeny-prigozhin-wagner-telegram.

38. Kaitlin Lewis, "Prigozhin Mansion Raid Reveals Guns, Gold Bars and Wardrobe of Wigs," *Newsweek*, July 6, 2023, www.newsweek.com/what-alleged-photos-video-wagner-group -leaders-estate-reveal-1811178.

39. Prigozhin posted his statement on Telegram on June 24, 2023, https://t.me/Prigozhin _hat/3814; see "Wagner Group Chief Says His Mercenaries Will Halt Their March on Moscow," NPR, June 24, 2023, www.npr.org/2023/06/24/1184166949/wagner-group-moscow -halting-march-russia.

40. Isabel van Brugen, "Who Is Aleksey Dyumin? Putin's Ex-bodyguard Tipped to Replace Shoigu," *Newsweek*, June 26, 2023, www.newsweek.com/who-aleksey-dyumin-putin -bodyguard-replace-shoigu-prigozhin-wagner-1809192.

41. "Putin Says Wagner Group Fully Financed by Russian Government," TASS, June 27, 2023, https://tass.com/defense/1639345.

CHAPTER 22: ICARUS DOWN

1. "Prigozhin Controlled Russian Media Group Shuts After Mutiny," Reuters, July 2, 2023, www.reuters.com/world/europe/prigozhin-controlled-russian-media-group-shuts-amid -mutiny-fallout-2023-07-02.

2. Suleiman Al-Khalidi and Maya Gebeily, "Syria Brought Wagner Fighters to Heel as Mutiny Unfolded in Russia," Reuters, July 7, 2023, www.reuters.com/world/syria-brought -wagner-group-fighters-heel-mutiny-unfolded-russia-2023-07-07.

3. "Russia Returns $111M Seized During Police Raids to Prigozhin," *Moscow Times*, July 4, 2023, www.themoscowtimes.com/2023/07/04/111m-seized-during-police-raids-returned-to -prigozhin-a81731.

4. "Pioneer, Asipovichy Base Commander for Wagner in Belarus," alleyesonwagner.org, July 19, 2023, https://alleyesonwagner.org/2023/07/19/pioneer-asipovichy-base-commander -for-wagner-in-belarus.

5. Interview with former Western military official, July 2023.

6. Joe Parkinson, Drew Hinshaw, Jack Gillum, and Benoit Faucon, "Prigozhin's Life on the

Run: Wagner Chief Used Jets to Evade Tracking for Years," *Wall Street Journal*, August 30, 2023, www.wsj.com/world/russia/prigozhin-wagner-jets-evade-tracking-61ba91e7.

7. The clip of the women who witnessed the plane crash circulated widely on Telegram; a sanitized excerpt of their reaction can be heard in this YouTube post: "Prigozhin's Plane Crash," *Meduza*, August 23, 2023, https://www.youtube.com/watch?v=u49_GWHrm9Q.

8. *The Sun* posted the video on July 19, 2023, several hours after it began circulating on Telegram channels. See www.youtube.com/watch?v=mmINJXYtRsE; see also Andrew Roth, "Video Appears to Show Wagner Chief for First Time Since Aborted Mutiny," *Guardian*, July 19, 2023, www.theguardian.com/world/2023/jul/19/video-appears-to-show-wagner-chief -yevgeny-prigozhin-addressing-fighters-in-belarus.

9. Parkinson, Hinshaw, Gillum, and Faucon, "Prigozhin's Life on the Run."

10. Jamie Dettmer, "Guns, Mercenaries, Minerals—Russia Embraces Africa," October 21, 2019, www.voanews.com/a/europe_guns-mercenaries-minerals-russia-embraces-africa/6177 907.html.

11. Irina Dolnina and Alesa Morovskaya, "Spets'i i Spetsii" ("Spies and Spices"), *Novaya Gazeta*, February 4, 2019, https://novayagazeta.ru/articles/2019/02/04/79417-spetsy-i-spetsii.

12. Carolina Pulice and Gabriel Araujo, "Yevgeny Prigozhin Plane Crash: Embraer Legacy 600 Jet Had Good Safety Record, Say Reports," Reuters, August 24, 2023, www.reuters.com/world/europe /embraer-whose-plane-reportedly-carried-prigozhin-says-its-compliant-russia-2023-08-23.

13. United Kingdom Companies House Registration Information for MNT Aero Ltd. can be found at https://find-and-update.company-information.service.gov.uk/company/07608743 /filing-history.

14. "She Collaborated with Rosoboronexport and Transneft" ("Сотрудничала с Рособоронэкспортом и «Транснефтью». Что известно о компании, которой принадлежит упавший под Тверью самолет"), *Chita.ru*, August 24, 2023, www.chita.ru/text/transport/2023 /08/24/72629444.

15. "She Collaborated with Rosoboronexport and Transneft."

16. "Blank Spots Revealed in Yevgeny Prigozhin's Death: Two Thought Provoking Facts" ("В смерти Евгения Пригожина вскрылись белые пятна: два факта, наталкивающих на раздумия"), *Dzen*, September 1, 2023, https://dzen.ru/a/ZPHXRrc8jSZxCxwq.

17. The IL-76 was first referenced in a story released by the BBC on August 24, 2023, which stated that the cargo jet's registered owner was Russia's Ministry of Emergency Services. See "Where Was Prigozhin Before the Crash?," *BBC News*, August 24, 2023, www.bbc.com/news /world-europe-66609273. The *Wall Street Journal* also mentioned that Prigozhin's last stop on the Africa flight was Mali but did not mention the tail number of the IL-76 cargo plane.

18. Mary Ilyushina, "Wagner Mercenary Group to Focus on Africa, Prigozhin Says in New Video," *Washington Post*, August 22, 2023, www.washingtonpost.com/world/2023/08/22 /prigozhin-africa-wagner-russia.

19. Pjotr Sauer and Graham Russell, "Prigozhin Points Finger at Putin as Prigozhin's Reported Death Seen as a Warning to 'Elites,'" *Guardian*, August 24, 2023, www.theguardian .com/world/2023/aug/24/wagner-boss-yevgeny-prigozhin-reported-killed-death-russia-biden -suggests-putin.

20. "A Turbo-fridge Is Under Suspicion," *Noviye Isvestiya*, August 25, 2023, https://newizv .ru/news/2023-08-25/pod-podozreniem-turboholodilnik-gde-mogli-zalozhit-bombu-v -samolete-prigozhina-417531.

21. Interview with Gleb Irisov, July 2023.

22. Andrius Sytas, "Lithuania Closes Two Belarus Border Crossings," Reuters, August 16, 2023, www.reuters.com/world/europe/lithuania-closes-two-belarus-border-crossings-2023-08-16.

23. The article has since been scrubbed from the web; the link resolves to a 404 error page on www.timeshub.in. Natasha Kumar, "Evgeny Prigozhin May Already Be Dead—Belarusian

Opposition Leader," August 8, 2023, https://thetimeshub.in/evgeny-prigozhin-may-already-be-dead-a-belarusian-opposition-leader/2285.

CHAPTER 23: SUCCESSION

1. Jaroslav Lukiv, "Putin Breaks Silence over Prigozhin's Death," *BBC News*, August 24, 2023, www.bbc.com/news/world-europe-66609678.

2. Guy Faulconbridge and Vladimir Soldatkin, "Putin Suggests Plane of Wagner Boss Prigozhin Was Blown Up by Hand Grenades on Board," Reuters, October 5, 2023, www.reuters.com/world/europe/putin-hand-grenade-fragments-found-bodies-prigozhin-plane-crash-2023-10-05.

3. Thomas Grove, Allen Cullison, and Bojan Pancevski, "How Putin's Right-Hand Man Took Out Prigozhin," *Wall Street Journal*, December 22, 2023, www.wsj.com/world/russia/putin-patrushev-plan-prigozhin-assassination-428d5ed8.

4. C4ADS, Evro Polis and subsidiaries data holdings.

5. "Who Is the New Head of Wagner? Who Exactly Is Andrei Averyanov—and Why Is the West Convinced He Is the New Head of the Orchestra?" ("У Вагнера новый глава? Кто такой Андрей Аверьянов и почему Запад выдвигает его на роль главы оркестрантов—есть ли еще кандидаты?"), *Kuryier Sreda*, August 23, 2023, https://dzen.ru/a/ZOwEK_thzAHx38nW.

6. "'Elite GRU Unit' from NY Times Article Turns Out to Be Intelligence Training Center" («Элитная часть ГРУ» из статьи NY Times оказалась курсами для разведчико), *Vedomosti*, October 9, 2019, www.vedomosti.ru/politics/articles/2019/10/09/813253-elitnaya-chast-ny-dlya.

7. Interview with former Western intelligence agent, August 2023.

8. "Czech President Says There Are Two Theories on 2014 Arms Depot Blast," RFE/RL, April 25, 2021, www.rferl.org/a/czech-president-arms-depot-blast-2014/31221891.html.

9. Michael Schwirtz, "The Arms Dealer in the Sights of Russia's Elite Assassination Squad," *New York Times*, April 24, 2021, www.nytimes.com/2021/04/24/world/europe/arms-merchant-russia-assassination-squad.html.

10. "A Hundred Grand and Hundreds of Betrayed Agents," *Meduza*, March 6, 2018, https://meduza.io/en/feature/2018/03/06/a-hundred-grand-and-hundreds-of-betrayed-agents.

11. Bellingcat Investigative Team, "Skripal Suspect Boshirov Identified as GRU Colonel Anatoliy Chepiga," Bellingcat.com, September 26, 2018, www.bellingcat.com/news/uk-and-europe/2018/09/26/skripal-suspect-boshirov-identified-gru-colonel-anatoliy-chepiga.

12. Andrew Osborn, "Prigozhin Hails Niger Coup, Touts Wagner Services," *Reuters*, July 29, 2023, www.reuters.com/world/europe/exiled-russian-mercenary-boss-prigozhin-hails-niger-coup-touts-services-2023-07-28.

13. Brett McDonald, "Exclusive: Viktor Bout Still Has His Eye on Africa," Defence Web, August 22, 2023, www.defenceweb.co.za/featured/exclusive-viktor-bout-still-has-his-eye-on-africa.

14. "Портфель Генштаба," VKontakte video post, May 2, 2023, https://vk.com/shtab24?w=wall-206639135_601722.

15. "Разгрузка Вагнера," Telegram post, June 11, 2023, https://t.me/razgruzka_vagnera/151.

16. @OrchestraW posted the note on the morning of August 26, 2023; https://t.me/orchestra_w/8621.

17. Interview with ex–Wagner Group and former Redut commander Marat Gabidullin, September 2023.

18. "'Ratibor' from PMC Wagner Faced Hate Online" ("«РАТИБОР» ИЗ ЧВК «ВАГНЕР» СТОЛКНУЛСЯ С ХЕЙТОМ В СЕТИ ПОСЛЕ ВСТУПЛЕНИЯ В «АХМАТ»"), *Dzen*, April 11, 2024, https://dzen.ru/b/ZhfCWRX_siM2XZLb.

19. Sofiia Syngaivska, "The UK Defense Intelligence Reveals Wagner Group's New Era," *Defense Express*, February 7, 2024, https://en.defence-ua.com/news/the_uk_defense_intelligence_reveals_wagner_groups_new_era-9436.html.

20. United Kingdom, Foreign Affairs Committee, House of Commons, "Written Evidence to Foreign Affairs Committee Inquiry into Wagner Group—Answers Provided by Anonymous Source to Committee Questions (WGN0026)," July 10, 2023, https://committees.parliament .uk/writtenevidence/122628/pdf.

21. "Relatives Are Dividing Prigozhin's Inheritance: What Belongs to the Head of the Vagners and Why, on the Eve of His Death, Did He Transfer the Companies to Other Owners?" ("Родственники делят наследство Пригожина: что принадлежит главе Вагнеров и зачем накануне смерти переписал компании на других собственников?"), *Ves Iskitim*, September 3, 2023, https://dzen.ru/a/ZPVBM45_Pwm5I5fb.

22. George Wright, "Putin Meets Former Wagner Commander Andrei Troshev," *BBC News*, September 29, 2023, www.bbc.com/news/world-europe-66957307.

23. "How Russia's GRU Set Up a Fake Private Military Company for Its War in Ukraine," Radio Free Europe/Radio Liberty, October 10, 2023, www.rferl.org/a/russia-gru-fake-private -military-company-ukraine-redut-investigation/32630705.html.

24. "Два майора," Telegram post, November 20, 2023, https://t.me/dva_majors/29354.

25. Jack Watling, Oleksandr V. Danylyuk, and Nick Reynolds, "The Threat from Russia's Unconventional Warfare Beyond Ukraine, 2022–24," Royal United Services Institute (RUSI), 2024, 20, https://static.rusi.org/SR-Russian-Unconventional-Weapons-final-web.pdf.

26. Claudia Chiappa, "From One Warlord to Another: Kadyrov Pays Tribute to Dead Wagner Chief," *Politico.eu*, August 25, 2023, www.politico.eu/article/ramzan-kadyrov-yevgeny -prigozhin-wagner-dead-russia-chechen-warlord-telegram.

27. "Dyumin About Prigozhin: He Did a Lot for the Country, and His Homeland Will Not Forget Him" (Дюмин о Пригожине: Он много сделал для страны, и Родина его не забудет), *Dzen*, August 25, 2023, https://dzen.ru/a/ZOguT-piblV8212y?utm_referer=www.google.com.

28. Konstantin Mityagin, "'We Were Asked to Remain Silent, We Remained Silent.' At the Porokhovskoe Cemetery They Told How Prigozhin Was Buried," *Fontanka*, August 29, 2023, www.fontanka.ru/2023/08/30/72653012.

29. "He Was Close to Prigozhin and Was Responsible for the Supply of Ammunition to Wagner. Valery Chekalov Was Buried at the Northern Cemetery" ("Был приближенным Пригожина, отвечал за поставку боеприпасов в «Вагнер». Валерия Чекалова похоронили на Северном кладбище"), *Moskovsky Komsomolets*, August 29, 2023, https://msk1.ru/text /incidents/2023/08/29/72649343.

30. "The Commander of the PMC 'Wagner' Utkin Was Buried in the Cemetery in Mytishchi," *Vedomosti*, August 31, 2023, www.kommersant.ru/doc/6186848.

31. "Security Forces in Three Rings. What's Happening at the Cemetery Where Prigozhin Was Secretly Buried—Online" ("Силовики в три цепи. Что происходит на кладбище, где тайно похоронили Пригожина—онлайн"), *Fontanka*, August 29, 2023, www.fontanka .ru/2023/08/29/72645755.

32. "Konnogvardeyskiy Manege (Horse Guards Riding School)," *St. Petersburg.com*, undated, www.saint-petersburg.com/buildings/konnogvardeyskiy-manege.

33. "Russian Horse Guards—Commemorative Manual, 1706–1931," www.allworldwars .com/Russian-Horse-Guards.html.

EPILOGUE: FALLOUT

1. "Arrested Russian Deputy Defense Minister Accused of Accepting $12 Mln Bribe, Lawyer Says," *Moscow Times*, May 9, 2024, www.themoscowtimes.com/2024/05/08/arrested-russian -deputy-defense-minister-accused-of-accepting-12-mln-bribe-lawyer-says-a85072.

2. Ryan Pickrell, "Putin Says He Hopes Prigozhin and His Wagner Mercenaries 'Didn't Steal Much' of the Billions Russia Spent on Them," *Business Insider*, June 27, 2023, www .businessinsider.com/putin-hopes-prigozhin-wagner-did-not-steal-much-of-billions-2023-6.

3. "The Temptation of Belousov" ("Искушение Белоусова"), Dossier Centre, May 21, 2024, https://dossier.center/belousov.

4. "Evgeny Minchenko: 'There Are Rumors That Mishustin and Most of His Team Will Remain, but for Two Years'" ("Евгений Минченко: «Ходят слухи, что Мишустин и большая часть его команды сохранятся, но на два года»"), *Bizness Online*, May 6, 2024, www.business-gazeta.ru/article/632072.

5. "Situation in Ukraine: ICC Judges Issue Arrest Warrants Against Sergei Kuzhugetovich Shoigu and Valery Vasilyevich Gerasimov," International Criminal Court, press release, June 25, 2024, www.icc-cpi.int/news/situation-ukraine-icc-judges-issue-arrest-warrants-against-sergei-kuzhugetovich-shoigu-and.

6. The 50,000 killed in action refers to the number identified by researchers as of April 2024; he estimated aggregate total Russian losses were about 120,000 at the time. *Mediazona* regularly updates its numbers as more casualties are identified; see "Russia's Losses in the War with Ukraine," *Mediazona*, May 11, 2024, https://en.zona.media/article/2022/05/11/casualties_eng.

7. "At Least 50,000 Russian Military Deaths, Likely Thousands More, Recorded in Ukraine War," Radio Free Europe/Radio Liberty, April 13, 2024, www.rferl.org/a/russia-war-ukraine-deaths/32903736.html.

8. Ben Dalton and Candace Rondeaux, "The Wagner Group Legacy: Reshaping Russia's Shadow Armies," *Future Frontlines–New America*, September 30, 2024, www.newamerica.org/future-frontlines/briefs/the-wagner-group-legacy.

9. "Mali Rebels Say They Killed 131 Soldiers and Russians in July Clashes," *Reuters*, August 1, 2024, www.reuters.com/world/africa/mali-rebels-say-they-killed-131-soldiers-russians-july-clashes-2024-08-01.

10. Rasima Musalimova, "Gold Mined in Mali Must Be Processed in Mali: Minister on Gold Processing Plant Project with Russia," *Sputnik*, March 26, 2024, https://en.sputniknews.africa/20240326/gold-mined-in-mali-must-be-processed-in-mali-minister-on-gold-processing-plant-project-with-russia-1065782130.html.

11. "Russian Mercenaries Pulled Out of Burkina Faso to Defend Kursk—Commander," *Moscow Times*, August 31, 2024, www.themoscowtimes.com/2024/08/31/russian-mercenaries-pulled-out-of-burkina-faso-to-defend-kursk-commander-a86214.

12. Dozens of anonymous posts of photos displaying the Wagner emblem have been uploaded to the @Razguzka_Vagner Telegram channel; see, for instance, https://ghostarchive.org/archive/ZNXXE.

INDEX

Credit: Ana Isabel Martinez Chamorro

Candace Rondeaux directs Future Frontlines, a public intelligence service for next-generation security and democratic resilience, and the Planetary Politics initiative at the New America Foundation. A writer and public-policy analyst, Rondeaux is a professor of practice and fellow at the Melikian Center for Russian, Eurasian, and East European Studies and the Future Security Initiative at Arizona State University. Before joining New America, Rondeaux served as a senior program officer at the US Institute of Peace, where she launched the RESOLVE Network, a global research consortium on conflict and violent extremism, and as a strategic adviser to the US Special Inspector General for Afghanistan Reconstruction. Rondeaux has documented and analyzed political violence in South Asia and around the world for the *Washington Post* and the International Crisis Group. Before going abroad for the *Post* in 2009, Rondeaux covered criminal justice in Maryland and Virginia, where she focused on capital punishment and was part of the Pulitzer Prize–winning team of *Post* reporters who covered the 2007 Virginia Tech massacre.

Rondeaux holds a BA in Russian area studies from Sarah Lawrence College, an MA in journalism from New York University, and an MPP in public policy from the Woodrow Wilson School of Public and International Affairs at Princeton University.